Plymouth Collection of Hymns and Tunes for the Use of Christian Congregations. Supplementary Hymns, Added by the Churches of the Miami Conference, 1856, 25P., at End

Henry Ward Beecher

Nabu Public Domain Reprints:

You are holding a reproduction of an original work published before 1923 that is in the public domain in the United States of America, and possibly other countries. You may freely copy and distribute this work as no entity (individual or corporate) has a copyright on the body of the work. This book may contain prior copyright references, and library stamps (as most of these works were scanned from library copies). These have been scanned and retained as part of the historical artifact.

This book may have occasional imperfections such as missing or blurred pages, poor pictures, errant marks, etc. that were either part of the original artifact, or were introduced by the scanning process. We believe this work is culturally important, and despite the imperfections, have elected to bring it back into print as part of our continuing commitment to the preservation of printed works worldwide. We appreciate your understanding of the imperfections in the preservation process, and hope you enjoy this valuable book.

PLYMOUTH COLLECTION

OF

HYMNS AND TUNES;

FOR THE

USE OF CHRISTIAN CONGREGATIONS.

[Henry Ward Beecher]

Beecher, Henry Ward. Plymouth Collection of Hymns and Tunes; for the Use of Christian Congregations (FACSIMILE). New York: Barnes, 1859. Print. [SGG-Indexed]

NEW YORK:
A. S. BARNES & COMPANY,
51 JOHN STREET.
1856.

CONTENTS OF THIS BOOK.

	PAGES
INTRODUCTION	iii—viii
GENERAL INDEX OF TUNES	ix—x
METRICAL INDEX	xi—xii
HYMNS	1—447
SABBATH AND SANCTUARY	1—20
THE BIBLE	21—22
GOD	
Manifested in Nature	23—32
Attributes	33—40
Adoration of	41—52
Government and Providence	53—58
Trinity	59—62
CHRIST	
Advent	63—70
Life and death	71—80
His resurrection and glory	81—98
WARNINGS AND INVITATIONS	99—132
CHRISTIAN EXPERIENCE	
Penitence and Consecration	133—156
Praise, Joy, and Conflict	157—216
Fellowship and Communion	217—234
Trials and Temptations	235—288
THE CHURCH	
Institutions and Ordinances	289—298
Missions and Reforms	299—340
TIME, ETERNITY, LIFE, DEATH	341—390
HEAVEN	391—414
TIMES AND SEASONS	415—438
CHILDREN'S HYMNS	439—445
DOXOLOGIES	446—447
INDEX OF SUBJECTS	448—450
INDEX OF FIRST LINES	451—462
INDEX OF HYMNS BY ANY VERSE BUT THE FIRST	463—482
INDEX OF PSALMS	482
INDEX OF AUTHORS	483—484

Entered according to Act of Congress, in the year 1855,
BY A. S. BARNES & CO.,
In the Clerk's Office of the District Court of the Southern District
of New York.

ELECTROTYPED BY
THOMAS B. SMITH,
82 & 84 Beekman Street.

PRINTED BY
GEORGE W. WOOD,
51 John St.

INTRODUCTION.

The book here presented to Christians and Churches numbers more than thirteen hundred hymns, and three hundred and sixty-seven tunes. The work is the result of a conviction that Congregational Singing best answers the end of worship by means of song. A choir should not sing *for* the congregation, but incite them to sing, and lead the way.

It is hoped that a book which shall present both the hymns and the music will contribute to the development of Congregational Singing, by providing the materials for it.

Although the work will not specially benefit those who have never been taught to read music, yet every year musical instruction in schools and in the community at large is increasing the number of those who can read plain music with facility. Already, and especially among the young, the number who might use such a work as this is very considerable.

It is desirable that every pew in the church should contain one or more copies of the Hymn and Tune Book. The Hymns have, however, been printed without the music, at a cheaper rate, for the use of those who wish only hymns.

We submit a few words in respect to the Hymns and the Music.

I.—THE HYMNS.

1. No pains have been spared in collecting materials for this work. The principal collections of Psalms and Hymns that have been published, either in America or Great Britain, have been carefully searched, and the fugitive pieces which have appeared in religious journals, or in collected poetical works of recent authors, have been made to contribute to the store.

A hymn is a lyrical discourse to the feelings. It should either excite or express feeling. The recitation of historical facts, descriptions of scenery, narrations of events, meditations, all may tend to inspire feeling. Hymns are not to be excluded, therefore, because they are deficient in lyrical form, or in feeling, if experience shows that they have power to excite pious emotions. Not many of Newton's hymns can be called poetical; yet there are few hymns in the English language that are more useful.

We have carefully avoided a narrow adherence to our own personal taste in the selection of hymns. Scarcely any two ministers would agree in the selection of hymns. A collection should be made so large and various that every one may find in it that which he needs. Neither should one complain of the multitude of hymns useless to *him*. They are not useless to others. A generously-spread table is not at fault because, in the profusion, each guest can not use every thing. Every one should have all the liberty and the means of following his own taste. Had we made this collection merely for our own use, it would not have numbered more than five hundred hymns.

Many Hymn-books have been so fastidiously made, as not only to exclude many hymns, as extravagant, that were not half so extravagant as are the Psalms of David, and as is all true and deep feeling which gives itself full expression; but also those retained have been abused by corrections, so called, and tamed down from their noble fervor and careless freedom, into flat and profitless propriety.

We have, as far as possible, avoided all changes, except those necessary to restore mutilated hymns to their original state. No language can well replace that which the original inspiration of the author suggested. Watts' hymns and psalms have been carefully compared with the original, and for the most part restored.

2. Great additions have been made to the hymns which celebrate Christ; to hymns of Christian experience, in its deeper and more tender moods; to hymns suitable for religious awakenings; and there will be found a great number of admirable pieces upon these topics, not combined in any other single collection.

Much attention has been given to the Great Humanities which the Gospel develops, whenever it is faithfully and purely preached. The hymns of Temperance, of Human Rights and Freedom, of Peace, and of Benevolence, will be found both numerous, energetic, and eminently Christian. No pains have been spared to secure a full expression to the whole religious feeling and activity of our times.

3. We have sought for hymns in the books of every denomination of Christians. There are certain hymns of the sacrifice of Christ, of utter and almost soul-dissolving yearning for the benefits of His mediation, which none could write so well as a devout and truly pious Roman Catholic. Some of the most touching and truly evangelical hymns in this collection

have been gathered from this source. It has been a matter of joy to us to learn, during our research, how much food for true piety is afforded through Catholic devotional books to the masses of darkened minds within that Church of Error.

We have gathered many exquisite hymns from the Moravian Collections, developing the most tender and loving views of Christ, of his personal presence, and gentle companionship. We know of no hymn-writers that equal their faith and fervor for Christ, as present with his people. Nor can any one conversant with these fail to recognize the fountain in which the incomparable Charles Wesley was baptized. His hymns are only Moravian hymns re-sung. Not alone are the favorite expressions used and the epithets which they loved, but, like them, he beholds all Christian truths through the medium of confiding love. The *love-element* of this school has never been surpassed.

To say that we have sought for hymns expressing the deepest religious feeling, and particularly the sentiments of love, and trust, and divine courage, and hopefulness, is only to say that we have drawn largely from the best Methodist hymns. The contributions of the Wesleys to Hymnology have been so rich as to leave the Christian world under an obligation which can not be paid so long as there is a struggling Christian brotherhood to sing and be comforted amid the trials of this world.

Charles Wesley was peculiarly happy in making the Scripture illustrate Christian experience, and personal experience throw light upon the deep places of the Bible. Some of his effusions have never been surpassed. Nor are there any hymns that could more nobly express the whole ecstacy of the apostolic writings in view of death and heaven.

Cowper, Stennet, Newton, Doddridge, Mrs. Steele, and many other familiar authors, will be found in this collection, as in every other that aspires to usefulness.

With whatever partiality to Dr. Watts we may have begun this compilation, a comparison of his hymns and psalms with the best effusions of the best hymn-writers has only served to increase our admiration, and our conviction that he stands incomparably above all other English writers. Nor do we believe any other man, in any department, has contributed so great a share of enjoyment, edification, and inspiration to struggling Christians as Dr. Watts. We have retained the greatest number of his versions of the Psalms, though under the title of Hymns. A table is prefixed by which the version of any particular psalm may be found.

II.—THE MUSIC.

1. As this work is designed for families, for social meetings, and for the lecture-room, as well as for the great congregation, so the music has been selected with reference to all these wants. But the tunes are chiefly for Congregational Singing. We have gathered up whatever we could find of merit, in old or new music, that seemed fitted for this end. Not the least excellent are the popular revival melodies, which, though often excluded from classic collections of music, have never been driven out from among the people. These have been gathered up, fitly arranged, and having already performed most excellent service, they are now sent forth with the best of all testimonials—the affection and admiration of thousands who have experienced their inspiration. Because they are homebred and popular, rather than foreign and stately, we like them none the less. And we can not doubt that many of them will carry up to heaven the devout fervor of God's people until the millennial day!

2. Congregational singing will never become general and permanent, until the churches employ tunes which have melodies that cling to the memory and touch the feelings or the imagination.

Music is not simply a vehicle for carrying a hymn. It is something in itself. No tune is fit to be sung to a hymn which would not be pleasant, in itself, without any words. Any other view of the function of music, if it shall prevail, will in the end bring music to such a tame and tasteless state that a reaction will be inevitable, and the public mind will go to the opposite extreme. Thus, those who are conscientiously anxious to make music a means of religious feeling, will, by an injudicious method, produce by and by the very mischief which they sought to cure.

A corruption of hymns will not be more fatal to public worship than will be a corruption of music. And any theory that denies to church music a power upon the imagination and the feelings, *as music*, and makes it a mere servile attendant upon words, will carry certain mischief upon its path, and put back indefinitely the cause of church music.

The tunes which burden our modern books, in hundreds and thousands, utterly devoid of character, without meaning or substance, may be sung a hundred times, and not a person in the congregation will remember them. There is nothing to remember. They are the very emptiness of fluent noise. But let a true tune be sung, and every person of sensibility, every person of feeling, every child even, is aroused and touched. The melody clings to them. On the way home snatches of it will be heard on this side and on that; and when, the next Sabbath, the same song is heard, one and another of the people fall in, and the volume grows with each verse, until at length the song, breaking forth as a many-rilled stream from the hills, grows deeper and flows on, broad as a mighty river! Such tunes are never forgotten. They cling to us through our whole life. We carry them with us upon our journey. We sing them in the forest. The workman follows the plow with sacred songs. Children catch them, and singing only for the joy it gives them now, are yet laying up for all their life food of the sweetest joy. Such tunes give new harmony and sweetness even to the hymns which float upon their current. And when some celestial hymn of Wesley, or of the scarcely less than inspired Watts, is wafted upon such music, the soul is lifted up above all its ailments, and rises into the very presence of God, with joys no longer unspeakable, though full of glory!

In selecting music, we should not allow any fastidiousness of taste to set aside the lessons of experience. A tune which has always interested a congregation, which inspires the young, and lends to enthusiasm a fit expression, ought not to be set aside because it does not follow the reigning fashion, or conform to the whims of technical science. There is such a thing as Pharasaism in music. Tunes may be very faulty in structure, and yet convey a full-hearted current that will sweep out of the way the worthless, heartless trash which has no merit except a literal correctness. And when, upon trial, a tune is found to do good work, it should be used for what it does, and can do.

3. We do not think that Congregational Singing will ever prevail with power, until *Pastors of Churches* appreciate its importance, and universally labor to secure it. If ministers regard singing as but a decorous kind of amusement, pleasantly relieving or separating the more solemn acts of worship, it will always be degraded. The pastor, in many cases, in small rural churches may be himself the leader. In larger societies, where a musical director is employed, the pastor should still be the animating center of the music, encouraging the people to take part in it, keeping before them their duty, and their benefit in participating in this most delightful part of public worship.

It is a very general impression that the pastor is to teach and to pray, but another man is to sing. Music is farmed out, and the unity of public services is marred by two systems of exercises conducted by different persons, and oftentimes without concord or sympathy with each other, and sometimes even with such contrariety that the organ and the choir effectually neutralize the pulpit. While it may not be needful that the pastor should perform the part of a musical leader, yet it is certain that there will not be a spirit of song, in the whole congregation, if he is himself indifferent to it, and the first step toward Congregational Singing must be in the direction of the ministry.

The musical department of this work has been under the joint care of Mr. John Zundel, and Rev. Charles Beecher. But by far the greatest part of the labor has devolved upon the latter gentleman, to whose diligence and enthusiasm the Christian public will be greatly indebted for the adaptation of words, and the arrangements and harmonies of the music.

Our task, which has occupied much time during a period of four years, is now concluded. We shall be disappointed if the judgment of the Christian churches shall set aside this collection, as adding nothing to those which have gone before. But even then we shall not regret our task. It has rewarded us at every step. Should it only prepare the way for another and better work, promotive of Congregational Singing, we shall rejoice to have wrought as a pioneer.

HENRY WARD BEECHER.

BROOKLYN, N. Y., August 10, 1855.

GENERAL INDEX OF TUNES.

A.
Tune	Page
Acacia	358
Advent	125
Agate	90
Alabaster	260
All Saints	297
All's Well	373
Amaland	64
Amazing Grace	180
Amelia	154
Amber	186
America	313
Amethyst	102
Amsterdam	370
Andover	66
Anemone	365
Angel's Call	108
Angel's Visit	365
Antigua	305
Antioch	68
Arcadia	246
Arnheim	84
Arnon	139
Aurora	23
Autumn	374
Avon	254
Axminster	358
Azrael	344

B.
Tune	Page
Baden	188
Balerma	183
Balmy Dew	99
Baltic	120
Baptismal Chant	295
Barby	354
Baron	268
Bartimeus	204
Basil	369
Bavaria	441
Bdellium	129
Beethoven	4
Behold the Lamb	79
Benevento	146
Bennet	68
Beryl	276
Bethesda	50
Birmingham	388
Bladenburg	322
Blendon	296
Bolton	183
Bowdoin	235
Boylston	81
Bradford	175
Bremen	202
Brentford	73
Bridgeport	413
Bristol	340
Brooklyn	116
Brown	140
Bruce	389
Burlington	323
Burns	256

C.
Tune	Page
Cambridge	93
Canaan	438
Carmel	377
Carnelian	99
Caspian	376
Cedron	181
Chalcedony	241
Charity	336
Chesterfield	186
Child of Sin and Sorrow	126
Child's Prayer	412
China	350
Christian Victor	411
Christmas	178
Christmas Eve	70
Christus Consolator	232
Chrome	20
Chrysolite	155
Clarendon	220
Clifford	238
Come Home	229
Come ye Disconsolate	269
Come ye Sinners	118
Conrad	94
Coral	206
Cornet	213
Coronation	174
Coventry	184
Cromwell	210
Cross and Crown	244
Crucifix	73
Crusader's Hymn	207
Cuba	421
Cuyler	205

D.
Tune	Page
Dalston	11
Darien	1
Darwell	19
David	291
Dawn	375
Daybreak	240
Dedham	153
De Call	435
Devizes	422
Diamond	287
Dies Iræ	364
Dort	338
Dover	262
Dresden	170
Duke Street	58
Dunbar	259
Dundee	290
Dunlapscreek	106
Dunstan	304

E.
Tune	Page
Easton	286
Eastport	10
Eden	409
Effingham	158
Eleu	228
Ellenthorpe	42
Emerald	430
Emilio	285
Emma	33
Empyrean	92
Essex	300
Erfurth	333
Eucharist	292
Eupator	408
Evening	439
Exeter	69
Expostulation	121

F.
Tune	Page
Far at Sea	369
Fisher	231
Florence	390
Foster	386
Freeland	144
Fulton	362

G.
Tune	Page
Ganges	148
Garnet	280
Geer	218
Geneva	54
Gennesaret	71
Gethsemane	76
Gilead	150
Glory	407
Golden Hill	256
Golden Shore	363
Gratitude	216
Greenville	16
Guardian	188

H.
Tune	Page
Hail to the Brightness	310
Hamburg	86
Happiness	239
Hark, those happy voices	129
Heber	223
Hebron	418
Hemans	79
Henry	86
Herald Angels	69
Herold	113
Hiding Place	173
Holstein	400
Holy City	406
Holyoke	252
Home	408
Hope	201
Howard	293
How calm and beautiful	91
Howitt	325
Hyacinth	268

I.
Tune	Page
I'm a Pilgrim	404
Invitation	122
Iowa	429

GENERAL INDEX OF TUNES.

	PAGE
Italian Hymn	60
Ives	402

J.
Jacinth	272
Jacksonville	207
Judah's Captive	233
Judgment	128

K.
Kalkbrenner	324
Kenaz	371
Kingsley	373
Kir	88

L.
Lafon	363
Lanesboro'	6
Lansingburgh	284
Latter Day	312
Lead thou me on	280
Lebanon	196
Leipzig	77
Lenox	82
Leyden	380
Lischer	212
Loro	368
Loving Kindness	172
Lucas	433
Lucius	444
Lyons	43

M.
Madison	387
Magdalen	281
Manning	427
Manoah	80
Mara	250
Marlow	426
Mary at the Cross, Chant	75
Martyn	112
May	328
Mear	8
Medina	306
Mendon	303
Meriden	21
Metropolis	396
Milton	67
Missionary Chant	300
Missionary Hymn	299
Monmouth	342
Montgomery	347
Morning Star	348
Mory	182
Moscow	321
Mother's Lament	357
Moyle	334
Mt. Blanc	407

N.
Nearer to Thee	283
Nebo	332
Newburgh	114
Newbury	436
Newcourt	329
Nowell	360
Night Thought	414
Nile	168
Nina	434
Norfolk	24
Northampton	420
Norwich	431
Nottingham	32
Nuremburg	331

O.
Ocean	20
Ocean Grave	348
Old Hundred	40
Olivet	222
Olmutz	194
Onyx	149
Opal	274
Oriel	30
Orion	22
Oriole	432
Ortonville	190

P.
Paddington	109
Paradise	405
Park Place	51
Park Street	166
Pearl	89
Pilesgrove	23
Pilgrim's Farewell	392
Pleading Saviour	119
Pleyel's Hymn	261
Plymouth	312
Plymouth Rock	319
Portugal	25
Portuguese Hymn	230
Praise	176

Q.
Quito	236

R.
Raphael	277
Rest	214
Resurgam	410
Retreat	234
Return	104
Requiem	366
Rhine	398
Rilda	132
Rock of Ages	110
Romaine	151
Rose	440
Rosefield	266
Rothwell	164
Ruby	265

S.
Sabbath	14
Salem	394
Sardius	273
Savannah	320
Schiller	29
Scotland	379
Sentinel	192
Seymour	219
Shepherd	158
Shepherd's Call	123
Shirland	12
Sicilian Hymn	279
Sigourney	392
Silent Land	356
Silver Street	294
Somerville	2
Southport	424
Spanish Hymn	367
St. Ann's	179
State Street	226
Stella	127
Stephens	51
Sterling	44
Sternhold	46
Stillwater	263
St. John's	84
Stonefield	417
Storrs	26
St. Petersburg	242
St. Thomas	198
Suffolk	327
Summer Morning	439
Sunshine	438
Swanwick	298
Sweet Story	442

T.
Tallis' Evening Hymn	416
Tamworth	115
Tappan	412
Thatcher	152
The Chariot	121
The Happy Land	410
The Last Beam	437
The Lord is Great	49
The Silent Land, Chant	356
To-day the Saviour Calls	138
Topaz	142
Triumph	85
Turner	224
Twilight	264

U.
Urmund	301
Utica	117
Uxbridge	160

V.
Vanhall's Hymn	41
Vesper	390
Violet	443
Vision	372

W.
Wales	270
Walnut Hills	352
Ward	52
Ware	162
Warner	72
Warning	122
Warwick	89
Washington	326
Watchman	227
Watchword	126
Waterbrook	277
Watts	311
Webb	316
Welcome	208
Weldon	61
Wells	100
Wesley	96
Westmoreland	307
What is Life	395
Whitfield	394
Whittier	328
Williams	74
Willis	206
Willow	367
Willowby	271
Will you go?	124
Wilmot	385
Wimborne	59
Windham	134
Woodland	248

Y.
York	56
Youth	440

Z.
Zephyr	346
Zion	314

METRICAL INDEX.

L. M.

	PAGE
All Saints	297
Amber	136
Antigua	305
Arnheim	84
Azrael	344
Baden	133
Balmy Dew	99
Beethoven	4
Blendon	296
Bowdoin	235
Brentford	73
Bristol	840
Carnelian	98
Chalcedony	211
Chrysolite	155
Darien	1
Daybreak	240
Dresden	170
Duke Street	58
Dunstan	304
Easton	286
Effingham	156
Ellenthorpe	42
Erfurth	388
Eucharist	292
Gethsemane	76
Gratitude	216
Hamburgh	86
Hebron	418
Hiding Place	178
Judah's Captive	288
Leipzig	77
Leyden	380
Loving Kindness	172
Manning	427
May	323
Mendon	303
Missionary Chant	300
Monmouth	342
Montgomery	347
Night Thought	414
Nile	168
Norfolk	24
Northampton	420
Old Hundred	40
Orion	22
Park Street	156
Pikesgrove	23
Pilgrim's Farewell	392
Plymouth	302
Portugal	25
Quito	236
Retreat	234
Ribla	152
Rothwell	164
Salem	394
Shepherd	158
Somerville	2
Sterling	44
Stonefield	417
St. Petersburgh	242
Tallis' Evening Hymn	416
Uxbridge	160
Urmund	301
Vanhall's Hymn	41
Ward	52
Ware	162
Warner	72
Wells	100
Williams	74
Wimborne	59
Windham	134
Zephyr	346

C. M.

	PAGE
Amazing Grace	130
Amethyst	102
Antioch	68
Arcadia	246
Avon	254
Balerma	138
Barby	354
Bennet	63
Bolton	188
Bradford	175
Brown	140
Burns	255
Cambridge	93
Charity	336
Chesterfield	186
China	350
Christmas	178
Clarendon	220
Clifford	283
Coronation	174
Coventry	184
Cross and Crown	244
Dedham	153
Devizes	422
Dundee	290
Dunlapscreek	106
Eastport	10
Exeter	69
Florence	890
Freeland	144
Geer	218
Geneva	54
Guardian	158
Heber	223
Henry	86
Holstein	400
Holyoke	252
Howard	298
Kalkbrenner	324
Lanesboro'	6
Lucius	444
Manoah	80
Mara	250
Marlow	426
Mear	8
Medina	306
Meriden	21
Metropolis	396
Mory	182
Nottingham	82
Ocean Grave	343
Oriel	30
Ortonville	190
Praise	176
Return	104
Rhine	398
Southport	424
St. Ann's	179
Stephens	81
Sternhold	46
St. John's	34
Swanwick	298
Tappan	419
Topaz	142
Turner	224
Walnut Hills	352
Warwick	89
Westmoreland	307
Whitfield	334
Woodland	248
York	56

S. M.

	PAGE
Acacia	358
Alabaster	260
Angel's Call	108
Baron	263
Bladenburg	322
Boylston	31
Dover	202
Dunbar	259
Empyrean	92
Eupator	428
Fisher	281
Golden Hill	258
Iowa	429
Lebanon	196
Nebo	332
Newell	360
Olmutz	194
Paddington	109
Plymouth Rock	319
Sentinel	192
Shirland	12
Silver Street	294
State Street	226
St. Thomas	198
Thatcher	152
Watchman	227

H. M.

	PAGE
Bethesda	50
Brooklyn	116
Christmas Eve	70
Cromwell	210
Darwell	18
Howitt	325
Lenox	82
Lischer	212
Newbury	436
Oriole	432
Park Place	51
Triumph	85
Watts	311

L. P. M.

	PAGE
Newcourt	329

L. C. M.

	PAGE
Axminster	353

C. P. M.

	PAGE
Advent	125
Arnon	130
Aurora	28
Bremen	202
Carmel	377
Caspian	376
Cedron	181
Emma	38
Ganges	148
Watchword	126
Willowby	271

C. H. M.

	PAGE
Bridgeport	418
Hemans	78
How calm and beautiful	91
Schiller	29

METRICAL INDEX.

S. P. M.
	PAGE
Dalston	11

S. H. M.
Requiem	366

12s.
Gennesaret	71
Scotland	379

12s & 11s.
Eden	409
Gennesaret	71

12s & 8s.
Warning	122

11s.
Agate	90
Expostulation	121
Gennesaret	71
Home	408
Kingsley	373
Portuguese Hymn	230

11s & 12s.
The Chariot	121

11s, 10s & 9s.
Moscow	321

11s & 10s.
Baltic	120
Come ye Disconsolate	269
Cuba	421
Hail to the Brightness	310
Rest	214
Still Water	283
Whittier	323

11s & 9s.
Sweet Story	442
Happiness	232

11s & 8s.
Chrome	20
Mt. Zion	49

10s.
Baltic	120
Christian Victor	411
Cuba	421
Rest	214
Savannah	320
Willow	367

10s & 11s.
Agate	90
Lyons	48

9s & 8s.
Dawn	375

8s.
Birmingham	388
Basil	369
Cuyler	205
Dies Iræ	364
Foster	336
Madison	397

8s & 7s.
Amaland	64
Andover	66
Autumn	374
Bavaria	441
Beryl	276
Come ye Sinners	118
David	291
Emerald	430
Golden Shore	383
Greenville	16
Jacinth	272
Jacksonville	207
Latter Day	312
Moyle	384
Opal	274
Pleading Saviour	119
Rose	410
Sicilian Hymn	279
Sigourney	382
Vesper	380
Wesley	96
What is Life	395

8s, 7s & 4s.
Far at Sea	360
Hyacinth	268
Newburgh	114
Sardius	273
Suffolk	327
Tamworth	115
Vesper	380
Welcome	278
Wesley	96
Zion	314

8s & 4s.
Axminster	353
Urmund	341
Wales	270

8s & 3s.
All's Well	378
Will you go	124

7s.
Bartimeus	204
Benevento	146
Come Home	229
David	291
Dies Iræ	364
Elen	228
Essex	290
Fulton	302
Herald Angels	62
Herold	113
Hope	201
Hyacinth	268
Ives	402
Kir	88
Lafon	368
Martyn	112
Morning Star	308
Norwich	431
Nuremburg	331
Pearl	89
Pleyell's Hymn	261
Rock of Ages	110
Rosefield	266
Sabbath	14
Seymour	219
Storrs	26
Twilight	264
Willis	206
Wilmot	335
Youth	440

7s & 6s.
Amelia	154
Amsterdam	370
Christus Consolator	282
Crucifix	79
De Call	435
Gilead	150
Holy City	406
Jacinth	272
Missionary Hymn	299
Nina	434
Ocean	20
Romaine	151
Stella	127
Utica	117
Vision	373
Webb	316
Weldon	61

6s.
Emilie	285
Invitation	122
Lansingburgh	284
Paradise	415
Shepherd's Call	123

6s & 5s.
Anemone	365
Child's Prayer	442
Emilie	285
Evening	439
Lansingburg	284
Loro	369
Mother's Lament	357
Spanish Hymn	367
Sunshine	438

6s & 4s.
America	318
Child of Sin and Sorrow	126
Conrad	94
Dort	339
Italian Hymn	60
Olivet	223
To-day the Saviour Calls	128
Washington	326

Peculiar.
Angel's Visits	363
Bdellium	129
Behold the Lamb	79
Bruce	359
Burlington	323
Canaan	433
Coral	206
Cornet	218
Crusaders' Hymn	207
Diamond	287
Garnet	230
Glory	407
Hark those happy voices	129
I'm a Pilgrim	404
Judgment	128
Kenaz	371
Lead Thou me on	280
Lucas	433
Magdalen	251
Merlin	404
Milton	67
Mt. Blanc	407
Nearer to Thee	232
Onyx	149
Raphael	277
Resurgam	410
Ruby	265
Shepherd's Call	123
Summer Morning	439
The Happy Land	410
The Last Beam	437
Waterbrook	377

Chants.
Baptismal Chant	295
Mary at the Cross	75
The Silent Land	356

PLYMOUTH COLLECTION.

DARIEN. L. M.   L. MASON.

1. Sweet is the work, my God, my King, To praise Thy name, give thanks, and sing; To show Thy love by morning light, And talk of all Thy truth at night.

1. L. M.

2. Sweet is the day of sacred rest,
No mortal care shall seize my breast;
O, may my heart in tune be found,
Like David's harp, of solemn sound!

3. My heart shall triumph in the Lord,
And bless His works, and bless His word;
Thy works of grace, how bright they shine;
How deep Thy counsels, how divine!

4. Fools never raise their thoughts so high;
Like brutes they live, like brutes they die;
Like grass they flourish, till Thy breath
Blasts them in everlasting death.

5. But I shall share a glorious part,
When grace hath well refined my heart,
And fresh supplies of joy are shed,
Like holy oil, to cheer my head.

6. Then shall I see, and hear, and know,
All I desired or wished below;
And every power find sweet employ
In that eternal world of joy.

                            WATTS.

2. L. M.

1. How pleasant, how divinely fair,
O, Lord of hosts, Thy dwellings are!
With long desire my spirit faints
To meet th' assemblies of Thy saints.

2. My flesh would rest in Thine abode,
My panting heart cries out for God;
My God, my King, why should I be
So far from all my joys and Thee!

3. Blest are the souls that find a place
Within the temple of Thy grace;
There they behold Thy gentler rays,
And seek Thy face, and learn Thy praise.

4. Blest are the men whose hearts are set
To find the way to Zion's gate:
God is their strength; and through the road
They lean upon their Helper, God.

5. Cheerful they walk with growing strength,
Till all shall meet in heaven at length;
Till all before Thy face appear,
And join in nobler worship there.

                            WATTS.

SOMERVILLE. L. M.
Templi Carmina.

1. My opening eyes with rapture see The dawn of Thy re-turning day; My thoughts, O God, as-cend to Thee, While thus my ear-ly vows I pay.

3. L. M.

1. My opening eyes with rapture see
   The dawn of thy returning day;
   My thoughts, O God, ascend to thee,
   While thus my early vows I pay.

2. Oh bid this trifling world retire,
   And drive each carnal thought away;
   Nor let me feel one vain desire—
   One sinful thought through all the day.

3. Then, to thy courts when I repair,
   My soul shall rise on joyful wing,
   The wonders of thy love declare,
   And join the strains which angels sing.

4. L. M.

1. Thine earthly Sabbaths, Lord, we love,
   But there's a nobler rest above;
   To that our longing souls aspire,
   With cheerful hope, and strong desire.

2. No more fatigue, no more distress,
   Nor sin, nor death shall reach the place;
   No groans shall mingle with the songs
   Which warble from immortal tongues;

3. No rude alarms of raging foes,
   No cares to break the long repose,
   No midnight shade—no clouded sun—
   But sacred, high, eternal noon.

4. Thine earthly Sabbaths, Lord, we love,
   But there's a nobler rest above;
   To that our longing souls aspire,
   With cheerful hope, and strong desire.
   DODDRIDGE.

5. L. M.

1. God in His temple let us meet;
   Low on our knees before Him bend;
   Here hath He fixed His mercy-seat;
   Here on His Sabbaths we attend.

2. Arise into Thy resting-place,
   Thou, and Thine ark of strength, O Lord!
   Shine through the vail, we seek Thy face;
   Speak, for we hearken to Thy word.

3. With righteousness Thy saints array;
   Joyful Thy chosen people be;
   Let those who teach and those who pray—
   Let all be holiness to Thee.
   MONTGOMERY.

6. L. M.

1. O sacred day of peace and joy,
   Thy hours are ever dear to me;
   Ne'er may a sinful thought destroy
   The holy calm I find in thee.

2. Dear are thy peaceful hours to me,
   For God has given them in his love,
   To tell how calm, how blest shall be
   The endless day of heaven above.

7. L. M.

1. Jesus, where'er Thy people meet,
There they behold Thy mercy-seat;
Where'er they seek Thee, Thou art found,
And every place is hallowed ground.

2. For Thou, within no walls confined,
Inhabitest the humble mind;
Such ever bring Thee where they come,
And going, take Thee to their home.

3. Great Shepherd of Thy chosen few!
Thy former mercies here renew;
Here to our waiting hearts proclaim
The sweetness of Thy saving name.
COWPER.

8. L. M.

1. Lord of the Sabbath and its light,
  I hail Thy hallowed day of rest;
It is my weary soul's delight,
  The solace of my care-worn breast.

2. Its dewy morn, its glowing noon,
  Its tranquil eve, its solemn night,
Pass sweetly; but they pass too soon,
  And leave me saddened at their flight.

3. Yet sweetly as they glide along,
  And hallowed tho' the calm they yield,
Transporting though their rapturous song,
  And heavenly visions seem revealed;—

4. My soul is desolate and drear,
  My silent harp untuned remains,
Unless, my Saviour, Thou art near,
  To heal my wounds and soothe my pains.

5. Oh! Jesus, let me ever hail
  Thy presence with the day of rest;
Then will Thy servant never fail
  To deem Thy Sabbath doubly blest.

9. L. M.

1. Another six day's work is done;
Another Sabbath is begun.
Return, my soul, enjoy the rest;
Improve the day thy God hath blest.

2. Come, bless the Lord, whose love assigns
So sweet a rest to wearied minds;
Provides an antepast of heaven,
And gives this day the food of seven.

3. O that our thoughts and thanks may rise
As grateful incense to the skies;
And draw from heaven that sweet repose
Which none but he that feels it knows.

4. This heavenly calm within the breast
Is the dear pledge of glorious rest
Which for the church of God remains,
The end of cares, the end of pains.

5. In holy duties let the day
In holy pleasures pass away.
How sweet a Sabbath thus to spend,
In hope of one that ne'er shall end.
STENNET.

10. L. M.

1. Be still! be still! for all around,
On either hand, is holy ground:
Here in His house, the Lord to-day
Will listen, while His people pray.

2. Thou, tossed upon the waves of care
Ready to sink with deep despair,
Here ask relief, with heart sincere,
And thou shalt find that God is here.

3. Thou who hast laid within the grave
Those whom thou hadst no power to save,
Believe their spirits now are near,
For angels wait while God is here.

4. Thou who hast dear ones far away,
In foreign lands, 'mid ocean's spray,
Pray for them now, and dry the tear,
And trust the God who listens here.

5. Thou who art mourning o'er thy sin,
Deploring guilt that reigns within,
The God of peace is ever near;
The troubled spirit meets Him here.

11. L. M.

1. Within Thy courts have millions met,
  Millions this day before Thee bowed;
Their faces heavenward were set,
  Their vows to Thee, O God! they vowed.

2. Still as the light of morning broke
  O'er island, continent, and deep,
Thy far-spread family awoke,
  Sabbath all round the world to keep.

3. From east to west the sun surveyed,
  From north to south, adoring throngs;
And still where evening stretched her shade,
  The stars came forth to hear their songs.

4. And not a prayer, a tear, a sigh,
  Hath failed this day some suit to gain;
To hearts that sought Thee Thou wast nigh,
  Nor hath one sought Thy face in vain.

5. The poor in spirit Thou hast fed,
  The feeble soul hath strengthened been,
The mourner Thou hast comforted,
  The pure in heart their God have seen.
MONTGOMERY.

BEETHOVEN, L. M. — Arranged by L. Mason.

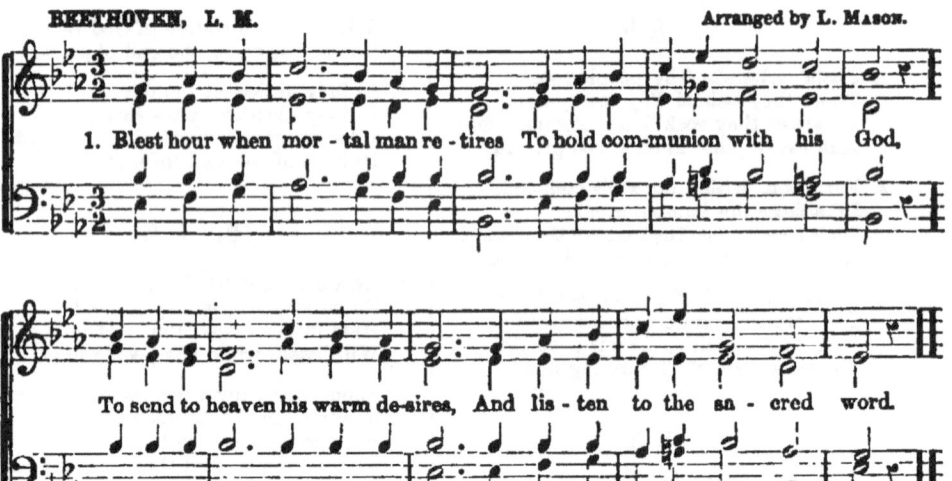

1. Blest hour when mortal man retires To hold communion with his God, To send to heaven his warm desires, And listen to the sacred word.

12. L. M.

2. Blest hour when earthly cares resign
   Their empire o'er his anxious breast,
   While all around the calm divine
   Proclaims the holy day of rest.

3. Blest hour when God himself draws nigh,
   Well pleased his people's voice to hear,
   To hush the penitential sigh,
   And wipe away the mourner's tear.

4. Blest hour, for where the Lord resorts—
   Foretastes of future bliss are given,
   And mortals find His earthly courts
   The house of God, the gate of Heaven.
   RAFFLES.

13. L. M.

1. How sweet to leave the world awhile,
   And seek the presence of our Lord!
   Dear Saviour! on thy people smile,
   And come, according to thy word.

2. From busy scenes we now retreat,
   That we may here converse with Thee:
   Ah! Lord! behold us at Thy feet;—
   Let this the "gate of heaven" be.

3. "Chief of ten thousand!" now appear,
   That we by faith may see Thy face:
   Oh! speak, that we Thy voice may hear,
   And let Thy presence fill this place.
   KELLY.

14. L. M.

1. When, as returns this solemn day,
   Man comes to meet his Maker, God,
   What rites, what honor shall we pay?
   How spread his sovereign name abroad?

2. From marble domes and gilded spires
   Shall curling clouds of incense rise,
   And gems, and gold, and garlands deck
   The costly pomp of sacrifice!

3. Vain, sinful man! creation's Lord
   Thy golden offerings well may spare,
   But give thy heart and thou shalt find
   Here dwells a God who heareth prayer.

4. O grant us, in this solemn hour,
   From earth and sin's allurements free,
   To feel Thy love, to own Thy power,
   And raise each raptured thought to
   Thee! MRS. BARBAULD.

15. L. M.

1. Another day has passed along,
   And we are nearer to the tomb,
   Nearer to join the heavenly song,
   Or hear the last eternal doom.

2. Sweet is the light of Sabbath eve,
   And soft the sunbeams lingering there;
   For these blest hours, the world I leave,
   Wafted on wings of faith and prayer.

3. The time how lovely and how still;
   Peace shines and smiles on all below—
   The plain, the stream, the wood, the hill—
   All fair with evening's setting glow.

4. Season of rest! the tranquil soul
   Feels the sweet calm, and melts to love—
   And while these sacred moments roll,
   Faith sees the smiling heaven above.

5. Nor will our days of toil be long,
   Our pilgrimage will soon be trod;
   And we shall join the ceaseless song—
   The endless Sabbath of our God.
   EDMESTON.

16. L. M.

1. Sweet Sabbath bells! I love your voice—
   You call me to the house of prayer;
   Oft have you made my heart rejoice,
   When I have gone to worship there.

2. But now, a prisoner of the Lord,
   His hand forbids, I can not go;
   Yet may I here His love record,
   And here the sweets of worship know.

3. Each place alike is holy ground,
   Where prayer from humble souls is [poured,
   Where praise awakes its silver sound,
   Or God is silently adored.

4. His sanctuary is the heart—
   There, with the contrite, will He rest;
   Lord, come, a Sabbath frame impart,
   And make Thy temple in my breast.
   SONGS IN THE NIGHT.

17. L. M.

1. Forth from the dark and stormy sky,
   Lord, to Thine altar's shade we fly;
   Forth from the world, its hope and fear,
   Saviour, we seek Thy shelter here:
   Weary and weak, Thy grace we pray;
   Turn not, O Lord! Thy guests away.

2. Long have we roamed in want and pain,
   Long have we sought Thy rest in vain;
   Wildered in doubt, in darkness lost,
   Long have our souls been tempest-tossed;
   Low at Thy feet our sins we lay;
   Turn not, O Lord! Thy guests away.
   WEBER.

18. L. M.

1. Lord! may Thy truth, upon the heart
   Now fall, and dwell as heavenly dew,
   And flowers of grace in freshness start
   Where once the weeds of error grew.

2. May prayer now lift her sacred wings,
   Contented with that aim alone
   Which bears her to the King of kings,
   And rests her at his sheltering throne.
   N. Y. COLL.

19. L. M.

1. While now upon this Sabbath eve,
   Thy house, Almighty God, we leave,
   'Tis sweet, as sinks the setting sun,
   To think on all our duties done.

2. Oh! evermore may all our bliss
   Be peaceful, pure, divine, like this;
   And may each Sabbath, as it flies,
   Fit us for joys beyond the skies.
   CHAPIN'S COLL.

20. L. M.

1. Dear is the hallowed morn to me,
   When Sabbath bells awake the day,
   And, by their sacred minstrelsy,
   Call me from earthly cares away.

2. And dear to me the wingéd hour
   Spent in Thy hallowed courts, O Lord!
   To feel devotion's soothing power,
   And catch the manna of Thy word.

3. And dear to me the loud Amen
   Which echoes through the blest abode,
   Which swells, and sinks, and swells again,
   Dies on the walls, but lives to God.

4. Oft when the world, with iron hands,
   Has bound me in its six days' chain,
   This bursts them, like the strong man's
   And lets my spirit loose again. [bands.

5. Go, man of pleasure, strike thy lyre,
   Of broken Sabbaths sing the charms;
   Ours be the prophet's car of fire
   That bears us to a Father's arms.
   CUNNINGHAM.

21. L. M.

1. Ere to the world again we go,
   Its pleasures, cares, and idle show,
   Thy grace, once more, O God, we crave,
   From folly and from sin to save.

2. May the great truths we here have heard—
   The lessons of Thy holy word—
   Dwell in our inmost bosoms deep,
   And all our souls from error keep.

3. O, may the influence of this day
   Long as our memory with us stay,
   And as an angel guardian prove,
   To guide us to our home above.

22. L. M.

1. Dismiss us with Thy blessing, Lord;
   Help us to feed upon Thy word;
   All that has been amiss, forgive,
   And let Thy truth within us live.

2. Though we are guilty, Thou art good;
   Wash all our works in Jesus' blood;
   Give every burdened soul release,
   And bid us all depart in peace.
   HART.

LANESBOROUGH. C. M.   Arranged by L. Mason.

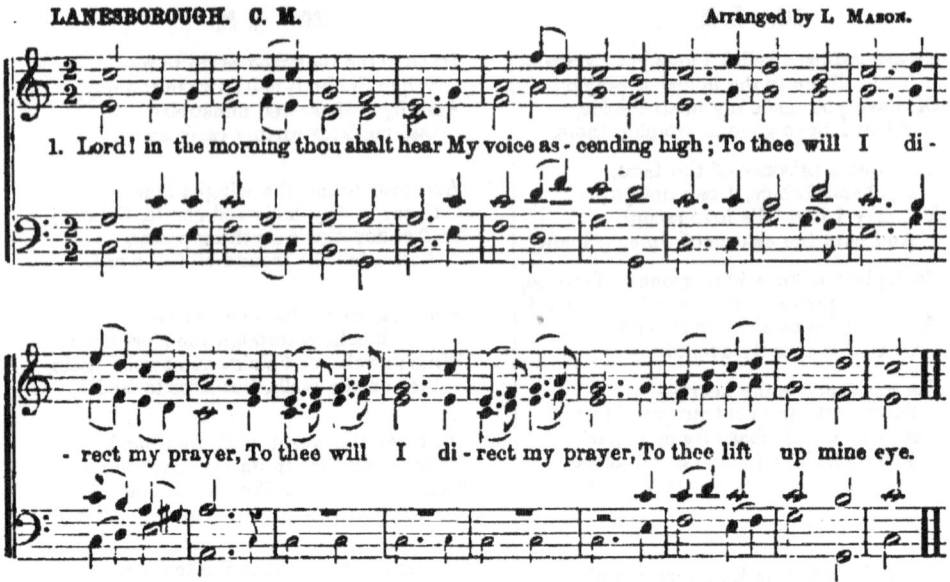

1. Lord! in the morning thou shalt hear My voice ascending high; To thee will I direct my prayer, To thee will I direct my prayer, To thee lift up mine eye.

23. C. M.

1. Lord! in the morning thou shalt hear
My voice ascending high;
To Thee will I direct my prayer,
To Thee lift up mine eye;

2. Up to the hills where Christ is gone
To plead for all his saints,
Presenting at his Father's throne
Our songs and our complaints.

3. Thou art a God before whose sight
The wicked shall not stand;
Sinners shall ne'er be Thy delight,
Nor dwell at Thy right hand.

4. But to Thy house will I resort,
To taste Thy mercies there;
I will frequent Thy holy court,
And worship in Thy fear.

5. Oh! may Thy spirit guide my feet,
In ways of righteousness;
Make every path of duty straight,
And plain before my face.   WATTS.

24. C. M.

1. Early, my God, without delay,
I haste to seek thy face;
My thirsty spirit faints away
Without Thy cheering grace.

2. So pilgrims on the scorching sand,
Beneath a burning sky,
Long for a cooling stream at hand,
And they must drink or die.

3. I've seen Thy glory and Thy power
Through all Thy temple shine:
My God, repeat that heavenly hour,
That vision so divine.

4. Not life itself, with all its joys,
Can my best passions move,
Or raise so high my cheerful voice,
As Thy forgiving love.

5. Thus, till my last expiring day,
I'll bless my God and King;
Thus will I lift my hands to pray,
And tune my lips to sing.   WATTS.

25. C. M.

1. This is the day the Lord hath made,
He calls the hours his own;
Let heaven rejoice, let earth be glad,
And praise surround the throne.

2. To-day he rose and left the dead,
And Satan's empire fell;
To-day the saints His triumph spread,
And all his wonders tell.

3. Hosanna to th' anointed King,
To David's holy Son;
Help us, O Lord—descend and bring
Salvation from Thy throne.

4. Blest be the Lord who comes to men
With messages of grace;
Who comes in God his Father's name
To save our sinful race.

5. Hosanna in the highest strains
The church on earth can raise;
The highest heavens in which he reigns
Shall give him nobler praise.   WATTS.

26. C. M.

1. WEARIED with earthly toil and care,
    The day of rest how sweet!
    To breathe the Sabbath's holy air,
    And sit at Jesus' feet.

2. What vain disturbing thoughts infest
    My bosom as their den;
    Oh that they knew the day of rest,
    Would they disturb me then?

3. Fain would I lay the burden down
    That wounds me with its weight,
    To gaze awhile at yonder crown,
    And press to heaven's gate.

4. I ask a foretaste of the peace,
    The rest, the joy, the love,
    Which, when their earthly Sabbaths cease,
    Await the saints above.
                    MRS. GILBERT.

27. C. M.

1. MY Sabbath suns may all have set,
    My Sabbath scenes be o'er,
    The place, at least, where we are met
    May know my steps no more;

2. The prophet of the cross may ne'er
    Again preach peace to me;
    The voice of interceding prayer,
    A farewell voice may be.

3. While yet the life-proclaiming word
    Doth through my conscience thrill,
    Breathe life; and lo! divinely stirred,
    I can repent, I will.

4. Thou that to will in me hast wrought,
    Haste, work in me to do;
    And, lest the purpose leave my thought,
    Now my whole heart renew.

5. Dying Redeemer, to thy breast,
    A dying wretch, I flee;
    Bid me be reconciled and blest,
    And born of God, through thee.
                    W. M. BUNTING.

28. C. M.

1. COME, dearest Lord, and feed thy sheep,
    On this sweet day of rest;
    O! bless this flock, and make this fold
    Enjoy a heavenly rest.

2. Welcome, and precious to my soul,
    Are these sweet days of love;
    But what a sabbath shall I keep
    When I shall rest above!

3. I come, I wait, I hear, I pray;
    Thy footsteps, Lord, I trace;
    Here, in thine own appointed way,
    I wait to see thy face.

4. These are the sweet and precious days
    On which my Lord I've seen,
    And oft, when feasting on his word,
    In raptures I have been.

5. O! if my soul, when death appears,
    In this sweet frame be found,
    I'll clasp my Saviour in mine arms,
    And leave this earthly ground.
                    MASON.

29. C. M.

1. WHEN the worn spirit wants repose,
    And sighs for God to seek,
    How sweet to hail the evening's close
    That ends the weary week!

2. How sweet will be the early dawn
    That opens on the sight,
    When first the soul-reviving morn
    Shall shed new rays of light.

3. Blest day! thine hours too soon will cease,
    Yet, while they gently roll,
    Breathe, heavenly Spirit, source of peace,
    A Sabbath o'er my soul.

4. When will my pilgrimage be done,
    The world's long week be o'er,
    That Sabbath dawn which needs no sun,
    That day which fades no more?
                    EDMESTON.

30. C. M.

1. BLEST day of God! most calm, most bright,
    The first and best of days;
    The laborer's rest, the saint's delight,
    The day of prayer and praise.

2. My Saviour's face made thee to shine;
    His rising thee did raise;
    And made thee heavenly and divine
    Beyond all other days.

3. The first-fruits oft a blessing prove
    To all the sheaves behind;
    And they who do the Sabbath love,
    A happy week will find.

4. This day I must to God appear;
    For, Lord, the day is thine;
    Help me to spend it in thy fear,
    And thus to make it mine.
                    CODMAN'S COLL.

MEAR. C. M.

1. How did my heart rejoice to hear My friends devoutly say, "In Zion let us all appear, And keep the solemn day."

31. C. M.

2. I love her gates, I love the road;
   The Church, adorned with grace,
   Stands like a palace, built for God,
   To show his milder face.

3. Up to her courts, with joys unknown,
   The holy tribes repair;
   The Son of David holds his throne,
   And sits in judgment there.

4. He hears our praises and complaints;
   And while His awful voice
   Divides the sinners from the saints,
   We tremble and rejoice.

5. Peace be within this sacred place,
   And joy a constant guest!
   With holy gifts and heavenly grace
   Be her attendants blest!

6. My soul shall pray for Zion still,
   While life or breath remains;
   There my best friends, my kindred, dwell,
   There God, my Saviour reigns.
                                    WATTS.

32. C. M.

1. O 'TWAS a joyful sound to hear
   Our tribes devoutly say,
   "Up, Israel, to the temple haste,
   And keep your festal day!"

2. At Salem's courts we must appear,
   With our assembled powers,
   In strong and beauteous order ranged,
   Like her united towers.   HEBER.

3. O pray we then for Salem's peace—
   For they shall prosp'rous be,
   Thou holy city of our God,
   Who bear true love to thee.
                            TATE AND BRADY.

33. C. M.

1. IN God's own house pronounce his praise
   His grace he there reveals;
   To heaven your joy and wonder raise,
   For there his glory dwells.

2. Let all your secret passions move
   While you rehearse his deeds;
   But the great work of saving love
   Your highest praise exceeds.

3. All that have motion, life, and breath,
   Proclaim your Maker blest;
   Yet, when my voice expires in death,
   My soul shall praise him best.
                                    WATTS.

34. C. M.

1. O GOD, by whom the seed is given,
   By whom the harvest blest; [heaven,
   Whose word, like manna showered from
   Is planted in our breast.

2. Preserve it from the passing feet,
   And plunderers of the air;
   The sultry sun's intenser heat,
   And weeds of worldly care!

3. Though buried deep, or thinly strewn,
   Do thou thy grace supply;
   The hope in earthly furrows sown
   Shall ripen in the sky.

35. C. M.

1. They pass refreshed the thirsty vale,
   The dry and barren ground,
   As through a fruitful, watery dale,
   Where springs and showers abound.

2. They journey on from strength to strength
   With joy and gladsome cheer,
   Till all before our God, at length,
   In Zion do appear.

3. For God the Lord, both sun and shield,
   Gives grace and glory bright;
   No good from them shall be withheld
   Whose ways are just and right.
   MILTON.

36. C. M.

1. How sweet, how calm, this Sabbath morn!
   How pure the air that breathes,
   And soft the sounds upon it borne,
   And light its vapor wreaths!

2. It seems as if the Christian's prayer,
   For peace, and joy, and love,
   Were answered by the very air
   That wafts its strain above.

3. Let each unholy passion cease,
   Each evil thought be crushed,
   Each anxious care that mars thy peace
   In Faith and Love be hushed.

37. C. M.

1. Come, Thou desire of all Thy saints!
   Our humble strains attend,
   While, with our praises and complaints,
   Low at Thy feet we bend.

2. How should our songs, like those above,
   With warm devotion rise!
   How should our souls, on wings of love,
   Mount upward to the skies!

3. Come, Lord! Thy love alone can raise
   In us the heavenly flame;
   Then shall our lips resound Thy praise,
   Our hearts adore Thy name.

4. Dear Saviour! let Thy glory shine
   And fill Thy dwellings here,
   Till life, and love, and joy divine
   A heaven on earth appear.

5. Then shall our hearts enraptured say,
   Come, great Redeemer! come,
   And bring the bright, the glorious day,
   That calls Thy children home.
   MRS. STEELE.

38. C. M.

1. With His rich gifts, the heavenly Dove
   Descends, and fills the place;
   While Christ reveals his wondrous love,
   And sheds abroad his grace.

2. My heart and flesh cry out for Thee
   While far from thine abode;
   When shall I tread Thy courts, and see
   My Saviour and my God?

3. To sit one day beneath Thine eye,
   And hear Thy gracious voice,
   Exceeds a whole eternity
   Employed in carnal joys.

4. Lord! at Thy threshhold I would wait,
   While Jesus is within,
   Rather than fill a throne of state,
   Or live in tents of sin.

5. Could I command the spacious land
   And the more boundless sea,
   For one blest hour at Thy right hand
   I'd give them both away.
   WATTS.

39. C. M.

1. Here cares and angry passions cease,
   For saints together meet
   To spend an hour of prayer and peace
   At their Redeemer's feet.

2. No sculptured wonders meet the sight,
   Nor pictured saints appear,
   Nor storied window's gorgeous light,
   For God himself is here.

3. And here are comrades in the war
   With Satan and with sin,
   Who now in God's own favor share,
   And soon their heaven will win.

4. Glory to God! who deigns to bless
   This consecrated day,
   Unfolds his wondrous promises
   And makes it sweet to pray.

5. Glory to God! who deigns to hear
   The humblest sigh we raise,
   And answers every heart-felt prayer,
   And hears our hymn of praise.
   NOEL'S COLL.

SABBATH AND SANCTUARY.

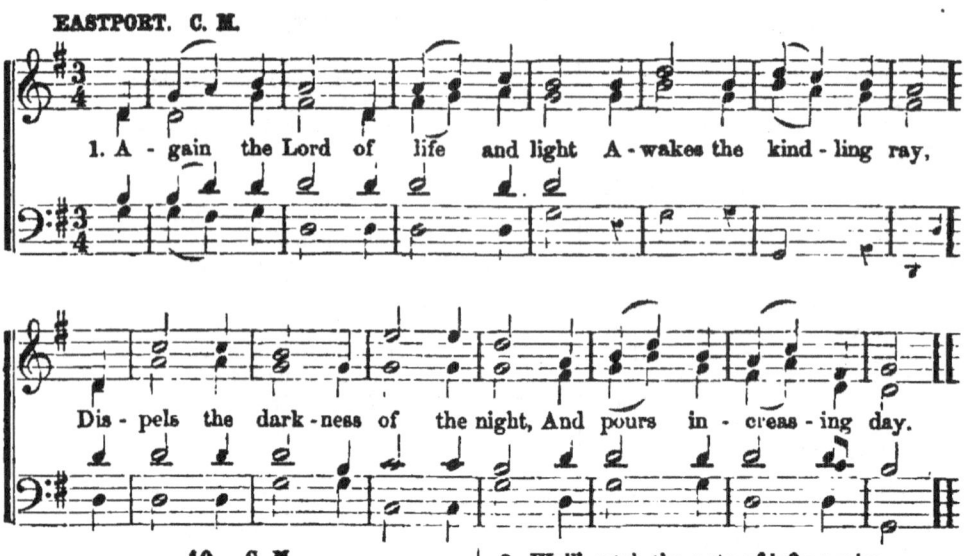

EASTPORT. C. M.

1. A-gain the Lord of life and light A-wakes the kind-ling ray, Dis-pels the dark-ness of the night, And pours in-creas-ing day.

40. C. M.

1. AGAIN the Lord of life and light
Awakes the kindling ray,
Dispels the darkness of the night,
And pours increasing day.

2. O what a night was that which wrapt
A guilty world in gloom!
O what a sun which broke this day
Triumphant from the tomb!

3. The powers of darkness leagued in vain
To bind our Lord in death;
He shook their kingdom, when He fell,
By his expiring breath.

4. And now His conquering chariot wheels
Ascend the lofty skies;
Broken beneath his powerful cross,
Death's iron scepter lies.

5. This day be grateful homage paid,
And loud hosannas sung;
Let gladness dwell in every heart,
And praise on every tongue.

6. Ten thousand thousand voices join
To hail this happy morn,
Which scatters blessings from its wings
On nations yet unborn.

MRS. BARBAULD.

41. C. M.

1. AND now another week begins,
This day we call the Lord's;
This day He rose, who bore our sins—
For so His word records.

2. Hark, how the angels sweetly sing!—
Their voices fill the sky;
They hail their great victorious King,
And welcome him on high.

3. We'll catch the note of lofty praise;
May we their rapture feel;
Our thankful songs with their's we'll raise,
And emulate their zeal.

4. Come, then, ye saints! and grateful sing
Of Christ, our risen Lord—
Of Christ, the everlasting King—
Of Christ, th' incarnate word.

5. Hail, mighty Saviour! Thee we hail!
High on thy throne above;
Till heart and flesh together fail,
We'll sing thy matchless love.

KELLY.

42. C. M.

1. BLEST morning, whose young dawning rays
Beheld our rising God,
That saw him triumph o'er the dust,
And leave his dark abode.

2. In the cold prison of the tomb
The dead Redeemer lay,
Till the revolving skies had brought
The third, th' appointed day.

3. Hell and the grave unite their force
To hold our Lord, in vain;
The sleeping conqueror arose,
And burst their feeble chain.

4. To Thy great name, almighty Lord,
These sacred hours we pay,
And loud hosannas shall proclaim
The triumph of the day.

5. Salvation and immortal praise
To our victorious King!
Let heaven and earth, and rocks and seas,
With glad hosannas ring.

WATTS.

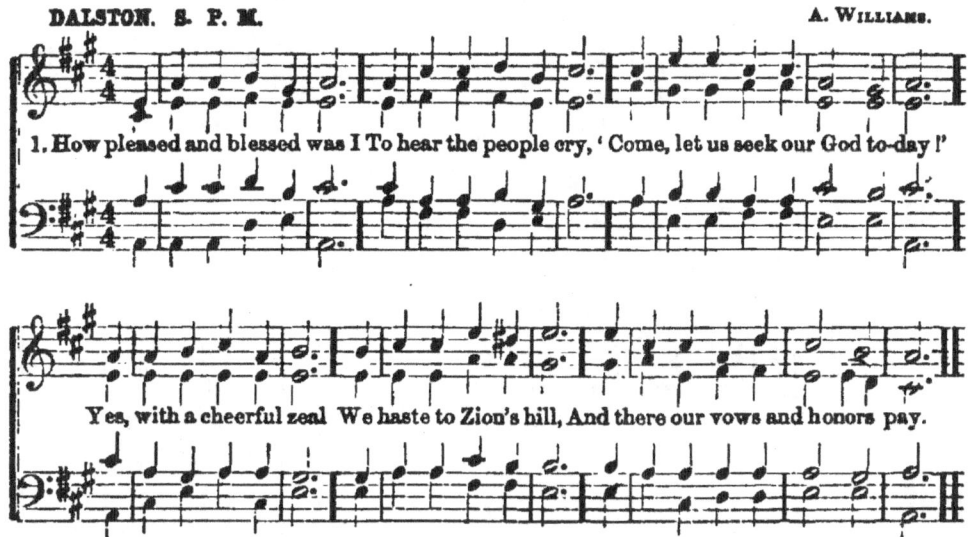

DALSTON. S. P. M.   A. WILLIAMS.

1. How pleased and blessed was I To hear the people cry, 'Come, let us seek our God to-day!'
Yes, with a cheerful zeal We haste to Zion's hill, And there our vows and honors pay.

43. S. P. M.

1. How pleased and blessed was I
 To hear the people cry—
   'Come, let us seek our God to-day!'
 Yes, with a cheerful zeal
 We haste to Zion's hill,
   And there our vows and honors pay.

2. Zion, thrice happy place,
 Adorned with wondrous grace,   [round.
   And walls of strength embrace thee
 In thee our tribes appear
 To pray, and praise, and hear
   The sacred Gospel's joyful sound.

3. May peace attend thy gate,
 And joy within thee wait
   To bless the soul of every guest:
 The man that seeks thy peace,
 And wishes thine increase,
   A thousand blessings on him rest!

4. My tongue repeats her vows—
 'Peace to this sacred house!'
   For here my friends and kindred dwell:
 And since my glorious God
 Makes thee his blest abode
   My soul shall ever love thee well.
                          WATTS.

DOXOLOGY. C. M.

To Father, Son, and Holy Ghost,
 One God, whom we adore,
Be glory as it was, is now,
 And shall be evermore.

44. S. P. M.

1. THE Lord Jehovah reigns,
 And royal state maintains,
   His head with awful glories crowned;
 Arrayed in robes of light,
 Begirt with sovereign might,
   And rays of majesty around.

2. Upheld by thy commands,
 The world securely stands,
   And skies and stars obey thy word;
 Thy throne was fixed on high
 Before the starry sky;
   Eternal is thy kingdom, Lord!

3. In vain the noisy crowd,
 Like billows fierce and loud,
   Against thine empire rage and roar;
 In vain, with angry spite,
 The surly nations fight,
   And dash like waves against the shore.

4. Let floods and nations rage,
 And all their powers engage—
   Let swelling tides assault the sky—
 The terrors of thy frown
 Shall beat their madness down;
   Thy throne forever stands on high.

5. Thy promises are true;
 Thy grace is ever new;   [move;
   There fixed, thy church shall ne'er re-
 Thy saints, with holy fear,
 Shall in thy courts appear,
   And sing thine everlasting love.
                          WATTS.

SHIELAND. S. M.   Stanley.

1. Welcome, sweet day of rest, That saw the Lord arise; Welcome to this reviving breast, And these rejoicing eyes.

45. S. M.

1. WELCOME, sweet day of rest,
   That saw the Lord arise,
   Welcome to this reviving breast,
   And these rejoicing eyes.

2. The King himself comes near,
   And feasts his saints to-day;
   Here may we sit, and see Him here,
   And love, and praise, and pray.

3. One day, amid the place
   Where God, my God, hath been,
   Is sweeter than ten thousand days
   Within the tents of sin.

4. My willing soul would stay
   In such a frame as this,
   And sit and sing herself away
   To everlasting bliss.
                   WATTS.

46. S. M.

1. BEHOLD, the morning sun
   Begins his glorious way;
   His beams through all the nations run,
   And life and light convey.

2. But where the Gospel comes,
   It spreads diviner light;
   It calls dead sinners from their tombs,
   And gives the blind their sight.

3. How perfect is Thy word!
   And all Thy judgments just!
   For ever sure Thy promise, Lord,
   And we securely trust.

4. My gracious God, how plain
   Are Thy directions given!
   O may I never read in vain,
   But find the path to heaven.
                   WATTS.

47. S. M.

1. SWEET is the task, O Lord,
   Thy glorious acts to sing,
   To praise Thy name, and hear Thy word,
   And grateful offerings bring.

2. Sweet, at the dawning hour,
   Thy boundless love to tell;
   And when the night-wind shuts the flower,
   Still on the theme to dwell.

3. Sweet, on this day of rest,
   To join in heart and voice
   With those who love and serve Thee best,
   And in Thy name rejoice.

4. To songs of praise and joy
   Be every Sabbath given,
   That such may be our best employ
   Eternally in heaven.
              SPIRIT OF THE PSALMS.

48. S. M.

1. Our willing feet shall stand
    Within the temple-door,
While young and old, in many a band,
    Shall throng the sacred floor.

2. Thither the tribes repair,
    Where all are wont to meet,
And, joyful in the house of prayer,
    Bend at Thy mercy-seat.

3. Within these walls may peace
    And harmony be found;
Zion, in all thy palaces,
    Prosperity abound!

4. For friends and brethren dear,
    Our prayer shall never cease;
Oft as they meet for worship here,
    God send His people peace.
                                MONTGOMERY.

49. S. M.

1. Lord, at this closing hour,
    Establish every heart
Upon Thy word of truth and power,
    To keep us when we part.

2. Peace to our brethren give;
    Fill all our hearts with love;
In faith and patience may we live,
    And seek our rest above.

3. Through changes, bright or drear
    We would Thy will pursue;
And toil to spread Thy kingdom here
    Till we its glory view.

4. To God, the Only Wise,
    In every age adored,
Let glory from the church arise
    Through Jesus Christ our Lord.
                                E. T. FITCH.

50. C. M.*

1. How blest Thy creature is, O God,
    When, with a single eye,
He views the luster of Thy word,
    The day-spring from on high!

2. Through all the storms that veil the skies,
    And frown on earthly things,
The Sun of Righteousness doth rise,
    With healing on His wings.

3. The soul, a dreary province once
    Of Satan's dark domain,
Feels a new empire formed within,
    And owns a heavenly reign.

4. The glorious orb, whose golden beams
    The fruitful year control,
Since first, obedient to Thy word,
    He started from the goal,

5. Has cheered the nations with the joys
    His orient rays impart;
But Jesus! 't is Thy light alone
    Can shine upon the heart.
                                COWPER.

51. S. M.

1. Come to the house of prayer!
    O thou afflicted, come;
The God of peace shall meet thee there;
    He makes that house His home.

2. Come to the house of praise!
    Ye who are happy now,
In sweet accord your voices raise,
    In kindred homage bow.

3. Ye aged, hither come!
    For ye have felt His love;
Soon shall your trembling tongues be dumb—
    Your lips forget to move.

4. Ye young! before His throne,
    Come, bow; your voices raise;
Let not your hearts His praise disown,
    Who gives the power to praise.

5. Thou, whose benignant eye
    In mercy looks on all,
Who seest the tear of misery,
    And hear'st the mourner's call,

6. Up to Thy dwelling-place
    Bear our frail spirits on,
Till they outstrip time's tardy pace,
    And heaven on earth be won.
                                E. TAYLOR.

DOXOLOGY. S. M.

Ye angels round the throne,
    And saints that dwell below,
Adore the Father, love the Son,
    And bless the Spirit, too.

* May be sung to Eastport page 10.

SABBATH AND SANCTUARY.

52. 7s.

1. SAFELY through another week
  God has brought us on our way;
  Let us now a blessing seek,
  Waiting in His courts to-day:
  Day of all the week the best,
  Emblem of eternal rest.

2. While we seek supplies of grace,
  Through the dear Redeemer's name,
  Show thy reconciling face—
  Take away our sin and shame;
  From our worldly cares set free—
  May we rest this day in Thee.

3. Here we come Thy name to praise;
  Let us feel Thy presence near;
  May Thy glories meet our eyes,
  While we in Thy house appear:
  Here afford us, Lord, a taste
  Of our everlasting rest.

4. May the Gospel's joyful sound
  Wake our minds to raptures new;
  Let Thy victories abound—
  Unrepenting souls subdue;
  Thus let all our Sabbaths prove
  Till we rest in Thee above. NEWTON.

53. 7s.

1. LIGHT of life, seraphic fire;
  Love divine, Thyself impart:
  Every fainting soul inspire;
  Enter every drooping heart:

2. Every mournful sinner cheer,
  Scatter all our guilty gloom;
  Father! in Thy grace appear,
  To Thy human temples come.

3. Come, in this accepted hour,
  Bring Thy heavenly kingdom in;
  Fill us with Thy glorious power,
  Rooting out the seeds of sin:

4. Nothing more can we require,
  We will covet nothing less:
  Be Thou all our heart's desire,
  All our joy, and all our peace.
  C. WESLEY.

54. 7s.

1. For the mercies of the day,
For this rest upon our way,
Thanks to Thee alone be given,
Lord of earth, and King of heaven.

2. Let these earthly Sabbaths prove
Foretastes of our joys above;
While their steps Thy children bend
To the rest which knows no end.

3. While to Thee our prayers ascend,
Let Thine ear in love attend;
Hear us when Thy Spirit pleads;
Hear, for Jesus intercedes.

4. While Thy word is heard with awe,
While we tremble at Thy law,
Let Thy gospel's wond'rous love
Every doubt and fear remove.

5. From Thy house when we return,
Let our hearts within us burn;
Then, at evening, we may say,
"We have walked with God to-day."
MONTGOMERY.

55. 7s.

1. Softly fades the twilight ray
Of the holy Sabbath day;
Gently as life's setting sun,
When the Christian's course is run.

2. Night her solemn mantle spreads
O'er the earth as daylight fades;
All things tell of calm repose
At the holy Sabbath's close.

3. Peace is on the world abroad;
'Tis the holy peace of God—
Symbol of the peace within,
When the spirit rests from sin.

4. Still the Spirit lingers near,
Where the evening worshipper
Seeks communion with the skies,
Pressing onward to the prize.

5. Saviour, may our Sabbaths be
Days of peace and joy in Thee,
Till in heaven our souls repose,
Where the Sabbath ne'er shall close.
S. F. SMITH.

56. 7s.

1. Now all chafing cares shall cease,
Now worn toil obtain release;
With the world we now have done,
Since "the Sabbath draweth on."

2. Early, at the break of day,
May we seek where Jesus lay;
Yet we know where He is gone,
Ere "the Sabbath draweth on."

3. At this hour, lo! from their place,
Myriad households seek Thy face;
We adore Thee not alone
That "the Sabbath draweth on."

4. When shall earth's blest Sabbath break?
When its rest all tribes partake?
See the brightening signal yon,
'Tis that "Sabbath drawing on."

5. And when nature sinks in death,
When heaves slow and faint our breath,
Brighter thou e'er day yet shone,
Heavenly "Sabbath" then draw on.
LEIFCHILD'S COLL.

57. 7s.

1. Thou who art enthroned above,
Thou by whom we live and move!
O how sweet, with joyful tongue,
To resound Thy praise in song!

2. When the morning paints the skies,
When the sparkling stars arise,
All Thy favors to rehearse,
And give thanks in grateful verse.

3. Sweet the day of sacred rest,
When devotion fills the breast,
When we dwell within Thy house,
Hear Thy word, and pay our vows;

4. Notes to heaven's high mansions raise
Fill its courts with joyful praise;
With repeated hymns proclaim
Great Jehovah's awful name.

5. From Thy works our joys arise,
O Thou only good and wise!
Who Thy wonders can declare?
How profound Thy counsels are!

6. Warm our hearts with sacred fire;
Grateful fervors still inspire;
All our powers, with all their might,
Ever in Thy praise unite.
SANDYS.

SABBATH AND SANCTUARY.

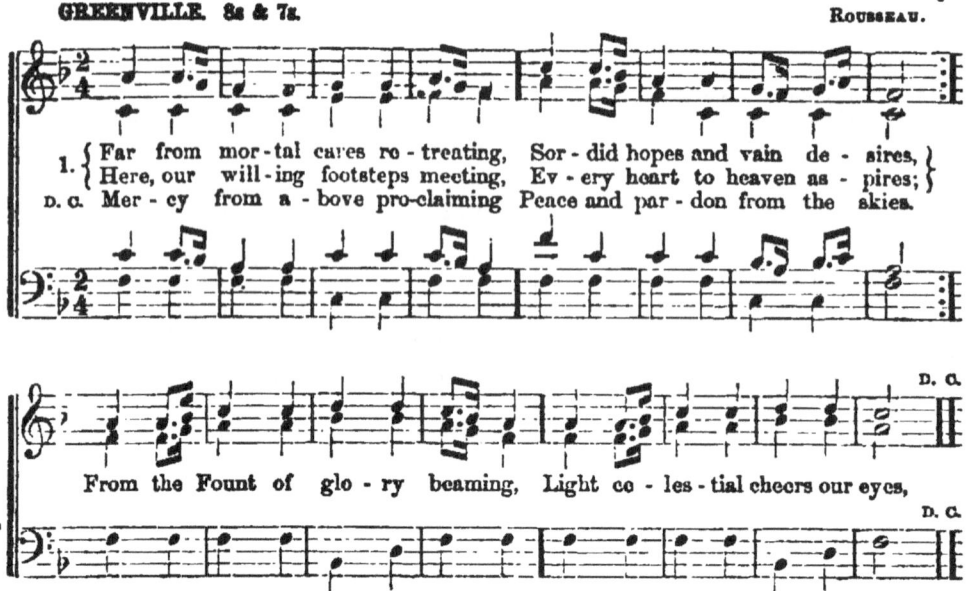

GREENVILLE. 8s & 7s.   ROUSSEAU.

1. Far from mor-tal cares re-treating, Sor-did hopes and vain de-sires,
Here, our will-ing footsteps meeting, Ev-ery heart to heaven as-pires;
D.C. Mer-cy from a-bove pro-claiming Peace and par-don from the skies.

From the Fount of glo-ry beaming, Light ce-les-tial cheers our eyes,

58.   8s & 7s.

1. Far from mortal cares retreating,
Sordid hopes and fond desires,
Here, our willing footsteps meeting,
Every heart to heaven aspires;
From the Fount of glory beaming,
Light celestial cheers our eyes,
Mercy from above proclaiming
Peace and pardon from the skies.

2. Who may share this great salvation?
Every pure and humble mind;
Every kindred, tongue, and nation,
From the dross of guilt refined:
Blessings all around bestowing,
God withholds His care from none;
Grace and mercy over flowing
From the fountain of His throne.

3. Every stain of guilt abhorring,
Firm and bold in virtue's cause,
Still Thy Providence adoring,
Faithful subjects to Thy laws;
Lord, with favor still attend us,
Bless us with Thy wondrous love;
Thou, our Sun, our Shield, defend us;
All our hope is from above.
                J. TAYLOR.

59.   8s & 7s.

1. May the grace of Christ, our Saviour,
And the Father's boundless love,
With the Holy Spirit's favor,
Rest upon us from above.

2. Thus may we abide in union
With each other and the Lord,
And possess, in sweet communion,
Joys which earth can not afford.
                NEWTON.

60.   8s & 7s.

1. Call Jehovah thy salvation,
Rest beneath th' Almighty's shade;
In His secret habitation
Dwell, nor ever be dismayed:
There no tumult can alarm thee,
Thou shalt dread no hidden snare,
Guile nor violence can harm thee,
In eternal safeguard there.

2. From the sword, at noonday wasting,
From the noisome pestilence,
In the depth of midnight, blasting,
God shall be thy sure defense:
Fear not thou the deadly quiver,
When a thousand feel the blow;
Mercy shall thy soul deliver,
Though ten thousand be laid low.

3. Since, with pure and firm affection,
Thou on God hast set thy love,
With the wings of His protection
He will shield thee from above;
Thou shalt call on Him in trouble,
He will hearken, He will save;
Here, for grief, reward thee double,
Crown with life beyond the grave.
                MONTGOMERY.

61. 8s & 7s.

1. WELCOME, welcome, quiet morning,
    Welcome is this holy day;
   Now the Sabbath morn, returning,
    Says a week has passed away.
   Let me think how time is passing;
    Soon the longest life departs;
   Nothing human is abiding
    Save the love of humble hearts.

2. Love to God, and to our neighbor,
    Makes our purest happiness;
   Vain the wish, the care, the labor,
    Earth's poor trifles to possess.
   Swift my life's vain dreams are passing;
    Like the startled dove they fly,
   Or the clouds, each other chasing
    Over yonder quiet sky.

3. Father, now one prayer I raise Thee;
    Give an humble, grateful heart;
   Never let me cease to praise Thee,
    Never from Thy fear depart;
   Then, when years have gathered o'er me,
    And the world is sunk in shade,
   Heaven's bright realm will rise before me;
    There my treasure will be laid.
                HYMNS FOR THE SANCTUARY.

62. 8s & 7s.

1. SEE the clouds upon the mountains,
    Rolling, rising, melt away,
   Light, forth flowing from its fountain,
    Pours an unobstructed ray.

2. So before Thy presence fading,
    Lord, may every shadow fly;
   Chase the gloom my soul invading,
    With the sunbeam of Thine eye.

3. Lo! it dawns, the Sabbath morning
    Streams with radiance all divine;
   Sanctify Thy courts adorning,
    Beautiful with grace they shine.

4. Holiness becomes Thy dwelling,
    Peerless Sovereign of the sky,
   Princely palaces excelling,
    Pomp of earthly majesty.

5. Rise, my soul, the day is breaking,
    Gladdened nature drinks the light;
   From the sleep of darkness waking,
    Put off all the clouds of night.

6. Take the rest this day is bringing,
    Best of all our earthly days,
   Enter thou His gates with singing,
    Tread the hallowed floor with praise.
                                COLLYER.

63. 8s, 7s & 4s.

1. LORD, dismiss us with Thy blessing,
    Fill our hearts with joy and peace;
   Let us each, Thy love possessing,
    Triumph in redeeming grace:
        O, refresh us,
    Traveling through this wilderness.

2. Thanks we give, and adoration,
    For Thy Gospel's joyful sound;
   May the fruits of Thy salvation
    In our hearts and lives abound;
        May Thy presence
    With us evermore be found.

3. Then, whene'er the signal's given
    Us from earth to call away,
   Borne, on angel's wings to heaven—
    Glad the summons to obey—
        May we ever
    Reign with Christ in endless day.
                                BURDER.

64. 8s & 7s.

1. LORD, with glowing heart I'll praise Thee,
    For the bliss Thy love bestows;
   For the pardoning grace that saves me,
    And the peace that from it flows:
   Help, O Lord, my weak endeavor,
    This dull soul to rapture raise:
   Thou must light the flame, or never
    Can my love be warm'd to praise.

2. Praise, my soul, the God that sought thee,
    Wretched wanderer, far astray;
   Found thee lost, and kindly brought thee
    From the paths of death away:
   Praise, with love's devoutest feeling,
    Him who saw thy guilt-born fear,
   And, the light of hope revealing,
    Bade the blood-stain'd cross appear.

3. Lord, this bosom's ardent feeling
    Vainly would my lips express:
   Low before Thy footstool kneeling,
    Deign Thy suppliant's prayer to bless:
   Let Thy grace, my soul's chief pleasure,
    Love's pure flame within me raise;
   And since words can never measure,
    Let my life show forth Thy praise.
                                S. F. KEY.

DOXOLOGY. 8s & 7s.

PRAISE the God of all creation;
    Praise the Father's boundless love;
Praise the Lamb, our expiation—
    Priest and King, enthroned above;
Praise the Fountain of salvation—
    Him by whom our spirits live;
Undivided adoration
    To the one Jehovah give.

DARWELL. H. M.

3. All hail, triumphant Lord! Heav'n with hosannas rings; While earth, in humbler strains, Thy praise responsive sings: Worthy art thou, who once wast slain, Thro' endless years to live and reign.

65. H. M.

1. AWAKE, our drowsy souls,
    And break each slothful band;
The wonders of this day
    Our noblest songs demand!
Auspicious morn, thy blissful rays
Bright seraphs hail in songs of praise.

2. At thy approaching dawn
    Reluctant death resigned
The glorious Prince of life,
    In dark domains confined:
Th' angelic host around him bends,
And mid their shouts the God ascends.

3. "All hail, triumphant Lord!"
    Heaven with hosannas rings;
While earth, in humbler strains,
    Thy praise responsive sings:
Worthy art thou, who once wast slain,
Through endless years to live and reign.

4. Gird on, great God, Thy sword,
    Ascend Thy conquering car,
While justice, truth, and love,
    Maintain the glorious war;
Victorious Thou, Thy foes shall tread,
And sin and hell in triumph lead.
E. SCOTT.

66. H. M.

1. ALL, from the sun's uprise
    Unto his setting rays,
Resound in jubilees
    The great Creator's praise.
Him serve alone; in triumph bring
Your gifts, and sing before his throne!

2. Man drew from man his birth;
    But God his noble frame,
Built of the ruddy earth,
    Filled with celestial flame.
His sons we are, by Him are led,
Preserved and fed with tender care.

3. Then to His portals press
    In your divine resorts;
With thanks his power profess,
    And praise him in his courts.
How good! how pure! His mercies last;
His promise past is ever sure.
SANDYS.

67. H. M.

1. REJOICE! the Lord is King!
    Your God and King adore;
Mortals! give thanks and sing,
    And triumph evermore:
Lift up the heart—lift up the voice—
Rejoice aloud, ye saints! rejoice.

2. His kingdom can not fail;
    He rules o'er earth and heaven;
The keys of death and hell
    Are to our Jesus given:
Lift up the heart—lift up the voice—
Rejoice aloud, ye saints! rejoice.

3. He all his foes shall quell—
    Shall all our sins destroy,
And every bosom swell
    With pure seraphic joy:
Lift up the heart—lift up the voice—
Rejoice aloud, ye saints! rejoice.

4. Rejoice in glorious hope;
   Jesus, the judge, shall come,
And take his servants up
   To their eternal home:
We soon shall hear th' archangel's voice;
The trump of God shall sound—Rejoice.
RIPPON.

68. H. M.

1. LORD of the worlds above,
   How pleasant and how fair
The dwellings of Thy love,
   Thine earthly temples are!
To Thine abode my heart aspires
With warm desires to see my God.

2. The sparrow for her young
   With pleasure seeks a nest;
And wandering swallows long
   To find their wonted rest;
My spirit faints, with equal zeal,
To rise and dwell among Thy saints.

3. O happy souls that pray
   Where God appoints to hear!
O happy men, that pay
   Their constant service there!
They praise Thee still; and happy they
That love the way to Zion's hill.

4. They go from strength to strength,
   Through this dark vale of tears,
Till each arrive at length,
   Till each in heaven appears.
O glorious seat, when God our King
Shall thither bring our willing feet.
WATTS.

69. H. M.

1. THE Lord Jehovah reigns;
   His throne is built on high;
The garments he assumes
   Are light and majesty:
     His glories shine
     With beams so bright,
     No mortal eye
     Can bear the sight.

2. The thunders of His hand
   Keep the wide world in awe;
His wrath and justice stand
   To guard His holy law:
     And where his love
     Resolves to bless,
     His truth confirms
     And seals the grace.

3. And can this mighty King
   Of glory condescend?
And will He write His name
   "My Father and my Friend?"
     I love His name,
     I love His word:
     Join, all my powers,
     And praise the Lord.
WATTS.

70. H. M.

1. WELCOME—delightful morn,
   Thou day of sacred rest;
I hail thy kind return;—
   Lord, make these moments blest:
From the low train of mortal toys,
I soar to reach immortal joys.

2. Now may the King descend
   And fill His throne with grace;
Thy scepter, Lord, extend,
   While saints address Thy face:
Let sinners feel Thy quickening word,
And learn to know and fear the Lord.

3. Descend, celestial Dove,
   With all Thy quickening powers;
Disclose a Saviour's love,
   And bless the sacred hours:
Then shall my soul new life obtain,
Nor Sabbaths be enjoyed in vain.
HAYWARD.

71. H. M.

1. ONE sole baptismal sign,
   One Lord, below, above—
Zion, one faith is thine,
   Only one watchword—love.
From different temples though it rise,
One song ascendeth to the skies.

2. Our sacrifice is one;
   One Priest before the throne—
The slain, the risen Son,
   Redeemer, Lord alone!
And sighs from contrite hearts that spring,
Our chief, our choicest offering.

3. Head of Thy church beneath!
   The catholic, the true,
On all her members breathe,
   Her broken frame renew!
Then shall Thy perfect will be done,
When Christians love and live as one.
G. ROBINSON.

SABBATH AND SANCTUARY.

OCEAN. 7s & 6s. *From the Psalmodist.*

1. The rosy light is dawning Upon the mountain's brow: It is the Sabbath morning, Arise, and pay thy vow, Arise, and pay thy vow.

72. 7s & 6s.

2. Lift up thy voice to heaven
   In sacred praise and prayer,
   While unto thee is given
   The light of life to share.

3. The landscape, lately shrouded
   By evening's paler ray,
   Smiles beauteous and unclouded
   Before the eye of day.

4. So let our souls, benighted
   Too long in folly's shade,
   By thy kind smiles be lighted
   To joys that never fade.

5. O see those waters streaming
   In crystal purity;
   While earth, with verdure teeming,
   Gives rapture to the eye.

6. Let rivers of salvation
   In larger currents flow,
   Till every tribe and nation
   Their healing virtues know.

T. HASTINGS.

CHROME. 11s & 8s.

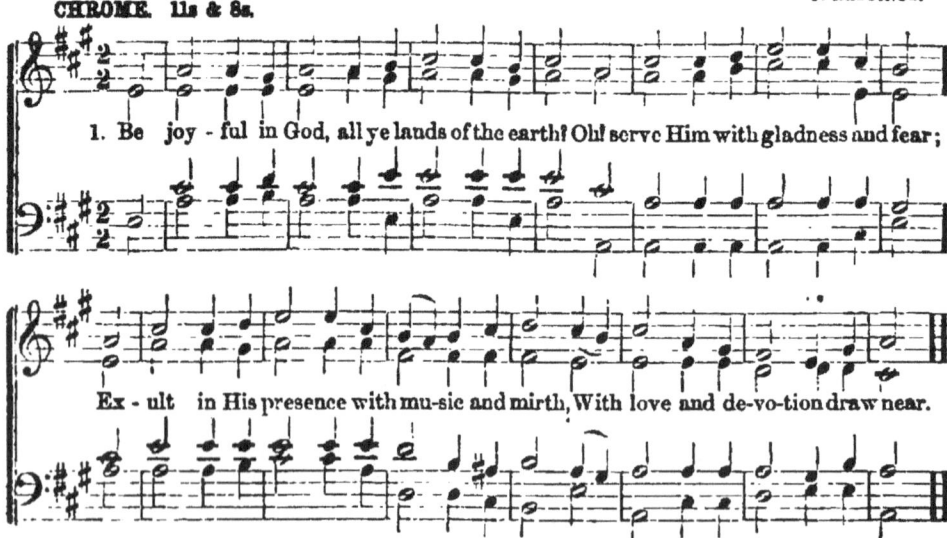

1. Be joyful in God, all ye lands of the earth! Oh! serve Him with gladness and fear; Exult in His presence with music and mirth, With love and devotion draw near.

73. 11s & 8s.

2. Jehovah is God, and Jehovah alone,
   Creator and Ruler o'er all;
   And we are His people—His sceptre we own;
   His sheep, and we follow His call.

3. Oh! enter his gates with thanksgiving and song,
   Your vows in His temple proclaim;
   His praise in melodious accordance prolong,
   And bless His adorable name

4. For good is the Lord, inexpressibly good,
   And we are the work of His hand;
   His mercy and truth from eternity stood,
   And shall to eternity stand.

MONTGOMERY.

THE BIBLE.

MERIDEN. C. M. Arranged from Thomas Clark of Canterbury by L. Mason.

1. What glory gilds the sacred page, Majestic, like the sun; It gives a light to every age; It gives, but borrows none, It gives, but borrows none, It gives, but, &c.

74. C. M.

2. The hand that gave it still supplies
   The gracious light and heat;
   Its truth upon the nations rise—
   They rise but never set.

3. Let everlasting thanks be Thine
   For such a bright display,
   As makes a world of darkness shine
   With beams of heavenly day.

4. My soul rejoices to pursue
   The steps of Him I love,
   Till glory breaks upon my view,
   In brighter worlds above.

   COWPER.

75. C. M.

1. How precious is the book divine,
   By inspiration given!
   Bright as a lamp its doctrines shine,
   To lead our souls to heaven.

2. O'er all the strait and narrow way
   Its radiant beams are cast;
   A light whose never weary ray
   Grows brightest at the last.

3. It sweetly cheers our fainting hearts
   In this dark vale of tears;
   Life, light, and comfort it imparts,
   And calms our anxious fears.

4. This lamp through all the dreary night
   Of life shall guide our way.
   Till we behold the clearer light
   Of an eternal day.

   RIPPON'S COLL.

76. C. M.

1. LAMP of our feet! whereby we trace
   Our path, when wont to stray;
   Stream from the Fount of heavenly grace!
   Brook by the traveler's way!

2. Bread of our souls! whereon we feed;
   True manna from on high!
   Our guide, our chart! wherein we read
   Of realms beyond the sky.

3. Pillar of fire, through watches dark!
   Or radiant cloud by day!
   When waves would whelm our tossing bark,
   Our anchor and our stay!

4. Childhood's preceptor! manhood's trust!
   Old age's firm ally!
   Our hope, when we go down to dust,
   Of immortality!

   BARTON.

77. C. M.

1. LADEN with guilt, and full of fears,
   I fly to Thee, my Lord;
   And not a ray of hope appears,
   But in Thy written word.

2. The volume of my Father's grace
   Does all my grief assuage;
   Here I behold my Saviour's face
   In almost ev'ry page.

3. This is the field where hidden lies
   The pearl of price unknown;
   That merchant is divinely wise
   Who makes the pearl his own.

4. This is the judge that ends the strife
   Where wit and reason fail;
   My guide to everlasting life
   Through all this gloomy vale.

   WATTS.

THE BIBLE.

ORION. L. M.   J. ZUNDEL.

1. The heavens declare thy glory, Lord! In every star thy wisdom shines; But when our eyes behold thy word, We read thy name in fairer lines; 2. The rolling sun, the changing light, And nights and days thy power confess; But the blest volume thou hast writ Reveals thy justice and thy grace.

78. L. M.

3. Sun, moon, and stars convey Thy praise
   Round the whole earth, and never stand;
So when Thy truth began its race
   It touched and glanced on every land.

4. Nor shall Thy spreading Gospel rest
   Till through the world Thy truth has run;
Till Christ has all the nations bless'd
   That see the light, or feel the sun.

5. Great Sun of Righteousness, arise;
   Bless the dark world with heavenly light;
Thy Gospel makes the simple wise,
   Thy laws are pure, Thy judgments right.

6. Thy noblest wonders here we view
   In souls renewed, and sins forgiven;
Lord, cleanse my sins, my soul renew,
   And make Thy word my guide to heaven.
                        WATTS.

79. L. M.

1. Upon the Gospel's sacred page
   The gathered beams of ages shine;
And, as it hastens, every age
   But makes its brightness more divine.

2. On mightier wing, in loftier flight,
   From year to year does knowledge soar;
And, as it soars, the Gospel light
   Adds to its influence more and more.

3. More glorious still as centuries roll, [furled,
   New regions blessed, new powers un-
Expanding with th' expanding soul,
   Its waters shall o'erflow the world—

4. Flow to restore, but not destroy;
   As when the cloudless lamp of day
Pours out its floods of light and joy,
   And sweeps each lingering mist away.
                        BOWRING.

80. L. M.

1. The starry firmament on high,
   And all the glories of the sky,
Yet shine not to Thy praise, O Lord,
   So brightly as Thy written word.

2. The hopes that holy word supplies,
   Its truths divine and precepts wise—
In each a heavenly beam I see,
   And every beam conducts to Thee.

3. Almighty Lord! the sun shall fail,
   The moon forget her nightly tale,
And deepest silence hush on high
   The radiant chorus of the sky—

4. But fixed for everlasting years,
   Unmoved amid the wreck of spheres,
Thy word shall shine in cloudless day
   When heaven and earth have passed away.
                       SIR R. GRANT.

GOD IN NATURE.

PILESGROVE. L. M. — N. MITCHELL.

1. Great Source of be-ing, and of love! Thou wa-terest all the worlds a-bove;
And all the joys we mor-tals know, From thine ex-haust-less fountain flow.

81. L. M.

2. A sacred spring, at Thy command,
From Zion's mount, in Canaan's land,
Beside Thy temple, cleaves the ground,
And pours its limpid stream around.

3. The limpid stream, with sudden force,
Swells to a river in its course:
Through desert realms its windings play,
And scatter blessings all the way.

4. Close by its banks, in order fair,
The blooming trees of life appear;
Their blossoms fragrant odors give,
And on their fruit the nations live.

5. Flow, wondrous stream, with glory crowned,
Flow on to earth's remotest bound;
And bear us, on thy gentle wave,
To Him who all thy virtues gave.
DODDRIDGE.

82. L. M. Peculiar. *

1. SINCE first Thy word awaked my heart
Like light new dawning o'er me,
Where'er I turn my eyes Thou art
All light and love before me.

2. Naught else I feel, or hear, or see,
All bonds of earth I sever;
Thee. Oh my Lord, and only Thee,
I live for, now, and ever.

3. Like him whose fetters dropped away
When light shone o'er his prison,
My soul, now touch'd by mercy's ray,
Hath from its chains arisen.

4. And shall the soul Thou bid'st be free
Return to bondage? Never!
Thee. Oh my God, and only Thee,
I live for, now, and ever.
MOORE.

83. L. M.

1. NATURE hath seasons of repose;
Her slumbering clouds and quiet sky;
And many a bright-faced stream that flows
Onward forever noiselessly.

2. The stormy winds are hushed to rest,
And hang self-poised upon their wings;
And, nursed on mother nature's breast,
Sweet flowers lie like sleeping things.

3. The ocean, that in mountains ran,
Spreads boundlessly without a wave;
And is it only said of man,
His peace is in the gloomy grave?

4. Oh! for the coming of the end,
The last long Sabbath-day of time
When peace from heaven shall descend
Like heaven's own light, on every clime.

5. When men in ships far off at sea
Shall hear the happy nations raise
The song of peace and liberty,
The chant of overflowing praise.

6. Mankind shall be one brotherhood;
One human soul shall fill the earth,
And God shall say, "The world is good
As in the day I gave it birth."

* Sung to Pilesgrove by slurring all the notes in measures (8) and (16).

GOD

NORFOLK. L. M. — From Root & Sweetser's Coll.

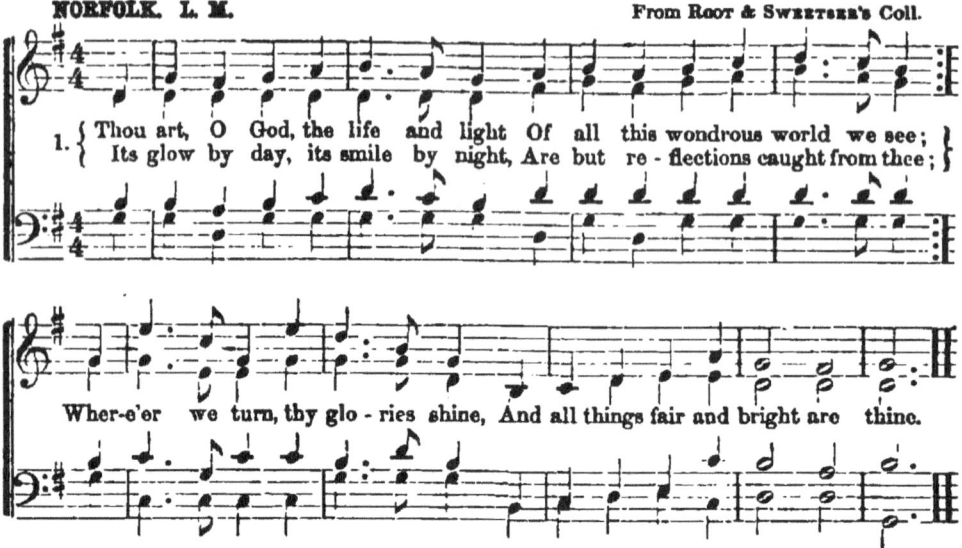

1. Thou art, O God, the life and light
Of all this wondrous world we see;
Its glow by day, its smile by night,
Are but reflections caught from thee;
Wher-e'er we turn, thy glories shine,
And all things fair and bright are thine.

84. L. M. 6 lines.

2. When day, with farewell beam, delays
Among the opening clouds of even,
And we can almost think we gaze,
Through opening vistas, into heaven—
Those hues that mark the sun's decline,
So soft, so radiant, Lord, are Thine.

3. When night, with wings of starry gloom,
O'ershadows all the earth and skies,
Like some dark, beauteous bird, whose plume
Is sparkling with unnumbered eyes—
That sacred gloom, those fires divine,
So grand, so countless, Lord, are Thine.

4. When youthful Spring around us breathes,
Thy Spirit warms her fragrant sigh;
And every flower that Summer wreathes
Is born beneath Thy kindling eye;
Where'er we turn, Thy glories shine,
And all things fair and bright are Thine.
MOORE.

85. L. M. 6 lines.

1. THE Lord my pasture shall prepare,
And feed me with a shepherd's care;
His presence shall my wants supply,
And guard me with a watchful eye:
My noonday walks he shall attend,
And all my midnight hours defend.

2. When in the sultry glebe I faint,
Or on the thirsty mountains pant,
To fertile vales and dewy meads
My weary, wandering steps he leads,
Where peaceful rivers, soft and slow,
Amid the verdant landscape flow.

3. Though in a bare and rugged way,
Through devious, lonely wilds I stray,
His bounty shall my pains beguile;
The barren wilderness shall smile,
With lively greens and herbage crowned,
And streams shall murmur all around.

4. Though in the paths of death I tread,
With gloomy horrors overspread,
My steadfast heart shall fear no ill,
For Thou, O Lord! art with me still;
Thy friendly crook shall give me aid,
And guide me through the dismal shade.
ADDISON.

86. L. M. 6 lines.

1. ABOVE—below—where'er I gaze,
Thy guiding finger, Lord, I view,
Traced in the midnight planets' blaze,
Or glistening in the morning dew;
Whate'er is beautiful or fair,
Is but Thine own reflection there.

2. I hear Thee in the stormy wind
That turns the ocean wave to foam;
Nor less Thy wondrous power I find
When summer airs around me roam;
The tempest and the calm declare
Thyself—for Thou art every where.

3. I find Thee in the noon of night,
And read Thy name in every star
That drinks in splendor from the light
That flows from mercy's beaming car:
Thy footstool, Lord, each starry gem
Composes—not Thy diadem.

IN NATURE.

PORTUGAL. L. M.   Thorley.

1. The spacious firmament on high, With all the blue, ethereal sky, And spangled heavens, a shining frame, Their great Original proclaim.

87. L. M.

1. The spacious firmament on high,
   With all the blue, ethereal sky,
   And spangled heavens, a shining frame,
   Their great Original proclaim.

2. The wearied sun, from day to day,
   Does his Creator's power display,
   And publishes to every land
   The work of an Almighty hand.

3. Soon as evening shades prevail,
   The moon takes up the wondrous tale,
   And nightly to the listening earth
   Repeats the story of her birth;

4. While all the stars that round her burn,
   And all the planets in their turn,
   Confirm the tidings as they roll,
   And spread the truth from pole to pole.

5. What though in solemn silence all
   Move round the dark, terrestrial ball?
   What though nor real voice nor sound
   Amidst their radiant orbs be found?

6. In reason's ear they all rejoice,
   And utter forth a glorious voice;
   For ever singing, as they shine—
   "The hand that made us is divine."
                         ADDISON.

88. L. M.

1. O Source divine, and Life of all,
   The Fount of being's wondrous sea!
   Thy depth would every heart appall,
   That saw not Love supreme in Thee.

2. We shrink before Thy vast abyss,
   Where worlds on worlds eternal brood;
   We know Thee truly but in this—
   That Thou bestowest all our good.

3. And so, 'mid boundless time and space,
   O, grant us still in Thee to dwell,
   And through the ceaseless web to trace
   Thy presence working all things well!

4. Nor let Thou life's delightful play
   Thy truth's transcendent vision hide;
   Nor strength and gladness lead astray
   From Thee, our nature's only guide.

5. Bestow on every joyous thrill
   Thy deeper tone of reverent awe;
   Make pure Thy children's erring will,
   And teach their hearts to love Thy law!
                         STERLING.

DOXOLOGY. L. M.

Praise God from whom all blessings flow;
Praise Him all creatures here below;
Praise Him above, ye heavenly host;
Praise Father, Son, and Holy Ghost.

STORRS. 7s.   J. ZUNDEL.

1. Source of being, source of light, With unfading beauties bright; Thee, when morning greets the skies, Blushing sweet with humid eyes; Thee, when soft, declining day Sinks in purple waves away; Thee, O parent, will I sing, To thy feet my tribute bring.

89. 7s. Double.

1. Source of being, source of light,
   With unfading beauties bright;
   Thee, when morning greets the skies,
   Blushing sweet with humid eyes;
   Thee, when soft declining day
   Sinks in purple waves away;
   Thee, O Parent, will I sing,
   To Thy feet my tribute bring!

2. Yonder azure vault on high,
   Yonder blue, low, liquid sky;
   Earth on its firm basis placed,
   And with circling waves embraced;
   All-creating power confess,
   All their mighty Maker bless;
   Shaking nature with Thy nod,
   Earth and heaven confess their God.

3. Source of light, Thou bid'st the sun
   On his burning axles run;
   Stars like dust around him fly,
   Strew the area of the sky;
   Fills the queen of solemn night
   From his vase her orb of light;
   Lunar luster, thus we see,
   Solar virtue shines by Thee.

4. Father, King, whose heavenly face
   Shines serene upon our race;
   Mindful of Thy guardian care,
   Slow to punish, prone to spare;
   We Thy majesty adore,
   We Thy well-known aid implore;
   Not in vain Thy aid we call,
   Nothing want, for Thou art all!

   WESLEY.

90. 7s.

1. Mighty One, before whose face
   Wisdom had her glorious seat,
   When the orbs that people space
   Sprang to birth beneath Thy feet!

2. Source of truth, whose rays alone
   Light the mighty world of mind!
   God of love, who from Thy throne
   Kindly watchest all mankind!

3. Shed on those who in Thy name
   Teach the way of truth and right,
   Shed that love's undying flame,
   Shed that wisdom's guiding light.

   BRYANT.

91. 7s.

1. Earth, with her ten thousand flowers,
Air, with all its beams and showers,
Ocean's infinite expanse,
Heaven's resplendent countenance;
All around, and all above,
Hath this record—God is love.

2. Sounds among the vales and hills,
In the woods and by the rills,
Of the breeze and of the bird,
By the gentle murmur stirr'd;
All these songs, beneath, above,
Have one burden—God is love.

3. All the hopes and fears that start
From the fountain of the heart;
All the quiet bliss that lies
In our human sympathies;
These are voices from above,
Sweetly whispering—God is love.

92. 7s.

1. To Thy pastures fair and large,
Heavenly Shepherd, lead Thy charge,
And my couch, with tenderest care,
Mid the springing grass prepare.

2. When I faint with summer's heat,
Thou shalt guide my weary feet
To the streams that, still and slow,
Through the verdant meadows flow.

3. Safe the dreary vale I tread,
By the shades of death o'erspread,
With Thy rod and staff supplied,
This my guard—and that my guide.

4. Constant to my latest end,
Thou my footsteps shalt attend;
And shalt bid Thy hallow'd dome
Yield me an eternal home.

MERRICK.

93. 7s. Double.

1. Let us with a joyful mind
Praise the Lord, for He is kind,
For His mercies shall endure,
Ever faithful, ever sure.
Let us sound His name abroad,
For of gods He is the God
Who by wisdom did create
Heaven's expanse and all its state;

2. Did the solid earth ordain
How to rise above the main;
Who, by His commanding might,
Filled the new-made world with light;
Caused the golden-tressèd sun
All the day his course to run;
And the moon to shine by night,
'Mid her spangled sisters bright.

3. All His creatures God doth feed,
His full hand supplies their need;
Let us therefore warble forth
His high majesty and worth.
He His mansion hath on high,
'Bove the reach of mortal eye;
And His mercies shall endure,
Ever faithful, ever sure.

MILTON.

94. 7s.

1. Father, they who Thee receive,
And in Thee begin to live,
Day and night they cry to Thee,
As Thou art, so let us be.

2. Fix, O, fix my wavering mind!
To the cross my spirit bind:
Earthly passions far remove;
Fill the soul with perfect love.

3. Who in heart on Thee believes,
He the promise now receives;
He with joy beholds Thy face,
Triumphs in Thy pardoning grace.

4. Boundless wisdom, power divine,
Love unspeakable, are thine:
Praise by all to Thee be given,
Sons of earth and hosts of heaven.

95. 7s.

1. Glorious in Thy saints appear;
Plant Thy heavenly kingdom here;
Light and life to all impart;
Shine on each believing heart;

2. And, in every grace complete,
Make us, Lord, for glory meet;
Till we stand before Thy sight,
Partners with the saints in light.

96. 7s.

1. All ye nations, praise the Lord,
All ye lands, your voices raise,
Heaven and earth with loud accord,
Praise the Lord, forever praise.

2. For His truth and mercy stand,
Past and present and to be,
Like the years of His right hand,
Like His own eternity.

3. Praise Him, ye who know His love,
Praise Him from the depths beneath;
Praise Him in the heights above;
Praise your Maker, all that breathe.

MONTGOMERY.

GOD

AURORA. C. P. M.   CH. BEECHER.

1. Be-gin, my soul, th' ex-alt-ed lay; Let each en-raptured thought o-bey, And praise th' Almighty name; Lo! heaven, and earth, and seas, and skies, In one melodious concert rise, To swell, ... th' in-spir-ing theme. To swell th' in-spir-ing theme, To swell th' in-spiring theme.

97. C. P. M.

1. BEGIN, my soul, th' exalted lay;
Let each enraptured thought obey,
   And praise the Almighty name;
Lo! heaven, and earth, and seas, and skies,
In one melodious concert rise,
   To swell th' inspiring theme.

2. Thou heaven of heavens, His vast abode,
Ye clouds, proclaim your Maker, God;
   Ye thunders, speak his power;
Lo! on the lightning's fiery wing,
In triumph rides th' eternal King;
   Th' astonished worlds adore.

3. Ye deeps, with roaring billows, rise
To join the thunders of the skies;
   Praise Him who bids you roll;
His praise in softer notes declare,
Each whispering breeze of yielding air,
   And breathe it to the soul.
                           OGILVIE.

98. C. P. M.

1. I SING of God, the mighty source
Of all things, the stupendous force
   On which all things depend; [eyes,
From whose right arm, beneath whose
All period, power, and enterprise
   Commence, and reign, and end.

2. The world, the clustering spheres, he made,
The glorious light, the soothing shade;
   Dale, plain, and grove and hill;
The multitudinous abyss,
Where nature joys in secret bliss,
   And wisdom hides her skill.

3. Tell them, I AM, Jehovah said
To Moses, while earth heard in dread,
   And, smitten to the heart,
At once above, beneath, around,
All nature, without voice or sound,
   Replied, O Lord, THOU ART!
                           SMART.

IN NATURE.

99. C. H. M.

1. Since o'er Thy footstool here below
   Such radiant gems are strown,
   O, what magnificence must glow,
   Great God, about Thy throne!
   So brilliant here these drops of light—
   There the full ocean rolls, how bright!

2. If night's blue curtain of the sky—
   With thousand stars inwrought,
   Hung like a royal canopy
   With glittering diamonds fraught—
   Be, Lord, Thy temple's outer vail,
   What splendor at the shrine must dwell!

3. The dazzling sun at noonday hour—
   Forth from his flaming vase
   Flinging o'er earth the golden shower
   Till vale and mountain blaze—
   But shows, O Lord, one beam of thine,
   What, then, the day where Thou dost shine.

4. O, how shall these dim eyes endure
   That noon of living rays!
   Or how our spirits, so impure,
   Upon Thy glory gaze!
   Anoint, O Lord, anoint our sight,
   And fit us for that world of light.

Doxology. C. P. M.

To Father, Son, and Holy Ghost,
The God whom Heaven's triumphant host,
    And saints on earth adore;
Be glory, as in ages past,
As now it is, and so shall last,
    When time shall be no more.

ORIEL. C. M.   CH. BEECHER.

100. C. M.

1. Praise ye the Lord, immortal choir
That fill the realms above;
Sing, for He formed you of His fire,
And feeds you with His love.

2. Thou restless globe of golden light,
Whose beams create our days,
Join with the silver queen of night,
To own your borrowed rays.

3. Thunder, and hail, and fires, and storms,
The troops of his command,
Appear in all your dreadful forms,
And speak His awful hand.

4. Winds, ye shall bear His name aloud
Through the ethereal blue;
For, when his chariot is a cloud,
He makes his wheels of you.

5. Shout to the Lord, ye surging seas,
In your eternal roar;
Let wave to wave resound his praise,
And shore reply to shore.

6. Thus, while the meaner creatures sing,
Ye mortals take the sound;
Echo the glories of your King
Through all the nations round.   WATTS.

101. C. M.

1. God, in the high and holy place,
Looks down upon the spheres;
Yet, in his providence and grace,
To every eye appears.

2. He bows the heavens; the mountains stand
A highway for our God;
He walks amidst the desert-land;
'T is Eden where He trod.

3. The forests in His strength rejoice;
Hark! on the evening breeze,
As once of old, Jehovah's voice
Is heard among the trees.

4. If God hath made this world so fair,
Where sin and death abound,
How beautiful beyond compare
Will paradise be found!   MONTGOMERY

IN NATURE.

BOYLSTON. S. M. — L. MASON.

1. My soul, repeat his praise, Whose mercies are so great; Whose anger is so slow to rise, So ready to abate.

102. S. M.

2. High as the heavens are raised
Above the ground we tread,
So far the riches of His grace
Our highest thoughts exceed.

3. His power subdues our sins,
And His forgiving love,
Far as the east is from the west,
Doth all our guilt remove.

4. The pity of the Lord,
To those that fear His name,
Is such as tender parents feel:
He knows our feeble frame.

5. Our days are as the grass,
Or like the morning flower:
If one sharp blast sweep o'er the field,
It withers in an hour.

6. But Thy compassions, Lord,
To endless years endure;
And children's children ever find
Thy words of promise sure.
WATTS.

103. S. M.

1. ALMIGHTY Maker, God!
How wondrous is Thy name!
Thy glories how diffused abroad
Through the creation's frame!

2. The lark mounts up the sky
With unambitious song,
And bears her Maker's praise on high
Upon her artless tongue.

3. My soul would rise and sing
To her Creator, too:
Fain would my tongue adore my King,
And pay the worship due.

4. And yet the songs I frame
Are faithless to Thy cause,
And steal the honors of Thy name
To build their own applause.

5. Create my soul anew,
Else all my worship's vain;
This wretched heart will ne'er be true
Untill 'tis formed again.
WATTS.

104. S. M.

1. Stand up, and bless the Lord,
Ye people of His choice;
Stand up, and bless the Lord your God,
With heart, and soul, and voice.

2. Though high above all praise,
Above all blessing high,
Who would not fear His holy name,
And laud, and magnify!

3. O for the living flame
From His own altar brought,
To touch our lips, our souls inspire,
And wing to heaven our thought!

4. God is our strength and song,
And His salvation ours;
Then be His love in Christ proclaimed
With all our ransomed powers.

5. Stand up, and bless the Lord;
The Lord your God adore;
Stand up, and bless His glorious name,
Henceforth, for evermore.
MONTGOMERY.

NOTTINGHAM. C. M.   I. CLARK.

1. Some seraph, lend your heavenly tongue, Or harp of golden string, That I may raise a lofty song To our eternal King.

105. C. M.

1. Some seraph, lend your heavenly tongue,
Or harp of golden string,
That I may raise a lofty song
To our eternal King.

2. Thy names, how infinite they be!
Great Everlasting One!
Boundless thy might and majesty,
And unconfined Thy throne.

3. Thy glory shines immensely bright;
Exhaustless is Thy grace;
Immortal day breaks from Thine eyes,
And Gabriel veils his face.

4. Thine essence is a vast abyss,
Which angels cannot sound;
An ocean of infinities
Where all our thoughts are drown'd.
WATTS.

106. C. M.

1. Beyond, beyond that boundless sea,
Above that dome of sky,
Farther than thought itself can flee,
Thy dwelling is on high;

2. Yet dear the awful thought to me,
That Thou, my God! art nigh;
Art here, and yet my laboring mind
Feels after Thee in vain—

3. Thee in these works of power to find,
Or to Thy seat attain;
Thy messenger—the stormy wind;
Thy path—the trackless main.

4. These speak of Thee with loud acclaim;
They thunder forth Thy praise—
The glorious honor of Thy name,
The wonders of Thy ways.

5. But Thou art not in tempest-flame,
Nor in the solar blaze.
We hear Thy voice, when thunders roll
Through the wild fields of air.

6. The waves obey Thy dread control;
Yet still Thou art not there:
Where shall I find Him, O my soul!
Who yet is every where?
CONDER.

107. C. M.

1. Great God, how infinite art Thou!
What worthless worms are we!
Let the whole race of creatures bow,
And pay their praise to Thee.

2. Thy throne eternal ages stood,
Ere seas or stars were made;
Thou art the ever-living God,
Were all the nations dead.

3. Eternity, with all its years,
Stands present in Thy view;
To Thee there's nothing old appears—
Great God, there's nothing new.

4. Our lives through various scenes are drawn,
And vexed with trifling cares;
While Thine eternal thoughts move on
Thine undisturbed affairs.

5. Great God, how infinite art Thou!
What worthless worms are we!
Let the whole race of creatures bow,
And pay their praise to Thee.   WATTS.

108. C. M.

1. 'Twas God who hurl'd the rolling spheres
   And stretch'd the boundless skies;
   Who form'd the plan of endless years,
   And bade the ages rise.

2. From everlasting is His might,
   Immense and unconfin'd:
   He pierces through the realms of light,
   And rides upon the wind.

3. He darts along the burning skies;
   Loud thunders round Him roar:
   All heav'n attends Him as He flies;
   All hell proclaims His pow'r.

4. Ye worlds, with ev'ry living thing,
   Fulfill His high command;
   Mortals, pay homage to your King,
   And own His ruling hand.
   WATTS.

109. C. M.

1. Great God, Thy penetrating eye
   Pervades my inmost powers;
   With awe profound my wandering soul
   Falls prostrate, and adores.

2. To be encompassed round with God,
   The holy and the just;
   Armed with omnipotence to save,
   Or crumble me to dust;

3. Oh, how tremendous is the thought!
   Deep may it be impressed;
   And may Thy Spirit firmly grave
   This truth within my breast.

4. By Thee observed, by Thee sustained,
   Should earth or hell oppose,
   I press with dauntless courage on
   To meet the proudest foes.

5. Begirt with Thee, my fearless soul
   The gloomy vale shall tread;
   And Thou wilt bind th' immortal crown
   Of glory on my head.
   E. SCOTT.

110. C. M.

1. Father! how wide Thy glory shines!
   How high Thy wonders rise! [signs—
   Known through the earth by thousand
   By thousand through the skies.

2. Those mighty orbs proclaim Thy power,
   Their motions speak Thy skill;
   And on the wings of every hour
   We read Thy patience still.

3. But when we view Thy strange design
   To save rebellious worms,
   Where vengeance and compassion join
   In their divinest forms.

4. Here the whole Deity is known;
   Nor dares a creature guess
   Which of the glories brightest shone,
   The justice, or the grace.

5. Now the full glories of the Lamb
   Adorn the heavenly plains:
   Bright seraphs learn Immanuel's name,
   And try their choicest strains.

6. Oh! may I bear some humble part,
   In that immortal song;
   Wonder and joy shall tune my heart,
   And love command my tongue.
   WATTS.

111. C. M.

1. Keep silence, all created things,
   And wait your Maker's nod;
   My soul stands trembling while she sings
   The honors of her God.

2. Life, death, and hell, and worlds unknown
   Hang on His firm decree;
   He sits on no precarious throne,
   Nor borrows leave to be.

3. Before His throne a volume lies,
   With all the fates of men;
   With every angel's form and size,
   Drawn by th' eternal pen.

4. His providence unfolds the book,
   And makes His counsels shine;
   Each opening leaf, and every stroke,
   Fulfills some deep design.

5. My God, I would not long to see
   My fate, with curious eyes—
   What gloomy lines are writ for me,
   Or what bright scenes may rise.

6. In Thy fair book of life and grace,
   O, may I find my name
   Recorded in some humble place,
   Beneath my Lord, the Lamb.
   WATTS.

ST. JOHN'S. C. M.

1. I sing th' al-might-y power of God, That made the moun-tains rise, That spread the flow-ing seas a-broad, And built the lof-ty skies.

112. C. M.

1. I SING th' almighty power of God,
   That made the mountains rise,
   That spread the flowing seas abroad,
   And built the lofty skies.

2. I sing the wisdom that ordained
   The sun to rule the day;
   The moon shines full at His command,
   And all the stars obey.

3. I sing the goodness of the Lord,
   That filled the earth with food;
   He formed the creatures with His word,
   And then pronounced them good.

4. Lord! how Thy wonders are displayed
   Where'er I turn mine eye!
   If I survey the ground I tread,
   Or gaze upon the sky!

5. There's not a plant or flower below
   But makes Thy glories known;
   And clouds arise, and tempests blow,
   By order from Thy throne.

6. Creatures that borrow life from Thee
   Are subject to Thy care;
   There's not a place where we can flee
   But God is present there.
   WATTS.

113. C. M.

1. LORD! when my raptured thought surveys
   Creation's beauties o'er,
   All nature joins to teach Thy praise,
   And bid my soul adore.

2. Where'er I turn my gazing eyes,
   Thy radiant footsteps shine;
   Ten thousand pleasing wonders rise,
   And speak their source divine.

3. On me Thy providence hath shone
   With gentle, smiling rays;
   Oh! let my lips and life make known
   Thy goodness and Thy praise.

4. All-bounteous Lord! Thy grace impart;
   Oh! teach me to improve
   Thy gifts, with ever-grateful heart,
   And crown them with Thy love.
   MRS. STEELE.

114. C. M.

1. How long, sometimes, a day appears!
   And weeks, how long are they!
   Months move on slow, as if the years
   Would never pass away.

2. But even years are passing by,
   And soon must all be gone;
   For day by day, as minutes fly,
   Eternity comes on.

3. Days, months, and years must have an end,
   Eternity has none;
   'Twill always have as long to spend
   As when it first begun.

4. Great God! a creature can not tell
   How such a thing can be,
   I only pray that I may dwell
   That long, long time with Thee.
   TAYLOR.

ATTRIBUTES.

TRIUMPH. H. M. — LOCKHART.

1. Sing to the Lord most high; Let every land adore; With grateful voice make known His goodness and his power: With cheerful songs Declare his ways, And let his praise inspire your tongues.

115. H. M.

2. Enter His courts with joy;
   With fear address the Lord;
   He formed us with His hand,
   And quickened by His word;
With wide command He spreads His sway,
O'er every sea and every land.

3. His hands provide our food,
   And every blessing give;
   We feed upon His care,
   And in His pastures live:
With cheerful songs declare His ways,
And let His praise inspire your tongues.

4. Good is the Lord our God,
   His truth and mercy sure;
   While earth and heaven shall last,
   His promises endure:
With wide command He spreads His sway,
O'er every sea and every land.

DWIGHT.

116. H. M.

1. COME, let us gladly sing
   To God, our Saviour-King;
   With thanks His presence seek,
   In psalms His praises speak;
He's God most high; let all draw nigh,
And crown Him—Lord of earth and sky.

2. He gave the mountains birth,
   He made this spacious earth;
   His are the sea and land—
   They rose at His command:
With reverence all before Him fall,
And on His name devoutly call.

3. Come, kneel before His throne,
   For He is God alone;
   We are the flock he leads—
   The sheep His bounty feeds:
To-day—to-day—His voice obey;
Grieve not the Holy Ghost away.

HATFIELD.

GOD.

HAMBURG. L. M. — Arranged by L. Mason.

1. Thro' every age, eternal God, Thou art our rest, our safe abode:
High was Thy throne ere heaven was made, Or earth Thy humble foot-stool laid.

117. L. M.

1. THROUGH every age, eternal God,
Thou art our rest, our safe abode:
High was Thy throne ere heaven was made,
Or earth Thy humble footstool laid.

2. Long hadst Thou reigned ere time began,
Or dust was fashioned into man;
And long Thy kingdom shall endure,
When earth and time shall be no more.

3. But man, weak man, is born to die,
Made up of guilt and vanity;
Thy dreadful sentence, Lord, was just—
"Return, ye sinners, to your dust."

4. Death, like an overflowing stream,
Sweeps us away; our life's a dream—
An empty tale—a morning flower,
Cut down and withered in an hour.

5. Teach us, O Lord, how frail is man;
And kindly lengthen out our span,
Till a wise care of piety
Fit us to die and dwell with Thee.
WATTS.

118. L. M.

1. YE nations round the earth, rejoice,
Before the Lord, your sovereign King;
Serve Him with cheerful heart and voice;
With all your tongues His glory sing.

2. The Lord is God; 'tis He alone
Doth life, and breath, and being give;
We are His work, and not our own;
The sheep that on His pastures live.

3. Enter His gates with songs of joy,
With praises to His courts repair;
And make it your divine employ
To pay your thanks and honors there.

4. The Lord is good, the Lord is kind,
Great is His grace, His mercy sure;
And the whole race of man shall find
His truth from age to age endure.
WATTS.

119. L. M.

1. O THOU, by long experience tried,
Near whom no grief can long abide;
My Lord, how full of sweet content
My years of pilgrimage are spent!

2. All scenes alike engaging prove,
To souls impressed with sacred love;
Where'er they dwell, they dwell in Thee,
In heaven, in earth, or on the sea.

3. To them remains nor place nor time;
Their country is in every clime;
They can be calm and free from care
On any shore, since God is there.

4. While place we seek, or place we shun,
The soul finds happiness in none;
But with our God to guide our way,
'Tis equal joy to go or stay.

5. Could I be cast where Thou art not,
That were indeed a dreadful lot;
But regions none remote I call,
Secure of finding God in all.

ATTRIBUTES.

120. L. M.

1. Jehovah reigns; He dwells in light,
Girded with majesty and might;
The world, created by His hands,
Still on its firm foundation stands.

2. But ere this spacious world was made
Or had its first foundation laid,
Thy throne eternal ages stood,
Thyself the ever-living God.

3. Like floods the angry nations rise,
And aim their rage against the skies;
Vain floods, that aim their rage so high;
At Thy rebuke the billows die.

4. Forever shall Thy throne endure;
Thy promise stands forever sure;
And everlasting holiness
Becomes the dwelling of Thy grace.
WATTS.

121. L. M.

1. With glory clad, with strength arrayed,
The Lord that o'er all nature reigns,
The world's foundation strongly laid,
And the vast fabric still sustains.

2. How sure established is Thy throne!
Which shall no change or period see;
For Thou, O Lord, and Thou alone,
Art God from all eternity.

3. The floods, O Lord, lift up their voice,
And toss the troubled waves on high;
But God above can still their noise,
And make the angry sea comply.
TATE AND BRADY.

122. L. M.

1. Lord, Thou hast searched and seen me through;
Thine eye commands, with piercing view,
My rising and my resting hours,
My heart and flesh, with all their powers.

2. My thoughts, before they are my own,
Are to my God distinctly known;
He knows the words I mean to speak
Ere from my opening lips they break.

3. Within Thy circling power I stand;
On every side I find Thy hand;
Awake, asleep, at home, abroad,
I am surrounded still with God.

4. Amazing knowledge, vast and great!
What large extent! what lofty height!
My soul, with all the powers I boast,
Is in the boundless prospect lost.

5. O, may these thoughts possess my breast,
Where'er I rove, where'er I rest,
Nor let my weaker passions dare
Consent to sin, for God is there. WATTS.

123. L. M.

1. What is our God, or what His name,
Nor men can learn, nor angels teach;
He dwells concealed in radiant flame,
Where neither eye nor thought can reach.

2. The spacious worlds of heavenly light,
Compared with Him, how short they fall!
They are too dark, and He too bright;
Nothing are they, and God is all.

3. He spake the wondrous word, and lo!
Creation rose at His command:
Whirlwinds and seas their limits know,
Bound in the hollow of His hand.

4. The tide of creatures ebbs and flows,
Measuring their changes by the moon:
No ebb His sea of glory knows;
His age is one eternal noon.

5. Then fly, my song, an endless round;
The lofty tune let angels raise:
All nature dwell upon the sound;
But we can ne'er fulfil the praise.
WATTS.

124. L. M.

1. Kingdoms and thrones to God belong;
Crown Him, ye nations, in your song;
His wondrous names and powers rehearse;
His honors shall enrich your verse.

2. He shakes the heavens with loud alarms;
How terrible is God in arms!
In Israel are His mercies known,
Israel is His peculiar throne.

3. Proclaim Him king, pronounce Him blest;
He's your defence, your joy, your rest;
When terrors rise, and nations faint,
God is the strength of every saint.
WATTS.

125. L. M.

1. Fairest of all the lights above, [spheres,
Thou sun, whose beams adorn the
And with unwearied swiftness move
To form the circles of our years—

2. Praise the Creator of the skies,
That dressed thine orb in golden rays;
Or may the sun forget to rise
If he forget his Maker's praise.

3. Ye twinkling stars, who gild the skies
When darkness has its curtains drawn,
Who keep your watch with wakeful eyes,
When business, cares, and day are gone—

4. Proclaim the glories of your Lord, [street,
Dispersed through all the heavenly
Whose boundless treasures can afford
So rich a pavement for His feet.

5. O God of glory, God of Love!
Thou art the sun that makes our days;
With all Thy shining works above,
Let earth and dust attempt Thy praise.
WATTS.

GOD.

EMMA. C. P. M.

1. The mighty God who rolls the spheres, And storm, and fire, and hail prepares, And guides this vast ma-chine; His powerful hand our life sustains, And scatters all those joys and pains That fill this checker'd scene, That fill this checker'd scene.

126. C. P. M.

1. THE mighty God who rolls the spheres,
And storm, and fire, and hail prepares,
   And guides this vast machine;
His powerful hand our life sustains,
And scatters all those joys and pains
   That fill this checkered scene.

2. His piercing eye at once surveys
Where thousand suns and systems blaze,
   And where the sparrow falls;
While seraphs tune their harps on high,
His ear attends the softest cry,
   When human misery calls.

3. Eternal God! who shall not fear,
And trust, and love with soul sincere,
   Thy awful, glorious name?
While man, Thy creature, swift decays,
Time has no measure for Thy days,
   Nor limit for Thy fame. J. TAYLOR.

127. C. P. M.

1. ALTHOUGH the vine its fruit deny,
The budding fig-trees droop and die,
   No oil the olives yield,

Yet will I trust me in my God,
Yea, bend rejoicing to His rod,
   And by His grace be heal'd.

2. Though fields, in verdure once array'd,
By whirlwinds desolate be laid,
   Or parch'd by scorching beam;
Still in the Lord shall be my trust,
My joy; for, though His frown is just,
   His mercy is supreme.

3. Though from the fold the flock decay,
Though herds lie famish'd o'er the lea
   And round the empty stall;
My soul above the wreck shall rise,
Its better joys are in the skies;
   There God is all in all.

4. In God my strength, howe'er distrest,
I yet will hope, and calmly rest,
   Nay, triumph in His love:
My ling'ring soul, my tardy feet,
Free as the hind He makes, and fleet,
   To speed my course above.
       H. U. ONDERDONK.

ATTRIBUTES.

WARWICK. C. M. — Stanley.

1. Come, ye that know and fear the Lord! And raise your souls above;
Let ev-ery heart and voice ac-cord, To sing that—God is love.

128. C. M.

1. Come, ye that know and fear the Lord!
   And raise your souls above;
   Let every heart and voice accord,
   To sing that—God is love.

2. This precious truth His word declares,
   And all His mercies prove;
   While Christ, th' atoning Lamb, appears,
   To show that—God is love.

3. Behold His loving-kindness waits
   For those who from Him rove,
   And calls for mercy reach their hearts,
   To teach them—God is love.

4. The work begun is carried on,
   By power from heaven above;
   And every step, from first to last,
   Proclaims that—God is love.

5. Oh! may we all, while here below,
   This best of blessings prove;
   Till warmer hearts, in brighter worlds,
   Shall shout that—God is love.

   G. BURDER.

129. C. M.

1. The Lord our God is full of might,
   The winds obey His will;
   He speaks, and, in His heavenly height,
   The rolling sun stands still.

2. Rebel, ye waves! and o'er the land
   With threatening aspect roar;
   The Lord uplifts His awful hand,
   And chains you to the shore.

3. Howl, winds of night! your force combine;
   Without His high behest
   Ye shall not, in the mountain-pine,
   Disturb the sparrow's nest.

4. His voice sublime is heard afar,
   In distant peals it dies;
   He yokes the whirlwind to His car,
   And sweeps the howling skies.

5. Ye nations! bend—in reverence bend;
   Ye monarchs! wait His nod,
   And bid the choral song ascend
   To celebrate your God.

   H. K. WHITE.

GOD.

OLD HUNDRED. L. M.

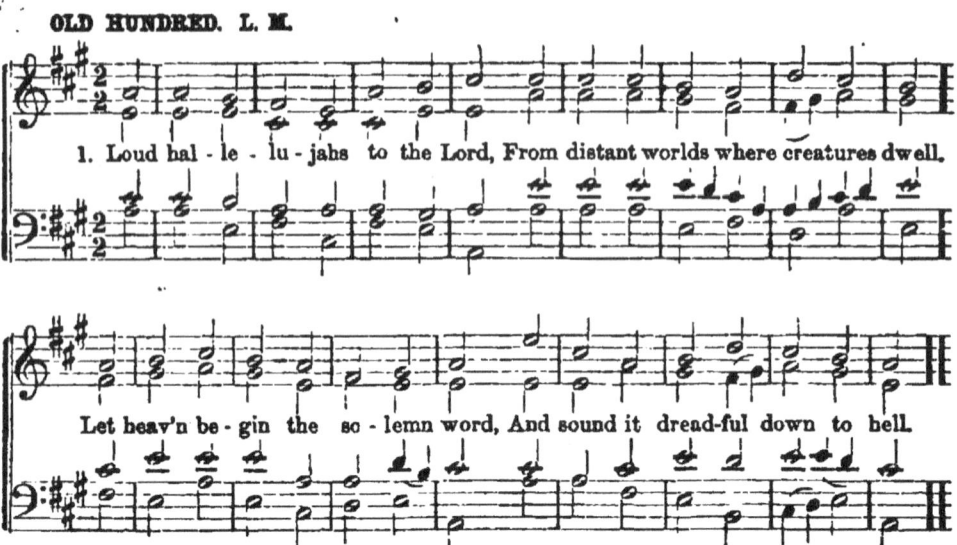

1. Loud hal-le-lu-jahs to the Lord, From distant worlds where creatures dwell.
Let heav'n be-gin the so-lemn word, And sound it dread-ful down to hell.

130. L. M.

1. Loud hallelujahs to the Lord, [dwell,
   From distant worlds where creatures
   Let heaven begin the solemn word,
   And sound it dreadful down to hell.

2. High on a throne His glories dwell,
   An awful throne of shining bliss:
   Fly through the world, O sun! and tell
   How dark thy beams compared to His.

3. Let clouds, and winds, and waves agree
   To join their praise with blazing fire;
   Let the firm earth and rolling sea,
   In this eternal song conspire.

4. Wide as His vast dominion lies,
   Make the Creator's name be known;
   Loud as His thunder shout His praise,
   And sound it lofty as His throne.

5. Jehovah—'t is a glorious word!
   O, may it dwell on every tongue!
   But saints, who best have known the Lord,
   Are bound to raise the noblest song.

6. Speak of the wonders of that love
   Which Gabriel plays on every chord;
   From all below, and all above,
   Loud hallelujahs to the Lord!
   WATTS.

131. L. M.

1. My God, my King, Thy various praise
   Shall fill the remnant of my days;
   Thy grace employ my humble tongue,
   Till death and glory raise the song.

2. The wings of every hour shall bear
   Some thankful tribute to Thine ear;
   And every setting sun shall see
   New works of duty, done for Thee.

3. Let distant times and nations raise
   The long succession of Thy praise;
   And unborn ages make my song
   The joy and labor of my tongue.

4. But who can speak Thy wondrous deeds?
   Thy greatness all my thoughts exceeds:
   Vast and unsearchable Thy ways,
   Vast and immortal be Thy praise.
   WATTS.

132. L. M.

1. Before Jehovah's awful throne,
   Ye nations bow, with sacred joy;
   Know that the Lord is God alone;
   He can create, and he destroy.

2. His sovereign power, without our aid,
   Made us of clay, and formed us men;
   And when, like wandering sheep, we strayed,
   He brought us to His fold again.

3. We are His people; we His care;
   Our souls, and all our mortal frame:
   What lasting honors shall we rear,
   Almighty Maker, to Thy name?

4. We'll crowd Thy gates, with thankful songs,
   High as the heaven our voices raise;
   And Earth, with her ten thousand tongues,
   Shall fill Thy courts with sounding praise.

5. Wide as the world is Thy command;
   Vast as eternity Thy love;
   Firm as a rock Thy truth shall stand,
   When rolling years shall cease to move,
   WATTS.

ADORATION.

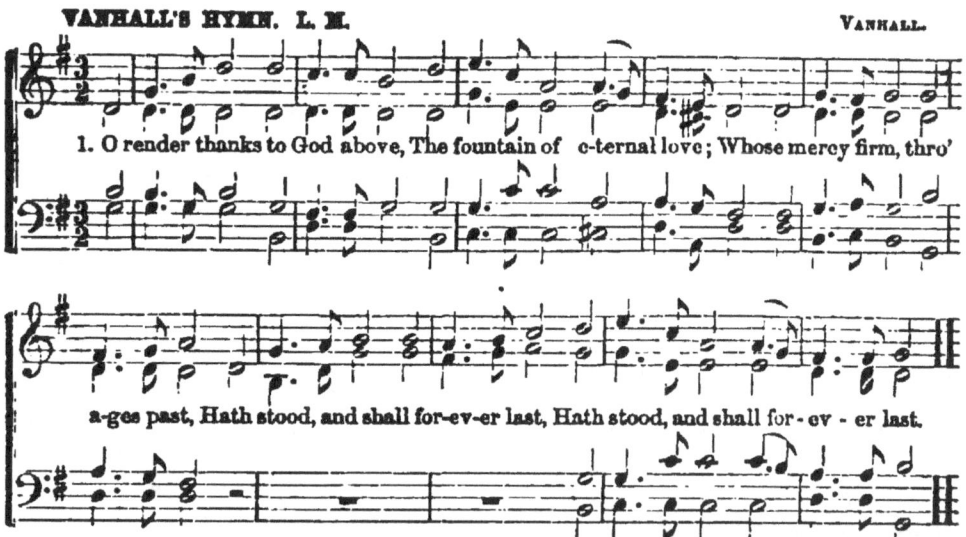

VANHALL'S HYMN. L. M. — Vanhall.

1. O render thanks to God above, The fountain of e-ternal love; Whose mercy firm, thro' a-ges past, Hath stood, and shall for-ev-er last, Hath stood, and shall for-ev-er last.

133. L. M.

2. Who can His mighty deeds express,
   Not only vast, but numberless?
   What mortal eloquence can raise
   His tribute of immortal praise?

3. Extend to me that favor, Lord,
   Thou to Thy chosen dost afford;
   When Thou return'st to set them free,
   Let Thy salvation visit me.

4. O render thanks to God above,
   The fountain of eternal love;
   His mercy firm, through ages past,
   Hath stood, and shall forever last.

134. L. M.

1. He reigns—the Lord, the Saviour reigns;
   Praise him in evangelic strains:
   Let the whole earth in songs rejoice;
   And distant islands join their voice.

2. Deep are His counsels, and unknown;
   But grace and truth support His throne:
   Though gloomy clouds His way surround,
   Justice is their eternal ground.

3. In robes of judgment, lo! He comes;
   Shakes the wide earth, and cleaves the tombs;
   Before Him burns devouring fire!
   The mountains melt, the seas retire!

4. His enemies, with sore dismay,
   Fly from the sight and shun the day:
   Then lift your heads, ye saints on high,
   And sing, for your redemption's nigh.
   WATTS.

135. L. M.

1. High on a hill of dazzling light
   The King of glory spreads His seat,
   And troops of angels, stretched for flight,
   Stand waiting round His awful feet.

2. Thy winged troops, O God of hosts,
   Wait on Thy wandering church below:
   Here we are sailing to Thy coasts;
   Let angels be our convoy too.

3. Are they not all Thy servants, Lord?
   At Thy command they go and come,
   With cheerful haste obey Thy word,
   And guard Thy children to their home.
   WATTS.

136. L. M.

1. Come, O my soul, in sacred lays,
   Attempt thy great Creator's praise:
   But, oh, what tongues can speak His fame!
   What mortal verse can reach the theme!

2. Enthroned amid the radiant spheres,
   He glory like a garment wears;
   To form a robe of light divine,
   Ten thousand suns around Him shine.

3. In all our Maker's grand designs,
   Omnipotence, with wisdom, shines;
   His works, through all this wondrous frame,
   Declare the glory of His name.

4. Raised on devotion's lofty wing,
   Do thou, my soul, His glories sing;
   And let His praise employ thy tongue,
   Till listening worlds shall join the song!
   BLACKLOCK.

GOD.

ELLENTHORPE. L. M.   Hymn 137.   LINLEY.

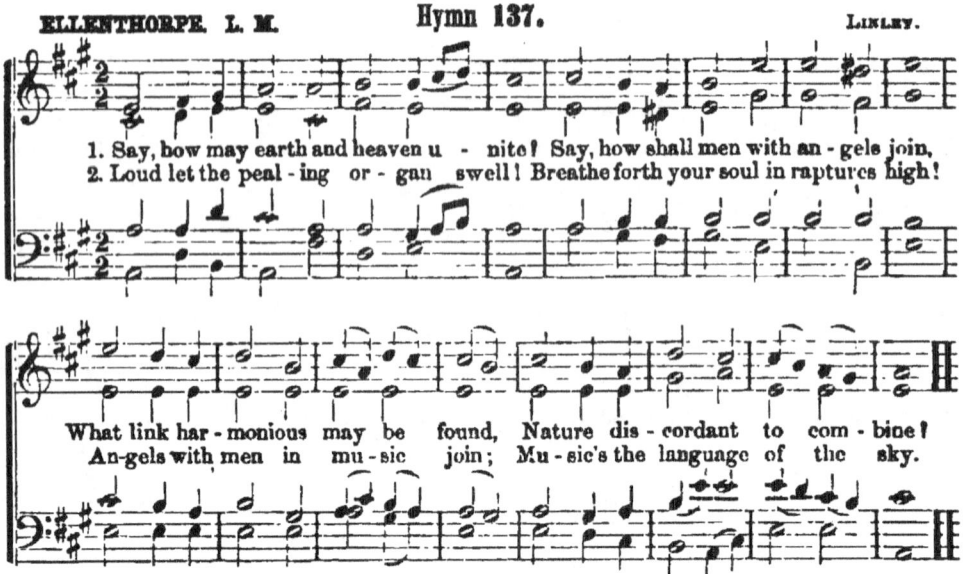

1. Say, how may earth and heaven unite! Say, how shall men with angels join, What link harmonious may be found, Nature discordant to combine!
2. Loud let the pealing organ swell! Breathe forth your soul in raptures high! Angels with men in music join; Music's the language of the sky.

138. L. M.

1. WITH all my powers of heart and tongue,
I'll praise my Maker in my song;
Angels shall hear the notes I raise,
Approve the song, and join the praise.

2. To God I cried when troubles rose;
He heard me, and subdued my foes:
He did my rising fears control,
And strength diffused through all my soul.

3. Amidst a thousand snares, I stand
Upheld and guarded by Thy hand;
Thy words my fainting word revive,
And keep my dying faith alive.

4. Grace will complete what grace begins,
To save from sorrow or from sins;
The work that wisdom undertakes,
Eternal mercy ne'er forsakes.

139. L. M.

1. O THE immense, the amazing height,
The boundless grandeur of our God,
Who treads the worlds beneath His feet,
And sways the nations with His nod!

2. He speaks, and lo! all nature shakes;
Heaven's everlasting pillars bow;
He rends the clouds with hideous cracks,
And shoots His fiery arrows through.

3. Let noise and flame confound the skies,
And drown the spacious realms below,
Yet will we sing the Thunderer's praise,
And send our loud hosannas through.

4. Celestial King! Thy blazing power
Kindles our hearts to flaming joys;
We shout to hear Thy thunders roar,
And echo to our Father's voice.

5. Thus shall the God our Saviour come,
And lightnings round His chariot play;
Ye lightnings, fly to make Him room!
Ye glorious storms, prepare His way!
                      WATTS.

140. L. M.

1. THE Lord, how wondrous are His ways!
How firm His truth! how large His grace!
He takes His mercy for His throne,
And thence He makes His glories known.

2. Not half so high His power hath spread
The starry heavens above our head
As His rich love exceeds our praise,
Exceeds the highest hopes we raise.

3. Not half so far has nature placed
The rising morning from the west
As His forgiving grace removes
The daily guilt of those He loves.

4. How slowly doth His wrath arise!
On swifter wings salvation flies:
And, if He lets His anger burn,
How soon His frowns to pity turn!
                      WATTS.

141. L. M.

1. Let God arise in all His might,
And put the hosts of hell to flight;
As smoke, that sought to cloud the skies,
Before the rising tempest flies.

2. He comes arrayed in burning flames;
Justice and vengeance are His names;
Behold His fainting foes expire
Like melting wax before the fire.

3. He rides and thunders through the sky;
His name, Jehovah, sounds on high;
Sing to His name, ye sons of grace;
Ye saints, rejoice before His face.

4. The widow and the fatherless
Fly to His aid in sharp distress;
In Him the poor and helpless find
A Judge that's just, a Father kind.

5. He breaks the captive's heavy chain,
And prisoners see the light again;
But rebels, who dispute His will,
Shall dwell in chains and darkness still.
WATTS.

142. L. M.

1. Sing to the Lord that built the skies,
The Lord that reared this stately frame;
Let all the nations sound His praise,
And lands unknown repeat His name.

2. He formed the seas, and formed the hills,
Made every drop and every dust,
Nature and time, with all their wheels,
And pushed them into motion first.

3. Now, from His high, imperial throne,
He looks far down upon the spheres;
He bids the shining orbs roll on,
And round he turns the hasty years.

4. Thus shall this moving engine last,
Till all His saints are gathered in;
Then for the trumpet's dreadful blast
To shake it all to dust again!

5. Yet, when the sound shall tear the skies,
And lightning burn the globe below,
Saints, you may lift your joyful eyes,
There's a new heaven and earth for you.
WATTS.

143. L. M.

1. Th' Almighty reigns, exalted high
O'er all the earth, o'er all the sky;
Though clouds and darkness vail His feet,
His dwelling is the mercy-seat.

2. O ye that love His holy name,
Hate every work of sin and shame:
He guards the souls of all His friends,
And from the snare of hell defends.

3. Immortal light, and joys unknown,
Are for the saints in darkness sown;
Those glorious seeds shall spring and rise,
And the bright harvest bless our eyes.

4. Rejoice, ye righteous, and record
The sacred honors of the Lord;
None but the soul that feels His grace
Can triumph in His holiness.
WATTS.

144. L. M.

1. No change of time shall ever shock
My firm affection, Lord, to Thee;
For Thou hast always been my rock,
A fortress and defence to me.

2. Thou my deliv'rer art, my God;
My trust is in Thy mighty power:
Thou art my shield from foes abroad;
At home my safeguard and my tower.

3. To Thee I will address my prayer,
To whom all praise we justly owe;
So shall I, by Thy watchful care,
Be guarded from my treacherous foe.
TATE AND BRADY.

145. L. M.

1. Thou, Lord, who rear'st the mountain's height,
And mak'st the cliffs with sunshine bright,
O, grant that we may own Thy hand
No less in every grain of sand!

2. With forests huge, of dateless time,
Thy will has hung each peak sublime;
But withered leaves beneath the tree
Have tongues that tell as loud of Thee.

3. Teach us that not a leaf can grow
Till life from Thee within it flow,
That not a grain of dust can be,
O Fount of being! save by Thee;

4. That every human word and deed,
Each flash of feeling, will, or creed,
Hath solemn meaning from above,
Begun and ended all in love.
STERLING.

GOD.

STERLING. L. M.

1. Oh! come, loud anthems let us sing, Loud thanks to our Almighty King; For we our voices high should raise, When our salvation's Rock we praise.

146. L. M.

1. O COME, loud anthems let us sing,
Loud thanks to our Almighty King;
For we our voices high should raise,
When our salvation's Rock we praise.

2. The depths of earth are in His hand,
Her secret wealth at His command;
The strength of hills, that threat the skies,
Subjected to His empire lies.

3. The rolling ocean's vast abyss
By the same sovereign right is His;
'T is moved by His almighty hand,
That formed and fixed the solid land.

4. O let us to His courts repair,
And bow with adoration there;
Down on our knees devoutly all
Before the Lord our Maker fall.
TATE AND BRADY.

147. L. M.

1. MY God, in whom are all the springs
Of boundless love and grace unknown,
Hide me beneath Thy spreading wings,
Till the dark cloud is overblown.

2. Up to the heavens I send my cry,
The Lord will my desires perform;
He sends His angels from the sky, [storm.
And saves me from the threatening

3. My heart is fixed: my song shall raise
Immortal honors to Thy name;
Awake, my tongue, to sound His praise,
My tongue, the glory of my frame.

4. High o'er the earth His mercy reigns,
And reaches to the utmost sky;
His truth to endless years remains,
When lower worlds dissolve and die.

5. Be Thou exalted, O my God!
Above the heavens where angels dwell;
Thy power on earth be known abroad,
And land to land Thy wonders tell.
WATTS.

148. L. M.

1. GIVE to the Lord ye sons of fame,
Give to the Lord renown and power;
Ascribe due honors to His name,
And His eternal might adore.

2. The Lord proclaims His power aloud
Over the ocean and the land:
His voice divides the watery cloud,
And lightnings blaze at His command.

3. To Lebanon He turns His voice,
And lo, the stately cedars break;
The mountains tremble at the noise,
The valleys roar, the deserts quake.

3. The Lord sits sovereign on the flood,
The Thunderer reigns forever king;
But makes His church His blest abode,
Where we His awful glories sing.
WATTS.

ADORATION.

149. L. M.

1. Praise, everlasting praise, be paid
To Him who earth's foundation laid;
Praise to the God whose strong decrees
Sway the creation as He please.

2. Firm are the words His prophets give,
Sweet words on which His children live;
Each of them is the voice of God,
Who spoke and spread the skies abroad.

3. Oh for a strong, a lasting faith,
To credit what th' Almighty saith;
T'' embrace the message of His Son,
And call the joys of heaven our own.

4. Then should the earth's old pillars shake,
And all the wheels of nature break,
Our steady souls shall fear no more
Than solid rocks when billows roar.
WATTS.

150. L. M.

1. God! the eternal, awful name
That the whole heavenly army fears,
That shakes the wide creation's frame,
And Satan trembles when He hears.

2. Like flames of fire His servants are,
And light surrounds His dwelling-place;
But, O ye fiery flames, declare
The brighter glories of His face.

3. Tell how He shows His smiling face,
And clothes all heaven in bright array:
Triumph and joy run through the place,
And songs eternal as the day.

4. Speak, for you feel His burning love,
What zeal it spreads through all your
That sacred fire dwells all above, [frame;
For we on earth have lost the name.

5. Proclaim His wonders from the skies,
Let every distant nation hear;
And while you sound His lofty praise,
Let humble mortals bow and fear.
WATTS.

151. L. M.

1. The Lord is King! lift up thy voice,
O earth, and all ye heavens, rejoice!
From world to world the joy shall ring:
The Lord omnipotent is King!

2. The Lord is King! child of the dust,
The Judge of all the earth is just:
Holy and true are all His ways;
Let every creature speak His praise.

3. Come, make your wants, your burdens known;
The contrite soul He'll ne'er disown;
And angel bands are waiting there,
His messages of love to bear.

4. O, when His wisdom can mistake,
His might decay, His love forsake;—
Then may His children cease to sing,
The Lord omnipotent is King!
CONDER.

152. L. M.

1. Let Zion in her King rejoice,
Though tyrants rage, and kingdoms rise,
He utters His almighty voice—
The nations melt—the tumult dies.

2. From sea to sea, through all the shores,
He makes the noise of battle cease;
When from on high His thunder roars,
He awes the trembling world to peace.

3. "Be still—and learn that I am God;
I'll be exalted o'er the lands;
I will be known and feared abroad,
But still my throne in Zion stands."

4. O Lord of hosts, Almighty King!
While we so near Thy presence dwell,
Our faith shall sit secure, and sing
Defiance to the gates of hell.
WATTS.

153. L. M.

1. Lo, God is here! let us adore,
And humbly bow before His face;
Let all within us feel His power,
Let all within us seek His grace.

2. Lo, God is here! Him, day and night,
United choirs of angels sing;
To Him, enthroned above all height,
Heaven's host their noblest praises bring.

3. Being of beings! may our praise
Thy courts with grateful incense fill;
Still may we stand before Thy face,
Still hear and do Thy sovereign will.
J. WESLEY.

154. L. M.

1. Infinite leagues beyond the sky
The great Eternal reigns alone,
Where neither wings nor souls can fly,
Nor angels climb the topless throne.

2. The Lord of glory builds His seat
Of gems insufferably bright,
And lays beneath His sacred feet
Substantial beams of gloomy night.

3. Yet, glorious Lord, Thy gracious eyes
Look through and cheer us from above;
Beyond our praise Thy grandeur flies;
Yet we adore, and yet we love.
WATTS.

46   GOD.

STERNHOLD. C. M.   Arranged from KENT by L. MASON.

1. The Lord descended from above, And bowed the heavens most high;
And underneath his feet he cast The darkness of the sky.

155. C. M.

1. THE Lord descended from above,
   And bowed the heavens most high;
   And underneath His feet He cast
   The darkness of the sky.

2. On cherub and on cherubim
   Full royally He rode;
   And on the wings of all the winds
   Came flying all abroad.

3. And like a den most dark He made
   His hid and secret place;
   With waters black and airy clouds
   Encompassed He was.

4. He sat serene upon the floods,
   Their fury to restrain;
   And He as sovereign Lord and King
   For evermore shall reign.
                            STERNHOLD.

156. C. M.

1. ARISE, ye people, and adore,
   Exulting strike the chord;
   Let all the earth—from shore to shore,
   Confess th' Almighty Lord.

2. Glad shouts aloud—wide echoing round,
   Th' ascending God proclaim;
   The angelic choir respond the sound.
   And shake creation's frame.

3. They sing of death and hell o'erthrown
   In that triumphant hour:
   And God exalts His conquering Son
   To His right hand of power.

4. O shout, ye people, and adore,
   Exulting strike the chord;
   Let all the earth—from shore to shore,
   Confess th' Almighty Lord.
                         SPIRIT OF THE PSALMS.

157. C. M.

1. O GOD! we praise Thee, and confess
   That Thou the only Lord
   And everlasting Father art,
   By all the earth adored.

2. To Thee, all angels cry aloud;
   To Thee the powers on high,
   Both cherubim and seraphim,
   Continually do cry:

3. O holy, holy, holy Lord,
   Whom heavenly hosts obey,
   The world is with the glory filled
   Of Thy majestic sway!

4. The apostles' glorious company,
   And prophets crowned with light,
   With all the martyrs' noble host,
   Thy constant praise recite.

5. The holy church throughout the world,
   O Lord! confesses Thee,
   That Thou the eternal Father art,
   Of boundless majesty.   PATRICK.

158. C. M.

1. Sing to the Lord Jehovah's name,
   And in His strength rejoice;
   When His salvation is our theme,
   Exalted be our voice.

2. With thanks approach His awful sight,
   And psalms of honor sing:
   The Lord 's a God of boundless might,
   The whole creation's King.

3. Let princes hear, let angels know,
   How mean their natures seem,
   Those gods on high, and gods below,
   When once compared with Him.

4. Earth, with its caverns dark and deep,
   Lies in His spacious hand;
   He fixed the sea what bounds to keep,
   And where the hills must stand.

5. Come, and with humble souls adore,
   Come, kneel before His face;
   O may the creatures of His power
   Be children of His grace!
   WATTS.

159. C. M.

1. The Lord—how fearful is His name!
   How wide is His command!
   Nature, with all her moving frame,
   Rests on His mighty hand.

2. Immortal glory forms His throne,
   And light His awful robe;
   While with a smile, or with a frown,
   He manages the globe.

3. A word of His almighty breath
   Can swell or sink the seas;
   Build the vast empires of the earth,
   Or break them as He please.

4. On angels, with unveiled face
   His glory beams above;
   On men, He looks with softest grace,
   And takes His title, Love.

5. Now let the Lord for ever reign,
   And sway us as He will;
   Sick or in health, in ease or pain,
   We are His favorites still.

6. No more shall peevish passion rise,
   The tongue no more complain;
   'T is sovereign love that lends our joys,
   And love resumes again.
   WATTS.

160. C. M.

1. When forth from Egypt's trembling strand
   The tribes of Israel sped,
   And Jacob in the stranger's land
   Departing banners spread;—

2. Then One, amid their thick array,
   His kingly dwelling made,
   And all along the desert way
   Their guiding scepter swayed.

3. The sea beheld, and struck with dread,
   Rolled all its billows back;
   And Jordan, through his deepest bed,
   Revealed their destined track.

4. What ailed thee, O thou mighty sea,
   And rolled thy waves in dread?
   What bade thy tide, O Jordan, flee,
   And bare its deepest bed?

5. O earth, before the Lord, the God
   Of Jacob, tremble still;
   Who makes the waste a watered sod,
   The flint a gushing rill.
   G. BURGESS.

161. C. M.

1. Begin, my tongue, some heavenly theme,
   And speak some boundless thing,—
   The mighty works, or mightier Name,
   Of our eternal King.

2. Tell of His wondrous faithfulness,
   And sound His power abroad;
   Sing the sweet promise of His grace,
   And the performing God.

3. Engraved, as in eternal brass,
   The mighty promise shines;
   Nor can the powers of darkness raze
   Those everlasting lines.

4. His very word of grace is strong,
   As that which built the skies;
   The voice that rolls the stars along
   Speaks all the promises.

5. O, might I hear Thy heavenly tongue
   But whisper, *Thou art mine!*
   Those gentle words should raise my song
   To notes almost divine.
   WATTS.

GOD.

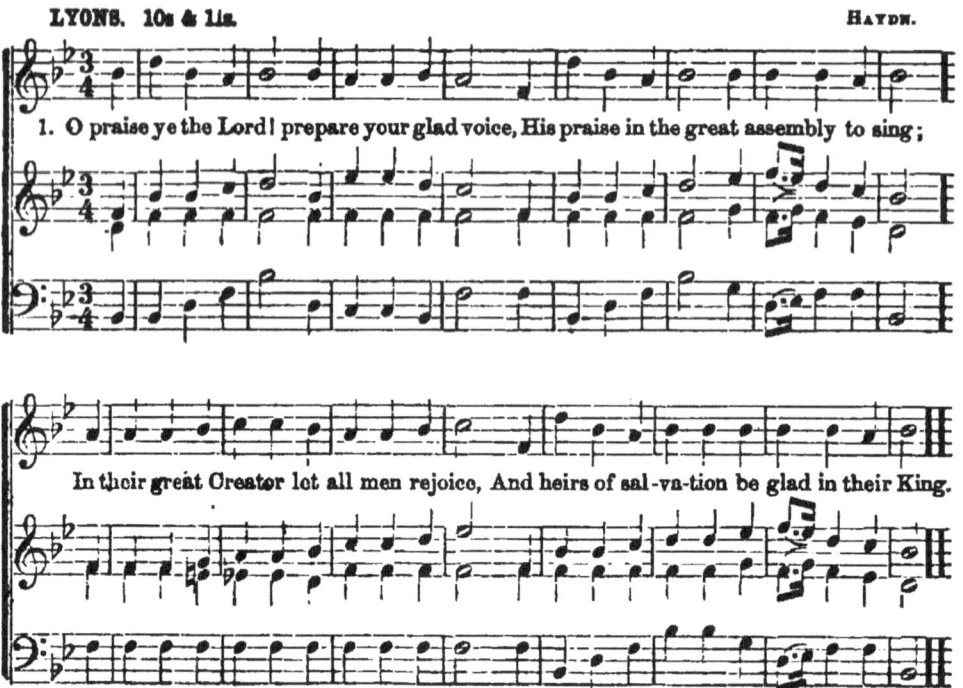

LYONS. 10s & 11s. — HAYDN.

1. O praise ye the Lord! prepare your glad voice, His praise in the great assembly to sing; In their great Creator let all men rejoice, And heirs of sal-va-tion be glad in their King.

162. 10s & 11s.

1. O PRAISE ye the Lord! prepare your glad voice,
 His praise in the great assembly to sing:
In their great Creator let all men rejoice,
 And heirs of salvation be glad in their King.

2. Let them His great name devoutly adore;
 In loud-swelling strains His praises express,
Who graciously opens His bountiful store,
 Their wants to relieve, and His children to bless.

3. With glory adorned, His people shall sing
 To God, who defence and plenty supplies;
Their loud acclamations to Him, their great King,
 Through earth shall be sounded, and reach to
 the skies.

4. Ye angels above, His glories who've sung,
 In loftiest notes, now publish His praise:
We mortals, delighted, would borrow your tongue—
 Would join in your numbers, and chant to your
 lays. TATE, VARIED.

163. 10s & 11s.

1. YE servants of God, your Master proclaim,
 And publish abroad His wonderful name;
The name all-victorious of Jesus extol;
 His kingdom is glorious; He rules over all.

2. God ruleth on high, almighty to save;
 And still He is nigh: His presence we have;
The great congregation His triumph shall sing,
 Ascribing salvation to Jesus, our King.

3. "Salvation to God, who sits on the throne,"
 Let all cry aloud, and honor the Son;
The praises of Jesus the angels proclaim,
 Fall down on their faces, and worship the Lamb.

4. Then let us adore, and give Him His right—
 All glory and power, and wisdom and might;
All honor and blessing, with angels above,
 And thanks never ceasing, for infinite love.

164. 11s.

1. How dear is the thought, that the angels of God
 May bow their bright wings to the world they
 once trod;
Will leave the sweet songs of the mansions
 above,
To breathe o'er our bosoms some message of love!

2. They come, on the wings of the morning they
 come,
Impatient to lead some poor wanderer home;
Some sinner to save from his darkened abode,
And lay him to rest in the arms of his God.

3. They come when we wander, they come when
 we pray,
In mercy to guard us wherever we stray;
A glorious cloud, their bright witness is given;
Encircling us here are these angels of heaven.

ADORATION. 49

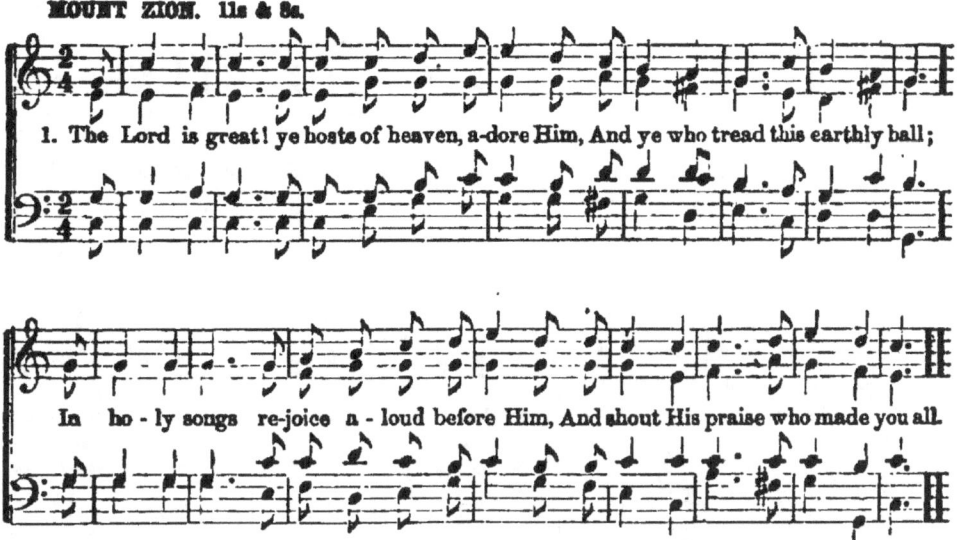

MOUNT ZION. 11s & 8s.

1. The Lord is great! ye hosts of heaven, adore Him, And ye who tread this earthly ball; In holy songs rejoice aloud before Him, And shout His praise who made you all.

165. 11s & 8s.

1. The Lord is great! ye hosts of heaven, adore Him,
And ye who tread this earthly ball;
In holy songs rejoice aloud before Him,
And shout His praise who made you all.

2. The Lord is great; His majesty, how glorious!
Resound His praise from shore to shore;
O'er sin, and death, and hell, now made victorious,
He rules and reigns for evermore.

3. The Lord is great; His mercy how abounding!
Ye angels, strike your golden chords;
O, praise our God, with voice and harp resounding,
The King of kings and Lord of lords.
CHURCH PSALMODY.

166. 10s & 11s.*

1. O, worship the King all-glorious above,
And gratefully sing His wonderful love—
Our Shield and Defender, the Ancient of Days,
Pavilioned in splendor, and girded with praise.

2. O tell of His might, and sing of His grace,
Whose robe is the light, whose canopy, space;
His chariots of wrath the deep thunder-clouds form,
And dark is His path on the wings of the storm.

3. Thy bountiful care what tongue can recite?
It breathes in the air, it shines in the light,
It streams from the hills, it descends to the plain,
And sweetly distills in the dew and the rain.

4. Frail children of dust, and feeble as frail,
In Thee do we trust, nor find Thee to fail,
Thy mercies how tender! how firm to the end!
Our Maker, Defender, Redeemer, and Friend!

5. Father Almighty, how faithful Thy love!
While angels delight to hymn Thee above,
The humbler creation, though feeble their lays,
With true adoration shall lisp to Thy praise.

DOXOLOGY. 11s & 8s.

All praise to the Father, all praise to the Son,
All praise to the Spirit, thrice blest,
The Holy, Eternal, Supreme Three in One,
Was, is, and shall be still addressed.

* Sung to Lyons.

4

GOD.

BETHESDA. H. M. — Dr. Green.

1. Angels! as-sist to sing The honors of your God; Touch every tune-ful string, And sound his name abroad: Come, pour the trembling notes along, And swell the grand, immortal song.

167. H. M.

1 Angels! assist to sing
   The honors of your God;
Touch every tuneful string,
   And sound His name abroad:
Come, pour the trembling notes along,
And swell the grand immortal song.

2 And ye of meaner birth!
   Your joyful voices raise;
Inhabitants of earth!
   Your great Creator praise:
Let your hosannas joyful rise,
And shake the earth, and pierce the skies.

3 Let day and dusky night,
   In solemn order, join
His praises to recite,
   And speak His power divine:
Let every hill and every vale
Re-echo with the sacred tale.

4 Let every creature sing
   The honors of our God;
Touch every tuneful string,
   And spread His praise abroad:
Come, pour the trembling notes along;
And swell the universal song.
                  GEMS.

168. H. M.

1 To your Creator, God,
   Your great Preserver, raise,
Ye creatures of His hand,
   Your highest notes of praise:
Let every voice proclaim His power,
His name adore, and loud rejoice.

2 Let every creature join
   To celebrate His name,
And all their various powers
   Assist th' exalted theme:
Let nature raise, from every tongue,
A general song of grateful praise.

3 But oh! from human tongues
   Should nobler praises flow;
And every thankful heart
   With warm devotion glow:
Your voices raise above the rest;
Ye highly blest! declare His praise.

4 Assist me, gracious God!
   My heart, my voice inspire;
Then shall I grateful join
   The universal choir:
Thy grace can raise my heart, my tongue,
And tune my song to lively praise.
                  MRS. STEELE.

169. H. M.

1 In Zion's sacred gates,
   Let hymns of praise begin,
Where acts of faith and love,
   In ceaseless beauty, shine:
In mercy there, while God is known,
Before His throne with songs appear.

2 The trumpet's martial voice,
   The timbrel's softer sound,
The organ's solemn peal,
   His praises shall resound:
To swell the song, with highest joy,
Let man employ his tuneful tongue.
                  DWIGHT.

ADORATION. 51

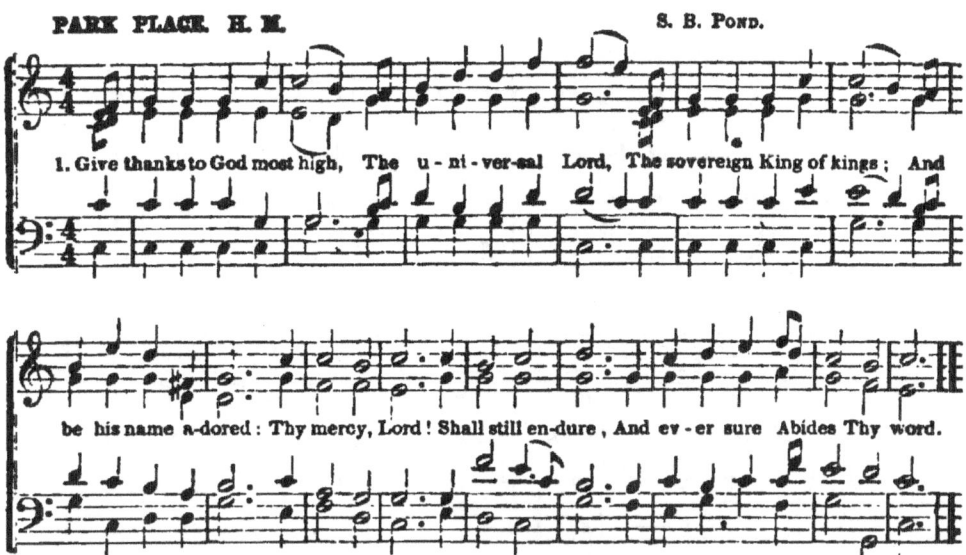

PARK PLACE. H. M.   S. B. POND.

1. Give thanks to God most high, The u-ni-ver-sal Lord, The sovereign King of kings; And be his name a-dored: Thy mercy, Lord! Shall still en-dure, And ev-er sure Abides Thy word.

170. H. M.

1. GIVE thanks to God most high,
   The universal Lord,
The sovereign King of kings;
   And be His name adored:
Thy mercy, Lord! shall still endure;
And ever sure abides Thy word.

2. How mighty is His hand!
   What wonders He hath done!
He formed the earth and seas,
   And spread the heavens alone:
His power and grace are still the same;
And let His name have endless praise.

3. He saw the nations lie
   All perishing in sin;
And pitied the sad state
   The ruined world was in:
Thy mercy, Lord! shall still endure:
And ever sure abides Thy word.

4. He sent His only Son
   To save us from our woe,
From Satan, sin, and death,
   And every hurtful foe:
His power and grace are still the same:
And let His name have endless praise.

5. Give thanks aloud to God,
   To God, the heavenly King;
And let the spacious earth
   His works and glories sing:
Thy mercy, Lord! shall still endure;
And ever sure abides Thy word.
                    WATTS.

171. H. M.

1. IN sweet exalted strains,
   The King of glory praise;
O'er heaven and earth He reigns,
   Through everlasting days:
He, at His will the world controls,
Sustains or sinks the distant poles.

2. To earth He bends His throne—
   His throne of grace divine;
Wide is his bounty known,
   And wide His glories shine:
Fair Salem, still His chosen rest,
Is with His smiles and presence blest.
                    B. FRANCIS.

172. H. M.

1. THE promises I sing,
   Which sovereign love hath spoke;
Nor will th' eternal King
   His words of grace revoke:
They stand secure and steadfast still;
Nor Zion's hill abides so sure.

2. The mountains melt away,
   When once the Judge appears;
And sun and moon decay
   That measure mortal years;
But still the same, in radiant lines,
The promise shines through all the flame.

3. Their harmony shall sound
   Through my attentive ears,
When thunders cleave the ground
   And dissipate the spheres;
'Mid all the shock of that dread scene,
I stand serene—Thy word my rock.
                    DODDRIDGE.

GOD.

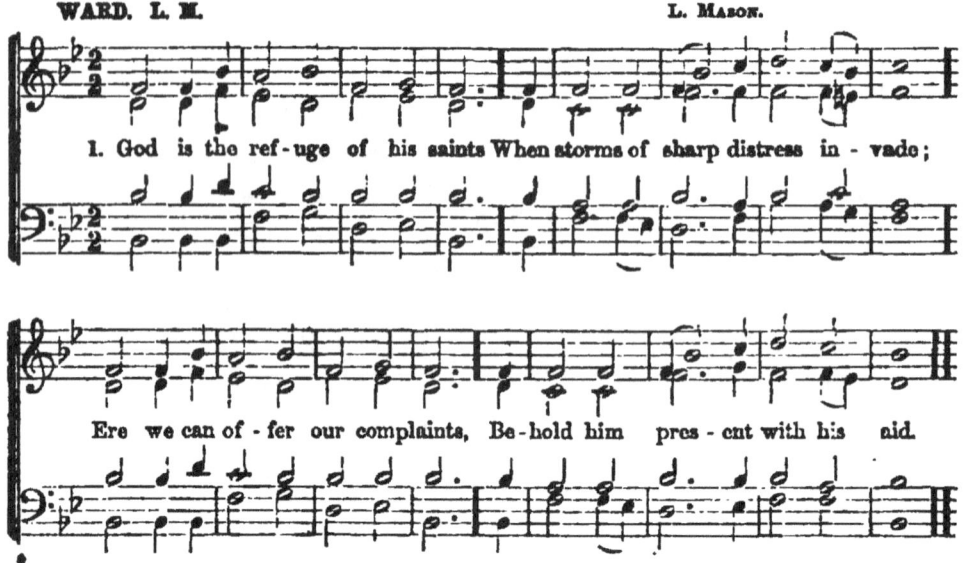

WARD. L. M.   L. Mason.

1. God is the refuge of his saints When storms of sharp distress invade; Ere we can offer our complaints, Behold him present with his aid.

173. L. M.

1. God is the refuge of His saints
   When storms of sharp distress invade;
   Ere we can offer our complaints,
   Behold Him present with His aid.

2. Let mountains from their seats be hurled
   Down to the deep, and buried there,
   Convulsions shake the solid world—
   Our faith shall never yield to fear.

3. Loud may the troubled ocean roar;
   In sacred peace our souls abide;
   While every nation, every shore,
   Trembles and dreads the swelling tide.

4. There is a stream whose gentle flow
   Supplies the city of our God,
   Life, love, and joy, still gliding through,
   And watering our divine abode.

5. That sacred stream, Thine holy word,
   Our grief allays, our fear controls;
   Sweet peace Thy promises afford,
   And give new strength to fainting souls.

6. Zion enjoys her Monarch's love,
   Secure against a threatening hour;
   Nor can her firm foundation move,
   Built on His truth, and armed with power.   WATTS.

174. L. M.

1. Up to the hills I lift mine eyes,
   Th' eternal hills beyond the skies;
   Thence all her help my soul derives,
   There my Almighty refuge lives.

2. He lives—the everlasting God
   That built the world, that spread the flood;
   The heavens with all their hosts He made,
   And the dark regions of the dead.

3. He guides our feet, he guards our way;
   His morning smiles bless all the day:
   He spreads the evening vail, and keeps
   The silent hours, while Israel sleeps.

4. Israel, a name divinely blest,
   May rise secure, securely rest;
   Thy holy guardian's wakeful eyes
   Admit no slumber, nor surprise.

5. No sun shall smite thy head by day;
   Nor the pale moon with sickly ray
   Shall blast thy couch; no baleful star
   Dart his malignant fire so far.

6. Should earth and hell with malice burn,
   Still thou shalt go, and still return,
   Safe in the Lord; His heavenly care
   Defends thy life from every snare.

7. On thee foul spirits have no power;
   And, in thy last departing hour,
   Angels, that trace the airy road,
   Shall bear thee homeward to thy God.   WATTS.

175. L. M.

1. They that have made their refuge God
Shall find a most secure abode;
Shall walk all day beneath His shade,
And there at night shall rest their head.

2. If burning beams of noon conspire
To dart a pestilential fire,
God is their life; His wings are spread,
To shield them 'midst ten thousand dead.

3. If vapors with malignant breath
Rise thick, and scatter midnight death;
Still they are safe; the poison'd air
Again grows pure, if God be there.

176. L. M.

1. There's nothing bright, above, below,
From flowers that bloom to stars that glow,
But in its light my soul can see
Some features of the Deity.

2. There's nothing dark, below, above,
But in its gloom I trace Thy love,
And meekly wait the moment when
Thy touch shall make all bright again.

3. The light, the dark, where'er I look,
Shall be one pure and shining book,
Where I may read, in words of flame,
The glories of Thy wondrous name.
MOORE.

177. L. M.

1. My God, I love and I adore;
But souls that love would know Thee more:
Wilt thou forever hide, and stand
Behind the labors of Thy hand?

2. Thy hand, great God, sustains the poles
On which this huge creation rolls;
The starry arch proclaims Thy power;
Thy pencil glows in every flower.

3. Across the waves, around the sky,
There's not a spot, or deep or high,
Where the Creator has not trod,
And left the footsteps of a God.

4. Fain would I trace the immortal way
That leads to courts of endless day,
Where the Creator stands confessed,
In His own fairest glories dressed.

178. L. M.

1. High in the heavens, eternal God,
Thy goodness in full glory shines;
Thy truth shall break through every cloud
That vails and darkens Thy designs.

2. Forever firm Thy justice stands,
As mountains their foundations keep;
Wise are the wonders of Thy hands;
Thy judgments are a mighty deep.

3. Thy providence is kind and large;
Both man and beast Thy bounty share;
The whole creation is Thy charge,
But saints are Thy peculiar care.

4. My God, how excellent Thy grace!
Whence all our hope and comfort springs;
The sons of Adam, in distress,
Fly to the shadow of Thy wings.

5. From the provisions of Thy house
We shall be fed with sweet repast;
There mercy like a river flows,
And brings salvation to our taste.

6. Life, like a fountain rich and free,
Springs from the presence of my Lord,
And in Thy light our souls shall see
The glories promised in Thy word.
WATTS.

179. L. M.

1. Jehovah reigns, His throne is high,
His robes are light and majesty;
His glory shines with beams so bright,
No mortal can sustain the sight.

2. His terrors keep the world in awe,
His justice guards His holy law,
His love reveals a smiling face,
His truth and promise seal the grace.

3. Through all His works what wisdom shines!
He baffles Satan's deep designs;
His power is sovereign to fulfill,
The noblest counsels of His will.

4. Thus glorious, will He condescend
To be my Father and my Friend?
Then let my songs with angels join,
Heaven is secure, if God is mine.
WATTS.

GENEVA. C. M. — J. Cole

1. When all thy mercies, O my God, My rising soul surveys,

Transported with the view I'm lost In wonder, love and praise.

180. C. M.

2. Unnumbered comforts on my soul
   Thy tender care bestowed,
   Before my infant heart conceived
   From whom those comforts flowed.

3. When in the slippery path of youth
   With heedless steps I ran,
   Thine arm, unseen, conveyed me safe,
   And led me up to man.

4. Ten thousand thousand precious gifts
   My daily thanks employ;
   'Nor is the least a cheerful heart,
   That tastes those gifts with joy.

5. Through every period of my life
   Thy goodness I'll pursue;
   And after death, in distant worlds,
   The glorious theme renew.

6. Through all eternity, to Thee
   A joyful song I'll raise:
   But oh! eternity's too short
   To utter all my praise!

   ADDISON.

181. C. M.

1. Soon as I heard my Father say,
   Ye children seek my face,
   My heart replied without delay,
   I'll seek my Father's face.

2. Let not Thy face be hid from me,
   Nor frown my soul away;
   God of my life! I fly to Thee
   In a distressing day.

3. Should friends and kindred, near and dear,
   Leave me to want, or die;
   My God would make my life His care,
   And all my need supply.

4. My fainting flesh had died with grief,
   Had not my soul believed
   To see Thy grace provide relief—
   Nor was my hope deceived.

5. Wait on the Lord, ye trembling saints!
   And keep your courage up:
   He'll raise your spirit when it faints,
   And far exceed your hope.

   WATTS.

182. C. M.

1. How rich Thy favors, God of grace!
   How various and divine!
   Full as the ocean they are poured,
   And bright as heaven they shine.

2. He to eternal glory calls,
   And leads the wondrous way
   To His own palace, where He reigns
   In uncreated day.

3. The songs of everlasting years
   That mercy shall attend,
   Which leads, through sufferings of an hour,
   To joys that never end.

   DODDRIDGE.

183. C. M.

1. We love Thee, Lord, and we adore;
   Now is Thine arm revealed;
   Thou art our strength, our heavenly tower,
   Our bulwark and our shield.

2. We fly to our eternal Rock,
   And find a sure defence;
   His holy name our lips invoke,
   And draw salvation thence.

3. When God, our leader, shines in arms,
   What mortal heart can bear
   The thunder of His loud alarms,
   The lightning of His spear?

4. He rides upon the winged wind,
   And angels in array,
   In millions, wait to know His mind,
   And swift as flames obey.

5. He speaks, and at His fierce rebuke
   Whole armies are dismayed;
   His voice, His frown, His angry look,
   Strikes all their courage dead.

6. Oft has the Lord whole nations blessed
   For His own children's sake;
   The powers that give His people rest
   Shall of His care partake.
                                        WATTS.

184. C. M.

1. That man, in life wherever placed,
   Has happiness in store,
   Who walks not in the wicked's way
   Nor learns their guilty lore;

2. Nor from the seat of scornful pride
   Casts forth his eyes abroad,
   But with humility and awe
   Still walks before his God.

3. That man shall flourish like the trees
   Which by the streamlet grow,
   Whose fruitful top is spread on high,
   And firm the root below.

4. But he whose blossom buds in guilt
   Shall to the ground be cast,
   And like the rootless stubble tossed
   Before the sweeping blast.

5. For God, that God the good adore,
   Will give them peace and joy;
   But all the hopes of wicked men
   Will utterly destroy.
                                        BURNS.

185. C. M.

1. How are Thy servants blest, O Lord,
   How sure is their defence!
   Eternal wisdom is their guide,
   Their help, omnipotence.

2. In foreign realms, and lands remote,
   Supported by Thy care,
   Through burning climes they pass unhurt,
   And breathe in tainted air.

3. When by the dreadful tempest borne
   High on the broken wave,
   They know Thou art not slow to hear,
   Nor impotent to save.

4. The storm is laid, the winds retire,
   Obedient to Thy will;
   The sea, that roars at Thy command,
   At Thy command is still.

5. In midst of dangers, fears, and deaths,
   Thy goodness we'll adore;
   We'll praise Thee for Thy mercies past,
   And humbly hope for more.

6. Our life, whilst Thou preserv'st that life,
   Thy sacrifice shall be;
   And death, when death shall be our lot,
   Shall join our souls to Thee.
                                        ADDISON.

186. C. M.

1. Why should the children of a King
   Go mourning all their days?
   Great Comforter, descend, and bring
   Some tokens of Thy grace.

2. Dost Thou not dwell in all the saints,
   And seal the heirs of heaven?
   When wilt Thou banish my complaints,
   And show my sins forgiven?

3. Assure my conscience of her part
   In the Redeemer's blood;
   And bear Thy witness with my heart
   That I am born of God.

4. Thou art the earnest of His love,
   The pledge of joys to come;
   And thy soft wings, celestial Dove,
   Will safe convey me home.
                                        WATTS.

GOD.

YORK. C. M.

1. O God! our help in a-ges past, Our hope for years to come,
Our shel-ter from the stormy blast, And our e-ter-nal home!

187. C. M.

1. O God! our help in ages past,
Our hope for years to come,
Our shelter from the stormy blast,
And our eternal home!

2. Before the hills in order stood,
Or earth received her frame,
From everlasting thou art God,
To endless years the same.

3. A thousand ages in Thy sight
Are like an evening gone—
Short as the watch that ends the night
Before the rising sun.

4. Time, like an ever-rolling stream,
Bears all its sons away;
They fly, forgotten, as a dream
Dies at the opening day.

5. O God! our help in ages past,
Our hope for years to come,
Be thou our guide while troubles last,
And our eternal home.
WATTS.

188. C. M.

1. As pants the hart for cooling streams,
When heated in the chase;
So longs my soul, O God for Thee,
And Thy refreshing grace.

2. For Thee, my God, the living God,
My thirsty soul doth pine;
Oh, when shall I behold Thy face,
Thou Majesty divine?

3. Why restless, why cast down, my soul?
Trust God; who will employ
His aid for thee, and change these sighs
To thankful hymns of joy.

4. God of my strength, how long shall I,
Like one forgotten, mourn;
Forlorn, forsaken, and exposed
To my oppressor's scorn?

5. I sigh to think of happier days,
When Thou, O Lord! wast nigh;
When every heart was tuned to praise,
And none more blessed than I.

6. Why restless, why cast down, my soul?
Hope still; and Thou shalt sing
The praise of Him who is Thy God,
Thy health's eternal spring.
TATE AND BRADY.

189. C. M.

1. Great Ruler of all nature's frame,
We own Thy power divine;
We hear Thy breath in every storm,
For all the winds are Thine.

2. Wide as they sweep their sounding way,
They work Thy sovereign will;
And, awed by Thy majestic voice,
Confusion shall be still.

3. Thy mercy tempers every blast
To them that seek Thy face,
And mingles with the tempest's roar
The whispers of Thy grace.

4. Those gentle whispers let me hear,
Till all the tumult cease;
And gales of paradise shall lull
My weary soul to peace.
DODDRIDGE.

190. C. M.

1. Let Zion and her sons rejoice—
   Behold the promised hour!
   Her God hath heard her mourning voice,
   And comes t' exalt His power.

2. Her dust and ruins that remain
   Are precious in our eyes;
   Those ruins shall be built again,
   And all that dust shall rise.

3. The Lord will raise Jerusalem,
   And stand in glory there;
   Nations shall bow before His name,
   And kings attend with fear.

4. He sits a Sovereign on His throne,
   With pity in His eyes;
   He hears the dying prisoners groan,
   And sees their sighs arise.

5. He frees the souls condemned to death;
   And, when his saints complain,
   It shan't be said that praying breath
   Was ever spent in vain.

6. This shall be known when we are dead,
   And left on long record,—
   That ages, yet unborn, may read,
   And trust and praise the Lord.
            WATTS.

191. C. M.

1. God! my supporter and my hope,
   My help for ever near,
   Thine arm of mercy held me up,
   When sinking in despair.

2. Thy counsels, Lord! shall guide my feet
   Through this dark wilderness:
   Thy hand conduct me near Thy seat,
   To dwell before Thy face.

3. Were I in heaven without my God,
   'T would be no joy to me;
   And while this earth is my abode,
   I long for none but Thee.

4. What if the springs of life were broke,
   And flesh and heart should faint?
   God is my soul's eternal rock,
   The strength of every saint.

5. But to draw near to Thee, my God!
   Shall be my sweet employ:
   My tongue shall sound Thy works abroad,
   And tell the world my joy.
            WATTS.

192. C. M.

1. Lord! where shall guilty souls retire,
   Forgotten and unknown?
   In hell they meet Thy dreadful fire,
   In heaven Thy glorious throne.

2. Should I suppress my vital breath
   To shun the wrath divine,
   Thy voice would break the bars of death,
   And make the grave resign.

3. If winged with beams of morning light,
   I fly beyond the west,
   Thy hand, which must support my flight,
   Would soon betray my rest.

4. If o'er my sins I think to draw
   The curtains of the night,
   Those flaming eyes that guard Thy law
   Would turn the shades to light.

5. The beams of noon, the midnight hour,
   Are both alike to Thee:
   Oh, may I ne'er provoke that power
   From which I can not flee.
            WATTS.

193. C. M.

1. God moves in a mysterious way
   His wonders to perform;
   He plants His footsteps in the sea,
   And rides upon the storm.

2. Deep in unfathomable mines
   Of never-failing skill,
   He treasures up His vast designs,
   And works His sovereign will.

3. Ye fearful saints, fresh courage take;
   The clouds ye so much dread
   Are big with mercy, and will break
   In blessings on your head.

4. Judge not the Lord by feeble sense,
   But trust Him for His grace;
   Behind a frowning providence
   He hides a smiling face.

5. His purposes will ripen fast,
   Unfolding every hour;
   The bud may have a bitter taste,
   But sweet will be the flower.

6. Blind unbelief is sure to err,
   And scan His work in vain;
   God is his own interpreter,
   And He will make it plain.
            COWPER.

GOD.

DUKE STREET. L. M. — J. HATTON.

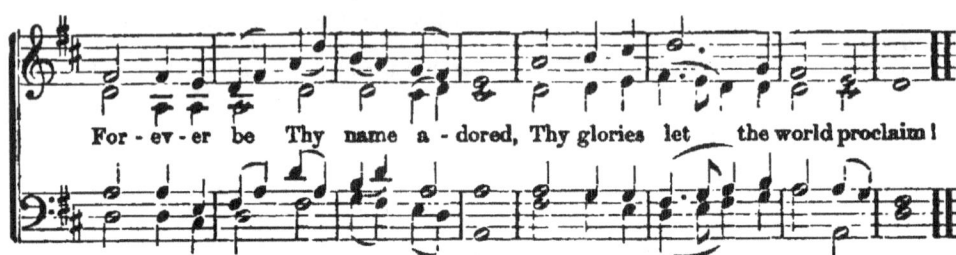

1. O ho-ly, ho-ly, ho-ly Lord! Bright in Thy deeds and in Thy name,
For-ev-er be Thy name a-dored, Thy glories let the world proclaim!

194. L. M.

1. O HOLY, holy, holy Lord!
   Bright in Thy deeds and in Thy name,
Forever be Thy name adored,
   Thy glories let the world proclaim!

2. O Jesus, Lamb once crucified
   To take our load of sins away,
Thine be the hymn that rolls its lay
   Along the realms of upper day!

3. O Holy Spirit from above,
   In streams of light and glory giv'n,
Thou source of ecstasy and love,
   Thy praises ring through earth and heav'n!

4. O God triune, to Thee we owe
   Our every thought, our every song;
And ever may Thy praises flow
   From saint and seraph's burning tongue!
                                J. W. EASTBURNE.

195. L. M.

1. GOD is a name my soul adores—
   Th' almighty Three, th' eternal One:
Nature and grace, with all their powers,
   Confess the Infinite Unknown.

2. Thy voice produced the sea and spheres;
   Bade the waves roar, the planets shine:
But nothing like Thyself appears
   Through all these spacious works of Thine.

3. Still restless nature dies and grows;
   From change to change the creatures run;
Thy being no succession knows,
   And all Thy vast designs are one.

4. A glance of Thine runs through the globes,
   Rules the bright worlds, and moves their frame;
Broad sheets of light compose Thy robes,
   Thy guards are formed of living flame.
                                WATTS.

196. L. M.

1. COME, O Creator Spirit blest!
   And in our souls take up Thy rest;
Come, with Thy grace and heavenly aid,
   To fill the hearts which Thou hast made.

2. Great Paraclete! to Thee we cry;
   O highest gift of God most high!
O fount of life! O fire of love!
   And sweet anointing from above!

3. Kindle our senses from above,
   And make our hearts o'erflow with love;
With patience firm, and virtue high,
   The weakness of our flesh supply.

4. Far from us drive the foe we dread,
   And grant us Thy true peace instead;
So shall we not, with Thee for guide
   Turn from the path of life aside.
                                LYRA CATH.

FATHER, SON AND HOLY SPIRIT.

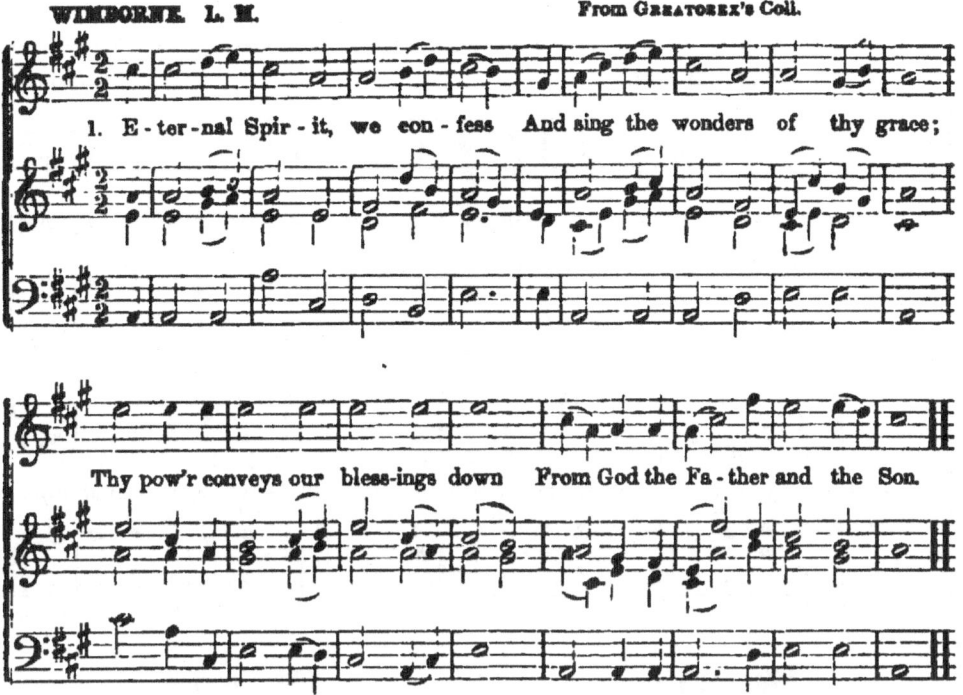

WIMBORNE. L. M.   From GREATOREX's Coll.

1. E-ter-nal Spir-it, we con-fess And sing the wonders of thy grace;
Thy pow'r conveys our bless-ings down From God the Fa-ther and the Son.

197. L. M.

1. ETERNAL Spirit, we confess
And sing the wonders of Thy grace;
Thy power conveys our blessings down
From God the Father and the Son.

2. Enlightened by Thy heavenly ray,
Our shades and darkness turn to day;
Thine inward teachings make us know
Our danger, and our refuge too.

3. Thy power and glory work within,
And break the chains of reigning sin;
Do our imperious lusts subdue,
And form our wretched hearts anew.

4. The troubled conscience knows Thy voice;
Thy cheering words awake our joys;
Thy words allay the stormy wind,
And calm the surges of the mind.
            WATTS.

198. L. M.

1. COME, gracious Spirit, heavenly Dove,
With light and comfort from above;
Be Thou our guardian, Thou our guide,
O'er every thought and step preside.

2. The light of truth to us display,
And make us know and choose Thy way;
Plant holy fear in every heart,
That we from God may ne'er depart.

3. Lead us to holiness, the road
That we must take to dwell with God;
Lead us to Christ, the living way,
Nor let us from His precepts stray.

4. Lead us to God, our final rest,
In His enjoyment to be bless'd;
Lead us to heaven, the seat of bliss,
Where pleasure in perfection is.
            BROWNE.

DOXOLOGY. L. M.

Lord! when the world is at its end,
And Christ to judgment shall descend,
May we be call'd those joys to see,
Prepared from all eternity.

Praise to the Father, with the Son,
And Holy Spirit, Three in One;
As ever was in ages past,
And shall be so while ages last.

GOD.

ITALIAN HYMN. 6s & 4s. GIARDINI.

1. Come, thou almighty King, Help us Thy name to sing, Help us to praise! Father all glorious, O'er all victorious, Come and reign over us, Ancient of days.

199. 6s & 4s.

2. Jesus, our Lord, descend;
From all our foes defend,
  Nor let us fall;
Let thine almighty aid
Our sure defence be made,
Our souls on Thee be stayed;
  Lord, hear our call.

3. Come, thou incarnate Word
Gird on Thy mighty sword;
  Our prayer attend;
Come, and Thy people bless;
Come, give Thy word success;
Spirit of holiness,
  On us descend.

4. Come, holy Comforter,
Thy sacred witness bear,
  In this glad hour;
Thou, who almighty art,
Now rule in every heart,
And ne'er from us depart,
  Spirit of power.

5. To Thee, great One in Three,
The highest praises be,
  Hence evermore;
Thy sovereign majesty
May we in glory see,
And to eternity
  Love and adore.

MADAN.

200. 6s & 4s.

1. Glory to God on high!
Let heaven and earth reply;
  Praise ye His name;
His love and grace adore,
Who all our sorrows bore;
And sing forevermore,
  "Worthy the Lamb."

2. Ye who surround the throne,
Join cheerfully in one,
  Praising His name;
Ye who have felt His blood
Sealing your peace with God,
Sound His dear name abroad:
  "Worthy the Lamb."

3. Join, all ye ransomed race,
Our Lord and God to bless;
  Praise ye His name;
In him we will rejoice,
And make a joyful noise,
Shouting with heart and voice,
  "Worthy the Lamb."

4. Soon must we change our place;
Yet will we never cease
  Praising His name;
To him our songs we'll bring,
Hail Him our gracious King,
And through all ages sing,
  "Worthy the Lamb."

FATHER, SON AND HOLY SPIRIT.

WELDON. 7s & 6s.

1. Meet and right it is to sing, In every time and place; Glory to our heavenly King, The God of truth and grace. Join we then with sweet accord, All in one thanksgiving join! Holy, holy, holy Lord, Eternal praise be Thine!

201. 7s & 6s.

1. MEET and right it is to sing,
   In every time and place;
   Glory to our heavenly King,
   The God of truth and grace.
   Join we then with sweet accord,
   All in one thanksgiving join!
   Holy, holy, holy Lord,
   Eternal praise be thine!

2. Thee, the first-born sons of light,
   In choral symphonies,
   Praise by day, day without night,
   And never, never cease;
   Angels and archangels, all
   Praise the mystic Three in One;
   Sing, and stop, and gaze, and fall,
   O'erwhelm'd before Thy throne!

3. Father, God, Thy love we praise,
   Which gave Thy Son to die;
   Jesus, full of truth and grace,
   Alike we glorify;
   Spirit, Comforter divine,
   Praise by all to Thee be given,
   Till we in full chorus join,
   And earth is turn'd to heaven.
   C. WESLEY.

202. 7s & 6s.

1. PRAISE the Lord, who reigns above,
   And keeps His courts below;
   Praise Him for His boundless love,
   And all His greatness show;
   Praise Him for His noble deeds;
   Praise Him for His matchless power;
   Him, from whom all good proceeds,
   Let earth and heaven adore.

2. Publish—spread to all around
   The great Immanuel's name;
   Let the gospel-trumpet sound;
   Him the Prince of Peace proclaim.
   Praise Him, every tuneful string!
   All the reach of heavenly art,
   All the power of music bring—
   The music of the heart.

3. Him, in whom they move and live,
   Let every creature sing;
   Glory to our Saviour give,
   And homage to our King.
   Hallowed be His name beneath,
   As in heaven, on earth adored;
   Praise the Lord in every breath—
   Let all things praise the Lord.

CHRIST.

HERALD ANGELS. 7s.   Arranged from Dr. Arnold.

1. Hark! the herald angels sing, Hark! the herald angels sing, "Glory to the new-born King; Peace on earth, and mercy mild,—God and sinners re-con-ciled.

203. 7s.

1. Hark! the herald-angels sing:
"Glory to the new-born King;
Peace on earth, and mercy mild;
God and sinners reconciled."

2. Joyful, all ye nations! rise,
Join the triumph of the skies;
With th' angelic host, proclaim:
"Christ is born in Bethlehem."

3. Mild He lays His glory by,
Born that man no more may die;
Born to raise the sons of earth;
Born to give them second birth.

4. Hail! the heaven-born Prince of peace!
Hail! the Sun of righteousness!
Light and life to all He brings,
Risen with healing in His wings.

5. Let us then with angels sing:
"Glory to the new-born King;
Peace on earth, and mercy mild;
God and sinners reconciled."

204. 8s & 7s.

1. Shepherds! hail the wondrous stranger;
Now to Bethle'm speed your way;
Lo! in yonder humble manger,
Christ, the Lord, is born to-day:

2. Christ, by prophets long-predicted,
Joy of Israel's chosen race;
Light to Gentiles long-afflicted,
Lost in error's darkest maze.

3. Bright the star of your salvation,
Pointing to His rude abode!
Rapturous news for every nation:
Mortals! now behold your God!

4. Glad, we trace th' amazing story,
Angels leave their bliss to tell;
Theme sublime, replete with glory:
Sinners saved from death and hell.

5. Love eternal moved the Saviour,
Thus to lay His radiance by;
Blessings on the Lamb for ever;
Glory be to God on high!

205. 7s.

1. O Thou holy God! come down,
God of spotless purity!
Claim and seize me for Thy own,
Consecrate my heart to Thee;

2. Under Thy protection take;
Songs in the night season give;
Let me sleep to Thee, and wake;
Let me die to Thee, and live.

3. Loose me from the chains of sense,
Set me from the body free;
Draw with stronger influence
My unfettered soul to Thee;

4. In me, Lord, Thyself reveal;
Fill me with a sweet surprise;
Let me Thee, when waking, feel,
Let me in Thy image rise.

METHODIST.

ADVENT.

BENNET. C. M. *English.*

1. While shepherds watch'd their flocks by night, All seated on the ground; The angel of the Lord came down, And glory shone around, And glory shone a-round.

206. C. M.

2. "Fear not," said he—for mighty dread
  Had seized their troubled mind—
  "Glad tidings of great joy I bring,
  To you and all mankind.

3. "To you, in David's town, this day,
  Is born of David's line,
  The Saviour, who is Christ, the Lord,
  And this shall be the sign:

4. "The heavenly babe you there shall find,
  To human view displayed,
  All meanly wrapped in swathing bands,
  And in a manger laid."

5. Thus spake the seraph; and forthwith
  Appeared a shining throng
  Of angels, praising God, who thus
  Addressed their joyful song:

6. "All glory be to God on high,
  And to the earth be peace;
  Good-will henceforth from heaven to men
  Begin, and never cease!"
  TATE.

207. C. M.

1. AWAKE—awake the sacred song
  To our incarnate Lord!
  Let every heart, and every tongue,
  Adore th' eternal Word.

2. That awful Word, that sovereign Power,
  By whom the worlds were made—
  Oh! happy morn—illustrious hour!—
  Was once in flesh arrayed.

3. Then shone almighty power and love,
  In all their glorious forms,
  When Jesus left his throne above,
  To dwell with sinful worms.

4. To dwell with misery here below,
  The Saviour left the skies,
  And sunk to wretchedness and wo,
  That worthless man might rise.

5. Adoring angels tuned their songs,
  To hail the joyful day;
  With rapture, then, let human tongues
  Their grateful homage pay.
  MRS. STEELE.

208. C. M.

1. ANGELS rejoiced and sweetly sung,
  At our Redeemer's birth;
  Mortals! awake; let every tongue
  Proclaim His matchless worth.

2. Glory to God, who dwells on high,
  And sent His only Son
  To take a servant's form, and die,
  For evils we had done!

3. Good-will to men; ye fallen race!
  Arise, and shout for joy;
  He comes, with rich, abounding grace
  To save, and not destroy.

4. Lord! send the gracious tidings forth,
  And fill the world with light,
  That Jew and Gentile, through the earth,
  May know Thy saving might.
  HURN.

CHRIST.

AMALAND. 8s & 7s. L. Mason.

1. Hark! what mean those holy voices, Sweetly sounding thro' the skies! Lo! th' angelic host rejoices; Heavenly hallelujahs rise.

2. Hear them tell the wondrous story, Hear them chant in hymns of joy, "Glory in the highest— glory! Glory be to God most high!"

209. 8s & 7s.

2. Hear them tell the wondrous story,
Hear them chant in hymns of joy:—
Glory in the highest, glory!
Glory be to God most high!

3. "Peace on earth, good-will from heaven,
Reaching far as man is found;
Souls redeemed, and sins forgiven!"—
Loud our golden harps shall sound.

4. "Christ is born, the great Anointed;
Heaven and earth His praises sing!
O receive whom God appointed,
For your Prophet, Priest, and King!

5. "Haste ye mortals, to adore him;
Learn His name, and taste His joy;
Till in heaven ye sing before Him,—
"Glory be to God most high!"

CAWOOD.

ADVENT.

210. 8s, 7s & 4s.

1. ANGELS, from the realms of glory,
    Wing your flight o'er all the earth,
   Ye who sang creation's story,
    Now proclaim Messiah's birth;
     Come and worship,
   Worship Christ the new-born King.

2. Shepherds, in the field abiding,
    Watching o'er your flocks by night,
   God with man is now residing,
    Yonder shines the infant-light;
     Come and worship,
   Worship Christ the new-born King.

3. Sages, leave your contemplations,
    Brighter visions beam afar;
   Seek the great Desire of nations;
    Ye have seen His natal star;
     Come and worship,
   Worship Christ the new-born King.

4. Saints, before the altar bending,
    Watching long in hope and fear,
   Suddenly the Lord, descending,
    In His temple shall appear;
     Come and worship,
   Worship Christ the new-born King.

5. Sinners, wrung with true repentance,
    Doomed for guilt to endless pains,
   Justice now revokes the sentence,
    Mercy calls you—break your chains;
     Come and worship,
   Worship Christ the new-born King.
                    MONTGOMERY.

211. 8s & 7s.
THRICE HOLY.

1. "LORD, Thy glory fills the heaven;
    Earth is with its fullness stored;
   Unto Thee be glory given,
    Holy, holy, holy Lord!"
   Heaven is still with anthems ringing:
    Earth takes up the angels' cry,
   "Holy, holy, holy," singing,
    "Lord of hosts, the Lord most High!"

2. Ever thus in God's high praises,
    Brethren, let our tongues unite,
   While our thoughts His greatness raises,
    And our love His gifts excite.
   With His seraph train before Him,
    With His holy church below,
   Thus unite we to adore Him,
    Bid we thus our anthem flow:

3. "Lord, Thy glory fills the heaven;
    Earth is with its fullness stored;
   Unto Thee be glory given,
    Holy, holy, holy Lord!
   Thus, Thy glorious name confessing,
    We adopt the angels' cry,
   "Holy, holy, holy"—blessing
    Thee, the Lord our God most High!"
                    ANCIENT HYMNS.

212. 8s & 7s. Double.

1. MIGHTY God! while angels bless Thee,
    May a mortal lisp Thy name?
   Lord of men, as well as angels!
    Thou art every creature's theme:
   Lord of every land and nation!
    Ancient of eternal days!
   Sounded through the wide creation,
    Be Thy just and lawful praise.

2. For the grandeur of Thy nature—
    Grand beyond a seraph's thought;
   For the wonders of creation,
    Works with skill and kindness wrought;
   For Thy providence, that governs
    Through Thine empire's wide domain,
   Wings an angel, guides a sparrow;
    Blessed be Thy gentle reign.

3. For Thy rich, Thy free redemption,
    Bright, though veiled in darkness long;
   Thought is poor, and poor expression,
    Who can sing that wondrous song?
   Brightness of the Father's glory!
    Shall Thy praise unuttered lie?
   Break, my tongue! such guilty silence,
    Sing the Lord who came to die:

4. From the highest throne of glory
    To the cross of deepest wo,
   Came to ransom guilty captives!
    Flow, my praise! forever flow:
   Re-ascend, immortal Saviour!
    Leave Thy footstool, take Thy throne;
   Thence return and reign for ever;
    Be the kingdom all Thine own!
                    ROBINSON.

213. 8s & 7s.

1. PRAISE the Lord! ye heavens, adore Him;
    Praise Him, angels in the height;
   Sun and moon, rejoice before Him;
    Praise Him, all ye stars of light!

2. Praise the Lord—for He hath spoken;
    Worlds His mighty voice obeyed;
   Laws which never shall be broken,
    For their guidance He hath made.

3. Praise the Lord—for He is glorious;
    Never shall His promise fail;
   God hath made His saints victorious,
    Sin and death shall not prevail.

4. Praise the God of our salvation,
    Hosts on high His power proclaim;
   Heaven and earth, and all creation,
    Laud and magnify His name!
            Hallelujah, Amen.
                    LIVERPOOL COLL.

ANDOVER. 8s & 7s. CH. BEECHER.

1. The scene around me disappears, And, borne to ancient regions, While time recalls the flight of years, I see an-gel-ic le-gions De-scending in an orb of light, A-midst the dark and silent night, I hear ce-lestial voi-ces, I hear ce-lestial voi-ces.

214. 8s & 7s. Peculiar.

1. THE scene around me disappears,
   And, borne to ancient regions,
 While time recals the flight of years,
   I see angelic legions
 Descending in an orb of light,
 Amidst the dark and silent night,
   I hear celestial voices.

2. Tidings, glad tidings from above,
   To every age and nation;
 Tidings, glad tidings,—God is love;
   To man He sends salvation;
 His Son beloved, His only Son,
 The work of mercy hath begun;
   Give to His name the glory!

3. Through David's city I am led;
   Here all around are sleeping;
 A light directs to yon poor shed,
   Where lonely watch is keeping:
 I enter;—ah! what glories shine!
 Is this Immanuel's earthly shrine?
   Messiah's infant temple?

4. It is; it is;—and I adore
   This Stranger meek and lowly,
 As saints and seraphs bow before
   The throne of God thrice holy;
 Faith through the vail of flesh can see
 The face of Thy divinity,
   My Lord, my God, my Saviour!
                    MONTGOMERY.

ADVENT.

MILTON. P. M.   J. ZUNDEL.

1. No war nor battle's sound Was heard the world a-round; No hostile chiefs to furious combat ran; But peaceful was the night, In which the Prince of light His reign of peace upon the earth began.

215. P. M.

1. No war nor battle's sound
   Was heard the world around;
No hostile chiefs to furious combat ran;
   But peaceful was the night,
   In which the Prince of light
His reign of peace upon the earth began.

2. The shepherds on the lawn,
   Before the point of dawn,
In social circle sat; while all around,
   The gentle, fleecy brood,
   Or cropped the flowery food,
Or slept, or sported on the verdant ground,—

3. When, lo! with ravished ears,
   Each swain delighted hears,
Sweet music, offspring of no mortal hand;
   Divinely-warbled voice,
   Answering the stringed noise, [band.
With blissful rapture charmed the listening

4. They saw a glorious light
   Burst on their wondering sight;
Harping in solemn choir, in robes arrayed,
   The helmed cherubim
   And sworded seraphim
Are seen in glittering ranks, with wings displayed.

5. Sounds of so sweet a tone
   Before were never known,
But when of old the sons of morning sung,
   While God disposed in air,
   Each constellation fair,
And the well-balanced world on hinges hung.

6. "Hail, hail, auspicious morn!
   The Saviour Christ is born!"
Such was th' immortal seraph's song sublime;
   "Glory to God in heaven!
   To man sweet peace be given,
Sweet peace and friendship to the end of time."

MILTON, VARIED.

CHRIST.

ANTIOCH. C. M. *Arranged by L. Mason.*

1. Joy to the world, the Lord is come! Let earth receive her King; Let ev-ery heart prepare him room, And heav'n and nature sing, And heav'n and nature sing, And heav'n and nature sing, And heav'n and nature sing.

216. C. M.

2. Joy to the world—the Saviour reigns,
Let men their songs employ;
While fields and floods—rocks, hills and plains
Repeat the sounding joy.

3. No more let sin and sorrow grow,
Nor thorns infest the ground;
He comes to make His blessings flow
Far as the curse is found.

4. He rules the world with truth and grace,
And makes the nations prove
The glories of His righteousness,
And wonders of His love.

WATTS.

217. C. M.

1. MORTALS, awake, with angels join,
And chant the solemn lay:
Joy, love, and gratitude, combine
To hail th' auspicious day.

2. In heaven the rapturous song began,
And sweet seraphic fire
Through all the shining legions ran,
And strung and tuned the lyre.

3. Swift through the vast expanse it flew,
And loud the echo rolled;
The theme, the song, the joy, was new,
'T was more than heaven could hold.

4. Down through the portals of the sky
Th' impetuous torrent ran;
And angels flew, with eager joy,
To bear the news to man.

5. Hark! the cherubic armies shout,
And glory leads the song;
'Good-will and peace are heard throughout
Th' harmonious angel throng.

6. Hail, Prince of life! forever hail,
Redeemer, brother, friend!
Though earth, and time, and life should fail,
Thy praise shall never end.

MEDLEY.

ADVENT.

EXETER. C. M.

1. Hark, the glad sound! the Saviour comes! The Saviour promised long! Let ev-ery heart pre-pare a throne, And ev-ery voice a song.

218. C. M.

2. On Him the Spirit, largely poured,
   Exerts its sacred fire;
   Wisdom and might, and zeal and love,
   His holy breast inspire.

3. He comes, the prisoner to release,
   In Satan's bondage held;
   The gates of brass before Him burst,
   The iron fetters yield.

4. He comes, from thickest films of vice
   To clear the mental ray,
   And on the eyeballs of the blind
   To pour celestial day.

5. He comes, the broken heart to bind,
   The bleeding soul to cure,
   And with the treasures of His grace
   To enrich the humble poor.

6. Our glad hosannas, Prince of Peace,
   The welcome shall proclaim,
   And heaven's eternal arches ring
   With Thy beloved name.

   DODDRIDGE.

219. C. M.

1. CALM on the listening ear of night
   Come heaven's melodious strains,
   Where wild Judea stretches far
   Her silver-mantled plains.

2. Celestial choirs, from courts above,
   Shed sacred glories there,
   And angels, with their sparkling lyres,
   Make music on the air.

3. The answering hills of Palestine
   Send back the glad reply;
   And greet, from all their holy heights,
   The day-spring from on high.

4. O'er the blue depths of Galilee
   There comes a holier calm,
   And Sharon waves, in solemn praise,
   Her silent groves of palm.

5. "Glory to God!" the sounding skies
   Loud with their anthems ring—
   "Peace to the earth, good-will to men,
   From heaven's eternal King!"

6. Light on thy hills, Jerusalem!
   The Saviour now is born!
   And bright on Bethlehem's joyous plains
   Breaks the first Christmas morn.

   E. H. SEARS.

220. C. M.

1. MESSIAH! at Thy glad approach
   The howling winds are still;
   Thy praises fill the lonely waste,
   And breathe from every hill.

2. The incense of the spring ascends
   Upon the morning gale;
   Red o'er the hill the roses bloom,
   The lilies in the vale.

3. Renew'd, the earth a robe of light,
   A robe of beauty wears;
   And in new heav'ns a brighter Sun
   Leads on the promis'd years.

4. Let Israel to the Prince of Peace
   The loud hosanna sing;
   With hallelujahs, and with hymns,
   O Zion, hail thy King.

   LOGAN.

CHRIST.

CHRISTMAS EVE. H. M.　　　　　　　　　　　　　　　　　　　　J. ZUNDEL.

1. Hark! what celestial sounds, What mu-sic fills the air! Soft war-bling to the morn, It

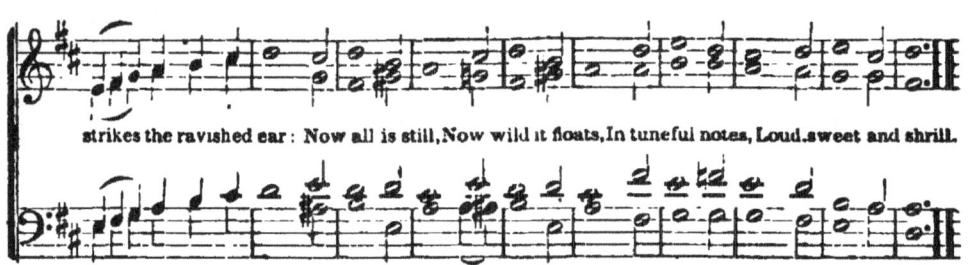

strikes the ravished ear: Now all is still, Now wild it floats, In tuneful notes, Loud, sweet and shrill.

221. H. M.

1. HARK! what celestial sounds,
　　What music fills the air!
　Soft warbling to the morn,
　　It strikes the ravished ear:
Now all is still; now wild it floats,
In tuneful notes, loud, sweet, and shrill.

2. Th' angelic hosts descend,
　　With harmony divine:
　See how from heaven they bend,
　　And in full chorus join:
"Fear not," say they; "Great joy we bring:
Jesus, your King, is born to-day."

3. He comes, your souls to save
　　From death's eternal gloom;
　To realms of bliss and light
　　He lifts you from the tomb:
Your voices raise, with sons of light;
Your songs unite of endless praise.

4. Glory to God, on high!
　　Ye mortals spread the sound,
　And let your raptures fly
　　To earth's remotest bound;
For peace on earth, from God in heaven,
To man is given, at Jesus' birth.
　　　　　　　　　SALISBURY COLL.

222. H. M.

1. HARK! hark!—the notes of joy
　　Roll o'er the heavenly plains,
　And seraphs find employ
　　For their sublimest strains:
Some new delight in heaven is known:
Loud sound the harp around the throne.

2. Hark! hark!—the sound draws nigh,
　　The joyful hosts descend;
　Jesus forsakes the sky,
　　To earth His footsteps bend;
He comes to bless our fallen race;
He comes with messages of grace.

3. Bear, bear the tidings round;
　　Let every mortal know
　What love in God is found,
　　What pity He can show;
Ye winds that blow! ye waves that roll!
Bear the glad news from pole to pole.

4. Strike, strike the harps again,
　　To great Immanuel's name;
　Arise, ye sons of men!
　　And all His grace proclaim;
Angels and men wake every string,
'Tis God the Saviour's praise we sing.
　　　　　　　　　REED'S COLL.

INCIDENTS IN HIS LIFE.

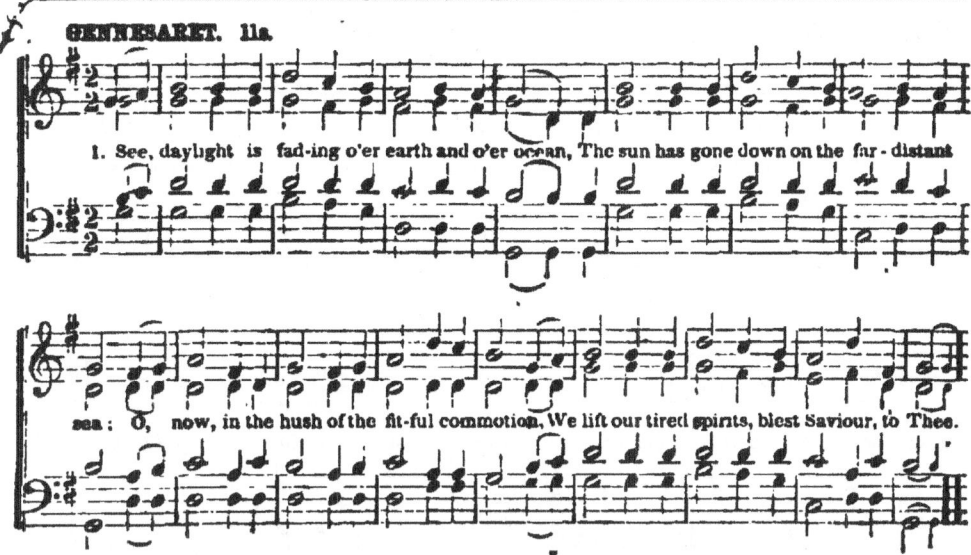

GENNESARET. 11s.

1. See, daylight is fading o'er earth and o'er ocean, The sun has gone down on the far-distant sea: O, now, in the hush of the fit-ful commotion, We lift our tired spirits, blest Saviour, to Thee.

223. 12s & 11s.

1. See, daylight is fading, o'er earth and o'er ocean,
   The sun has gone down on the far-distant sea;
   Oh, now in the hush of the fitful commotion
   We lift our tired spirits, blest Saviour, to Thee.

2. Full oft wast thou found afar on the mountain,
   As eventide spread her dark wing o'er the wave:
   Thou Son of the Highest, and life's endless fountain,
   Be with us, we pray Thee, to bless and to save.

3. And oft as the tumult of life's heaving billow
   Shall toss our frail bark, driving wild o'er night's deep,
   Let Thy healing wing be stretched over our pillow,
   And guard us from evil, though Death watch our sleep.

4. To God our great Father, whose throne is in heaven
   Who dwells with the lowly and humble in heart,
   To the Son and the Spirit all glory be given:
   One God, ever blessed and praised, Thou art.
   HEBER.

224. 12s.

1. WHEN through the torn sail the wild tempest is streaming,
   When o'er the dark wave the red lightning is gleaming,
   Nor hope lends a ray the poor sailors to cherish,
   They fly to their Master, "Save, Lord, or we perish."

2. O Jesus, once rocked on the breast of the billow,
   Aroused by the shriek of despair from Thy pillow,
   Now seated in glory, the poor sinner cherish,
   Who cries in his anguish, "Save, Lord, or we perish."

3. And, O when the whirlwind of passion is raging,
   When sin in our hearts its wild warfare is waging,
   Then send down Thy grace, thy redeemed to cherish.
   Rebuke the destroyer: "Save, Lord, or we perish."

225. 11s.

1. WHILE nature was sinking in stillness to rest,
   The last beam of daylight shone dim in the west,
   O'er fields by pale moonlight or stars' trembling ray,
   In deep meditation, I wandered away.

2. While passing a garden I paused to hear,
   A voice faint and plaintive, from One that was there;
   The voice of the sufferer affected my heart,
   While pleading in anguish the poor sinner's part.

3. So deep were His sorrows, so fervent His prayers,
   That down o'er His bosom rolled sweat, blood, and tears!
   I wept to behold Him!—I asked Him His name,
   He answered, "'Tis JESUS! from heaven I came!"

4. How sweet was that moment He bade me rejoice!
   His smile, O how pleasant! How pleasant His voice!
   I flew from the garden to spread it abroad!
   I shouted Salvation! and Glory to God!

5. I'm now on my journey to mansions above;
   My soul's full of glory, of light, grace, and love!
   I think of the garden, the prayers, and the tears,
   Of that loving Stranger, who banished my fears!

6. The day of bright glory is rolling around,
   When Gabriel descending, the trumpet shall sound;
   My soul then in raptures of glory shall rise
   To gaze on the Stranger with unclouded eyes.

226. 11s.

1. THOU sweet gliding Kedron, by thy silver streams,
   Our Saviour, at midnight, when moonlight's pale beams
   Shone bright on thy waters, would frequently stray,
   And lose, in thy murmurs, the toils of the day.

2. How damp were the vapors that fell on His head!
   How hard was His pillow, how humble His bed!
   The angels, astonished, grew sad at the sight,
   And followed their Master with solemn delight.

3. O garden of Olivet, thou dear honored spot,
   The fame of thy wonders shall ne'er be forgot;
   The theme most transporting to seraphs above;
   The triumph of sorrow,—the triumph of love!

4. Come, saints, and adore Him; come, bow at His feet:
   O, give Him the glory, the praise that is meet;
   Let joyful hosannahs unceasing arise,
   And join the full chorus that gladdens the skies.
   MARIE DE FLEURY.

CHRIST.

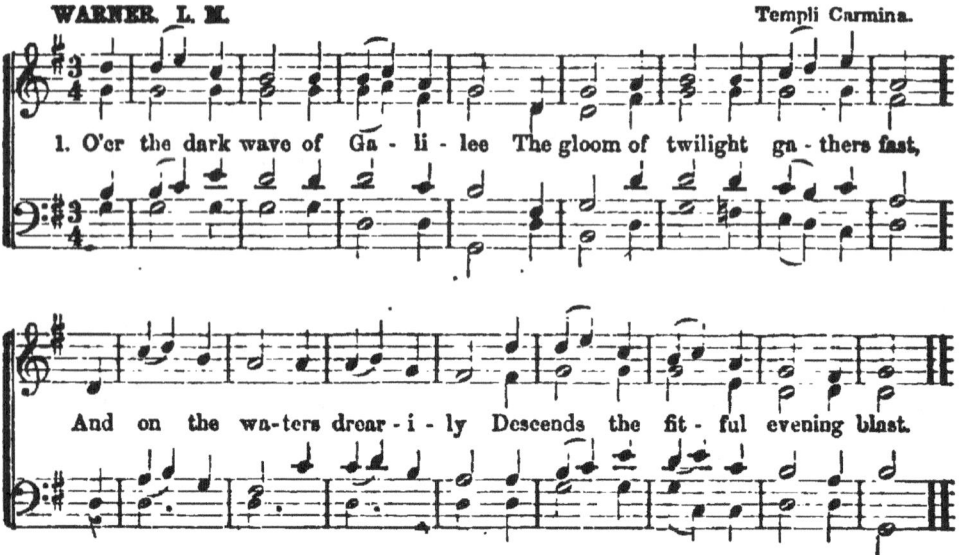

WARNER. L. M.   Templi Carmina.

1. O'er the dark wave of Ga-li-lee The gloom of twilight ga-thers fast, And on the wa-ters drear-i-ly Descends the fit-ful evening blast.

227. L. M.

2. The weary bird hath left the air,
   And sunk into his sheltered nest;
   The wandering beast has sought his lair,
   And laid him down his welcome rest.

3. Still near the lake, with weary tread,
   Lingers a form of human kind;
   And on His lone, unsheltered head,
   Flows the chill night-damp of the wind.

4. Why seeks He not a home of rest?
   Why seeks He not a pillowed bed?
   Beasts have their dens, the bird its nest;
   He hath not where to lay His head.

5. Such was the lot He freely chose,
   To bless, to save the human race;
   And through His poverty there flows
   A rich, full stream of heavenly grace.
                   RUSSELL.

228. L. M.

1. When Jordan hushed his waters still,
   And silence slept on Zion's hill,
   When Bethlehem's shepherds, through the [night,
   Watched o'er their flocks by starry light,—

2. Hark! from the midnight hills around,
   A voice of more than mortal sound,
   In distant hallelujahs stole,
   Wild murmuring o'er the raptured soul.

3. On wheels of light, on wings of flame,
   The glorious hosts of Zion came;
   High heaven with songs of triumph rung,
   While thus they struck their harps and sung:

4. "O Zion, lift thy raptured eye;
   The long-expected hour is nigh;
   The joys of nature rise again;
   The Prince of Salem comes to reign.

5. "See, Mercy, from her golden urn,
   Pours a rich stream to them that mourn;
   Behold, she binds, with tender care,
   The bleeding bosom of despair.

6. He comes to cheer the trembling heart;
   Bids Satan and his host depart;
   Again the day-star gilds the gloom,
   Again the bowers of Eden bloom."
                   T. CAMPBELL.

229. L. M.

1. How sweetly flowed the gospel sound
   From lips of gentleness and grace,
   When listening thousands gathered round,
   And joy and gladness filled the place!

2. From heaven He came, of heaven He spoke,
   To heaven He led his followers' way;
   Dark clouds of gloomy night He broke,
   Unveiling an immortal day.

3. "Come, wanderers, to my Father's home;
   Come, all ye weary ones, and rest:"
   Yes, sacred Teacher, we will come,
   Obey Thee, love Thee, and be blest.

4. Decay, then, tenements of dust;
   Pillars of earthly pride, decay:
   A nobler mansion waits the just,
   And Jesus has prepared the way.
                   BOWRING.

LIFE AND DEATH OF CHRIST.

BRENTFORD. L. M.

1. How beauteous were the marks divine, That in Thy meekness used to shine; That lit Thy lonely pathway, trod In wondrous love, O Son of God!

230. L. M.

2. O, who like Thee—so calm, so bright,
So pure, so made to live in light?
O, who like Thee did ever go
So patient through a world of woe?

3. O, who like Thee so humbly bore
The scorn, the scoffs of men, before?
So meek, forgiving, godlike, high,
So glorious in humility?

4. The bending angels stooped to see
The lisping infant clasp Thy knee,
And smile, as in a father's eye,
Upon Thy mild divinity.

5. And death, which sets the prisoner free,
Was pang, and scoff, and scorn to Thee;
Yet love through all Thy torture glowed,
And mercy with Thy life-blood flowed.

6. O, in Thy light be mine to go,
Illuming all my way of woe;
And give me ever on the road
To trace Thy footsteps, Son of God!
A. C. COXE.

231. L. M.

1. LORD! in Thy garden agony,
No light seemed on Thy soul to break,
No form of seraph lingered nigh,
Nor yet the voice of comfort spake,—

2. Till, by Thine own triumphant word,
The victory over ill was won;
Till the sweet, mournful cry was heard,
"Thy will, O God, not mine, be done!"

3. Lord, bring those precious moments back,
When, fainting, against sin we strain;
Or in Thy counsels fail to track
Aught but the present grief and pain.

4. In weakness, help us to contend;
In darkness, yield to God our will;
And true hearts, faithful to the end,
Cheer by Thine holy angels still!

232. L. M.

1. HAVE we no tears to shed for Him,
While soldiers scoff, and Jews deride?
Ah! look, how patiently He hangs—
Jesus, our love, is crucified!

2. What was Thy crime, my dearest Lord?
By earth, by heaven, Thou hast been tried,
And guilty found of too much love;
Jesus, our Love, is crucified!

3. Found guilty of excess of love,
It was Thine own sweet will that tied
Thee tighter far than helpless nails;
Jesus, our Love, is crucified!

4. O break, O break, hard heart of mine!
Thy weak self-love and guilty pride
His Pilate and his Judas were;
Jesus, our Love, is crucified!

5. A broken heart, a fount of tears—
Ask, and they will not be denied;
A broken heart love's cradle is;
Jesus, our Love, is crucified!
LYRA. CATH.

CHRIST.

WILLIAMS. L. M. Arranged from Templi Carmina.

1. When I sur-vey the wondrous cross, On which the Prince of Glo-ry died,

My rich-est gain I count but loss, And pour contempt on all my pride.

233. L. M.

1. WHEN I survey the wondrous cross,
   On which the Prince of glory died,
   My richest gain I count but loss,
   And pour contempt on all my pride.

2. Forbid it, Lord, that I should boast,
   Save in the death of Christ, my God;
   All the vain things that charm me most,
   I sacrifice them to His blood.

3. See, from His head, His hands, His feet,
   Sorrow and love flow mingled down:
   Did e'er such love and sorrow meet,
   Or thorns compose so rich a crown?

4. Were the whole realm of nature mine,
   That were a present far too small;
   Love so amazing, so divine,
   Demands my soul, my life, my all.
   WATTS.

234. L. M.

1. RIDE on, ride on in majesty!
   Hark! all the tribes hosanna cry!
   Thy humble beast pursues his road,
   With palms and scattered garments strowed.

2. Ride on, ride on in majesty!
   In lowly pomp ride on to die!
   O Christ! thy triumphs now begin,
   O'er captive death and conquered sin.

3. Ride on, ride on in majesty!
   The winged squadrons of the sky
   Look down with sad and wondering eyes,
   To see the approaching sacrifice.

4. Ride on, ride on in majesty!
   Thy last and fiercest strife is nigh;
   The Father on his sapphire throne
   Expects his own anointed Son!
   MILMAN.

235. L. M.

1. HE dies!—the friend of sinners dies;
   Lo! Salem's daughters weep around;
   A solemn darkness veils the skies;
   A sudden trembling shakes the ground.

2. Here's love and grief beyond degree;
   The Lord of glory dies for men;
   But lo! what sudden joys we see!
   Jesus, the dead, revives again.

3. The rising God forsakes the tomb;
   Up to His Father's court He flies;
   Cherubic legions guard Him home,
   And shout Him welcome to the skies.

4. Break off your tears, ye saints, and tell
   How high our great Deliverer reigns;
   Sing how He spoiled the hosts of hell,
   And led the tyrant death in chains.

5. Say—live forever, glorious King,
   Born to redeem, and strong to save!
   Where now, O Death, where is thy sting?
   And where thy victory, boasting Grave?
   WATTS.

LIFE AND DEATH OF CHRIST.

MARY AT THE CROSS. 8s & 7s.

236. 8s & 7s.

1. Jews were wrought to cruel madness,
Christians fled in fear and sadness, |
Mary stood the cross beside; |
At its foot, her foot she planted,
By the dreadful scene undaunted, |
Till the gentle Suff'rer died. |
Poets oft have sung her story,
Painters decked her brow with glory, |
Priests her name have | dei | fied. |

2. But no worship, song, or glory,
Touches like the simple story, |
Mary stood the cross beside. |
And when under fierce oppression,
Goodness suffers like transgression, |
Christ again is crucified. |
But if love be there, true-hearted,
By no grief or terror parted, |
Mary stands the | cross be | side. |

237. 8s & 7s.

1. At the cross her station keeping, |
Stood the mournful mother weeping, |
Close to Jesus to the | last: |
Through her heart, His sorrow sharing, |
All His bitter anguish bearing,
Now at length the | sword had | pass'd.

2. Oh, how sad and sore distress'd, |
Was that mother highly blest,
Of the sole-begotten | One! |
Christ above in torment hangs, |
She beneath beholds the pangs
Of her dying, | glorious | Son.

3. Let me mingle tears with thee, |
Mourning Him who mourned for me, |
All the days that I may | live; |
By the cross with Him to stay, |
There with thee to weep and pray,
Is all I ask of | Christ to | give.

4. Christ, when Thou shalt call me hence, |
Be Thou only my defence, |
Be Thy cross my victo | ry; |
While my body here decays, |
May my soul Thy goodness praise,
Safe in Para | dise with | Thee. |

238. 8s & 7s.

1. See the Lord of glory dying, |
See Him gasping, hear Him crying, |
See His burthened bosom | heave; |
Look, ye sinners, ye that hung Him,
See how deep your sins have stung Him,
Dying sinners, | look and | live. |

2. See the rocks and mountains shaking, |
Earth unto her center quaking, |
Nature's groans awake the | dead. |
Veiled the sun in awful wonder, |
While the veil is rent asunder,
And the victim | bows His | head. |

3. Heaven's bright melodious legions, |
Chanting thro' those lofty regions, |
Cease to thrill the quivering | string; |
Songs seraphic all suspended, |
Till the tragic woe is ended,
By the all a | toning | King. |

4. Hell and all the powers infernal, |
Rage against the Lamb Eternal, |
While He pours the vital | flood; |
And their empire's deep foundation—
Rocks in frightful consternation,
As earth feels that | warm life- | blood. |

5. Shout, ye saints, with exultation, |
Fill with song the wide creation. |
See! He rises from the | tomb! |
Vain the bars of Death's dominion! |
Marble bond, and midnight pinion,
Part for aye your | reign of | doom.

6. Lo! the heavens are bursting o'er us, |
Hark, the wide out-rushing chorus |
Everlasting numbers | rise— |
Songs immortal sweetly sounding, |
Myriad lyres and harps resounding,
As the Conqueror | mounts the | skies!

CHRIST.

GETHSEMANE. L. M.   Arranged by CH. BEECHER.

1. 'Tis midnight, and on Olive's brow, The star is dimm'd that lately shone; 'Tis midnight, in the garden now The suffering Saviour prays a-lone, The suffering Saviour prays a-lone.

239. L. M.

2. 'Tis midnight—and, from all removed,
   Immanuel wrestles lone, with fears;
E'en the disciple that he loved
   Heeds not his Master's grief and tears.

3. 'T is midnight—and, for others' guilt,
   The Man of sorrows weeps in blood;
Yet He, who hath in anguish knelt,
   Is not forsaken by His God.

4. 'T is midnight—and, from ether-plains,
   Is borne the song that angels know;
Unheard by mortals are the strains
   That sweetly soothe the Saviour's woe.

240. L. M.

1. BEHOLD the Man! how glorious He!
   Before His foes He stands unaw'd,
And, without wrong or blasphemy,
   He claims equality with God.

2. Behold the Man! by all condemn'd,
   Assaulted by a host of foes;
His person and His claims contemn'd,
   A Man of sufferings and of woes.

3. Behold the Man! He stands alone,
   His foes are ready to devour;
Not one of all His friends will own
   Their Master in this trying hour.

4. Behold the Man! though scorn'd below,
   He bears the greatest name above;
The angels at His footstool bow,
   And all His royal claims approve.
                 CHRISTIAN PSALMIST.

241. L. M.

1. FROM Calvary a cry was heard—
   A bitter and heart-rending cry:
My Saviour! every mournful word
   Bespeaks Thy soul's deep agony.

2. A horror of great darkness fell
   On Thee, Thou spotless, holy One!
And all the swarming hosts of hell
   Conspired to tempt God's only Son.

3. The scourge, the Thorns, the deep disgrace—
   These Thou could'st bear, nor once repine;
But when Jehovah veiled His face,
   Unutterable pangs were Thine.

4. Let the dumb world its silence break;
   Let pealing anthems rend the sky;
Awake, my sluggish soul, awake!
   He died, that we might never die.

5. Lord! on Thy cross I fix mine eye;
   If e'er I lose its strong control,
Oh! let that dying, piercing cry,
   Melt and reclaim my wandering soul.
                 MONTGOMERY.

242. L. M.

1. 'Tis finished!—so the Saviour cried,
And meekly bowed His head, and died;
'Tis finished!—yes, the race is run,
The battle fought, the vict'ry won.

2. 'Tis finished!—let the joyful sound
Be heard through all the nations round:
'T is finished!—let the echo fly,
Through heaven and hell, through earth and sky
                 STENNET.

LIFE AND DEATH OF CHRIST.

LEIPZIG. L. M. — From the Psalmodist.

1. Lord, what a heaven of saving grace, Shines in the beauties of Thy face; And lights our passions to a flame! Lord! how we love Thy charming name!

243. L. M.

1. Lord! what a heaven of saving grace
Shines through the beauties of Thy face,
And lights our passions to a flame!
Lord! how we love Thy charming name!

2. When I can say, my God is mine—
When I can feel Thy glories shine—
I tread the world beneath my feet,
And all that earth calls good or great.

3. While such a scene of sacred joys
Our raptured eyes and souls employs,
Here we could sit, and gaze away
A long, an everlasting day.

4. Well, we shall quickly pass the night,
To the fair coasts of perfect light;
Then shall our joyful senses rove
O'er the dear object of our love.
WATTS.

244. L. M.

1. 'Twas on that dark, that doleful night,
When powers of earth and hell arose,
Against the Son of God's delight,
And friends betrayed Him to His foes:

2. Before the mournful scene began, [brake;
He took the bread, and blessed, and
What love through all His actions ran!
What wondrous words of grace He spake!

3. "This is my body, broke for sin;
Receive and eat the living food;"
Then took the cup, and blessed the wine:
"'Tis the new covenant in my blood."

4. "Do this," He cried, "till time shall end,
In mem'ry of your dying Friend;
Meet at my table, and record
The love of your departed Lord."

5. Jesus! Thy feast we celebrate;
We show Thy death, we sing Thy name,
Till Thou return, and we shall eat
The marriage-supper of the Lamb.
WATTS.

245. L. M.

1. The morning dawns upon the place
Where Jesus spent the night in prayer;
Through yielding glooms behold His face!
Nor form, nor comeliness is there.

2. Brought forth to judgment, now He stands
Arraigned, condemned, at Pilate's bar;
Here, spurned by fierce prætorian bands,
There, mocked by Herod's men of war.

3. He bears their buffeting and scorn—
Mock-homage of the lip, the knee—
The purple robe, the crown of thorn—
The scourge, the nail, th' accursed tree.

4. No guile within His mouth is found;
He neither threatens, nor complains;
Meek as a lamb for slaughter bound,
Dumb, 'mid His murderers He remains.

5. But hark! He prays: 't is for His foes:
He speaks: 't is comfort to His friends;
Answers: and paradise bestows;
He bows His head: the conflict ends.
MONTGOMERY.

CHRIST.

HEMANS. C. H. M.

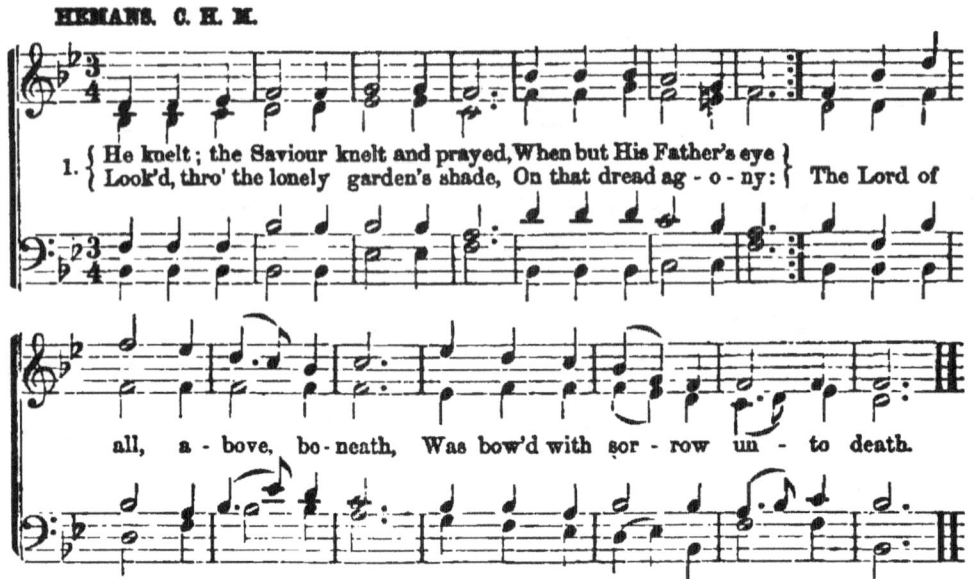

1. He knelt; the Saviour knelt and prayed, When but His Father's eye
Look'd, thro' the lonely garden's shade, On that dread ag-o-ny:
The Lord of all, a-bove, be-neath, Was bow'd with sor-row un-to death.

246. C. H. M.

2. The sun went down in fearful hour;
   The heavens might well grow dim,
When this mortality had power
   To thus o'ershadow Him;
That He who gave man's breath might know
The very depths of human woe.

3. He knew them all—the doubt, the strife,
   The faint, perplexing dread:
The mists that hang o'er parting life
   All darkened round His head;
And the Deliverer knelt to pray;
Yet passed it not, that cup, away.

4. It passed not, though the stormy wave
   Had sunk beneath His tread;
It passed not, though to Him the grave
   Had yielded up its dead;
But there was sent Him, from on high,
A gift of strength, for man to die.

5. And was His mortal hour beset
   With anguish and dismay?
How may we meet our conflict yet
   In the dark, narrow way?
How, but through Him that path who trod?
"Save, or we perish, Son of God."
                                    HEMANS.

CRUCIFIX. 7s & 6s.   Greek Melody.

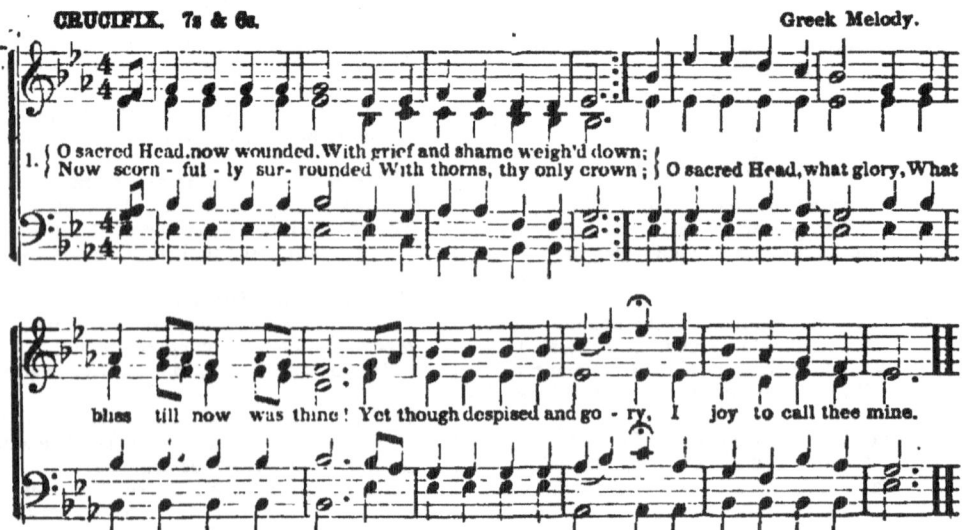

1. O sacred Head, now wounded, With grief and shame weigh'd down;
Now scorn-ful-ly sur-rounded With thorns, thy only crown;
O sacred Head, what glory, What bliss till now was thine! Yet though despised and go-ry, I joy to call thee mine.

LIFE AND DEATH OF CHRIST.

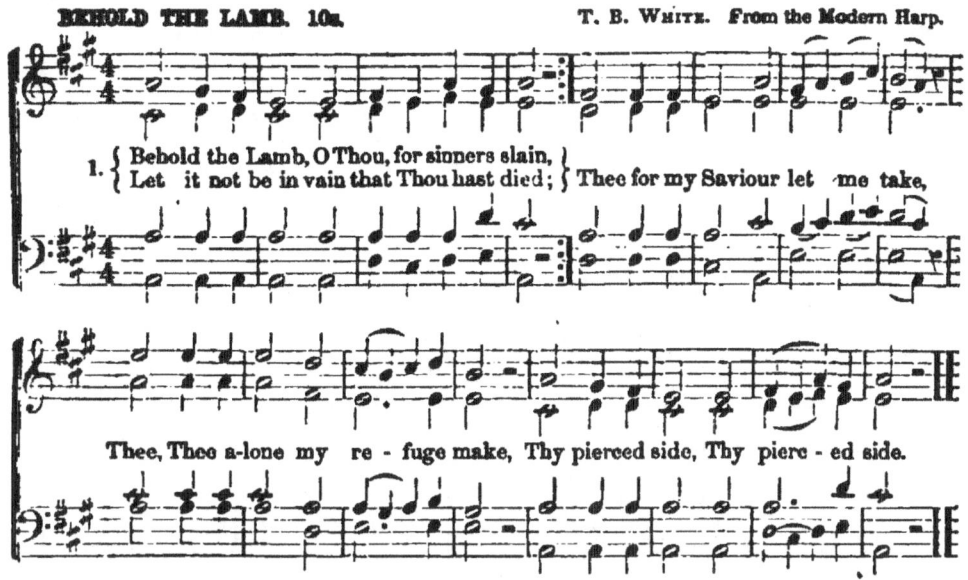

BEHOLD THE LAMB. 10s.   T. B. WHITE. From the Modern Harp.

1. Behold the Lamb, O Thou, for sinners slain,
Let it not be in vain that Thou hast died;
Thee for my Saviour let me take,
Thee, Thee alone my refuge make, Thy pierced side, Thy pierced side.

* 247.   7s & 6s.

2. O noblest brow and dearest,
   In other days the world
All fear'd when Thou appearedst;
   What shame on Thee is hurl'd;
How art Thou pale with anguish,
   With sore abuse and scorn;
How does that visage languish,
   Which once was bright as morn.

3. What language shall I borrow,
   To thank Thee, dearest Friend,
For this Thy dying sorrow,
   Thy pity without end!
O make me Thine for ever,
   And should I fainting be,
Lord, let me never, never,
   Outlive my love to thee.

4. If I, a wretch, should leave Thee,
   O Jesus, leave not me;
In faith may I receive Thee,
   When death shall set me free.
When strength and comfort languish,
   And I must hence depart,
Release me then from anguish,
   By thine own wounded heart.

5. Be near when I am dying,
   O, show Thy cross to me!
And for my succor flying,
   Come, Lord, to set me free.
These eyes new faith receiving,
   From Jesus shall not move;
For he who dies believing,
   Dies safely—through Thy love.
              PAUL GERHARDT, 1659.

248.   8s, 7s & 4s.

2. Behold the Lamb!
Archangels—fold your wings—
Seraphs—hush all the strings
   Of million lyres:
The Victim, veil'd on earth, in love—
Unveil'd—enthroned—adored above,
   All heaven admires!

3. Behold the Lamb!
Drop down, ye glorious skies—
He dies—He dies—He dies—
   For man once lost!
Yet lo! He lives—He lives—He lives—
And to his church Himself He gives—
   Incarnate Host!

4. Behold the Lamb!
All hail—Eternal Word!—
Thou universal Lord—
   Purge out our leaven:
Clothe us with godliness and good,
Feed us with Thy celestial food—
   Manna from heaven!

5. Behold the Lamb!
Saints, wrapt in blissful rest—
Souls—waiting to be blest—
   Oh! Lord—how long!   [tears,
Thou church on earth, o'erwhelm'd with
Still in this vale of woe and tears,
   Swell the full song.

6. Behold the Lamb!
Worthy is He alone,
To sit upon the throne
   Of God above!
One with the Ancient of all days—
One with the Paraclete in praise—
   All light—all love!   BRYDGES.

* This is a continuation of page 78.

CHRIST.

MANOAH. C. M.   From Greatorex's Coll.

1. The Saviour, what a noble flame Was kindled in His breast, When, hasting to Jerusalem, He marched before the rest!

249. C. M.

1. The Saviour, what a noble flame
   Was kindled in His breast,
   When, hasting to Jerusalem,
   He marched before the rest!

2. Good-will to men, and zeal for God,
   His every thought engross;
   He longs to be baptized with blood,
   He pants to reach the cross.

3. With all His sufferings full in view,
   And woes to us unknown,
   Forth to the task His spirit flew;
   'T was love that urged Him on.

4. Lord, we return Thee what we can;
   Our hearts shall sound abroad,
   Salvation to the dying man,
   And to the rising God!

5. And while Thy bleeding glories here
   Engage our wondering eyes,
   We learn our lighter cross to bear,
   And hasten to the skies.
   COWPER.

250. C. M.

1. Behold, where, in a mortal form
   Appears each grace divine;
   The virtues, all in Jesus met,
   With mildest radiance shine.

2. To spread the rays of heavenly light,
   To give the mourner joy,
   To preach glad tidings to the poor,
   Was His divine employ.

3. 'Midst keen reproach, and cruel scorn,
   Patient and meek He stood;
   His foes, ungrateful, sought His life;
   He labored for their good.

4. In the last hour of deep distress,
   Before His Father's throne,
   With soul resigned, He bowed, and said,
   "Thy will, not mine, be done!"

5. Be Christ our pattern and our guide;
   His image may we bear;
   O, may we tread His holy steps,
   His joy and glory share!
   ENFIELD.

251. C. M.

1. Behold the Saviour of mankind
   Nailed to the shameful tree!
   How vast the love that Him inclined
   To bleed and die for me.

2. Hark! how He groans, while nature shakes,
   And earth's strong pillars bend!
   The temple's veil asunder breaks,
   The solid marbles rend.

3. 'Tis finished! now the ransom's paid,
   "Receive my soul!" He cries:
   See—how He bows His sacred head!
   He bows His head and dies!

4. But soon He'll break death's iron-chain,
   And in full glory shine;
   O Lamb of God! was ever pain—
   Was ever love like Thine?

HIS RESURRECTION AND GLORY.

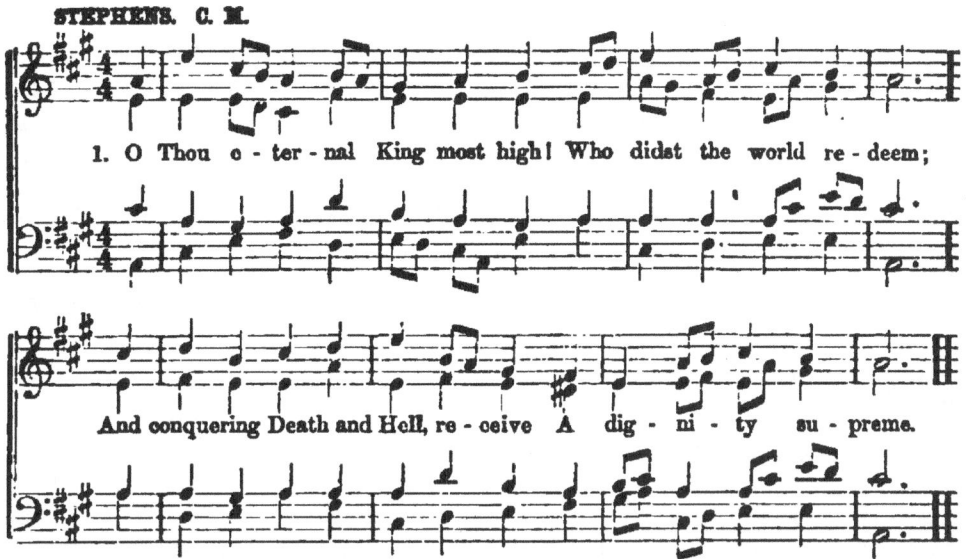

STEPHENS. C. M.

1. O Thou eternal King most high! Who didst the world redeem;
And conquering Death and Hell, receive A dignity supreme.

252. C. M.

2. Thou, through the starry orbs, this day,
   Didst to Thy throne ascend;
   Thenceforth to reign in sovereign power,
   And glory without end.

3. There, seated in Thy majesty,
   To Thee submissive bow
   The Heav'n of Heav'ns, the spacious earth,
   The depths of Hell below.

4. When Thou shinest on the clouds,
   With Thy angelic train.
   May we be saved from vengeance due,
   And our lost crowns regain.

5. Glory to Jesus, who returns
   Triumphantly to Heaven;
   Praise to the Father evermore,
   And Holy Ghost, be given.
   LYRA CATH.

253. C. M.

1. JESUS, our Lord, ascend Thy throne,
   And near Thy Father sit:
   In Zion shall Thy power be known,
   And make Thy foes submit.

2. What wonders shall Thy gospel do!
   Thy converts shall surpass
   The numerous drops of morning dew,
   And own Thy sovereign grace.

3. God hath pronounced a firm decree,
   Nor changes what he swore;—
   "Eternal shall Thy priesthood be,
   When Aaron is no more."

4. Jesus, our Priest, forever lives,
   To plead for us above;
   Jesus, our King, forever gives
   The blessings of His love.

5. God will exalt His glorious head,
   His lofty throne maintain,
   And strike the powers and princes dead,
   Who dare oppose His reign.
   WATTS.

254. C. M.

1. WHY is thy face so lit with smiles,
   Mother of Jesus! why?
   And wherefore is thy beaming look
   So fixed upon the sky?

2. His rising form on Olivet
   A summer's shadow cast!
   The branches of the hoary trees
   Droop'd as the shadow pass'd.

3. And as He rose with all His train
   Of righteous souls around,
   His blessing fell into thine heart,
   Like dew into the ground.

4. Down stoop'd a silver cloud from heaven,
   The Eternal Spirit's car,
   And on the lessening vision went,
   Like some receding star.

5. The silver cloud hath sail'd away,
   The skies are blue and free;
   The road that vision took is now
   Sunshine and vacancy.
   FABER.

LENOX. H. M. — EDSON.

255. H. M.

1. YES, the Redeemer rose;
   The Saviour left the dead;
   And o'er our hellish foes
   High raised His conquering head.
   In wild dismay, the guards around,
   Fall to the ground, and sink away.

2. Lo! the angelic bands
   In full assembly meet,
   To wait His high commands,
   And worship at His feet;
   Joyful they come, and wing their way,
   From realms of day, to Jesus' tomb.

3. Then back to heaven they fly,
   The joyful news to bear:
   Hark! as they soar on high,
   What music fills the air!
   Their anthems say,—'Jesus, who bled,
   Hath left the dead, He rose to-day.'

4. Ye mortals, catch the sound,
   Redeemed by Him from hell;
   And send the echo round
   The globe on which you dwell;
   Transported cry,—'Jesus who bled,
   Hath left the dead, no more to die.

5. All hail, triumphant Lord,
   Who sav'st us with Thy blood!
   Wide be Thy name adored,
   Thou, rising, reigning God.
   With Thee we rise, with Thee we reign,
   And empires gain beyond the skies.

DODDRIDGE.

256. H. M.

1. God is gone up on high,
    With a triumphant noise;
  The clarions of the sky
    Proclaim th' angelic joys:
  Join, all on earth! rejoice and sing,
  Glory ascribe to glory's King.

2. All power to our great Lord
    Is by the Father given,
  By angel-hosts adored,
    He reigns supreme in heaven:
  Join, all on earth! rejoice and sing,
  Glory ascribe to glory's King.

3. High on His holy seat,
    He bears the righteous sway;
  His foes beneath His feet
    Shall sink and die away:
  Join, all on earth! rejoice and sing,
  Glory ascribe to glory's King.

4. Then all the earth, renewed
    In righteousness divine,
  With all the hosts of God,
    In one great chorus join:
  Join, all on earth! rejoice and sing,
  Glory ascribe to glory's King.
          C. WESLEY.

257. H. M.

1. Ye saints! your music bring,
    And swell the rapturous sound;
  Strike every trembling string,
    Till earth and heaven resound:
  The triumphs of the cross we sing—
  Awake, ye saints! each joyful string.

2. The cross—the cross alone—
    Subdued the powers of hell;
  Like lightning from his throne,
    The prince of darkness fell;
  The triumphs of the cross we sing—
  Awake, ye saints, each joyful string.

3. The cross hath power to save,
    From all the foes that rise;
  The cross hath made the grave
    A passage to the skies;
  The triumphs of the cross we sing—
  Awake, ye saints! each joyful string.
          REED.

258. H. M.

1. Join all the glorious names
    Of wisdom, love, and power,
  That ever mortals knew,
    That angels ever bore:
  All are too mean to speak His worth,
  Too mean to set my Saviour forth.

2. Great prophet of our God!
    Our tongues would bless Thy name;
  By Thee the joyful news
    Of our salvation came;
  The joyful news of sins forgiven,
  Of hell subdued, and peace with heaven.

3. Jesus, our great High Priest,
    Offered His blood and died;
  My guilty conscience needs
    No sacrifice beside;
  His powerful blood did once atone,
  And now it pleads before the throne.

4. Oh thou almighty Lord,
    Our conqueror and our King!
  Thy sceptre and Thy sword,
    Thy reigning grace we sing;
  Thine is the power; Behold, we sit,
  In willing bonds, beneath Thy feet.
          WATTS.

259. H. M.

1. Jesus—transporting name!
    It charms the hosts above;
  They evermore proclaim,
    And wonder at His love;
  They look upon His heavenly face,
  And study His mysterious grace.

2. His name the sinner hears,
    And is from sin set free,
  'T is music in his ears,
    'T is life and victory;
  New songs do now his lips employ,
  And dances his glad heart for joy.

3. Stung by the scorpion sin,
    My poor expiring soul
  The balmy sound drinks in,
    And is at once made whole;
  I see my Lord upon the tree,
  I know, I feel He died for me.

4. Oh, for a trumpet voice,
    On all the world to call;
  To bid their hearts rejoice
    In Him, who died for all;
  Inspire with praise each human tongue,
  And wake a universal song.
          C. WESLEY.

ARNHEIM. L. M.   S. HOLYOKE.

1. Our Lord is ris-en from the dead, Our Jesus is gone up on high;
The powers of hell are cap-tive led, Dragged to the portals of the sky.

260. L. M.

2. There His triumphal chariot waits,
   And angels chant the solemn lay:
"Lift up your heads, ye heavenly gates!
   Ye everlasting doors! give way."

3. Loose all your bars of massy light,
   And wide unfold the ethereal scene;
He claims these mansions as His right;
   Receive the King of glory in.

4. "Who is the King of glory, who?"—
   The Lord that all our foes o'ercame;
That sin, and death, and hell o'erthrew;
   And Jesus is the Conqueror's name.

5. Lo! His triumphal chariot waits,
   And angels chant the solemn lay:—
"Lift up your heads, ye heavenly gates!
   Ye everlasting doors! give way."

6. "Who is the King of glory, who?"
   The Lord of boundless power possessed;
The King of saints and angels too;
   God over all, for ever blessed.
                    C. WESLEY.

261. L. M.

1. HAIL! morning known among the blest,—
   Morning of hope, and joy, and love,—
Of heavenly peace, and holy rest,
   Pledge of the endless rest above.

2. Blest be the Father of our Lord,
   Who from the dead hath brought His Son,
Hope to the lost was then restored,
   And everlasting glory won.

3. Scarce morning twilight had begun
   To chase the shades of night away,
When Christ arose—unsetting sun—
   The dawn of joy's eternal day.

4. Mercy looked down with smiling eye,
   When our Immanuel left the dead;
Faith marked His bright ascent on high,
   And Hope, with gladness, raised her head.

5. Descend, O Spirit of the Lord!
   Thy fire to every bosom bring,
Then shall our ardent hearts accord,
   And teach our lips God's praise to sing.
                    WARDLAW.

262. L. M.

1. HOSANNA to the living Lord!
Hosanna to th' incarnate Word!
To Christ, Creator, Saviour, King,
Let earth, let heaven, Hosanna sing.

2. Hosanna, Lord! Thine angels cry;
Hosanna, Lord! Thy saints reply:
Above, beneath us, and around,
The dead and living swell the sound.

3. O Saviour! with protecting care,
Return to this, Thy house of prayer:
Assembled in Thy sacred name,
Here we Thy parting promise claim.

4. But, chiefest, in our cleansed breast,
Eternal! bid Thy Spirit rest,
And make our secret soul to be
A temple pure, and worthy Thee!

5. So, in the last and dreadful day,
When earth and heaven shall melt away,
Thy flock, redeemed from sinful stain,
Shall swell the sound of praise again.
                    HEBER.

HIS RESURRECTION AND GLORY.

263. L. M.

1. Now for a tune of lofty praise,
   To great Jehovah's equal Son!
   Awake, my voice, in heavenly lays,
   Tell the loud wonders He hath done.

2. Sing, how He left the worlds of light,
   And the bright robes He wore above;
   How swift and joyful was the flight,
   On wings of everlasting love.

3. Deep in the shades of gloomy death,
   Th' almighty captive Prisoner lay;
   Th' almighty Captive left the earth,
   And rose to everlasting day.

4. Lift up your eyes, ye sons of light,
   Up to His throne of shining grace;
   See what immortal glories sit—
   Round the sweet beauties of His face.

5. Amongst a thousand harps and songs,
   Jesus the God exalted reigns;
   His sacred name fills all their tongues,
   And echoes through the heavenly plains!
   WATTS.

264. L. M.

1. When I the holy grave survey,
   Where once my Saviour deigned to lie,
   I see fulfilled what prophets say,
   And all the power of death defy.

2. This empty tomb shall now proclaim,
   How weak the bands of conquered death:
   Sweet pledge that all who trust His name
   Shall rise, and draw immortal breath.

3. Jesus, once numbered with the dead,
   Unseals His eyes to sleep no more;
   And ever lives their cause to plead,
   For whom the pains of death He bore.

4. Thy risen Lord, my soul! behold;
   See the rich diadem He wears!
   Thou too shalt bear a harp of gold—
   A crown of joy, when He appears.

5. Though in the dust I lay my head,
   Yet, gracious God! Thou wilt not leave
   My flesh for ever with the dead,
   Nor lose Thy children in the grave.
   WALLIN.

265. L. M.

1. Where high the heavenly temple stands,
   The house of God not made with hands,
   A great High Priest our nature wears,
   The guardian of mankind appears.

2. Though now ascended up on high,
   He bends to earth a brother's eye;
   Partaker of the human name,
   He knows the frailty of our frame.

3. Our fellow-sufferer yet retains
   A fellow-feeling of our pains;
   And still remembers, in the skies,
   His tears, His agonies, and cries.

4. In every pang that rends the heart,
   The Man of sorrows had a part;
   He sympathizes with our grief,
   And to the sufferer sends relief.

5. With boldness, therefore, at the throne,
   Let us make all our sorrows known;
   And ask the aid of heavenly power,
   To help us in the evil hour.
   LOGAN.

266. L. M.

1. Hail to the Prince of life and peace,
   Who holds the keys of death and hell!
   The spacious world unseen is His,
   And sovereign power becomes Him well.

2. In shame and anguish once He died;
   But now He lives for evermore;
   Bow down, ye saints, around His seat,
   And all ye angel-bands adore.

3. So live forever, glorious Lord,
   To crush Thy foes, and guard Thy friends;
   While all Thy chosen tribes rejoice,
   That Thy dominion never ends.

4. Worthy Thy hand to hold the keys,
   Guided by wisdom and by love;
   Worthy to rule o'er mortal life,
   O'er worlds below, and worlds above.

5. Forever reign, victorious King, [known;
   Wide through the earth Thy name be
   And call my longing soul to sing
   Sublimer anthems near Thy throne.
   DODDRIDGE.

CHRIST.

1. Oh! for a shout of sacred joy To God, the sovereign King; Let every land their tongues employ, And hymns of triumph sing.

267. C. M.

2. Jesus, our God, ascends on high;
   His heavenly guards around
   Attend Him rising through the sky,
   With trumpets' joyful sound.

3. While angels shout and praise their King,
   Let mortals learn their strains;
   Let all the earth his honor sing;—
   O'er all the earth he reigns.

4. Rehearse his praise, with awe profound;
   Let knowledge lead the song;
   Nor mock Him with a solemn sound
   Upon a thoughtless tongue.

5. In Israel stood His ancient throne:—
   He loved that chosen race;
   But now He calls the world His own;
   The heathen taste His grace.
   WATTS.

268. C. M.

1. TRIUMPHANT, Christ ascends on high,
   The glorious work complete;
   Sin, death, and hell, low vanquished lie,
   Beneath His awful feet.

2. There, with eternal glory crowned,
   The Lord, the Conqueror reigns;
   His praise the heavenly choirs resound,
   In their immortal strains.

3. Amid the splendors of His throne,
   Unchanging love appears;
   The names He purchased for His own
   Still on His heart He bears.

4. O, the rich depths of love divine!
   Of bliss, a boundless store:
   Dear Saviour, let me call Thee mine;
   I can not wish for more.

5. On Thee alone, my hope relies;
   Beneath Thy cross I fall,
   My Lord, my Life, my Sacrifice,
   My Saviour, and my All.
   MRS. STEELE.

269. C. M.

1. THE head that once was crown'd with thorns
   Is crowned with glory now;
   A royal diadem adorns
   The mighty Victor's brow.

2. The highest place that heaven affords,
   Is His by sovereign right;
   The King of kings, and Lord of lords,
   He reigns in glory bright;—

3. The joy of all who dwell above,
   The joy of all below,
   To whom He manifests His love,
   And grants His name to know.

4. To them, the cross, with all its shame,
   With all its grace is given;
   Their name, an everlasting name,
   Their joy—the joy of heaven.

5. They suffer with their Lord below,
   They reign with Him above;
   Their profit and their joy to know
   The mystery of His love.

6. To them the cross is life and health,
   Though shame and death to Him;
   His people's hope, His people's wealth,
   Their everlasting theme.
   KELLY.

HIS RESURRECTION AND GLORY.

270. C. M.

1. He, who on earth as man was known,
   And bore our sins and pains,
   Now, seated on th' eternal throne,
   The God of glory reigns.

2. His hands the wheels of nature guide,
   With an unerring skill,
   And countless worlds, extended wide,
   Obey His sovereign will.

3. While harps unnumbered sound His praise
   In yonder world above,
   His saints on earth admire His ways,
   And glory in His love.

4. When troubles, like a burning sun,
   Beat heavy on their head,
   To this almighty Rock they run,
   And find a pleasant shade.

5. How glorious He! how happy they,
   In such a glorious Friend!
   Whose love secures them all the way,
   And crowns them at the end.
   NEWTON.

271. C. M.

1. Now let our cheerful eyes survey
   Our great High Priest above,
   And celebrate His constant care,
   And sympathetic love.

2. Though raised to a superior throne,
   Where angels bow around,
   And high o'er all the shining train,
   With matchless honors crowned;—

3. The names of all His saints He bears,
   Deep graven on His heart;
   Nor shall a name once treasured there,
   E'er from His care depart.

4. Those characters shall fair abide,
   Our everlasting trust,
   When gems, and monuments, and crowns,
   Are mouldered down to dust.

5. So, gracious Saviour, on my breast,
   May Thy dear name be worn,
   A sacred ornament and guard,
   To endless ages borne.
   DODDRIDGE.

272. C. M.

1. With joy we meditate the grace
   Of our High Priest above;
   His heart is made of tenderness,
   His bosom glows with love.

2. Touched with a sympathy within,
   He knows our feeble frame;
   He knows what sore temptations mean,
   For He hath felt the same.

3. He in the days of feeble flesh
   Poured out His cries and tears;
   And in His measure feels afresh
   What every member bears.

4. Then let our humble faith address
   His mercy and His power;
   We shall obtain delivering grace
   In the distressing hour.
   WATTS.

273. C. M.

1. Ye humble souls, that seek the Lord,
   Chase all your fears away;
   And bow with reverence down, to see
   The place where Jesus lay.

2. Thus low the Lord of life was brought—
   Such wonders love can do!
   Thus cold in death that bosom lay,
   Which throbbed and bled for you.

3. If ye have wept at yonder cross,
   And still your sorrows rise,
   Stoop down and view the vanquished
       grave,
   Then wipe your weeping eyes.

4. But dry your tears, and tune your songs,
   The Saviour lives again;
   Not all the bolts and bars of death
   The Conqueror could detain.

5. High o'er th' angelic band He rears
   His once dishonored head;
   And through unnumbered years He reigns,
   Who dwelt among the dead.
   DODDRIDGE.

CHRIST.

XIII. 7s. L. MASON.

1. Ho-ly, ho-ly, ho-ly Lord! Live by heaven and earth a-dored!
Filled with Thee let all things cry, Glo-ry be to God most high.

274. 7s.

2. Mixt with those beyond the sky,
   Chanters to the Lord, most high,
We our hearts and voices raise,
   Echoing Thy eternal praise.

3. Thee, while dust and ashes sings,
   Angels shrink within their wings;
Prostrate seraphim above
   Breathe unutterable love.

4. Happy they who never rest,
   With Thy heavenly presence blest!
They the heights of glory see,
   Sound the depth of Deity.

5. Fain with them our souls would vie;
   Sink as low, and mount as high;
Fall, o'erwhelmed with love, or soar,
   Shout, or silently adore.   C. WESLEY.

275. 7s.

1. HOLY, holy, holy Lord!
   Be Thy glorious name adored;
   Lord! Thy mercies never fail;
   Hail, celestial goodness, hail!

2. Though unworthy, Lord, Thine ear,
   Deign our humble songs to hear;
   Purer praise we hope to bring,
   When around Thy throne we sing.

3. While on earth ordained to stay,
   Guide our footsteps in Thy way;
   Then on high we'll joyful raise
   Songs of everlasting praise.

4. Lord! Thy mercies never fail;
   Hail, celestial goodness, hail!
   Be Thy glorious name adored,
   Holy, holy, holy Lord!
                  SALISBURY COLL.

276. 7s.

1. MORNING breaks upon the tomb,
   Jesus scatters all its gloom;
   Day of triumph through the skies—
   See the glorious Saviour rise!

2. Ye, who are of death afraid,
   Triumph in the scattered shade;
   Drive your anxious cares away;
   See the place where Jesus lay!

3. Christian! dry your flowing tears,
   Chase your unbelieving fears;
   Look on His deserted grave;
   Doubt no more His power to save.
                         COLLYER.

HIS RESURRECTION AND GLORY.

PEARL. 7s. Arranged from RIPPON.

1. Angels, roll the rock away! Death, yield up the mighty prey! See, the Saviour quits the tomb— Glowing with immortal bloom.

277. 7s.

2. Shout, ye seraphs; Gabriel, raise
Thine eternal trump of praise;
Let the earth's remotest bound
Echo to the blissful sound.

3. Now, ye saints, lift up your eyes;
See the Conqueror mount the skies;
Troops of angels on the road,
Hail, and sing the incarnate God.

4. Heaven unfolds its portals wide—
Glorious Hero, through them ride;
King of glory, mount Thy throne;
Boundless empire is Thine own.

5. Praise Him, ye celestial choirs,
Praise, and sweep your golden lyres;
Praise Him in the noblest songs,
From ten thousand thousand tongues.
GIBBONS.

278. 7s.

1. CHRIST, the Lord, is risen to-day,
Our triumphant holy day:
He endured the cross and grave,
Sinners to redeem and save.

2. Lo! He rises, mighty King!
Where, O death! is now thy sting?
Lo! He claims His native sky!
Grave! where is thy victory?

3. Sinners, see your ransom paid,
Peace with God, for ever made:
With your risen Saviour rise;
Claim with Him the purchased skies.

4. Christ, the Lord, is risen to-day,
Our triumphant holy day;
Loud the song of victory raise;
Shout the great Redeemer's praise.

279. 7s, 6 lines.

1. GLORY, glory to our King!
Crowns unfading wreath His head;
Jesus, is the name we sing—
Jesus, risen from the dead;
Jesus, Conqueror o'er the grave;
Jesus, mighty now to save.

2. Now behold Him high enthroned,
Glory beaming from His face,
By adoring angels owned,
God of holiness and grace:
O for hearts and tongues to sing,
Glory, glory to our King!
KELLY.

280. 7s.

1. HAIL the day that sees Him rise,
Glorious, to His native skies!
Christ, awhile to mortals given,
Enters now the gates of heaven.

2. There the glorious triumph waits;
Lift your heads, eternal gates!
Christ hath vanquished death and sin;
Take the King of glory in.

3. See, the heaven its Lord receives!
Yet He loves the earth He leaves:
Though returning to His throne,
Still He calls mankind His own.

4. Still for us He intercedes,
His prevailing death He pleads;
Near Himself prepares our place,
Great Forerunner of our race.

5. What, though parted from our sight,
Far above yon starry height;
Thither our affections rise,
Foll'wing Him beyond the skies.
MADAN.

CHRIST.

AGATE. 11s, or 10s & 11s.

1. The Lord is my Shepherd, no want shall I know; I feed in green pastures, safe folded to rest, He leadeth my soul where the still waters flow, Restores me when wandering, redeems when oppress

281. 11s.

1. The Lord is my Shepherd, no want shall I know;
I feed in green pastures, safe-folded to rest;
He leadeth my soul where the still waters flow,
Restores me when wandering, redeems when oppress'd.

2. Through the valley and shadow of death though I stray,
Since Thou art my Guardian, no evil I fear;
Thy rod shall defend me, Thy staff be my stay;
No harm can befall with my Comforter near.

3. In the midst of affliction my table is spread;
With blessings unmeasured my cup runneth o'er;
With perfume and oil Thou anointest my head;
O what shall I ask of Thy providence more.

4. Let goodness and mercy, my bountiful God!
Still follow Thy steps till I meet Thee above;
I seek—by the path which my forefathers trod,
Through the land of their sojourn—Thy kingdom of love.

MONTGOMERY.

282. 11s & 10s.

1. Brightest and best of the sons of the morning!
Dawn on our darkness, and lend us thine aid;
Star of the East, the horizon adorning,
Guide where our infant Redeemer is laid.

2. Cold on His cradle the dew-drops are shining;
Low lies His head with the beasts of the stall;
Angels adore Him in slumber reclining—
Maker, and Monarch, and Saviour of all.

3. Say, shall we yield Him, in costly devotion,
Odors of Edom, and offerings divine!
Gems of the mountain, and pearls of the ocean,
Myrrh from the forest, or gold from the mine?

4. Vainly we offer each ample oblation,
Vainly with gold would His favor secure;
Richer, by far, is the heart's adoration,—
Dearer to God are the prayers of the poor.

5. Brightest and best of the sons of the morning!
Dawn on our darkness, and lend us thine aid;
Star of the East, the horizon adorning,
Guide where our infant Redeemer is laid.

HEBER.

283. 10s & 11s.

1. Lift your glad voices in triumph on high,
For Jesus hath risen, and man can not die,
Vain were the terrors that gathered around Him,
And short the dominion of death and the grave;
He burst from the fetters of darkness that bound Him,
Resplendent in glory to live and to save.
Loud was the chorus of angels on high,—
"The Saviour hath risen, and man shall not die."

2. Glory to God, in full anthems of joy;
The being He gave us, death can not destroy.
Sad were the life we must part with to-morrow,
If tears were our birthright, and death were our end;
But Jesus hath cheered the dark valley of sorrow,
And bade us, immortal, to heaven ascend.
Lift, then, your voices in triumph on high,
Jesus hath risen, and man shall not die.

HIS RESURRECTION AND GLORY.

HOW CALM AND BEAUTIFUL. C. L. M. — Hastings.

1. How calm and beautiful the morn That gilds the sacred tomb, Where once the Crucified was borne, And veiled in midnight gloom! Oh! weep no more the Saviour slain; The Lord is risen—He lives again.

284. C. L. M.

2. Ye mourning saints! dry every tear
   For your departed Lord;
   "Behold the place—He is not there,"
   The tomb is all unbarred:
   The gates of death were closed in vain:
   The Lord is risen—He lives again.

3. Now cheerful to the house of prayer
   Your early footsteps bend,
   The Saviour will Himself be there,
   Your advocate and friend:
   Once by the law your hopes were slain,
   But now in Christ ye live again.

4. How tranquil now the rising day!
   'Tis Jesus still appears,
   A risen Lord to chase away
   Your unbelieving fears:
   Oh! weep no more your comforts slain,
   The Lord is risen—He lives again.

5. And when the shades of evening fall,
   When life's last hour draws nigh,
   If Jesus shine upon the soul,
   How blissful then to die:
   Since He has risen who once was slain,
   Ye die in Christ to live again.
   T. HASTINGS.

285. C. L. M.

1. O SING unto my soul, my love,
   That all-entrancing lay,
   Such as the seraphim above
   Are singing far away;
   It comes as some familiar strain,
   Once heard in heaven, now heard again.

2. For, sure as olden sages tell,
   We are not all of earth;
   The soul, by some mysterious spell,
   Has glimpses of its birth,
   And memories of things divine,
   Thrill o'er me at that voice of thine.

3. They come as half-forgotten dreams
   From that eternal land,
   The sound of its celestial streams,
   And shores of silver sand.
   The angel faces in the air,
   O sing—and waft my spirit there.

EMPYREAN. S. M.   J. ZUNDEL.

1. Beyond the starry skies, Far as th' eternal hills, There, in the boundless world of light, Our great Redeemer dwells, Our great Redeemer dwells.

286. S. M.

1. BEYOND the starry skies,
 Far as th' eternal hills,
There in the boundless world of light,
 Our great Redeemer dwells.

2. Around Him angels fair,
 In countless armies shine;
And ever, in exalted lays,
 They offer songs divine.

3. "Hail, Prince of life!" they cry,
 "Whose unexampled love,
Moved Thee to quit these glorious realms
 And royalties above."

4. And when He stooped to earth,
 And suffered rude disdain,
They cast their honors at His feet,
 And waited in His train.

5. They saw Him on the cross,
 While darkness veiled the skies,
And when He burst the gates of death,
 They saw the Conqueror rise.

6. They thronged His chariot wheels,
 And bore Him to His throne;
Then swept their golden harps and sung—
 "The glorious work is done."
                        TURNER.

287. S. M.

1. "THE Lord is risen indeed;"
 The grave hath lost its prey;
With Him shall rise the ransomed seed
 To reign in endless day.

2. "The Lord is risen indeed;"
 He lives, to die no more;
He lives His people's cause to plead,
 Whose curse and shame He bore.

3. "The Lord is risen indeed;"
 Attending angels, hear;
Up to the courts of heaven, with speed,
 The joyful tidings bear.

4. Then take your golden lyres,
 And strike each cheerful chord;
Join all the bright, celestial choirs,
 To sing our risen Lord.
                        KELLY.

288. S. M.

1. ENTHRONED is Jesus now,
 Upon His heavenly seat;
The kingly crown is on His brow,
 The saints are at His feet.

2. In shining white they stand—
 A great and countless throng;
A palmy sceptre in each hand,
 On every lip a song.

3. They sing the Lamb of God,
 Once slain on earth for them;
The Lamb, through whose atoning blood
 Each wears his diadem.

4. Thy grace, O Holy Ghost,
 Thy blessed help supply,
That we may join that radiant host,
 Triumphant in the sky.
                        JUDKIN.

HIS RESURRECTION AND GLORY.

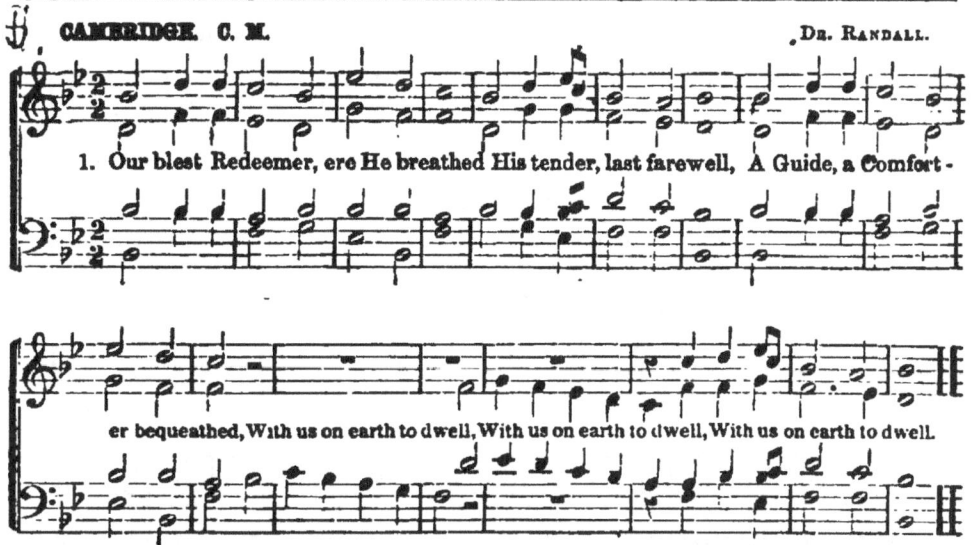

CAMBRIDGE. C. M. — Dr. Randall.

1. Our blest Redeemer, ere He breathed His tender, last farewell, A Guide, a Comforter bequeathed, With us on earth to dwell, With us on earth to dwell, With us on earth to dwell.

289. C. M.

2. He came in tongues of living flame,
   To teach, convince, subdue;
   All-powerful as the wind He came,
   And all as viewless, too.

3. He came, sweet influence to impart,
   A gracious, willing Guest,
   While He can find one humble heart
   Wherein to fix his rest.

4. And His that gentle voice we hear,
   Soft as the breath of even,
   That checks each fault, that calms each fear,
   And whispers us of heaven.

5. And every virtue we possess,
   And every virtue won,
   And every thought of holiness
   Are His and his alone.

6. Spirit of purity and grace,
   Our weakness pitying see;
   O, make our hearts Thy dwelling-place,
   Purer and worthier Thee.
   SPIRIT OF THE PSALMS.

290. C. M.

1. When God of old came down from heav'n,
   In power and wrath He came;
   Before His feet the clouds were riven,
   Half darkness, and half flame.

2. But when He came the second time,
   He came in power and love;
   Softer than gales at morning prime
   Hovered His holy Dove.

3. The fires that rushed on Sinai down
   In sudden torrents dread,
   Now gently light a glorious crown
   On every sainted head.

4. Like arrows went those lightnings forth,
   Winged with the sinner's doom;
   But these, like tongues, o'er all the earth
   Proclaiming life to come.
   KEBLE.

291. C. M.

1. No track is on the sunny sky,
   No footprints on the air:
   Jesus hath gone; the face of earth
   Is desolate and bare.

2. That Upper Room is heaven on earth;
   Within its precincts lie
   All that earth has of faith, or hope,
   Or heaven-born charity.

3. One moment—and the silentness
   Was breathless as the grave;
   The flutter'd earth forgot to quake,
   The troubled trees to wave.

4. He comes! He comes! that mighty Breath
   From heaven's eternal shores;
   His uncreated freshness fills
   His Bride, as she adores.

5. Earth quakes before that rushing blast,
   Heaven echoes back the sound,
   And mightily the tempest wheels
   That Upper Room around.

6. One moment—and the Spirit hung
   O'er all with dread desire;
   Then broke upon the heads of all
   In cloven tongues of fire.
   FABER.

CHRIST.

CONRAD. 6s & 4s.   CONRAD TREUER.

1. Rise, glorious Conqueror, rise Into Thy native skies, Assume Thy right; And where, in many a fold, The clouds are backward rolled, Pass thro' those gates of gold, And reign in light.

292. 6s & 4s.

1. RISE, glorious Conqueror, rise,
  Into Thy native skies,—
    Assume Thy right:
  And where, in many a fold,
  The clouds are backward roll'd—
  Pass through those gates of gold,
    And reign in light!

2. Victor o'er death and hell!
  Cherubic legions swell
    The radiant train:
  Praises all heaven inspire;
  Each angel sweeps his lyre,
  And claps his wings of fire,—
    Thou Lamb, once slain!

3. Enter, incarnate God!
  No feet but Thine have trod
    The serpent down:
  Blow the full trumpets, blow!
  Wider yon portals throw!
  Saviour, triumphant, go
    And take Thy crown!

4. Lion of Judah—Hail!—
  And let Thy name prevail
    From age to age:
  Lord of the rolling years—
  Claim for Thine own the spheres,
  For Thou hast bought with tears
    Thy heritage.

5. Yet, who are those behind,
  In numbers more than mind
    Can count or say—
  Clothed in immortal stoles,
  Illumining the poles—
  A galaxy of souls
    In white array?

6. And then was heard afar
  Star answering to star—
    "Lo! these have come,
  Followers of Him who gave
  His life their lives to save;
  And now their palms they wave,
    Brought safely home."

7. O Lord! ascend Thy throne!
 For Thou shalt rule alone
  Beside Thy Sire,
 With the great Paraclete,
 The Three in One complete—
 Before whose awful feet
  All foes expire! BRYDGES.

293. 6s & 4s.

1. HEAD of the hosts in glory!
 We joyfully adore Thee,—
  Thy church below,
 Blending with those on high,—
 Where through the azure sky
 Thy saints in ecstasy
  For ever glow!

2. Angels! archangels! glorious
 Guards of the church victorious!
  Worship the Lamb!
 Crown Him with crowns of light,
 One of the Three by right,—
 Love, Majesty, and Might—
  The great I AM!

3. Martyrs! whose mystic legions
 March o'er yon heavenly regions
  In triumph round:
 Wave high your banners, wave!
 Your God, our Saviour, clave
 For Death itself a grave,—
  In hell profound!

4. Saints! in fair circles, casting
 Rich trophies everlasting
  At Jesus' feet,—
 Amidst our rude alarms,
 We stretch forth suppliant arms,
 That we, too, safe from harms,
  In heaven may meet!

5. Then raise the song of gladness,
 To dissipate our sadness,
  And dry our tears;
 We wind our weary way
 Up to the realms of day,
 And watch, and wait, and pray,
  Through hopes and fears!

6. Saviour in glory beaming
 With radiance brightly streaming,
  Enthron'd in power,
 Grant by Thy awful name
 That we thro' flood and flame
 The Gospel may proclaim,
  Till life's last hour. BRYDGES.

294. 6s & 4s.

1. SING, sing His lofty praise,
 Whom angels cannot raise,
  But whom they sing;
 Jesus, who reigns above,
 Object of angels' love.
 Jesus, whose grace we prove,
  Jesus, our King.

2. Rich is the grace we sing,
 Poor is the praise we bring,
  Not as we ought:
 But when we see His face,
 In yonder glorious place,
 Then we shall sing His grace,
  Sing without fault.

295. 6s & 4s.

1. LET us awake our joys;
 Strike up with cheerful voice;
  Each creature, sing:
 Angels, begin the song;
 Mortals, the strain prolong,
 In accents sweet and strong,
  "Jesus is King."

2. Proclaim abroad His name;
 Tell of His matchless fame;
  What wonders done;
 Above, beneath, around,
 Let all the earth resound,
 'Till heaven's high arch rebound,
  "Victory is won."

3. He vanquished sin and hell,
 And our last foe will quell;
  Mourners, rejoice:
 His dying love adore;
 Praise Him, now raised in power;
 Praise Him for evermore,
  With joyful voice.

4. All hail the glorious day,
 When, through the heavenly way,
  Lo, He shall come,
 While they who pierced Him wail;
 His promise shall not fail;
 Saints, see your King prevail:
  Great Saviour, come. KINGSBURY.

CHRIST.

WESLEY. 8s & 7s, or 8s, 7s & 4s. — CH. BEECHER.

1. Hark! ten thousand harps and voices Sound the note of praise above; Jesus reigns, and heaven rejoices; Jesus reigns, the God of love: See, he sits on yonder throne; Jesus rules the world alone. Hallelujah, Hallelujah, Hallelujah, Amen.

296. 8s & 7s.

1. HARK! ten thousand harps and voices
   Sound the notes of praise above;
   Jesus reigns, and heaven rejoices;
   Jesus reigns, the God of love:
   See He sits on yonder throne;
   Jesus rules the world alone.

2. Jesus, hail! whose glory brightens
   All above, and gives it worth;
   Lord of life, Thy smile enlightens,
   Cheers, and charms Thy saints on earth:
   When we think of love like Thine,
   Lord, we own it love divine.

3. King of glory, reign for ever;
   Thine an everlasting crown:
   Nothing from Thy love shall sever
   Those whom Thou hast made Thine own;
   Happy objects of Thy grace,
   Destined to behold Thy face.

4. Saviour, hasten Thine appearing;
   Bring, O, bring the glorious day,
   When, the awful summons hearing,
   Heaven and earth shall pass away:
   Then, with golden harps, we'll sing,
   "Glory, glory to our King."

KELLY.

297. 8s, 7s & 4.

1. LOOK, ye saints;—the sight is glorious;—
   See the Man of sorrows now,
   From the fight returned victorious,
   Every knee to Him shall bow;
   Crown Him, crown Him;
   Crowns become the Victor's brow.

2. Crown the Saviour, angels, crown Him;
   Rich the trophies Jesus brings;
   In the seat of power enthrone Him,
   While the heavenly concert rings:
   Crown Him, crown Him;
   Crown the Saviour King of kings.

3. Sinners in derision crowned Him,
   Mocking thus the Saviour's claim;
   Saints and angels crowd around Him,
   Own His title, praise His name:
   Crown Him, crown Him;
   Spread abroad the Victor's fame.

4. Hark! those bursts of acclamation!
   Hark! those loud, triumphant chords!
   Jesus takes the highest station;
   O, what joy the sight affords!
   Crown Him, crown Him,
   King of kings, and Lord of lords.

KELLY.

HIS RESURRECTION AND GLORY.

298. 8s, 7s & 4.

1. Hail, thou happy morn, so glorious!
   Come, ye saints, your griefs give o'er;
   Sing how Jesus rose victorious,
   By His own almighty power:
      Hallelujah!
   To the glorious Son of God.

2. Countless bands of angels glorious,
   Cloth'd in bright ethereal blue;
   Straight the sound of Christ victorious
   From their silver trumpets flew:
      Christ triumphant
   Rises, Conqueror o'er the tomb.

3. Is that He who died on Calvary,
   Who was pierc'd with many a spear?
   Clad with countless suns of glory,
   See, He rises through the air:
      Hallelujah!
   Zion's mourner, now rejoice.

4. Tremble, ye who Him rejected,
   Lo! He breaks through yonder cloud;
   Rise, ye saints, and shout triumphant,
   Victory! through Jesus' blood:
      Hark! the trumpet
   Sounds the resurrection morn.

299. 8s & 7s.

1. Hail, thou once despised Jesus!
   Crowned in mockery a king!
   Thou didst suffer to release us;
   Thou didst free salvation bring.
   Hail, thou agonizing Saviour,
   Bearer of our sin and shame!
   By Thy merits we find favor;
   Life is given through Thy name.

2. Jesus, hail! enthroned in glory,
   There for ever to abide;
   All the heavenly hosts adore Thee,
   Seated at Thy Father's side:
   There for sinners Thou art pleading;
   There Thou dost our place prepare:
   Ever for us interceding,
   Till in glory we appear.

3. Worship, honor, power, and blessing
   Thou art worthy to receive;
   Loudest praises, without ceasing,
   Meet it is for us to give.
   Help, ye bright angelic spirits;
   Bring your sweetest, noblest lays;
   Help to sing our Saviour's merits;
   Help to chant Immanuel's praise.
                              BAKEWELL.

300. 8s, 7s & 4.

1. Hark! the voice of love and mercy
   Sounds aloud from Calvary;
   See! it rends the rocks asunder,
   Shakes the earth, and veils the sky:
      "It is finished!"
   Hear the dying Saviour cry.

2. "It is finished!" Oh! what pleasure
   Do these charming words afford!
   Heavenly blessings, without measure,
   Flow to us through Christ, the Lord:
      "It is finished!"
   Saints! the dying words record.

3. Tune your harps anew, ye seraphs!
   Join to sing the pleasing theme;
   All in earth and heaven, uniting,
   Join to praise Immanuel's name:
      Hallelujah!
   Glory to the bleeding Lamb!
                              EVANS.

301. 8s, 7s & 4.

1. God the Lord a King remaineth,
   Robed in His own glorious light;
   God hath robed Him, and He reigneth—
   He hath girded Him with might:
      Hallelujah!
   God is King in depth and height.

2. Lord! the water-floods have lifted,
   Ocean-floods have raised their roar,
   Now they pause where they have drifted,
   Now they burst upon the shore:
      Hallelujah!
   From the ocean's sounding store.

3. With all tones of waters blending
   Glorious is the breaking deep;
   Glorious, beauteous without ending,
   God who reigns on heaven's high steep.
      Hallelujah!
   Songs of ocean never sleep.

4. Lord! the words Thy lips are telling
   Are the perfect verity;
   Of Thine high, eternal dwelling
   Holiness shall inmate be:
      Hallelujah!
   Pure is all that lives with Thee.
                              OXFORD PSALTER.

WARNING AND INVITATION.

CARNELIAN. L. M. — CH. BEECHER.

1. That day of wrath! that dread-ful day, When heaven and earth shall pass a-way! What power shall be the sin-ner's stay? How shall he meet that dreadful day?

302. L. M.

2. When, shrivelling like a parched scroll,
The flaming heavens together roll;
When, louder yet, and yet more dread,
Swells the high trump that wakes the dead;

3. O, on that day, that dreadful day,
When man to judgment wakes from clay,
Be thou, O God, the sinner's stay,
Though heaven and earth shall pass away.
    SIR WALTER SCOTT.

303. L. M.

1. GOD of eternity, from Thee
 Did infant Time its being draw;
Moments, and days, and months, and years,
 Revolve, by Thine unvaried law.

2. Silent and slow, they glide away;
 Steady and strong the current flows,
Lost in eternity's wide sea,—
 The boundless gulf from whence it rose.

3. With it the thoughtless sons of men
 Before the rapid stream are borne
On to that everlasting home,
 Whence not one soul can e'er return.

4. Great Source of wisdom, teach my heart
 To know the price of every hour,
That time may bear me on to joys
 Beyond its measure and its power.
    DODDRIDGE.

304. L. M.

1. BEHOLD a Stranger at the door!
He gently knocks, has knocked before;
Has waited long—is waiting still;
You treat no other friend so ill.

2. Oh! lovely attitude—He stands
With melting heart, and loaded hands:
Oh! matchless kindness—and He shows
This matchless kindness to His foes!

3. But will He prove a friend indeed?
He will—the very Friend you need;
The Friend of sinners—yes, 'tis He,
With garments dyed on Calvary.

4. Rise, touched with gratitude divine,
Turn out His enemy and thine,
That soul-destroying monster, sin,—
And let the heavenly Stranger in.

5. Admit Him, ere His anger burn,—
His feet, departed, ne'er return;
Admit Him,—or the hour's at hand,
You'll at His door rejected stand.
    GRIGG.

305. L. M.

1. "COME hither, all ye weary souls!
 Ye heavy-laden sinners! come!
I'll give you rest from all your toils,
 And raise you to My heavenly home.

2. "They shall find rest who learn of Me,—
 I'm of a meek and lowly mind;
But passion rages like the sea,
 And pride is restless as the wind.

3. "Blessed is the man, whose shoulders take
 My yoke, and bear it with delight;
My yoke is easy to his neck,
 My grace shall make the burden light.

4. Jesus! we come at Thy command,
 With faith, and hope, and humble zeal,
Resign our spirits to Thy hand,
 To mould and guide us at Thy will.
    WATTS.

WARNING AND INVITATION.

BALMY DEW. L. M.*   Arranged by Ch. Beecher.

1. Come children, drink the balmy dew, O glory, hal-le-lu-jah, For Christ hath shed his blood for you, O glo-ry, hal-le-lu-jah, His blood can cleanse the vilest soul, O glory, hal-le-lu-jah, O see the purple torrent roll, O glory, hal-le-lu-jah!

1. Come, wea-ry souls! with sin distressed, Come and accept the promised rest: The Saviour's gracious call o-bey, And cast your gloomy fears a-way. 2. Here mercy's boundless ocean flows, To cleanse your guilt and heal your woes; Pardon and life, and endless peace, How rich the gift, how free [the grace!

* May be sung as a duet, with hallelujah responses. Or as a L. M. double.

306. L. M.

1. Come, children, drink the balmy dew,
For Christ hath shed His blood for you,
That blood can cleanse the vilest soul,—
O see the purple torrent roll!

2. Behold the Lamb on Calvary,
He sighs, and groans, and dies for thee;
The rocks are rent, the sleeping dead
Awake because their Jesus bled.

3. Behold the body in the tomb,
The soldiers watching in the gloom;
But angels come, at dawn of day,
And bear the Lord of life away.

4. Behold Him rise from Olive's brow,
The clouds His form are hiding now;
He's gone to stand before the throne
And pray for ever for His own.

5. Yet see the sign among the stars,
One like the Son of Man appears:
Now all the tribes of Israel mourn,
To see the Crucified return.

6. Come, sinner, drink the balmy dew,
And let that blood avail for you,
Then say when His bright hour you see,
"It is my Lord, He comes for me."

307. L. M.

1. Come, weary souls! with sins distress'd,
Come, and accept the promised rest;
The Saviour's gracious call obey,
And cast your gloomy fears away.

2. Here mercy's boundless ocean flows,
To cleanse your guilt and heal your woes;
Pardon, and life, and endless peace,—
How rich the gift, how free the grace!

3. Dear Saviour! let Thy powerful love
Confirm our faith,—our fears remove;
Oh! sweetly reign in every breast,
And guide us to eternal rest.   MRS. STEELE.

WARNING AND INVITATION.

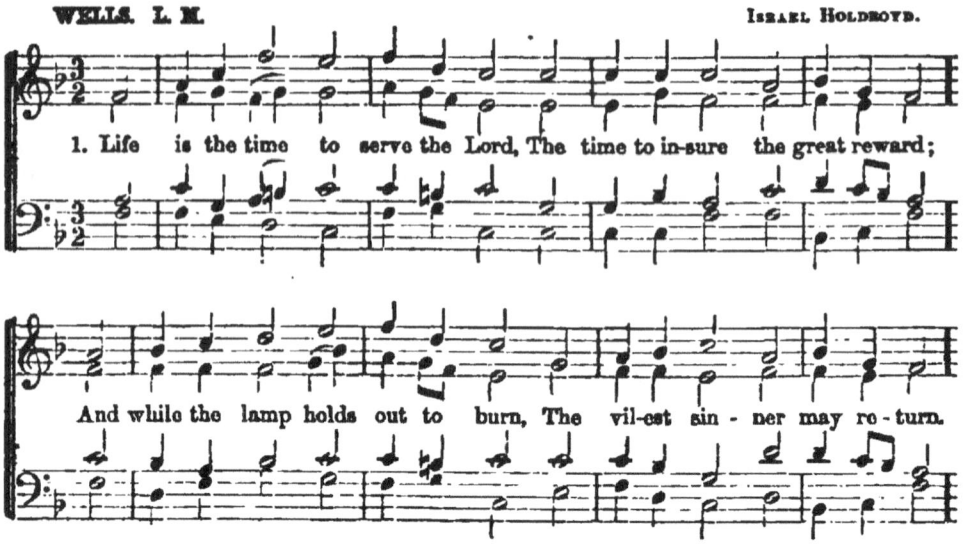

WELLS. L. M.   Israel Holdroyd.

1. Life is the time to serve the Lord, The time to insure the great reward; And while the lamp holds out to burn, The vilest sinner may return.

308. L. M.

1. LIFE is the time to serve the Lord,
The time to insure the great reward;
And while the lamp holds out to burn,
The vilest sinner may return.

2. The living know that they must die;
But all the dead forgotten lie;
Their memory and their sense are gone,
Alike unknowing and unknown.

3. Their hatred, and their love, is lost,
Their envy buried in the dust;
They have no share in all that's done
Beneath the circuit of the sun.

4. Then what my thoughts design to do,
My hands, with all your might pursue,
Since no device, no work, is found,
Nor faith, nor hope, beneath the ground.

5. There are no acts of pardon passed
In the cold grave to which we haste;
But darkness, death, and long despair
Reign in eternal silence there.
WATTS.

309. L. M.

1. WHILE life prolongs its precious light,
Mercy is found, and peace is given;
But soon, ah soon, approaching night
Shall blot out every hope of heaven.

2. Soon, borne on time's most rapid wing,
Shall death command you to the grave,
Before His bar your spirits bring,
And none be found to hear or save.

3. In that lone land of deep despair,
No Sabbath's heavenly light shall rise,—
No God regard your bitter prayer,
No Saviour call you to the skies.

4. Silence, and solitude, and gloom,
In those forgetful realms appear;
Deep sorrows fill the dismal tomb,
And hope shall never enter there.

5. Now God invites; how blest the day!
How sweet the Gospel's charming sound!
Come, sinners, haste, O haste away,
While yet a pard'ning God is found.
DWIGHT.

310. L. M.

1. BROAD is the road that leads to death,
And thousands walk together there;
But wisdom shows a narrow path,
With here and there a traveler.

2. "Deny thyself, and take thy cross,"
Is the Redeemer's great command;
Nature must count her gold but dross,
If she would gain this heavenly land.

3. The fearful soul that tires and faints,
And walks the ways of God no more,
Is but esteemed almost a saint,
And makes his own destruction sure.

4. Lord! let not all my hopes be vain;
Create my heart entirely new,
Which hypocrites could ne'er attain;
Which false apostates never knew.
WATTS.

311. L. M.

1. BEHOLD the path that mortals tread
Down to the regions of the dead!
Nor will the fleeting moments stay,
Nor can we measure back our way.

2. Our kindred and our friends are gone;
Know, O my soul, this doom thine own:
Feeble as theirs, my mortal frame,
The same my way, my house the same.

3. And must I, from the cheerful light,
Pass to the grave's perpetual night,—
From scenes of duty, means of grace,
Must I to God's tribunal pass?

4. Awake, my soul, thy way prepare,
And lose, in this, each mortal care;
With steady feet that path be trod,
Which through the grave conducts to God.
WARDLAW'S COLL.

312. L. M.

1. LORD! what a thoughtless wretch was I
To mourn, and murmur, and repine;
To see the wicked, placed on high,
In pride and robes of honor shine!

2. But Oh! their end, their dreadful end!
Thy sanctuary taught me so;
On slippery rocks I see them stand,
And fiery billows roll below.

3. Their fancied joys—how fast they flee!
Just like a dream when man awakes;
Their songs of softest harmony
Are but a prelude to their plagues.

4. Now I esteem their mirth and wine
Too dear to purchase with my blood;
Lord! 't is enough that Thou art mine,
My life, my portion, and my God.
WATTS.

313. L. M.

1. SAY, sinner! hath a voice within
Oft whispered to thy secret soul,
Urged thee to leave the ways of sin,
And yield thy heart to God's control?

2. Sinner! it was a heavenly voice,—
It was the Spirit's gracious call;
It bade thee make the better choice,
And haste to seek in Christ thine all.

3. Spurn not the call to life and light;
Regard, in time, the warning kind;
That call thou may'st not always slight,
And yet the gate of mercy find.

4. God's Spirit will not always strive
With hardened, self-destroying man;
Ye who persist His love to grieve,
May never hear His voice again.

5. Sinner! perhaps, this very day,
Thy last accepted time may be:
Oh! should'st thou grieve Him now away,
Then hope may never beam on thee.
HYDE.

314. L. M.

1. Now, in the heat of youthful blood,
Remember your Creator, God;
Behold! the months come hastening on,
When you shall say, "My joys are gone."

2. Behold! the aged sinner goes,
Laden with guilt and heavy woes,
Down to the regions of the dead,
With endless curses on his head.

3. The dust returns to dust again;
The soul, in agonies of pain,
Ascends to God—not there to dwell—
But hears her doom, and sinks to hell.

4. Eternal King! I fear Thy name;
Teach me to know how frail I am;
And when my soul must hence remove,
Give me a mansion in Thy love.
WATTS.

315. L. M.

1. MAN has a soul of vast desires;
He burns within with restless fires;
Tossed to and fro, his passions fly
From vanity to vanity.

2. In vain on earth we hope to find
Some solid good to fill the mind;
We try new pleasures, but we feel
The inward thirst and torment still.

3. So, when a raging fever burns,
We shift from side to side, by turns;
And 't is a poor relief we gain,
To change the place, but keep the pain.

4. Great God, subdue this vicious thirst,
This love to vanity and dust;
Cure the vile fever of the mind,
And feed our souls with joys refined.
WATTS.

WARNING AND INVITATION.

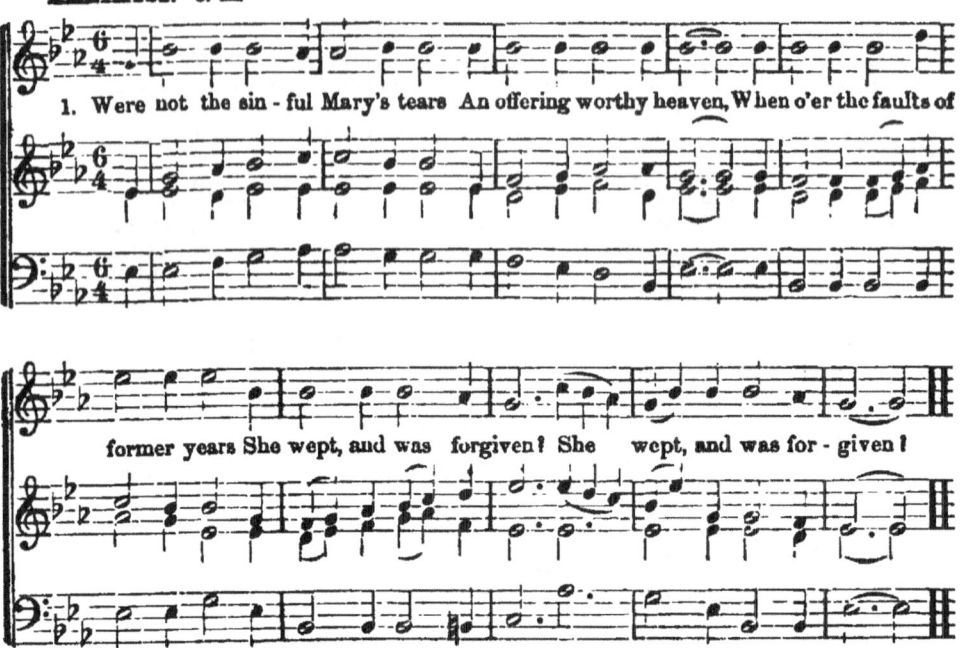

AMETHYST. C. M.   CH. BEECHER.

1. Were not the sinful Mary's tears An offering worthy heaven, When o'er the faults of former years She wept, and was forgiven! She wept, and was forgiven!

316. C. M.

2. WHEN, bringing every balmy sweet
   Her day of luxury stored,
   She o'er her Saviour's hallowed feet
   The precious perfume poured,—

3. Were not those sweets so humbly shed,
   That hair, those weeping eyes,
   And the sunk heart which inly bled,
   Heaven's noblest sacrifice?

4. Thou that hast slept in error's sleep,
   O, wouldst thou wake to heaven,
   Like Mary kneel, like Mary weep;
   "Love much," and be forgiven!

   MOORE.

317. C. M.

1. SWEET day! so cool, so calm, so bright,
   Bridal of earth and sky;
   The dew shall weep thy fall to-night,
   For thou, alas! must die.

2. Sweet rose! in air whose odors wave,
   And colors charm the eye;
   Thy root is ever in the grave,
   And thou, alas! must die.

3. Sweet spring! of days and roses made,
   Whose charms for beauty vie,
   Thy days depart, thy roses fade,
   Thou, too, alas! must die.

4. Only a sweet and holy soul
   Hath tints that never fly:
   While flowers decay, and seasons roll,
   It lives, and can not die.

   HERBERT.

318. C. M.

1. IN evil long I took delight,
   Unawed by shame or fear,
   Till a new object struck my sight,
   And stopped my wild career.

2. I saw One hanging on a tree,
   In agony and blood;
   Who fixed His languid eyes on me,
   As near the cross I stood.

3. Sure never, till my latest breath,
   Can I forget that look;
   It seemed to charge me with His death,
   Though not a word He spoke.

4. Alas, I knew not what I did,
   But all my tears were vain;
   Where could my trembling soul be hid,
   For I the Lord had slain.

5. A second look He gave, that said,
   "I freely all forgive;
   This blood is for thy ransom paid,—
   I die that thou may'st live."

   NEWTON.

WARNING AND INVITATION. 108

319. C. M.

1. YE wretched, hungry, starving poor,
  Behold a royal feast!
 Where mercy spreads her bounteous store,
  For every humble guest.

2. See, Jesus stands with open arms;
  He calls, He bids you come;
 Guilt holds you back, and fear alarms;
  But see, there yet is room—

3. Room in the Saviour's bleeding heart;
  There love and pity meet;
 Nor will He bid the soul depart
  That trembles at His feet.

4. O come, and with His children taste
  The blessings of His love;
 While hope attends the sweet repast
  Of nobler joys above.

5. There, with united heart and voice,
  Before th' eternal throne,
 Ten thousand thousand souls rejoice
  In ecstasies unknown.

6. And yet ten thousand thousand more
  Are welcome still to come:
 Ye longing souls, the grace adore;
  Approach, there yet is room.
  MRS. STEELE.

320. C. M.

1. OH! what amazing words of grace
  Are in the gospel found,
 Suited to every sinner's case
  Who hears the joyful sound!

2. Come, then, with all your wants and
  Your every burden bring; [wounds,
 Here love, unchanging love, abounds,—
  A deep, celestial spring.

3. This spring with living water flows,
  And heavenly joy imparts;
 Come, thirsty souls! your wants disclose,
  And drink, with thankful hearts.

4. Millions of sinners, vile as you,
  Have here found life and peace;
 Come then, and prove its virtues too,
  And drink, adore, and bless.
  MEDLEY.

321. C. M.

1. THE Saviour calls; let every ear
  Attend the heavenly sound;
 Ye doubting souls, dismiss your fear;
  Hope smiles reviving round.

2. For every thirsty, longing heart,
  Here streams of bounty flow,
 And life, and health, and bliss impart,
  To banish mortal woe.

3. Ye sinners, come; 'tis mercy's voice;
  That gracious voice obey;
 'Tis Jesus calls to heavenly joys;
  And can you yet delay?

4. Dear Saviour, draw reluctant hearts;
  To Thee let sinners fly,
 And take the bliss Thy love imparts,
  And drink, and never die.
  MRS. STEELE.

322. C. M.

1. COME, sinner, to the gospel feast;
  O, come without delay;
 For there is room in Jesus' breast
  For all who will obey.

2. There's room in God's eternal love
  To save thy precious soul;
 Room in the Spirit's grace above
  To heal and make thee whole.

3. There's room within the church, redeemed
  With blood of Christ divine;
 Room in the white-robed throng, convened
  For that dear soul of thine.

4. There's room in heaven among the choir,
  And harps and crowns of gold,
 And glorious palms of victory there,
  And joys that ne'er were told.

5. There's room around thy Father's board
  For thee and thousands more:
 O, come and welcome to the Lord;
  Yea, come this very hour.
  HUNTINGDON.

323. C. M.

1. OH, if my soul were formed for woe,
  How would I vent my sighs!
 Repentance should like rivers flow
  From both my streaming eyes.

2. 'Twas for my sins my dearest Lord
  Hung on the cursed tree,
 And groaned away a dying life
  For thee, my soul, for thee.

3. Oh, how I hate those lusts of mine
  That crucified my Lord; [flesh
 Those sins that pierced and nailed His
  Fast to the fatal wood!

4. Yes, my Redeemer—they shall die;
  My heart has so decreed;
 Nor will I spare the guilty things
  That made my Saviour bleed.

5. While with a melting, broken heart,
  My murdered Lord I view,
 I'll raise revenge against my sins,
  And slay the murd'rers too.
  WATTS.

WARNING AND INVITATION.

324. C. M. Peculiar.

1. RETURN, O wand'rer, to thy home.
Thy Father calls for thee;
No longer now an exile roam,
In guilt and misery:
Return, return!

2. Return, O wand'rer, to thy home,
'Tis Jesus calls for thee;
The Spirit and the Bride say—come;
Oh! now for refuge flee;
Return, return!

3. Return, O wand'rer, to thy home,
'Tis madness to delay;
There are no pardons in the tomb,
And brief is mercy's day:
Return, return! T. HASTINGS.

325. C. M.

1. RETURN, O wanderer, return,
And seek thy Father's face;
Those new desires which in thee burn
Were kindled by His grace.

2. Return, O wanderer, return;
He hears thy humble sigh:
He sees thy soften'd spirit mourn,
When no one else is nigh.

3. Return, O wanderer, return;
Thy Saviour bids thee live:
Come to His cross, and, grateful, learn
How Jesus can forgive.

4. Wretched wanderer, now return,
And wipe the falling tear:
Thy Father calls—no longer mourn;
'Tis love invites thee near.

5. From all thy wanderings, now return,
Regain thy long-sought rest:
The Saviour's melting mercies yearn
To clasp thee to His breast.
  COLLYER.

326. C. M.

1. BEHOLD, my soul, the narrow bound
Of the revolving year:
How swift the weeks complete their round,
How short the months appear.

2. So fast eternity comes on,
And that important day,
When all that mortal life has done,
God's judgment shall survey.

3. Yet, like an idle tale, we spend
The swift-advancing year;
And study artful ways to mend
The speed of its career.

4. Waken, O God! my trifling heart,
Its great concern to see;
That I may act the Christian part,
And give the year to Thee.

5. So shall their course more grateful roll,
If future years arise;
Or this shall bear my happy soul
To joy that never dies.
  DODDRIDGE.

327. C. M.

1. PROSTRATE, dear Jesus! at Thy feet
A guilty rebel lies;
And upward to the mercy-seat
Presumes to lift his eyes.

2. If tears of sorrow would suffice
   To pay the debt I owe,
   Tears should from both my weeping eyes
   In ceaseless torrents flow.

3. But no such sacrifice I plead
   To expiate my guilt;
   No tears, but those which thou hast shed—
   No blood, but Thou hast spilt.

4. Think of Thy sorrows, dearest Lord!
   And all my sins forgive:
   Justice will well approve the word
   That bids the sinner live.
   STENNETT.

328. C. M.

1. REPENT! the voice-celestial cries,
   No longer dare delay:
   The soul that scorns the mandate dies,
   And meets a fiery day.

2. No more the sovereign eye of God
   O'erlooks the crimes of men;
   His heralds now are sent abroad
   To warn the world of sin.

3. O sinners! in His presence bow,
   And all your guilt confess;
   Accept the offered Saviour now,
   Nor trifle with His grace.

4. Soon, will the awful trumpet sound,
   And call you to His bar;
   His mercy knows th' appointed bound,
   And yields to justice there.

5. Amazing love—that yet will call,
   And yet prolong our days!
   Our hearts, subdued by goodness, fall,
   And weep, and love, and praise.
   DODDRIDGE.

329. C. M.

1. SINNERS, the voice of God regard;
   His mercy speaks to-day:
   He calls you, by His sovereign word,
   From sin's destructive way.

2. Like the rough sea that can not rest,
   You live devoid of peace;
   A thousand stings within your breast
   Deprive your souls of ease.

3. Your way is dark, and leads to hell;
   Why will you persevere?
   Can you in endless sorrows dwell,
   Shut up in black despair?

4. Why will you in the crooked ways
   Of sin and folly go?
   In pain you travel all your days,
   To reap eternal wo!

5. But he that turns to God shall live,
   Through His abounding grace;
   His mercy will the guilt forgive
   Of those that seek His face.

6. His love exceeds your highest thoughts;
   He pardons like a God;
   He will forgive your numerous faults,
   Through a Redeemer's blood.
   FAWCETT.

330. C. M.

1. How short and hasty is our life!
   How vast our soul's affairs!
   Yet senseless mortals vainly strive
   To lavish out their years.

2. Our days run thoughtlessly along,
   Without a moment's stay;
   Just like a story, or a song,
   We pass our lives away.

3. God from on high invites us home,
   But we march heedless on,
   And, ever hastening to the tomb,
   Stoop downward as we run.

4. How we deserve the deepest hell,
   Who slight the joys above!
   What chains of vengeance should we feel,
   Who break such cords of love!

5. Draw us, O God! with sovereign grace,
   And lift our thoughts on high,
   That we may end this mortal race,
   And see salvation nigh.
   WATTS.

331. C. M.

1. YE hearts, with youthful vigor warm,
   In smiling crowds draw near,
   And turn from every mortal charm
   A Saviour's voice to hear.

2. He, Lord of all the worlds on high,
   Stoops to converse with you,
   And lays His radiant glories by,
   Your friendship to pursue.

3. "The soul that longs to see My face,
   Is sure My love to gain;
   And those that early seek My grace,
   Shall never seek in vain."

4. What object, Lord, my soul should move,
   If once compared with Thee?
   What beauty should command my love,
   Like what in Christ I see?

5. Away, ye false, delusive toys,
   Vain tempters of the mind!
   'Tis here I fix my lasting choice,
   For here true bliss I find. DODDRIDGE.

WARNING AND INVITATION.

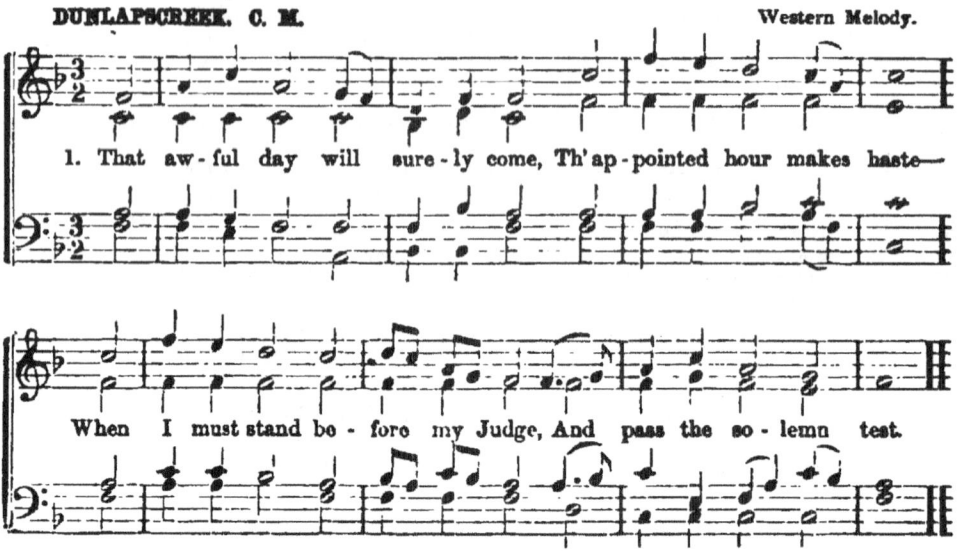

DUNLAPSCREEK. C. M. — Western Melody.

1. That awful day will surely come, Th' appointed hour makes haste—
When I must stand before my Judge, And pass the solemn test.

332. C. M.

2. Thou lovely Chief of all my joys,
    Thou Sovereign of my heart,
  How could I bear to hear Thy voice
    Pronounce the sound *Depart!*

3. The thunder of that dismal word
    Would so distress my ear,
  'T would tear my soul asunder, Lord,
    With most tormenting fear.

4. Oh, wretched state of deep despair,
    To see my God remove —
  And fix my doleful station where
    I must not taste His love!

5. Jesus, I throw my arms around,
    And hang upon Thy breast,
  Without a gracious smile from Thee,
    My spirit can not rest.

6. Oh! tell me that my worthless name
    Is graven on Thy hands;
  Show me some promise in Thy book,
    Where my salvation stands.

7. Give me one kind, assuring word,
    To sink my fears again:
  And cheerfully my soul shall wait
    Her threescore years and ten.
                    WATTS.

333. C. M.

1. THE Lord, the Judge, before His throne
    Bids the whole earth draw nigh,
  The nations near the rising sun,
    And near the western sky.

2. No more shall bold blasphemers say—
    "Judgment will ne'er begin;"
  No more abuse His long delay,
    To impudence and sin.

3. Throned on a cloud our God shall come;
    Bright flames prepare His way;
  Thunder and darkness, fire and storm,
    Lead on the dreadful day.

4. Heaven from above His call shall hear,
    Attending angels come,
  And earth and hell shall know and fear
    His justice and their doom.

5. "But gather all my saints," He cries,
    "That made their peace with God
  By the Redeemer's sacrifice,
    And sealed it with His blood."
                    WATTS.

334. C. M.

1. THE day approacheth, Oh my soul,
    The great decisive day,
  Which from the verge of mortal life,
    Shall bear thee far away.

2. Another day, more awful, dawns;
   And, lo, the Judge appears;
   Ye heavens, retire before His face,
   And sink, ye darkened stars.

3. Yet does one short, preparing hour,
   One precious hour remain;
   Rouse thee, my soul, with all thy power,
   Nor let it pass in vain.

4. For this, Thy temple, Lord, we throng,
   For this, Thy board surround;
   Here may our service be approved,
   And in Thy presence crowned.
   DODDRIDGE.

335. C. M.

1. My thoughts on awful subjects roll,
   Damnation and the dead;
   What horrors seize the guilty soul
   Upon a dying bed!

2. Ling'ring about these mortal shores,
   She makes a long delay;
   Till, like a flood, with rapid force,
   Death sweeps the wretch away.

3. Then swift and dreadful she descends
   Down to the fiery coast,
   Among abominable fiends,
   Herself a frighted ghost.

4. There endless crowds of sinners lie,
   And darkness makes their chains;
   Tortured with keen despair they cry,
   Yet wait for fiercer pains.

5. Amazing grace! that kept my breath,
   Nor bade my soul remove,
   Till I had learned my Saviour's death,
   And well ensured his love!
   WATTS.

336. C. M.

1. Sin, like a venomous disease,
   Infects our vital blood;
   The only balm is sovereign grace,
   And the physician, God.

2. Our beauty and our strength are fled,
   And we draw near to death;
   But Christ, the Lord, recalls the dead,
   With His almighty breath.

3. Madness, by nature reigns within,
   The passions burn and rage,
   Till God's own Son, with skill divine,
   The inward fire assuage.

4. We lick the dust, we grasp the wind,
   And solid good despise:
   Such is the folly of the mind,
   Till Jesus makes us wise.

5. We give our souls the wounds they feel,
   We drink the poisonous gall,
   And rush with fury down to hell;
   But heaven prevents the fall.
   WATTS.

337. C. M.

1. Stoop down my thoughts, that use to rise,
   Converse awhile with death;
   Think how a gasping mortal lies,
   And pants away his breath.

2. But Oh, the soul that never dies!
   At once it leaves the clay,
   Ye thoughts pursue it where it flies,
   And trace its wondrous way.

3. And must my body faint and die?
   And must this soul remove?
   Oh for some guardian angel nigh
   To bear it safe above.

5. Jesus, to thy dear faithful hand,
   My naked soul I trust;
   And my flesh waits for thy command,
   To drop into the dust.
   WATTS.

338. C. M.

1. Thee we adore, eternal Name!
   And humbly own to Thee,
   How feeble is our mortal frame,
   What dying worms are we!

2. The year rolls round, and steals away
   The breath, that first it gave;
   Whate'er we do, whate'er we be,
   We're traveling to the grave.

3. Dangers stand thick through all the ground,
   To push us to the tomb;
   And fierce diseases wait around,
   To hurry mortals home.

4. Great God! on what a slender thread
   Hang everlasting things!
   Th' eternal state of all the dead,
   Upon life's feeble strings.

5. Infinite joy, or endless woe,
   Attends on every breath;
   And yet, how unconcerned we go
   Upon the brink of death!

6. Waken, O Lord, our drowsy sense,
   To walk this dangerous road;
   And if our souls are hurried hence,
   May they be found with God.
   WATTS.

WARNING AND INVITATION.

ANGELS' CALL. S. M. — Ch. Beecher.

1. Come to the land of peace, From shadows come a-way, Where all the sounds of weeping cease. And storms no more have sway, And storms no more have sway.

339. S. M.

2. Fear hath no dwelling here;
But pure repose and love
Breathe through the bright, celestial air,
The spirit of the dove.

3. Come to the bright and blest,
Gathered from every land;
For here thy soul shall find its rest,
Amidst the shining band.

4. In this divine abode
Change leaves no saddening trace;
Come, trusting spirit, to thy God,
Thy holy resting-place!

BRIGGS' COLL.

340. S. M.

1. The Spirit, in our hearts,
Is whispering, "Sinner, come:"
The bride, the church of Christ, proclaims
To all His children, "Come!"

2. Let him that heareth say
To all about him, "Come!"
Let him that thirsts for righteousness,
To Christ, the fountain, come!

3. Yes, whosoever will,
O let him freely come,
And freely drink the stream of life;
'T is Jesus bids him come.

4. Lo! Jesus, who invites,
Declares, "I quickly come;"
Lord, even so! we wait Thine hour;
O blest Redeemer, come!

H. U. ONDERDONK.

341. S. M.

1. Ye trembling captives! hear;
The gospel-trumpet sounds;
No music more can charm the ear,
Or heal your heart-felt wounds.

2. 'T is not the trump of war,
Nor Sinai's awful roar;
Salvation's news it spreads afar,
And vengeance is no more.

3. Forgiveness, love, and peace,
Glad heaven aloud proclaims;
And earth, the jubilee's release,
With eager rapture claims.

4. Far, far to distant lands
The saving news shall spread;
And Jesus all His willing bands,
In glorious triumph lead.

PRATT'S COLL.

342. S. M.

1. In true and patient hope,
My soul, on God attend;
And calmly, confidently look
Till He salvation send.

2. I shall His goodness see,
While on His name I call;
He will defend and strengthen me,
And I shall never fall.

3. Jesus, to Thee I fly,
My refuge, and my tower;
Upon Thy faithful love rely,
And find Thy saving power.

C. WESLEY.

WARNING AND INVITATION.

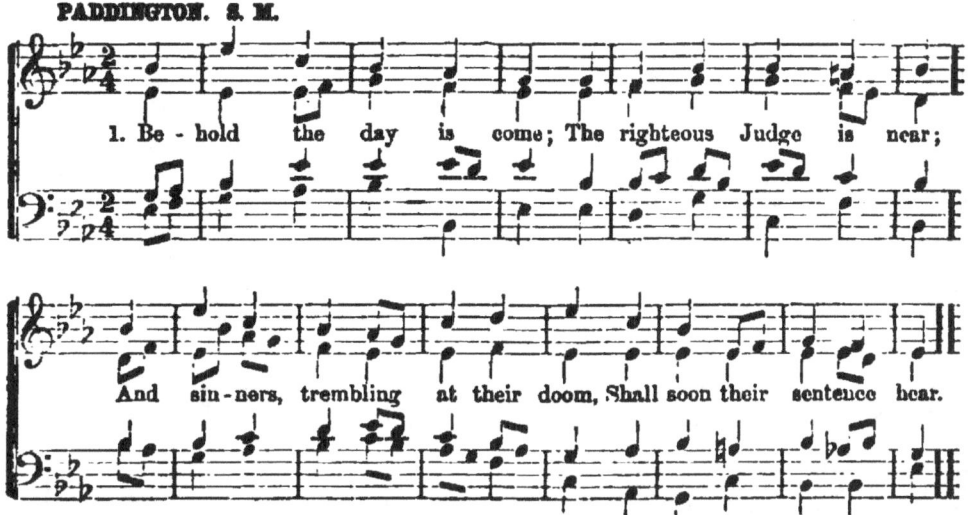

PADDINGTON. S. M.

1. Behold the day is come; The righteous Judge is near;
And sinners, trembling at their doom, Shall soon their sentence hear.

343. S. M.

2. Angels, in bright attire,
   Conduct Him through the skies;
Darkness and tempest, smoke and fire,
   Attend Him as He flies.

3. How awful is the sight!
   How loud the thunders roar!
The sun forbears to give his light,
   And stars are seen no more.

4. The whole creation groans;
   But saints arise and sing:
They are the ransomed of the Lord,
   And He their God and King.
                              BEDDOME.

344. S. M.

1. O WHERE shall rest be found—
   Rest for the weary soul?
'T were vain the ocean depths to sound,
   Or pierce to either pole.

2. The world can never give
   The bliss for which we sigh:
'T is not the whole of life to live,
   Nor all of death to die.

3. Beyond this vale of tears
   There is a life above,
Unmeasured by the flight of years;
   And all that life is love.

4. There is a death whose pang
   Outlasts the fleeting breath:
O what eternal horrors hang
   Around the second death!

5. Lord God of truth and grace,
   Teach us that death to shun,
Lest we be banished from Thy face,
   And evermore undone.
                              MONTGOMERY.

345. S. M.

1. THOU Judge of quick and dead,
   Before whose bar severe,
With holy joy, or guilty dread,
   We all shall soon appear.

2. Our cautioned souls prepare
   For that tremendous day;
O, fill us now with watchful care,
   And stir us up to pray.

3. To damp our earthly joys,
   To wake our gracious fears,
For ever let th' archangel's voice
   Be sounding in our ears.

4. The solemn, midnight cry—
   " Ye dead, the Judge is come!
Arise, and meet Him in the sky,
   And meet your instant doom!"

5. O may we thus be found,
   Obedient to Thy word;
Attentive to the trumpet's sound,
   And looking for our Lord!

6. O may we thus insure
   Our lot among the blest;
And watch a moment to secure
   An everlasting rest.   C. WESLEY.

WARNING AND INVITATION.

346. 7s.

1. Rock of Ages, cleft for me,
   Let me hide myself in Thee!
   Let the water and the blood,
   From Thy riven side which flowed,
   Be of sin the double cure,
   Cleanse me from its guilt and power.

2. Not the labors of my hands
   Can fulfill Thy law's demands:
   Could my zeal no respite know,
   Could my tears for ever flow,
   All for sin could not atone;
   Thou must save, and Thou alone!

3. Nothing in my hand I bring;
   Simply to Thy cross I cling;
   Naked, come to Thee for dress;
   Helpless, look to Thee for grace;
   Foul, I to Thy fountain fly;
   Wash me, Saviour, or I die!

4. While I draw this fleeting breath,
   When my eyelids close in death,
   When I soar to worlds unknown,
   See Thee on Thy judgment-throne,
   Rock of Ages, cleft for me,
   Let me hide myself in Thee.
   TOPLADY.

347. 7s.

1. Go to dark Gethsemane,
   Ye that feel the tempter's power,
   Your Redeemer's conflict see,
   Watch with Him one bitter hour;
   Turn not from His griefs away,
   Learn of Jesus Christ to pray.

2. Follow to the judgment-hall;
   View the Lord of life arraigned;
   O the wormwood and the gall!
   O the pangs His soul sustained!
   Shun not suffering, shame, or loss;
   Learn of Him to bear the cross.

3. Calvary's mournful mountain climb;
   There, adoring at his feet,
   Mark that miracle of time,
   God's own sacrifice complete:
   "It is finished"—hear Him cry;
   Learn of Jesus Christ to die.

4. Early hasten to the tomb,
   Where they laid His breathless clay;
   All is solitude and gloom,
   —Who hath taken Him away?
   Christ is risen; He meets our eyes;
   Saviour, teach us so to rise.
   MONTGOMERY.

348. 7s.

1. From the cross uplifted high,
   Where the Saviour deigns to die,
   What melodious sounds we hear,
   Bursting on the ravished ear!—
   "Love's redeeming work is done;
   Come and welcome, sinner, come.

2. "Sprinkled now with blood the throne,
   Why beneath thy burdens groan?
   On My pierced body laid,
   Justice owns the ransom paid;
   Bow the knee, and kiss the Son;
   Come and welcome, sinner, come.

3. "Spread for thee, the festal board
   See with richest dainties stored;
   To thy Father's bosom pressed,
   Yet again a child confessed,
   Never from His house to roam,
   Come and welcome, sinner, come.

4. "Soon the days of life shall end;
   Lo, I come, your Saviour, Friend,
   Safe your spirits to convey
   To the realms of endless day,
   Up to My eternal home;
   Come and welcome, sinner, come."

   HAWES.

349. 7s.

1. Sinner, art thou still secure?
     Wilt thou still refuse to pray?
   Can thy heart or hands endure
     In the Lord's avenging day?
   See His mighty arm made bare!
     Awful terrors clothe His brow!
   For His judgment now prepare,
     Thou must either break or bow.

2. At His presence nature shakes,
     Earth affrighted hastes to flee;
   Solid mountains melt like wax,
     What will then become of thee?
   Who His coming may abide?
     You that glory in your shame,
   Will you find a place to hide
     When the world is wrapt in flame?

3. Then the great, the rich, the wise,
     Trembling, guilty, self-condemned,
   Must behold the wrathful eyes
     Of the Judge they once blasphemed.
   Where are now their haughty looks?
     O! their horror and despair,
   When they see the opened books,
     And their dreadful sentence hear!

4. Lord, prepare us by Thy grace,
     Soon we must resign our breath,
   And our souls be called to pass
     Through the iron gate of death.
   Let us now our day improve,
     Listen to the gospel voice;
   Seek the things that are above;
     Scorn the world's pretended joys.

   NEWTON.

350. 7s.

1. When thy mortal life is fled,
   When the death-shades o'er thee spread,
   When is finished thy career,
   Sinner, where wilt thou appear?

2. When the world has passed away,
   When draws near the judgment-day,
   When the awful trump shall sound,
   Say, O, where wilt thou be found?

3. When the Judge descends in light,
   Clothed in majesty and might,
   When the wicked quail with fear,
   Where, O, where wilt thou appear?

4. What shall soothe thy bursting heart,
   When the saints and thou must part?
   When the good with joy are crowned,
   Sinner, where wilt thou be found?

5. While the Holy Ghost is nigh,
   Quickly to the Saviour fly;
   Then shall peace thy spirit cheer;
   Then in heaven shalt thou appear.

   S. F. SMITH.

351. 7s.

1. Depth of mercy! can there be
   Mercy still reserved for me?
   Can my God His wrath forbear?
   Me, the chief of sinners, spare?

2. I have long withstood His grace;
   Long provoked Him to His face;
   Would not hearken to His calls;
   Grieved Him by a thousand falls.

3. Kindled His relentings are;
   Me He now delights to spare;
   Cries, How shall I give thee up?—
   Lets the lifted thunder drop.

4. There for me the Saviour stands;
   Shows His wounds, and spreads His hands;
   God is love! I know, I feel;
   Jesus weeps, and loves me still.

   C. WESLEY.

WARNING AND INVITATION.

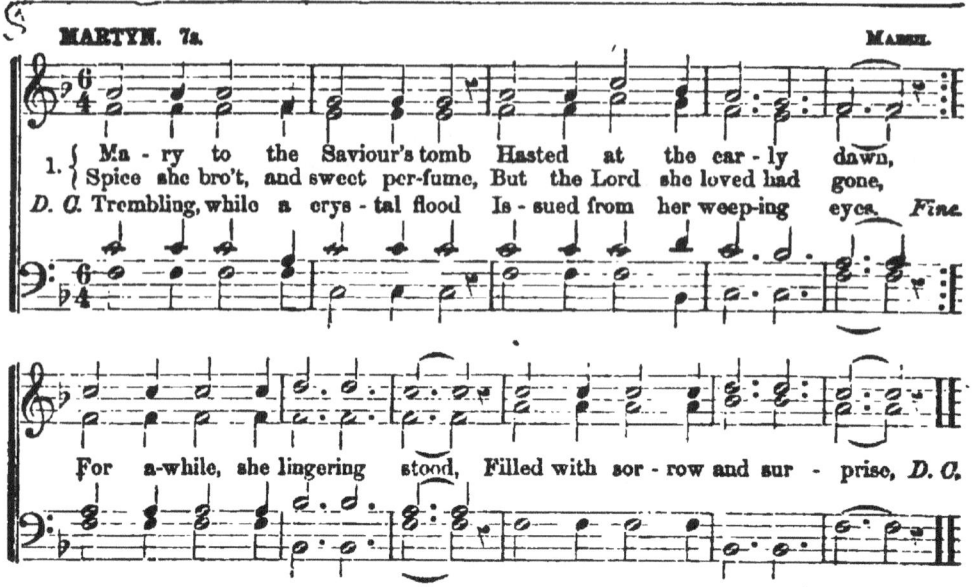

MARTYN. 7s.

1. Mary to the Saviour's tomb
Hasted at the early dawn,
Spice she bro't, and sweet perfume,
But the Lord she loved had gone,
For awhile, she lingering stood,
Filled with sorrow and surprise,
D.C. Trembling, while a crystal flood
Issued from her weeping eyes.

352. 7s.

2. But her sorrows quickly fled
When she heard His welcome voice;
Christ had risen from the dead,
Now He bids her heart rejoice;
What a change His word can make,
Turning darkness into day;
Ye who weep for Jesus' sake
He will wipe your tears away.

353. 7s.

1. Pilgrim. burdened with thy sin,
Come the way to Zion's gate;
There, till mercy speaks within,
Knock, and weep, and watch, and wait:
Knock—He knows the sinner's cry;
Weep—He loves the mourners's tears;
Watch, for saving grace is nigh;
Wait, till heavenly grace appears.

2. Hark. it is the Saviour's voice!
"Welcome, pilgrim, to thy rest!"
Now within the gate rejoice,
Safe, and owned, and bought, and blest:
Safe, from all the lures of vice;
Owned, by joys the contrite know;
Bought by love, and life the price;
Blest, the mighty debt to owe.

3. Holy pilgrim! what for thee
In a world like this remains?
From thy guarded breast shall flee
Fear, and shame, and doubts, and pains:
Fear—the hope of heaven shall fly,
Shame, from glory's view retire;
Doubt, in full belief shall die;
Pain, in endless bliss expire.

354. 7s.

1. Hearts of stone! relent, relent,
Break, by Jesus' cross subdued;
See His body, mangled, rent,
Covered with a gore of blood!
Sinful soul! what hast thou done?
Crucified God's only Son!

2. Yes, thy sins have done the deed,
Driven the nails that fixed Him there,
Crowned with thorns His sacred head,
Pierced Him with the bloody spear,
Made His soul a sacrifice—
While for sinful man He dies.

3. Wilt thou let Him bleed in vain—
Still to death thy Lord pursue?
Open all His wounds again,
And the shameful cross renew?
No; with all my sins I'll part,
Break, Oh! break, my bleeding heart!
TIEBOUT'S COLL.

355. 7s.

1. Weary souls, that wander wide
From the central point of bliss,
Turn to Jesus crucified,
Fly to those dear wounds of His;
Sink into the purple flood;
Rise into the life of God.

2. Oh believe the record true,
God to you His Son hath given;
Ye may now be happy, too—
Find on earth the life of heaven,
Live the life of heaven above,
All the life of glorious love.
C. WESLEY.

WARNING AND INVITATION.

1. Come, ye weary souls, oppressed,
Answer to the Saviour's call:
"Come, and I will give you rest;
Come, and I will save you all."

356. 7s.

2. Jesus—full of truth and love,
   We Thy kindest call obey,
Faithful let Thy mercies prove,
   Take our load of guilt away.

3. Weary of this war within,
   Weary of this endless strife,
Weary of ourselves and sin,
   Weary of a wretched life,

4. Burdened with a world of grief,
   Burdened with our sinful load,
Burdened with this unbelief,
   Burdened with the wrath of God,

5. Lo, we come to Thee for ease,
   True and gracious as Thou art;
Now our weary souls release,
   Write forgiveness on our heart.

357. 7s.

1. Come! said Jesus' sacred voice,
Come, and make my paths your choice:
I will guide you to your home:
Weary wanderer, hither come.

2. Thou, who homeless and forlorn,
Long hast borne the proud world's scorn,
Long hast roamed the barren waste,
Weary wanderer, hither haste.

3. Ye, who tossed on beds of pain
Seek for ease, but seek in vain;
Ye, by fiercer anguish torn,
In remorse for guilt who mourn:—

4. Hither come, for here is found
Balm that flows for every wound!
Peace, that ever shall endure,
Rest eternal, sacred, sure.

BARBAULD.

358. 7s.

1. HASTE, O sinner! to be wise,
Stay not for the morrow's sun;
Wisdom warns thee, from the skies,
All the paths of death to shun.

2. Haste, and mercy now implore;
Stay not for the morrow's sun;
Thy probation may be o'er
Ere this evening's work is done.

3. Haste, O sinner! now return;
Stay not for the morrow's sun;
Lest thy lamp should cease to burn
Ere salvation's work is done.

4. Haste, while yet thou canst be blest;
Stay not for the morrow's sun,
Death may thy poor soul arrest
Ere the morrow is begun.

T. SCOTT.

WARNING AND INVITATION.

NEWBURGH. 8s, 7s & 4.   From Root & Sweetser's Coll.

1. Lo! He comes with clouds descending, Once for favor'd sinners slain : Thousand—thousand saints at-

tending, Swell the triumph of his train: Hal-le-lu-jah! Je-sus Christ shall e-ver reign!

359.   8s, 7s & 4s.

2. See the universe in motion,
   Sinking on her funeral pyre—
Earth dissolving, and the ocean
   Vanishing in final fire:—
     Hark, the trumpet!
Loud proclaims that Day of Ire!

3. Graves have yawn'd in countless numbers,
   From the dust the dead arise:
Millions, out of silent slumbers,
   Wake in overwhelm'd surprise;
     Where creation,
Wreck'd and torn in ruin lies!

4. See the Judge our nature wearing,
   Pure, ineffable, divine:—
See the great Archangel bearing
   High in heaven the mystic sign:
     Cross of Glory!
Christ be in that moment mine!

5. Every eye shall then behold Him
   Robed in awful majesty:—
Those that set at naught, and sold Him,
   Pierced and nail'd Him to a tree—
     Deeply wailing,
Shall the true Messiah see!

6. Lo! the last long separation!
   As the cleaving crowds divide;
And one dread adjudication
   Sends each soul to either side!
     Lord of mercy!
How shall I that day abide!

7. O, may Thine own Bride and Spirit
   Then avert a dreadful doom—
And me summon to inherit
   An eternal blissful home:—
     Ah! come quickly!
Let Thy second Advent come!

8. Yea, Amen! Let all adore Thee
   On Thine amaranthine throne!
Saviour—take the power and glory,
   Claim the kingdom for Thine own!
     Men and angels
Kneel and bow to Thee alone!
                       BRYDGES.

360.   8s, 7s & 4s.

1. Day of judgment, day of wonders!
   Hark! the trumpet's awful sound,
Louder than a thousand thunders,
   Shakes the vast creation round:
     How the summons
Will the sinner's heart confound!

2. At His call, the dead awaken,
   Rise to life from earth and sea;
All the powers of nature, shaken
   By His looks, prepare to flee;
     Careless sinner,
What will then become of thee?

3. But to those who have confessed,
   Loved and served the Lord below,
He will say, "Come near, ye blessed!
   See the kingdom I bestow:
     You for ever
Shall my love and glory know."
                       NEWTON.

WARNING AND INVITATION.

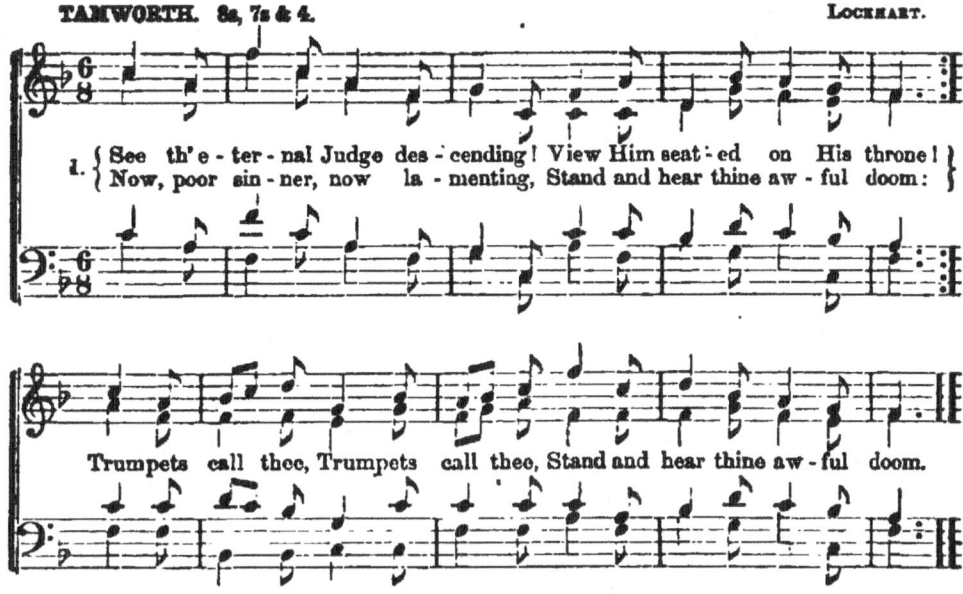

TAMWORTH. 8s, 7s & 4.   LOCKHART.

1. See th' e-ter-nal Judge des-cending! View Him seat-ed on His throne!
   Now, poor sin-ner, now la-menting, Stand and hear thine aw-ful doom:
   Trumpets call thee, Trumpets call thee, Stand and hear thine aw-ful doom.

361. 8s, 7s & 4.

2. Hear the cries he now is venting,
   Fill'd with dread of fiercer pain;
   While in anguish thus lamenting
   That he ne'er was born again—
   Greatly mourning
   That he ne'er was born again.

3. "Yonder sits my slighted Saviour,
   With the marks of dying love;
   O that I had sought His favor,
   When I felt His Spirit move—
   Golden moments,
   When I felt His Spirit move."

4. Now, despisers, look and wonder!
   Hope and sinners here must part;
   Louder than a peal of thunder,
   Hear the dreadful sound, "Depart!"
   Lost for ever,
   Hear the dreadful sound, "Depart!"

362. 8s, 7s & 4.

1. HEAR, O sinner! mercy hails you;
   Now with sweetest voice she calls;
   Bids you haste to seek the Saviour,
   Ere the hand of justice falls:
   Hear, O sinner!
   'Tis the voice of mercy calls.

2. See! the storm of vengeance gathering
   O'er the path you dare to tread!
   Hark! the awful thunder rolling
   Loud and louder o'er your head!
   Turn, O sinner!
   Lest the lightning strike you dead.

3. Haste, O sinner! to the Saviour;
   Seek His mercy while you may;
   Soon the day of grace is over;—
   Soon your life will pass away;
   Haste, O sinner!
   You must perish if you stay.
   REED.

363. 8s, 7s & 4.

1. HEAR the heralds of the Gospel
   News from Zion's King proclaim:—
   "To each rebel sinner pardon;
   Free forgiveness in His name:"
   Oh, what mercy!
   "Free forgiveness in His name."

2. Sinners, will you scorn the message
   Sent in mercy from above?
   Every sentence, O how tender!
   Every line is full of love:
   Listen to it;
   Every line is full of love.

3. Tempted souls, they bring you succor;
   Fearful hearts, they quell your fears;
   And with news of consolation
   Chase away the falling tears;
   Tender heralds—
   Chase away the falling tears.

4. O, ye angels, hovering round us,
   Waiting spirits, speed your way;
   Hasten to the court of heaven;
   Tidings bear without delay;
   Rebel sinners
   Glad the message will obey.
   ALLEN.

364. H. M.

1. Fair shines the morning star,
 The silver trumpets sound,
Their notes reëchoing far,
 While dawns the day around:
Joy to the slave; the slave is free;
It is the year of jubilee.

2. Prisoners of hope, in gloom
 And silence left to die,
With Christ's unfolding tomb,
 Your portals open fly;
Rise with your Lord; He sets you free;
It is the year of jubilee.

3. Ye, who yourselves have sold
 For debts to justice due,
Ransomed, but not with gold,
 He gave Himself for you!
The blood of Christ hath made you free;
It is the year of jubilee.

4. Captives of sin and shame,
 O'er earth and ocean, hear
An angel's voice proclaim
 The Lord's accepted year;
Let Jacob rise, be Israel free;
It is the year of jubilee.

MONTGOMERY.

365. H. M.

1. Blow ye the trumpet, blow,
 The gladly-solemn sound;
Let all the nations know,
 To earth's remotest bound,
The year of jubilee is come;
Return, ye ransomed sinners home.

2. Exalt the Lamb of God,
 The sin-atoning Lamb;
Redemption by His blood,
 Through all the lands proclaim.
 The year, &c.

3. Ye slaves of sin and hell,
 Your liberty receive,
And safe in Jesus dwell,
 And blest in Jesus live.
 The year, &c.

4. The gospel trumpet hear,
 The news of pardoning grace;
Ye happy souls, draw near,
 Behold your Saviour's face.
 The year, &c.

5. Jesus, our great High Priest,
 Has full atonement made;
Ye weary spirits, rest;
 Ye mourning souls, be glad.
 The year, &c.

TOPLADY.

WARNING AND INVITATION.

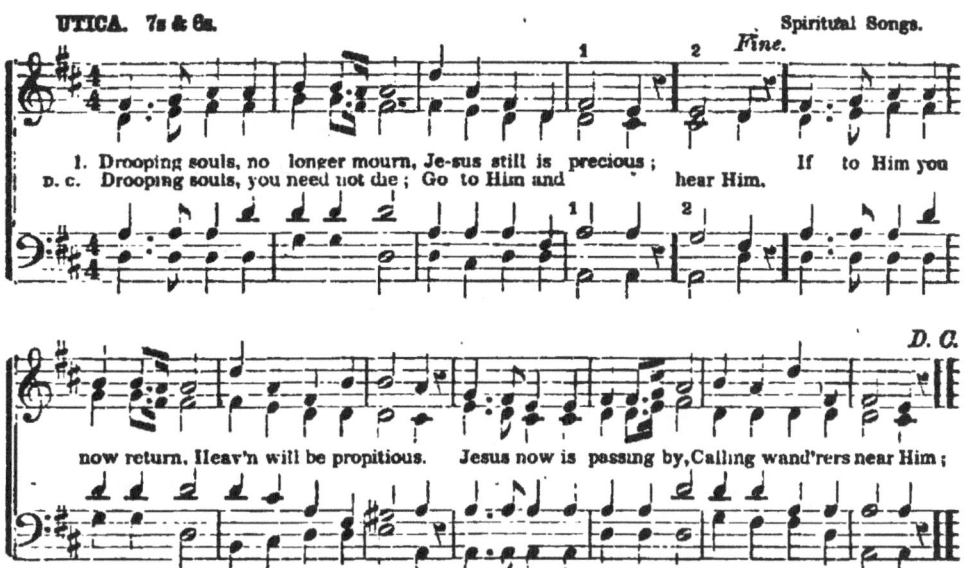

366. 7s & 6s.

1. DROOPING souls, no longer mourn,
    Jesus still is precious;
   If to Him you now return,
    Heaven will be propitious.
   Jesus now is passing by,
    Calling wanderers near Him;
   Drooping souls, you need not die,
    Go to Him and hear Him.

2. He has pardons, full and free,
    Drooping souls to gladden;
   Still He cries—"Come unto me,
    Weary, heavy laden"
   Though your sins like mountains high,
    Rise, and reach to heaven.
   Soon as you on Him rely,
    All shall be forgiven.

3. Precious is the Saviour's name,
    Dear to all that love Him;
   He to save the dying came;
    Go to Him and prove Him.
   Wand'ring sinners, now return;
    Contrite souls, believe Him!
   Jesus calls you, cease to mourn;
    Worship Him; receive Him.

367. 7s & 6s.

1. DYING souls, fast bound in sin,
    Trembling and repining,
   With no ray of light divine
    On your pathway shining;
   Why in darkness wander on,
    Filled with condemnation?
   Jesus lives; in Him alone
    Can you find salvation.

2. Prostrate bow; confess your guilt;
    Own your lost condition;
   Yield to Him whose blood was spilt,
    Unreserved submission.
   Then no more in anguish groan;
    See His mediation;
   Jesus lives; in Him alone
    Can you find salvation.

3. Linger not in all the plain;
    Vengeance is pursuing;
   'Mid the dying and the slain,
    Save your souls from ruin.
   Flee to Him who can atone;
    Flee from condemnation;
   Jesus lives; in Him alone
    Can you find salvation.

DOXOLOGY. H. M.

To God the Father's throne
 Perpetual honors raise;
Glory to God the Son!
 To God the Spirit, praise!
  With all our powers,
   Eternal King,
  Thy name we sing,
   While faith adores.

WARNING AND INVITATION.

368. 8s & 7s.

2. Now, ye needy, come and welcome,
    God's free bounty glorify;
   True belief and true repentance,
    Every grace that brings you nigh.

3. Let not conscience make you linger,
    Nor of fitness fondly dream;
   All the fitness He requireth,
    Is to feel your need of Him.

4. Come ye weary, heavy laden,
    Bruised and mangled by the fall,
   If you tarry till you're better,
    You will never come at all.

5. Agonizing in the garden,
    Lo! your Maker prostrate lies!
   On the bloody tree behold Him—
    Hear Him cry before He dies.

369. 8s, 7s & 4s.

1. Come, ye sinners, heavy laden,
    Lost and ruined by the fall,
   If you wait till you are better,
    You will never come at all;
      Sinners only,
    Christ, the Saviour, came to call.

2. Let no sense of guilt prevent you,
    Nor of fitness fondly dream;
   All the fitness He requireth,
    Is to feel your need of Him;
      This He gives you—
    'T is the Spirit's rising beam.

3. Agonizing in the garden,
    Lo! your Saviour prostrate lies;
   On the bloody tree behold Him,
    There He groans, and bleeds, and dies,
      "It is finished"—
    Heaven accepts the sacrifice.

4. Lo! th' incarnate God ascending
    Pleads the merit of His blood;
   Venture on Him—venture wholly,
    Let no other trust intrude;
      None but Jesus
    Can do helpless sinners good.

5. Saints and angels, joined in concert,
    Sing the praises of the Lamb;
   While the blissful seats of heaven
    Sweetly echo with His name;
      Hallelujah!—
    Sinners here may sing the same.
                                    HART.

370. 8s & 7s.

1. Tell us, wanderer! wildly roving
    From the path that leads to peace,
   Pleasure's false enchantment loving—
    When will thy delusion cease?

2. Once, like thee, by joys surrounded,
    We could kneel at pleasure's shrine;
   Then our brightest hopes were bounded
    By delights as false as thine.

3. But those visions never blessed us—
    Soon their fleeting day was o'er;
   Then the world that had caressed us,
    Charmed us with its smiles no more.

4. Such is pleasure's transient story;
    Lasting happiness is known
   Only in the path to glory,
    In the Saviour's love alone.

WARNING AND INVITATION.

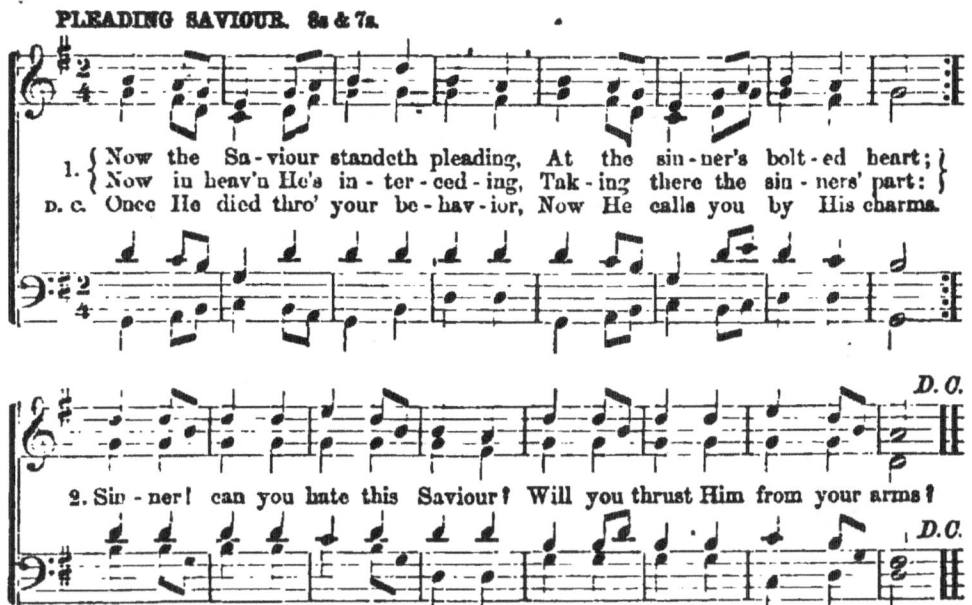

PLEADING SAVIOUR. 8s & 7s.

1. Now the Saviour standeth pleading, At the sinner's bolted heart;
   Now in heav'n He's interceding, Taking there the sinners' part:
D.C. Once He died thro' your behavior, Now He calls you by His charms.

2. Sinner! can you hate this Saviour? Will you thrust Him from your arms?

371. 8s & 7s.

1. Now the Saviour standeth pleading
   At the sinner's bolted heart;
   Now in heaven He 's interceding,
   Taking there the sinner's part.

2. Sinner! can you hate this Saviour?
   Will you thrust Him from your arms?
   Once He died through your behavior,
   Now he calls you by His charms.

3. Sinner! hear your God and Saviour,
   Hear His gracious voice to-day,
   Turn from all your vain behavior,
   O repent, return and pray!

4. Now He 's waiting to be gracious,
   Now He stands and looks on thee:
   See what kindness, love, and pity,
   Shine around on you and me.

5. Come, for all things now are ready,
   Yet there 's room for many more:
   O ye blind, ye lame and needy,
   Come to wisdom's boundless store!

372. 8s, 7s & 4s.

1. Come, ye souls by sin afflicted,
   Bow'd with fruitless sorrow down;
   By the perfect law convicted,
   Through the cross behold the crown!
   Look to Jesus—
   Mercy flows thro' Him alone.

2. Take His easy yoke, and wear it,
   Love will make obedience sweet;
   Christ will give you strength to bear it,
   While His wisdom guides your feet,
   Safe to glory,
   Where His ransom'd captives meet.

3. Sweet as home to pilgrims weary,
   Light to newly-opened eyes,
   Or full springs in deserts dreary,
   Is the rest the cross supplies:
   All who taste it,
   Shall to rest immortal rise.

4. While the wounds of woe are healing,
   While the heart is all resigned,
   'T is the solemn feast of feeling,
   'T is the Sabbath of the mind.
   None but Jesus
   Can the broken heart up-bind.

5. But to sing the rest of glory,
   Mortal tongues far short must fall;
   Tongues celestial strive to reach it,
   But it soars beyond them all:
   Faith believes it, Hope expects it,
   Love desires it—
   But it overwhelms them all.

WARNING AND INVITATION.

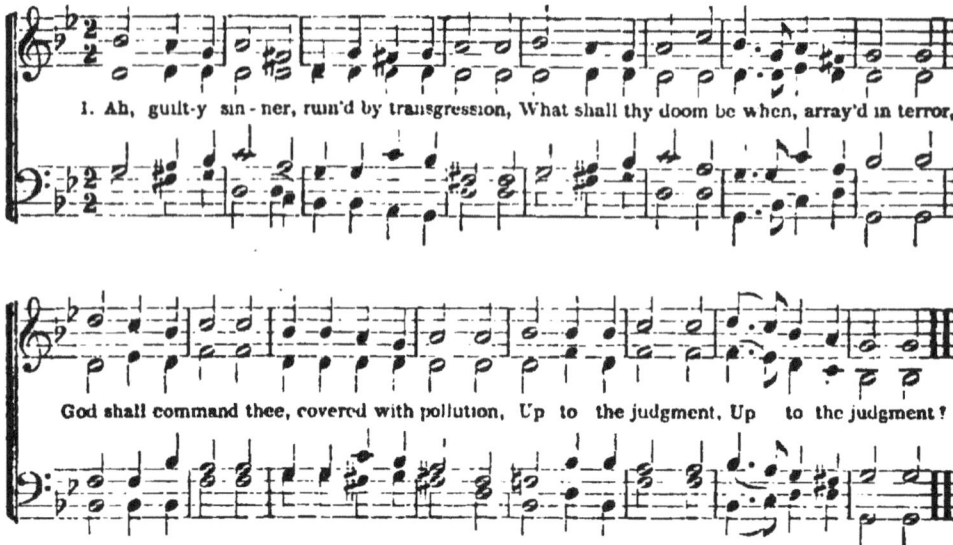

BALTIC. 10s. or 10s & 11s.

1. Ah, guilty sinner, ruin'd by transgression, What shall thy doom be when, array'd in terror, God shall command thee, covered with pollution, Up to the judgment, Up to the judgment!

373. 11s & 5s.

1. Ah, guilty sinner, ruin'd by transgression,
   What shall thy doom be when, array'd in terror,
   God shall command thee, cover'd with pollution,
      Up to the judgment!

2. Stop, thoughtless sinner, stop awhile and ponder,
   Ere death arrest thee, and the Judge, in vengeance,
   Hurl from His presence thine affrighted spirit,
      Swift to perdition.

3. Oft has He called thee, but thou wouldst not hear Him,
   Mercies and judgments have alike been slighted;
   Yet He is gracious, and with arms unfolded,
      Waits to embrace thee.

4. But, if you trifle with His gracious message,
   Cleave to the world and love its guilty pleasures,
   Mercy, grown weary, shall in righteous judgment
      Quit you for ever.

5. Where the worm dies not? and the fire eternal,
   Fills the lost soul with anguish and with terror,
   There shall the sinner spend a long for ever,
      Dying unpardoned.

6. Oh! guilty sinner, hear the voice of warning;
   Fly to the Saviour, and embrace His pardon;
   So shall your spirit meet, with joy triumphant,
      Death and the judgment.

374. 11s & 5s.

1. From the recesses of a lowly spirit,
   Our humble prayer ascends: O Father! hear it,
   Upsoaring on the wings of awe and meekness;
      Forgive its weakness!

2. We see Thy hand; it leads us, it supports us;
   We hear Thy voice; it counsels and it courts us;
   And then we turn away; and still Thy kindness
      Forgives our blindness.

3. O, how long-suffering, Lord! but Thou delightest
   To win with love the wandering: Thou invitest,
   By smiles of mercy, not by frowns or terrors,
      Man from his errors.

4. Father and Saviour! plant within each bosom
   The seeds of holiness, and bid them blossom
   In fragrance and in beauty bright and vernal,
      And spring eternal.
                                    BOWRING.

375. 10s.

1. Thou hast been called to God, rebellious heart,
   By many an awful and neglected sign,
   By many a joy which came and did depart
   For that thou didst not fear to call them thine.

2. Thou hast been called when o'er thy trembling head
   The storm in all its fury hath swept by,
   And whelmed with greedy roar the struggling dead,
   Who never more may meet thy anxious eye.

3. Thou hast been called when by some early grave
   Thou stoodest, yearning for what might not be,
   And murmuring against the God that gave,
   Because He claims His gifts again from thee.

4. Oh hear it, sinner—hear that warning voice
   Which vainly yet hath struck thy hardened ear,
   Hear, and glad troops of angels shall rejoice
   Over the sinner's warm, repentant tear.

5. Lest when thy struggling soul would quit the frame,
   Which bound it here by sin and passion lost,
   Thy Saviour's voice should wake despairing shame;
   "I call'd thee, and thou wouldst not—and art lost."
                                    MRS. NORTON.

WARNING AND INVITATION. 121

THE CHARIOT. 12s. — J. WILLIAMS.

1. The Chariot! the chariot! its wheels roll in fire, As the Lord cometh down in the pomp of His ire, Lo, self-moving, it drives on its path-way of cloud, And the heav'ns with the bur-den of God-head are bow'd.

376. 12s.

2. The glory! the glory! around Him are poured
Mighty hosts of the angels that wait on the Lord.
And the glorified saints, and the martyrs are there,
And there all who the palm-wreaths of victory wear

3. The trumpet! the trumpet! the dead have all heard;
Lo, the depths of the stone-covered charnel are stirred!
From sea, from the earth, from the south, from the north,
All the vast generations of man are come forth.

4. The judgment! the judgment! the thrones are all set,
Where the Lamb, and the white-vested elders are met:
There all flesh is at once in the sight of the Lord,
And the doom of eternity hangs on His word.

MILMAN.

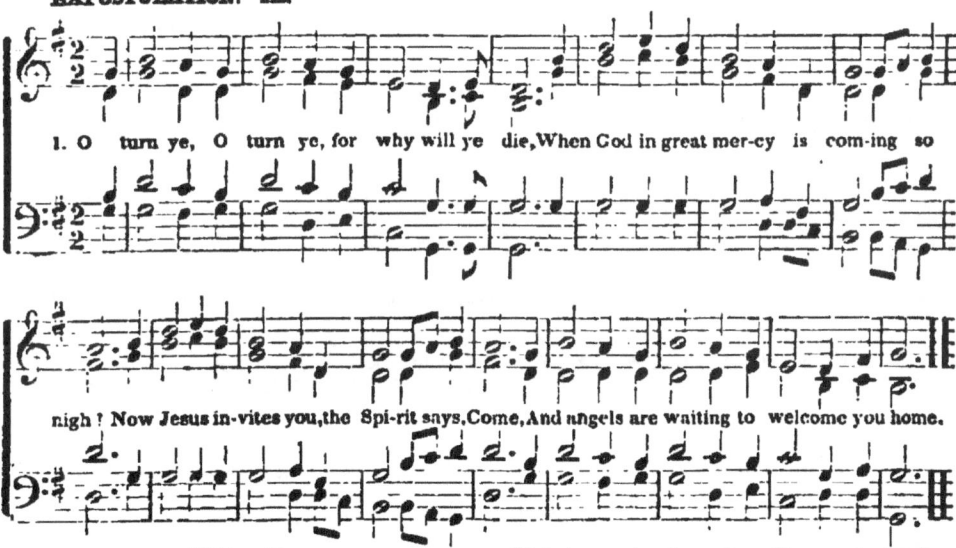

EXPOSTULATION. 11s.

1. O turn ye, O turn ye, for why will ye die, When God in great mer-cy is com-ing so nigh! Now Jesus in-vites you, the Spi-rit says, Come, And angels are waiting to welcome you home.

377. 11s.

2. How vain the delusion, that while you delay,
Your hearts may grow better by staying away;
Come wretched, come starving, come just as you be,
While streams of salvation are flowing so free.

3. And now Christ is ready your souls to receive,
O how can you question if you will believe!
If sin is your burden, why will you not come?
'Tis you He bids welcome; He bids you come home.

4. Come, give us your hand, and the Saviour your heart
And trusting in Heaven, we never shall part;
O how can we leave you? why will you not come?
We'll journey together, and soon be at home.

WARNING AND INVITATION.

378. 6s.

1. Sinner! come, 'mid thy gloom,
   All thy guilt confessing;
   Trembling now, contrite bow,
   Take the offered blessing.

2. Sinner! come, while there's room—
   While the feast is waiting;
   While the Lord, by His word,
   Kindly is inviting.

3. Sinner! come, ere thy doom
   Shall be sealed forever;
   Now return, grieve and mourn,
   Flee to Christ, the Saviour.

4. Sinner! come to thy home,
   High in heaven gleaming;
   To the sky lift thine eye,
   With true sorrow streaming.

5. Sinner! haste, time fleets fast,
   And the grave is yawning;
   Win renown, seize the crown,
   Eternity is dawning.

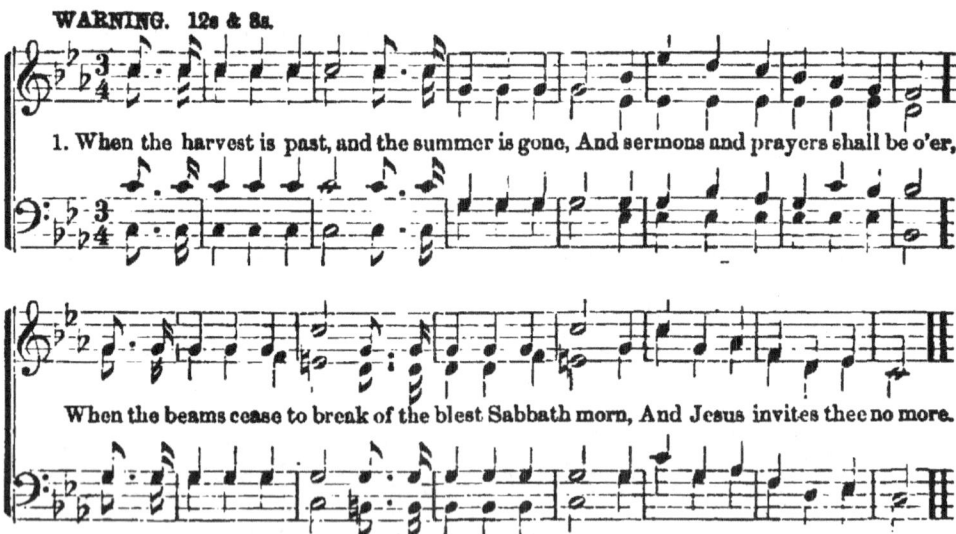

379. 12s & 8s.

2. When the rich gales of mercy no longer shall blow,
   The gospel no message declare,—
   Sinner, how canst thou bear the deep wailing of woe,
   How suffer the night of despair?

3. When the holy have gone to the regions of peace,
   To dwell in the mansions above;
   When their harmony wakes, in the fullness of bliss,
   Their song to the Saviour of love,—

4. Say, O sinner, that livest at rest and secure,
   Who fearest no trouble to come,
   Can thy spirit the swellings of sorrow endure,
   Or bear the impenitent's doom?

S. F. SMITH.

WARNING AND INVITATION.

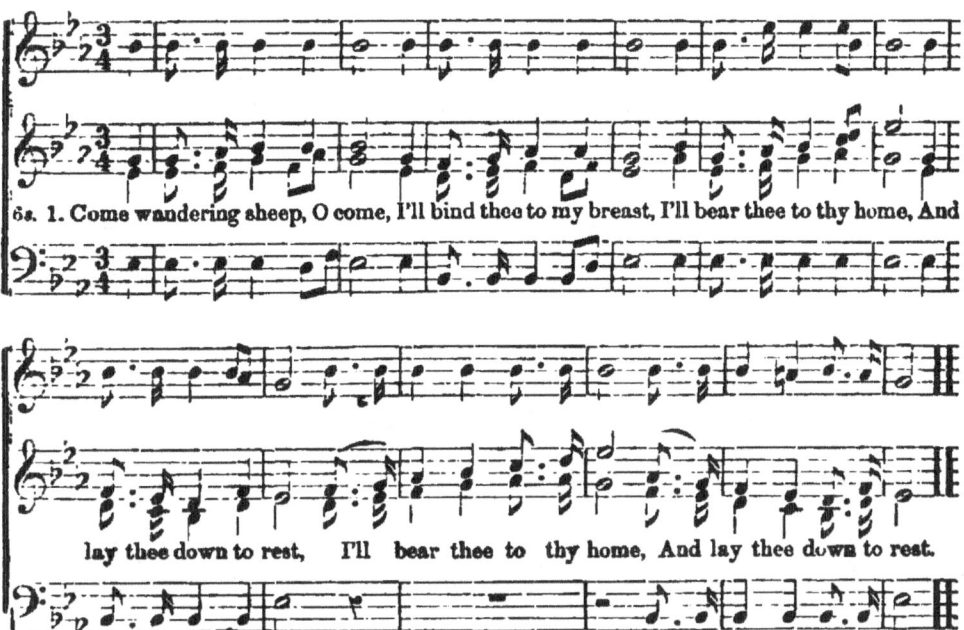

SHEPHERD'S CALL. 6s. Or 6s & 7s.   CH. BEECHER.

6s. 1. Come wandering sheep, O come, I'll bind thee to my breast, I'll bear thee to thy home, And lay thee down to rest, I'll bear thee to thy home, And lay thee down to rest.

380. 6s.

1. Come, wandering sheep, O come!
   I'll bind thee to My breast;
   I'll bear thee to thy home,
   And lay thee down to rest.

2. I saw thee stray forlorn,
   And heard thee faintly cry,
   And on the tree of scorn
   For thee I deign'd to die—

3. I shield thee from alarms,
   And wilt thou not be blest?
   I bear thee in My arms;
   Thou, bear me in thy breast!

381. 6s & 7s.

1. Love, Love, on earth appears!
   The wretched throng His way;
   He beareth all their griefs,
   And wipes their tears away:
   Soft and sweet the strain should be,
   Saviour, when I sing of Thee.

2. He saw me as He passed,
   In hopeless sorrow lie,
   Condemned and doomed to death,
   And no salvation nigh:
   Long and loud the strain should be,
   When I sing His love to me.

3. "I die for thee," He said—
   Behold the cross arise!
   And lo! He bows His head—
   He bows His head, and dies!
   Soft, my harp, thy breathings be,
   Let me weep on Calvary.

4. Now in the grave He's laid,
   In death's funereal gloom;
   Stern watchmen in the shade,
   A seal upon the tomb:
   Hush'd, my harp, thy murmurs be,
   Christ is sleeping there for thee!

5. The angels come at dawn,
   The stone is rolled away;
   The living Dead is gone,
   And bursts eternal day:
   Loud, loud the strain should be
   Jesus conquers death for me.

6. He lives! again He lives!
   I hear the voice of Love—
   He comes to soothe my fears,
   And draw my soul above:
   Joyful now the strain should be,
   When I sing of Calvary.

MRS. SOUTHEY.

WARNING AND INVITATION.

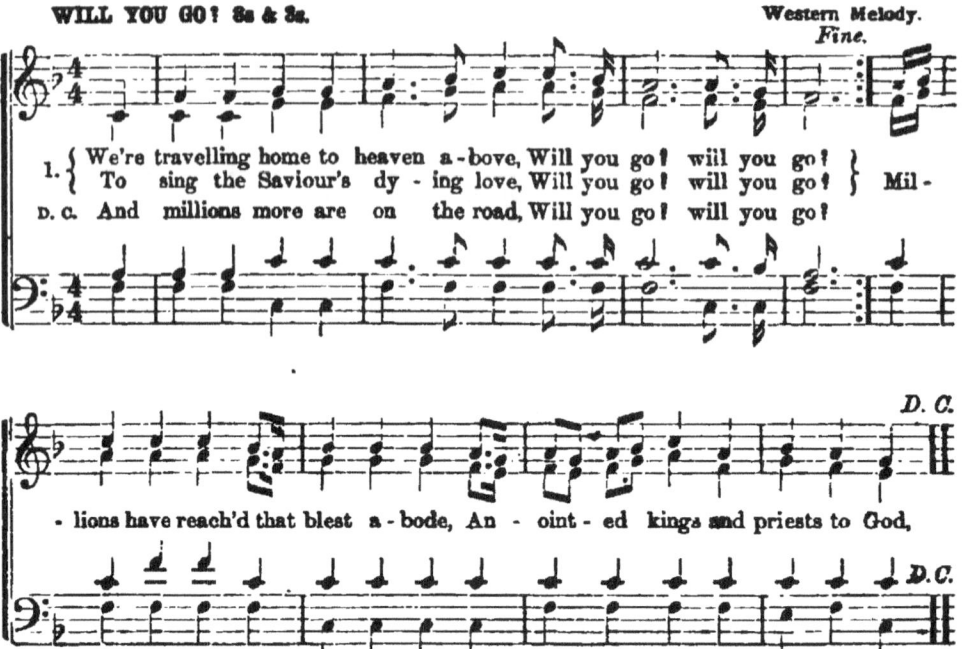

WILL YOU GO? 8s & 3s. Western Melody.

382. 8s & 3s.

1. We 're travelling home to heaven above,
      Will you go?
   To sing the Saviour's dying love,
      Will you go?
   Millions have reached that blest abode,
   Anointed kings and priests to God,
   And millions more are on the road,
      Will you go?

2. We 're going to see the bleeding Lamb,
      Will you go?
   In rapturous strains to praise His name,
      Will you go?
   The crown of life we there shall wear,
   The conqueror's palms our hands shall bear,
   And all the joys of heaven we'll share,
      Will you go?

3. We 're going to join the heavenly choir,
      Will you go?
   To raise our voice and tune the lyre,
      Will you go?
   There saints and angels gladly sing
   Hosanna to their God and King,
   And make the heavenly arches ring,
      Will you go?

4. Ye weary, heavy-laden, come,
      Will you go?
   In the blest house there still is room,
      Will you go?
   The Lord is waiting to receive,
   If thou wilt on Him now believe,
   He'll give thy troubled conscience ease,
      Come, believe.

5. The way to heaven is straight and plain,
      Will you go?
   Repent, believe, be born again,
      Will you go?
   The Saviour cries aloud to thee,
   "Take up thy cross and follow Me,
   And thou shalt My salvation see,
      Come to Me."

6. O, could I hear some sinner say,
      I will go,
   I 'll start this moment, clear the way,
      Let me go!
   My old companions, fare you well,
   I will not go with you to hell,
   With Jesus Christ I mean to dwell,
      Let me go! fare you well.

WARNING AND INVITATION.

ADVENT. C. P. M. — Western Melody.

1. When Thou, my righteous Judge, shalt come To take Thy ransomed people home, Shall I among them stand? Shall such a worthless worm as I, Who sometimes am afraid to die, Be found at Thy right hand?

2. I love to meet Thy people now, Before Thy feet with them to bow, Though vilest of them all; But, can I bear the piercing tho't, What if my name should be left out, When Thou for them shalt call?

383. C. P. M.

3. O Lord, prevent it by Thy grace,
Be Thou my only hiding-place,
  In this th' accepted day;
Thy pardoning voice, O let me hear,
To still my unbelieving fear,
  Nor let me fall, I pray.

4. Among Thy saints let me be found,
Whene'er th' archangel's trump shall
  To see Thy smiling face; [sound,
Then loudest of the throng I'll sing,
While heaven's resounding mansions ring,
  With shouts of sovereign grace.

OVINGTON'S COLL.

384. C. P. M.

1. Lo! on a narrow neck of land,
'Twixt two unbounded seas, I stand,
  Secure! insensible!
A point of time, a moment's space
Removes me to that heavenly place,
  Or shuts me up in hell.

2. O God, mine inmost soul convert,
And deeply on my thoughtful heart
  Eternal things impress!
Give me to feel their solemn weight,
And save me ere it be too late,
  Wake me to righteousness.

3. Before me place, in dread array,
The pomp of that tremendous day,
  When Thou with clouds shalt come
To judge the nations at Thy bar;
And tell me, Lord, shall I be there
  To meet a joyful doom?

4. Be this my one great business here,
With holy diligence and fear,
  To make my calling sure;
Thine utmost counsel to fulfill,
And suffer all Thy righteous will,
  And to the end endure.

5. Then, Saviour, then my soul receive,
Transported from this earth, to live
  And reign with Thee above;
Where faith is sweetly lost in sight,
And hope, in full, supreme delight,
  And everlasting love.   C. WESLEY.

WARNING AND INVITATION.

CHILD OF SIN AND SORROW. 6s & 4s.
TH. HASTINGS.

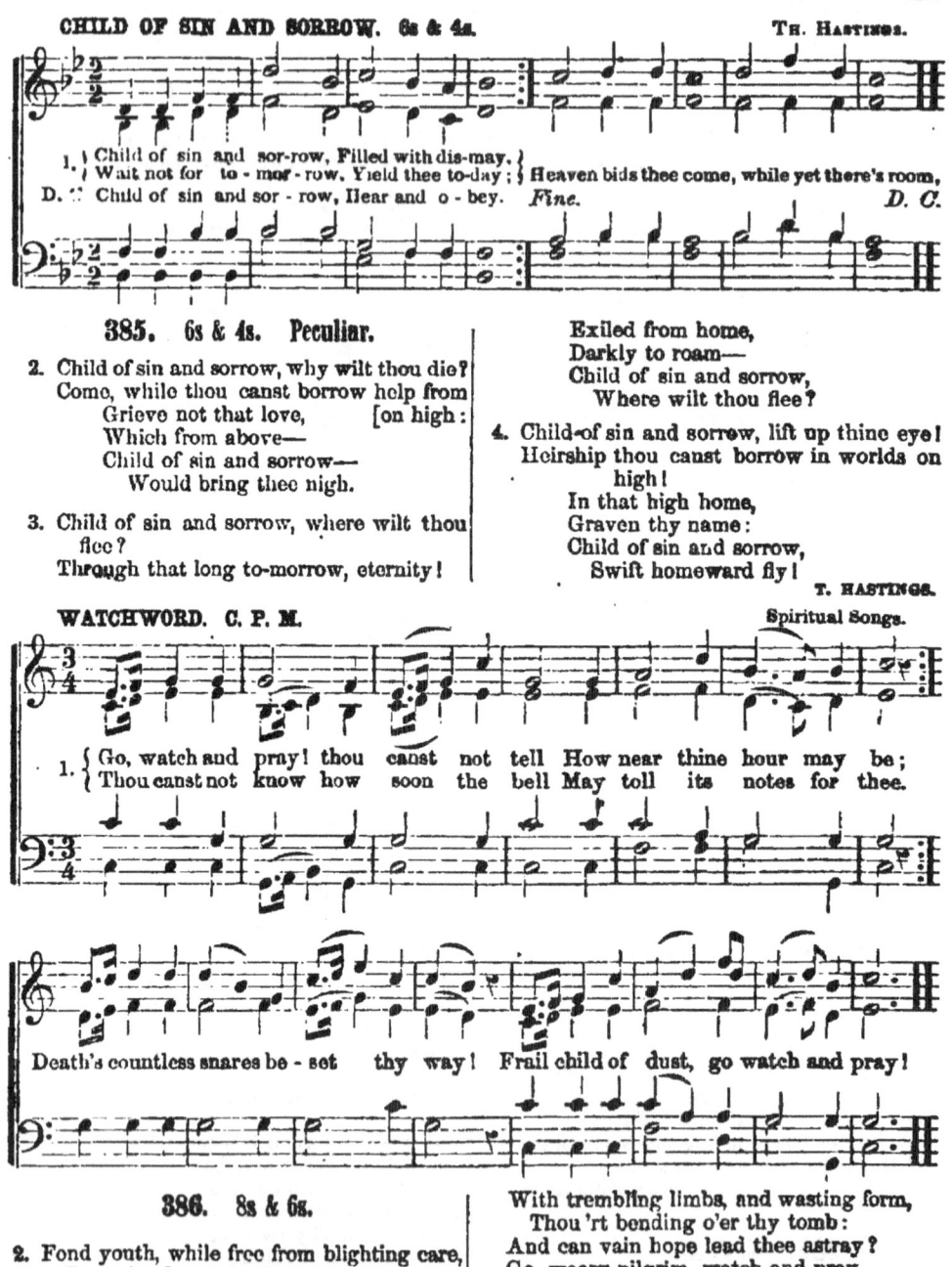

1. Child of sin and sor-row, Filled with dis-may.
Wait not for to-mor-row. Yield thee to-day; Heaven bids thee come, while yet there's room,
D.C. Child of sin and sor-row, Hear and o-bey. *Fine.* D. C.

385. 6s & 4s. Peculiar.

2. Child of sin and sorrow, why wilt thou die?
Come, while thou canst borrow help from on high:
Grieve not that love,
Which from above—
Child of sin and sorrow—
Would bring thee nigh.

3. Child of sin and sorrow, where wilt thou flee?
Through that long to-morrow, eternity!
Exiled from home,
Darkly to roam—
Child of sin and sorrow,
Where wilt thou flee?

4. Child of sin and sorrow, lift up thine eye!
Heirship thou canst borrow in worlds on high!
In that high home,
Graven thy name:
Child of sin and sorrow,
Swift homeward fly!

T. HASTINGS.

WATCHWORD. C. P. M.
Spiritual Songs.

1. Go, watch and pray! thou canst not tell How near thine hour may be;
Thou canst not know how soon the bell May toll its notes for thee.
Death's countless snares be-set thy way! Frail child of dust, go watch and pray!

386. 8s & 6s.

2. Fond youth, while free from blighting care,
Does thy firm pulse beat high?
Do hope's glad visions, bright and fair,
Dilate before thine eye?
Soon these must change, must pass away;
Frail child of dust, go watch and pray.

3. Thou aged man, life's wintry storm
Hath seared thy vernal bloom;
With trembling limbs, and wasting form,
Thou 'rt bending o'er thy tomb:
And can vain hope lead thee astray?
Go, weary pilgrim, watch and pray.

4. Ambition, stop thy panting breath!
Pride, sink thy lifted eye!
Behold the caverns, dark with death,
Before you open lie:
The heavenly warning now obey;
Ye sons of pride, go watch and pray.

SPIR. SONGS.

WARNING AND INVITATION.

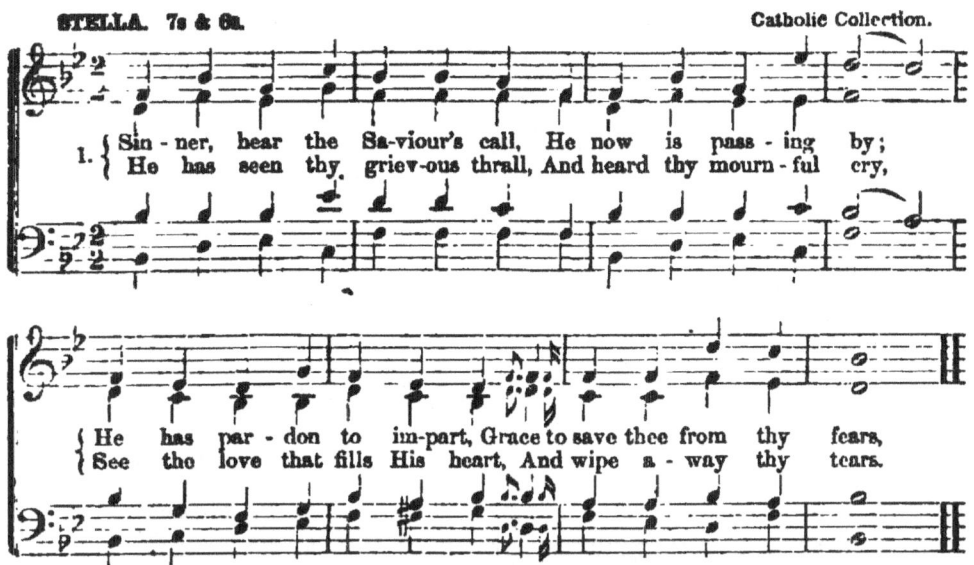

STELLA. 7s & 6s. — Catholic Collection.

1. Sinner, hear the Saviour's call, He now is passing by;
He has seen thy grievous thrall, And heard thy mournful cry,
He has pardon to impart, Grace to save thee from thy fears,
See the love that fills His heart, And wipe away thy tears.

387. 7s & 6s.

2. Why art thou afraid to come,
    And tell Him all thy case?
He will not pronounce thy doom,
    Nor frown thee from His face:
Wilt thou fear Immanuel?
    Wilt thou dread the Lamb of God
Who, to save thy soul from hell,
    Has shed His precious blood?

3. Think how on the cross He hung,
    Pierced with a thousand wounds!
Hark! from each, as with a tongue,
    The voice of pardon sounds!
See from all His bursting veins
    Blood of wondrous virtue flow!
Shed to wash away thy stains,
    And ransom thee from woe.

4. Though His majesty be great,
    His mercy is no less;
Though He thy transgressions hate,
    He feels for thy distress:
By Himself the Lord has sworn,
    He delights not in thy death,
But invites thee to return,
    That thou mayest live by faith.

5. Raise thy downcast eyes, and see
    What throngs His throne surround!
These, though sinners once, like thee,
    Have full salvation found:
Yield not then to unbelief,
    While He says, "There yet is room;"
Though of sinners thou art chief,
    Since Jesus calls thee, come.
        NEWTON.

388. 7s & 6s.

1. Stop, poor sinner, stop and think,
    Before you farther go;
Will you sport upon the brink
    Of everlasting wo?
Can you stand in that dread day,
    When He judgment shall proclaim,
And the earth shall melt away,
    Like wax before the flame?

2. Soon relentless death will come,
    To drag you to His bar;
Then, to hear your awful doom
    Will fill you with despair;
All your sins will round you crowd,
    Sins of a blood-crimson dye,
Each for vengeance crying loud—
    And what can you reply?

3. Though your heart be made of steel,
    Your forehead lined with brass,
God at length will make you feel;
    He will not let you pass.
Sinners then in vain will call,
    Though they now despise His grace,
"Rocks and mountains, on us fall,
    And hide us from His face."
        NEWTON.

WARNING AND INVITATION.

TO-DAY THE SAVIOUR CALLS. 6s & 4s.
L. Mason.

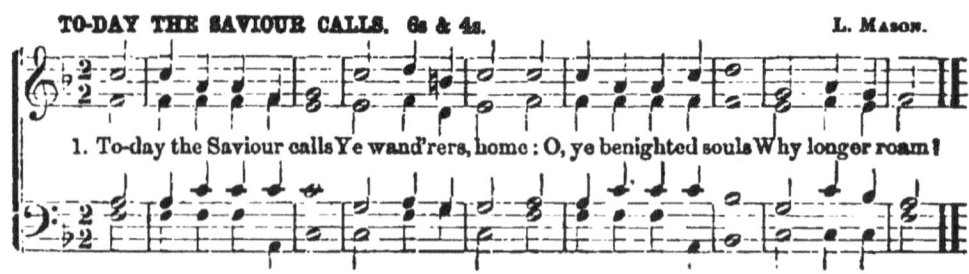

389. 6s & 4s.

2. To-day the Saviour calls;
   O, hear Him now;
   Within these sacred walls
   To Jesus bow.

3. To-day the Saviour calls;
   For refuge fly;
   The storm of justice falls,
   And death is nigh.

4. The Spirit calls to-day:
   Yield to His power;
   O, grieve Him not away:
   'Tis mercy's hour.

SACRED SONGS.

JUDGMENT. 6s & 7s.
Spiritual Songs.

390. 6s & 7s.

2. O, there will be mourning
   Before the judgment seat!
   When the trumpet's warning
   The sinner's ear shall greet!

3. O, there will be mourning
   Before the judgment seat!
   When, from dust returning,
   The lost their doom shall meet.

4. O, there will be mourning
   Before the judgment seat;
   Justice, ever frowning,
   Shall seal the sinner's fate.

WARNING AND INVITATION.

HARK! THOSE HAPPY VOICES.
Spiritual Songs.

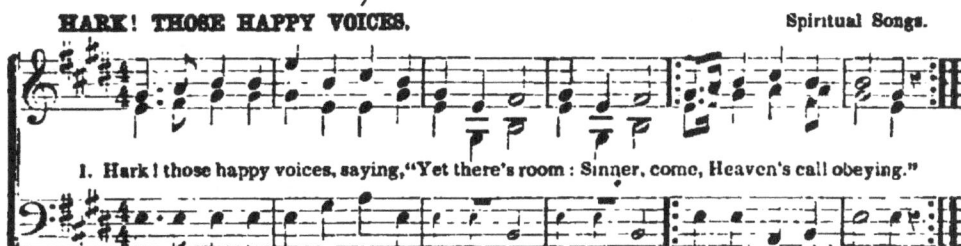

1. Hark! those happy voices, saying, "Yet there's room: Sinner, come, Heaven's call obeying."
2. Now the feast is spread before thee, Wait no more, Grace implore, Peace shall then come o'er thee.

391.

3. Bless the Lord of life for ever,
    O, my soul,
    Bountiful,
    Infinite His favor.

4. Bless the Lord of Thy salvation,
    Who in love
    From above,
    Heard thy supplication.

5. Bless the Lord of earth and heaven
    Through His blood
    That freely flow'd,
    Are thy sins forgiven.

6. Bless the Lord, whose love abounding,
    Fills thy days,
    With joy and praise,
    Songs of triumph sounding.

BDELLIUM. 10, 7s & 9s.

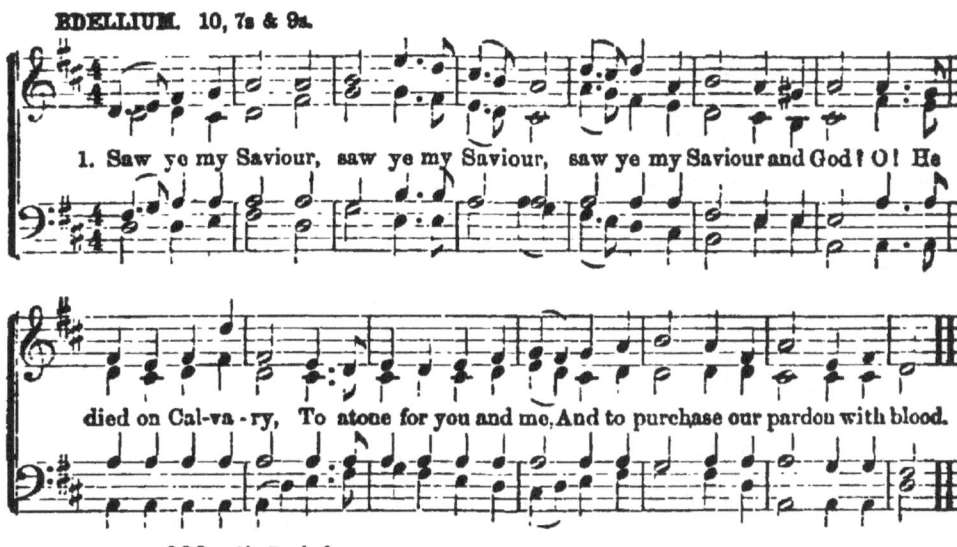

1. Saw ye my Saviour, saw ye my Saviour, saw ye my Saviour and God! O! He died on Cal-va-ry, To atone for you and me, And to purchase our pardon with blood.

392. 10, 7s & 9s.

2. He was extended, He was extended,
    Painfully nail'd to the cross;
    Here He bow'd His head and died,
    Thus my Lord was crucified,
    To atone for a world that was lost.

3. Darkness prevailed, darkness prevailed,
    Darkness prevail'd o'er the land,
    And the sun refused to shine,
    When His majesty divine
    Was derided, insulted, and slain.

4. Hail, mighty Saviour! Hail, mighty Saviour,
    Prince, and the Author of peace!
    O! He burst the bars of death,
    And, triumphant from the earth,
    He ascended to mansions of bliss.

5. There interceding, there interceding,
    Pleading that sinners may live,
    Crying, "Father, I have died,
    O, behold My hands and side,
    O, forgive them, I pray Thee, forgive."

6. "I will forgive them—I will forgive them
    When they repent and believe,
    Let them now return to Thee,
    And be reconciled to Me,
    And salvation they all shall receive."

WARNING AND INVITATION.

393. C. P. M.

1. O Thou that hear'st the prayer of faith,
Wilt Thou not save a soul from death,
That casts itself on Thee:
I have no refuge of my own,
But fly to what my God hath done,
And suffered once for all.

2. Slain in the guilty sinner's stead,
His spotless righteousness I plead,
And his availing blood;
That righteousness my robe shall be,
That merit shall atone for me,
And bring me near to God.

3. Then save me from eternal death,
The spirit of adoption breathe,
His consolations send:
By Him some word of life impart,
And sweetly whisper to my heart—
"Thy Maker is thy Friend."

4. The king of terrors then would be
A welcome messenger to me,
To bid me come away:
Unclogged by earth, or earthly things,
I'd mount, I'd fly, with eager wings,
To everlasting day.
TOPLADY.

394. C. P. M.

1. My days, my weeks, my months, my years,
Fly rapid as the whirling spheres
Around the steady pole;
Time, like the tide, its motion keeps,
And I must launch through endless deeps,
Where endless ages roll.

2. The grave is near the cradle seen,
How swift the moments pass between!
And whisper as they fly—
Unthinking man, remember this,
Thou, 'midst thy sublunary bliss,
Must groan, and gasp, and die!

3. But shall my soul be then extinct,
And cease to be, or cease to think?
Great God! it can not be;
Thou! my immortal, can not die,
What wilt thou do, or whither fly,
When death shall set thee free?

4. My soul, attend the solemn call,
Thine earthly tent must quickly fall,
And thou must take thy flight,
Beyond the vast ethereal blue,
To love and sing as angels do,
Or sink in endless night.
GREEN.

395. C. P. M.

1. What is the world?—a wildering maze,
Whose sin hath track'd ten thousand ways,
Her victims to ensnare;
All broad and winding, and aslope,
All tempting with perfidious hope,
All ending in despair.

2. Millions of pilgrims throng these roads,
Bearing their baubles or their loads
Down to eternal night;
One only path that never bends,
Narrow, and rough, and steep, ascends
From darkness into light.

3. Is there no guide to show that path?
The Bible! He alone that hath
The Bible need not stray;
But he who hath and will not give
The light of life to all that live,
Himself shall lose the way.
MONTGOMERY.

WARNING AND INVITATION.

CEDRON. C. P. M.   Th. Hastings.

1. Beyond, where Cedron's waters flow, Behold the suffering Saviour go To sad Gethsemane; His countenance is all divine, Yet grief appears in every line.

396. C. P. M.

1. Beyond where Cedron's waters flow,
Behold the suffering Saviour go
  To sad Gethsemane;
His countenance is all divine,
Yet grief appears in every line.

2. He bows beneath the sins of men;
He cries to God, and cries again,
  In sad Gethsemane;
He lifts His mournful eyes above—
"My Father can this cup remove?"

3. With gentle resignation still,
He yielded to His Father's will
  In sad Gethsemane;
"Behold Me here, thine only Son;
And, Father, let Thy will be done."

4. The Father heard; and angels, there,
Sustained the Son of God in prayer,
  In sad Gethsemane;
He drank the dreadful cup of pain—
Then rose to life and joy again.

5. When storms of sorrow round us sweep,
And scenes of anguish make us weep,
  To sad Gethsemane
We'll look, and see the Saviour there,
And humbly bow, like Him, in prayer.

               S. F. SMITH.

397. C. P. M.*

1. O Lord! how happy should we be
If we could cast our care on Thee—
  If we from self could rest;
And feel at heart, that One above,
In perfect wisdom, perfect love,
  Is working for the best.

2. How far from this our daily life!
Ever disturbed by anxious strife,
  By sudden, wild alarms;
Oh, could we but relinquish all
Our earthly props, and simply fall
  On Thy almighty arms!

3. Could we but kneel, and cast our load,
E'en while we pray, upon our God,
  Then rise with lightened cheer—
Sure that the Father, who is nigh
To still the famished raven's cry,
  Will hear, in that we fear!

4. We can not trust Him as we should,
So chafes fallen nature's restless mood
  To cast its peace away;
Yet birds and flow'rets round us preach,
All, all the present evil teach,
  Sufficient for the day.

5. Lord, make these faithless hearts of ours
Such lesson learn from birds and flowers
  Make them from self to cease;
Leave all things to a Father's will,
And taste, before Him lying still,
  E'en in affliction, peace.

     * Sing Arnon.

CHRISTIAN EXPERIENCE.

RILDA. L. M. — Melody by Mrs. M. De L. Love.

1. Just as I am—without one plea, But that Thy blood was shed for me, And that Thou bid'st me come to Thee, O Lamb of God, I come, I come!

398. L. M.

2. Just as I am—and waiting not
   To rid my soul of one dark blot,
   To Thee whose blood can cleanse each spot,
      O Lamb of God, I come! I come!

3. Just as I am—though tossed about
   With many a conflict, many a doubt,
   "Fightings within, and fears without,
      O Lamb of God, I come! I come!

4. Just as I am—poor, wretched, blind;
   Sight, riches, healing of the mind,
   Yea, all I need, in Thee to find,
      O Lamb of God, I come! I come!

5. Just as I am—Thou wilt receive;
   Wilt welcome, pardon, cleanse, relieve;
   Because Thy promise I believe,
      O Lamb of God, I come! I come!

6. Just as I am—Thy love unknown
   Has broken every barrier down;
   Now, to be Thine, yea, Thine alone,
      O Lamb of God, I come! I come!

399. L. M.

1. God of my life! Thy boundless grace,
   Chose, pardoned, and adopted me;
   My rest, my home, my dwelling-place;
      Father! I come, I come to Thee.

2. Jesus, my hope, my rock, my shield!
   Whose precious blood was shed for me,
   Into Thy hands my soul I yield;
      Saviour! I come, I come to Thee.

3. Spirit of glory and of God!
   Long hast Thou deigned my guide to be;
   Now be Thy comfort sweet bestowed;
      My God! I come, I come to Thee.

4. I come to join that countless host,
   Who praise Thy name unceasingly;
   Blest Father, Son, and Holy Ghost!
      My God! I come, I come to Thee.

400. L. M.

1. Thou only Sovereign of my heart,
      My Refuge, my almighty Friend—
   And can my soul from Thee depart,
      On whom alone my hopes depend!

2. Whither, ah! whither shall I go,
      A wretched wanderer from my Lord?
   Can this dark world of sin and wo
      One glimpse of happiness afford?

3. Eternal life Thy words impart;
      On these my fainting spirit lives;
   Here sweeter comforts cheer my heart,
      Than all the round of nature gives.

4. Let earth's alluring joys combine;
      While Thou art near, in vain they call;
   One smile, one blissful smile of Thine,
      My dearest Lord, outweighs them all.

5. Thy name my inmost powers adore;
      Thou art my life, my joy, my care;
   Depart from Thee—'t is death—'t is more—
      'T is endless ruin, deep despair!

6. Low at Thy feet my soul would lie;
      Here safety dwells, and peace divine;
   Still let me live beneath Thine eye,
      For life, eternal life, is Thine.
                                    MRS. STEELE.

PENITENCE AND CONSECRATION.

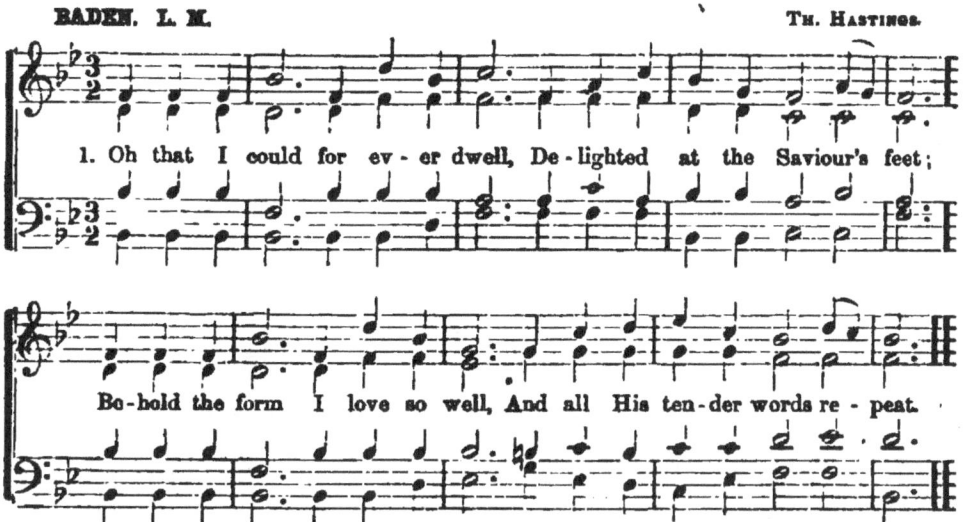

BADEN. L. M. — Th. Hastings.

1. Oh that I could for ev-er dwell, De-lighted at the Saviour's feet;
Be-hold the form I love so well, And all His ten-der words re-peat.

401. L. M.

2. The world shut out from all my soul,
   And heaven brought in with all its bliss;
   Oh! is there aught from pole to pole,
   One moment to compare with this?

3. This is the hidden life I prize,
   A life of penitential love;
   When most my follies I despise,
   And raise my highest thoughts above.

4. When all I am I clearly see,
   And freely own, with deepest shame;
   When the Redeemer's love to me
   Kindles within a deathless flame.

5. Thus would I live till nature fail,
   And all my former sins forsake;
   Then rise to God, within the vail,
   And of eternal joys partake.
   REED.

402. L. M.

1. Oh! the sweet wonders of that cross,
   Where my Redeemer loved and died!
   Her noblest life my spirit draws
   From His dear wounds, and bleeding side.

2. I would for ever speak His name,
   In sounds to mortal ears unknown;
   With angels join to praise the Lamb,
   And worship at His Father's throne.
   WATTS.

403. L. M.

1. Come, now, ye wanderers, to your God,
   Through love, to purity restored;
   The proffered benefit embrace,
   The plenitude of Heavenly grace:

2. The seeing eye, the feeling sense,
   The mystic joys of penitence;
   The tears that tell your sins forgiven;
   The sighs that waft your souls to heaven;

3. The guiltless shame, the sweet distress,
   The unutterable tenderness;
   The genuine meek humility,
   The wonder—"Why such love to me?"

4. The o'erwhelming power of saving grace,
   The sight that veils the seraph's face;
   The speechless awe that dares not move,
   And all the silent heaven of love.
   C. WESLEY.

404. L. M.

1. Though all the world my choice deride,
   Yet Jesus shall my portion be;
   For I am pleased with none beside;
   The fairest of the fair is He.

2. Sweet is the vision of Thy face,
   And kindness o'er Thy lips is shed;
   Lovely art Thou, and full of grace,
   And glory beams around Thy head.

3. Thy sufferings I embrace with Thee,
   Thy poverty and shameful cross;
   The pleasures of the world I flee,
   And deem its treasures only dross.

4. Be daily dearer to my heart,
   And ever let me feel Thee near;
   Then willingly with all I'd part,
   Nor count it worthy of a tear.
   G. TERSTEEGEN.

CHRISTIAN EXPERIENCE.

WINDHAM. L. M. — READ.

1. Stay, Thou insulted Spirit, stay! Though I have done Thee such despite, Cast not a sinner quite away, Nor take Thine everlasting flight.

405. L. M.

1. Stay, thou insulted Spirit, stay!
   Though I have done Thee such despite,
   Cast not a sinner quite away,
   Nor take Thine everlasting flight.

2. Though I have most unfaithful been
   Of all whoe'er Thy grace received;
   Ten thousand times Thy goodness seen,
   Ten thousand times Thy goodness grieved;—

3. Yet O! the chief of sinners spare,
   In honor of my great High Priest;
   Nor, in Thy righteous anger, swear
   I shall not see Thy people's rest.

4. O Lord, my weary soul release,
   And raise me by Thy gracious hand;
   Guide me into Thy perfect peace,
   And bring me to the promised land.
   C. WESLEY.

406. L. M.

1. Show pity, Lord, O Lord, forgive;
   Let a repenting rebel live.
   Are not Thy mercies large and free?
   May not a sinner trust in Thee?

2. My crimes are great, but don't surpass
   The power and glory of Thy grace;
   Great God, Thy nature hath no bound—
   So let Thy pard'ning love be found.

3. O wash my soul from every sin,
   And make my guilty conscience clean;
   Here on my heart the burden lies,
   And past offences pain my eyes.

4. My lips with shame my sins confess,
   Against Thy law, against Thy grace;
   Lord, should Thy judgments grow severe,
   I am condemn'd, but Thou art clear.

5. Should sudden vengeance seize my breath,
   I must pronounce Thee just, in death;
   And if my soul were sent to hell,
   Thy righteous law approves it well.

6. Yet, save a trembling sinner, Lord,
   Whose hope, still hov'ring round Thy word,
   Would light on some sweet promise there,
   Some sure support against despair.
   WATTS.

407. L. M.

1. When Jesus' friend had ceased to be,
   Still Jesus' heart its friendship kept—
   "Where have ye laid him?" "Come and see,"
   But ere His eyes could see, they wept.

2. Lord! not in sepulchres alone
   Corruption's worm is rank and free;
   The shroud of death our bosoms own—
   The shades of sorrow! come and see.

3. Come, Lord! God's image can not shine
   Where sin's funereal darkness lowers—
   Come! turn those weeping eyes of Thine
   Upon these sinning souls of ours!

4. And let those eyes, with shepherd care,
   Their moving watch above us keep;
   Till love the strength of sorrow wear,
   And as Thou weepedst, we may weep.

5. For surely we may weep to know,
   So dark and deep our spirit's stain,
   That had Thy *blood* refused to flow,
   Thy very tears had flowed in vain.
   MRS. BROWNING.

PENITENCE AND CONSECRATION.

408. L. M.

1. My suff'rings all to Thee are known,
   Tempted in every point like me;
   Regard my grief, regard Thine own:
   Jesus, remember Calvary!

2. For whom didst Thou the cross endure?
   Who nail'd Thy body to the tree?
   Did not Thy death my life procure?
   O let Thy mercy answer me.

3. Art Thou not touched with human woe?
   Hath pity left the Son of man?
   Dost thou not all my sorrows know,
   And claim a share in all my pain?

4. Thou wilt not break a bruised reed,
   Or quench the smallest spark of grace,
   Till through the soul Thy power is spread,
   Thy all-victorious righteousness.

5. The day of small and feeble things,
   I know Thou never wilt despise;
   I know, with healing in His wings,
   The Sun of righteousness shall rise.
                                C. WESLEY.

409. L. M.

1. Here at Thy cross, my dying Lord,
   I lay my soul beneath Thy love,
   Beneath the droppings of Thy blood,
   Jesus, nor shall it e'er remove.

2. Not all that tyrants think or say,
   With rage and lightning in their eyes,
   Nor hell shall fright my heart away,
   Should hell with all its legions rise.

3. Should worlds conspire to drive me thence,
   Moveless and firm this heart should lie;
   Resolved, for that's my last defence
   If I must perish, there to die.

4. But speak, my Lord, and calm my fear;
   Am I not safe beneath Thy shade?
   Thy vengeance will not strike me here,
   Nor Satan dare my soul invade.

5. Yes, I'm secure beneath Thy blood,
   And all my foes shall lose their aim;
   Hosanna to my dying Lord,
   And my best honors to His name.
                                WATTS.

410. L. M.

1. I asked the Lord that I might grow
   In faith, and love, and every grace;
   Might more of His salvation know,
   And seek more earnestly His face.

2. I hoped that in some favored hour
   At once He'd answer my request;
   And, by His love's constraining power,
   Subdue my sins, and give me rest.

3. Instead of this, He made me feel
   The hidden evils of my heart,
   And let the angry powers of hell
   Assault my soul in every part.

4. Yea more, with His own hand He seemed
   Intent to aggravate my woe;
   Crossed all the fair designs I schemed,
   Blasted my hopes, and laid me low.

4. "Lord, why is this," I trembling cried—
   "Wilt Thou pursue Thy worm to death?"
   "'T is in this way," the Lord replied,
   "I answer prayer for grace and faith.

4. "These inward trials I employ,
   From self, and pride, to set thee free;
   And break thy schemes of earthly joy,
   That thou may'st seek thy all in Me."
                                NEWTON.

411. L. M.

1. O that my load of sin were gone,
   O that I could at last submit
   At Jesus' feet to lay it down,
   To lay my soul at Jesus' feet!

2. Rest for my soul I long to find;
   Saviour of all, if mine Thou art,
   Give me Thy meek and lowly mind,
   And stamp Thine image on my heart.

3. Break off the yoke of inbred sin,
   And fully set my spirit free;
   I can not rest, till pure within,
   Till I am wholly lost in Thee.

4. Fain would I learn of Thee, my God;
   Thy light and easy burden prove,
   The cross, all stain'd with hallow'd blood,
   The labor of Thy dying love.

5. I would, but Thou must give the power,
   My heart from every sin release;
   Bring near, bring near the joyful hour,
   And fill me with Thy perfect peace.
                                C. WESLEY.

Doxology. L. M.

Glory to Jesus, who returns
In pomp triumphant to the sky,
With Thee, O Father, and with Thee,
O Holy Ghost, eternally.

CHRISTIAN EXPERIENCE.

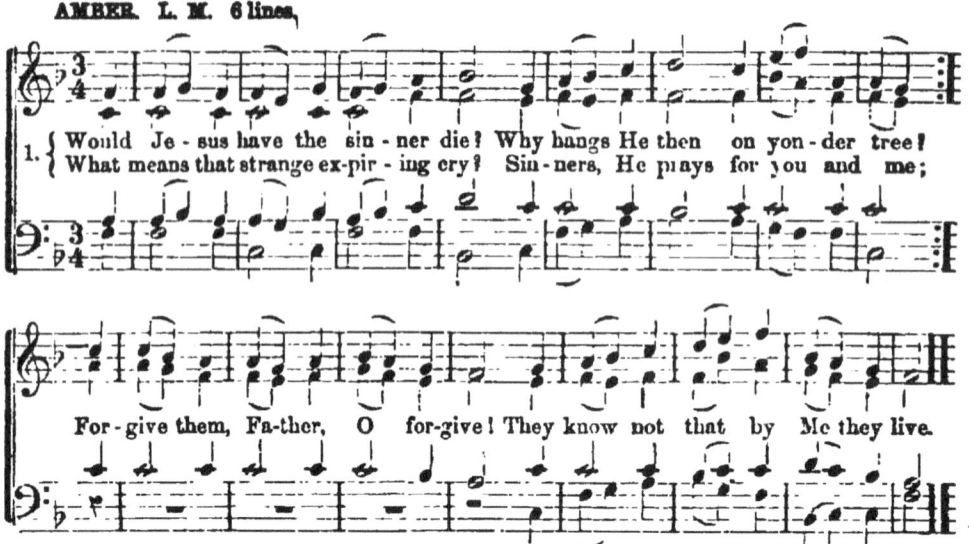

AMBER. L. M. 6 lines.

1. Would Jesus have the sinner die? Why hangs He then on yonder tree?
What means that strange expiring cry? Sinners, He prays for you and me;
Forgive them, Father, O forgive! They know not that by Me they live.

412. L. M. 6 lines.

2. Thou loving, all-atoning Lamb—
Thee, by Thy painful agony,
Thy bloody sweat, Thy grief and shame,
Thy cross and passion on the tree,
Thy precious death and life—I pray,
Take all, take all my sins away.
C. WESLEY.

413. L. M. 6 lines.

1. WEARY of wandering from my God,
And now made willing to return,
I hear, and bow me to the rod:
Yet not in hopeless grief I mourn;
I have an Advocate above,
A Friend before the throne of love.

2. O Jesus, full of truth and grace—
More full of grace than I of sin;
Yet once again I seek Thy face,
Open Thine arms, and take me in!
And freely my backslidings heal,
And love Thy faithless servant still.

3. Thou know'st the way to bring me back,
My fallen spirit to restore;
O, for Thy truth and mercy's sake,
Forgive, and bid me sin no more:
The ruins of my soul repair,
And make my heart a house of prayer.
C. WESLEY.

414. L. M. 6 lines.

1. LOOSED from my God, and far removed,
Long have I wandered to and fro;
O'er earth in endless circles roved,
Nor found whereon to rest below:
But now, my God, to Thee I fly,
For, Oh! estranged from Thee, I die.

2. Selfish pursuits, and nature's maze,
The things of sense, for Thee I leave:
Put forth Thy hand, Thy hand of grace;
Into the ark of love receive;
Take my poor, fluttering soul to rest,
And still it, Father, on Thy breast.

3. Endow me with my Saviour's peace,
Confirm and keep my longing heart;
In Thee may all my wanderings cease;
From Thee may I no more depart:
Never again from Thee remove,
Loved with an everlasting love!
MORAVIAN.

415. L. M. 6 lines.

1. O LOVE, of pure and heavenly birth!
O simple Truth, scarce known on earth!
Whom men resist with stubborn will,
And, more perverse and daring still,
Smother and quench with reasonings vain,
While error and deception reign!

2. Whence comes it, that, your power the same
As His on high, from whom you came,
Ye rarely find a listening ear,
Or heart, that makes you welcome here?
Because ye bring reproach and pain,
Where'er ye visit, in your train.

3. Then let the price be what it may,
Though poor, I am prepared to pay:
Come shame, come sorrow; spite of tears,
Weakness, and heart-oppressing fears;
One soul, at least, shall not repine
To give you room; come, reign in mine!
MADAME GUION.

PENITENCE AND CONSECRATION.

416. L. M. 6 lines.

1. Thou hidden love of God, whose height,
   Whose depth, unfathomed, no man knows,
   I see from far Thy beauteous light;
   Inly I sigh for Thy repose;
   My heart is pained; nor can it be
   At rest till it find rest in Thee.

2. Thy secret voice invites me still
   The sweetness of Thy yoke to prove;
   And fain I would; but though my will
   Seem fixed, yet wide my passions rove;
   Yet hindrances strow all the way;
   I aim at Thee, yet from Thee stray.

3. 'T is mercy all, that Thou hast brought
   My mind to seek her peace in Thee;
   Yet, while I seek, but find Thee not,
   No peace my wandering soul shall see.
   O, when shall all my wanderings end,
   And all my steps to Thee-ward tend?

4. Is there a thing beneath the sun
   That strives with thee my heart to share?
   Ah, tear it thence, and reign alone,
   The Lord of every motion there;
   Then shall my heart from earth be free,
   When it hath found repose in Thee.

5. O Love, Thy sov'reign aid impart,
   To save me from low-thoughted care;
   Chase this self-will through all my heart,
   Through all its latent mazes there;
   Make me Thy duteous child, that I,
   Ceaseless, may Abba, Father, cry.
   J. WESLEY.

417. L. M. 6 lines.

1. Saviour of all, what hast Thou done?
   What hast Thou suffer'd on the tree?
   Why didst Thou groan Thy mortal groan,
   Obedient unto death for me?
   The myst'ry of Thy passion show—
   The end of all Thy griefs below.

2. Pardon, and grace, and heaven to buy,
   My bleeding sacrifice expired;
   But didst Thou not my pattern die,
   That, by Thy glorious Spirit fired,
   Faithful to death I might endure,
   And make the crown by suff'ring sure?

3. Thou didst the meek example leave,
   That I might in Thy footsteps tread;
   Might like the Man of Sorrows grieve,
   And groan, and bow with Thee my head:
   Thy dying in my body bear,
   And all Thy state of suff'ring share.
   C. WESLEY.

418. L. M. 6 lines.

1. I thank thee, uncreated Sun,
   That Thy bright beams on me have shined;
   I thank Thee, who hast overthrown
   My foes, and heal'd my wounded mind;
   I thank Thee, whose enlivening voice
   Bids my freed heart in Thee rejoice.

2. Uphold me in the doubtful race,
   Nor suffer me again to stray;
   Strengthen my feet, with steady pace
   Still to press forward in Thy way;
   My soul and flesh, O Lord of might,
   Fill, satiate, with Thy heavenly light.

3. Thee will I love, my joy, my crown;
   Thee will I love, my Lord, my God;
   Thee will I love, beneath Thy frown
   Or smile, Thy sceptre or Thy rod.
   What though my flesh and heart decay;
   Thee shall I love in endless day.
   J. WESLEY.

419. L. M. 6 lines.

1. Around Bethesda's healing wave,
   Waiting to hear the rustling wing,
   Which spoke the angel nigh, who gave
   Its virtue to that holy spring,
   With patience and with hope endued,
   Were seen the gathered multitude.

2. Bethesda's pool has lost its power!
   No angel, by his glad descent,
   Dispenses that diviner dower,
   Which with its healing waters went.
   But He, whose word surpassed its wave,
   Is still omnipotent to save.

3. Saviour! Thy love is still the same
   As when that healing word was spoke;
   Still in Thine all-redeeming name
   Dwells power to burst the strongest yoke!
   O, be that power, that love displayed,
   Help those whom Thou alone canst aid!
   BARTON.

420. L. M.

1. Health of the weak, to make them strong!
   Refuge of sinners, and their song!
   Comfort of each afflicted breast!
   Haven of hope in realms of rest!

2. Lord of the patriarchs gone before!
   Light of the prophets' learned lore!
   Deign from Thy throne to look on me,
   And hear my lowly litany.

3. Lead me, O Spirit, to the Son,
   To taste and feel what He has done;
   To lay me low before His cross,
   And reckon all besides as dross;

4. To speak, and think, and will, and move,
   And love, as Thou wouldst have me love:
   O, look upon this bended knee,
   And hear my heart's own litany!
   LYRA CATH.

CHRISTIAN EXPERIENCE.

SALERMA. C. M.

1. Come, trembling sinner, in whose breast
A thousand thoughts revolve—
Come, with your guilt and fear oppressed,
And make this last resolve:

421. C. M.

2. I'll go to Jesus, though my sin
Hath like a mountain rose;
I know His courts, I'll enter in,
Whatever may oppose.

3. Prostrate I'll lie before His throne,
And there my guilt confess;
I'll tell Him I'm a wretch undone,
Without His sovereign grace.

4. Perhaps He will admit my plea,
Perhaps will hear my prayer;
But if I perish, I will pray,
And perish only there.

5. I can but perish if I go;
I am resolved to try;
For if I stay away, I know
I must for ever die. JONES.

422. C. M.

1. WHAT shall I render to my God
For all His kindness shown?
My feet shall visit Thine abode,
My songs address Thy throne.

2. Among the saints that fill Thy house,
My offerings shall be paid;
There shall my zeal perform the vows
My soul in anguish made.

3. How much is mercy Thy delight,
Thou ever-blessed God!
How dear Thy servants in Thy sight!
How precious is their blood!

4. How happy all Thy servants are
How great Thy grace to me!

My life, which Thou hast made Thy care,
Lord, I devote to Thee.

5. Now I am Thine, for ever Thine,
Nor shall my purpose move;
Thy hand hath loosed my bonds of pain,
And bound me with Thy love.

6. Here in Thy courts I leave my vow,
And Thy rich grace record;
Witness, ye saints, who hear me now,
If I forsake the Lord. WATTS.

423. C. M.

1. SON of the Carpenter! receive
This humble work of mine,
Worth to my meanest labor give,
By joining it to Thine.

2. Servant of all, to toil for man
Thou wouldst not, Lord, refuse;
Thy majesty did not disdain
To be employed for us.

3. Thy bright example I pursue,
To Thee in all things rise;
And all I think, or speak, or do,
Is but one sacrifice.

4. Careless, through outward cares I go,
From all distraction free:
My hands are but engaged below,
My heart is still with Thee.

5. Oh! when wilt Thou, my Life, appear!
How gladly would I cry—
"'T is done, the work Thou gav'st me here,
"'T is finished, Lord!" and fly.
  MORAVIAN.

424. C. M.

1. Thou, O my Jesus, Thou didst me
   Upon the cross embrace;
   For me didst bear the nails and spear,
   And manifold disgrace;

2. And griefs and torments numberless,
   And sweat of agony,
   Yea, death itself; and all for one
   That was Thine enemy.

3. Then, why, O blessed Jesus Christ,
   Should I not love Thee well?
   Not for the hope of winning heaven,
   Nor of escaping hell;

4. Not with the hope of gaining aught,
   Not seeking a reward;
   But as Thyself hast loved me,
   O ever-loving Lord.

5. E'en so I love Thee, and will love,
   And in thy praise will sing;
   Solely because Thou art my God,
   And my eternal King.
   F. XAVIER.

425. C. M.

1. O that I knew the secret place
   Where I might find my God!
   I'd spread my wants before His face,
   And pour my woes abroad.

2. I'd tell Him how my sins arise;
   What sorrows I sustain;
   How grace decays, and comfort dies,
   And leaves my heart in pain.

3. Arise, my soul, from deep distress,
   And banish every fear;
   He calls thee to His throne of grace,
   To spread thy sorrows there.
   WATTS.

426. C. M.

1. Thou Lamb once slain! whose flaming eyes
   Sparkle with dazzling light,
   How can a sinner choose but bow,
   And sink beneath Thy sight?

2. But I am Thine, my ransom paid—
   The price, Thy precious blood;
   And Thine and mine are made one heart,
   O my Redeemer, God!

3. How did love seize me—that pure fire
   That flamed within Thy breast
   When Thou, before Thy Father's throne,
   Wert pleased to name me bless'd!

4. Let me to Thee, in all my wants,
   Child-like, still closer fly,
   In all my course regarding still
   The guiding of Thine eye.
   MORAVIAN.

427. C. M.

1. Let worldly minds the world pursue;
   It has no charms for me;
   Once I admired its trifles, too,
   But grace has set me free.

2. Its pleasures now no longer please,
   No more content afford;
   Far from my heart be joys like these,
   Now I have seen the Lord.

3. As by the light of opening day
   The stars are all concealed;
   So earthly pleasures fade away
   When Jesus is revealed.

4. Creatures no more divide my choice;
   I bid them all depart;
   His name, and love, and gracious voice
   Have fixed my roving heart.
   NEWTON.

428. C. M.

1. Witness, ye men and angels now,
   Before the Lord we speak;
   To Him we make our solemn vow,
   A vow we dare not break:

2. That long as life itself shall last,
   Ourselves to Christ we yield,
   Nor from His cause will we depart,
   Or ever quit the field.

3. We trust not in our native strength,
   But on His grace rely,
   That, with returning wants, the Lord
   Will all our need supply.
   BEDDOME.

429. C. M.

1. And must I part with all I have,
   My dearest Lord, for Thee?
   It is but right! since Thou hast done
   Much more than this for me.

2. Yes, let it go! One look from Thee
   Will more than make amends
   For all the losses I sustain
   Of credit, riches, friends.

3. Ten thousand worlds, ten thousand lives,
   How worthless they appear,
   Compared with Thee, supremely good!
   Divinely bright and fair!
   BEDDOME.

430. C. M.

1. Sweet was the time when first I felt
The Saviour's pard'ning blood,
Applied to cleanse my soul from guilt,
And bring me home to God.

2. Soon as the morn the light revealed,
His praises tuned my tongue;
And, when the evening shade prevailed,
His love was all my song.

3. In prayer, my soul drew near the Lord,
And saw His glory shine;
And when I read His holy word,
I called each promise mine.

4. Now when the evening shade prevails,
My soul in darkness mourns;
And, when the morn the light reveals,
No light to me returns.

5. Rise, Saviour! help me to prevail,
And make my soul Thy care;
I know Thy mercy can not fail,
Let me that mercy share.

NEWTON.

431. C. M.

1. The winds were howling o'er the deep,
Each wave a watery hill;
The Saviour wakened from His sleep:
He spake, and all was still.

2. The madman in a tomb had made
His mansion of despair:
Woe to the traveler who strayed,
With heedless footsteps, there

3. He met that glance so thrilling sweet,
He heard those accents mild;
And melting at Messiah's feet,
Wept like a weaned child.

4. Oh, madder than the raving man!
Oh, deafer than the sea!
How long the time since Christ began
To call in vain to me!

5. Yet could I hear Him once again,
As I have heard of old,
Methinks He should not call in vain
His wanderer to the fold.

HEBER.

432. C. M.

1. Dear Saviour, when my thoughts recall
The wonders of Thy grace,
Low at Thy feet ashamed, I fall,
And hide this wretched face.

2. Shall love like Thine be thus repaid?
Ah, vile, ungrateful heart!
By earth's low cares so oft betrayed,
From Jesus to depart.

3. But He, for His own mercy's sake,
My wandering soul restores;
He bids the mourning heart partake
The pardon it implores.

4. Oh, while I breathe to Thee, my Lord,
The deep, repentant sigh,
Confirm the kind, forgiving word,
With pity in Thine eye.

5. Then shall the mourner at Thy feet,
Rejoice to seek Thy face;
And grateful, own how kind, how sweet,
Thy condescending grace.

MRS. STEELE.

433. C. M.

1. Why is my heart so far from Thee,
My God, my chief delight?
Why are my thoughts no more by day
With Thee, no more by night?

2. When my forgetful soul renews
The savor of Thy grace,
My heart presumes, I can not lose
The relish all my days.

3. But ere one fleeting hour is past,
The flattering world employs
Some sensual bait to seize my taste,
And to pollute my joys.

4. Wretch that I am to wander thus,
In chase of false delight!
Let me be fastened to Thy cross,
Rather than lose Thy sight.

5. Make haste, my days, to reach the goal,
And bring my heart to rest
On the dear center of my soul,
My God, my Saviour's breast.
WATTS.

434. C. M.

1. Amidst thy wrath, remember love,
Restore thy servant, Lord;
Nor let a father's chastening prove
Like an avenger's sword.

2. My sins a heavy load appear,
And o'er my head are gone;
Too heavy they for me to bear,
Too hard for me t' atone.

3. All my desire to Thee is known,
Thine eye counts every tear,
And every sigh and every groan
Is noticed by Thine ear.

4. But I'll confess my guilt to Thee,
And grieve for all my sin;
I'll mourn how weak my graces be,
And beg support divine.

5. My God! forgive my follies past,
And be for ever nigh;
O Lord of my salvation! haste,
Before Thy servant die.
WATTS.

435. C. M.

1. Mercy alone can meet my case,
For mercy, Lord, I cry;
Jesus, Redeemer, show thy face
In mercy, or I die.

2. Save me, for none beside can save,
At Thy command I tread,
With failing steps, life's stormy wave;
The wave goes o'er my head.

3. I perish, and my doom were just;
But wilt Thou leave me?—No!
I hold Thee fast, my hope, my trust;
I will not let Thee go.

4. To Thee, Thee only will I cleave;
Thy word is all my plea;
That word is truth, and I believe—
Have mercy, Lord, on me.
MONTGOMERY.

436. C. M.

1. And will the Lord thus condescend
To visit sinful worms?
Thus at the door shall mercy stand,
In all her winning forms.

2. Shall Jesus for admittance plead,
His charming voice unheard?
And this vile heart, for which he bled,
Remain forever barred?

3. 'T is sin, alas! with tyrant power,
The lodging has possessed,
And crowds of traitors bar the door,
Against the heavenly guest.

4. Lord! rise in Thine all-conquering grace,
Thy mighty power display;
One beam of glory from Thy face
Can drive my foes away.

5. Ye vile seducers! hence, depart;
Dear Saviour! enter in;
Oh! guard the passage to my heart,
And keep out every sin.
MRS. STEELE.

437. C. M.

1. Our Christ hath reached His heavenly seat,
Through sorrows and through scars;
The golden lamps are at His feet,
And in His hand the stars.

2. O Lord of life, and truth, and grace,
Ere nature was begun!
Make welcome to our erring race
Thy Spirit and Thy Son.

3. We hail the Church, built high o'er all
The heathens' rage and scoff;
Thy Providence its fenced wall,
"The Lamb the light thereof."

4. O, may He walk among us here,
With His rebuke and love,—
A brightness o'er this lower sphere,
A ray from worlds above!
FROTHINGHAM.

438. C. M.

2. This pilgrim-path by Thee was trod,
   Jesus! my King! by Thee—
   Traced by Thy feet, Thy tears, Thy blood,
   In love, in death, for me—
   O! bring my soul nearer to Thee!

3. Let every step, let every thought,
   Sweet memories bear of Thee!
   And hear the soul Thy love hath bought,
   Whose every cry shall be
   "Nearer to Thee!" "Nearer to Thee!"

4. Thou wilt! Thou dost!—a still small voice
   Whispers of faith in Thee,
   Of hope that might in grief rejoice,
   If still the way-cry be—
   "Nearer to Thee!" "Nearer to Thee!"

5. Yet a few days to me, perhaps,
   And time shall no more be—
   But boundless love can know no lapse,
   Thou art eternity!
   Draw then, my soul, "Nearer to Thee!"

439. C. M.

1. Jesus, the very thought of Thee,
   With sweetness fills my breast;
   But sweeter far Thy face to see,
   And in Thy presence rest.

2. Nor voice can sing, nor heart can frame,
   Nor can the memory find,
   A sweeter sound than Thy blest name,
   O Saviour of mankind!

3. O hope of every contrite heart!
   O joy of all the meek!
   To those who fall, how kind Thou art!
   How good to those who seek!

4. But what to those who find? Ah! this,
   Nor tongue nor pen can show,
   The love of Jesus, what it is,
   None but His loved ones know.
   ST. BERNARD.

440. C. M.

1. Lord, see what floods of sorrow rise,
   And beat upon my soul:
   One trouble to another cries;
   Billows on billows roll.

2. From fear to hope, from hope to fear,
   My shipwrecked soul is tost,
   Till I am tempted, in despair,
   To give up all for lost.

3. Yet through the stormy clouds I'll look
   Once more to Thee, my God;
   O, fix my feet upon the rock,
   Beyond the raging flood.

4. One look of mercy from Thy face
   Will set my heart at ease;
   One all-commanding word of grace
   Will make the tempest cease.
   STENNETT.

PENITENCE AND CONSECRATION.

441. C. M.

1. OH, my dear Saviour, when Thy cares,
Thy toils for me I read,
My eyes run o'er with grateful tears,
And I bow down my head.

2. Thy suffering life I can not trace,
Or read Thy sacred word;
But I'm o'ercome with thankfulness
To Thee, my gracious Lord.

3. What am I, Lord, that Thou so much
Should'st love and value me?
Vile dust I am, yet Thou for such
Didst bear Thy misery.
MORAVIAN.

442. C. M.

1. THE Lord will happiness divine
On contrite hearts bestow:
Then tell me, gracious God, is mine,
A contrite heart, or no?

2. I hear, but seem to hear in vain,
Insensible as steel;
If aught is felt, 'tis only pain
To find I can not feel.

3. My best desires are faint and few:
Fain would I strive for more;
But, when I cry, "My strength renew,"
Seem weaker than before.

4. Thy saints are comforted, I know,
And love the house of prayer;
I therefore go where others go,
But find no comfort there.

5. Oh! make this heart rejoice or ache;
Decide this doubt for me;
And if it be not broken, break—
And heal it, if it be.
COWPER.

443. C. M.

1. How oft, alas! this wretched heart
Has wandered from the Lord!
How oft my roving thoughts depart—
Forgetful of His word!

2. Yet sovereign mercy calls—"Return!"
Dear Lord! and may I come?
My vile ingratitude I mourn;
Oh! take the wanderer home.

3. And canst Thou—wilt Thou yet forgive,
And bid my crimes remove!
And shall a pardoned rebel live
To speak Thy wondrous love?

4. Almighty grace! Thy healing power,
How glorious—how divine!
That can to life and bliss restore
A heart so vile as mine!

5. Thy pard'ning love—so free, so sweet—
Dear Saviour! I adore;
Oh! keep me at Thy sacred feet,
And let me rove no more.
MRS. STEELE.

444. C. M.

1. WITH tears of anguish I lament,
Here, at Thy feet, my God,
My passion, pride, and discontent,
And vile ingratitude.

2. Sure there was ne'er a heart so base,
So false as mine has been;
So faithless to its promises,
So prone to every sin!

3. My reason tells me Thy commands
Are holy, just, and true;
Tells me whate'er my God demands
Is His most righteous due.

4. Reason, I hear, her counsels weigh,
And all her words approve;
But still I find it hard t' obey,
And harder yet to love.

5. How long, dear Saviour, shall I feel
These struggles in my breast?
When wilt Thou bow my stubborn will,
And give my conscience rest?

6. Break, Sovereign Grace, O break the charm,
And set the captive free;
Reveal, Almighty God, Thine arm,
And haste to rescue me.
STENNETT.

445. C. M.

1. MY God! the covenant of Thy love
Abides forever sure;
And in its matchless grace I feel
My happiness secure.

2. Since Thou, the everlasting God,
My Father art become,
Jesus my guardian and my friend,
And heaven my final home;—

3. I welcome all thy sovereign will,
For all that will is love;
And when I know not what Thou dost,
I wait the light above.

4. Thy covenant in the darkest gloom
Shall heavenly rays impart,
And when my eyelids close in death,
Sustain my fainting heart.
DODDRIDGE.

CHRISTIAN EXPERIENCE.

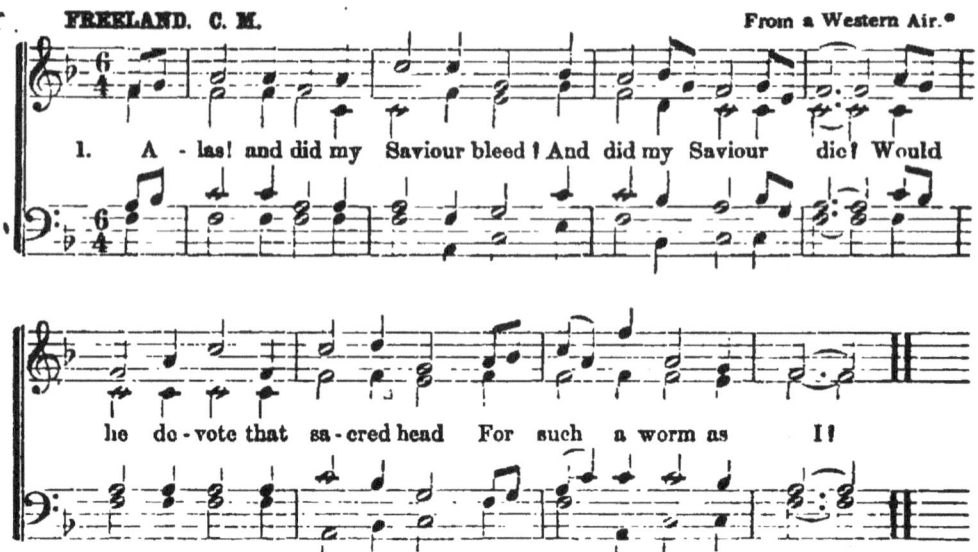

FREELAND. C. M. From a Western Air.*

1. Alas! and did my Saviour bleed? And did my Saviour die? Would he devote that sacred head For such a worm as I?

* The first two strains of this melody were heard in the camp ground, sung by hundreds of voices. It was written down from memory, and the other strains added.

446. C. M.

1. ALAS! and did my Saviour bleed?
   And did my Sovereign die?
   Would He devote that sacred head
   For such a worm as I?

2. Was it for crimes that I had done
   He groaned upon the tree?
   Amazing pity! grace unknown!
   And love beyond degree!

3. Well might the sun in darkness hide,
   And shut his glories in,
   When God, the mighty Maker, died
   For man the creature's sin.

4. Thus might I hide my blushing face
   While His dear cross appears,
   Dissolve my heart in thankfulness,
   And melt mine eyes to tears.

5. But drops of grief can ne'er repay
   The debt of love I owe:
   Here, Lord, I give myself away;
   'T is all that I can do.
                              WATTS.

447. C. M.

1. JESUS! Thou art the sinner's Friend;
   As such I look to Thee;
   Now, in the fullness of Thy love,
   O Lord! remember me.

2. Remember Thy pure word of grace—
   Remember Calvary;
   Remember all Thy dying groans,
   And, then, remember me.

3. Thou wondrous Advocate with God!
   I yield myself to Thee;
   While Thou art sitting on Thy throne,
   Dear Lord! remember me.

4. Lord! I am guilty—I am vile,
   But Thy salvation 's free;
   Then, in Thine all-abounding grace,
   Dear Lord! remember me.

5. And, when I close my eyes in death,
   When creature-helps all flee,
   Then, O my dear Redeemer-God!
   I pray, remember me.
                         PARKINSON SELEC.

448. C. M.

1. JESUS, and didst Thou condescend,
   When vailed in human clay,
   To heal the sick, the lame, the blind,
   And drive disease away?

2. Didst Thou regard the beggar's cry,
   And give the blind to see?
   Jesus, Thou Son of David, hear—
   Have mercy, too, on me.

3. And didst Thou pity mortal woe,
   And sight and health restore?
   Then pity, Lord, and save my soul,
   Which needs Thy mercy more.

4. Didst Thou regard Thy servant's cry,
   When sinking in the wave?
   I perish, Lord—oh save my soul,
   For Thou alone canst save.
                              BRADLEY.

PENITENCE AND CONSECRATION.

449. C. M.

1. Welcome, O Saviour! to my heart;
   Possess Thine humble throne;
   Bid every rival hence depart,
   And claim me for Thine own.

2. The world and Satan I forsake—
   To Thee, I all resign;
   My longing heart, O Jesus! take,
   And fill with love divine.

3. Oh! may I never turn aside,
   Nor from Thy bosom flee;
   Let nothing here my heart divide—
   I give it all to Thee.
   BOURNE'S COLL.

450. C. M.

1. My Saviour, can I follow Thee,
   When all is dark before?
   While midnight rests upon the sea,
   How can I reach the shore?

2. Oh, let Thy star of love but shine,
   Though with the faintest ray;
   'T will gild with light the foaming brine,
   And light my stormy way.

3. Then gladly will I follow Thee,
   Though hurricanes appear;
   Singing with rapture o'er the sea;
   "What can I have to fear?"
   LEIFCHILD'S COLL.

451. C. M.

1. Thy gracious presence, O my God!
   All that I wish contains;
   With this, beneath affliction's load,
   My heart no more complains.

2. This can my every care control,
   Gild each dark scene with light;
   This is the sunshine of the soul,
   Without it all is night.

3. O happy scenes above the sky,
   Where Thy full beams impart
   Unclouded beauty to the eye,
   And rapture to the heart.

4. Her portion in those realms of bliss,
   My spirit longs to know;
   My wishes terminate in this,
   Nor can they rest below.

5. Lord! Shall the breathings of my heart
   Aspire in vain to Thee?
   Confirm my hope, that where Thou art,
   I shall for ever be.

6. Then shall my cheerful spirit sing
   The darksome hours away,
   And rise on faith's expanded wing
   To everlasting day.
   STEELE.

452. C. M.

1. Approach, my soul! the mercy-seat,
   Where Jesus answers prayer:
   There humbly fall before His feet,
   For none can perish there.

2. Thy promise is my only plea,
   With this I venture nigh:
   Thou callest burdened souls to Thee,
   And such, O Lord! am I.

3. Bowed down beneath a load of sin,
   By Satan sorely pressed,
   By wars without, and fears within,
   I come to Thee for rest.

4. Be Thou my shield and hiding-place,
   That, sheltered near Thy side,
   I may my fierce accuser face,
   And tell Him—"Thou hast died."

5. Oh! wondrous Love—to bleed and die,
   To bear the cross and shame,
   That guilty sinners, such as I,
   Might plead Thy gracious name!
   NEWTON.

453. C. M.

1. My soul, review the trembling days
   In which my God I sought,
   I cried aloud for aid divine,
   And aid divine He brought.

2. Thro' all my weak and fainting heart
   His secret strength He spread,
   And clasped me in His arms of love,
   And raised my drooping head.

3. He called Himself my covenant God;
   His promises He shewed;
   And wide displayed their solemn seal
   In the great-Surety's blood.

4. I heard His people shout around,
   And joined their cheerful song;
   And saw from far the shining seats—
   Which to His saints belong.

5. My God, what inward strength thou givest
   I to Thy service vow;
   And in Thy strength would upward march,
   Till at Thy throne I bow.
   DODDRIDGE.

BENEVENTO. 7s.

1. Saviour, when in dust to Thee,
Low we bow th' adoring knee:
When, repentant, to the skies
Scarce we lift our streaming eyes;
O, by all Thy pains and woe,
Suffered once for man below,
Bending from thy throne on high,
Hear our solemn litany.

454. 7s.

2. By Thy birth and early years,
By Thy human griefs and fears,
By Thy fasting and distress
In the lonely wilderness,
By Thy vict'ry in the hour
Of the subtle tempter's power:
Jesus, look with pitying eye;
Hear our solemn litany.

3. By Thine hour of dark despair,
By Thine agony of prayer,
By the purple robe of scorn,
By Thy wounds, Thy crown of thorn,
By Thy cross, Thy pangs and cries,
By Thy perfect sacrifice:
Jesus, look with pitying eye;
Hear our solemn litany.

4. By Thy deep expiring groan,
By the seal'd sepulchral stone,
By Thy triumph o'er the grave,
By Thy power from death to save:
Mighty God, ascended Lord,
To Thy throne in heaven restored,
Prince and Saviour, hear our cry,
Hear our solemn litany.

ROBERT GRANT.

455. 7s.

1. While with ceaseless course the sun
Hasted through the former year,
Many souls their race have run,
Never more to meet us here.
Fixed in an eternal state,
They have done with all below;
We a little longer wait,
But how little, none can know.

2. Spared to see another year,
Let Thy blessing meet us here;
Come, Thy dying work revive,
Bid Thy drooping garden thrive:
Sun of Righteousness, arise!
Warm our hearts and bless our eyes;
Let our prayer Thy pity move,
Make this year a time of love.

3. Thanks for mercies past receive,
Pardon of our sins renew;
Teach us henceforth how to live,
With eternity in view:
Bless Thy word to old and young,
Fill us with a Saviour's love;
When our life's short race is run,
May we dwell with Thee above.

NEWTON.

456. 7s.

1. Does the Gospel word proclaim
    Rest for those that weary be?
   Then, my soul, put in thy claim—
    Sure that promise speaks to thee:
   Marks of grace I can not show,
    All polluted is my best;
   But I weary am, I know,
    And the weary long for rest.

2. Burdened with a load of sin,
    Harassed with tormenting doubt,
   Hourly conflicts from within,
    Hourly crosses from without;
   All my little strength is gone,
    Sink I must without supply;
   Sure upon the earth is none
    Can more weary be than I.

3. In the ark the weary dove
    Found a welcome resting-place;
   Thus my spirit longs to prove
    Rest in Christ, the Ark of grace:
   Tempest-tossed I long have been,
    And the flood increases fast;
   Open, Lord, and take me in,
    Till the storm be overpast!
                                NEWTON.

457. 7s.

1. Gracious Jesus, Lord most dear,
   Guilty though I am, give ear;
   Show Thine own sweet clemency;
   Spurn me not, though vile I be,

2. Here before Thee, fallen, weeping,
   And with tears these torn feet steeping;
   Jesus, for Thy mercy's sake,
   Pity on my misery take.

3. Sharing now Thy wounds, I pray Thee,
   Let me love for love repay Thee,—
   Thou, whose soul for sinners smarted,
   Healer of the broken-hearted!

4. On my heart each stripe be written,
   Wherewith Thou for me wert smitten;
   Each deep wound, that I may be
   Wholly crucified with Thee.

5. From the cross uplifted high,
   My beloved, cast Thine eye;
   Turn me to Thee, heart and soul,
   Speak the word of power—"Be whole!"

458. 7s.

1. 'T is my happiness below,
    Not to live without the cross,
   But the Saviour's power to know,
    Sanctifying every loss.

2. Trials must and will befall;
    But, with humble faith to see
   Love inscribed upon them all—
    This is happiness to me.

3. God, in Israel, sows the seeds
    Of affliction, pain, and toil;
   These spring up, and choke the weeds
    Which would else o'erspread the soil.

4. Trials make the promise sweet;
    Trials give new life to prayer;
   Trials bring me to His feet—
    Lay me low, and keep me there.
                                COWPER.

459. 7s.

1. Once I thought my mountain strong,
    Firmly fixed, no more to move;
   Then my Saviour was my song,
    Then my soul was filled with love:
   Those were happy, golden days,
   Sweetly spent in prayer and praise.

2. Little, then, myself I knew,
    Little thought of Satan's power;
   Now I feel my sins renew,
    Now I feel the stormy hour;
   Sin has put my joys to flight—
   Sin has turned my day to night.

3. Saviour! shine, and cheer my soul;
    Bid my dying hopes revive;
   Make my wounded spirit whole;
    Far away the tempter drive;
   Speak the word, and set me free—
   Let me live alone to Thee.
                                NEWTON.

460. 7s.

1. Lord, for ever at Thy side
    Let my place and portion be;
   Strip me of the robe of pride;
    Clothe me with humility.

2. Meekly may my soul receive
    All Thy Spirit hath revealed;
   Thou hast spoken; I believe,
    Though the oracle be sealed.

3. Humble as a little child,
    Weaned from the mother's breast,
   By no subtleties beguiled,
    On Thy faithful word I rest.

4. Israel, now and evermore
    In the Lord Jehovah trust;
   Him in all His ways adore,
    Wise, and powerful, and just.
                                MONTGOMERY.

CHRISTIAN EXPERIENCE.

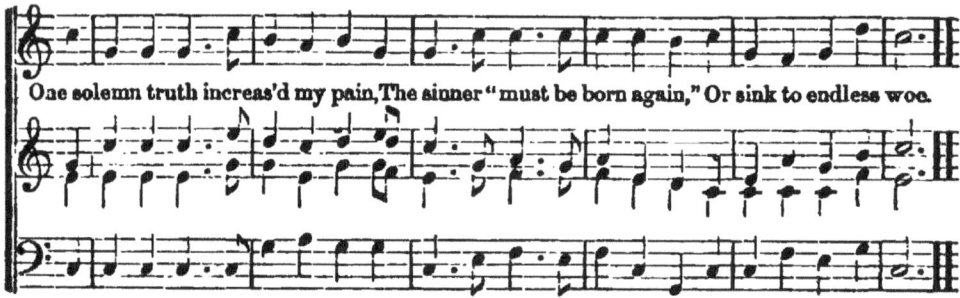

461. C. P. M.

1. Awaked by Sinai's awful sound,
My soul in bonds of guilt I found,
 And knew not where to go;
One simple truth increased my pain,
The sinner "must be born again,"
 Or sink to endless woe.

2. I heard the law its thunders roll,
While guilt lay heavy on my soul—
 A vast oppressive load;
All creature-aid I saw was vain;
The sinner "must be born again,"
 Or drink the wrath of God.

3. The saints I heard with rapture tell—
How Jesus conquered death and hell
 To bring salvation near;
Yet still I found this truth remain—
The sinner "must be born again,"
 Or sink in deep despair.

4. But while I thus in anguish lay,
The bleeding Saviour passed that way,
 My bondage to remove;
The sinner, once by justice slain,
Now by His grace is born again,
 And sings redeeming love.
OCKUM.

462. C. P. M.

1. That warning voice, O sinner hear!
And while salvation lingers near,
 The heav'nly call obey;
Flee from destruction's downward path,
Flee from the threat'ning storm of wrath,
 That rises o'er thy way.

2. Soon night comes on with thick'ning shade,
The tempest hovers o'er thy head,
 The winds their fury pour:
The lightnings rend the earth and skies,
The thunders roar, the flames arise;
 What terrors fill that hour.

3. That warning voice, O sinner, hear,
Whose accents linger on thine ear;
 Thy footsteps now retrace;
Renounce thy sins and be forgiv'n,
Believe, become an heir of heav'n,
 And sing redeeming grace.

4. Then, while a voice of pardon speaks,
The storm is hush'd, the morning breaks,
 The heav'ns are all serene;
Fresh verdure clothes the beauteous fields,
Joy echoes on the distant hills,
 New wonders fill the scene.
T. HASTINGS.

PENITENCE AND CONSECRATION.

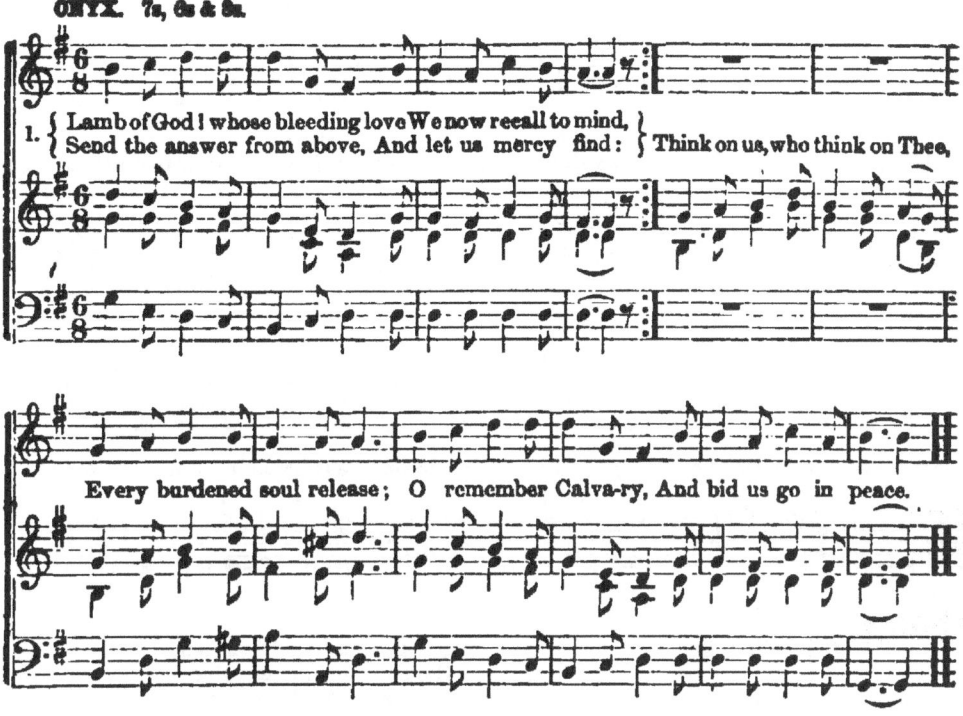

ONYX. 7s, 6s & 8s.

1. Lamb of God! whose bleeding love We now recall to mind,
Send the answer from above, And let us mercy find:
Think on us, who think on Thee, Every burdened soul release;
O remember Calvary, And bid us go in peace.

463. 7s & 6s.

1. LAMB of God! whose bleeding love
   We now recall to mind,
   Send the answer from above,
   And let us mercy find;
   Think on us, who think on Thee,
   Every burdened soul release;
   O remember Calvary,
   And bid us go in peace!

2. By thine agonizing pain,
   And bloody sweat, we pray;
   By Thy dying love to man,
   Take all our sins away;
   Burst our bonds and set us free,
   From all sin do Thou release;
   O remember Calvary,
   And bid us go in peace!

3. Let Thy blood, by faith applied,
   The sinner's pardon seal;
   Own us freely justified,
   And all our sickness heal;
   By Thy passion on the tree,
   Let our griefs and troubles cease;
   O remember Calvary,
   And bid us go in peace!

   C. WESLEY.

464. 7s, 6s & 8s.

1. THOU, O Lord, in tender love,
   Dost all my burdens bear;
   Lift my heart to things above,
   And fix it ever there.
   Calm on tumult's wheel I sit,
   'Midst busy multitudes alone;
   Sweetly waiting at Thy feet,
   Till all Thy will be done.

2. Careful without care I am,
   Nor feel my happy toil;
   Kept in peace by Jesus' name,
   Supported by His smile.
   Joyful thus my faith to show,
   I find His service my reward;
   Every work I do below,
   I do it to the Lord.

3. To the desert or the cell,
   Let others blindly fly,
   In this evil world I dwell,
   Unhurt, unspotted I.
   Here I find a house of prayer,
   To which I inwardly retire;
   Walking unconcerned in care,
   And unconsumed in fire.

   C. WESLEY.

CHRISTIAN EXPERIENCE.

GILEAD. 7s & 6s.   Arranged by CH. BEECHER.

1. How lost was my con-di-tion, Till Jesus made me whole! / There is but one Physician Can cure a sin-sick soul. / Next door to death he

found me, And snatched me from the grave, To tell to all around me His wondrous power to save.

465. 7s & 6s.

2. The worst of all diseases
   Is light compared with sin;
On every part it seizes,
   But rages most within;
'T is palsy, plague, and fever,
   And madness, all combined;
And none but a believer
   The least relief can find.

3. From men, great skill professing,
   I thought a cure to gain;
But this proved more distressing,
   And added to my pain.
Some said that nothing ailed me,
   Some gave me up for lost;
Thus every refuge failed me,
   And all my hopes were crossed.

4. At length, this great Physician—
   How matchless is His grace!
Accepted my petition,
   And undertook my case;
First gave me sight to view Him—
   For sin my sight had sealed—
Then bade me look unto Him;
   I looked, and I was healed.

5. A dying, risen Jesus,
   Seen by the eye of faith,
At once from anguish frees us,
   And saves the soul from death.

Come, then, to this Physician;
   His help He'll freely give;
He makes no hard condition;
   'Tis only—look and live!
                  NEWTON.

466. 7s & 6s.

1. O WHEN shall I see Jesus,
   And reign with Him above;
And from that flowing fountain,
   Drink everlasting love?
When shall I be delivered
   From this vain world of sin,
And with my blessed Jesus,
   Drink endless pleasures in?

2. But now I am a soldier,
   My Captain's gone before;
He's given me my orders,
   And bid me not give o'er;
And since He has proved faithful,
   A righteous crown He'll give,
And all His valiant soldiers
   Eternal life shall have.

3. Whene'er you meet with troubles
   And trials on your way,
O! cast your care on Jesus,
   And don't forget to pray.
Gird on the heavenly armor
   Of faith, and hope, and love;
Then, when the combat's ended,
   He'll carry you above.

PENITENCE AND CONSECRATION.

467. 7s & 6s.

1. To Thee, my God and Saviour,
   My heart exulting springs,
   Rejoicing in Thy favor,
   Almighty King of kings:
   I'll celebrate Thy glory
   With all the saints above,
   And tell the joyful story
   Of Thy redeeming love.

2. Soon as the morn with roses
   Bedecks the dewy east,
   And when the sun reposes
   Upon the ocean's breast;
   My voice in supplication,
   Jehovah, Thou shalt hear;
   O grant me Thy salvation,
   And to my soul draw near.

3. By Thee, through life supported,
   I pass the dangerous road,
   With heavenly hosts escorted
   Up to their bright abode;
   There cast my crown before Thee,
   My toils and conflicts o'er,
   And day and night adore Thee—
   What can an angel more?

   HAWES.

468. 7s & 6s.

1. From ev'ry earthly pleasure,
   From ev'ry transient joy,
   From ev'ry mortal treasure
   That soon will fade and die;
   No longer these desiring,
   Upward our wishes tend,
   To nobler bliss aspiring,
   And joys that never end.

2. What though we are but strangers,
   And sojourners below,
   And countless snares and dangers
   Surround the path we go?
   Though painful and distressing,
   Yet there's a rest above,
   And onward still we're pressing
   To reach that land of love.

CHRISTIAN EXPERIENCE.

THATCHER. S. M. — HANDEL. Arranged by L. MASON.

1. Is this the kind return? Are these the thanks we owe? Thus to abuse eternal Love, Whence all our blessings flow!

469. S. M.

2. To what a stubborn frame
   Has sin reduced our mind!
What strange, rebellious wretches we,
   And God as strangely kind!

3. On us He bids the sun
   Shed his reviving rays;
For us the skies their circles run,
   To lengthen out our days.

4. Turn, turn us, mighty God,
   And mould our souls afresh;
Break, sovereign grace, these hearts of stone,
   And give us hearts of flesh.

5. Let past ingratitude
   Provoke our weeping eyes,
And hourly, as new mercies fall,
   Let hourly thanks arise.
                               WATTS.

470. S. M.

1. AH! whither should I go,
   Burdened, and sick, and faint?
To whom should I my troubles show,
   And pour out my complaint?

2. My Saviour bids me come,
   Ah! why do I delay?
He calls the weary sinner home,
   And yet from Him I stay!

3. What worldy tie must break?
   What idol yet depart,
Which will not let the Saviour take
   Possession of my heart?

4. Jesus, the hindrance show
   Which I have feared to see;
And let me now consent to know
   What keeps me back from Thee.

5. Oh! break the fatal chain,
   And all my bonds remove;
Nor let one bosom-sin remain,
   To keep me from Thy love.
                               C. WESLEY.

471. S. M.

1. WHERE, O my soul, O where
   Thy image shall I view?
In the light cloud that melts in air,
   Or in the early dew.

2. This hour, with flowing tears,
   My follies I bewail:
The next, my heart a waste appears,
   Where all the fountains fail.

3. To-day, her glimmering light
   Hope kindles in my breast;
The morrow, with despair's black night,
   Has all my soul oppressed.

4. O my unsteadfast mind,
   Tossed between good and ill!
While brutes, with instinct sure, though blind,
   Their Maker's law fulfill.

5. O wavering, wretched state,
   Of hope by fear subdued!
On Thee, O Lord, for help I wait—
   Fix, fix my soul in good.
                               T. SCOTT.

PENITENCE AND CONSECRATION.

DEDHAM. C. M.   Arranged by L. Mason, from Gardner.

1. Come, Holy Spirit, Heavenly Dove, With all thy quickening powers,
Kindle a flame of sacred love In these cold hearts of ours.

472. C. M.

2. Look! how we grovel here below,
Fond of these trifling toys!
Our souls can neither fly nor go
To reach eternal joys.

3. In vain we tune our formal songs;
In vain we strive to rise;
Hosannas languish on our tongues,
And our devotion dies.

4. Dear Lord, and shall we ever live
At this poor, dying rate,—
Our love so faint, so cold to Thee,
And Thine to us so great?

5. Come, Holy Spirit, heavenly Dove,
With all Thy quickening powers,
Come, shed abroad a Saviour's love,
And that shall kindle ours.
                            WATTS.

473. S. M.

1. Like sheep we went astray,
And broke the fold of God;
Each wandering in a different way,
But all the downward road.

2. How dreadful was the hour,
When God our wanderings laid,
And did at once His vengeance pour
Upon the Shepherd's head!

3. How glorious was the grace,
When Christ sustained the stroke!
His life and blood the Shepherd pays,
A ransom for the flock.

4. But God shall raise His head
O'er all the sons of men,
And make Him see a numerous seed,
To recompense His pain.   WATTS.

474. C. M.

1. My Father, God! how sweet the sound,
How tender and how dear!
Not all the melody of heaven
Could so delight the ear.

2. Come, sacred Spirit, seal the name
On my expanding heart,
And show, that in Jehovah's grace
I share a filial part.

3. Cheered by a signal so divine,
Unwavering I believe;
My spirit Abba, Father, cries,
Nor can the sign deceive.
                            DODDRIDGE.

475. C. M.

1. Speak with us, Lord; Thyself reveal,
While here on earth we rove;
Speak to our hearts, and let us feel
The kindlings of Thy love.

2. With Thee conversing, we forget
All toil, and time, and care;
Labor is rest, and pain is sweet,
If Thou art present there.

3. Here then, my God, be pleased to stay,
And bid my heart rejoice;
My bounding heart shall own Thy sway,
And echo to Thy voice.

4. Thou callest me to seek Thy face;
Thy face, O God, I seek,
Attend the whispers of Thy grace,
And hear Thee inly speak.
                            C. WESLEY.

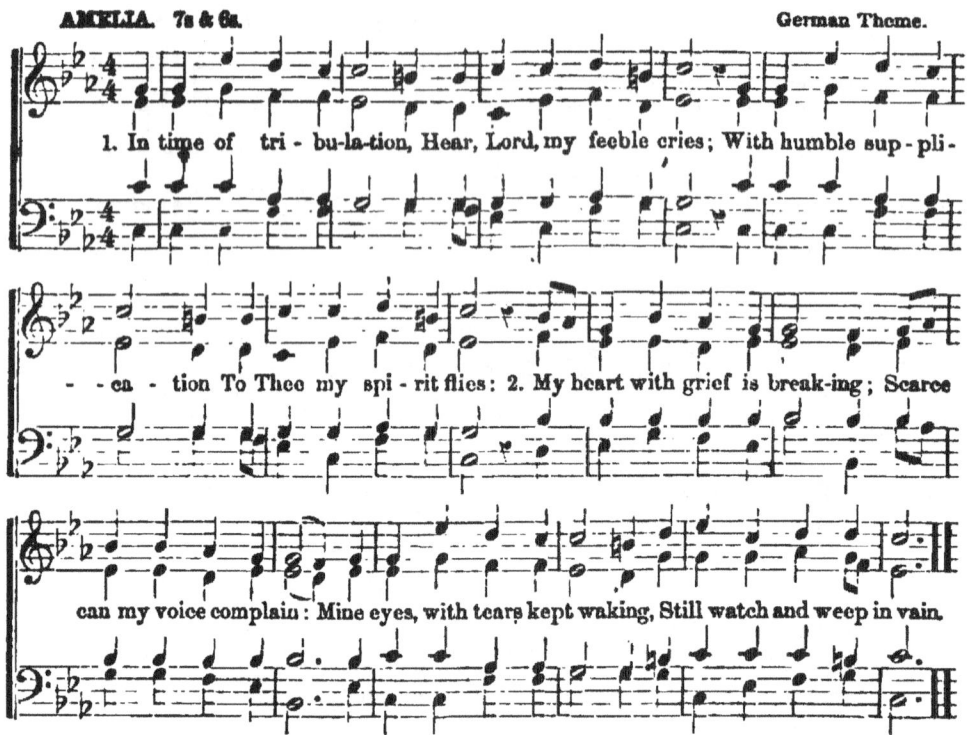

AMELIA. 7s & 6s. German Theme.

1. In time of tribulation, Hear, Lord, my feeble cries; With humble supplication To Thee my spirit flies: 2. My heart with grief is breaking; Scarce can my voice complain: Mine eyes, with tears kept waking, Still watch and weep in vain.

476. 7s & 6s.

3. The days of old, in vision,
    Bring vanished bliss to view:
  The years of lost fruition
    Their joys in pangs renew:

4. Remembered songs of gladness,
    Through night's lone silence brought,
  Strike notes of deeper sadness,
    And stir desponding thought.
                    MONTGOMERY.

477. 7s & 6s.

1. HATH God cast off for ever?
    Can time His truth impair?
  His tender mercy, never
    Shall I presume to share?

2. Hath He his loving kindness
    Shut up in endless wrath?
  No: this is mine own blindness,
    That can not see His path.

3. I call to recollection
    The years of His right hand;
  And, strong in His protection,
    Again through faith I stand.

4. Thy deeds, O Lord, are wonder,
    Holy are all Thy ways;
  The secret place of thunder
    Shall utter forth Thy praise.
                    MONTGOMERY.

478. 7s & 6s.

1. THEE, with the tribes assembled,
    O God! the billows saw;
  They saw Thee, and they trembled,
    Turned, and stood still, with awe:

2. The clouds shot hail, they lightened;
    The earth reeled to and fro;
  The fiery pillar brightened
    The gulf of gloom below.

3. Thy way is in great waters,
    Thy footsteps are not known:
  Let Adam's sons and daughters
    Confide in Thee alone.

4. Through the wild sea Thou leddest
    Thy chosen flock of yore:
  Still on the waves Thou treadest,
    And Thy redeemed pass o'er.
                    MONTGOMERY.

PENITENCE AND CONSECRATION.

CHRYSOLITE. L. M. — S. B. POND.

1. I left the God of truth and light, I left the God who gave me breath, To wander in the wilds of night, And perish in the snares of death.

479. L. M.

2. I dream'd of bliss in pleasure's bowers,
   While pillowing roses stayed my head;
But serpents hiss'd amongst the flowers:
   I 'woke, and thorns were all my bed.

3. In riches when I sought for joy,
   And placed in sordid gains my trust,
I found that gold was all alloy,
   And worldly treasures fleeting dust.

4. I wooed ambition, climb'd the pole,
   And shone among the stars—but fell
Headlong in all my pride of soul,
   Like Lucifer, from heaven to hell.

5. Heart-broken, friendless, poor, cast-down,
   Where shall the chief of sinners fly,
Almighty Vengeance, from Thy frown?—
   Eternal Justice, from Thine eye?

6. Lo, through the gloom of guilty fears,
   My faith discerns a dawn of grace;
The sun of righteousness appears
   In Jesus' reconciling face.

7. My suffering, slain, and risen Lord,
   In sore distress I turn to Thee;
I claim acceptance on Thy word;
   My God! my God! forsake not me!

8. Prostrate before the mercy seat,
   I dare not, if I would, despair;
None ever perish'd at Thy feet,
   And I will lie for ever there.

MONTGOMERY.

480. L. M.

1. LORD, I am vile, conceived in sin,
   And born unholy and unclean;
Sprung from the man, whose guilty fall
Corrupts the race, and taints us all.

2. Soon as we draw our infant breath,
   The seeds of sin grow up for death:
Thy law demands a perfect heart—
But we're defiled in every part.

3. Great God, create my heart anew,
   And form my spirit pure and true;
No outward rites can make me clean,—
The leprosy lies deep within.

4. No bleeding bird, nor bleeding beast,
   Nor hyssop branch, nor sprinkling priest,
Nor running brook, nor flood, nor sea,
Can wash the dismal stain away.

5. Jesus, my God, Thy blood alone,
   Hath power sufficient to atone:
Thy blood can make me white as snow,
No Jewish types could cleanse me so.

6. While guilt disturbs and breaks my peace,
   Nor flesh nor soul hath rest or ease;
Lord, let me hear Thy pardoning voice,
And make my broken bones rejoice.

WATTS.

DOXOLOGY. L. M.

1. To God, the Father,—God, the Son,—
   And God, the Spirit—Three in One,
Be honor, praise, and glory given,
By all on earth, and all in heaven.

CHRISTIAN EXPERIENCE.

EFFINGHAM. L. M.

1. At an-chor laid, re-mote from home, Toiling I cry, "Sweet Spi-rit, come, Ce-les-tial breeze, no long-er stay, But swell my sails, and speed my way."

481. L. M.

2. "Fain would I mount, fain would I glow,
And loose my cable from below;
But I can only spread my sail;
Thou, Thou must breathe the auspicious gale."

482. L. M.

1. Up to the fields where angels lie,
And living waters gently roll,
Fain would my thoughts leap out and fly,
But sin hangs heavy on my soul.

2. O might I once mount up and see
The glories of the eternal skies,
What little things these worlds would be,
How despicable to my eyes!

3. Had I a glance of Thee, my God,
Kingdoms and men would vanish soon;
Vanish as though I saw them not,
As a dim candle dies at noon.

4. Then they might fight, and rage, and rave,
I should perceive the noise no more
Than we can hear a shaking leaf,
While rattling thunders round us roar.

5. Great All in All, Eternal King!
Let me but view Thy lovely face,
And all my powers shall bow and sing
Thine endless grandeur and Thy grace.
WATTS.

483. L. M.

1. Like morning,—when her early breeze
Breaks up the surface of the seas,
That, in their furrows, dark with night,
Her hand may sow the seeds of light—

2. Thy grace can send its breathings o'er
The spirit dark and lost before;
And, freshening all its depths, prepare
For truth divine to enter there.

3. Till David touched his sacred lyre,
In silence lay the unbreathing wire;
But when he swept its chords along,
Then angels stooped to bear the song.

4. So sleeps the soul, till Thou, O Lord,
Shalt deign to touch its lifeless chord;
Till, waked by Thee, its breath shall rise
In music worthy of the skies.
MOORE.

484. L. M.

1. Lord, how secure and blest are they,
Who feel the joys of pardoned sin!
Should storms of wrath shake earth and sea
Their minds have heaven and peace within.

2. The day glides swiftly o'er their heads,
Made up of innocence and love;
And soft and silent as the shades,
Their nightly minutes gently move.

3. Quick as their thoughts their joys come on,
But fly not half so swift away;
Their souls are ever bright as noon,
And calm as summer evenings be.

4. How oft they look to heavenly hills,
Where groves of living pleasures grow;
And longing hopes and cheerful smiles
Sit undisturbed upon their brow!

5. They scorn to seek our golden toys,
But spend the day, and share the night,
In numbering o'er the richer joys
That heaven prepares for their delight.
WATTS.

485. L. M.

1. O Thou, to whose all-searching sight
The darkness shineth as the light,
Search, prove my heart, it pants for Thee;
O burst these bonds, and set it free.

2. Wash out its stains, refine its dross;
Nail my affections to the cross;
Hallow each thought; let all within
Be clean, as Thou, my Lord, art clean.

3. If in this darksome wild I stray,
Be Thou my light, be Thou my way:
No foes, no violence I fear,
No fraud, while Thou, my God, art near.

4. When rising floods my soul o'erflow,
When sinks my heart in waves of woe—
Jesus, Thy timely aid impart,
And raise my head, and cheer my heart.

5. Saviour, where'er Thy steps I see,
Dauntless, untired, I follow Thee;
O let Thy hand support me still,
And lead me to Thy holy hill.
                                C. WESLEY.

486. L. M.

1. God of my life, through all its days
My grateful powers shall sound Thy praise,
The song shall wake with opening light,
And warble to the silent night.

2. When anxious cares would break my rest,
And griefs would tear my throbbing breast,
Thy tuneful praises, raised on high,
Shall check the murmur and the sigh.

3. When death o'er nature shall prevail,
And all its powers of language fail,
Joy through my swimming eyes shall break,
And mean the thanks I cannot speak.

4. But oh! when that last conflict 's o'er,
And I am chained to flesh no more,
With what glad accents shall I rise,
To join the music of the skies!

5. The cheerful tribute will I give,
Long as a deathless soul can live,
A work so sweet, a theme so high,
Demands, and crowns eternity!
                                DODDRIDGE.

487. L. M.

1. Trembling, before Thine awful throne,
O Lord! in dust my sins I own:
Justice and Mercy for my life
Contend!—O smile, and heal the strife.

2. The Saviour smiles! upon my soul
New tides of hope tumultuous roll—
His voice proclaims my pardon found—
Seraphic transport wings the sound!

3. Earth has a joy unknown in heaven—
The new-born peace of sins forgiven!
Tears of such pure and deep delight,
Ye angels! never dimmed your sight.

4. Ye saw of old, on chaos rise
The beauteous pillars of the skies;
Ye know where morn exulting springs,
And evening folds her drooping wings.

5. Bright heralds of th' Eternal Will,
Abroad His errands ye fulfill;
Or, throned in floods of beamy day,
Symphonious, in His presence play.

6. Loud is the song, the heavenly plain
Is shaken by the choral strain,
And dying echoes, floating far,
Draw music from each chiming star.

7. But I amid your choirs shall shine,
And all your knowledge will be mine;
Ye on your harps must lean to hear
A secret chord that *mine* will bear.
                                HILLHOUSE.

488. L. M.

1. God named Love, whose fount Thou art,
Thy crownless church before Thee stands,
With too much hating in her heart,
And too much striving in her hands.

2. "Love as I loved you"—was the sound
That on Thy lips expiring sate!
Sweet words in bitter strivings drowned!
We hated as the wordly hate.

3. Yet, Lord, Thy wronged love fulfill,
Thy church, though fallen, before Thee
    stands;
Behold, the voice is Jacob's still,
Albeit the hands are Esau's hands.

4. Hast thou no tears, like those bespent
Upon thy Zion's ancient part?
No moving looks, like those which sent
Their softness through a traitor's heart?

5. No touching tale of anguish dear,
Whereby like children we may creep,
All trembling to each other near,
And view each other's face, and weep?

6. Oh, move us—Thou hast power to move—
One in the One Beloved to be;
Teach us the hights and depths of love:
Give Thine—that we may love like
    Thee!   MRS. BROWNING.

CHRISTIAN EXPERIENCE.

SHEPHERD. L. M. Arranged from Marot & Beza's Psalms.

1. Thou, whom my soul admires above All earthly joy and earthly love—Tell me, dear Shepherd, let me know, Where do Thy sweetest pastures grow, Where do Thy sweetest pastures grow?

489. L. M.

1. Thou, whom my soul admires above
All earthly joy and earthly love—
Tell me, dear Shepherd, let me know,
Where do thy sweetest pastures grow?

2. Where is the shadow of that rock,
That from the sun defends thy flock?
Fain would I feed among thy sheep,
Among them rest, among them sleep.

3. Why should thy bride appear like one,
That turns aside to paths unknown?
My constant feet would never rove,
Would never seek another love.

4. The footsteps of thy flock I see;
Thy sweetest pastures here they be;
A wondrous feast thy love prepares,
Bought with Thy wounds, and groans and tears.

5. His dearest flesh He makes my food,
And bids me drink His richest blood;
Here to these hills, my soul would come,
Till my Beloved leads me home.
WATTS.

490. L. M.

1. My Lord, if Thou one moment leave,
That moment I from Thee depart,—
Fall into sin, Thy Spirit grieve,
And to the tempter yield my heart.

2. O, do not at a distance stand,
Or from my helpless soul remove;
Trouble and sin are hard at hand,
And nought can save me but Thy love.

3. Exposed continually to shame,
To fiends, and men, and passion's power:
O pluck the brand from out the flame,
Or turn aside the fiery hour.

4. I feel throughout my evil day
Temptation intimately near:
Oh could I without ceasing pray,
And always watch, and always fear!

5. Jesus, for this to Thee I cry;
Upon my thirsty, gasping soul,
Pour out Thy Spirit from on high,
And floods o'er all the desert roll.
C. WESLEY.

491. L. M.

1. Jesus! my Lord, my God, my All!
How can I love Thee as I ought!
And how revere this wondrous gift,
So far surpassing hope or thought?

2. O earth! grow flowers beneath His feet,
And thou, O sun, shine bright this day!
He comes! He comes! O Heaven on earth!
Our Jesus comes upon His way.

3. He comes! He comes! The Lord of Hosts,
Borne on His throne triumphantly!
We see Thee, and we know Thee, Lord,
And yearn to shed our blood for Thee!

4. Our hearts leap up; our trembling song
Grows fainter still; we can no more;
Silence! and let us weep—and die
Of very love, while we adore.
LYRA CATH.

PRAISE, JOY, CONFLICT, ETC.

492. L. M.

1. Jesus! and shall it ever be,
A mortal man ashamed of Thee?
Ashamed of Thee, whom angels praise,
Whose glories shine through endless days?

2. Ashamed of Jesus! sooner far
Let evening blush to own a star;
He sheds the beams of light divine
O'er this benighted soul of mine.

3. Ashamed of Jesus! that dear Friend
On whom my hopes of heaven depend!
No; when I blush—be this my shame,
That I no more revere His name.

4. Ashamed of Jesus! yes, I may,
When I've no guilt to wash away;
No tear to wipe, no good to crave,
No fears to quell, no soul to save.

5. Till then—nor is my boasting vain—
Till then I boast a Saviour slain!
And O may this my glory be,
That Christ is not ashamed of me!
GRIGG.

493. L. M.

1. Faith, hope, and charity, these three,
Yet is the greatest charity;
Father of lights, these gifts impart
To mine and every human heart.

2. Faith, that in prayer can never fail,
Hope, that o'er doubting must prevail,
And charity, whose name above
Is God's own name, for God is love.

3. The morning star is lost in light,
Faith vanishes at perfect sight,
The rainbow passes with the storm,
And hope with sorrow's fading form.

4. But charity, serene, sublime,
Beyond the reach of death and time,
Like the blue sky's all-abounding space,
Holds heaven and earth in its embrace.
MONTGOMERY.

494. L. M.

1. God of my life, whose gracious power
Through varied deaths my soul hath led,
Or turn'd aside the fatal hour,
Or lifted up my sinking head;

2. In all my ways Thy hand I own,
Thy ruling providence I see;
Assist me still my course to run,
And still direct my paths to Thee.

3. Whither, O whither should I fly,
But to my loving Saviour's breast!
Secure within Thine arms to lie,
And safe beneath Thy wings to rest.

4. I have no skill the snare to shun,
But Thou, O Christ my wisdom art;
I ever into ruin run,
But Thou art greater than my heart.

5. Foolish, and impotent, and blind,
Lead me a way I have not known;
Bring me where I my heaven may find—
The heaven of loving Thee alone.
C. WESLEY.

495. L. M.

1. How high Thou art! Our songs can own
No music Thou couldst stoop to hear;
But still the Son's expiring groan
Is vocal in the Father's ear.

2. How pure Thou art! Our hands are dyed
With curses, red with murder's hue;
But He hath stretched His hands to hide
The sins, that pierced them, from Thy view.

3. How strong Thou art! We tremble lest
The thunders of Thine arm be moved;
But He is lying on Thy breast,
And Thou must clasp thy Best-beloved!

4. How kind Thou art! Thou didst not choose
To joy in Him forever so;
But that embrace Thou wouldst not lose
For vengeance, didst for love forego!

5. High God, and pure, and strong, and kind!
The low, the foul, the feeble, spare!
The brightness in His face we find,—
Behold our darkness only there!
MRS. BROWNING.

496. L. M.

1. The Word, descending from above,
Though with the Father still on high,
Went forth upon His work of love,
And soon to life's last eve drew nigh.

2. At birth, our brother He became;
Ever Himself as food He gives;
To ransom us He died in shame;
As our reward, in bliss He lives.

3. O saving Leader! opening wide
The gate of heaven to man below!
Our foes press on from every side;
Thine aid supply, Thy strength bestow.
BREVIARY.

CHRISTIAN EXPERIENCE.

UXBRIDGE. L. M. — L. MASON.

1. What sin-ners val-ue I re-sign; Lord! 'tis enough that Thou art mine; I shall be-hold Thy bliss-ful face, And stand complete in righteous-ness.

497. L. M.

2. This life's a dream—an empty show;
But the bright world, to which I go,
Hath joys substantial and sincere;
When shall I wake, and find me there?

3. Oh! glorious hour!—Oh! blest abode!
I shall be near, and like my God;
And flesh and sin no more control
The sacred pleasures of the soul.

4. My flesh shall slumber in the ground,
Till the last trumpet's joyful sound;
Then burst the chains, with sweet surprise,
And in my Saviour's image rise.
WATTS.

498. L. M.

1. Now let our souls on wings sublime,
Rise from the vanities of time,
Draw back the parting vail, and see
The glories of eternity.

2. Born by a new celestial birth,
Why should we grovel here on earth?
Why grasp at transitory toys,
So near to heaven's eternal joys?

3. Shall aught beguile us on the road,
When we are walking back to God?
For strangers into life we come,
And dying is but going home.

4. Welcome, sweet hour of full discharge,
That sets our longing souls at large;
Unbinds our chains, breaks up our cell;
And gives us with our God to dwell.

5. To dwell with God, to feel His love,
Is the full heaven enjoyed above;
And the sweet expectation now,
Is the young dawn of heaven below.
GIBBONS.

499. L. M.

1. "WE 'VE no abiding city here,"
This may distress the worldly mind;
But should not cost a saint a tear,
Who hopes a better rest to find.

2. "We 've no abiding city here,"
Sad truth, were this to be our home;
But let this thought our spirits cheer,
"We seek a city yet to come."

3. "We 've no abiding city here,"
Then let us live as pilgrims do;
Let not the world our rest appear,
But let us haste from all below.

4. "We 've no abiding city here,"
We seek a city out of sight,
Zion its name—the Lord is there—
It shines with everlasting light.

5. O sweet abode of peace and love,
Where pilgrims freed from toil are blest!
Had I the pinions of the dove,
I'd flee to Thee, and be at rest.

6. But hush, my soul, nor dare repine!
The time my God appoints is best:
While here, to do His will be *mine*;
And *His* to fix my time of rest.
KELLY.

500. L. M.

1. I send the joys of earth away;
   Away, ye tempters of the mind,
   False as the smooth, deceitful sea,
   And empty as the whistling wind.

2. Your streams were floating me along,
   Down to the gulf of dark despair;
   And while I listened to your song, [there.
   Your streams had e'en conveyed me

3. Lord, I adore Thy matchless grace,
   Which warned me of that dark abyss,
   Which drew me from those treacherous
   And bade me seek superior bliss. [seas,

4. Now to the shining realms above,
   I stretch my hands and glance my eyes;
   O for the pinions of a dove,
   To bear me to the upper skies!

5. There, from the bosom of my God,
   Oceans of endless pleasure roll;
   There would I fix my last abode,
   And drown the sorrows of my soul.
   WATTS.

501. L. M.

1. Jesus, Thou everlasting King!
   Accept the tribute which we bring;
   Accept the well-deserved renown,
   And wear our praises as Thy crown.

2. Let every act of worship be
   Like our espousals, Lord, to Thee:
   Like the dear hour, when from above
   We first received Thy pledge of love.

3. The gladness of that happy day!
   Our hearts would wish it long to stay;
   Nor let our faith forsake its hold,
   Nor comfort sink, nor love grow cold.

4. Each following minute, as it flies,
   Increase Thy praise, improve our joys,
   Till we are raised to sing Thy name,
   At the great supper of the Lamb.
   WATTS.

502. L. M.

1. Around the Saviour's lofty throne,
   Ten thousand times ten thousand sing;
   They worship Him as God alone,
   And crown Him everlasting King.

2. Approach, ye saints! this God is yours!
   'Tis Jesus fills the throne above:
   Ye can not want, while God endures;
   Ye can not fail, while God is love.

3. Jesus, Thou everlasting King!
   To Thee the praise of heaven belongs;
   Yet smile on us, who fain would bring
   The tribute of our humble songs.

4. Though sin defile our worship here,
   We hope ere long Thy face to view;
   And, when our souls in heaven appear,
   We'll praise Thy name as angels do.
   KELLY.

503. L. M.

1. Lord, when I quit this earthly stage,
   Where shall I fly, but to Thy breast?
   For I have sought no other home;
   For I have learned no other rest.

2. I can not live contented here,
   Without some glimpses of Thy face;
   And heaven, without Thy presence there,
   Will be a dark and tiresome place.

3. When earthly cares engross the day,
   And hold my thoughts aside from Thee,
   The shining hours of cheerful light
   Are long and tedious years to me.

4. And if no evening visit's paid
   Between my Saviour and my soul,
   How dull the night! how sad the shade!
   How mournfully the minutes roll!

5. My God! and can an humble child,
   Who loves Thee with a flame so high,
   Be ever from Thy face exiled,
   Without the pity of Thine eye?

6. Impossible!—for Thine own hands
   Have tied my heart so fast to Thee;
   And in Thy book the promise stands,
   That where Thou art, Thy friends must be.
   WATTS.

504. L. M.

1. My God, accept my early vows,
   Like morning incense in Thy house;
   And let my nightly worship rise,
   Sweet as the evening sacrifice.

2. Watch o'er my lips, and guard them, Lord,
   From every rash and heedless word;
   Nor let my feet incline to tread
   The guilty path where sinners lead.

3. O may the righteous, when I stray,
   Smite and reprove my wand'ring way!
   Their gentle words, like ointment shed,
   Shall never bruise, but cheer my head.

4. When I behold them pressed with grief,
   I'll cry to heaven for their relief;
   And by my warm petitions prove
   How much I prize their faithful love.
   WATTS.

CHRISTIAN EXPERIENCE.

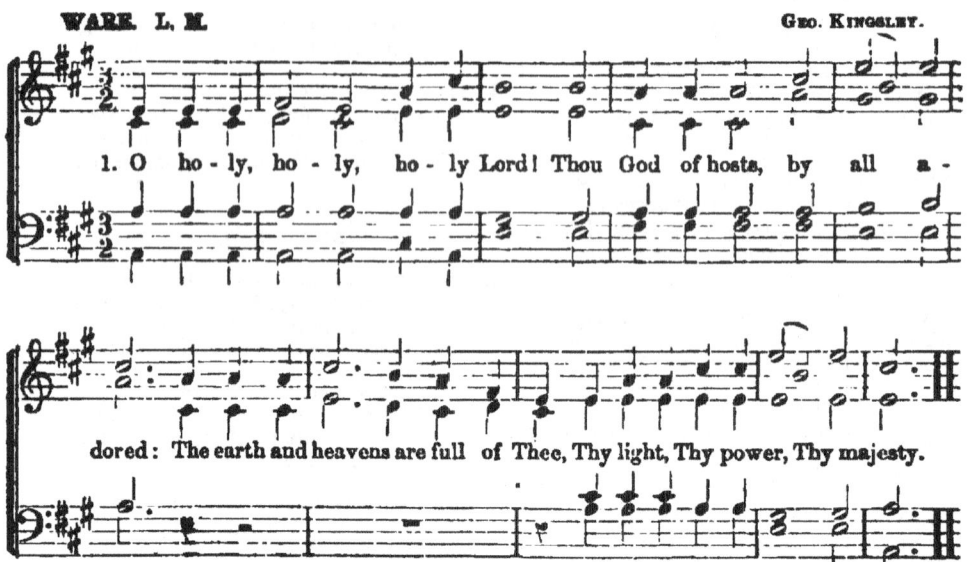

WARE. L. M. — Geo. Kingsley.

1. O ho-ly, ho-ly, ho-ly Lord! Thou God of hosts, by all a-dored: The earth and heavens are full of Thee, Thy light, Thy power, Thy majesty.

505. L. M.

2. Loud hallelujahs to Thy name,
Angels and Seraphim proclaim:
By all the powers and thrones in heaven
Eternal praise to Thee is given.

3. Apostles join the glorious throng,
And swell the loud, triumphant song:
Prophets and martyrs hear the sound,
And spread the hallelujahs round.

4. Glory to Thee, O God most high!
Father, we praise Thy majesty:
The Son, the Spirit we adore—
One Godhead, blest for evermore.

CONDER.

506. L. M.

1. Both heaven and earth do worship Thee,
Thou Father of eternity!
With splendor from Thy glory spread,
Are heaven and earth replenished.

2. To Thee all angels loudly cry,
The heavens, and all the powers on high,
The apostles' glorious company,
The prophets' fellowship praise Thee.

3. The noble and victorious host
Of martyrs make of Thee their boast;
The holy church, in every place
Throughout the earth exalts Thy praise.

4. From day to day, O Lord, do we
Highly exalt and honor Thee:
Thy name we worship and adore,
World without end, for evermore.

ST. AMBROSE.

507. L. M.

1. Lo! what a glorious corner-stone
The Jewish builders did refuse;
But God has built his church thereon,
In spite of envy and the Jews.

2. Great God! the work is all divine,
The joy and wonder of our eyes;
This is the day that proves it thine,
The day that saw our Saviour rise.

3. Sinners, rejoice, and saints, be glad;
Hosanna, let his name be blest;
A thousand honors on his head,
With peace, and light, and glory rest!

WATTS.

508. L. M.

1. 'T is not the skill of human art,
Which gives me power my God to know;
The sacred lessons of the heart
Come not from instruments below.

2. Love is my teacher; He can tell
The wonders that He learnt above:
No other Master knows so well;
'T is Love alone can tell of Love.

3. Love is my Master; when it breaks,—
The morning light, with rising ray,
To Thee, O God! my spirit wakes,
And Love instructs it all the day.

4. And when the gleams of day retire,
And midnight spreads its dark control,
Love's secret whispers still inspire
Their holy lessons in the soul.

MADAME GUION.

509. L. M.

1. Now to the Lord a noble song!
   Awake, my soul! awake, my tongue!
   Hosanna to th' eternal Name,
   And all His boundless love proclaim!

2. See where it shines in Jesus' face,
   The brightest image of His grace;
   God, in the person of His Son,
   Has all His mightiest works outdone.

3. The spacious earth, and spreading flood,
   Proclaim the wise and powerful God;
   And Thy rich glories from afar
   Sparkle in every rolling star.

4. But in His looks a glory stands,
   The noblest labor of Thine hands:
   The pleasing lustre of His eyes
   Outshines the wonders of the skies.

5. Grace! 't is a sweet, a charming theme;
   My thoughts rejoice at Jesus' name!
   Ye angels, dwell upon the sound;
   Ye heavens, reflect it to the ground!

6. O may I live to reach the place
   Where He unveils His lovely face!
   Where all His beauties you behold,
   And sing His name to harps of gold!
   WATTS.

510. L. M.

1. Of all the joys we mortals know,
   Jesus, Thy love exceeds the rest;
   Love, the best blessing here below,
   And nearest image of the blest.

2. While I am held in Thine embrace,
   There's not a thought attempts to rove;
   Each smile He wears upon His face
   Fixes, and charms, and fires my love.

3. While of Thy absence we complain,
   And long, and weep, in all we do,
   There's a strange pleasure in the pain,
   And tears have their own sweetness too.

4. If He withdraws a moment's space,
   He leaves a sacred pledge behind;
   Here in this breast His image stays,
   The grief and comfort of my mind.

5. When round Thy courts by day I rove,
   Or ask the watchman of the night
   For some kind tidings of my Love,
   His very name creates delight.

6. Jesus, my God, but rather come!
   Our eyes would dwell upon Thy face;
   'T is best to see our Lord at home,
   And feel the presence of His grace.
   WATTS.

511. L. M.

1. From all that dwell below the skies
   Let the Creator's praise arise;
   Let the Redeemer's name be sung
   Through every land, by every tongue.

2. Eternal are Thy mercies, Lord;
   Eternal truth attends Thy word;
   Thy praise shall sound from shore to shore,
   Till suns shall rise and set no more.
   WATTS.

512. L. M.

1. What equal honors shall we bring
   To Thee, O Lord our God, the Lamb,
   When all the notes that angels sing
   Are far inferior to Thy name?

2. Worthy is He that once was slain,
   The Prince of Life, who groaned and died,
   Worthy to rise, and live, and reign
   At His almighty Father's side.

3. Honor immortal must be paid,
   Instead of scandal and of scorn;
   While glory shines around His head,
   And a bright crown without a thorn.

4. Blessings for ever on the Lamb,
   Who bore the curse for wretched men;
   Let angels sound His sacred name,
   And every creature say, Amen.
   WATTS.

513. L. M.

1. Jesus shall reign where'er the sun
   Does his successive journeys run;
   His kingdom stretch from shore to shore,
   Till moons shall wax and wane no more.

2. For Him shall endless prayer be made,
   And praises throng to crown His head;
   His name, like sweet perfume, shall rise
   With every morning sacrifice.

3. People and realms of every tongue
   Dwell on His love with sweetest song;
   And infant voices shall proclaim
   Their early blessings on His name.

4. Blessings abound where'er He reigns;
   The prisoner leaps to lose His chains;
   The weary find eternal rest,
   And all the sons of want are blest.

5. Let every creature rise, and bring
   Peculiar honors to their King:
   Angels descend with songs again,
   And earth repeat the long amen.
   WATTS.

CHRISTIAN EXPERIENCE.

ROTHWELL. L. M. — Arranged by L. Mason.

1. He lives, the great Redeemer lives, What joy the blest assurance gives: And now, before His Father, God, Pleads the full mer-it of His blood, Pleads the full mer-it of His blood.

514. L. M.

2. Repeated crimes awake our fears,
And justice armed with frowns appears;
But in the Saviour's lovely face,
Sweet mercy smiles, and all is peace.

3. Hence then, ye black, despairing thoughts;
Above our fears, above our faults,
His powerful intercessions rise,
And guilt recedes, and terror dies.

4. In every dark, distressful hour,
When sin and Satan join their power,
Let this dear hope repel the dart,
That Jesus bears us on His heart.

5. Great Advocate, almighty Friend!
On Him our humble hopes depend;
Our cause can never, never fail,
For Jesus pleads, and must prevail.
MRS. STEELE.

515. L. M.

1. GREAT God, we sing that mighty hand,
By which supported still we stand;
The opening year Thy mercy shows;
Let mercy crown it till it close.

2. By day, by night, at home, abroad,
Still we are guarded by our God;
By His incessant bounty fed,
By His unerring counsel led.

3. With grateful hearts the past we own;
The future, all to us unknown,
We to Thy guardian care commit,
And peaceful leave before Thy feet.

4. In scenes exalted or depressed,
Be Thou our joy, and Thou our rest;
Thy goodness all our hopes shall raise,
Adored through all our changing days.

5. When death shall interrupt these songs,
And seal in silence mortal tongues,
Our Helper, God, in whom we trust,
In better worlds, our souls shall boast.
DODDRIDGE.

516. L. M.

1. THE deluge, at th' Almighty's call,
In what impetuous streams it fell!
Swallowed the mountains in its rage,
And swept a guilty world to hell.

2. Yet Noah, humble, happy saint,
Surrounded with the chosen few,
Sat in his ark secure from fear,
And sang the grace that steered him through.

3. So I may sing, in Jesus safe,
While storms of vengeance round me fall,
Conscious how high my hopes are fixed,
Beyond what shakes this earthly ball.

4. Enter thine ark, while patience waits,
Nor ever quit that sure retreat!
Then the wide flood, which buries earth,
Shall waft thee to a fairer seat.

5. Nor wreck, nor ruin, there is seen;
There not a wave of trouble rolls;
But the bright rainbow round the throne
Seals endless life to all their souls.
DODDRIDGE.

517. L. M.

1. O Jesus! life-spring of the soul!
   The Father's Power, and Glory bright!
   Thee with the angels we extol;
   From Thee they draw their life and light.

2. Thy thousand thousand hosts are spread,
   Embattled o'er the azure sky;
   And Thou dost lift Thy standard dread,
   And wave the mighty cross on high.

3. Thou in that sign the rebel powers
   Didst with their dragon prince expel;
   And hurl them from the heaven's high towers,
   Down like a thunderbolt to hell.

4. Glory to Jesus, who returns
   In pomp triumphant to the sky,
   With Thee, O Father, and with Thee,
   O Holy Ghost, eternally.
   LYRA CATH.

518. L. M.

1. Stand up, my soul, shake off thy fears,
   And gird the gospel armor on;
   March to the gates of endless joy,
   Where Jesus, thy great Captain's gone.

2. Hell and thy sins resist thy course;
   But hell and sin are vanquished foes;
   Thy Jesus nailed them to the cross,
   And sung the triumph when He rose.

3. Then let my soul march boldly on—
   Press forward to the heavenly gate;
   There peace and joy eternal reign,
   And glittering robes for conquerors wait.

4. There shall I wear a starry crown;
   And triumph in almighty grace,
   While all the armies of the skies
   Join in my glorious Leader's praise.
   WATTS.

519. L. M.

1. Awake our souls, away our fears,
   Let every trembling thought be gone;
   Awake and run the heavenly race,
   And put a cheerful courage on.

2. True, 't is a straight and thorny road
   And mortal spirits tire and faint;
   But they forget the mighty God,
   That feeds the strength of every saint:

3. The mighty God, whose matchless power
   Is ever new and ever young,
   And firm endures, while endless years
   Their everlasting circles run.

4. From Thee, the overflowing spring,
   Our souls shall drink a fresh supply,
   While such as trust their native strength
   Shall melt away, and droop, and die.

5. Swift as an eagle cuts the air
   We'll mount aloft to Thine abode;
   On wings of love our souls shall fly,
   Nor tire amid the heavenly road.
   WATTS.

520. L. M.

1. Thou art the Way; and he who sighs,
   Amid this starless waste of woe,
   To find a pathway to the skies,
   A light from heaven's eternal glow,

2. By Thee must come. Thou Gate of love,
   Through which the saints undoubting trod,
   Till faith discovers, like the dove,
   An ark, a resting-place in God.

521. L. M.

1. If on our daily course our mind
   Be set, to hallow all we find,
   New treasures still, of countless price,
   God will provide for sacrifice.

2. Old friends, old scenes, will lovelier be,
   As more of heaven in each we see;
   Some softening gleam of love and prayer
   Shall dawn on every cross and care.

3. O could we learn that sacrifice,
   What light would all around us rise!
   How would our hearts with wisdom talk,
   Along life's dullest, dreariest walk!

4. The trivial round, the common task,
   Will furnish all we ought to ask;—
   Room to deny ourselves, a road
   To bring us daily nearer God.

522. L. M.

1. When Israel, of the Lord beloved,
   Out from the land of bondage came,
   Her father's God before her moved,
   An awful guide in smoke and flame.

2. By day, along th' astonished lands,
   The cloudy pillar glided slow;
   By night, Arabia's crimsoned sands
   Returned the fiery column's glow.

3. Thus present still, though now unseen,
   When brightly shines the prosperous day,
   Be thoughts of Thee a cloudy screen,
   To temper the deceitful ray!

4. And, O, when gathers on our path,
   In shade and storm, the frequent night,
   Be Thou, long suffering, slow to wrath,
   A burning and a shining light!
   WALTER SCOTT.

CHRISTIAN EXPERIENCE.

PARK STREET. L. M.   VENUA.

1. O for a glance of heaven-ly day, To take this stubborn heart a-way; And thaw, with beams of love divine, This heart, this frozen heart of mine. This heart, this frozen heart of mine.

523. L. M.

2. The rocks can rend; the earth can quake;
The seas can roar; the mountains shake:
Of feeling, all things show some sign,
But this unfeeling heart of mine.

3. To hear the sorrows Thou hast felt,
O Lord, an adamant would melt:
But I can read each moving line,
And nothing moves this heart of mine.

4. Thy judgments, too, which devils fear—
Amazing thought!—unmoved I hear;
Goodness and wrath in vain combine
To stir this stupid heart of mine.

5. But Power Divine can do the deed;
And, Lord, that power I greatly need:
Thy Spirit can from dross refine,
And melt and change this heart of mine.
          HART.

524. L. M.

1. JESUS, whose glory's streaming rays,
  Though duteous to Thy high command,
Not seraphs view with open face,
  But veil'd before Thy presence stand;—

2. How shall weak eyes of flesh, weigh'd down
  With sin, and dim with error's night,
Dare to behold Thy awful throne,
  Or view Thy unapproached light?

3. Thy golden sceptre from above
  Reach forth; lo! my whole heart I bow;
Say to my soul,—"thou art my love,—
  My chosen, 'midst ten thousand, thou."

4. O Jesus, full of grace! the sighs
  Of a sick heart with pity view;
Hark, how my silence speaks, and cries,—
  Mercy, Thou God of mercy, show!
          J. WESLEY.

525. L. M.

1. Oh! if my Lord would leave the skies,
Drest in the rays of mildest grace,
My soul should hasten to my eyes
To meet the pleasures of His face.

2. In vain the tempter's flattering tongue,
The world in vain should bid me move,
In vain, for I should gaze so long,
'Till I were all transformed to love.

3. Then, mighty God, I'd sing and say,
What empty names are crowns and kings;
Amongst them give these worlds away—
These little despicable things.

4. I would not ask to climb the sky,
Nor envy angels their abode;
I have a heaven as bright and high,
In the blest vision of my God.
          WATTS.

526. L. M.

1. AWAKE, my soul! lift up thine eyes;
See where thy foes against thee rise,
In long array, a numerous host;
Awake, my soul! or thou art lost.

2. See where rebellious passions rage,
And fierce desires and lusts engage;
The meanest foe of all the train
Has thousands and ten thousands slain.

3. Thou treadest on enchanted ground;
Perils and snares beset thee round;
Beware of all, guard every part,—
But most the traitor in thy heart.

4. Put on the armor, from above,
Of heavenly truth, and heavenly love,
The terror and the charm repel,
And powers of earth, and powers of hell.
MRS. BARBAULD.

527. L. M.

1. Thy happy ones a strain begin:
Dost thou not, Lord, glad souls possess?
Thy cheerful Spirit dwells within;
We feel Thee in our joyfulness.

2. Our mirth is not afraid of Thee;
Our life rejoices to be bright;
We would not from our gladness flee,
But give full welcome to delight.

3. Thou wilt not, Lord, our smiles deny:
Dost Thou not deem them of rich worth?
Our cheer flows on beneath Thine eye;
We feel accepted in our mirth.

4. We turn to Thee a smiling face.
Thou sendest us the smile again;
Our joy, the richness of Thy grace,—
Thine own, the cheer of this glad strain.
T. H. GILL.

528. L. M.

1. Soft be the gently breathing notes,
That sing the Saviour's dying love;
Soft as the ev'ning zephyr floats,
Soft as the tuneful lyres above:

2. Soft as the morning dews descend,
While the sweet lark exulting soars,
So soft to your Almighty Friend,
Be ev'ry sigh your bosom pours.

3. Pure as the sun's enliv'ning ray,
That scatters life and joy abroad;
Pure as the lucid car of day,
That wide proclaims its Maker, God.

4. True as the magnet to the pole,
So true let your contrition be—
So true let all your sorrows roll
To Him, who bled upon the tree.
COLLIER.

529. L. M.

1. When sins and fears prevailing rise,
And fainting hope almost expires,
Jesus, to Thee I lift mine eyes—
To Thee I breathe my soul's desires.

2. If my immortal Saviour lives,
Then my immortal soul is sure;
His word a firm foundation gives;
Here let me build, and rest secure.

3. Here let my faith unshaken dwell;
Immovable the promise stands;
Not all the powers of earth or hell
Can e'er dissolve the sacred bands.

4. Here, O my soul, thy trust repose!
If Jesus is for ever mine,
Not death itself, that last of foes,
Shall break a union so divine.
MRS. STEELE.

530. L. M.

1. I thirst, but not as once I did,
The vain delights of earth to share;
Thy wounds, Immanuel, all forbid,
That I should seek my pleasure there.

2. It was the sight of Thy dear cross,
First weaned my soul from earthly things;
And taught me to esteem as dross
The mirth of fools, and pomp of kings.

3. I want that grace that springs from Thee,
That quickens all things where it flows,
And makes a wretched thorn like me
Bloom as the myrtle, or the rose.

4. For sure, of all the plants that share
The notice of my Father's eye,
None proves less grateful to His care,
Or yields Him meaner fruit than I.
COWPER.

531. L. M.

1. Fountain of grace, rich, full, and free,
What need I, that is not in Thee?
Full pardon, strength to meet the day,
And peace which none can take away.

2. Doth sickness fill the heart with fear?
'Tis sweet to know that Thou art near;
Am I with dread of justice tried?
'Tis sweet to feel that Christ hath died.

3. In life, Thy promises of aid
Forbid my heart to be afraid;
In death, peace gently veils the eyes;
Christ rose, and I shall surely rise.

4. O, all-sufficient Saviour! be
This all-sufficiency to me;
Nor pain, nor sin, nor death can harm
The weakest, shielded by Thine arm.

CHRISTIAN EXPERIENCE.

NILE. L. M. — English Melody.

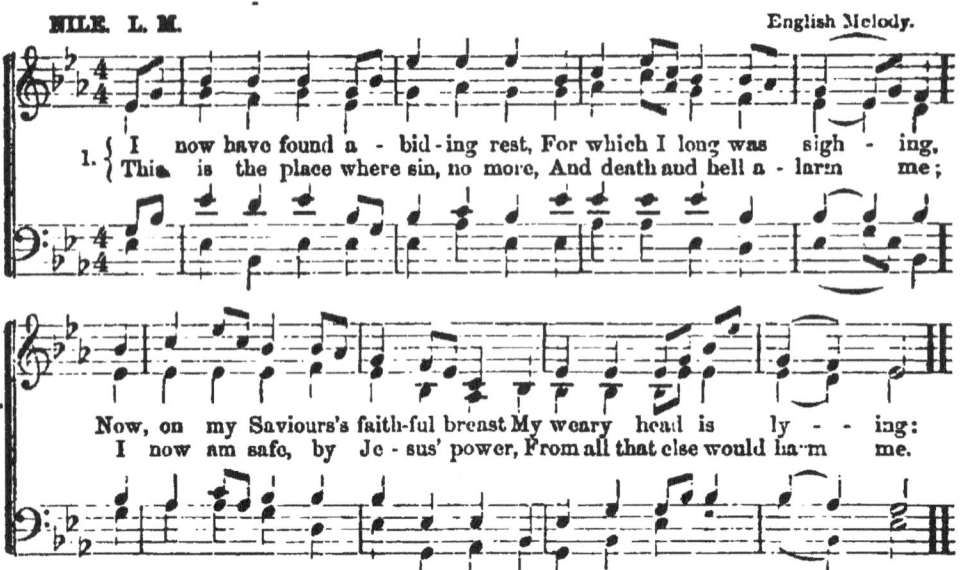

1. I now have found abiding rest, For which I long was sighing,
Now, on my Saviour's faithful breast My weary head is lying:
This is the place where sin, no more, And death and hell alarm me;
I now am safe, by Jesus' power, From all that else would harm me.

532. L. M. Peculiar.

2. He whispers me—"I'm wholly thine,
And thou art Mine for ever;
Henceforth all fear and doubt resign,
Confiding in My favor!
Thy ev'ry want shall find supply
From My exhaustless treasures;
I'll fill thy spirit with My joy,
The pledge of endless pleasures."

3. From Jesus and His love, who now,
By terrors to divide me,
My great and many sins would show?
His wounds from vengeance hide me:
My sins are great—I'll not despair,
Though conscience, too, arraigns me,
Nor doubt my Saviour's watchful care—
His arm of love sustains me.

4. I thank Thee, God's beloved Son,
Thy boundless grace adoring,
Which brought Thee from Thy glorious throne,
Our peace with God restoring.
O make my heart a shrine, where peace
Shall keep her constant dwelling;
Where grateful praise shall never cease
Abroad Thy glories telling.

533. L. M.

1. When marshalled on the nightly plain,
The glittering host bestud the sky,
One star alone, of all the train,
Can fix the sinner's wandering eye.

2. Hark! hark! to God the chorus breaks,
From every host, from every gem;
But one alone the Saviour speaks—
It is the Star of Bethlehem.

3. Once on the raging seas I rode,
The storm was loud, the night was dark;
The ocean yawned, and rudely blowed
The wind that tossed my foundering bark.

4. Deep horror then my vitals froze,
Death-struck, I ceased the tide to stem;
When suddenly a Star arose—
It was the Star of Bethlehem.

5. It was my guide, my light, my all;
It bade my dark forebodings cease;
And through the storm, and danger's thrall,
It led me to the port of peace.

6. Now safely moored—my perils o'er,
I'll sing, first in night's diadem,
For ever and for evermore,
The Star—the Star of Bethlehem!

H. KIRKE WHITE.

534. L. M.

1. None loves me, Saviour, with Thy love,
None else can meet such needs as mine;
O, grant me, as Thou shalt approve,
All that befits a child of Thine!

2. Give me a faith shall never fail,
One that shall always work by love;
And then, whatever foes assail,
They shall but higher courage move.

3. A heart that, when my days are glad,
May never from Thy way decline,
A heart that loves to trust in Thee,
A patient heart, create in me!

GERMAN.

535. L. M.

1. Though sorrows rise, and dangers roll
   In waves of darkness o'er my soul;
   Though friends are false, and love decays,
   And few and evil are my days;
   Though conscience, fiercest of my foes,
   Swells with remembered guilt my woes;
   Yet even in nature's utmost ill,
   I love Thee, Lord! I love Thee still!

2. Though Sinai's curse, in thunder dread,
   Peals o'er mine unprotected head,
   And memory points, with busy pain,
   To grace and mercy given in vain;
   Till nature, shrinking in the strife,
   Would fly to hell to 'scape from life;
   Though every thought has power to kill,
   I love Thee, Lord! I love Thee still!

3. O, by the pangs Thyself hast borne,
   The ruffian's blow, the tyrant's scorn;
   By Sinai's curse, whose dreadful doom
   Was buried in Thy guiltless tomb;
   By these my pangs, whose healing smart
   Thy grace hath planted in my heart—
   I know, I feel Thy bounteous will,
   Thou lov'st me, Lord! Thou lov'st me still.

536. L. M.

1. A poor way-faring man of grief
   Hath often crossed me on my way,
   Who sued so humbly for relief,
   That I could never answer nay.

2. I had no power to ask His name,
   Whither He went, or whence He came;
   Yet there was something in His eye
   That won my love, I knew not why.

3. Once when my scanty meal was spread,
   He entered; not a word He spake;
   Just perishing for want of bread—
   I gave Him all; He blessed and brake,

4. And ate, but gave me part again:
   Mine was an angel's portion then!
   And while I fed with eager haste,
   The crust was manna to my taste!

5. I spied Him where a fountain burst
   Clear from the rock; His strength was gone;
   The heedless water mocked His thirst:
   He heard it, saw it hurrying on.

6. I ran and raised the Sufferer up;
   Thrice from the stream He drained my cup,
   Dipped, and returned it running o'er;
   I drank, and never thirsted more!

7. In prison I saw Him next, condemned
   To meet a traitor's doom at morn;
   The tide of lying tongues I stemmed,
   And honored Him 'mid shame and scorn.

8. My friendship's utmost zeal to try,
   He ask'd if I for Him would die?
   The flesh was weak, my blood ran chill,
   But the free spirit cried, "I will!"

9. Then, in a moment, to my view,
   The Stranger started from disguise;
   The tokens in His hands I knew—
   My Saviour stood before my eyes!

10. He spake, and my poor name He named:
    "Of Me thou hast not been ashamed;
    These deeds shall thy memorial be;
    Fear not, thou didst it unto Me!"
    MONTGOMERY.

537. L. M.

1. Abide with us, the evening shades
   Begin already to prevail,
   And as the evening twilight fades,
   Dark clouds around the horizon sail.

2. Abide with us, and still unfold
   Thy sacred though prophetic lore,
   What wond'rous things of Jesus told—
   Stranger, we thirst, we pant for more.

3. O stay with us, and still converse
   Of Him that late on Calvary died—
   Of Him the prophecies rehearse—
   It was our Friend they crucified.

4. Our souls are faint, our hearts are cold,
   We thought that Israel He'd restore;
   But sweet the truths Thy lips have told
   And, Stranger, we complain no more.

5. Thus while they prayed, at their request,
   The Stranger bows with smile divine;
   Then round the board the unknown Guest,
   And weary travelers recline.

6. Abide with us, amaz'd they cried,
   As suddenly, while breaking bread,
   Their own lost Jesus met their eyes,
   With radiant glories round His head!

7. Abide with us, Thou heavenly Friend,
   Leave not Thy followers alone.
   The sweet communion here must end—
   The heavenly Visitant is gone.

CHRISTIAN EXPERIENCE.

DRESDEN. L. M.

1. Come, O Thou Traveler unknown, Whom still I hold, but cannot see,
My company before is gone, And I am left alone with Thee:
D.C. With Thee all night I mean to stay, And wrestle till the break of day.

538. L. M. (Part 1.) *

2. I need not tell Thee who I am;
My sin and misery declare;
Thyself hast call'd me by my name,
Look on Thy hands and read it there;
But who, I ask Thee, who art Thou?
Tell me Thy name, and tell me now.

3. In vain Thou strugglest to get free,
I never will unloose my hold!
Art Thou the Man that died for me?
The secret of Thy love unfold:
Wrestling, I will not let Thee go,
Till I Thy name, Thy nature know.

4. Wilt Thou not yet to me reveal
Thy new, unutterable name?
Tell me, I still beseech Thee, tell;
To know it now resolved I am:
Wrestling, I will not let Thee go,
Till I Thy name, Thy nature know.
C. WESLEY.

539. L. M. (Part 2.)

1. YIELD to me now, for I am weak,
But confident in self-despair;
Speak to my heart, in blessings speak:
Be conquer'd by my instant prayer:
Speak, or Thou never hence shalt move,
And tell me if Thy name be Love.

2. 'Tis Love! 'tis Love! Thou diedst for me;
I hear Thy whisper in my heart;
The morning breaks, the shadows flee;
Pure, universal Love Thou art:
To me, to all, Thy bowels move—
Thy nature and Thy name is Love.

3. My prayer hath power with God; the grace
Unspeakable I now receive;
Through faith I see Thee face to face;
I see Thee face to face, and live!
In vain I have not wept and strove;
Thy nature and Thy name is Love.

4. I know Thee, Saviour, who Thou art—
Jesus, the feeble sinner's Friend:
Nor wilt Thou with the night depart,
But stay and love me to the end:
Thy mercies never shall remove;
Thy nature and Thy name is Love.
C. WESLEY.

540. L. M. (Part 3.)

1. THE Sun of Righteousness on me
Hath risen with healing in His wings:
Wither'd my nature's strength, from Thee
My soul its life and succor brings;
My help is all laid up above,
Thy nature and Thy name is Love.

2. Contented now, upon my thigh
I halt, till life's short journey end;
All helplessness, all weakness, I
On Thee alone for strength depend:
Nor have I power from Thee to move;
Thy nature and Thy name is Love.

3. Lame as I am, I take the prey;
Hell, earth, and sin, with ease o'ercome;
I leap for joy, pursue my way,
And, as a bounding hart, fly home,
Through all eternity to prove
Thy nature and Thy name is Love.
C. WESLEY.

* Genesis 32 : 24—30.

541. L. M. 6 lines.

1. Jesus, Thy boundless love to me
   No thought can reach, no tongue declare;
   O knit my thankful heart to Thee,
   And reign without a rival there:
   Thine wholly, Thine alone, I am;
   Be Thou alone my constant flame.

2. O grant that nothing in my soul
   May dwell, but Thy pure love alone:
   O may Thy love possess me whole—
   My, joy, my treasure, and my crown:
   Strange flames far from my heart remove,
   My every act, word, thought, be love.

3. Unwearied may I this pursue;
   Dauntless to the high prize aspire;
   Hourly within my soul renew
   This holy flame, this heavenly fire:
   And day and night, be all my care
   To guard the sacred treasure there.

4. In suff'ring be Thy love my peace;
   In weakness be Thy love my power;
   And when the storms of life shall cease,
   Jesus, in that important hour,
   In death, as life, be Thou my Guide,
   And save me, who for me hast died.
   C. WESLEY.

542. L. M. 6 lines.

1. My Saviour, Thou Thy love to me,
   In want, in pain, in shame, hast shown,
   For me upon the accursed tree,
   Didst by Thy precious death atone;
   Thy death upon my heart impress,
   That nothing may it thence erase.

2. O that I, like a little child,
   May follow Thee; nor ever rest
   Till sweetly Thou hast poured Thy mild
   And lowly mind into my breast.
   Oh may I now and ever be
   One spirit, dearest Lord, with Thee!

3. What in Thy love possess I not?
   My Star by night, my Sun by day,
   My spring of life when parched with drought,
   My wine to cheer, my bread to stay;
   My strength, my shield, my safe abode,
   My robe before the throne of God.

4. From all eternity with love
   Unchangeable thou hast me viewed;
   Ere knew this beating heart to move,
   Thy tender mercies me pursued.
   Ever with me may they abide,
   And close me in on every side.
   C. WESLEY.

543. L. M. 6 lines.

1. Now I have found the ground wherein
   Sure my soul's anchor may remain;
   The wounds of Jesus, for my sin,
   Before the world's foundation slain;
   Whose mercy shall unshaken stay,
   When heaven and earth are fled away.

2. O Love, thou bottomless abyss!
   My sins are swallowed up in Thee;
   Cover'd is my unrighteousness,
   From condemnation now I'm free;
   While Jesus' blood through earth and skies,
   Mercy, free, boundless mercy! cries.

3. With faith I plunge me in this sea,
   Here is my hope, my joy, my rest;
   Hither, when hell assails, I flee,
   I look into my Saviour's breast.
   Away, sad doubt, and anxious fear!
   Mercy is all that's written here.

4. Tho' waves and storms go o'er my head,
   Tho' strength, and health, and friends be gone;
   Tho' joys be withered all, and dead;
   Tho' every comfort be withdrawn—
   Steadfast on this my soul relies:
   Father, Thy mercy never dies.
   MORAVIAN.

544. L. M. 6 lines.

1. Thou hidden Source of calm repose,
   Thou all-sufficient Love divine,
   My help and refuge from my foes,
   Secure I am while Thou art mine:
   And lo! from sin, and grief, and shame,
   I hide me, Jesus, in Thy name.

2. Jesus, my all in all Thou art;
   My rest in toil, my ease in pain;
   The med'cine of my broken heart;
   In war, my peace; in loss, my gain;
   My smile beneath the tyrant's frown;
   In shame, my glory and my crown.

3. In want, my plentiful supply;
   In weakness, my almighty power;
   In bonds, my perfect liberty;
   My light in Satan's darkest hour;
   In grief, my joy unspeakable;
   My life in death, my all in all.
   C. WESLEY.

172 CHRISTIAN EXPERIENCE.

LOVING KINDNESS. L. M.

1. Awake, my soul, in joyful lays, And sing thy great Redeemer's praise; He justly claims a song from me, His loving kind-ness, O how free! Loving kindness, Loving kindness, His lov-ing kind-ness, O how free!

545. L. M.

2. When trouble, like a gloomy cloud,
 Has gather'd thick and thunder'd loud,
 He near my soul has always stood,
 His loving-kindness, O how good!

3. Often I feel my sinful heart
 Prone from my Jesus to depart;
 But though I have him oft forgot,
 His loving-kindness changes not.

4. Soon shall I pass the gloomy vale,
 Soon all my mortal powers must fail;
 O may my last expiring breath,
 His loving-kindness sing in death.

5. Then let me mount and soar away
 To the bright world of endless day;
 And sing, with rapture and surprise,
 His loving-kindness in the skies.
  MEDLEY.

546. L. M.

1. Lord, I will bless Thee all my days;
 Thy praise shall dwell upon my tongue;
 My soul shall glory in Thy grace,
 While saints rejoice to hear the song.

2. Come, magnify the Lord with me;
 Let every heart exalt His name;
 I sought the eternal God, and He
 Has not exposed my hope to shame.

3. I told Him all my silent grief,
 My secret groaning reached His ears;
 He gave my inward pains relief,
 And calmed the tumult of my fears.

4. His holy angels pitch their tents
 Around the men who serve the Lord;
 Oh, fear and love Him all His saints,
 Accept His grace and trust His word.
  WATTS.

547. L. M.

1. Jesus, my all, to heaven is gone,
 He whom I fix my hopes upon;
 His track I see, and I'll pursue
 The narrow way till Him I view.

2. The way the holy prophets went,
 The way that leads from banishment;
 The King's highway of holiness,
 I'll go, for all His paths are peace.

3. This is the way I long had sought,
 And mourned because I found it not;
 My grief a burden long had been,
 Oppressed with unbelief and sin.

4. The more I strove against their power,
 I sinned and stumbled but the more;
 Till late I heard my Saviour say,
 "Come hither, soul, I am the way."

5. Lo! glad I come, and Thou, blest Lamb,
 Shalt take me to Thee, as I am:
 Nothing but sin I Thee can give;
 Nothing but love shall I receive.

6. Then will I tell to sinners round,
 What a dear Saviour I have found;
 I'll point to Thy redeeming blood,
 And say, "Behold the way to God."
  CENNICK.

PRAISE, JOY, CONFLICT, ETC.

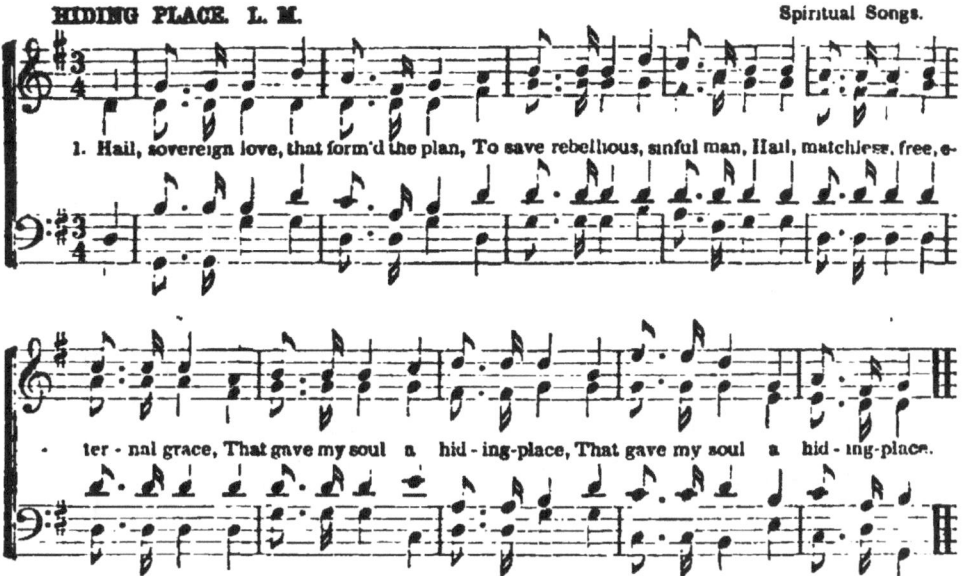

HIDING PLACE. L. M. — Spiritual Songs.

1. Hail, sovereign love, that form'd the plan, To save rebellious, sinful man, Hail, matchless, free, eternal grace, That gave my soul a hiding-place, That gave my soul a hiding-place.

548. L. M.

1. HAIL, sov'reign love, that form'd the plan
To save rebellious, ruin'd man,
Hail, matchless, free, eternal grace,
That gave my soul a hiding-place.

2. Against the God that rules the sky
I fought, with weapons lifted high,
I madly ran the sinful race,
Regardless of a hiding-place.

3. Yet when God's justice rose in view,
To Sinai's burning mount I flew;
Keen were the pangs of my distress,—
The mountain was no hiding-place.

4. But a celestial voice I heard,
A bleeding Saviour then appear'd,
Led by the Spirit of His grace,—
I found in Him a hiding-place.

5. On Him the weight of vengeance fell,
That else had sunk a world to hell;
Then, O my soul, for ever praise
Thy Saviour God, thy hiding-place.
SPIR. SONGS.

549. L. M.

1. MY gracious Lord, I own Thy right
To every service I can pay;
And call it my supreme delight
To hear Thy dictates and obey.

2. What is my being, but for Thee,
Its sure support, its noblest end?
I live Thy smiling face to see,
And serve the cause of such a Friend.

3. I would not breathe for worldly joy,
Or to increase my worldly good,
Nor future days or powers employ
To spread a sounding name abroad.

4. 'Tis to my Saviour I would live;
To Him who for my ransom died;
Nor could the bowers of Eden give
Such bliss as blossoms at His side.

5. His work my hoary age shall bless,
When youthful vigor is no more;
And my last hour of life confess
His dying love's constraining power.
DODDRIDGE.

550. L. M.

1. JESUS! Thy robe of righteousness
My beauty is, my glorious dress;
Mid flaming worlds, in this arrayed,
With joy shall I lift up my head.

2. When from the dust of death I rise,
To claim my mansion in the skies,
E'en then shall this be all my plea—
"Jesus hath lived and died for me."

3. This spotless robe the same appears,
When ruined nature sinks in years;
No age can change its lovely hue;
Its glory is for ever new.

4. O let the dead now hear Thy voice;
Now bid Thy banished ones rejoice;
Their beauty this, their glorious dress,—
Jesus, the Lord, our righteousness.
C. WESLEY.

CHRISTIAN EXPERIENCE.

CORONATION. C. M. — OLIVER HOLDEN.

1. All hail! the power of Jesus' name! Let angels prostrate fall, Bring forth the royal di-a-dem, And crown Him Lord of all, Bring forth the roy-al di-adem, And crown Him Lord of all.

551. C. M.

1. All hail! the power of Jesus' name!
   Let angels prostrate fall,
   Bring forth the royal diadem,
   And crown Him Lord of all.

2. Crown Him, ye morning stars of light,
   Who fix'd this floating ball;
   Now hail the strength of Israel's might,
   And crown Him Lord of all.

3. Crown Him, ye martyrs of our God,
   Who from His altar call;
   Extol the stem of Jesse's rod,
   And crown Him Lord of all.

4. Ye chosen seed of Israel's race,
   Ye ransom'd from the fall,
   Hail Him, who saves you by His grace,
   And crown Him Lord of all.

5. Hail Him, ye heirs of David's line,
   Whom David, Lord, did call;
   The God incarnate! Man divine!
   And crown Him Lord of all.

6. Sinners, whose love can ne'er forget
   The wormwood and the gall:
   Go, spread your trophies at His feet,
   And crown Him Lord of all.

7. Let every kindred, every tribe,
   On this terrestrial ball,
   To Him all majesty ascribe,
   And crown Him Lord of all.

8. O that with yonder sacred throng,
   We at His feet may fall;
   We'll join the everlasting song,
   And crown Him Lord of all.
                                   DUNCAN.

552. C. M.

1. ARISE, my soul, my joyful powers,
   And triumph in my God;
   Awake, my voice, and loud proclaim
   His glorious grace abroad.

2. He raised me from the deeps of sin,
   The gates of gaping hell;
   And fixed my standing more secure
   Than 't was before I fell.

3. The arms of everlasting love
   Beneath my soul He placed;
   And on the Rock of Ages set
   My slippery footsteps fast.

4. The city of my blest abode
   Is walled around with grace;
   Salvation for a bulwark stands
   To shield the sacred place.

5. Satan may vent his sharpest spite,
   And all his legions roar;
   Almighty mercy guards my life,
   And bounds his raging power.

6. Arise, my soul! awake, my voice!
   And tunes of pleasure sing;
   Loud hallelujahs shall address
   My Saviour and my King.
                                   WATTS.

PRAISE, JOY, CONFLICT, ETC.

BRADFORD. C. M.   HANDEL.

1. Thou dear Redeemer, dying Lamb, We love to hear of Thee; No music's like thy charming name, Nor half so sweet can be.

553. C. M.

2. O may we ever hear Thy voice,
In mercy to us speak;
And in our Priest will we rejoice,
Thou great Melchisedec.

3. Our Saviour shall be still our theme,
While in this world we stay;
We'll sing our Jesus' lovely name,
When all things else decay.

4. When we appear in yonder cloud,
With all the favored throng,
Then will we sing more sweet, more loud,
And Christ shall be our song.
MADAN'S COLL.

554. C. M.

1. When God revealed His gracious name,
And changed my mournful state,
My rapture seemed a pleasing dream,
The grace appeared so great.

2. The world beheld the glorious change,
And did Thy hand confess;
My tongue broke out in unknown strains,
And sung surprising grace.

3. "Great is the work," my neighbors cried,
And owned Thy power divine;
"Great is the work," my heart replied,
"And be the glory Thine."

4. The Lord can clear the darkest skies,
Can give us day for night;
Make drops of sacred sorrow rise
To rivers of delight.

5. Let those that sow in sadness wait
Till the fair harvest come;
They shall confess their sheaves are great,
And shout the blessings home.

6. Though seed lie buried long in dust,
'T will not deceive their hope;
The precious grain can ne'er be lost,
For grace insures the crop.
WATTS.

555. C. M.

1. How dread are thine eternal years,
O everlasting Lord!
By prostrate spirits day and night
Incessantly adored!

2. Yet I may love thee too, O Lord!
Almighty as Thou art,
For Thou hast stooped to ask of me,
The love of my poor heart.

3. No earthly father loves like Thee,
No mother half so mild
Bears and forbears, as Thou hast done
With me, Thy sinful child.

4. Only to sit and think of God—
O what a joy it is!
To think the thought, to breathe the name,
Earth has no higher bliss!

5. Father of Jesus! love's reward!
What rapture will it be,
Prostrate before Thy throne to lie,
And gaze and gaze on Thee!
LYRA CATH.

PRAISE. C. M.

English.

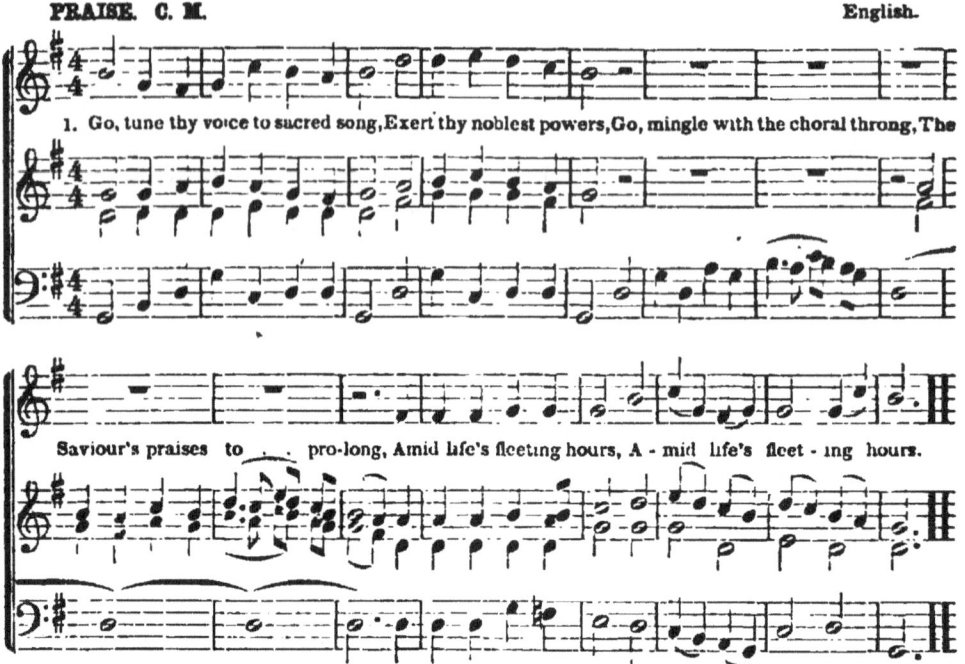

1. Go, tune thy voice to sacred song, Exert thy noblest powers, Go, mingle with the choral throng, The Saviour's praises to prolong, Amid life's fleeting hours, A-mid life's fleeting hours.

556. C. M.

2. O! hast thou felt a Saviour's love,
That flame of heavenly birth?
Then let thy strains melodious prove,
With raptures soaring far above
  The trifling toys of earth.

3. Hast found the pearl of price unknown,
That cost a Saviour's blood?
Heir of a bright celestial crown,
That sparkles near th' eternal throne,
  O sing the praise of God!

4. Sing of the Lamb that once was slain
That man might be forgiven;
Sing how He broke death's bars in twain,
Ascending high in bliss to reign,
  The God of earth and heaven.

557. C. M.

1. Sing, ye redeemed of the Lord,
Your great Deliverer sing,
Pilgrims for Zion's city bound,
  Be joyful in your King.

2. A hand divine shall lead you on
Through all the blissful road,
Till to the sacred mount you rise,
  And see your smiling God.

3. Bright garlands of immortal joy
Shall bloom on every head;
While sorrow, sighing, and distress,
  Like shadows, all are fled.

4. March on in your Redeemer's strength;
Pursue His footsteps still;
And let the prospect cheer your eye,
  While laboring up the hill.

DODDRIDGE.

558. C. M.

1. Come, ye that love the Saviour's name,
And joy to make it known,
The Sovereign of your hearts proclaim,
  And bow before His throne.

2. Behold your King, your Saviour crowned
With glories all divine;
And tell the wondering nations round,
  How bright those glories shine.

3. When in His earthly courts we view
The beauties of our King,
We long to love as angels do,
  And with their voice to sing.

4. O for the day, the glorious day!
When heaven and earth shall raise,
With all their powers, the raptured lay,
  To celebrate Thy praise.

MRS. STEELE.

559. C. M.

1. COME, let us lift our joyful eyes
   Up to the courts above,
   And smile to see our Father there,
   Upon a throne of love.

2. Now we may bow before His feet,
   And venture near the Lord;
   No fiery cherub guards His seat,
   Nor double-flaming sword.

3. The peaceful gates of heavenly bliss
   Are opened by the Son;
   High let us raise our notes of praise,
   And reach th' almighty throne.

4. To Thee, ten thousand thanks we bring,
   Great Advocate on high,
   And glory to th' eternal King,
   Who lays His anger by.
   WATTS.

560. C. M.

1. YE lands and isles of every sea,
   Rejoice—the Saviour reigns;
   His word, like fire, prepares His way,
   And mountains melt to plains.

2. His presence sinks the proudest hills,
   And makes the valleys rise;
   The humble soul enjoys His smiles,
   The haughty sinner dies.

3. The heavens His rightful power proclaim;
   The idol-gods around
   Fill their own worshippers with shame,
   And totter to the ground.

4. Adoring angels at His birth
   Make the Redeemer known;
   Thus shall He come to judge the earth,
   And angels guard His throne.

5. His foes shall tremble at the sight,
   And hills and seas retire;
   His children take their unknown flight,
   And leave the world on fire.

6. The seeds of joy and glory sown,
   For saints in darkness here,
   Shall rise and spring in worlds unknown,
   And a rich harvest bear.
   WATTS.

561. C. M.

1. HOSANNA to the Prince of light,
   That clothed Himself in clay;
   Entered the iron gates of death,
   And tore the bars away.

2. See how the Conqueror mounts aloft,
   And to His Father flies,
   With scars of honor in His flesh,
   And triumph in His eyes.

3. There our exalted Saviour reigns,
   And scatters blessings down;
   Our Jesus fills the middle seat
   Of the celestial throne.

4. Raise your devotion, mortal tongues,
   To reach His bless'd abode;
   Sweet be the accents of your songs
   To our incarnate God.

5. Bright angels, strike your loudest strings,
   Your sweetest voices raise;
   Let heaven, and all created things,
   Sound our Immanuel's praise.
   WATTS.

562. C. M.

1. O FOR a thousand tongues to sing
   My dear Redeemer's praise—
   The glories of my God and King,
   The triumphs of His grace!

2. My gracious Master and my God,
   Assist me to proclaim,
   To spread through all the earth abroad,
   The honors of Thy name.

3. Jesus! the name that calms our fears,
   That bids our sorrows cease;
   'Tis music in the sinner's ears;
   'Tis life, and health, and peace.

4. He breaks the power of reigning sin;
   He sets the prisoner free;
   His blood can make the foulest clean;
   His blood availed for me.
   C. WESLEY.

563. C. M.

1. I'M not ashamed to own my Lord,
   Or to defend His cause;
   Maintain the honor of His word,
   The glory of His cross.

2. Jesus, my God!—I know His name,
   His name is all my trust;
   Nor will He put my soul to shame,
   Nor let my hope be lost.

3. Firm as His throne, His promise stands,
   And He can well secure
   What I've committed to His hands,
   Till the decisive hour.

4. Then will He own my worthless name,
   Before His Father's face,
   And in the new Jerusalem
   Appoint my soul a place.
   WATTS.

CHRISTMAS. C. M. — HANDEL.

1. Awake, my soul, stretch every nerve, And press with vigor on: A heavenly race demands thy zeal, And an immortal crown, And an immortal crown.

564. C. M.

2. A cloud of witnesses around
Hold thee in full survey;
Forget the steps already trod,
And onward urge thy way.

3. 'Tis God's all-animating voice,
That calls thee from on high;
'T is His own hand presents the prize
To thine aspiring eye.

4. That prize with peerless glories bright,
Which shall new lustre boast,
When victor's wreaths and monarch's gems
Shall blend in common dust.

5. Blest Saviour, introduced by Thee,
Have I my race begun;
And, crowned with victory, at Thy feet
I'll lay my honors down.
DODDRIDGE.

565. C. M.

1. RISE, O my soul—pursue the path
By ancient worthies trod;
Aspiring, view those holy men,
Who lived and walked with God.

2. Though dead, they speak in reason's ear,
And in example live;
Their faith, and hope, and mighty deeds,
Still fresh instruction give.

3. 'T was through the Lamb's most precious blood,
They conquered every foe;
To His almighty power and grace,
Their crowns of life they owe.

4. Lord, may I ever keep in view
The patterns Thou hast given,
And ne'er forsake the blessed road
That led them safe to heaven.
NEEDHAM.

566. C. M.

1. AM I a soldier of the cross?
A follower of the Lamb?
And shall I fear to own His cause,
Or blush to speak His name?

2. Must I be carried to the skies
On flowery beds of ease?
While others fought to win the prize,
And sailed through bloody seas?

3. Are there no foes for me to face?
Must I not stem the flood?
Is this vile world a friend to grace,
To help me on to God?

4. Sure I must fight, if I would reign;
Increase my courage, Lord;
I'll bear the toil, endure the pain,
Supported by Thy word.

5. Thy saints, in all this glorious war,
Shall conquer, though they die;
They view the triumph from afar,
And seize it with their eye.

6. When that illustrious day shall rise,
And all Thy armies shine
In robes of victory through the skies—
The glory shall be Thine.
WATTS.

PRAISE, JOY, CONFLICT, ETC.

ST. ANN'S. C. M. — DR. CROFT.

1. In all my Lord's appointed ways, My journey I'll pursue;
Hinder me not, ye much-loved saints! For I must go with you.

567. C. M.

2. Through floods and flames, if Jesus leads,
I'll follow where He goes;
Hinder me not!—shall be my cry,
Though earth and hell oppose.

3. Through duty, and through trials, too,
I'll go at His command;
Hinder me not, for I am bound
To my Immanuel's land.

4. And when my Saviour calls me home,
Still this my cry shall be—
Hinder me not—come, welcome death!
I'll gladly go with Thee.
     RYLAND.

568. C. M.

1. Alas, what hourly dangers rise!
What snares beset my way!
To heaven O let me lift mine eyes,
And hourly watch and pray.

2. How oft my mournful thoughts complain,
And melt in flowing tears!
My weak resistance!—ah, how vain!
How strong my foes and fears!

3. O gracious God! in whom I live,
My feeble efforts aid;
Help me to watch, and pray, and strive,
Though trembling and afraid.

4. Increase my faith—increase my hope,
When foes and fears prevail;
And bear my fainting spirit up,
Or soon my strength will fail.

5. O keep me in Thy heavenly way,
And bid the tempter flee;
And let me never, never stray
From happiness and Thee.
     MRS. STEELE.

569. C. M.

1. Through all the changing scenes of life,
In trouble, and in joy,
The praises of my God shall still
My heart and tongue employ.

2. Of His deliverance I will boast,
Till all, who are distress'd,
From my example comfort take,
And charm their griefs to rest.

3. Oh! magnify the Lord with me,
With me exalt His name;
When in distress to Him I called,
He to my rescue came.

4. The hosts of God encamp around
The dwellings of the just;
Deliverance He affords to all
Who on His succor trust.

5. Oh! make but trial of His love;
Experience will decide—
How blest are they, and only they,
Who in His truth confide.

6. Fear Him, ye saints! and ye will then
Have nothing else to fear;
Make ye His service your delight—
He'll make your wants His care.
     TATE AND BRADY.

CHRISTIAN EXPERIENCE.

* The *D. C. al Segno* signifies that the voices go back to the sign 𝄋.

570. C. M.

2. 'T was grace that taught my heart to fear,
   And grace my fears relieved:
   How precious did that grace appear,
   The hour I first believed!

3. Through many dangers, toils, and snares,
   I have already come;
   'T is grace has brought me safe thus far,
   And grace will lead me home.

4. The Lord has promised good to me,
   His word my hope secures;
   He will my shield and portion be,
   As long as life endures.

5. Yes, when this flesh and heart shall fail,
   And mortal life shall cease,
   I shall possess, within the vail,
   A life of joy and peace.

6. The earth shall soon dissolve like snow,
   The sun forbear to shine;
   But God, who call'd me here below,
   Will be for ever mine.

   NEWTON.

571. C. M.

1. Come, let us join our songs of praise
   To our ascended Priest;
   He entered heaven, with all our names
   Engraven on His breast.

2. Below He washed our guilt away
   By His atoning blood;
   Now He appears before the throne,
   And pleads our cause with God.

3. Clothed with our nature still, He knows
   The weakness of our frame,
   And how to shield us from the foes
   Whom He Himself o'ercame.

4. Nor time, nor distance, e'er shall quench
   The fervor of His love;
   For us He died in kindness here,
   For us He lives above.

5. O may we ne'er forget His grace,
   Nor blush to bear His name;
   Still may our hearts hold fast His faith—
   Our lips His praise proclaim.

   CAMPBELL'S COLL.

572. C. M.

1. Salvation! Oh! the joyful sound;
   'T is pleasure to our ears;
   A sovereign balm for every wound,
   A cordial for our fears.

2. Buried in sorrow and in sin,
   At hell's dark door we lay;
   But we arise, by grace divine,
   To see a heavenly day.

3. Salvation!—let the echo fly
   The spacious earth around;
   While all the armies of the sky
   Conspire to raise the sound.

   WATTS.

573. C. M.

1. There is a fountain filled with blood
   Drawn from Immanuel's veins;
   And sinners plunged beneath that flood
   Lose all their guilty stains.

2. The dying thief rejoiced to see
   That fountain in his day;
   And there may I, as vile as he,
   Wash all my sins away.

3. Dear, dying Lamb, Thy precious blood
   Shall never lose its power
   Till all the ransomed church of God
   Be saved, to sin no more.

4. E'er since, by faith, I saw the stream
   Thy flowing wounds supply,
   Redeeming love has been my theme,
   And shall be, till I die.

5. Then in a nobler, sweeter song,
   I'll sing Thy power to save,
   When this poor, lisping, stammering tongue
   Lies silent in the grave.

   COWPER.

574. C. M.

1. To our Redeemer's glorious name
   Awake the sacred song!
   O, may His love—immortal flame—
   Tune every heart and tongue.

2. His love what mortal thought can reach!
   What mortal tongue display!
   Imagination's utmost stretch
   In wonder dies away.

3. Dear Lord, while we, adoring, pay
   Our humble thanks to Thee,
   May every heart with rapture say,
   "The Saviour died for me."

4. O, may the sweet, the blissful theme
   Fill every heart and tongue,
   Till strangers love Thy charming name,
   And join the sacred song.

   MRS. STEELE.

575. C. M.

1. Awake, my heart, arise, my tongue,
   Prepare a tuneful voice;
   In God, the life of all my joys,
   Aloud will I rejoice.

2. 'T is He adorned my naked soul,
   And made salvation mine;
   Upon a poor, polluted worm
   He makes His graces shine.

3. And, lest the shadow of a spot
   Should on my soul be found,
   He took the robe the Saviour wrought,
   And cast it all around.

4. How far this heavenly robe exceeds
   What earthly princes wear!
   These ornaments, how bright they shine!
   How white the garments are!

5. The Spirit wrought my faith, and love,
   And hope, and every grace;
   But Jesus spent His life to work
   The robe of righteousness.

6. Strangely, my soul, art thou arrayed,
   By the great sacred Three!
   In sweetest harmony of praise,
   Let all thy powers agree.

   WATTS.

576. C. M.

1. Come, let us join our cheerful songs
   With angels round the throne;
   Ten thousand thousand are their tongues,
   But all their joys are one.

2. "Worthy the Lamb that died," they cry,
   "To be exalted thus;"
   "Worthy the Lamb," our lips reply,
   "For He was slain for us."

3. Jesus is worthy to receive
   Honor and power divine;
   And blessings, more than we can give,
   Be, Lord, for ever thine.

4. Let all that dwell above the sky,
   And air, and earth, and seas,
   Conspire to lift Thy glories high,
   And speak Thine endless praise.

5. The whole creation join in one,
   To bless the sacred name
   Of Him that sits upon the throne,
   And to adore the Lamb.

   WATTS.

CHRISTIAN EXPERIENCE.

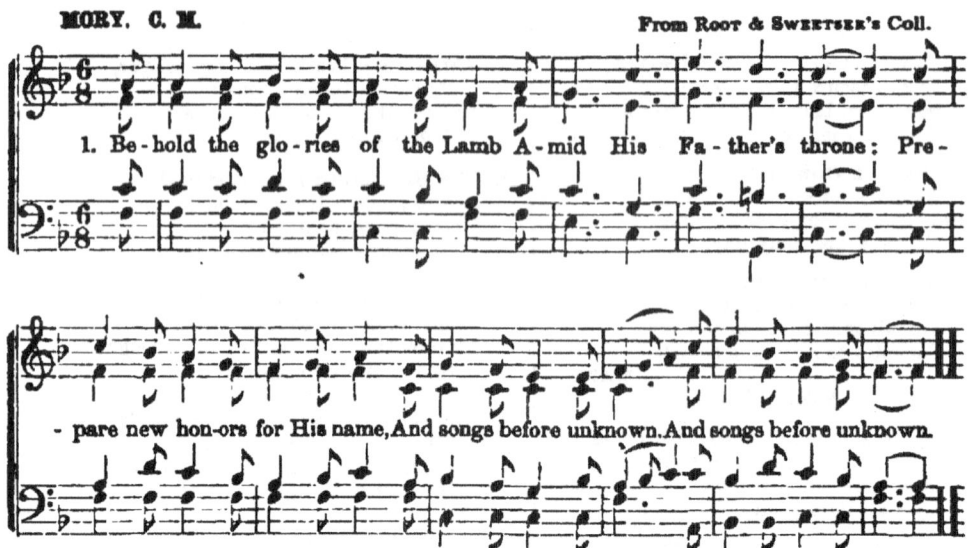

MORY. C. M.   From Root & Sweetser's Coll.

1. Behold the glories of the Lamb Amid His Father's throne; Prepare new honors for His name, And songs before unknown, And songs before unknown.

577. C. M.

2. Let elders worship at His feet,
   The church adore around,
   With vials full of odors sweet,
   And harps of sweeter sound.

3. Now to the Lamb that once was slain,
   Be endless blessings paid;
   Salvation, glory, joy, remain
   For ever on Thy head.

4. Thou hast redeemed our souls with blood,
   Hast set the prisoners free,
   Hast made us kings and priests to God,
   And we shall reign with Thee.

5. The worlds of nature and of grace
   Are put beneath Thy power;
   Then shorten these delaying days,
   And bring the promised hour.
   WATTS.

578. C. M.

1. My Saviour! my almighty Friend!
   When I begin Thy praise,
   Where will the growing numbers end—
   The numbers of Thy grace?

2. Thou art my everlasting trust;
   Thy goodness I adore;
   And since I knew Thy graces first,
   I speak Thy glories more.

3. My feet shall travel all the length
   Of the celestial road;
   And march, with courage, in Thy strength,
   To see my Father-God.

4. When I am filled with sore distress
   For some surprising sin,
   I'll plead Thy perfect righteousness,
   And mention none but Thine.

5. How will my lips rejoice to tell
   The vict'ries of my King!
   My soul, redeemed from sin and hell,
   Shall Thy salvation sing.

6. Awake, awake, my tuneful powers!
   With this delightful song,
   I'll entertain the darkest hours,
   Nor think the season long.
   WATTS.

579. C. M.

1. PLUNGED in a gulf of dark despair,
   We wretched sinners lay,
   Without one cheerful beam of hope,
   Or spark of glimmering day.

2. With pitying eyes the Prince of grace
   Beheld our helpless grief;
   He saw, and—O amazing love!—
   He ran to our relief.

3. Down from the shining seats above,
   With joyful haste He fled,
   Entered the grave in mortal flesh,
   And dwelt among the dead.

4. O for this love let rocks and hills
   Their lasting silence break;
   And all harmonious human tongues
   The Saviour's praises speak.

5. Angels! assist our mighty joys;
   Strike all your harps of gold:
   But when you raise your highest notes,
   His love can ne'er be told.
   WATTS.

PRAISE, JOY, CONFLICT, ETC.

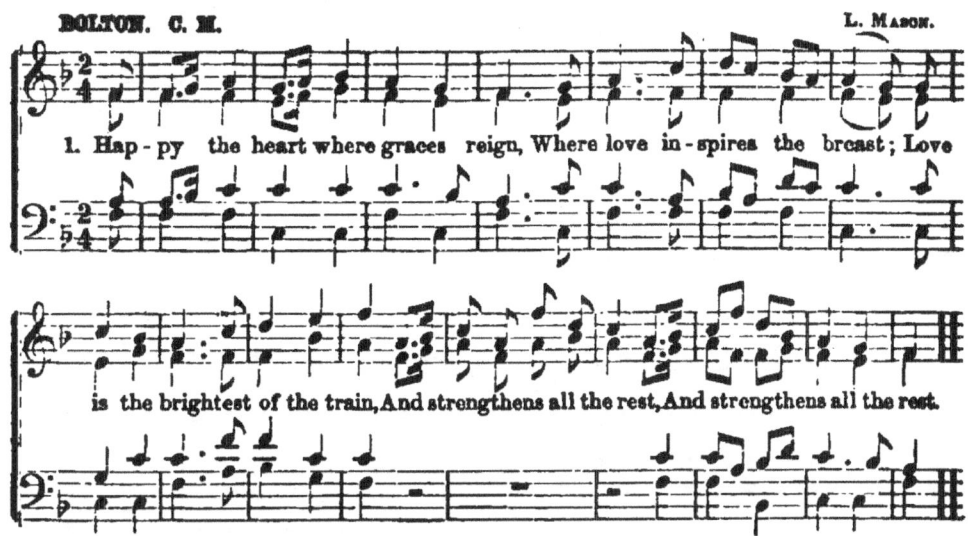

BOLTON. C. M.   L. MASON.

1. Happy the heart where graces reign, Where love inspires the breast; Love is the brightest of the train, And strengthens all the rest, And strengthens all the rest.

580. C. M.

2. Knowledge, alas, 't is all in vain,
   And all in vain our fear;
   Our stubborn sins will fight and reign,
   If love be absent there.

3. This is the grace that lives and sings,
   When faith and hope shall cease;
   T 'is this shall strike our joyful strings,
   In the sweet realms of bliss.

4. Before we quite forsake our clay,
   Or leave this dark abode,
   The wings of love bear us away,
   To see our smiling God.
                     WATTS.

581. C. M.

1. Come, shout aloud the Father's grace,
   And sing the Saviour's love;
   Soon shall you join the glorious theme,
   In loftier strains above.

2. God, the eternal, mighty God,
   To dearer names descends;
   Calls you His treasure and His joy,
   His children and His friends.

3. My Father, God! and may these lips
   Pronounce a name so dear?
   Not thus could heaven's sweet harmony
   Delight my listening ear.

4. Thanks to my God for every gift
   His bounteous hands bestow;
   And thanks eternal for that love
   Whence all those comforts flow.
                 HIGINBOTHAM.

582. C. M.

1. Lord! 't is an infinite delight
   To see Thy lovely face,
   To dwell whole ages in Thy sight,
   And feel Thy vital rays.

2. While the bright nation sounds Thy praise
   From each eternal hill,
   Sweet odors of exhaling grace,
   The happy region fill.

3. Thy love a sea without a shore,
   Spreads life and joy abroad—
   Oh, 't is a heaven worth dying for,
   To see a smiling God!

4. Show me Thy face, and I 'll away
   From all inferior things;
   Speak Lord, and here I quit my clay,
   And stretch my airy wings.   WATTS.

583. C. M.

1. Jesus—the name high over all,
   In hell, or earth, or sky—
   Angels and men before it fall,
   And devils fear and fly.

2. Jesus—the name to sinners dear,
   The name to sinners given—
   It scatters all their guilt and fear;
   It turns their hell to heaven.

3. Oh that a dying world might know
   The glory of His name;
   My voice shall His salvation show,
   And cry—"Behold the Lamb!"

4. Happy, if with my latest breath
   I may but gasp His name;
   Proclaim His love, and cry in death—
   "Behold, behold the Lamb!"
                 C. WESLEY.

COVENTRY. C. M.   Arranged by L. Mason.

584. C. M.

1. O could our thoughts and wishes fly
Above these gloomy shades,
To those bright worlds beyond the sky,
Which sorrow ne'er invades!

2. There joys, unseen by mortal eyes,
Or reason's feeble ray,
In ever-blooming prospect rise,
Unconscious of decay.

3. Lord, send a beam of light divine,
To guide our upward aim!
With one reviving touch of Thine,
Our languid hearts inflame.

4. Then shall, on faith's sublimest wing,
Our ardent wishes rise
To those bright scenes where pleasures spring,
Immortal in the skies.
            MRS. STEELE.

585. C. M.

1. O could I find, from day to day,
A nearness to my God,
Then would my hours glide sweet away,
While leaning on His word.

2. Lord, I desire with Thee to live
Anew from day to day,
In joys the world can never give,
Nor ever take away.

3. Blest Jesus, come, and rule my heart,
And make me wholly Thine,
That I may never more depart,
Nor grieve Thy love divine.

4. Thus, till my last expiring breath,
Thy goodness I'll adore;
And when my frame dissolves in death,
My soul shall love Thee more.
            HARTFORD SELECTION.

586. C. M.

1. From Thee, my God, my joys shall rise,
And run eternal rounds,
Beyond the limits of the skies,
And all created bounds.

2. The holy triumphs of my soul
Shall death itself outbrave,
Leave dull mortality behind,
And fly beyond the grave.

3. There, where my blessed Jesus reigns,
In heaven's unmeasured space,
I'll spend a long eternity
In pleasure and in praise.

4. Millions of years my wondering eyes
Shall o'er thy beauties rove,
And endless ages I'll adore
The glories of Thy love.

5. My Saviour, every smile of Thine
Shall fresh endearments bring,
And thousand tastes of new delight
From all Thy graces spring.

6. Haste, my Beloved, fetch my soul
Up to Thy blest abode;
Fly, for my spirit longs to see
My Saviour and my God.
            WATTS.

587. C. M.

1. My God, my portion, and my love,
    My everlasting all,
   I've none but Thee in heaven above,
    Or on this earthly ball.

2. In vain the bright, the burning sun
    Scatters his feeble light;
   'T is thy sweet beams create my noon—
    If thou withdraw, 't is night.

3. And while upon my restless bed
    Through midnight hours I roll,
   If my Redeemer shows His head,
    'T is morning with my soul.

4. To Thee I owe my wealth and friends,
    My health and safe abode;
   Thanks to Thy name for meaner things,
    But they are not my God.

5. Were I possessor of the earth,
    And called the stars my own,
   Without Thy graces and Thyself,
    I were a wretch undone.

6. Let others stretch their arms like seas,
    And grasp in all the shore,
   Grant me the visits of Thy face,
    And I desire no more.
                         WATTS.

588. C. M.

1. The bird let loose in Eastern skies,
    Returning fondly home,
   No'er stoops to earth her wing, nor flies
    Where idler warblers roam.

2. But high she shoots through air and light,
    Above all low delay,
   Where nothing earthly bounds her flight,
    Nor shadow dims her way.

3. So grant me, Lord, from every snare
    Of sinful passion free,
   Aloft through faith's serener air
    To hold my course to Thee.

4. No sin to cloud, no lure to stay
    My soul, as home she springs;
   Thy sunshine on her joyful way,
    Thy freedom in her wings.
                         MOORE.

589. C. M.

1. Thy home is with the humble, Lord!
    The simplest are the best;
   Thy lodging is in child-like hearts;
    Thou makest there Thy rest.

2. Dear Comforter! Eternal Love!
    If Thou wilt stay with me,
   Of lowly thoughts and simple ways
    I'll build a house for Thee.

3. Who made this beating heart of mine
    But Thou, my heavenly Guest?
   Let no one have it, then, but Thee,
    And let it be Thy rest.
                         LYRA CATH.

590. C. M.

1. My Saviour, let me hear Thy voice
    Pronounce the word of peace,
   And all my warmest powers shall join
    To celebrate Thy grace.

2. With gentle smiles call me Thy child,
    And speak my sins forgiven;
   The accents mild shall charm my ear
    Like the sweet harps of heaven.

3. Cheerful, where'er Thy hand shall lead,
    The darkest path I'll tread;
   Cheerful I'll quit these mortal shores,
    And mingle with the dead.

4. When dreadful guilt is done away,
    No other fears we know;
   That hand which scatters pardons down
    Shall crowns of life bestow.
                         DODDRIDGE.

591. C. M.

1. Unite, my roving thoughts, unite,
    In silence soft and sweet;
   And thou, my soul, sit gently down
    At thy great Sov'reign's feet.

2. Jehovah's awful voice is heard,
    Yet gladly I attend;
   For lo! the everlasting God
    Proclaims Himself my Friend.

3. Harmonious accents to my soul,
    The sounds of peace convey;
   The tempest at His word subsides,
    And winds and seas obey.

4. By all its joys, I charge my heart
    To grieve His love no more;
   But, charm'd by melody divine,
    To give its follies o'er.
                         DODDRIDGE.

Doxology. C. M.

Praise, honor, to the Father be,
 Praise to His only Son;
Praise to the Spirit Paraclete,
 While ceaseless ages run.

CHRISTIAN EXPERIENCE.

592. C. M.

1. O FOR the happy days gone by,
   When love ran smooth and free,
   Days when my Spirit so enjoy'd
   More than earth's liberty!

2. O for the times when on my heart
   Long prayer had never pall'd—
   Times when the ready thought of God
   Would come when it was call'd!

3. Then when I knelt to meditate,
   Sweet thoughts came o'er my soul,
   Countless, and bright, and beautiful,
   Beyond my own control.

4. O who hath lock'd those fountains up?
   Those visions who hath stay'd?
   What sudden act hath thus transform'd
   My sunshine into shade?

5. This freezing heart, O Lord! this will
   Dry as the desert sand,
   Good thoughts that will not come, bad thoughts
   That come without command,—

6. A faith that seems not faith, a hope
   That cares not for its aim,
   A love that none the warmer grows
   At Jesus' blessed name;—

7. If this drear change be Thine, O Lord!
   If it be Thy sweet will,
   Spare not, but to the very brim
   The bitter chalice fill.

8. But if it hath been sin of mine,
   O show that sin to me,
   Not to get back the sweetness lost,
   But to make peace with Thee.

9. One thing alone, dear Lord! I dread—
   To have a secret spot
   That separates my soul from Thee,
   And yet to know it not.

10. But if this weariness hath come
    A present from on high,
    Teach me to find the hidden wealth
    That in its depths may lie.

11. So in this darkness I can learn
    To tremble and adore,
    To sound my own vile nothingness,
    And thus to love Thee more.

12. O blessed be this darkness then,
    This deep in which I lie,
    And blessed be all things that teach
    God's dread Supremacy!   FABER.

593. C. M.

1. O Jesus! Light of all below!
    Thou Fount of life and fire!
   Surpassing all the joys we know,
    All that we can desire:

2. O Jesus! Thou the beauty art
    Of angel worlds above;
   Thy name is music to the heart,
    Enchanting it with love.

3. Poor souls! that know not how to love;
    They feel not Jesus near;
   And they who know not how to love
    Still less know how to fear.

4. The majesty of God ne'er broke
    On them like fire at night,
   Flooding their stricken souls, while they
    Lay trembling in the light.

5. Stay with us, Lord, and with Thy light
    Illume the soul's abyss;
   Scatter the darkness of our night,
    And fill the world with bliss.
                    LYRA CATH.

594. C. M.

1. GLORY to God! whose witness-train,
    Those heroes bold in faith,
   Could smile on poverty and pain,
    And triumph even in death.

2. O, may that faith our hearts sustain,
    Wherein they fearless stood,
   When, in the power of cruel men,
    They poured their willing blood.

3. God, whom we serve, our God, can save,
    Can damp the scorching flame,
   Can build an ark, can smooth the wave,
    For such as love his name.

4. Lord! if thine arm support us still
    With its eternal strength,
   We shall o'ercome the mightiest ill,
    And conquerors prove at length.

595. C. M.

1. DEAR Friend, whose presence in the house,
    Whose gracious word benign
   Could once, at Cana's wedding feast,
    Change water into wine,

2. Come, visit us! and when dull work
    Grows weary, line on line,
   Revive our souls, and let us see
    Life's water turned to wine.

3. Gay mirth shall deepen into joy,
    Earth's hopes grow half divine,
   When Jesus visits us, to make
    Life's water glow as wine.

4. The social talk, the evening fire,
    The homely household shrine,
   Grow bright with angel visits, when
    The Lord pours out the wine.

5. For when self-seeking turns to love,
    Not knowing mine nor thine,
   The miracle again is wrought,
    And water turned to wine.
                    J. F. CLARKE.

596. C. M.

1. DEAR Jesus! ever at my side,
    How loving must Thou be
   To leave Thy home in heaven to guard
    A little child like me.

2. Thy beautiful and shining face
    I see not, though so near;
   The sweetness of Thy soft low voice
    I am too deaf to hear.

3. I can not feel Thee touch my hand
    With pressure light and mild,
   To check me, as my mother did
    When I was but a child.

4. But I have felt Thee in my thoughts
    Fighting with sin for me;
   And when my heart loves God, I know
    The sweetness is from Thee.

5. And when, dear Saviour! I kneel down
    Morning and night to prayer,
   Something there is within my heart
    Which tells me Thou art there.

6. Yes! when I pray, Thou prayest too—
    Thy prayer is all for me;
   But when I sleep, Thou sleepest not,
    But watchest patiently.
                    FABER.

DOXOLOGY. C. M.

To God the Father, glory be,
 And to His only Son;
The same, O Holy Ghost! to Thee,
 While ceaseless ages run.

CHRISTIAN EXPERIENCE.

GUARDIAN. C. M. — A. Brown.

1. My God, the spring of all my joys, The life of my delights, The glory of my brightest days, And comfort of my nights, And comfort of my nights.

597. C. M.

1. My God! the spring of all my joys,
   The life of my delights,
   The glory of my brightest days,
   And comfort of my nights.

2. In darkest shades if He appear,
   My dawning is begun!
   He is my soul's sweet morning star,
   And He my rising sun.

3. The opening heavens around me shine
   With beams of sacred bliss,
   While Jesus shows His heart is mine,
   And whispers, "I am His!"

4. My soul would leave this heavy clay
   At that transporting word,
   Run up with joy the shining way,
   T' embrace my dearest Lord.

5. Fearless of hell, and ghastly death,
   I'd break through every foe;
   The wings of love, and arms of faith,
   Should bear me conqueror through.
   WATTS.

598. C. M.

1. Do not I love Thee, O my Lord?
   Behold my heart and see;
   And turn the dearest idol out
   That dares to rival Thee.

2. Is not Thy name melodious still
   To mine attentive ear?
   Doth not each pulse with pleasure bound,
   My Saviour's voice to hear?

3. Hast Thou a lamb in all Thy flock
   I would disdain to feed?
   Hast Thou a foe before whose face
   I fear Thy cause to plead?

4. Would not my heart pour forth its blood
   In honor of Thy name?
   And challenge the cold hand of death
   To damp th' immortal flame?

5. Thou knowest I love Thee, dearest Lord;
   But O! I long to soar
   Far from the sphere of mortal joys,
   And learn to love Thee more.
   DODDRIDGE.

599. C. M.

1. Dearest of all the names above,
   My Saviour and my God,
   Who can resist Thy heavenly love,
   Or trifle with Thy blood?

2. 'Tis by the merits of Thy death
   Thy Father smiles again;
   'Tis by Thine interceding breath
   The Spirit dwells with men.

3. Till God in human flesh I see,
   My thoughts no comfort find;
   The holy, just, and sacred Three
   Are terrors to my mind.

4. But if Immanuel's face appear,
   My hope, my joy, begin;
   His name forbids my slavish fear;
   His grace removes my sin.

5. While Jews on their own law rely,
   And Greeks of wisdom boast,
   I love th' incarnate mystery,
   And there I fix my trust.
   WATTS.

600. C. M.

1. O HOW the thought of God attracts
   And draws the heart from earth,
   And sickens it of passing shows
   And dissipating mirth!

2. God only is the creature's home,
   Though long and rough the road;
   Yet nothing less can satisfy
   The love that longs for God.

3. O utter but the name of God
   Down in your heart of hearts,
   And see how from the world at once
   All tempting light departs.

4. A trusting heart, a yearning eye,
   Can win their way above;
   If mountains can be moved by faith,
   Is there less power in love?

5. How little of that road, my soul!
   How little hast Thou gone!
   Take heart, and let the thought of God
   Allure thee further on.

6. Dole not thy duties out to God,
   But let thy hand be free;
   Look long at Jesus; His sweet blood,
   How was it dealt to Thee?

7. The perfect way is hard to flesh;
   It is not hard to love;
   If thou wert sick for want of God
   How swiftly wouldst thou move!

   FABER.

601. C. M.

1. O SINNER, bring not tears alone,
   Or outward form of prayer,
   But let it in thy heart be known
   That penitence is there.

2. To smite the breast, the clothes to rend,
   God asketh not of thee;
   Thy secret soul He bids thee bend
   In true humility.

3. O, let us, then, with heartfelt grief,
   Draw near unto our God,
   And pray to Him to grant relief,
   And stay the lifted rod.

4. O righteous Judge, if Thou wilt deign
   To grant us what we need,
   We pray for time to turn again,
   And grace to turn indeed.

   BREVIARY.

602. C. M.

1. O GIFT of gifts! O grace of faith!
   My God! how can it be
   That Thou, who hast discerning love,
   Shouldst give that gift to me?

2. How many hearts thou mightst have had
   More innocent than mine!
   How many souls more worthy far
   Of that sweet touch of Thine!

3. Ah, grace! into unlikeliest hearts
   It is thy boast to come,
   The glory of thy light to find
   In darkest spots a home.

4. The crowd of cares, the weightiest cross,
   Seem trifles less than light—
   Earth looks so little and so low
   When faith shines full and bright.

5. O, happy, happy that I am!
   If thou canst be, O faith,
   The treasure that thou art in life,
   What wilt thou be in death?

   LYRA CATH.

603. C. M.

1. O dearest Lamb, take Thou my heart!
   Where can such sweetness be,
   As I have tasted in Thy love,
   As I have found in Thee?

2. If there's a fervor in my soul,
   And fervor sure there is,
   Now it shall be at thy control,
   And but to serve Thee rise.

3. If love, that mildest flame can rest
   In hearts so hard as mine,
   Come, gentle Saviour to my breast,
   Its love shall all be Thine.

4. Now the gay world with treacherous art
   Shall tempt thy heart in vain
   I have conveyed away that heart,
   Ne'er to return again.

5. 'Tis heaven on earth to taste His love,
   To feel His quickening grace,
   And all the heaven I hope above,
   Is but to see His face.

   MORAVIAN.

190   CHRISTIAN EXPERIENCE.

ORTONVILLE. C. M.   THOMAS HASTINGS.

1. Majestic sweetness sits enthroned Upon the Saviour's brow; His head with radiant glo-ries crowned, His lips with grace o'er-flow, His lips with grace o-er-flow.

604. C. M.

2. No mortal can with Him compare,
    Among the sons of men;
Fairer is He than all the fair
    Who fill the heavenly train.

3. He saw me plunged in deep distress,
    And flew to my relief;
For me He bore the shameful cross,
    And carried all my grief.

4. To Him I owe my life and breath,
    And all the joys I have;
He makes me triumph over death,
    And saves me from the grave.

5. To heaven, the place of His abode,
    He brings my weary feet,
Shows me the glories of my God,
    And makes my joys complete.

6. Since from His bounty I receive
    Such proofs of love divine,
Had I a thousand hearts to give,
    Lord! they should all be thine.
                  S. STENNETT.

605. C. M.

1. Jesus! I love Thy charming name,
    'T is music to mine ear;
Fain would I sound it out so loud,
    That earth and heaven should hear.

2. Yes!—Thou art precious to my soul,
    My transport and my trust;
Jewels, to Thee, are guilty toys,
    And gold is sordid dust.

3. All my capacious powers can wish,
    In Thee doth richly meet;
Not to mine eyes is light so dear,
    Nor friendship half so sweet.

4. Thy grace still dwells upon my heart,
    And sheds its fragrance there;—
The noblest balm of all its wounds,
    The cordial of its care.

5. I'll speak the honors of Thy name,
    With my last lab'ring breath;
Then, speechless, clasp Thee in mine arms,
    The antidote of death.
                  DODDRIDGE.

606. C. M.

1. To Thee, my Shepherd, and my Lord,
    A grateful song I'll raise;
O let the humblest of Thy flock
    Attempt to speak thy praise.

2. My life, my joy, my hope, I owe
    To Thine amazing love;
Ten thousand thousand comforts here,
    And nobler bliss above.

3. To Thee my trembling spirit flies,
    With sin and grief oppress'd;
Thy gentle voice dispels my fears,
    And lulls my cares to rest.

4. Lead on, dear Shepherd!—led by Thee,
    No evil shall I fear;
Soon shall I reach Thy fold above,
    And praise Thee better there.
                  HIGGINBOTHAM.

607. C. M.

1. How sweet the name of Jesus sounds
   In a believer's ear!
   It soothes his sorrows, heals his wounds,
   And drives away his fear.

2. It makes the wounded spirit whole,
   And calms the troubled breast;
   'T is manna to the hungry soul,
   And for the weary, rest.

3. By Thee, my prayers acceptance gain,
   Although with sin defiled;
   Satan accuses me in vain,
   And I am owned a child.

4. Jesus! my Shepherd, Guardian, Friend,
   My Prophet, Priest, and King;
   My Lord, my Life, my Way, my End,
   Accept the praise I bring.

5. Weak is the effort of my heart,
   And cold my warmest thought;
   But when I see Thee as Thou art,
   I 'll praise Thee as I ought.

6. Till then, I would Thy love proclaim,
   With every fleeting breath;
   And may the music of Thy name,
   Refresh my soul in death.
   NEWTON.

608. C. M.

1. GRACE, like an uncorrupted seed,
   Abides and reigns within;
   Immortal principles forbid
   The sons of God to sin.

2. Not by the terrors of a slave
   Do they perform His will,
   But, with the noblest powers they have,
   His sweet commands fulfill.

3. They find access at every hour,
   To God within the vail;
   Hence they derive a quickening power,
   And joys that never fail.

4. O happy souls! O glorious state
   Of overflowing grace!
   To dwell so near their Father's seat,
   And see His lovely face!

5. Lord, I address Thy heavenly throne,
   Call me a child of Thine;
   Send down the Spirit of Thy Son,
   To form my heart divine.

6. There shed Thy choicest love abroad,
   And make my comforts strong;
   Then shall I say—"My Father, God,"
   With an unwavering tongue.
   WATTS.

609. C. M.

1. As once the Saviour took His seat—
   Attracted by His fame,
   And lowly bending at His feet,
   An humble suppliant came.

2. Ashamed to lift her streaming eyes
   His holy glance to meet,
   She poured her costly sacrifice
   Upon the Saviour's feet.

3. Oppressed with sin and sorrow's weight,
   And sinking in despair,
   With tears she washed His sacred feet,
   And wiped them with her hair.

4. "Depart in peace," the Saviour said,
   "Thy sins are all forgiven!"
   The trembling sinner raised her head,
   In peaceful hope of heaven.
   MRS. BROWN.

610. C. M.

1. LET every mortal ear attend,
   And every heart rejoice;
   The trumpet of the gospel sounds
   With an inviting voice.

2. Ho! all ye hungry, starving souls,
   That feed upon the wind,
   And vainly strive with earthly toys
   To fill an empty mind!—

3. Eternal wisdom has prepared
   A soul-reviving feast,
   And bids your longing appetites
   The rich provision taste.

4. Ho! ye that pant for living streams,
   And pine away and die!
   Here you may quench your raging thirst
   With springs that never dry.

5. Rivers of love and mercy, here,
   In a rich ocean join;
   Salvation in abundance flows,
   Like floods of milk and wine.

6. The happy gates of gospel-grace
   Stand open night and day;—
   Lord! we are come to seek supplies,
   And drive our wants away.
   WATTS.

DOXOLOGY. C. M.

PRAISE Him, who with the Father sits
Enthroned upon the skies;
Whose blood redeems our souls from guilt,
Whose Spirit sanctifies.

CHRISTIAN EXPERIENCE.

SENTINEL. S. M.   From Templi Carmina.

1. My soul, be on thy guard; Ten thousand foes arise;
The hosts of sin are pressing hard To draw thee from the skies.

611. S. M.

2. O watch, and fight, and pray;
   The battle ne'er give o'er;
Renew it boldly every day,
   And help divine implore.

3. Ne'er think the victory won,
   Nor lay thine armor down;
Thy arduous work will not be done,
   Till thou obtain thy crown.

4. Fight on, my soul, till death
   Shall bring thee to thy God;
He'll take thee, at thy parting breath,
   To His divine abode.
                        HEATH.

612. S. M.

1. SOLDIERS of Christ, arise,
   And gird your armor on,
Strong in the strength which God supplies
   Through his eternal Son.

2. Strong in the Lord of hosts,
   And in His mighty power,
Who in the strength of Jesus trusts
   Is more than conqueror.

3. Leave no unguarded place,
   No weakness of the soul;
Take every virtue, every grace,
   And fortify the whole.

4. But above all lay hold
   On faith's victorious shield;
Armed with that adamant and gold,
   Be sure to win the field.

5. Stand, then, in His great might,
   With all His strength endued,
And take, to arm you for the fight,
   The panoply of God;—

6. That, having all things done,
   And all your conflicts past,
You may o'ercome through Christ alone,
   And stand complete at last.

7. From strength to strength go on;
   Wrestle, and fight, and pray;
Tread all the powers of darkness down,
   And win the well-fought day.

8. Still let the Spirit cry,
   In all his soldiers, "Come,"
Till Christ the Lord descends from high,
   And takes the conquerors home.
                        C. WESLEY.

613. S. M.

1. SOLDIERS of Christ! arise!
   The God of armies calls
Unto His mansions in the skies—
   His everlasting halls:

2. The angel host appears
   To welcome you to bliss;
Oh! what is earth, its sighs and tears,
   Its joys, compared to this!

3. Crush'd is the haughty foe,
   His might, his glory gone;
But ye, with victory crown'd, shall go
   To Christ's eternal throne.

4. There shall the conqueror rest,
   And in that bright abode
For ever reign amid the blest,
   Triumphant with his God.
                        LYRA CATH.

614. S. M.

1. I STAND on Zion's mount,
   And view my starry crown;
No power on earth my hope can shake,
   Nor hell can thrust me down.

2. The lofty hills and towers,
   That lift their heads on high,
Shall all be leveled low in dust—
   Their very names shall die.

3. The vaulted heavens shall fall,
   Built by Jehovah's hands;
But firmer than the heavens, the Rock
   Of my salvation stands.
                              SWAIN.

615. S. M.

1. GRACE! 'tis a charming sound,
   Harmonious to the ear;
Heaven with the echo shall resound;
   And all the earth shall hear.

2. Grace first contrived a way
   To save rebellious man;
And all the steps that grace display,
   Which drew the wondrous plan.

3. Grace led my roving feet
   To tread the heavenly road;
And new supplies each hour I meet,
   While pressing on to God.

4. Grace all the work shall crown,
   Through everlasting days;
It lays in heaven the topmost stone,
   And well deserves the praise.
                              DODDRIDGE.

616. S. M.

1. Now let our voices join
   To form a sacred song;
Ye pilgrims, in Jehovah's ways,
   With music pass along.

2. How straight the path appears,
   How open and how fair!
No lurking gins t' entrap our feet;
   No fierce destroyer there.

3. But flowers of paradise
   In rich profusion spring;
The Sun of glory gilds the path,
   And dear companions sing.

4. See Salem's golden spires
   In beauteous prospect rise;
And brighter crowns than mortals wear
   Which sparkle through the skies.

5. All honor to His name,
   Who marks the shining way;
To Him, who leads the wanderer on
   To realms of endless day.
                              DODDRIDGE.

617. S. M.

1. REJOICE in God alway;
   When earth looks heavenly bright,
When joy makes glad the livelong day,
   And peace shuts in the night.

2. Rejoice when care and woe
   The fainting soul oppress;
When tears at wakeful midnight flow,
   And morn brings heaviness.

3. Rejoice in hope and fear;
   Rejoice in life and death;
Rejoice when threatening storms are near,
   And comfort languisheth.

4. When should not they rejoice,
   Whom Christ His brethren calls;
Who hear and know His guiding voice,
   When on their hearts it falls?

5. So, though our path is steep,
   And many a tempest lowers,
Shall His own peace our spirits keep,
   And Christ's dear love be ours.

618. S. M.

1. JESUS' tremendous name
   Puts all our foes to flight;
Jesus, the meek, the gentle Lamb
   A Lion is, in fight.

2. By all Hell's host withstood,
   We all Hell's host o'erthrow;
And conquering them in Jesus' blood
   We still to conquer go.

3. Our Captain leads us on;
   He beckons from the skies,
And reaches out a starry crown,
   And bids us take the prize;

4. "Be faithful unto death;
   Partake My victory;
And thou shalt wear this glorious wreath,
   And thou shalt reign with Me."
                              C. WESLEY.

DOXOLOGY. S. M.

Blest Trinity! vouchsafe
   That, to Thy guidance true,
What Thou forbiddest, we may shun;
   What Thou commandest, do.

CHRISTIAN EXPERIENCE.

OLMUTZ. S. M. *Arranged by L. Mason.*

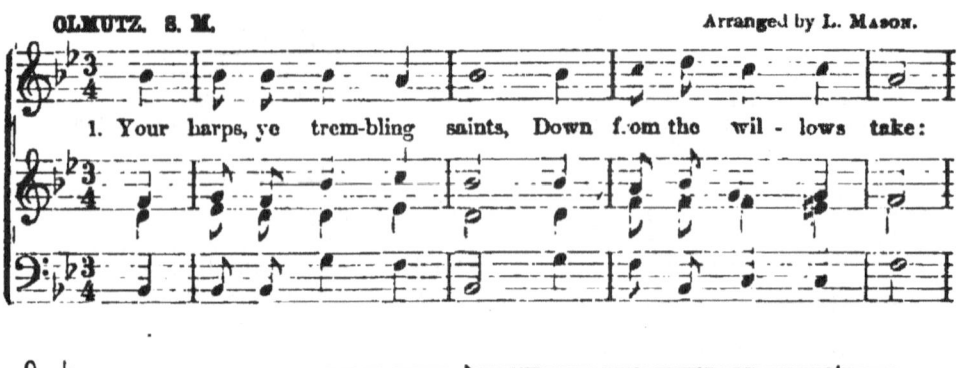

1. Your harps, ye trembling saints, Down from the willows take:

Loud to the praise of Love divine Bid every string awake.

619. S. M.

2. Though in a foreign land,
      We are not far from home,
   And nearer to our house above
      We every moment come.

3. His grace will to the end
      Stronger and brighter shine,
   Nor present things, nor things to come,
      Shall quench the spark divine.

4. When we in darkness walk,
      Nor feel the heavenly flame,
   Then is the time to trust our God,
      And rest upon His name.

5. Soon shall our doubts and fears
      Subside at His control;
   His loving-kindness shall break through
      The midnight of the soul.

6. Blest is the man, O God,
      That stays himself on Thee!
   Who waits for Thy salvation, Lord,
      Shall Thy salvation see.
                              TOPLADY.

620. S. M.

1. How heavy is the night
      That hangs upon our eyes,
   Till Christ, with His reviving light,
      Over our souls arise!

2. Our guilty spirits dread
      To meet the wrath of Heaven;
   But in His righteousness arrayed,
      We see our sins forgiven.

3. Unholy and impure
      Are all our thoughts and ways;
   His hands infected nature cure,
      With sanctifying grace.

4. The powers of hell agree
      To hold our souls in vain;
   He sets the sons of bondage free,
      And breaks the accursed chain.

5. Lord, we adore Thy ways,
      To bring us near to God;
   Thy sovereign Power, Thy healing grace,
      And Thy atoning blood.
                              WATTS.

621. S. M.

1. "For ever, with the Lord!"—
      So, Jesus! let it be;
   Life from the dead is in that word;
      'Tis immortality.

2. Here, in the body pent,
      Absent from Thee I roam;
   Yet nightly pitch my moving tent,
      A day's march nearer home

3. "For ever with the Lord!"
   Saviour, if 'tis Thy will
The promise of that faithful word
   E'en here to me fulfill.

4. So when my latest breath
   Shall rend the vail in twain,
By death I shall escape from death,
   And life eternal gain.

5. Knowing as I am known,
   How shall I love that word,
And oft repeat before the throne—
   "For ever with the Lord!"
                                MONTGOMERY.

622. S. M.

1. A CHARGE to keep I have;
   A God to glorify;
A never-dying soul to save,
   And fit it for the sky.

2. To serve the present age,
   My calling to fulfill;
O may it all my powers engage
   To do my Master's will.

3. Arm me with jealous care,
   As in Thy sight to live;
And O thy servant, Lord, prepare
   A strict account to give.

4. Help me to watch and pray,
   And on Thyself rely;
Assured if I my trust betray,
   I shall for ever die.
                                C. WESLEY.

623. S. M.

1. TEACH me, my God and King,
   Thy will in all to see;
And what I do in any thing,
   To do it as for Thee!

2. To scorn the senses' sway,
   While still to Thee I tend;
In all I do, be Thou the way,
   In all, be Thou the end.

3. All may of Thee partake;
   Nothing so small can be
But draws, when acted for Thy sake
   Greatness and worth from Thee.

4. If done beneath Thy laws
   E'en servile labors shine;
Hallowed is toil, if this the cause;
   The meanest work, divine.
                                HERBERT.

624. S. M.

1. COME, Holy Spirit, come;
   Let Thy bright beams arise;
Dispel the sorrow from our minds,
   The darkness from our eyes.

2. Convince us of our sin;
   Then lead to Jesus' blood,
And to our wondering view reveal
   The secret love of God.

3. Revive our drooping faith,
   Our doubts and fears remove,
And kindle in our breasts the flame
   Of never-dying love.

4. 'T is Thine to cleanse the heart,
   To sanctify the soul,
To pour fresh life in every part,
   And new-create the whole.

5. Come, Holy Spirit, come;
   Our minds from bondage free;
Then shall we know, and praise, and love,
   The Father, Son, and Thee.
                                BEDDOME.

625. S. M.

1. THE harvest dawn is near,
   The year delays not long;
And he who sows with many a tear,
   Shall reap with many a song.

2. Sad to his toil he goes,
   His seed with weeping leaves;
But He shall come, at twilight's close,
   And bring His golden sheaves.
                                G. BURGESS.

626. S. M.

1. YE servants of the Lord,
   Each in His office wait,
Observant of His heavenly word,
   And watchful at His gate.

2. Let all your lamps be bright,
   And trim the golden flame;
Gird up your loins as in His sight,
   For awful is His name.

3. Watch—'t is your Lord's command;
   And while we speak, He's near;
Mark the first signal of His hand,
   And ready all appear.

4. O happy servant he
   In such a posture found!
He shall his Lord with rapture see,
   And be with honor crowned.
                                DODDRIDGE.

627. S. M. Double.

1. I was a wandering sheep,
   I did not love the fold:
   I did not love my Father's voice,
   I would not be controll'd;
   I was a wayward child,
   I did not love my home,
   I did not love my Shepherd's voice,
   I loved afar to roam.

2. The Shepherd sought His sheep,
   The Father sought His child;
   They followed me o'er vale and hill,
   O'er deserts waste and wild:
   They found me nigh to death,
   Famish'd, and faint, and lone;
   They bound me with the bands of love,
   They saved the wandering one.

3. They spoke in tender love,
   They raised my drooping head;
   They gently closed my bleeding wounds,
   My fainting soul they fed:
   They washed my filth away,
   They made me clean and fair;
   They brought me to my home in peace,
   The long-sought wanderer.

4. Jesus my Shepherd is,
   'T was He that loved my soul,
   T was He that wash'd me in His blood,
   'T was He that made me whole:
   'T was He that sought the lost,
   That found the wandering sheep,
   'T was He that brought me to the fold—
   'T is He that still doth keep.

5. No more a wand'ring sheep,
   I love to be controll'd,
   I love my tender Shepherd's voice,
   I love the peaceful fold:
   No more a wayward child,
   I seek no more to roam,
   I love my heavenly Father's voice—
   I love, I love His home.

628. S. M.

1. The Lord my Shepherd is;
   I shall be well supplied:
Since He is mine, and I am His,
   What can I want beside?

2. He leads me to the place
   Where heavenly pasture grows,
Where living waters gently pass,
   And full salvation flows.

3. If e'er I go astray,
   He doth my soul reclaim,
And guides me, in His own right way,
   For His most holy name.

4. While He affords His aid,
   I can not yield to fear;
Tho' I should walk thro' death's dark shade,
   My Shepherd's with me there.

5. In sight of all my foes,
   Thou dost my table spread;
My cup with blessings overflows,
   And joy exalts my head.

6. The bounties of Thy love
   Shall crown my future days;
Nor from Thy house will I remove,
   Nor cease to speak Thy praise.
                                    WATTS.

629. S. M.

1. Our heavenly Father calls,
   And Christ invites us near;
With both, our friendship shall be sweet,
   And our communion dear.

2. God pities all our griefs:
   He pardons every day;
Almighty to protect our souls,
   And wise to guide our way.

3. How large His bounties are!
   What various stores of good,
Diffused from our Redeemer's hand,
   And purchased with His blood!

4. Jesus, our living Head,
   We bless Thy faithful care;
Our Advocate before the throne,
   And our forerunner there.

5. Here fix, my roving heart!
   Here wait, my warmest love!
Till the communion be complete,
   In nobler scenes above.
                                DODDRIDGE.

630. S. M.

1. My God, my Life, my Love,
   To Thee, to Thee I call;
I can not live, if Thou remove,
   For Thou art all in all.

2. Thy shining grace can cheer
   This dungeon where I dwell;
'T is paradise when Thou art here;
   If Thou depart, 't is hell.

3. To Thee, and Thee alone,
   The angels owe their bliss;
They sit around Thy gracious throne,
   And dwell where Jesus is.

4. Not all the harps above
   Can make a heavenly place,
If God His residence remove,
   Or but conceal His face.

5. Nor earth, nor all the sky,
   Can one delight afford,
No, not a drop of real joy,
   Without Thy presence, Lord.

6. Thou art the sea of love,
   Where all my pleasures roll;
The circle where my passions move,
   And centre of my soul.
                                    WATTS.

631. S. M. Double.

1. I want a heart to pray,—
      To pray, and never cease;
   Never to murmur at Thy stay,
      Or wish my suff'rings less.
   This blessing, above all,—
      Always to pray—I want;
   Out of the deep on Thee to call,
      And never, never faint.

2. I want a true regard,
      A single, steady aim,—
   Unmoved by threat'ning or reward,
      To Thee and Thy great name;
   A jealous, just concern,
      For Thine immortal praise;
   A pure desire that all may learn
      And glorify Thy grace.

3. I rest upon Thy word,—
      The promise is for me;
   My succor and salvation, Lord,
      Shall surely come from Thee:
   But let me still abide,
      Nor from my hope remove,
   Till Thou my patient spirit guide
      Into Thy perfect love.
                                    C. WESLEY.

CHRISTIAN EXPERIENCE.

ST. THOMAS. S. M.

1. A-wake, and sing the song Of Moses and the Lamb; Wake every heart, and every tongue, To praise the Saviour's name.

632. S. M.

2. Sing, till we feel our heart
   Ascending with our tongue;
Sing, till the love of sin depart;
   And grace inspire our song.

3. Sing, on your heavenly way,
   Ye ransomed sinners, sing;
Sing on, rejoicing every day
   In Christ, the heavenly King.

4. Soon shall we hear him say,
   "Ye blessed children, come!"
Soon will He call us hence away
   To our eternal home.

5. There shall our raptured tongue
   His endless praise proclaim,
And sweeter voices tune the song
   Of Moses and the Lamb.

HAMMOND.

633. S. M.

1. HARK, how the watchmen cry!
   Attend the trumpet's sound;
Stand to your arms, the foe is nigh,—
   The powers of hell surround.

2. Who bow to Christ's command,
   Your arms and hearts prepare;
The day of battle is at hand,—
   Go forth to glorious war.

3. See on the mountain top
   The standard of your God;
In Jesus' name 't is lifted up,
   All stain'd with hallow'd blood.

4. His standard-bearers, now
   To all the nations call:
To Jesus' cross, ye nations, bow;
   He bore the cross for all.

5. Go up with Christ your Head;
   Your Captain's footsteps see;
Follow your Captain, and be led
   To certain victory.

6. All power to Him is given;
   He ever reigns the same:
Salvation, happiness, and heaven,
   Are all in Jesus' name.

C. WESLEY.

634. S. M.

1. NOT all the blood of beasts,
   On Jewish altars slain.
Could give the guilty conscience peace,
   Or wash away the stain.

2. But Christ, the heavenly Lamb,
   Takes all our sins away;
A sacrifice of nobler name,
   And richer blood than they.

3. My faith would lay her hand
   On that dear head of Thine,
While like a penitent I stand,
   And there confess my sin.

4. My soul looks back, to see
   The burdens Thou didst bear,
When hanging on the cursed tree,
   And hopes her guilt was there.

5. Believing, we rejoice
   To see the curse remove;
We bless the Lamb with cheerful voice,
   And sing His bleeding love.

WATTS.

635. S. M.

1. Raise your triumphant songs
   To an immortal tune;
Let all the earth resound the deeds
   Celestial grace has done.

2. Sing how eternal love
   Its chief Beloved chose,
And bade Him raise our wretched race
   From their abyss of woes.

3. His hand no thunder bears;
   No terror clothes His brow;
No bolts to drive our guilty souls
   To fiercer flames below.

4. 'T was mercy filled the throne,
   And wrath stood silent by,
When Christ was sent with pardons down
   To rebels doomed to die.

5. Now, sinners, dry your tears;
   Let hopeless sorrow cease;
Bow to the sceptre of His love,
   And take the offered peace.

6. Lord, we obey Thy call;
   We lay an humble claim
To the salvation Thou hast brought,
   And love and praise Thy name.
                              WATTS.

636. S. M.

1. Behold, what wondrous grace
   The Father has bestowed
On sinners of a mortal race,
   To call them sons of God!

2. Nor doth it yet appear
   How great we must be made;
But when we see our Saviour here,
   We shall be like our Head.

3. A hope so much divine
   May trials well endure;
May purify our souls from sin,
   As Christ, the Lord, is pure.

4. If in my Father's love
   I share a filial part,
Send down Thy Spirit, like a dove,
   To rest upon my heart.

5. We would no longer lie
   Like slaves beneath the throne;
Our faith shall Abba, Father, cry,
   And Thou the kindred own.
                              WATTS.

637. S. M.

1. To God the only wise,
   Our Saviour and our King,
Let all the saints below the skies
   Their humble praises bring.

2. 'T is His almighty love,
   His counsel and His care,
Preserves us safe from sin and death,
   And every hurtful snare.

3. He will present our souls,
   Unblemished and complete,
Before the glory of His face,
   With joys divinely great.

4. Then all the chosen seed
   Shall meet around the throne,
Shall bless the conduct of His grace,
   And make His wonders known.

5. To our Redeemer God
   Wisdom and power belongs,
Immortal crowns of majesty,
   And everlasting songs.
                              WATTS.

638. S. M.

1. Come, ye that love the Lord,
   And let your joys be known;
Join in a song with sweet accord,
   And thus surround the throne.

2. Let those refuse to sing,
   That never knew our God;
But favorites of the heavenly King
   May speak their joys abroad.

3. The men of grace have found
   Glory begun below:
Celestial fruits on earthly ground
   From faith and hope may grow.

4. The hill of Zion yields
   A thousand sacred sweets,
Before we reach the heavenly fields,
   Or walk the golden streets.

5. Then let our songs abound,
   And every tear be dry;
We're marching through Immanuel's ground
   To fairer worlds on high.
                              WATTS.

Doxology. S. M.

To God, the Father, Son,
   And Spirit, glory be:
As, and is, and shall be so,
   Through all eternity.

CHRISTIAN EXPERIENCE.

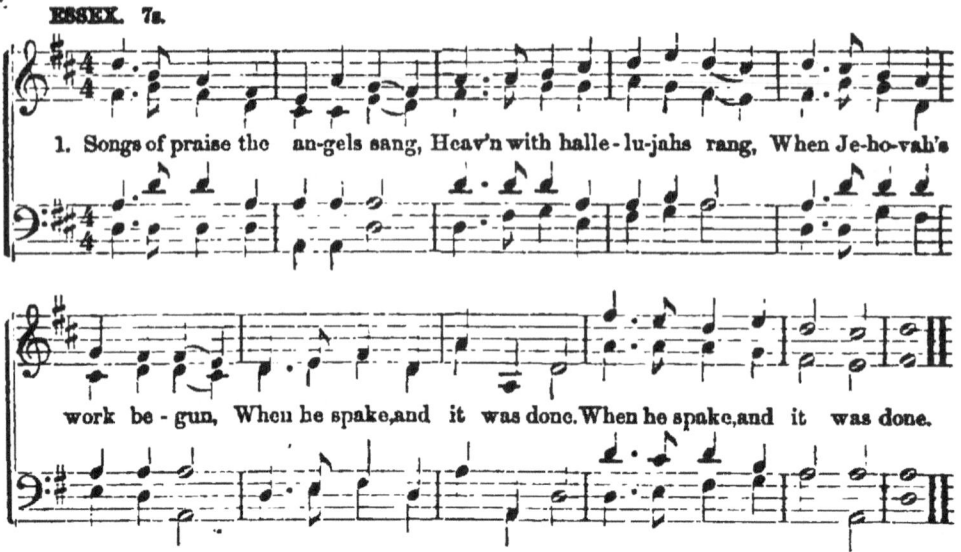

ESSEX. 7s.

1. Songs of praise the an-gels sang, Heav'n with halle-lu-jahs rang, When Je-ho-vah's work be-gun, When he spake, and it was done. When he spake, and it was done.

639. 7s.

1. Songs of praise the angels sang,
Heaven with hallelujahs rang,
When Jehovah's work begun,
When He spake, and it was done.

2. Songs of praise awoke the morn,
When the Prince of Peace was born;
Songs of praise arose, when He
Captive led captivity.

3. Heaven and earth must pass away,—
Songs of praise shall crown that day;
God will make new heavens and earth,—
Songs of praise shall hail their birth.

4. And shall man alone be dumb,
Till that glorious kingdom come?
No; the Church delights to raise
Psalms and hymns and songs of praise.

5. Saints below, with heart and voice,
Still in songs of praise rejoice;
Learning here, by faith and love,
Songs of praise to sing above.

6. Borne upon the latest breath,
Songs of praise shall conquer death;
Then, amidst eternal joy,
Songs of praise their powers employ.
MONTGOMERY.

640. 7s.*

1. Jesus lives, and so shall I.
Death! thy sting is gone for ever!
He, who deigned for me to die,

* Sung to Essex, by repeating the two first strains.

Lives, the bands of death to sever.
He shall raise me with the just:
Jesus is my Hope and Trust.

2. Jesus lives and reigns supreme;
And, His kingdom still remaining,
I shall also be with him,
Ever living, ever reigning.
God has promised; be it must:
Jesus is my Hope and Trust.

3. Jesus lives, and God extends
Grace to each returning sinner;
Rebels He receives as friends,
And exalts to highest honor.
God is True as He is Just;
Jesus is my Hope and Trust.

4. Jesus lives, and by His grace
Victory o'er my passions giving,
I will cleanse my heart and ways,
Ever to His glory living.
The weak He raises from the dust:
Jesus is my Hope and Trust.

5. Jesus lives, and I am sure
Nought shall e'er from Jesus sever.
Satan's wiles, and Satan's power,
Pain or pleasure—ye shall never!
Christian armor can not rust:
Jesus is my Hope and Trust.

6. Jesus lives, and death is now
But my entrance into glory.
Courage! then, my soul, for thou
Hast a crown of life before thee;
Thou shalt find thy hopes were just—
Jesus is the Christian's Trust.
GELLERT.

PRAISE, JOY, CONFLICT, ETC.

HOPE. 7s. H. POND.

1. { "Joy to those that love the Lord!" Saith the sure e-ter-nal word;
     Not of earth the joy it brings, Tempered in ce - - - - - les-tial springs.
D.C. 'Tis the joy that fills the breast, When the pas-sions - - - - - sink to rest.

2. 'Tis the joy of par-doned sin, When we feel 'tis well with-in.

641. 7s.

3. 'Tis a joy, that seated deep,
   Leaves not when we sigh and weep;
   Spreads itself in virtuous deeds,
   Sighs for woe, in pity bleeds.

4. Stern and awful are its tones
   When the patriot martyr groans,
   And the death-pulse beating high,
   Rapture blends with agony.

5. Tend'rer is the form it wears,
   Touch'd in love, dissolved in tears,
   When, subdued, at Jesus' feet,
   Sinners clasp the mercy-seat.

6. Joy e'en here! a budding flower,
   Struggling with the storm and shower,
   Till its season to expand,
   Planted in its native land.

642. 7s. Single.

1. CHRIST, of all my hopes the ground—
   Christ, the spring of all my joy!
   Still in Thee let me be found,
   Still for Thee my powers employ.

2. Fountain of o'erflowing grace!
   Freely from Thy fullness give;
   Till I close my earthly race,
   Be it "Christ for me to live!"

3. Firmly trusting in Thy blood,
   Nothing shall my heart confound;
   Safely I shall pass the flood,
   Safely reach Immanuel's ground.

4. When I touch the blessed shore,
   Back the closing waves shall roll;
   Death's dark stream shall never more
   Part from Thee my ravished soul.

5. Thus—O thus an entrance give
   To the land of cloudless sky;
   Having known it, "Christ to live,"
   Let me know it "gain to die."
   WINDHAM.

643. 7s. 6 lines.

1. CHRIST, whose glory fills the skies,
   Christ, the true, the only light,
   Sun of Righteousness, arise,
   Triumph o'er the shades of night;
   Day-spring from on high be near,
   Day-star in my heart appear.

2. Dark and cheerless is the morn,
   If Thy light is hid from me;
   Joyless is the day's return,
   Till Thy mercy's beams I see;
   Till they inward light impart,
   Warmth and gladness to my heart.

3. Visit, then, this soul of mine;
   Pierce the gloom of sin and grief;
   Fill me, radiant Sun divine;
   Scatter all my unbelief;
   More and more Thyself display,
   Shining to the perfect day.
   C. WESLEY.

CHRISTIAN EXPERIENCE.

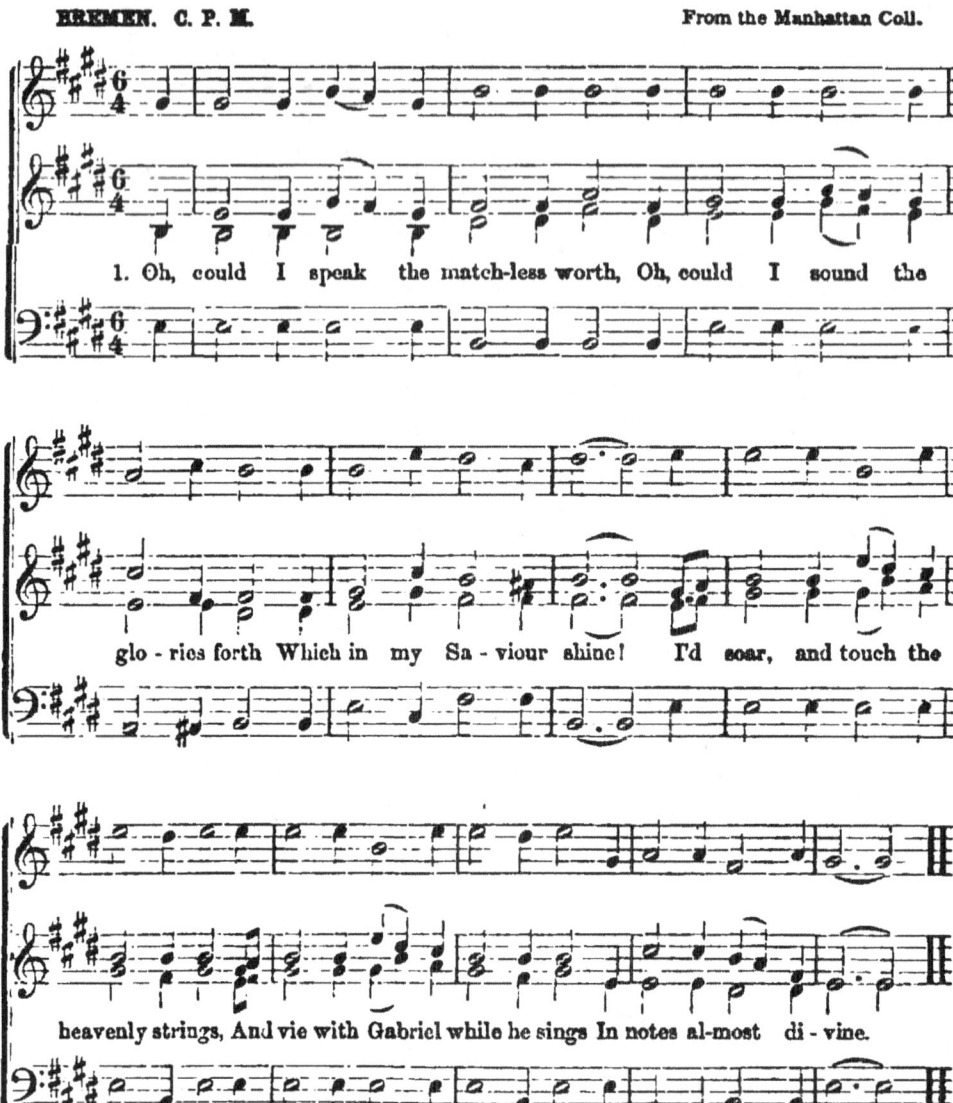

BREMEN. C. P. M.   From the Manhattan Coll.

1. Oh, could I speak the matchless worth, Oh, could I sound the glories forth Which in my Saviour shine! I'd soar, and touch the heavenly strings, And vie with Gabriel while he sings In notes almost divine.

614. C. P. M.

2. I'd sing the precious blood He spilt,
My ransom from the dreadful guilt
  Of sin and wrath divine:
I'd sing His glorious righteousness,
In which all perfect, heavenly dress,
  My soul shall ever shine.

3. I'd sing the characters He bears,
And all the forms of love He wears,
  Exalted on His throne:
In loftiest songs of sweetest praise,
I would to everlasting days
  Make all His glories known.

4. Well, the delightful day will come
When my dear Lord will bring me home,
  And I shall see His face;
Then with my Saviour, Brother, Friend,
A blest eternity I'll spend,
  Triumphant in His grace.

MEDLEY.

615. C. P. M.

1. How happy are the new-born race,
Partakers of adopting grace!
  How pure the bliss they share!
Hid from the world and all its eyes,
Within their heart the blessing lies,
  And conscience feels it there.

2. The moment we believe, 't is ours;
And if we love with all our powers
  The God from whom it came,
And if we serve with hearts sincere,
'T is still discernable and clear,
  An undisputed claim.

3. O messenger of dear delight!
Whose voice dispels the deepest night,
  Sweet, peace-proclaiming Dove!
With thee at hand to soothe our pains,
No wish unsatisfied remains,
  No task but that of love.
              MADAME GUION.

616. C. P. M.

1. LORD, thou hast won—at length I yield;
My heart, by mighty grace compelled,
  Surrenders all to Thee:
Against Thy terrors long I strove,
But who can stand against Thy love?—
  Love conquers even me.

2. But since Thou hast Thy love reveal'd,
And shown my soul a pardon seal'd,
  I can resist no more;
Couldst Thou for such a sinner bleed?
Canst Thou for such a rebel plead?
  I wonder and adore!

3. If Thou hadst bid Thy thunders roll,
And lightnings flash to blast my soul,
  I still had stubborn been:
But mercy has my heart subdued,
A bleeding Saviour I have viewed,
  And now, I hate my sin.

4. Now, Lord, I would be Thine alone—
Come, take possession of Thine own,
  For Thou hast set me free;
Released from Satan's hard command,
See all my powers in waiting stand,
  To be employed by Thee.
              NEWTON.

617. C. P. M.

1. O LOVE divine, how sweet Thou art!
When shall I find my willing heart
  All taken up in Thee?
I thirst, I faint, I die to prove
The greatness of redeeming love,
  The love of Christ to me.

2. Stronger his love than death or hell;
Its riches are unsearchable:
  The first-born sons of light
Desire in vain its depths to see;
They can not reach the mystery,
  The length, the breadth, the height.

3. God only knows the love of God;
O that it now were shed abroad
  In this poor stony heart!
For this I sigh; for Thee I pine;
This only portion, Lord, be mine,
  Be mine the better part!

4. O that I could for ever sit,
With Mary at the Master's feet!
  Be this my happy choice,
My only care, delight, and bliss,
My joy, my heaven on earth be this,
  To hear the Bridegroom's voice!

5. O that I could, with favor'd John,
Recline my weary head upon
  The dear Redeemer's breast:
From care, and sin, and sorrow free,
Give me! O Lord, to find in Thee
  My everlasting rest!
              C. WESLEY.

618. C. P. M.

1. SELF-LOVE no grace in sorrow sees,
Consults her own peculiar ease—
  'T is all the bliss she knows;
But nobler aims true Love employ—
In self-denial is her joy,
  In suffering her repose.

2. Sorrow and Love go side by side;
Nor height nor depth can e'er divide
  Their heaven-appointed bands;
Those dear associates still are one,
Nor, till the race of life is run,
  Disjoin their wedded hands.

3. Thy choice and mine shall be the same,
Inspirer of that holy flame,
  Which must for ever blaze!
To take the cross and follow Thee,
Where love and duty lead, shall be
  My portion and my praise.
              MADAME GUION.

DOXOLOGY. C. P. M.

To Father, Son, and Holy Ghost,
Be praise amid the heavenly host,
  And in the church below;
From whom all creatures draw their breath,
By whom redemption blessed the earth,
  From whom all comforts flow.

BARTIMEUS. 7s.

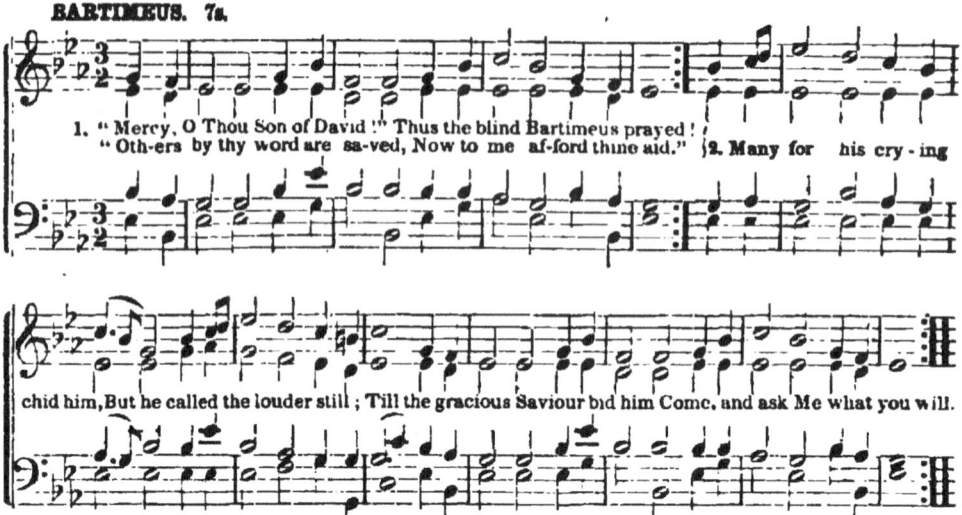

1. "Mercy, O Thou Son of David!" Thus the blind Bartimeus prayed!
"Others by thy word are saved, Now to me afford thine aid."
2. Many for his crying chid him, But he called the louder still; Till the gracious Saviour bid him Come, and ask Me what you will.

649. 8s & 7s.

3. Money was not what he wanted,
   Though by begging used to live;
But he asked, and Jesus granted
   Alms which none but He could give.

4. "Lord, remove this grievous blindness,
   Let my eyes behold the day!"
Straight he saw, and, won by kindness,
   Followed Jesus in the way.

5. Oh! methinks I hear him praising,
   Publishing to all around:
"Friends, is not my case amazing?
   What a Saviour I have found!

6. "Oh! that all the blind but knew Him,
   And would be advised by me!
Surely they would hasten to him,
   He would cause them all to see."
                                    NEWTON.

650. 8s & 7s.

1. Come, thou Fount of every blessing,
   Tune my heart to sing Thy grace;
Streams of mercy never ceasing,
   Call for songs of loudest praise.

2. Teach me some melodious sonnet,
   Sung by flaming tongues above:
Praise, the mount—I'm fixed upon it—
   Mount of God's unchanging love.

3. Here I raise my Ebenezer;
   Hither by Thine help I'm come;
And I hope, by Thy good pleasure,
   Safely to arrive at home.

4. Jesus sought me when a stranger,
   Wandering from the fold of God;
He, to save my soul from danger,
   Interposed His precious blood.

5. Oh! to grace how great a debtor
   Daily I'm constrained to be!
Let that grace now, like a fetter,
   Bind my wandering heart to Thee.

6. Prone to wander, Lord, I feel it—
   Prone to leave the God I love—
Here's my heart—O take and seal it;
   Seal it from Thy courts above.
                                    ROBINSON.

651. 8s & 7s.

1. God is love; His mercy brightens
   All the path in which we rove;
Bliss He wakes, and woe He lightens;
   God is wisdom, God is love.

2. Chance and change are busy ever;
   Man decays, and ages move;
But His mercy waneth never;
   God is wisdom, God is love.

3. E'en the hour that darkest seemeth,
   Will His changeless goodness prove;
From the gloom His brightness streameth;
   God is wisdom, God is love.

4. He with earthly cares entwineth
   Hope and comfort from above:
Every where His glory shineth;
   God is wisdom, God is love.
                                    BOWRING.

PRAISE, JOY, CONFLICT, ETC.

CUYLER. 8s.   T. HASTINGS.

1. My gracious Redeemer I love, His praises aloud I'll proclaim:
And join with the armies above, To shout His adorable name.

2. To gaze on His glories divine Shall be my eternal employ;
To see them incessantly shine, My boundless, ineffable joy.

652. 8s.

3. He freely redeemed, with His blood,
My soul from the confines of hell,
To live on the smiles of my God,
And in His sweet presence to dwell.

4. To shine with the angels in light,
With saints and with seraphs to sing,
To view, with eternal delight,
My Jesus, my Saviour, my King.

5. Ye palaces, sceptres, and crowns,
Your pride with disdain I survey;
Your pomps are but shadows and sounds,
And pass in a moment away.

6. The crown that my Saviour bestows,
Yon permanent sun shall outshine;
My joy everlastingly flows—
My God, my Redeemer is mine.

FRANCIS.

653. 8s.

1. INSPIRER and hearer of prayer,
Thou Shepherd and Guardian of Thine,
My all to Thy covenant care
I sleeping or waking resign.

2. If Thou art my shield and my sun,
The night is no darkness to me;
And, fast as my moments roll on,
They bring me but nearer to Thee.

3. Thy ministering spirits descend
To watch while Thy saints are asleep;
By day and by night they attend,
The heirs of salvation to keep.

4. Bright seraphs, dispatched from the throne,
Repair to their stations assigned;
And angels elect are sent down
To guard the elect of mankind.

5. Their worship no interval knows;
Their fervor is still on the wing;
And, while they protect my repose,
They chant to the praise of my King.

6. I, too, at the season ordained,
Their chorus for ever shall join,
And love and adore, without end,
Their faithful Creator and mine.

TOPLADY.

654. 8s.

1. THE winter is over and gone,
The thrush whistles sweet on the spray,
The turtle breathes forth her soft moan,
The lark mounts and warbles away.

2. Shall every creature around
Their voices in concert unite,
And I, the most favored, be found
In praising to take less delight?

3. Awake, then, my harp, and my lute!
Sweet organs your notes softly swell!
No longer my lips shall be mute,
The Saviour's high praises to tell.

4. His love in my heart shed abroad,
My graces shall bloom as the spring;
This temple, His spirit's abode;
My joy as my duty to sing.

HAWES.

CHRISTIAN EXPERIENCE.

WILLIS. 7s. — R. Storrs Willis.

1. Now begin the heavenly theme, Sing aloud in Jesus' name! Ye, who His salvation prove, Triumph in redeeming love, Triumph in redeeming love.

655. 7s.

1. Now begin the heavenly theme,
Sing aloud in Jesus' name!
Ye, who His salvation prove,
Triumph in redeeming love.

2. Ye who see the Father's grace
Beaming in the Saviour's face,
As to Canaan on ye move,
Praise and bless redeeming love.

3. Mourning souls dry up your tears;
Banish all your guilty fears;
See your guilt and curse remove,
Cancelled by redeeming love.

4. Hither, then, your tribute bring,
Strike aloud each joyful string;
Saints below, and saints above,
Join to praise redeeming love.

LANGFORD.

CORAL. 12s & 11s.

1. As down in the sunless retreats of the ocean, Sweet flowers are springing no mortal can see, So, deep in my heart, the still pray'r of devotion, Unheard by the world, rises silent to Thee, My God! Silent to Thee, Pure, warm, silent to Thee.

656. 12s & 11s.

1. As down in the sunless retreats of the ocean,
Sweet flowers are springing no mortal can see,
So, deep in my heart, the still prayer of devotion,
Unheard by the world, rises silent to Thee,
My God! silent to Thee—
Pure, warm, silent to Thee.

2. As still to the star of its worship, though clouded,
The needle points faithfully o'er the dim sea,
So, dark as I roam, through this wintry world shrouded,
The hope of my spirit turns trembling, to Thee,
My God! trembling to Thee—
True, fond, trembling to Thee.

MOORE.

PRAISE, JOY, CONFLICT, ETC.

JACKSONVILLE. 8s & 7s.   Hymn 657.

1. Thro' the day Thy love has spared us, Now we lay us down to rest,
2. Pilgrims thro' this world and strangers, Toil-ing in the midst of foes,

Thro' the si-lent watches guard us, Let no foe our peace molest;
Us and ours pre-serve from dangers, And our trust in Thee re-pose;

Je-sus now our Sa-viour be, Sweet it is to trust in Thee.
And when life's short day is past, Rest with Thee in heav'n at last.

CRUSADER'S HYMN. 5s, 6s & 8s.   Hymn 658.   Arranged by R. STORRS WILLIS.

1. Fairest Lord Je-sus! Ruler of all nature! O Thou of God and man the Son!
2. Fair are the meadows, Fairer still the woodlands, Rob'd in the blooming garb of spring;
3. Fair is the sunshine, Fairer still the moonlight, And the twinkling star-ry host;

Thee will I cher-ish, Thee will I hon-or, Thou! my soul's glory, joy, and crown.
Je-sus is fair-er, Je-sus is pur-er, Who makes the woful heart to sing.
Je-sus shines brighter, Je-sus shines purer Than all the angels heav'n can boast.

CHRISTIAN EXPERIENCE.

659. 8s, 7s & 4s.

1. Welcome, welcome, dear Redeemer,
    Welcome to this heart of mine;
   Lord, I make a full surrender,
    Every power and thought be Thine;
     Thine entirely,
    Through eternal ages, Thine.

2. Known to all to be Thy mansion,
    Earth and hell will disappear;
   Or in vain attempt possession,
    When they find the Lord is near—
     Shout, O Zion!
    Shout, ye saints, the Lord is here!

660. 8s & 7s.

1. Love divine, all love excelling,
    Joy of heaven, to earth come down!
   Fix in us Thy humble dwelling,
    All Thy faithful mercies crown;

2. Jesus! Thou art all compassion,
    Pure, unbounded love Thou art;
   Visit us with Thy salvation,
    Enter every trembling heart.

3. Breathe, O breathe Thy loving Spirit
    Into every troubled breast!
   Let us all in Thee inherit,
    Let us find Thy promised rest.

4. Come, Almighty to deliver,
    Let us all Thy grace receive!
   Suddenly return, and never,
    Never more Thy temples leave!

5. Finish then Thy new creation,
    Pure, and spotless may we be;
   Let us see our whole salvation
    Perfectly secured by Thee!

6. Changed from glory into glory,
    Till in heaven we take our place;
   Till we cast our crowns before Thee,
    Lost in wonder, love, and praise.
                                        C. WESLEY.

661. 8s & 7s.

1. Come, Thou long-expected Jesus,
    Born to set Thy people free;
   From our fears and sins release us,
    Let us find our rest in Thee.

2. Israel's Strength and Consolation,
    Hope of all the saints Thou art;
   Dear Desire of every nation,
    Joy of every longing heart.

3. Born, Thy people to deliver;
    Born a child—and yet a King;
   Born to reign in us for ever,
    Now Thy precious kingdom bring.

4. By Thine own eternal Spirit,
    Rule in all our hearts alone;
   By Thine all-sufficient merit,
    Raise us to Thy glorious throne.

   MADAN'S COLL.

662. 8s & 7s.

1. Jesus, who on Calvary's mountain
    Poured Thy precious blood for me,
   Wash me in its flowing fountain,
    That my soul may spotless be.

2. I have sinned, but Oh, restore me;
    For unless Thou smile on me,
   Dark is all the world before me,
    Darker yet eternity!

3. In Thy word I hear Thee saying,
    Come and I will give you rest;
   And the gracious call obeying,
    See, I hasten to Thy breast.

4. Grant, Oh grant Thy Spirit's teaching,
    That I may not go astray,
   Till the gate of heaven reaching,
    Earth and sin are passed away.

663. 8s & 7s.

1. Sweet the moments, rich in blessing,
    Which before the cross I spend;
   Life, and health, and peace possessing,
    From the sinner's dying Friend.

2. Here I'll sit, for ever viewing
    Mercy streaming in His blood;
   Precious drops! my soul bedewing,
    Plead and claim my peace with God.

3. Truly blessed is this station,
    Low before His cross to lie;
   While I see divine compassion
    Floating in His languid eye.

4. Here it is I find my heaven,
    While upon the cross I gaze;
   Love I much? I've much forgiven,
    I'm a miracle of grace.

5. Love and grief my heart dividing,
    With my tears His feet I'll bathe;
   Constant still in faith abiding,
    Life deriving from His death.

6. Lord! in ceaseless contemplation,
    Fix my heart and eyes on Thine,
   Till I taste Thy whole salvation,
    Where, unveiled, Thy glories shine.

   BEATTY.

664. 8s & 7s.

1. Crown His head with endless blessing,
    Who, in God the Father's name,
   With compassion never ceasing,
    Comes, salvation to proclaim.

2. Lo, Jehovah, we adore Thee—
    Thee, our Saviour—Thee, our God;
   From Thy throne let beams of glory
    Shine through all the world abroad.

3. Jesus! Thee our Saviour hailing,
    Thee our God in praise we own;
   Highest honors, never failing,
    Rise eternal round Thy throne.

4. Now, ye saints, His power confessing,
    In your grateful strains adore;
   For His mercy, never ceasing,
    Flows, and flows for evermore.

   PRATT'S COLL.

665. 8s & 7s. 6 lines.

1. One there is, above all others,
    Well deserves the name of Friend;
   His is love beyond a brother's,
    Costly, free, and knows no end;
   They who once His kindness prove,
   Find it everlasting love.

2. Which of all our friends, to save us,
    Could or would have shed his blood?
   But our Jesus died to have us
    Reconciled in Him to God;
   This was boundless love indeed,
   Jesus is a Friend in need!

3. When He lived on earth abased,
    Friend of sinners was His name;
   Now above all glory raised,
    He rejoices in the same;
   Still He calls them "Brethren—friends,"
   And to all their wants attends.

4. O, for grace our hearts to soften!
    Teach us, Lord, at length to love;
   We alas! forget too often,
    What a Friend we have above;
   But when home our souls are brought,
   We will love Thee as we ought.

   NEWTON.

666. H. M.

1. Come, every pious heart,
    That loves the Saviour's name!
   Your noblest powers exert
    To celebrate His fame;
   Tell all above, and all below,
   The debt of love to Him you owe.

2. He left His starry crown,
    And laid His robes aside;
   On wings of love came down,
    And wept, and bled, and died:
   What He endured, no tongue can tell,
   To save our souls from death and hell.

3. From the dark grave He rose,—
    The mansion of the dead;
   And thence His mighty foes
    In glorious triumph led;
   Up through the sky the conqueror rode,
   And reigns on high, the Saviour-God.

4. From thence He'll quickly come,—
    His chariot will not stay,—
   And bear our spirits home
    To realms of endless day:
   There shall we see His lovely face,
   And ever be in His embrace.

STENNETT.

667. H. M.

1. Ye dying sons of men.—
    Immerged in sin and woe,
   The gospel's voice attend,
    While Jesus sends to you;
   Ye perishing and guilty, come;
   In Jesus' arms there yet is room.

2. No longer now delay,
    Nor vain excuses frame:
   He bids you come to-day,
    Though poor, and blind, and lame:
   All things are ready; sinners, come;
   For every trembling soul there's room.

3. Believe the heavenly word
    His messengers proclaim;
   He is a gracious Lord,
    And faithful is His name.
   Backsliding souls, return and come;
   Cast off despair; there yet is room.

4. Compelled by bleeding love,
    Ye wandering sheep, draw near;
   Christ calls you from above;
    His charming accents hear;
   Let whosoever will now come:
   In mercy's breast there still is room.

BODEN.

668. H. M.

1. Jesus, at thy command,
    I launch into the deep,
And leave my native land,
    Where sin lulls all asleep.
For Thee I would the world resign,
And sail to heaven with Thee and Thine.

2. Thou art my pilot—wise,
    My compass is Thy word:
My soul each storm defies,
    While I have such a Lord;
I'll trust Thy faithfulness and power,
To save me in the trying hour.

3. Though rocks and quicksands deep,
    Through all my passage lie,
Yet Christ will safely keep,
    And guide me with His eyes:
My anchor-hope, will firm abide,
And ev'ry bois'trous storm outride.

4. Whene'er becalm'd I lie,
    And storms forbear to toss,
Be Thou, dear Lord, still nigh,
    Lest I should suffer loss;
For more the treach'rous calm I dread,
Than tempests bursting o'er my head.

5. By faith I see the land,
    The port of endless rest;
My soul, thy sails expand,
    And fly to Jesus' breast!
Oh may I reach the heavenly shore
Where winds and waves disturb no more
TOPLADY.

669. H. M.

1. Arise, my soul, arise,
    Shake off thy guilty fears;
The bleeding Sacrifice
    In my behalf appears;
Before the throne my Surety stands;
My name is written on His hands.

2. He ever lives above,
    For me to intercede,
His all-redeeming love,
    His precious blood to plead;
His blood atoned for all our race,
And sprinkles now the throne of grace.

3. My God is reconciled;
    His pardoning voice I hear;
He owns me for his child,—
    I can no longer fear;
His Spirit answers to the blood,
And tells me "Thou art born of God."
C. WESLEY.

670. H. M.

1. My Shepherd's name is Love—
    Jehovah, God above;
Where tender herbage grows,
    And peaceful water flows,
He gently leads, He kindly feeds,
And lulls me then to sweet repose.

2. If e'er I heedless stray,
    He shows my feet the way;
Yea, though through dreary glades,
    I walk in dismal shades,
No harm I fear, for Thou art near,
Thy faithful staff my progress aids.

3. When raging foes surround,
    My comforts still abound;
I breath a fragrant air,
    And feed on sweetest fare;
Thus in Thy fold, when worn and old,
I'll dwell secure beneath Thy care.
HATFIELD.

671. H. M.

1. Come, my fond, fluttering heart!
    Come, struggle to be free;
Thou and the world must part,
    However hard it be:
My trembling spirit owns it just,
But cleaves yet closer to the dust.

2. Ye tempting sweets! forbear;
    Ye dearest idols! fall;
My love ye must not share,
    Jesus shall have it all:
'Tis bitter pain,—'tis cruel smart,—
But, ah! thou must consent, my heart!

3. Ye fair, enchanting throng!
    Ye golden dreams! farewell!
Earth has prevailed too long,
    And now I break the spell:
Farewell, ye joys of early years!
Jesus! forgive these parting tears.

4. In Gilead there is balm,
    A kind Physician there
My fevered mind to calm,
    And bid me not despair:
Aid me, dear Saviour! set me free;
My all I would resign to Thee.

5. Oh! may I feel Thy worth,
    And let no idol dare—
No vanity of earth
    With Thee, my Lord! compare:
Now bid all worldly joys depart,
And reign supremely in my heart.
JANE TAYLOR.

LISCHER. H. M.   From the German by L. Mason

1. O, Zion, tune thy voice, And raise thy hands on high;
Tell all the earth thy joys, And boast salvation nigh.
Cheerful in God, arise and shine, While rays divine stream all abroad, While rays divine stream all abroad.

672. H. M.

2. He gilds thy mourning face
  With beams that can not fade;
His all-resplendent grace
  He pours around thy head;
The nations round thy form shall view,
With lustre new divinely crowned.

3. In honor to His name
  Reflect that sacred light;
And loud that grace proclaim,
  Which makes thy darkness bright;
Pursue His praise till sovereign love,
In worlds above, the glory raise.

4. There on His holy hill
  A brighter sun shall rise,
And with His radiance fill
  Those fairer, purer skies;
While round His throne ten thousand stars,
In nobler spheres, His influence own.
                 DODDRIDGE.

673. H. M.

1. To heaven I lift mine eyes;
  From God is all my aid—
The God who built the skies,
  And earth and nature made;
God is the tower to which I fly;
His grace is nigh in every hour.

2. My feet shall never slide,
  And fall in fatal snares,
Since God, my Guard and Guide,
  Defends me from my fears.
Those wakeful eyes, which never sleep,
Shall Israel keep when dangers rise.

3. No burning heats by day,
  Nor blasts of evening air,
Shall take my health away,
  If God be with me there;
Thou art my sun, and Thou my shade,
To guard my head by night or noon.

4. Hast Thou not pledged Thy word
  To save my soul from death?
And I can trust my Lord
  To keep my mortal breath.
I'll go and come, nor fear to die,
Till from on high Thou call me home.
                 WATTS.

PRAISE, JOY, CONFLICT, ETC.

674.

1. O Thou Almighty Father,
   Come help me now to praise Thy glory,
      Methinks I hear, &c.

2. O come, Thou living Saviour,
   Come help me now to love Thee truly,
      Methinks I hear, &c.

3. O come, Thou Holy Spirit,
   Inflame my soul with heav'nly fire,
      Methinks, &c.

4. O angels and archangels,
   Come help me chant Jehovah's praises,
      Methinks, &c.

5. O all ye Christian heroes,
   Come help me fight the mighty battle,
      Methinks, &c.

6. Burst wide, ye heavenly portals,
   Room for the host of blood-bought conquerors,
      Methinks, &c.

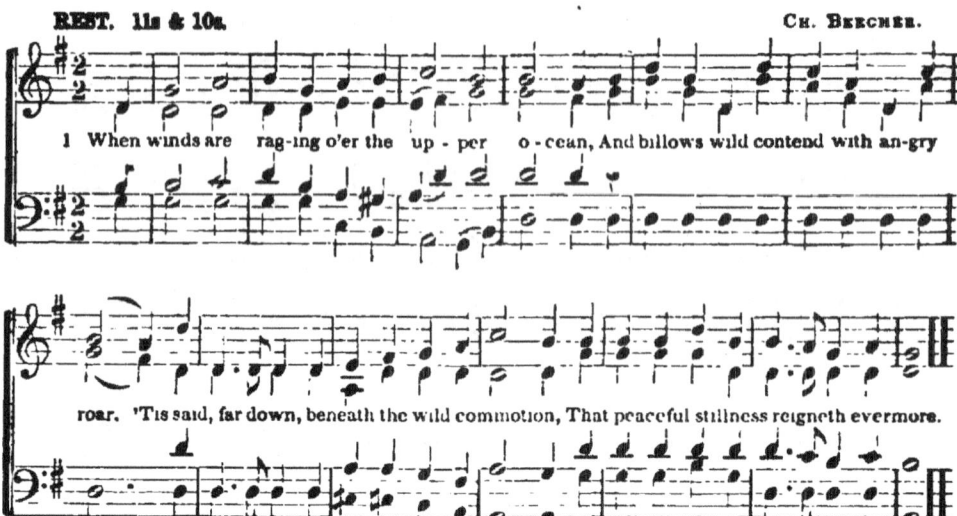

REST. 11s & 10s.   CH. BEECHER.

1. When winds are raging o'er the upper ocean, And billows wild contend with angry roar. 'Tis said, far down, beneath the wild commotion, That peaceful stillness reigneth evermore.

675. 11s & 10s.

2. Far, far beneath, the noise of tempests dieth,
   And silver waves chime ever peacefully,
   And no rude storm, how fierce so e'er it flieth,
   Disturbs the Sabbath of that deeper sea.

3. So to the heart that knows Thy love, O Purest!
   There is a temple, sacred evermore,
   And all the babble of life's angry voices
   Dies in hushed stillness at its peaceful door.

4. Far, far away, the roar of passion dieth,
   And loving thoughts rise calm and peacefully,
   And no rude storm, how fierce so e'er it flieth,
   Disturbs the soul that dwells, O Lord, in Thee.

5. O Rest of rests! O Peace, serene, eternal!
   Thou ever livest, and Thou changest never;
   And in the secret of Thy presence dwelleth
   Fullness of joy, for ever and for ever.
                   MRS. STOWE.

676. 11s & 10s.

1. STILL, still with Thee—when purple morning breaketh,
   When the bird waketh, and the shadows flee;
   Fairer than morning, lovelier than the daylight,
   Dawns the sweet consciousness, I am with Thee!

2. Alone with Thee—amid the mystic shadows,
   The solemn hush of nature newly born;
   Alone with Thee in breathless adoration,
   In the calm dew and freshness of the morn.

3. As in the dawning, o'er the waveless ocean,
   The image of the morning star doth rest,
   So in this stillness, Thou beholdest only
   Thine image in the waters of my breast.

4. Still, still with Thee! as to each new-born morning
   A fresh and solemn splendor still is given,
   So doth this blessed consciousness awaking,
   Breathe, each day, nearness unto Thee and Heaven.

5. When sinks the soul, subdued by toil, to slumber,
   Its closing eye looks up to Thee in prayer,
   Sweet the repose beneath Thy wings o'ershading,
   But sweeter still, to wake and find Thee there.

6. So shall it be at last, in that bright morning,
   When the soul waketh, and life's shadows flee;
   Oh! in that hour, fairer than daylight dawning,
   Shall rise the glorious thought—I am with Thee.
                   MRS. STOWE.

677. 11s.

"Abide in me."

1. THAT mystic word of Thine, O Sovereign Lord!
    Is all too pure, too high, too deep for me;
Weary of striving, and with longing faint,
    I breathe it back again in prayer to Thee.

2. Abide in me—o'ershadow by Thy love,
    Each half-formed purpose and dark thought of sin
Quench, ere it rise, each selfish, low desire,
    And keep my soul as Thine—calm and divine.

3. As some rare perfume in a vase of clay
    Pervades it with a fragrance not its own—
So, when thou dwellest in a mortal soul,
    All heaven's own sweetness seems around it thrown.

4. The soul alone, like a neglected harp,
    Grows out of tune, and needs that Hand divine;
Dwell Thou within it, tune and touch the chords,
    Till every note and string shall answer Thine.

5. Abide in me: there have been moments pure,
    When I have seen Thy face and felt Thy power;
Then evil lost its grasp, and, passion hushed,
    Owned the divine enchantment of the hour.

6. These were but seasons beautiful and rare;
    Abide in me—and they shall ever be;
I pray Thee now fulfill my earnest prayer,
    Come and abide in me, and I in Thee.
    MRS. STOWE.

678. 10s.

1. ABIDE with me! Fast falls the eventide,
    The darkness deepens—Lord, with me abide!
When other helpers fail, and comforts flee,
    Help of the helpless, O abide with me!

2. Swift to its close ebbs out life's little day;
    Earth's joys grow dim, its glories pass away;
Change and decay in all around I see;
    O Thou who changest not, abide with me!

3. I need Thy presence every passing hour:
    What but Thy grace can foil the tempter's power?
Who like Thyself my guide and stay can be?
    On to the close, O Lord, abide with me!
    LYTE.

679. 10s.

1. MY feet are worn and weary with the march
    Over the rough road and up the steep hill-side;
O city of our God! I fain would see
    Thy pastures green, where peaceful waters glide.

2. My hands are weary, toiling on,
    Day after day, for perishable meat;
O city of our God! I fain would rest,—
    I sigh to gain Thy glorious mercy-seat.

3. My garments, travel-worn and stained with dust,
    Oft rent by briers and thorns that crowd my way,
Would fain be made, O Lord, my righteousness!
    Spotless and white in heaven's unclouded ray.

4. My eyes are weary looking at the sin,
    Impiety, and scorn upon the earth;
O city of our God! within Thy walls
    All—all are clothed again with Thy new birth.

5. My heart is weary of its own deep sin,—
    Sinning, repenting, sinning still again;
When shall my soul Thy glorious presence feel,
    And find, dear Saviour, it is free from stain?

6. Patience, poor soul! the Saviour's feet were worn;
    The Saviour's heart and hands were weary too;
His garments stained, and travel-worn, and old;
    His vision blinded with a pitying dew.

7. Love thou the path of sorrow that He trod;
    Toil on, and wait in patience for thy rest;
O city of our God! we soon shall see
    Thy glorious walls,—Home of the loved and blest.

CHRISTIAN EXPERIENCE.

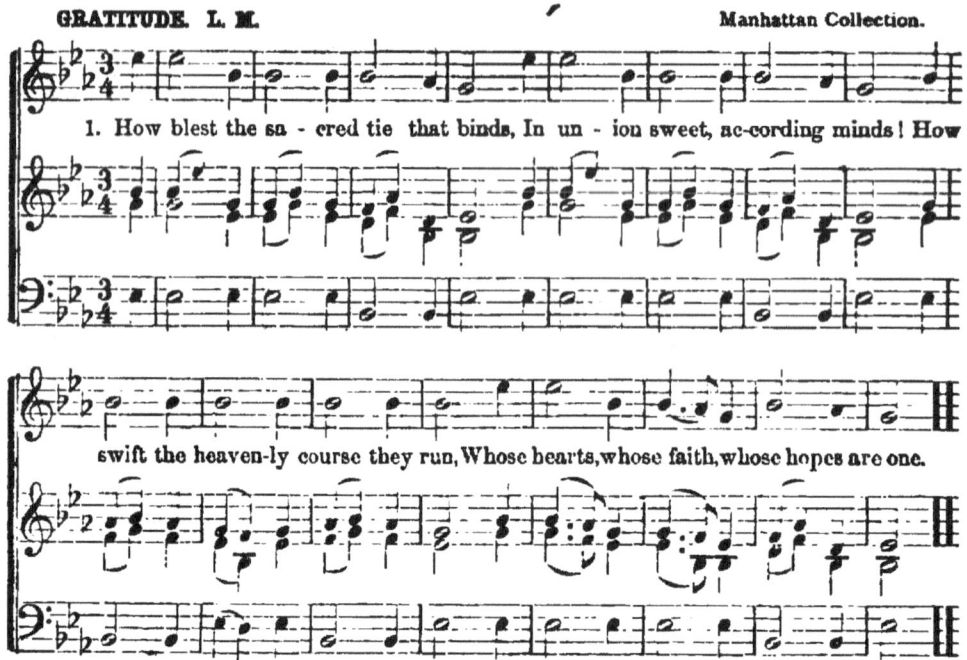

GRATITUDE. L. M. — Manhattan Collection.

1. How blest the sa-cred tie that binds, In un-ion sweet, ac-cording minds! How swift the heaven-ly course they run, Whose hearts, whose faith, whose hopes are one.

680. L. M.

2. To each, the soul of each how dear!
What watchful love, what holy fear!
How doth the gen'rous flame within
Refine from earth, and cleanse from sin!

3. Their streaming eyes together flow
For human guilt and mortal woe;
Their ardent prayers together rise,
Like mingling flames in sacrifice.

4. Together oft they seek the place
Where God reveals His awful face;
How high, how strong their raptures swell,
There's none but kindred souls can tell.

5. Nor shall the glowing flame expire
'Midst nature's drooping, sick'ning fire:
Soon shall they meet in realms above,
A heaven of joy, because of love.
MRS. BARBAULD.

681. L. M.

1. Come in, thou blessed of our God,
In Jesus' name we bid thee come;
No more thy feet shall roam abroad,
Henceforth a brother,—welcome home.

2. Those joys which earth can not afford,
We'll seek in fellowship to prove,
Joined in one spirit to our Lord,
Together bound by mutual love.

3. And while we pass this vale of tears,
We'll make our joys and sorrows known;
We'll share each other's hopes and fears,
And count a brother's cares our own.

4. Once more our welcome we repeat;
Receive assurance of our love;
O may we all together meet
Around the throne of God above!
KELLY.

682. L. M.

1. How blest is he whose tranquil mind,
When life declines, recalls again
The years that time has cast behind,
And reaps delight from toil and pain.

2. So, when the transient storm is past,
The sudden gloom and driving shower,
The sweetest sunshine is the last;
The loveliest is the evening hour.

FELLOWSHIP AND COMMUNION. 217

683. L. M.

1. My God, permit me not to be
A stranger to myself and Thee;
Amid a thousand thoughts I rove,
Forgetful of my highest love.

2. Why should my passions mix with earth,
And thus debase my heavenly birth?
Why should I cleave to things below,
And let my God, my Saviour, go?

3. Call me away from flesh and sense;
One sovereign word can draw me thence;
I would obey the voice divine,
And all inferior joys resign.

4. Be earth, with all her scenes withdrawn;
Let noise and vanity be gone:
In secret silence of the mind
My heaven, and there my God, I find.
WATTS.

684. L. M.

1. Great Shepherd of Thine Israel,
Who didst between the cherubs dwell,
And lead the tribes, Thy chosen sheep,
Safe through the desert and the deep:—

2. Thy church is in the desert now;
Shine from on high and guide us through;
Turn us to Thee, Thy love restore,—
We shall be saved and sigh no more.

3. Great God, whom heavenly hosts obey,
How long shall we lament and pray,
And wait in vain Thy kind return?
How long shall thy fierce anger burn?

4. Instead of wine and cheerful bread,
Thy saints with their own tears are fed;
Turn us to Thee, Thy love restore,—
We shall be saved and sigh no more.
WATTS.

685. L. M.

1. Kindred in Christ! for His dear sake
A hearty welcome here receive;
May we together now partake
The joys which only He can give.

2. May He, by whose kind care we meet,
Send His good Spirit from above;
Make our communications sweet,
And cause our hearts to burn with love.

3. Forgotten be each worldly theme,
When Christians meet together thus;
We only wish to speak of Him,
Who lived, and died, and reigns, for us.

4. We'll talk of all He did and said,
And suffered for us here below;—
The path He marked for us to tread,
And what He's doing for us now.

5. Thus,—as the moments pass away,—
We'll love, and wonder, and adore;
And hasten on the glorious day,
When we shall meet to part no more.
NEWTON.

686. L. M.

1. What various hind'rances we meet,
In coming to a mercy seat!
Yet who that knows the worth of prayer,
But wishes to be often there?

2. Prayer makes the darkened clouds withdraw;
Prayer climbs the ladder Jacob saw,
Gives exercise to faith and love,
Brings every blessing from above.

3. Restraining prayer, we cease to fight;
Prayer makes the Christian's armor bright;
And Satan trembles when he sees
The weakest saint upon his knees.

4. Have you no words? Ah, think again;
Words flow apace when you complain,
And fill a fellow-creature's ear
With the sad tale of all your care.

5. Were half the breath thus vainly spent,
To heaven in supplication sent,
Our cheerful song would oftener be,
"Hear what the Lord hath done for me."
COWPER.

Doxology. L. M.

Oh, may Thy grace on us bestow,
The Father and the Son to know,
And Thee through endless times confess'd
Of Both th' eternal Spirit blest.

All glory while the ages run
Be to the Father, and the Son
Who rose from death; the same to Thee,
O Holy Ghost, eternally.

CHRISTIAN EXPERIENCE.

GEER. C. M. — Greatorex's Coll.

1. While Thee I seek, protecting Power, Be my vain wishes still'd;
And may this consecrated hour With better hopes be fill'd.

687. C. M.

2. Thy love the powers of thought bestowed!
To Thee my thoughts would soar;
Thy mercy o'er my life has flowed;
That mercy I adore.

3. In each event of life, how clear
Thy ruling hand I see!
Each blessing to my soul more dear,
Because conferred by Thee.

4. In every joy that crowns my days,
In every pain I bear,
My heart shall find delight in praise,
Or seek relief in prayer.

5. When gladness wings my favored hour,
Thy love my thoughts shall fill;
Resigned, when storms of sorrow lower,
My soul shall meet Thy will.

6. My lifted eye, without a tear,
The gathering storm shall see;
My steadfast heart shall know no fear;
That heart shall rest on Thee.
MISS H. M. WILLIAMS.

688. C. M.

1. O God of Bethel! by whose hand
Thy people still are fed;
Who through this weary pilgrimage
Hast all our fathers led!

2. Our vows our prayers we now present
Before Thy throne of grace;
God of our fathers! be the God
Of their succeeding race.

3. Through each perplexing path of life
Our wandering footsteps guide,
Give us each day our daily bread,
And raiment fit provide.

4. O spread Thy covering wings around,
Till all our wanderings cease,
And, at our Father's loved abode,
Our souls arrive in peace.

5. Such blessings from Thy gracious hand
Our humble prayers implore;
And Thou shalt be our chosen God
And portion evermore.
LOGAN.

689. C. M.

1. How deep and tranquil is the joy
Which Thou hast kindly given
To those who seek Thy presence, Lord,
And tread the path to heaven.

2. 'T is in the silence of the shade
My sober thoughts begin,
And earth's illusive charms appear
But vanity and sin.

3. 'T is here the troubled springs of life
Are calmed to sweetest rest;
The stillness of this hour expels
The tumult of my breast.

4. Far, far above all mortal things
I walk with God alone;
And while He names celestial joys,
I call them all my own.

5. Then let the noisy world pursue
The trifles of a day,—
Mine be the silent, secret joys
That never fade away.
REED.

FELLOWSHIP AND COMMUNION. 219

SEYMOUR. 7s. GREATOREX'S COLL.

1. Come, my soul, thy suit prepare, Jesus loves to answer prayer; He Himself invites thee near, Bids thee ask Him—waits to hear.

690. 7s.

2. With my burden I begin:—
Lord, remove this load of sin!
Let Thy blood, for sinners spilt,
Set my conscience free from guilt!

3. Lord, I come to Thee for rest;
Take possession of my breast;
There, Thy blood-bought right maintain,
And without a rival reign.

4. While I am a pilgrim here,
Let Thy love my spirit cheer;
As my Guide, my Guard, my Friend,
Lead me to my journey's end!

5. Show me what I have to do;
Every hour my strength renew;
Let me live a life of faith,
Let me die Thy people's death.
                                NEWTON.

691. 7s.

1. THEY who seek the throne of grace
Find that throne in every place;
If we live a life of prayer,
God is present every where.

2. In our sickness and our health,
In our want, or in our wealth,
If we look to God in prayer,
God is present every where.

3. When our earthly comforts fail,
When the woes of life prevail,
'Tis the time for earnest prayer;
God is present every where.

4. Then, my soul, in every strait,
To Thy Father come, and wait;
He will answer every prayer:
God is present every where.

692. C. M.

1. To heaven I lift my waiting eyes;
There all my hopes are laid;
The Lord that built the earth and skies
Is my perpetual aid.

2. Their feet shall never slide to fall
Whom He designs to keep;
His ear attends the softest call;
His eyes can never sleep.

3. He will sustain our weakest powers
With His almighty arm,
And watch our most unguarded hours
Against surprising harm.

4. Israel, rejoice, and rest secure;
Thy keeper is the Lord;
His wakeful eyes employ His power
For thine eternal guard.

5. Nor scorching sun, nor sickly moon,
Shall have his leave to smite;
He shields thy head from burning noon,
From blasting damps at night.

6. He guards thy soul, he keeps thy breath,
Where thickest dangers come;
Go and return, secure from death,
Till God commands thee home.
                                WATTS.

CLARENDON. C. M.　　　　　　　　　　I. TUCKER.

1. O for a closer walk with God! A calm and heav'nly frame!
A light to shine upon the road That leads me to the Lamb!

693. C. M.

2. Where is the blessedness I knew
  When first I saw the Lord?
  Where is the soul-refreshing view
  Of Jesus and His word?

3. What peaceful hours I once enjoyed!
  How sweet their memory still!
  But they have left an aching void
  The world can never fill.

4. Return, O holy Dove, return
  Sweet messenger of rest;
  I hate the sins that made Thee mourn,
  And drove Thee from my breast.

5. The dearest idol I have known,
  Whate'er that idol be,
  Help me to tear it from Thy throne,
  And worship only Thee.

6. So shall my walk be close with God,
  Calm and serene my frame;
  So purer light shall mark the road
  That leads me to the Lamb.
  COWPER.

694. C. M.

1. PRAYER is the soul's sincere desire,
  Unuttered or expressed;
  The motion of a hidden fire
  That trembles in the breast.

2. Prayer is the burden of a sigh,
  The falling of a tear;
  The upward glancing of an eye
  When none but God is near.

3. Prayer is the simplest form of speech
  That infant lips can try;
  Prayer the sublimest strains that reach
  The Majesty on high.

4. Prayer is the contrite sinner's voice
  Returning from His ways,
  While angels in their songs rejoice,
  And say—"Behold, he prays"

5. Prayer is the Christian's vital breath,
  The Christian's native air,
  His watchword at the gate of death;
  He enters heaven with prayer.
  MONTGOMERY.

695. C. M.

1. FAR from the world, O Lord, I flee,
  From strife and tumult far;
  From scenes where Satan wages still
  His most successful war.

2. The calm retreat, the silent shade,
  With prayer and praise agree;
  And seem by Thy sweet bounty made
  For those who follow Thee.

3. There, if Thy Spirit touch the soul,
  And grace her mean abode,
  O with what peace, and joy and love,
  She communes with her God!

4. There, like the nightingale she pours
  Her solitary lays;
  Nor asks a witness of her song,
  Nor thirsts for human praise.

5. Author and Guardian of my life!
  Sweet source of light divine,
  And—all harmonious names in one—
  My Saviour, Thou art mine!

6. What thanks I owe Thee, and what love—
  A boundless, endless store—
  Shall echo through the realms above,
  When time shall be no more. COWPER.

696. C. M.

1. SWEET is the prayer whose holy stream
In earnest pleading flows:
Devotion dwells upon the theme,
And warm and warmer glows.

2. Faith grasps the blessing she desires,
Hope points the upward gaze;
And love, untrembling love, inspires
The eloquence of praise.

3. But sweeter far the still small voice,
Heard by no human ear,
When God hath made the heart rejoice,
And dried the bitter tear.

4. Nor accents flow, nor words ascend;
All utterance faileth there;
But listening spirits comprehend,
And God accepts the prayer.

697. C. M.

1. THE bud will soon become a flower,
The flower become a seed,
Then seize, O youth, the present hour,
Of that thou hast most need.

2. Do thy best always—do it now—
For in the present time,
As in the furrows of a plow,
Fall seeds of good or crime.

3. The sun and rain will ripen fast
Each seed that thou hast sown,
And every act and word at last
By its own fruit be known.

4. And soon the harvest of thy toil,
Rejoicing, thou shalt reap,
Or o'er thy wild neglected soil,
Go forth in shame to weep.
JONES VERY.

698. C. M.

1. THOU art my hiding-place, O Lord,
In Thee I fix my trust,
Encouraged by Thy holy word,
A feeble child of dust.

2. I have no argument beside
I urge no other plea,
And 't is enough—the Saviour died,
The Saviour died for me.

3. When storms of fierce temptation beat,
And furious foes assail,
My refuge is the mercy-seat,
My hope within the vail.

4. From strife of tongues and bitter words,
My spirit flies to Thee;
Joy to my heart the thought affords—
My Saviour died for me.

5. And when Thy awful voice commands
This body to decay,
And life, in its last lingering sands,
Is ebbing fast away—

6. Then, though it be in accents weak,
My voice shall call on Thee,
And ask for strength in death to speak—
"My Saviour died for me."
RAFFLES.

699. C. M.

1. GREAT Shepherd of Thy people, hear;
Thy presence now display;
As Thou hast given a place for prayer,
So give us hearts to pray.

2. Show us some token of Thy love,
Our feeble hope to raise;
And pour Thy blessing from above,
That we may render praise.

3. Within these walls let holy peace,
And love and concord dwell;
Here give the troubled conscience ease,
The wounded spirit heal.

4. The hearing ear, the watchful eye,
The contrite heart bestow:
And shine upon us from on high,
To make our graces grow.

5. May we in faith receive Thy word,
In faith address our prayers;
And in the presence of the Lord
Unbosom all our cares.

6. And may Thy Gospel's joyful sound,
Enforced by grace divine,
Awaken many sinners round,
And bend their wills to Thine.
NEWTON.

DOXOLOGY. C. M.

1. HAVE mercy on us, God Most High!
Have mercy upon me,
Have mercy on us worms of earth,
Most Holy Trinity!

2. Most ancient of all mysteries!
Before Thy throne we lie;
Have mercy now, most merciful,
Most Holy Trinity!

CHRISTIAN EXPERIENCE.

OLIVET. 6s & 4s.   Spiritual Songs.

1. My faith looks up to Thee, Thou Lamb of Calvary, Saviour divine: Now hear me while I pray; Take all my guilt away; O let me from this day Be wholly Thine.

700. 6s & 4s.

2. May Thy rich grace impart
Strength to my fainting heart,
  My zeal inspire;
As Thou hast died for me,
O may my love to Thee,
Pure, warm, and changeless be—
  A living fire.

3. While life's dark maze I tread,
And griefs around me spread,
  Be Thou my guide;
Bid darkness turn to day,
Wipe sorrow's tears away,
Nor let me ever stray
  From Thee aside.

4. When ends life's transient dream,
When death's cold, sullen stream
  Shall o'er me roll;
Blest Saviour, then, in love,
Fear and distrust remove;
O bear me safe above—
  A ransomed soul.

                RAY PALMER.

701. 6s & 4s. *

1. Lowly and solemn be
Thy children's cry to Thee,
  Father Divine;
A hymn of suppliant breath,
Owning that life and death
  Alike are Thine!

2. O Father, in that hour,
When earth all helping power
  Shall disavow,—
When spear, and shield, and crown,
In faintness are cast down,—
  Sustain us, Thou!

3. By Him who bowed to take
The death-cup for our sake,
  The thorn, the rod,—
From whom the last dismay
Was not to pass away,
  Aid us, O God!

              MRS. SIGOURNEY.

702. 6s & 4s.

1. Come, all ye saints of God;
Wide through the earth abroad
  Spread Jesus' fame;
Tell what His love has done;
Trust in His name alone;
Shout to His lofty throne,
  "Worthy the Lamb."

2. Hence, gloomy doubts and fears!
Dry up your mournful tears;
  Swell the glad theme;
Praise ye our gracious King,
Strike each melodious string;
Join heart and voice to sing,
  "Worthy the Lamb."

3. Hark! how the choirs above,
Filled with the Saviour's love,
  Dwell on His name!
There, too, may we be found,
With light and glory crowned,
While all the heavens resound,
  "Worthy the Lamb."

              PRATT'S COLL.

* Repeat the fifth line of each verse.

FELLOWSHIP AND COMMUNION.

HEBER. C. M.   GEO. KINGSLEY.

1. Hail, sweetest, dearest tie that binds Our glowing hearts in one;
Hail, sacred hope that tunes our minds To harmony divine.

703. C. M.

1. Hail, sweetest, dearest tie, that binds
Our glowing hearts in one;
Hail, sacred hope! that tunes our minds
To harmony divine.

2. What though the northern wintry blast
Shall howl around our cot;
What though beneath an eastern sun
Be cast our distant lot;

3. No lingering look, no parting sigh,
Our future meeting knows;
There friendship beams from every eye,
And love immortal glows.

4. O sacred hope! O blissful hope!
Which Jesus' grace has given—
The hope, when days and years are past,
We all shall meet in heaven.
    SUTTON.

704. C. M.

1. Let saints below in concert sing
With those to glory gone:
For all the servants of our King,
In earth and heaven are one.

2. One family, we dwell in Him,
One church above, beneath,
Though now divided by the stream,
The narrow stream of death:—

3. One army of the living God,
To his command we bow;
Part of the host have crossed the flood,
And part are crossing now.

4. Some to their everlasting home
This solemn moment fly;
And we are to the margin come,
And soon expect to die.

5. Oh that we now might see our Guide!
O that the word were given!
Come, blessed Lord! the waves divide,
And land us all in heaven.
    C. WESLEY.

705. C. M.

1. Not to the terrors of the Lord,
The tempest, fire, and smoke,—
Not to the thunder of that word
Which God on Sinai spoke,—

2. But we are come to Sion's hill,
The city of our God,
Where milder words declare His will,
And spread His love abroad.

3. Behold the innumerable host
Of angels clothed in light!
Behold the spirits of the just,
Whose faith is turned to sight!

4. Behold the blest assembly there,
Whose names are writ in heaven!
And God, the Judge of all, declare
Their vilest sins forgiven!

5. The saints on earth and all the dead
But one communion make;
All join in Christ, their living Head,
And of His grace partake.

6. In such society as this
My weary soul would rest;
The man that dwells where Jesus is,
Must be for ever blest.
    WATTS.

CHRISTIAN EXPERIENCE.

706. C. M.

1. Our souls, by love together knit,
Cemented, mixed in one,
One hope, one heart, one mind, one voice,
'T is heaven on earth begun.

2. Our hearts have often burned within,
And glowed with sacred fire,
While Jesus spoke, and fed, and bless'd,
And filled the enlarged desire.

3. The little cloud increases still,
The heavens are big with rain;
We haste to catch the teeming shower,
And all its moisture drain.

4. A rill, a stream, a torrent flows!
But pour a mighty flood;
O sweep the nations, shake the earth,
'Till all proclaim Thee, God!

5. And when Thou mak'st Thy jewels up,
And sett'st Thy starry crown;
When all Thy sparkling gems shall shine,
Proclaimed by Thee Thine own;

6. May we, a little band of love,
We sinners, saved by grace,
From glory unto glory changed,
Behold Thee face to face.

MILLER.

707. C. M.

1. BLESS'D be the dear, uniting love,
That will not let us part;
Our bodies may far off remove—
We still are one in heart.

2. Joined in one Spirit to our head,
Where He appoints, we go;
And still in Jesus' footsteps tread,
And show His praise below.

3. Partakers of the Saviour's grace,
The same in mind and heart—
Nor joy, nor grief, nor time, nor place,
Nor life, nor death, can part.

4. But let us hasten to the day
Which shall our flesh restore,
When death shall all be done away,
And we shall part no more.

C. WESLEY.

708. C. M.

1. The glorious universe around,
   The heavens with all their train,
   Sun, moon, and stars, are firmly bound
   In one mysterious chain.

2. The earth, the ocean, and the sky,
   To form one world agree,
   Where all that walk, or swim, or fly,
   Compose one family.

3. In one fraternal bond of love,
   One fellowship of mind,
   The saints below and saints above
   Their bliss and glory find.

4. Here in their house of pilgrimage,
   Thy statutes are their song;
   There, through one bright, eternal age,
   Thy praises they prolong.

   MONTGOMERY.

709. C. M.

1. O, it is joy in one to meet
   Whom one communion blends,
   Council to hold in converse sweet,
   And talk as Christian friends.

2. 'T is joy to think the angel train,
   Who 'mid heaven's temple shine,
   To seek our earthly temples deign,
   And in our anthems join.

3. But chief 't is joy to think that He,
   To whom His church is dear,
   Delights her gathered flock to see,
   Her joint devotions hear.

4. Then who would choose to walk abroad,
   While here such joys are given?
   "This is indeed the house of God,
   And this the gate of heaven!"

   ANCIENT HYMNS.

710. C. M.

1. How sweet and heav'nly is the sight,
   When those that fear the Lord,
   In mutual love and peace unite,
   And thus fulfill His word.

2. When each can feel his brother's sigh,
   And with him bear a part;
   When sorrow flows from eye to eye,
   And joy from heart to heart.

3. When love in one delightful stream
   Through every bosom flows,
   And union sweet, with fond esteem,
   In every action glows.

4. Love is the golden chain that binds
   The happy souls above;
   And he's an heir of heav'n that finds
   His bosom fill'd with love.

   SWAIN.

711. C. M.

1. What poor despised company
   Of travelers are these,
   Who walk in yonder narrow way,
   Along the rugged maze?

2. Ah, those are of a royal line,
   All children of a King;
   Heirs of immortal crowns divine,
   And lo, for joy they sing!

3. But some of them seem poor, distressed,
   And lacking daily bread;
   Ah! they 're of boundless wealth possessed,
   With hidden manna fed.

4. But why keep they that narrow road,
   That rugged, thorny maze?
   Why?—that 's the way their Leader trod;
   They love and keep His ways.

5. Why must they shun the pleasant path,
   That worldlings love so well?
   Because that is the road to death,
   The open road to hell.

712. C. M.

1. How happy every child of grace,
   Who knows His sins forgiven!
   This earth, He cries, is not my place,
   I seek my home in heaven.

2. A country far from mortal sight,
   Yet O, by faith I see
   The land of rest, the saints' delight,
   The heaven prepared for me.

3. O, what a blessed hope is ours!
   While here on earth we stay,
   We more than taste the heavenly powers,
   And ante-date that day.

4. We feel the resurrection near,
   Our life in Christ concealed,
   And with His glorious presence here
   Our earthen vessels filled.

5. O, would He all of heaven bestow!
   Then like our Lord we 'll rise;
   Our bodies, fully ransomed, go
   To take the glorious prize.

6. On Him with rapture then I 'll gaze,
   Who bought the bliss for me,
   And shout and wonder at His grace
   Through all eternity.

   C. WESLEY.

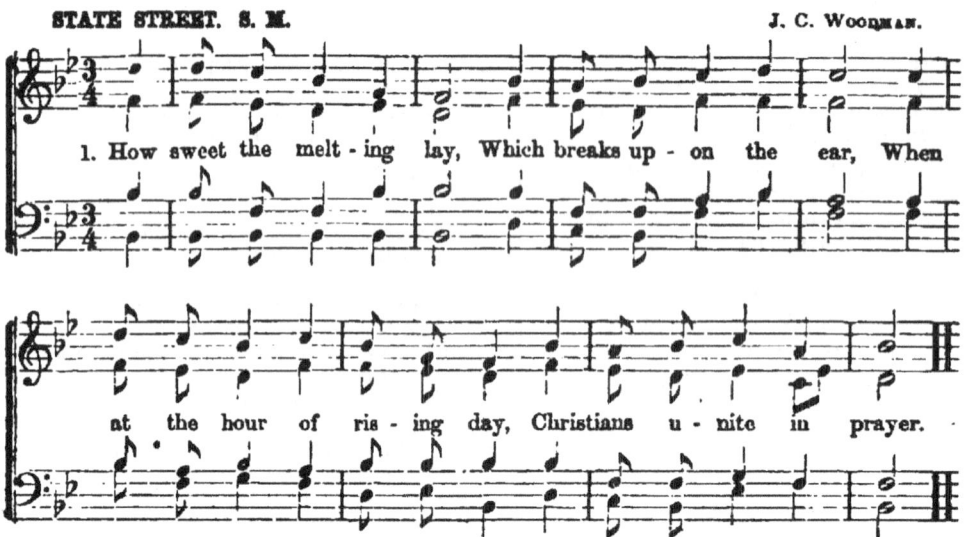

STATE STREET. S. M.   J. C. Woodman.

1. How sweet the melt-ing lay, Which breaks up-on the ear, When at the hour of ris-ing day, Christians u-nite in prayer.

713. S. M.

2. The breezes waft their cries
    Up to Jehovah's throne;
He listens to their humble sighs,
    And sends His blessings down.

3. So Jesus rose to pray,
    Before the morning light,—
Once on the chilling mount did stay,
    And wrestle all the night.

4. So Jesus still doth pray,
    Before the morning bright,
On heavenly mountains far away,
    While we toil here in night.

5. Leave, Lord, Thy vigil there,
    Descend upon life's wave;
Come to the bark through midnight air—
    The storm shall cease to rave.

714. S. M.

1. How charming is the place
    Where my Redeemer God
Unvails the beauties of His face,
    And sheds His love abroad!

2. Not the fair palaces
    To which the great resort,
Are once to be compared with this,
    Where Jesus holds His court.

3. Here on the mercy-seat,
    With radiant glory crowned,
Our joyful eyes behold Him sit,
    And smile on all around.

4. To Him their prayers and cries
    Each humble soul presents;
He listens to their broken sighs,
    And grants them all their wants.

5. Give me, O Lord, a place
    Within Thy bless'd abode,
Among the children of Thy grace,
    The servants of my God.
                                STENNETT.

715. S. M.

1. Jesus, who knows full well
    The heart of every saint,
Invites us all our griefs to tell,
    To pray, and never faint.

2. He bows His gracious ear,
    We never plead in vain:
Yet we must wait till He appear,
    And pray, and pray again.

3. Jesus the Lord will hear
    His chosen when they cry;
Yes, though He may a while forbear,
    He'll help them from on high.

4. His nature, truth, and love,
    Engage Him on their side;
When they are grieved, His bowels move,
    And can they be denied?

5. Then let us earnest be,
    And never faint in prayer;
He loves our importunity,
    And makes our cause His care.
                                WESTON.

FELLOWSHIP AND COMMUNION.

WATCHMAN. S. M.

1. Blest be the tie that binds Our hearts in Christian love; The fellowship of kindred minds Is like to that above.

716. S. M.

2. Before our Father's throne
   We pour our ardent prayers;
Our fears, our hopes, our aims are one,
   Our comforts and our cares.

3. We share our mutual woes,
   Our mutual burdens bear;
And often for each other flows
   The sympathizing tear.

4. When we asunder part,
   It gives us inward pain;
But we shall still be joined in heart,
   And hope to meet again.

5. This glorious hope revives
   Our courage by the way;
While each in expectation lives,
   And longs to see the day.

6. From sorrow, toil, and pain,
   And sin, we shall be free,
And perfect love and friendship reign
   Through all eternity.
                        FAWCETT.

717. S. M.

1. I LOVE Thy kingdom, Lord,
   The house of Thine abode,
The Church, our blest Redeemer saved
   With His own precious blood.

2. I love Thy church, O God!
   Her walls before Thee stand,
Dear as the apple of Thine eye,
   And graven on Thy hand.

3. For her my tears shall fall,
   For her my prayers ascend;
To her my cares and toils be given,
   Till toils and cares shall end.

4. Beyond my highest joy
   I prize her heavenly ways,
Her sweet communion, solemn vows,
   Her hymns of love and praise.

5. Jesus, Thou Friend divine,
   Our Saviour, and our King,
Thy hand from every snare and foe,
   Shall great deliverance bring.

6. Sure as Thy truth shall last,
   To Zion shall be given
The brightest glories earth can yield,
   And brighter bliss of heaven.
                        DWIGHT.

718. S. M.

1. LET party names no more
   The Christian world o'erspread;
Gentile and Jew, and bond and free,
   Are one in Christ, their Head.

2. Among the saints on earth
   Let mutual love be found;
Heirs of the same inheritance,
   With mutual blessings crowned.

3. Thus will the Church below
   Resemble that above,
Where streams of pleasure ever flow,
   And every heart is love.
                        BEDDOME.

CHRISTIAN EXPERIENCE.

719. P. M. 7s.

1. WHEN shall we all meet again?
   When shall we all meet again?
   Oft shall glowing hope expire;
   Oft shall wearied love retire,
      Oft shall death and sorrow reign,
      Ere we all shall meet again.

2. Though on foreign shore we sigh,
   Far remote our native sky;
   Though the depth between us roll,
   Hope shall anchor there our soul,
      And in faith's well known domain,
      Within the vail, we'll meet again.

3. When the dreams of life are fled,
   When its wasted lamps are dead,
   When in cold oblivion's shade
   Beauty, wealth, and fame, are laid,
      Where immortal spirits reign,
      Thither soar, to meet again!

720. 7s.

1. CHILDREN of the heavenly King,
   As ye journey, sweetly sing;
   Sing your Saviour's worthy praise,
   Glorious in His works and ways.

2. Ye are traveling home to God,
   In the way the fathers trod;
   They are happy now—and ye
   Soon their happiness shall see.

3. Shout, ye little flock, and blest;
   You on Jesus' throne shall rest:
   There your seat is now prepared—
   There your kingdom and reward.

4. Fear not, brethren, joyful stand
   On the borders of your land;
   Jesus Christ, your Father's Son,
   Bids you undismayed go on.

5. Lord, submissive make us go,
   Gladly leaving all below;
   Only Thou our leader be,
   And we still will follow Thee.
   CENNICK.

721. 7s.

1. JESUS, Lord, we look to Thee;
   Let us in Thy name agree;
   Show thyself the Prince of Peace;
   Bid our jars for ever cease.

2. By thy reconciling love,
   Every stumbling-block remove:
   Each to each unite, endear;
   Come, and spread Thy banner here.

3. Make us of one heart and mind,—
   Courteous, pitiful, and kind;
   Lowly, meek, in thought and word,—
   Altogether like our Lord.

4. Let us for each other care;
   Each the other's burden bear;
   To Thy Church the pattern give;
   Show how true believers live.

5. Free from anger and from pride,
   Let us thus in God abide;
   All the depths of love express,—
   All the heights of holiness.

6. Let us then with joy remove
   To the family above;
   On the wings of angels fly;
   Show how true believers die.
   C. WESLEY.

FELLOWSHIP AND COMMUNION.

COME HOME. 7s.

1. Brethren, while we sojourn here, Fight we must, but should not fear;
Foes we have, but we've a Friend, One that loves us to the end.
Forward, then, with courage go, Long we shall not dwell below;
Soon the joyful news will come, "Child, your Father calls—come home!"

722. 7s.

2. In the way a thousand snares
Lie, to take us unawares;
Satan, with malicious art,
Watches each unguarded part:
But, from Satan's malice free,
Saints shall soon victorious be;
Soon the joyful news will come,
"Child, your Father calls—come home!"

3. But of all the foes we meet,
None so oft mislead our feet,
None betray us into sin,
Like the foes that dwell within;
Yet let nothing spoil our peace,
Christ shall also conquer these;
Soon the joyful news will come,
"Child, your Father calls—come home!"

723. 7s.

1. WHEN, my Saviour, shall I be
Perfectly resigned to thee?
Poor and vile in my own eyes,
Only in Thy wisdom wise?

2. Only Thee content to know,
Ignorant of all below?
Only guided by Thy light?
Only mighty in Thy might?

3. Fully in my life express
All the heights of holiness;
Sweetly let my spirit prove
All the depths of humble love.

C. WESLEY.

724. 7s.

1. FOR a season called to part,
Let us now ourselves commend
To the gracious eye and heart
Of our ever-present Friend.

2. Jesus, hear our humble prayer:
Tender Shepherd of Thy sheep,
Let Thy mercy and Thy care
All our souls in safety keep.

3. In Thy strength may we be strong;
Sweeten every cross and pain;
Spare us, that we may, ere long,
Meet and worship Thee again.

NEWTON.

CHRISTIAN EXPERIENCE.

PORTUGUESE HYMN. 11s.

1. How firm a foundation, ye saints of the Lord, Is laid for your faith in his excellent word; What more can he say than to you he hath said—Who unto the Saviour, for refuge have fled, Who unto the Saviour for refuge have fled.

725. 11s.

2. Fear not, I am with thee, Oh! be not dismayed;
For I am thy God, and will still give thee aid:
I'll strengthen thee, help thee, and cause thee to stand,
Upheld by My righteous, omnipotent hand.

3. When through the deep waters I call thee to go,
The rivers of sorrow shall not overflow;
For I will be with thee thy trials to bless,
And sanctify to thee thy deepest distress.

4. When through fiery trials thy pathway shall lie,
My grace, all-sufficient, shall be thy supply,
The flame shall not hurt thee; I only design
Thy dross to consume, and thy gold to refine.

5. E'en down to old age all My people shall prove
My sovereign, eternal, unchangeable love;
And then, when gray hairs shall their temples adorn,
Like lambs they shall still in My bosom be borne.

6. The soul that on Jesus hath leaned for repose,
I will not—I will not desert to his foes:
That soul—though all hell should endeavor to shake,
I'll never—no never—no never forsake!
KENNEDY.

726. 11s.

1. DAUGHTER of Zion! awake from thy sadness;
Awake!—for thy foes shall oppress thee no more:
Bright o'er thy hills dawns the day-star of gladness;
Arise!—for the night of thy sorrow is o'er.

2. Strong were thy foes; but the arm that subdued them,
And scattered their legions, was mightier far;
They fled, like the chaff, from the scourge that pursued them;
Vain were their steeds and their chariots of war!

3. Daughter of Zion! the Power that hath saved thee,
Extolled with the harp and the timbrel should be;
Shout!—for the foe is destroyed that enslaved thee,
Th' oppressor is vanquished, and Zion is free.
FITZGERALD'S COLL.

FELLOWSHIP AND COMMUNION.

727. S. M.

1. AND are we yet alive,
   And see each other's face?
   Glory and praise to Jesus give,
   For His redeeming grace.

2. What troubles have we seen!
   What conflicts have we past!
   Fightings without, and fears within,
   Since we assembled last!

3. But out of all, the Lord
   Hath brought us by His love;
   And still He doth His help afford,
   And hides our life above.

4. Then let us make our boast
   Of His redeeming power,
   Which saves us to the uttermost,
   Till we can sin no more.

5. Let us take up the cross,
   Till we the crown obtain;
   And gladly reckon all things loss,
   So we may Jesus gain.

C. WESLEY.

728. S. M.

1. To keep the lamp alive,
   With oil we fill the bowl;
   'T is water makes the willow thrive,
   And grace that feeds the soul.

2. The Lord's unsparing hand
   Supplies the living stream;
   It is not at our own command,
   But still derived from Him.

3. Man's wisdom is to seek
   His strength in God alone;
   And e'en an angel would be weak,
   Who trusted in his own.

4. Retreat beneath His wings,
   And in His grace confide;
   This more exalts the King of kings,
   Than all your works beside.

5. In Jesus is our store;
   Grace issues from His throne;
   Whoever says, "I want no more,"
   Confesses he has none.

COWPER.

CHRISTIAN EXPERIENCE.

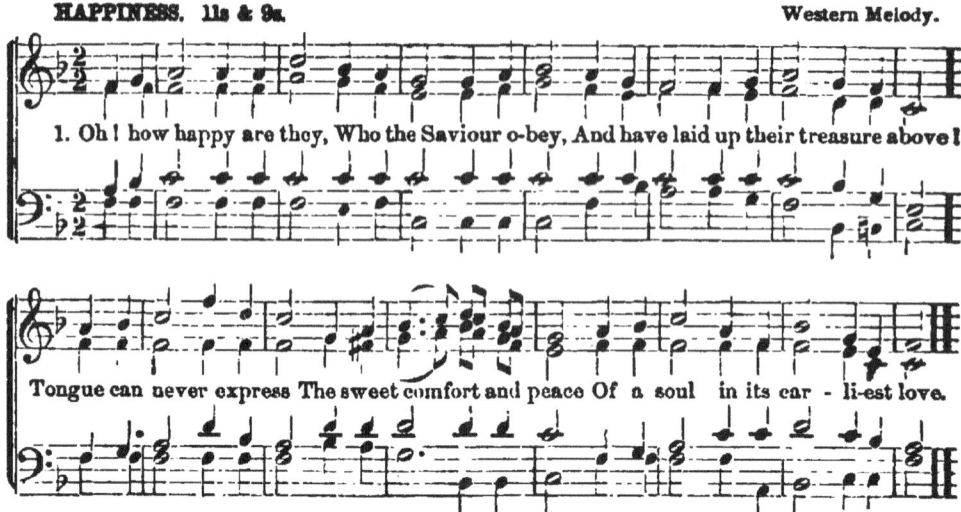

HAPPINESS. 11s & 9s.   Western Melody.

1. Oh! how happy are they, Who the Saviour obey, And have laid up their treasure above! Tongue can never express The sweet comfort and peace Of a soul in its earliest love.

729. 11s & 9s.

1. OH! how happy are they,
Who the Saviour obey,
And have laid up their treasures above!
O what tongue can express
The sweet comfort and peace
Of a soul in its earliest love.

2. It was heaven below
My Redeemer to know!
And the angels could do nothing more,
Than to fall at His feet,
And the story repeat,
And the Lover of sinners adore.

3. O the rapturous height
Of that holy delight,
Which I felt in the life-giving blood!
Of my Saviour possess'd,
I was perfectly blest,
As if filled with the fullness of God.

4. Then, all the day long,
Was my Jesus my song,
And redemption through faith in His name;
O that all might believe,
And salvation receive,
And their song and their joy be the same.

730. 11s & 8s.

1. O THOU, in whose presence
My soul takes delight,
On whom in affliction I call,
My comfort by day,
And my song in the night,
My hope, my salvation, my all.

2. Where dost Thou, dear Shepherd,
Resort with Thy sheep,
To feed them in pastures of love;
Say, why in the valley
Of death should I weep,
Or alone in this wilderness rove.

3. O! why should I wander
An alien from Thee,
Or cry in the desert for bread?
Thy foes will rejoice when
My sorrows they see,
And smile at the tears I have shed.

4. Ye daughters of Zion,
Declare, have you seen
The star that on Israel shone?
Say, if in your tents
My Beloved has been,
And where with His flocks He is gone?

5. Love sits in His eyelids,
And scatters delight
Through all the bright mansions on high!
Their faces the cherubims
Veil in His sight,
And tremble with fullness of joy.

6. He looks! and ten thousands
Of angels rejoice,
And myriads wait for His words;
He speaks! and eternity,
Filled with His voice,
Re-echoes the praise of the Lord.

7. Dear Shepherd! I hear, and
Will follow Thy call;
I know the sweet sound of Thy voice;
Restore and defend me,
For Thou art my all,
And in Thee I will ever rejoice.

FELLOWSHIP AND COMMUNION. 233

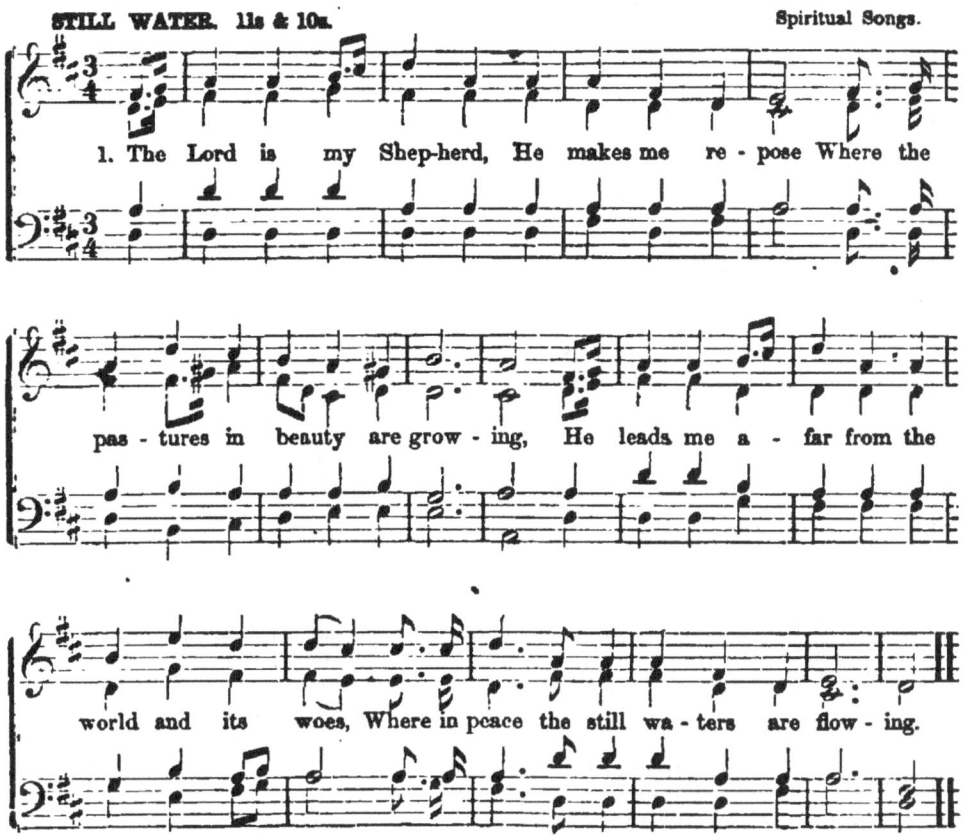

STILL WATER. 11s & 10s. — Spiritual Songs.

1. The Lord is my Shepherd, He makes me repose Where the pastures in beauty are growing, He leads me afar from the world and its woes, Where in peace the still waters are flowing.

731. 11s & 10s.

2. He strengthens my spirit, He shows me the path,
Where the arms of His love shall enfold me,
And when I walk through the dark valley of death,
His rod and His staff will uphold me!

732. 11s & 10s.

1. O! tell me, Thou life and delight of my soul,
Where the flock of Thy pasture are feeding;
I seek Thy protection, I need Thy control,
I would go where my Shepherd is leading

2. O! tell me the place where Thy flock are at rest,
Where the noontide will find them reposing?
The tempest now rages, my soul is distress'd,
And the pathway of peace I am losing.

3. O! why should I stray with the flocks of Thy foes,
'Mid the desert where now they are roving,
Where hunger and thirst, where affliction and woes,
And temptations their ruin are proving?

4. O! when shall my foes and my wandering cease?
And the follies that fill me with weeping!
Thou Shepherd of Israel, restore me that peace
Thou dost give to the flock Thou art keeping.

5. A voice from the Shepherd now bids thee return
By the way where the footprints are lying:
No longer to wander, no longer to mourn;
O fair one, now homeward be flying!

T. HASTINGS.

CHRISTIAN EXPERIENCE.

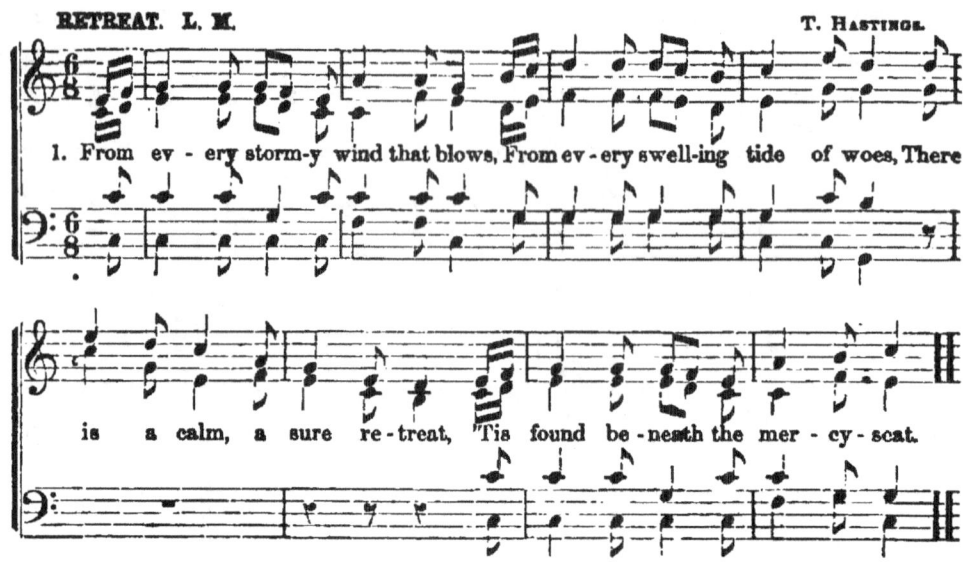

RETREAT. L. M. — T. HASTINGS.

1. From every stormy wind that blows, From every swelling tide of woes, There is a calm, a sure retreat, 'Tis found beneath the mercy-seat.

733. L. M.

1. From every stormy wind that blows,
From every swelling tide of woes,
There is a calm, a sure retreat,
'Tis found beneath the mercy-seat.

2. There is a place where Jesus sheds
The oil of gladness on our heads,
A place of all on earth most sweet;
It is the blood-bought mercy-seat.

3. There is a scene where spirits blend,
Where friend holds fellowship with friend,
Though sundered far, by faith we meet
Around one common mercy-seat.

4. There, there, on eagle wings we soar,
And sense and sin becloud no more;
And heaven comes down our souls to greet,
And glory crowns the mercy-seat.

5. Oh! let my hand forget her skill,
My tongue be silent, cold, and still,
This throbbing heart forget to beat,
If I forget the mercy-seat.
STOWELL.

734. L. M.

1. All mortal vanities, be gone,
Nor tempt my eyes, nor tire my ears;
Behold, amidst the eternal throne,
A vision of the Lamb appears!

2. Lo, He receives a sealed book
From Him that sits upon the throne!
Jesus, my Lord, prevails to look
On dark decrees and things unknown!

3. All the assembling saints around
Fall worshiping before the Lamb,
And in new songs of gospel sound
Address their honors to His name.

4. The joy, the shout, the harmony,
Flies o'er the everlasting hills—
"Worthy art Thou alone," they cry,
"To read the book, to loose the seals."

5. Our voices join the heavenly strain,
And with transporting pleasure sing,
"Worthy the Lamb, that once was slain,
To be our Teacher and our King!"
WATTS.

735. L. M.

1. The turf shall be my fragrant shrine;
My temple, Lord, that arch of Thine;
My censer's breath the mountain airs,
And silent thoughts my only prayers.

2. My choir shall be the moon-lit waves,
When murmuring homeward to their caves,
Or when the stillness of the sea,
E'en more than music, breathes of Thee.

3. I'll seek, by day, some glade unknown,
All light and silence, like Thy throne;
And the pale stars shall be, at night,
The only eyes that watch my rite.

4. Thy heaven, on which 'tis bliss to look,
Shall be my pure and shining book,
Where I can read, in words of flame,
The glories of Thy wondrous name.

5. There's nothing bright, above, below,
From flowers that bloom, to stars that glow,
But in its light my soul can see
Some feature of Thy Deity.

6. There's nothing dark, below, above,
But in its gloom I trace Thy love,
And meekly wait that moment when
Thy touch shall turn all bright again.
MOORE.

TRIALS AND TEMPTATIONS. 235

BOWDOIN. L. M.   CH. BEECHER.

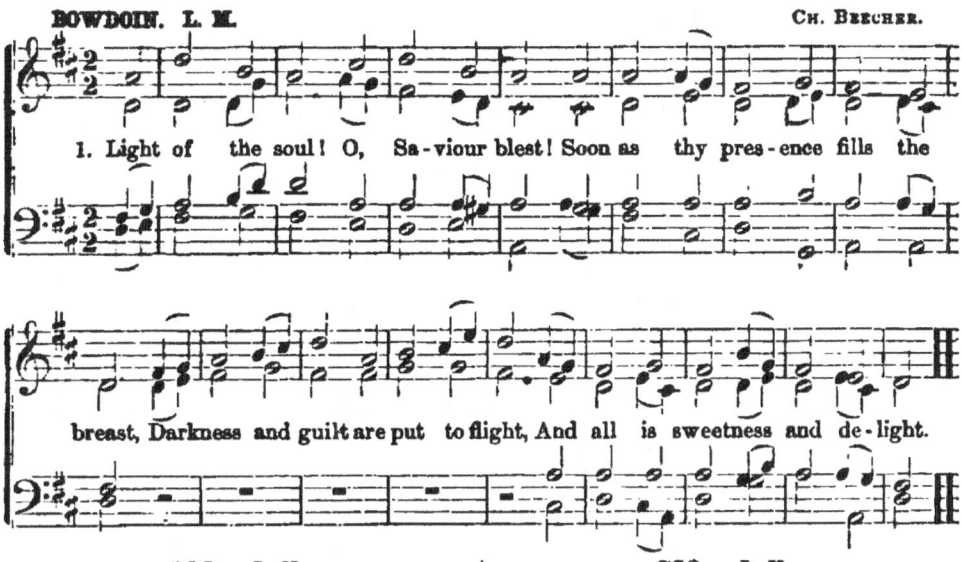

1. Light of the soul! O, Saviour blest! Soon as thy presence fills the breast, Darkness and guilt are put to flight, And all is sweetness and delight.

736. L. M.

2. Son of the Father! Lord most high!
How glad is he who feels Thee nigh!
Come in Thy hidden majesty;
Fill us with love, fill us with Thee.

3. Jesus is from the proud concealed,
But evermore to babes revealed,
Through Him, unto the Father be
Glory and praise eternally.

737. L. M.

1. Nor seldom, clad in radiant vest,
   Deceitfully goes forth the morn;
Not seldom evening in the west
   Sinks sweetly, smilingly forsworn.

2. The smoothest seas will sometimes prove,
   To the confiding bark, untrue;
And if she trust the stars above,
   They can be false and treacherous too.

3. The umbrageous oak, in pomp outspread,
   Full oft, when storms the welkin rend,
Draws lightnings down upon the head
   It promised surely to defend.

4. But Thou art true, incarnate Lord,
   Who didst vouchsafe for man to die;
Thy smile is sure, Thy plighted word
   No change can break or falsify.

5. I bent before Thy gracious throne,
   And asked for peace with suppliant knee;
And peace was given,—nor peace alone,
   But faith, and hope, and ecstasy!
                  WORDSWORTH.

738. L. M.

1. WHEN groves by moonlight silence keep,
   And winds the vexed waves release,
And fields are hushed, and cities sleep,—
   Lord, is not that the hour of peace?

2. When infancy at evening tries,
   By turns to climb each parent's knees,
And gazing, meets their raptured eyes:
   Lord, is not that the hour of peace?

3. In golden pomp, when autumn smiles,
   And hill and dale, its rich increase
By man's full barns, exulting piles:
   Lord, is not that the hour of peace?

4. When mercy points where Jesus pleads,
   And faith beholds Thine anger cease,
And hope to black despair succeeds:
   This, Father, this alone is peace!
                  GISBORNE.

739. L. M.

1. FAR from my thoughts, vain world! be gone,
Let my religious hours alone:
Fain would mine eyes my Saviour see;
I wait a visit, Lord! from Thee.

2. My heart grows warm with holy fire,
And kindles with a pure desire;
Come, my dear Jesus! from above,
And feed my soul with heavenly love.

3. Blest Saviour! what delicious fare—
How sweet Thine entertainments are!
Never did angels taste above
Redeeming grace and dying love.

4. Hail, great Immanuel, all-divine!
In Thee Thy Father's glories shine:
Thou brightest, sweetest, fairest One,
That eyes have seen, or angels known!
                  WATTS.

CHRISTIAN EXPERIENCE.

QUITO. L. M. — English arranged by L. Mason.

1. Who is this fair one in distress, That travels from the wilderness? And pressed with sorrows and with sins, On her beloved Lord she leans, On her beloved Lord she leans.

740. L. M.

2. This is the spouse of Christ our God,
Bought with the treasures of His blood;
And her request, and her complaint,
Is but the voice of every saint.

3. "O let my name engraven stand,
Both on Thy heart, and on Thy hand;
Seal me upon Thine arm, and wear
That pledge of love for ever there.

4. "Stronger than death Thy love is known,
Which floods of wrath could never drown;
And hell and earth in vain combine
To quench a fire so much divine.

5. "But I am jealous of my heart,
Lest it should once from Thee depart;
Then let Thy name be well impress'd,
As a fair signet, on my breast.

6. "Come, my Beloved, haste away,
Cut short the hours of Thy delay;
Fly, like a youthful hart or roe,
Over the hills where spices grow."
WATTS.

741. L. M.

1. Be still, my heart! these anxious cares
To thee are burdens, thorns, and snares;
They cast dishonor on thy Lord,
And contradict His gracious word.

2. Brought safely by His hand thus far,
Why wilt thou now give place to fear?
How canst thou want if He provide,
Or lose thy way with such a Guide?

3. When first before His mercy-seat
Thou didst to Him thy all commit,
He gave thee warrant from that hour
To trust His wisdom, love, and power.

4. Did ever trouble yet befall,
And He refuse to hear thy call?
And has He not His promise past,
That thou shalt overcome at last?

5. He who has helped me hitherto,
Will help me all my journey through,
And give me daily cause to raise
New trophies to His endless praise.

6. Though rough and thorny be the road,
It leads thee home, apace, to God;
Then count thy present trials small,
For heaven will make amends for all.
NEWTON.

742. L. M.

1. With tearful eyes I look around,
Life seems a dark and stormy sea;
Yet, 'midst the gloom, I hear a sound,
A heavenly whisper, "Come to Me."

2. It tells me of a place of rest—
It tells me where my soul may flee;
O! to the weary, faint, oppress'd,
How sweet the bidding, "Come to Me."

3. When nature shudders, loth to part
   From all I love, enjoy, and see;
   When a faint chill steals o'er my heart,
   A sweet voice utters, "Come to Me."

4. Come, for all else must fail and die;
   Earth is no resting-place for thee;
   Heavenward direct thy weeping eye,
   I am thy portion, "Come to Me."

5. O, voice of mercy! voice of love!
   In conflict, grief, and agony,
   Support me, cheer me from above!
   And gently whisper, "Come to Me."

743. L. M.

1. THE darkened sky, how thick it lowers!
   Troubled with storms, and big with showers,
   No cheerful gleam of light appears,
   But nature pours forth all her tears.

2. Yet let the sons of Grace revive;
   He bids the soul that seeks Him, live;
   And from the gloomiest shade of night
   Calls forth a morning of delight.

3. The seeds of ecstasy unknown
   Are in these watered furrows sown;
   See the green blades, how thick they rise,
   And with fresh verdure bless our eyes!

4. In secret foldings they contain
   Unnumbered ears of golden grain;
   And heaven shall pour its beams around,
   Till the ripe harvest load the ground.

5. Then shall the trembling mourner come,
   And bind his sheaves, and bear them home;
   The voice long broke with sighs shall sing,
   Till heaven with hallelujahs ring!
   DODDRIDGE.

744. L. M.

1. GOD of my life, to Thee I call;
   Afflicted, at Thy feet I fall;
   When the great water-floods prevail,
   Leave not my trembling heart to fail.

2. Friend of the friendless and the faint,
   Where should I lodge my deep complaint?
   Where—but with Thee, whose open door
   Invites the helpless and the poor?

3. Did ever mourner plead with Thee,
   And Thou refuse that mourner's plea?
   Does not the word still fixed, remain,
   That none shall seek Thy face in vain?

4. Poor tho' I am—despised, forgot,
   Yet God, my God, forgets me not;
   And he is safe, and must succeed,
   For whom the Lord vouchsafes to plead.
   COWPER.

745. L. M.

1. WAIT, O my soul, thy Maker's will;
   Tumultuous passions, all be still!
   Nor let a murmuring thought arise;
   His ways are just, His counsels wise.

2. He in the thickest darkness dwells,
   Performs His work, the cause conceals;
   But, though His methods are unknown,
   Judgment and truth support His throne.

3. In heaven, and earth, and air, and seas,
   He executes His firm decrees;
   And by His saints it stands confessed,
   That what He does is ever best.

4. Wait, then, my soul, submissive wait,
   Prostrate before His awful seat;
   And, 'mid the terrors of His rod,
   Trust in a wise and gracious God.
   BEDDOME.

746. L. M.

1. THE waters of Bethesda's pool
   Were to the outward eye as clear,
   And to the outward touch as cool,
   Before the Visitant drew near.

2. But while untroubled, they possess'd
   No healing virtue: gentle Friend,
   Is there no fount within the breast
   To which an angel may descend?

3. O, while the soul unruffled lies,
   Its mirror only can display,
   However beautiful their dyes,
   The forms of things that pass away.

4. But when its troubled waters own
   A Saviour's presence, in the wave
   The healing power of grace is known,
   And found omnipotent to save.

5. A glimpse of glories far more bright
   Than earth can give is mirrored there;
   And perfect purity and light
   The presence of its God declare.
   BARTON.

DOXOLOGY. L. M.

1. THE peace, which God alone reveals,
   And by His word of grace imparts,
   Which only the believer feels,
   Direct, and keep, and cheer our hearts.

2. And may the holy Three in One,
   The Father, Word, and Comforter,
   Pour an abundant blessing down,
   On every soul assembled here.

CHRISTIAN EXPERIENCE.

JUDAH'S CAPTIVE. L. M. — Arranged by J. ZUNDEL.

1. When we, our wearied limbs to rest, Sat down by proud Euphrates' stream, We wept with doleful thoughts oppressed, And Zion was our mournful theme. 2. Our harps that, when with joy we sung, Were wont their tuneful parts to bear, With silent strings neglected hung On willow trees that withered there.

747. L. M.

3. How shall we tune our voice to sing,
Or touch our harps with skillful hands?
Shall hymns of joy, to God our King,
Be sung by slaves in foreign lands?

4. O Salem! our once happy seat,
When I of thee forgetful prove,
Let then my trembling hand forget
The tuneful strings with art to move.

5. If I to mention thee forbear,
Eternal silence seize my tongue;
Or if I sing one cheerful air,
Till thy deliverance is my song.
TATE AND BRADY.

748. L. M.

1. 'Tis by the faith of joys to come,
We walk through deserts dark as night;
Till we arrive at heaven, our home,
Faith is our guide, and faith our light.

2. The want of sight she well supplies,
She makes the pearly gates appear;
Far into distant worlds she pries,
And brings eternal glories near.

3. Cheerful we tread the desert through,
While faith inspires a heavenly ray,
Though lions roar, and tempests blow,
And rocks and dangers fill the way.

4. So Abra'm, by divine command,
Left his own house to walk with God;
His faith beheld the promised land,
And fired his zeal along the road.
WATTS.

749. L. M.

1. WHEN power divine, in mortal form,
Hushed with a word the raging storm,
In soothing accents Jesus said—
"Lo! it is I; be not afraid."

2. Blessed be the voice that breathes from heaven,
To every heart in sunder riven,
When love, and joy, and hope are fled—
"Lo! it is I; be not afraid."

3. And when the last dread hour is come,
While shuddering nature waits her doom,
This voice shall call the pious dead—
"Lo! it is I; be not afraid."
J. R. SMITH.

750. L. M.

1. THE billows swell, the winds are high,
Clouds overcast my wintry sky;
Out of the depths to Thee I call;
My fears are great, my strength is small.

2. O Lord, the pilot's part perform,
And guide and guard me through the storm;
Defend me from each threatening ill;
Control the waves; say, "Peace! be still."

3. Amidst the roaring of the sea,
My soul still hangs her hopes on Thee;
Thy constant love, Thy faithful care,
Is all that saves me from despair.

4. Though tempest-tossed, and half a wreck,
My Saviour through the floods I seek;
Let neither winds nor stormy main
Force back my shattered bark again.
COWPER.

751. L. M.

1. WHILE to its grief my soul gave way,
To see the work of God decline,
Methought I heard the Saviour say—
"Dismiss thy fears, the ark is Mine.

2. "Though for a time I hid My face,
Rely upon My love and power;
Still wrestle at the throne of grace,
And wait for a reviving hour.

3. "Take down thy long-neglected harp,
I've seen thy tears, and heard thy prayer;
The winter season has been sharp,
But spring shall all its wastes repair."

4. Lord! I obey, my hopes revive;
Come, join with me, ye saints, and sing:
Our foes in vain against us strive,
For God will help and triumph bring.
NEWTON.

752. L. M.

1. THY will be done! I will not fear
The fate provided by Thy love;
Though clouds and darkness shroud me here,
I know that all is bright above.

2. The stars of heaven are shining on,
Though these frail eyes are dimmed with tears;
The hopes of earth indeed are gone,
But are not ours the immortal years?

3. Father! forgive the heart that clings,
Thus trembling, to the things of time;
And bid my soul, on angel wings,
Ascend into a purer clime.

4. There shall no doubts disturb its trust,
No sorrows dim celestial love;
But these afflictions of the dust,
Like shadows of the night, remove.

5. E'en now, above, there's radiant day,
While clouds and darkness brood below;
Then, Father, joyful on my way
To drink the bitter cup I go.
J. ROSCOE.

753. L. M.

1. IF life in sorrow must be spent,
So be it; I am well content;
And meekly wait my last remove,
Desiring only trustful love.

2. No bliss I'll seek, but to fulfill
In life, in death, Thy perfect will;
No succors in my woes I want,
But what my Lord is pleased to grant.

3. Our days are numbered: let us spare
Our anxious hearts a needless care:
'T is Thine to number out our days;
'T is ours to give them to Thy praise.

4. Faith is our only business here,—
Faith simple, constant, and sincere;
O blessed days Thy servants see!
Thus spent, O Lord! in pleasing Thee.
MADAME GUION.

754. L. M.

1. MY heart lies dead; and no increase
Doth my dull husbandry improve:
O let Thy graces, without cease,
Drop from above.*

2. Thy dew doth every morning fall:
And shall the dew outstrip Thy Dove?
The dew, for which earth can not call,
"Drop from above!"

3. The world is tempting still my heart
Unto a hardness void of love;
Let heavenly grace, to cross its art,
Drop from above.

4. O come! for Thou dost know the way!
Or if to me Thou wilt not move,
Remove me where I need not say,
"Drop from above!"
HERBERT.

*The last line is to be repeated in singing.

240   CHRISTIAN EXPERIENCE.

DAYBREAK. L. M. — JOHN ZUNDEL.

1. O God, thou art my God alone; Early to Thee my soul shall cry, A pilgrim in a land unknown, A thirsty land where springs are dry.

755. L. M.

2. Yet, through this rough and thorny maze,
I follow hard on Thee, my God;
Thy hand unseen upholds my ways,
I safely tread where Thou hast trod.

3. Thee, in the watches of the night,
When I remember on my bed,
Thy presence makes the darkness light;
Thy guardian wings are round my head.

4. Better than life itself Thy love,
Dearer than all beside to me;
For whom have I in heaven above,
Or what on earth compared with Thee?
MONTGOMERY.

756. L. M.

1. The floods, O Lord, lift up their voice,
The mighty floods lift up their roar;
The floods in tumult loud rejoice,
And climb in foam the sounding shore.

2. But mightier than the mighty sea,
The Lord of glory reigns on high;
Far o'er its waves we look to Thee,
And see their fury break and die.

3. Thy word is true, Thy promise sure,
That ancient promise sealed in love;
Here be Thy temple ever pure,
As Thy pure mansions shine above.
G. BURGESS.

757. L. M.

1. O Lord, Thy counsels and Thy care
My safety and my comfort are;
And Thou shalt guide me all my days,
Till glory crown the work of grace.

2. In whom but Thee, in heaven above,
Can I repose my trust, my love?
And shall an earthly object be
Loved in comparison with Thee?

3. My flesh is hastening to decay;
Soon shall the world have passed away;
And what can mortal friends avail,
When heart, and strength, and life shall fail?

4. But O! my Saviour, be Thou nigh,
And I will triumph when I die;
My strength, my portion is divine;
And Jesus is for ever mine!

758. L. M.

1. My spirit sinks within me, Lord—
But I will call Thy name to mind;
And times of past distress record,
When I have found my God was kind.

2. Huge troubles, with tumultuous noise,
Swell like a sea, and round me spread;
The water-spouts drown all my joys,
And rising waves roll o'er my head.

3. Yet will the Lord command His love,
When I address His throne by day;
Nor in the night His grace remove;
The night shall hear me sing and pray.

4. I'll cast myself before His feet,
And say, "My God, my heavenly Rock,
"Why doth Thy love so long forget
The soul that groans beneath Thy stroke?"

5. Thy light and truth shall guide me still;
Thy word shall my best thoughts employ,
And lead me to Thine heavenly hill,
My God, my most exceeding joy!
WATTS.

TRIALS AND TEMPTATIONS.

CHALCEDONY. L. M.

1. Ho-ly Saviour, Friend unseen, Since on Thine arm Thou bid'st me lean, Help me throughout life's varying scene, By faith to cling a-lone to Thee, By faith to cling a-lone to Thee!

759. L. M.

2. Blest with this fellowship divine,
   Take what Thou wilt, I'll ne'er repine;
   E'en as the branches to the vine,
   My fainting soul would cling to Thee!

3. Far from her home, fatigued, opprest,
   Here she has found her place of rest;
   An exile still, yet not unblest,
   While she can closely cling to Thee!

4. Oft, when I seem to tread alone
   Some barren waste with thorns o'ergrown,
   Thy voice of love, in tenderest tone,
   Still whispers softly, "Cling to me!"

5. Though faith and hope may oft be tried,
   I ask not, need not, aught beside;
   How safe, how calm, how satisfied,
   The soul that only clings to Thee!

760. L. M.

1. Thee will I love, O Lord, my strength,
   My rock, my tower, my high defense;
   Thy mighty arm shall be my trust,
   For I have found salvation thence.

2. Death, and the terrors of the grave,
   Stood round me with their dismal shade;
   While floods of high temptations rose,
   And made my sinking soul afraid.

3. I saw the opening gates of hell,
   With endless pains and sorrows there,
   Which none but they that feel can tell—
   While I was hurried to despair.

4. In my distress I called my God,
   When I could scarce believe Him mine,
   He bowed His ear to my complaint;
   Then did His grace appear divine.

5. With speed He flew to my relief,
   As on a cherub's wing He rode;
   Awful and bright as lightning shone
   The face of my Deliverer, God!

6. Temptations fled at His rebuke—
   The blast of His almighty breath;
   He sent salvation from on high,
   And drew me from the deeps of death.

7. My song for ever shall record
   That terrible, that joyful hour!
   And give the glory to the Lord,
   Due to His mercy and His power.
   WATTS.

761. L. M.

1. The tempter to my soul hath said—
   "There is no help in God for Thee;"
   Lord! lift Thou up Thy servant's head;
   My glory, shield, and solace be.

2. Thus to the Lord I raised my cry,
   He heard me from His holy hill:
   At His command the waves rolled by;
   He beckoned—and the winds were still.

3. I laid me down and slept—I woke—
   Thou, Lord! my spirit didst sustain;
   Bright from the east the morning broke—
   Thy comforts rose on me again.

4. I will not fear, though armed throngs
   Compass my steps in all their wrath;
   Salvation to the Lord belongs;
   His presence guards His people's path.
   MONTGOMERY.

CHRISTIAN EXPERIENCE.

ST. PETERSBURGH. L. M. — BORTNIANSKY.

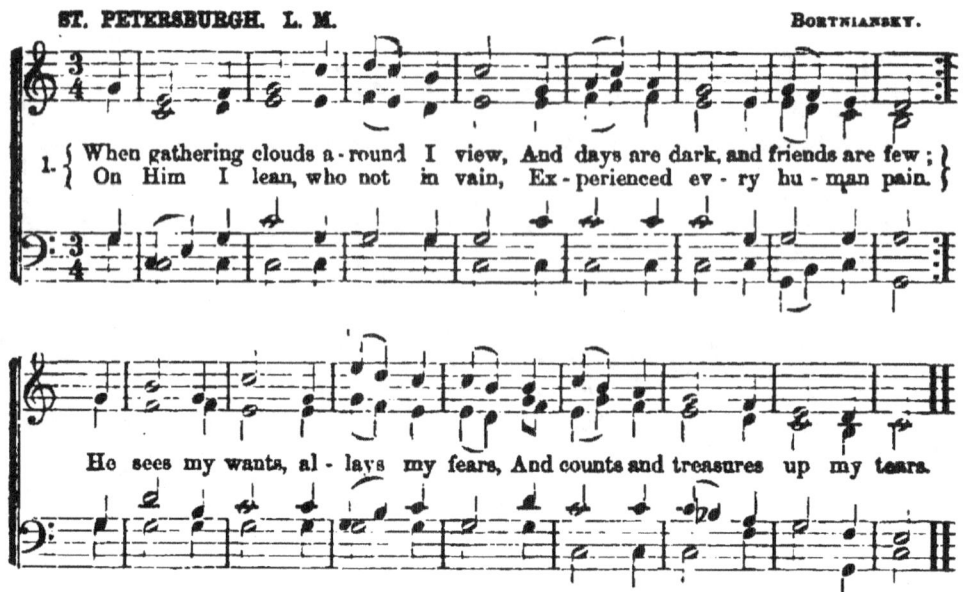

1. When gathering clouds a-round I view, And days are dark, and friends are few;
On Him I lean, who not in vain, Ex-perienced ev-ry hu-man pain.
He sees my wants, al-lays my fears, And counts and treasures up my tears.

762. L. M.

2. If aught should tempt my soul to stray
From heavenly wisdom's narrow way,
To fly the good I would pursue,
Or do the ill I would not do;
Still, He who felt temptation's power,
Will guard me in that dangerous hour.

3. When, sorrowing, o'er some stone I bend,
Which covers all that was a friend;
And from His hand, His voice, His smile,
Divides me for a little while—
My Saviour marks the tears I shed,
For "Jesus wept" o'er Lazarus dead.

4. And, O! when I have safely pass'd
Through every conflict but the last,
Still, Lord, unchanging, watch beside
My dying bed, for Thou hast died;
Then point to realms of cloudless day,
And wipe the latest tear away.
ROBERT GRANT.

763. L. M.

1. To weary hearts, to mourning homes,
God's meekest angel gently comes;
No power hath he to banish pain,
Or give us back our lost again,
And yet, in tenderest love, our dear
And Heavenly Father sends him here.

2. Angel of patience! sent to calm
Our feverish brows with cooling balm,
To lay with hope the storms of fear,
And reconcile life's smile and tear,
The throbs of wounded pride to still,
And make our own our Father's will!

3. O thou, who mournest on thy way,
With longings for the close of day,
He walks with Thee, that angel kind,
And gently whispers, "Be resign'd!
Bear up, bear on, the end shall tell,
The dear Lord ordereth all things well."
GERMAN TR. WHITTIER.

764. L. M.

1. O, LET my trembling soul be still,
While darkness veils this mortal eye,
And wait Thy wise, Thy holy will,
Wrapped yet in fears and mystery;
I can not, Lord, Thy purpose see;
Yet all is well, since ruled by Thee.

2. When mounted on Thy clouded car,
Thou send'st Thy darker spirits down,
I can discern Thy light afar—
Thy light, sweet beaming through Thy frown;
And, should I faint a moment, then
I think of Thee, and smile again.

3. So, trusting in Thy love, I tread
The narrow path of duty on;
What though some cherished joys are fled?
What though some flattering dreams are gone?
Yet purer, brighter joys remain;
Why should my spirit, then, complain?

765. L. M.

1. When adverse winds and waves arise,
And in my heart despondence sighs;
When life her throng of cares reveals,
And weakness o'er my spirit steals,
Grateful I hear the kind decree,
That "as my day, my strength shall be."

2. When, with sad footsteps, memory roves
'Mid smitten joys and buried loves,
When sleep my tearful pillow flies,
And dewy morning drinks my sighs,
Still to Thy promise, Lord! I flee,
That "as my day, my strength shall be."

3. One trial more must yet be past,
One pang—the keenest and the last;
And when, with brow convulsed and pale,
My feeble, quivering heart-strings fail,
Redeemer! grant my soul to see
That "as her day, her strength shall be."
MRS. SIGOURNEY.

766. L. M.

1. Peace, troubled soul, whose plaintive moan
Hath taught each scene the notes of woe;
Cease thy complaint, suppress thy groan,
And let thy tears forget to flow;
Behold, the precious balm is found,
To lull thy pain, to heal thy wound.

2. Come, freely come, by sin oppress'd;
On Jesus cast thy weighty load;
In Him thy refuge find, thy rest,
Safe in the mercy of thy God;
Thy God's thy Saviour—glorious word!
For ever love and praise the Lord.

3. As spring the winter—day, the night,
So peace thy gloom shall chase away,
And smiling joy, a seraph bright,
Shall tend thy steps and near thee stay;
While glory weaves the immortal crown,
And waits to claim thee for her own.

767. L. M.

1. Though waves and storms go o'er my head,
Though strength, and health, and friends be gone;
Though joys be withered all, and dead,
Though every comfort be withdrawn;
On this my steadfast soul relies—
Father, thy mercy never dies.

2. Fix'd on this ground will I remain,
Though my heart fail, and flesh decay;
This anchor shall my soul sustain,
When earth's foundations melt away;
Mercy's full power I then shall prove,
Loved with an everlasting love.
J. WESLEY.

768. L. M.

1. "Perfect in love!"—Lord, can it be,
Amidst this state of doubt and sin?
While foes so thick without, I see,
With weakness, pain, disease within;
Can perfect love inhabit here,
And, strong in faith, extinguish fear?

2. O, Lord! amidst this mental night,
Amidst the clouds of dark dismay,
Arise! arise! shed forth Thy light,
And kindle love's meridian day.
My Saviour God to me appear,
So love shall triumph over fear.

769. L. M.

1. As oft, with worn and weary feet,
We tread earth's rugged valley o'er,
The thought—how comforting and sweet!
Christ trod this very path before!
Our wants and weaknesses He knows,
From life's first dawning to its close.

2. Do sickness, feebleness, or pain,
Or sorrow in our path appear,
The recollection will remain,
More deeply did He suffer here!
His life, how truly sad and brief,
Filled up with suff'ring and with grief!

3. If Satan tempt our hearts to stray,
And whisper evil things within,
So did he, in the desert way,
Assail our Lord with thoughts of sin;
When worn, and in a feeble hour,
The tempter came with all his power.

4. Just such as I, this earth He trod,
With every human ill but sin;
And, though indeed the very God,
As I am now, so He has been.
My God, my Saviour, look on me
With pity, love, and sympathy.

Doxology. L. M.

Now to the Father, and the Son
Who rose from death, be glory given;
With Thee, O holy Comforter!
Henceforth by all in earth and heaven.

CROSS AND CROWN. C. M.
Western Melody.

1. Must Jesus bear the cross alone, And all the world go free?
No, there's a cross for every one, And there's a cross for me.

770. C. M.

2. How happy are the saints above,
   Who once went sorrowing here;
   But now they taste unmingled love,
   And joy without a tear.

3. The consecrated cross I'll bear,
   Till death shall set me free,
   And then go home my crown to wear,—
   For there's a crown for me.
   G. N. ALLEN.

1. Upon the crystal pavement down
   At Jesus' pierced feet,
   Joyful, I'll cast my golden crown,
   And His dear name repeat.

2. And palms shall wave, and harps shall ring
   Beneath heaven's arches high,
   The Lord that lives, the ransomed sing,
   That lives no more to die.

3. O precious cross! O glorious crown!
   O resurrection day!
   Ye angels! from the stars flash down,
   And bear my soul away.

771. C. M.

1. Now to the haven of Thy breast,
   O Son of man, I fly;
   Be Thou my refuge and my rest,
   For O! the storm is high.

2. Protect me from the furious blast;
   My shield and shelter be:
   Hide me, my Saviour, till o'erpast
   The storm of sin I see.

3. As welcome as the water-spring
   Is to a barren place,
   Jesus, descend on me, and bring
   Thy sweet, refreshing grace.

4. As o'er a parched and weary land,
   A rock extends its shade,
   So hide me, Saviour, with Thy hand,
   And screen my naked head,

5. In all the times of my distress
   Thou hast my succor been;
   And, in my utter helplessness,
   Restraining me from sin.

6. How swift to save me didst Thou move,
   In every trying hour;
   O! still protect me with Thy love,
   And shield me with Thy power.
   C. WESLEY.

772. C. M.

1. Jesus! Thy love shall we forget,
   And never bring to mind
   The grace that paid our hopeless debt,
   And bade us pardon find.

2. Shall we Thy life of grief forget,
   Thy fasting and Thy prayer;
   Thy locks with mountain vapors wet,
   To save us from despair?

3. Gethsemane can we forget—
   Thy struggling agony;
   When night lay dark on Olivet,
   And none to watch with Thee?

4. Our sorrows and our sins were laid
   On Thee, alone on Thee:
   Thy precious blood our ransom paid—
   Thine all the glory be!

5. Life's brightest joys we may forget—
   Our kindred cease to love;
   But He who paid our hopeless debt,
   Our constancy shall prove.
   CHRISTIAN LYRE.

TRIALS AND TEMPTATIONS.

773. C. M.

1. Come to the ark—come to the ark,
   To Jesus come away;
   The pestilence walks forth by night,
   The arrow flies by day.

2. Come to the ark—the waters rise,
   The seas their billows rear;
   While darkness gathers o'er the skies,
   Behold a refuge near!

3. Come to the ark—all, all that weep
   Beneath the sense of sin;
   Without, deep calleth unto deep,
   But all is peace within.

4. Come to the ark—ere yet the flood
   Your lingering steps oppose;
   Come, for the door which open stood,
   Is now about to close.

774. C. M.

1. O Thou, who driest the mourner's tear,
   How dark this world would be,
   If, when deceived and wounded here,
   We could not fly to Thee!

2. But Thou wilt heal the broken heart,
   Which, like the plants that throw
   Their fragrance from the wounded part,
   Breathes sweetness out of woe.

3. When joy no longer soothes or cheers,
   And e'en the hope that threw
   A moment's sparkle o'er our tears
   Is dimmed and vanished too;

4. O, who would bear life's stormy doom,
   Did not Thy wing of love
   Come, brightly wafting through the gloom
   Our peace-branch from above?

5. Then sorrow, touched by Thee, grows
   With more than rapture's ray; [bright,
   As darkness shows us worlds of light
   We never saw by day.

   MOORE.

775. C. M.

1. When grief and anguish press me down,
   And hope and comfort flee,
   I cling, O Father, to Thy throne,
   And stay my heart on Thee.

2. When death invades my peaceful home,
   The sundered ties shall be
   A closer bond, in time to come,
   To bind my heart to Thee.

3. Lord, not my will, but Thine, be done!
   My soul, from fear set free,
   Her faith shall anchor at Thy throne,
   And trust alone in Thee.

776. C. M.

1. Our pathway oft is wet with tears,
   Our sky with clouds o'ercast,
   And worldly cares and worldly fears
   Go with us to the last;—
   Not to the last! God's word hath said,
   Could we but read aright:
   O pilgrim! lift in hope thy head,
   At eve it shall be light!

2. Though earth-born shadows now may,
   Our toilsome path awhile, [shroud
   God's blessed word can part each cloud,
   And bid the sunshine smile.
   If we but trust in living faith,
   His love and power divine,
   Then, though our sun may set in death,
   His light shall round us shine.

3. When tempest clouds are dark on high,
   His bow of love and praise
   Shines beauteous in the vaulted sky,
   Token that storms shall cease.
   Then keep we on with hope unchill'd
   By faith and not by sight,
   And we shall own His word fulfill'd—
   At eve there shall be light!

   BARTON.

777. C. M.

1. Dear Refuge of my weary soul,
   On Thee, when sorrows rise—
   On Thee, when waves of trouble roll,
   My fainting hope relies.

2. To Thee I tell each rising grief,
   For Thou alone canst heal;
   Thy word can bring a sweet relief
   For every pain I feel.

3. But O! when gloomy doubts prevail,
   I fear to call Thee mine;
   The springs of comfort seem to fail,
   And all my hopes decline.

4. Yet, gracious God, where shall I flee?
   Thou art my only trust:
   And still my soul would cleave to Thee,
   Though prostrate in the dust.

5. Thy mercy-seat is open still,
   Here let my soul retreat,
   With humble hope attend Thy will,
   And wait beneath Thy feet.

   MRS. STEELE.

CHRISTIAN EXPERIENCE.

ARCADIA. C. M. — T. Hastings.

1. In time of fear, when trouble's near, I look to Thine abode; Tho' helpers fail, and foes prevail, I'll put my trust in God, I'll put my trust in God.

778. C. M.

2. And what is life, 'mid toil and strife?
   What terror has the grave?
   Thine arm of power, in peril's hour,
   The trembling soul will save.

3. In darkest skies, though storms arise,
   I will not be dismay'd:
   O God of light, and boundless might,
   My soul on Thee is stay'd!

   T. HASTINGS.

779. C. M.

1. WHEN waves of trouble round me swell,
   My soul is not dismay'd;
   I hear a voice I know full well,—
   "'T is I; be not afraid."

2. When black the threatening skies appear,
   And storms my path invade,
   Those accents tranquillize each fear,—
   "'T is I; be not afraid."

3. There is a gulf that must be cross'd;
   Saviour, be near to aid!
   Whisper, when my frail bark is toss'd,—
   "'T is I; be not afraid."

4. There is a dark and fearful vale,
   Death hides within its shade;
   O say, when flesh and heart shall fail,—
   "'T is I; be not afraid."

780. C. M.

1. WHERE shall the child of sorrow find
   A place for calm repose?
   Thou! Father of the fatherless,
   Pity the orphan's woes!

2. What Friend have I in heaven or earth,
   What Friend to trust but Thee?
   My father's dead, my mother's dead;
   My God! "remember me."

3. Thy gracious promise now fulfill,
   And bid my trouble cease;
   In Thee the fatherless shall find
   Pure mercy, grace, and peace.

4. I've not a secret care or pain
   But He that secret knows;
   Thou Father of the fatherless,
   Pity the orphan's woes!

781. C. M.

1. THOUGH faint and sick, and worn away
   With poverty and woe,
   My widowed feet are doomed to stray
   'Mid thorny paths below,—

2. Be Thou, O Lord, my Father still,
   My confidence and guide;
   I know that perfect is Thy will,
   Whate'er that will decide.

3. I know the soul that trusts in Thee
   Thou never wilt forsake;
   And though a bruised reed I be,
   That reed Thou wilt not break.

4. Then keep me, Lord, where'er I go,
   Support me on my way,
   Though, worn with poverty and woe,
   My widowed footsteps stray.

5. To give my weakness strength, O God,
   Thy staff shall yet avail;
   And, though Thou chasten with Thy rod,
   That staff shall never fail.

782. C. M.

1. 'T was in the watches of the night
   I thought upon Thy power;
   I kept Thy lovely face in sight,
   Amid the darkest hour.

2. While I lay resting on my bed
   My thoughts arose on high;
   My God, my Life, my Hope, I said,
   Bring Thy salvation nigh.

3. I strive to mount Thy holy hill,
   And climb the heav'nly road;
   And Thy right hand upholds me still,
   When I commune with God.

4. Thy mercy stretches o'er my head
   The shadow of Thy wing;
   My heart rejoices in Thine aid,
   And I Thy praises sing.

   WATTS.

783. C. M.

1. THOUSANDS, O Lord of Hosts, to-day
   Within Thy temple meet;
   And tens of thousands throng to pay
   Their homage at Thy feet.

2. They sing Thy deeds, as I have sung,
   In sweet and solemn lays;
   Were I among them, my glad tongue
   Might learn new themes of praise.

3. The dew lies thick on all the ground,—
   Shall my poor fleece be dry?
   The manna rains from heaven around,—
   Shall I of hunger die?

4. Behold Thy prisoner, loose my bands,
   If 't is Thy gracious will;
   If not, contented in Thy hands
   Behold Thy prisoner still.

5. I may not to Thy courts repair,
   Yet here Thou surely art;
   O give me here a house of prayer;
   Here Sabbath joys impart.

   MONTGOMERY.

784. C. M.

1. I WORSHIP Thee, sweet Will of God!
   And all Thy ways adore;
   And every day I live, I long
   To love Thee more and more.

2. Man's weakness, waiting upon God,
   Its end can never miss,
   For men on earth no work can do
   More angel-like than this.

3. He always wins who sides with God,
   To him no chance is lost;
   God's will is sweetest to him when
   It triumphs at his cost.

4. Ill, that God blesses, is our good,
   And unblest good is ill;
   And all is right that seems most wrong,
   If it be His dear will!

5. When obstacles and trials seem
   Like prison-walls to be,
   I do the little I can do,
   And leave the rest to Thee.

6. I have no cares, O blessed Will!
   For all my cares are Thine;
   I live in triumph, Lord! for Thou
   Hast made Thy triumphs mine.

   LYRA CATH.

785. C. M.

1. AUTHOR of good, we rest on Thee;
   Thine ever watchful eye
   Alone our real wants can see,
   Thy hand alone supply.

2. In Thine all-gracious providence
   Our cheerful hopes confide;
   O let Thy power be our defence,
   Thy love our footsteps guide!

3. And since, by passion's force subdued,
   Too oft, with stubborn will,
   We blindly shun the latent good,
   And grasp the specious ill,—

4. Not what we wish, but what we want,
   Thy mercy still supply!
   The good unasked, O Father, grant;
   The ill, though asked, deny!

   MERRICK.

786. C. M.

1. FIRM as the earth Thy gospel stands,
   My Lord, my Hope, my Trust;
   If I am found in Jesus' hands,
   My soul can ne'er be lost.

2. His honor is engaged to save
   The meanest of His sheep;
   All whom His heavenly Father gave,
   His hands securely keep.

3. Nor death nor hell shall e'er remove
   His favorites from His breast;
   In the dear bosom of His love
   They must for ever rest.

   WATTS.

CHRISTIAN EXPERIENCE.

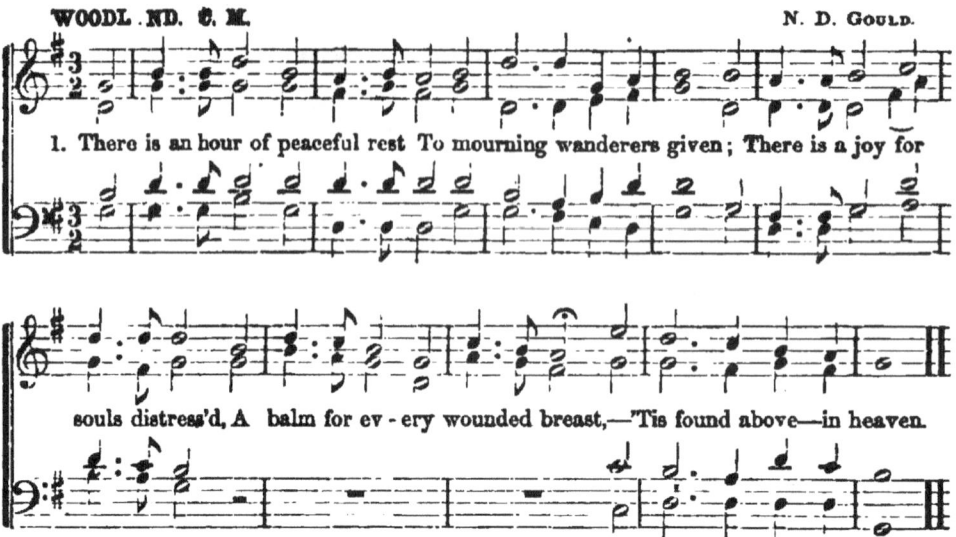

WOODLAND. C. M. N. D. GOULD.

1. There is an hour of peaceful rest To mourning wanderers given; There is a joy for souls distress'd, A balm for ev-ery wounded breast,—'Tis found above—in heaven.

787. C. M. Peculiar.

1. THERE is an hour of peaceful rest
   To mourning wanderers given;
   There is a joy for souls distress'd,
   A balm for every wounded breast—
   'T is found above—in heaven.

2. There is a soft, a downy bed,
   'T is fair as breath of even;
   A couch for weary mortals spread,
   Where they may rest the aching head,
   And find repose—in heaven.

3. There is a home for weary souls,
   By sin and sorrow driven;
   When toss'd on life's tempestuous shoals,
   Where storms arise, and ocean rolls,
   And all is drear—but heaven.

4. There, faith lifts up her cheerful eye,
   To brighter prospects given;
   And views the tempest passing by,
   The evening shadows quickly fly,
   And all serene—in heaven.

5. There, fragrant flowers immortal bloom,
   And joys supreme are given:
   There, joys divine disperse the gloom—
   Beyond the confines of the tomb
   Appears the dawn of heaven.
   W. B. TAPPAN.

788. C. M. Peculiar.

1. THIS world is poor from shore to shore,
   And, like a baseless vision,
   Its lofty domes and brilliant ore,
   Its gems and crowns are vain and poor;
   There 's nothing rich but heaven.

2. Empires decay, and nations die,
   Our hopes to winds are given;
   The vernal blooms in ruin lie,
   Death reigns o'er all beneath the sky;
   There 's nothing sure but heaven.

3. Creation's mighty fabric all
   Shall be to atoms riven.—
   The skies consume, the planets fall,
   Convulsions rock this earthly ball;
   There 's nothing firm but heaven.

4. A stranger, lonely here I roam,
   From place to place am driven;
   My friends are gone, and I 'm in gloom,
   This earth is all a dismal tomb;
   I have no home but heaven.

5. The clouds disperse—the light appears,
   My sins are all forgiven:
   Triumphant grace has quelled my fears;
   Roll on, thou sun! fly swift, my years!
   I 'm on my way to heaven.

789. C. M.

1. I CAN not call affliction sweet;
   And yet 't was good to bear:
   Affliction brought me to Thy feet,
   And I found comfort there.

2. My wearied soul was all resign'd
   To Thy most gracious will:
   O had I kept that better mind,
   Or been afflicted still!

3. Where are the vows which then I vow'd?
   The joys which then I knew?
   Those, vanished like the morning cloud;
   These, like the early dew.

4. Lord, grant me grace for every day,
   Whate'er my state may be,
   Through life, in death, with truth to say,
   "My God is all to me."
   MONTGOMERY.

790. C. M.

1. In trouble and in grief, O God,
   Thy smile hath cheered my way;
   And joy hath budded from each thorn
   That round my footsteps lay.

2. The hours of pain have yielded good,
   Which prosperous days refused;
   As herbs, though scentless when entire,
   Spread fragrance when they 're bruised.

3. The oak strikes deeper, as its boughs
   By furious blasts are driven;
   So life's tempestuous storms the more
   Have fixed my heart in heaven.

4. All-gracious Lord, whate'er my lot
   In other times may be,
   I 'll welcome still the heaviest grief
   That brings me near to Thee.

791. C. M.

1. Christ leads me through no darker rooms
   Than He went through before:
   He that into God's kingdom comes
   Must enter by this door.

2. Come, Lord, when grace hath made me
   Thy blessed face to see; [meet
   For if Thy work on earth be sweet,
   What must Thy glory be?

3. Then I shall end my sad complaints,
   And weary, sinful days,
   And join with those triumphant saints
   That sing Jehovah's praise.

4. My knowledge of that life is small;
   The eye of faith is dim;
   But 't is enough that Christ knows all,
   And I shall be with Him!

   R. BAXTER.

792. C. M.

1. It is the Lord—enthroned in light,
   Whose claims are all divine,
   Who has an undisputed right
   To govern me and mine.

2. It is the Lord—who gives me all,
   My wealth, my friends, my ease;
   And of His bounties may recall
   Whatever part He please.

3. It is the Lord—my covenant God—
   Thrice blessed be His name;
   Whose gracious promise, sealed with blood,
   Must ever be the same.

4. Can I, with hopes so firmly built,
   Be sullen, or repine?
   No, gracious God! take what Thou wilt—
   To Thee I all resign.

   T. GREENE.

793. C. M.

1. Affliction is a stormy deep,
   Where wave resounds to wave;
   Though o'er our heads the billows roll,
   We know the Lord can save.

2. When darkness, and when sorrows rose,
   And pressed on every side,
   The Lord hath still sustained our steps,
   And still hath been our Guide.

3. Perhaps, before the morning dawn,
   He will restore our peace;
   For He who bade the tempest roar,
   Can bid the tempest cease.

4. Here will we rest, here build our hopes,
   Nor murmur at His rod;
   He 's more to us than all the world,
   Our Health, our Life, our God.

   COTTON.

794. C. M.

1. O God, my Refuge, hear my cries,
   Behold my flowing tears;
   For earth and hell my hurt devise,
   And triumph in my fears.

2. O were I like some gentle dove,
   And innocence had wings,
   I'd fly, and make a long remove
   From all these restless things.

3. Let me to some wild desert go,
   And find a peaceful home,
   Where storms of malice never blow,
   Temptations never come.

4. God shall preserve my soul from fear,
   And shield me when afraid:
   Ten thousand angels must appear,
   If He command their aid.

5. I cast my burdens on the Lord,
   The Lord sustains them all;
   My courage rests upon His word,
   That saints shall never fall.

   WATTS.

CHRISTIAN EXPERIENCE.

MARA. C. M.   CH. BEECHER.

1: Father, whate'er of earthly bliss Thy sovereign will denies, Accepted at Thy throne of grace, Let this petition rise:—

795. C. M.

1. Father! whate'er of earthly bliss
   Thy sovereign will denies,
   Accepted at Thy throne of grace,
   Let this petition rise.

2. "Give me a calm, a thankful heart,
   From every murmur free!
   The blessings of Thy grace impart,
   And make me live to Thee.

3. "Let the sweet hope that Thou art mine
   My life and death attend;
   Thy presence through my journey shine,
   And crown my journey's end."
   MRS. STEELE.

796. C. M.

1. My God, my Father—blissful name—
   O may I call Thee mine?
   May I with sweet assurance claim
   A portion so divine?

2. This only can my fears control,
   And bid my sorrows fly;
   What harm can ever reach my soul
   Beneath my Father's eye?

3. Whate'er Thy providence denies,
   I calmly would resign;
   For Thou art good, and just, and wise;
   O bend my will to Thine.

4. Whate'er Thy sacred will ordains,
   O give me strength to bear;
   And let me know my Father reigns,
   And trust His tender care.
   MRS. STEELE.

797. C. M.

1. O Lord! I would delight in Thee,
   And on Thy care depend;
   To Thee in every trouble flee,
   My best, my only Friend.

2. When all created streams are dried,
   Thy fullness is the same;
   May I with this be satisfied,
   And glory in Thy name!

3. No good in creatures can be found,
   But may be found in Thee;
   I must have all things, and abound,
   While God is God to me.

4. O Lord! I cast my care on Thee;
   I triumph and adore;
   Henceforth my great concern shall be
   To love and please Thee more.
   RYLAND.

798. C. M.

1. Unshaken as the sacred hill,
   And fixed as mountains be,
   Firm as a rock the soul shall rest,
   That leans, O Lord! on Thee.

2. Not walls, nor hills, could guard so well
   Old Salem's happy ground,
   As those eternal arms of love,
   That every saint surround.

3. Deal gently, Lord! with souls sincere,
   And lead them safely on
   To the bright gates of paradise,
   Where Christ, their Lord, is gone.
   WATTS.

799. C. M.

1. O Lord, hadst Thou been here! but when
   Is not the Saviour nigh?
   His power and love were present then,
   Though Lazarus needs must die.

2. And when the Master seems to stay,
   Regardless of our grief,
   His tarrying never is delay,
   But well-timed, sure relief.

3. He loves to come when others flee,
   Or, coming, can not aid;
   To save in faith's extremity,
   When hope's last glimmerings fade.

4. The house of mourning He prefers
   With voice of love to cheer;
   And sorrows are the harbingers
   That say, The Lord is near.

5. Lord, not in sorrow's hour alone,
   We ask to feel Thy grace;
   The hearts that once Thy love have known,
   Would be Thy dwelling-place.
   CONDER.

800. C. M.

1. Not for the pious dead we weep;
   Their sorrows now are o'er;
   The sea is calm, the tempest past,
   On that eternal shore.

2. Their peace is sealed, their rest is sure,
   Within that better home;
   Awhile we weep and linger here,
   Then follow to the tomb.

3. O, might some dream of visioned bliss,
   Some trance of rapture, show
   Where, on the bosom of their God,
   They rest from human woe!

4. Jesus! our shadowy path illume,
   And teach the chastened mind
   To welcome all that's left of good,
   To all that's lost resigned.
   BARBAULD.

801. C. M.

1. Bright were the mornings first impearl'd
   O'er earth, and sea, and air;
   The birth-days of a rising world—
   For Power divine was there.

2. But fairer shone the tears of God,
   For Lazarus, o'er his grave—
   Since love divine bedew'd the sod
   Of one He sought to save.

3. Sweet drops of grace, the pledges given,
   Of mercy's mighty plan—
   That He, who was the Prince of heaven,
   Had pity upon man!

4. Let us Thy dear example, Lord!
   Fixed in our memories keep—
   That we, obedient to Thy word,
   May weep with those that weep.

802. C. M.

1. Jesus, united by Thy grace,
   And each to each endeared.
   With confidence we seek Thy face,
   And know our prayer is heard.

2. Make us into one spirit drink;
   Baptize into Thy name;
   And let us always kindly think,
   And sweetly speak, the same.

3. Touched by the loadstone of Thy love,
   Let all our hearts agree;
   And ever towards each other move,
   And ever move toward Thee.
   C. WESLEY.

803. C. M.

1. When I can read my title clear
   To mansions in the skies,
   I bid farewell to every fear,
   And wipe my weeping eyes.

2. Should earth against my soul engage,
   And hellish darts be hurled,
   Then I can smile at Satan's rage,
   And face a frowning world.

3. Let cares like a wild deluge come,
   And storms of sorrow fall;
   May I but safely reach my home,
   My God, my Heaven, my All.

4. There shall I bathe my weary soul
   In seas of heavenly rest;
   And not a wave of trouble roll
   Across my peaceful breast.
   WATTS.

Doxology. C. M.

The God of mercy be adored,
Who calls our souls from death,
Who saves by His redeeming word
And new-creating breath;

To praise the Father and the Son
And Spirit all-divine,—
The One in Three, and Three in One,—
Let saints and angels join.

804. C. M.

2. They bid us be in mirthful mood,
   And dry those tears so sad;
   But Judah's hearths are desolate,
   And how can we be glad?

3. Silent our harps o'er Babel's stream
   Are hung on willows wet;
   And Zion, though we no more see,
   We never can forget.

4. Sad be the notes, the plaintive wail,
   Our lyres must falter here;
   Echoes of songs within the vail,
   Celestial, sweet, and clear.

5. O memory! can those strains on high
   Grow silent, and unknown?
   Can death's deep pall enshroud our eyes,
   And hide yon glitt'ring throne.

6. Jerusalem! thy banished ones—
   Prove anguish and regret—
   But endless curses wait on them,
   If thee they can forget!

805. C. M.

1. Jesus, in sickness and in pain,
   Be near to succor me,
   My sinking spirit still sustain;
   To Thee I turn, to Thee.

2. When cares and sorrows thicken round,
   And nothing bright I see,
   In Thee alone can help be found;
   To Thee I turn, to Thee.

3. Should strong temptations fierce assail,
   As if to ruin me,
   Then in Thy strength will I prevail,
   While still I turn to Thee.

4. Through all my pilgrimage below,
   Whate'er my lot may be,
   In joy or sadness, weal or wo,
   Jesus, I'll turn to Thee.

   T. H. GALLAUDET.

806. C. M.

1. WHEN languor and disease invade
   This trembling house of clay,
   'T is sweet to look by faith abroad,
   And long to fly away;

2. Sweet to look inward, and attend
   The whispers of His love;
   Sweet to look upward to the place
   Where Jesus pleads above;

3. Sweet on His faithfulness to rest,
   Whose love can never end;
   Sweet on His covenant of grace,
   For all things to depend;

4. Sweet in the confidence of faith,
   To trust His firm decrees;
   Sweet to lie passive in His hands,
   And know no will but His.

5. If such the sweetness of the streams,
   What must the fountain be,
   Where saints and angels draw their bliss
   Immediately from Thee?

   TOPLADY.

807. C. M.

1. WHEN musing sorrow weeps the past,
   And mourns the present pain,
   'T is sweet to think of peace at last,
   And feel that death is gain.

2. 'T is not that murmuring thoughts arise,
   And dread a Father's will;
   'T is not that meek submission flies,
   And would not suffer still.

3. It is that heaven-born faith surveys
   The path that leads to light,
   And longs her eagle plumes to raise,
   And lose herself in sight.

4. O let me wing my hallowed flight
   From earthborn woe and care,
   And soar above these clouds of night,
   My Saviour's bliss to share.
   B. W. NOEL.

808. C. M.

1. WHENCE do our mournful thoughts arise,
   And where 's our courage fled?
   Has restless sin, and raging hell,
   Struck all our comforts dead?

2. Have we forgot the almighty Name
   That formed the earth and sea?
   And can an all-creating arm
   Grow weary or decay?

3. Treasures of everlasting might
   In our Jehovah dwell;
   He gives the conquest to the weak,
   And treads their foes to hell.

4. Mere mortal power shall fade and die,
   And youthful vigor cease;
   But those that wait upon the Lord,
   Shall feel their strength increase.

5. The saints shall mount on eagles' wings,
   And taste the promised bliss,
   Till their unwearied feet arrive
   Where perfect pleasure is. WATTS.

809. C. M.

1. ONE prayer I have—all prayers in one—
   When I am wholly Thine;
   Thy will, my God, Thy will be done,
   And let that will be mine.

2. All-wise, almighty, and all-good,
   In Thee I firmly trust;
   Thy ways, unknown or understood,
   Are merciful and just.

3. May I remember that to Thee
   Whate'er I have I owe;
   And back, in gratitude, from me
   May all Thy bounties flow.

4. And though Thy wisdom takes away,
   Shall I arraign Thy will?
   No, let me bless Thy name, and say,
   " The Lord is gracious still."

5. A pilgrim through the earth I roam,
   Of nothing long possess'd,
   And all must fail when I go home,
   For this is not my rest.
   MONTGOMERY.

810. C. M.

1. MY times of sorrow and of joy,
   Great God! are in Thy hand;
   My choicest comforts come from Thee,
   And go at Thy command.

2. If Thou should'st take them all away,
   Yet would I not repine;
   Before they were possessed by me,
   They were entirely Thine.

3. Nor would I drop a murmuring word,
   Though the whole world were gone,
   But seek enduring happiness,
   In Thee, and Thee alone.
   BEDDOME.

811. C. M.

1. O LORD! my best desires fulfill,
   And help me to resign
   Life, health, and comfort to Thy will,
   And make Thy pleasure mine.

2. Why should I shrink at Thy command,
   Whose love forbids my fears?
   Or tremble at the gracious hand
   That wipes away my tears?

3. No! rather let me freely yield
   What most I prize to Thee,
   Who never hast a good withheld,
   Or wilt withhold from me.

4. Thy favor, all my journey through,
   Thou art engaged to grant:
   What else I want, or think I do,
   'T is better still to want.

5. Wisdom and mercy guide my way,—
   Shall I resist them both;
   A poor, blind creature of a day,
   And crushed before the moth?

6. But, ah! my inward spirit cries,
   Still bind me to Thy sway;
   Else the next cloud, that vails my skies,
   Drives all these thoughts away.
   COWPER.

CHRISTIAN EXPERIENCE.

AVON. C. M. — Scottish.

1. O Thou, whose tender mercy hears Contrition's humble sigh;
Whose hand, indulgent, wipes the tears From sorrow's weeping eye,—

812. C. M.

2. See, low before Thy throne of grace,
A wretched wanderer mourn;
Hast Thou not bid me seek Thy face?
Hast Thou not said—"Return?"

3. And shall my guilty fears prevail
To drive me from Thy feet?
O let not this dear refuge fail,
This only safe retreat?

4. O shine on this benighted heart,
With beams of mercy shine!
And let Thy healing voice impart
A taste of joys divine.

MRS. STEELE.

813. C. M.

1. YE trembling souls, dismiss your fears;
Be mercy all your theme;
Mercy, which like a river flows
In one continued stream.

2. Fear not the powers of earth and hell:
God will these powers restrain;
His mighty arm their rage repel,
And make their efforts vain.

3. Fear not the want of outward good:
He will for His provide;
Grant them supplies of daily food,
And give them heaven beside.

4. Fear not that He will e'er forsake,
Or leave His work undone:
He's faithful to His promises,
And faithful to His Son.

5. Fear not the terrors of the grave,
Or death's tremendous sting:
He will from endless wrath preserve,
To endless glory bring.

6. You, in His wisdom, power, and grace,
May confidently trust;
His wisdom guides, His power protects,
His grace rewards the just.

BEDDOME.

814. C. M.

1. How vain are all things here below!
How false, and yet how fair!
Each pleasure hath its poison, too,
And every sweet a snare.

2. The brightest things below the sky
Give but a flattering light;
We should suspect some danger nigh,
Where we possess delight.

3. Our dearest joys, and nearest friends,—
The partners of our blood,
How they divide our wavering minds,
And leave but half for God!

4. The fondness of a creature's love,
How strong it strikes the sense!
Thither the warm affections move,
Nor can we call them thence.

5. Dear Saviour! let Thy beauties be
My soul's eternal food;
And grace command my heart away
From all created good.

WATTS.

815. C. M.

1. Angel of God! whate'er betide,
   Thy summons I obey;
   Jesus! I take Thee for my guide,
   And walk in Thee my way.

2. Secure from danger and from dread,
   Nor earth nor hell shall move,
   Since over me Thine hand hath spread
   The banner of Thy love.

3. To leave my Saviour I disdain,
   Behind I will not stay,
   Though shame, and loss, and bonds, and pain,
   And death obstruct the way.

4. Me to Thy suffering self conform,
   And arm me with Thy power,
   Then burst the cloud, descend the storm,
   And come the fiery hour.

   C. WESLEY.

816. C. M.

1. Children of God, who, faint and slow,
   Your pilgrim-path pursue,
   In strength and weakness, joy and wo,
   To God's high calling true!—

2. Why move ye thus, with lingering tread,
   A doubting, mournful band?
   Why faintly hangs the drooping head?
   Why fails the feeble hand?

3. Oh! weak to know a Saviour's power,
   To feel a Father's care;
   A moment's toil, a passing shower,
   Is all the grief ye share.

4. The orb of light, though clouds awhile
   May hide his noon-tide ray,
   Shall soon in lovelier beauty smile
   To gild the closing day,—

5. And, bursting through the dusky shroud
   That dared his power invest,
   Ride throned in light o'er every cloud,
   Triumphant to his rest.

6. Then, Christian, dry the falling tear,
   The faithless doubt remove;
   Redeemed at last from guilt and fear,
   O wake thy heart to love.

   BOWDLER.

817. C. M.

1. And can my heart aspire so high,
   To say—"My Father God!"
   Lord, at Thy feet I long to lie,
   And learn to kiss the rod.

2. I would submit to all Thy will,
   For Thou art good and wise;
   Let every anxious thought be still,
   Nor one faint murmur rise.

3. Thy love can cheer the darksome gloom,
   And bid me wait serene;
   Till hopes and joys immortal bloom,
   And brighten all the scene.

4. My Father! O permit my heart
   To plead her humble claim;
   And ask the bliss those words impart,
   In my Redeemer's name.

   MRS. STEELE.

818. C. M.

1. God of my life and all my powers,
   The everlasting Friend!
   Shall life, so favored in its dawn,
   Be fruitless in its end?

2. To Thee, O Lord, my tender years
   A trembling duty paid,
   With glimpses of the mighty God
   Delighted and afraid.

3. From parent's eye, and paths of men,
   Thy touch I ran to meet;
   It swelled the hymn, and sealed the prayer;
   'T was calm, and strange, and sweet!

4. Oft when beneath the work of sin
   Trembling and dark I stood,
   And felt the edge of eager thought,
   And felt the kindling blood;—

5. Thy dew came down—my heart was Thine;
   It knew nor doubt nor strife;
   Cool now, and peaceful as the grave,
   And strong to second life.

6. Still will I hope for voice and strength
   To glorify Thy name;
   Though I must die to all that's mine,
   And suffer all my shame.

   C. WESLEY.

819. C. M.

1. O Thou eternal Source of love!
   Ruler of nature's scheme!
   In Substance One, in Persons Three!
   Omniscient and Supreme!

2. For Thy dear mercy's sake receive
   The strains and tears we pour,
   And purify our hearts to taste
   Thy sweetness more and more.

3. Our flesh, our reins, our spirits, Lord,
   In Thy clear fire refine;
   Break down the self-indulgent will;
   Gird us with strength divine.

   CASWELL.

BURNS. C. M.
Robert Burns.

1. O Thou, from whom all goodness flows, I lift my soul to Thee;
In all my sorrows, conflicts, woes, O Lord, remember me.

820. C. M.

2. If, for Thy sake, upon my name
Reproach and shame shall be,
I'll hail reproach, and welcome shame;
O Lord, remember me!

3. When worn with pain, disease, and grief,
This feeble body see;
Grant patience, rest, and kind relief;
O Lord, remember me!

4. When, in the solemn hour of death,
I wait Thy just decree,
Be this the prayer of my last breath,—
O Lord, remember me!

5. And when before Thy Throne I stand,
And lift my soul to Thee,
Thou, with the saints at Thy right hand,
O Lord, remember me!

HAWES.

821. C. M.

1. OH Thou, the first, the greatest Friend
Of all the human race!
Whose strong right hand has ever been
Their stay and dwelling place!

2. Before the mountains heav'd their heads
Beneath thy forming hand,
Before this ponderous globe itself
Arose at Thy command.

3. That Power, which raised, and still upheld
This universal frame,
From countless, unbeginning time,
Was ever still the same.

4. Those mighty periods of years
Which seem to us so vast,
Appear no more before Thy sight
Than yesterday that's past.

5. Thou givs't the word; Thy creature man
Is to existence brought,
Again Thou say'st, " Ye sons of men
Return ye into naught!"

6. Thou layest them, with all their cares,
In everlasting sleep;
As in a flood, Thou tak'st them off,
With overwhelming sweep.

7. They flourish like the morning flower,
In beauty's pride array'd;
But long ere night cut down it lies,
All withered and decayed.

ROBERT BURNS.

822. C. M.

1. My Father! to Thy mercy-seat
My soul for shelter flies;
'T is here I find a safe retreat,
When storms and tempests rise.

2. My cheerful hope can never die,
If Thou, my God, art near;
Thy grace can raise my comforts high,
And banish every fear.

3. My great Protector and my Lord,
Thy constant aid impart;
And let Thy kind, Thy gracious word
Sustain my trembling heart.

4. O never let my soul remove
From this divine retreat;
Still let me trust Thy power and love,
And dwell beneath Thy feet.
MRS. STEELE.

823. C. M.

1. Walk in the light! so shalt thou know
That fellowship of love,
His Spirit only can bestow,
Who reigns in light above.

2. Walk in the light! and thou shalt find
Thy heart made truly His,
Who dwells in cloudless light enshrined,
In whom no darkness is.

3. Walk in the light! and thou shalt own
Thy darkness passed away,
Because that Light hath on thee shone
In which is perfect day.

4. Walk in the light! and e'en the tomb
No fearful shade shall wear;
Glory shall chase away its gloom,
For Christ hath conquered there.

5. Walk in the light! thy path shall be
Peaceful, serene, and bright:
For God, by grace, shall dwell in thee,
And God himself is Light.
BERNARD BARTON.

824. C. M.

1. Lord! what a wretched land is this,
That yields us no supply,
No cheering fruits, no wholesome trees,
Nor streams of living joy!

2. Yet the dear path to Thine abode
Lies through this weary land;
Lord! we would keep that heavenly road,
And run at Thy command.

3. Our journey is a thorny maze,
But we march upward still;
Forget these troubles of the ways,
And reach at Zion's hill.

4. See the kind angels at the gates
Inviting us to come!
There Jesus, the forerunner, waits
To welcome travelers home!

5. There, on a green and flowery mount,
Our weary souls shall sit,—
And, with transporting joys, recount
The labors of our feet.

6. Eternal glory to the King,
That brought us safely through;
Our tongue shall never cease to sing,
And endless praise renew.
WATTS.

825. C. M.

1. Let others boast how strong they be,
Nor death nor danger fear;
But we 'll confess, O Lord! to Thee,
What feeble things we are.

2. Fresh as the grass our bodies stand,
And flourish bright and gay;
A blasting wind sweeps o'er the land,
And fades the grass away.

3. Our life contains a thousand springs,
And dies, if one be gone;
Strange! that a harp of thousand strings
Should keep in tune so long.

4. But 't is our God supports our frame,—
The God who built us first;
Salvation to th' Almighty Name
That reared us from the dust.
WATTS.

826. C. M.

1. Few are thy days, and full of woe,
O man of woman born!
Thy doom is written—'Dust thou art,
And shalt to dust return!'

2. Determined are the days that fly
Successive o'er thy head;
The numbered hour is on the wing,
Which lays thee with the dead.

3. Gay is thy morning: flattering hope
Thy sprightly steps attends;
But soon the tempest howls behind,
And the dark night descends!

4. Before its splendid hour, the cloud
Comes o'er the beam of light;
A pilgrim in a weary land,
Man tarries but a night!
LOGAN.

GOLDEN HILL. S. M.   Western Melody.

1. O throw a-way Thy rod! O throw a-way Thy wrath! My gra-cious Sa-viour and my God, O take the gen-tle path.

827. S. M.

2. Thou seest my heart's desire
Still unto Thee is bent;
Still does my longing soul aspire
To an entire consent.

3. Although I fail, I weep;
Although I halt in pace,
Yet still with trembling steps I creep
Unto the throne of grace.

4. O then let wrath remove;
For love will do the deed;
Love will the conquest gain; with love
E'en stony hearts will bleed.

5. O throw away thy rod!
What though man frailties hath?
Thou art my Saviour and my God;
O throw away thy wrath!

828. S. M.

1. My former hopes are fled,
My terror now begins;
I feel, alas! that I am dead
In trespasses and sins.

2. Ah! whither shall I fly?
I hear the thunder roar;
The law proclaims destruction nigh,
And vengeance at the door.

3. When I review my ways,
I dread impending doom;
But sure a friendly whisper says—
"Flee from the wrath to come."

4. I see, or think I see,
A glimmering from afar;
A beam of day that shines for me
To save me from despair.

5. Forerunner of the sun,
It marks the pilgrim's way;
I'll gaze upon it while I run,
And watch the rising day.

COWPER.

829. C. M.*

1. WHEN on the giddy cliff I stand,
I see the billows roar,
And, breaking on the coral strand,
Whiten with foam the shore.

2. But 'tis in vain they strive to break
Beyond the bounds decreed;
"No farther come!" let God but speak,
No farther they proceed.

3. Though furiously their heads they rear,
And mingle sea and skies,
They smooth as polished glass appear,
If "Peace, be still!" He cries.

4. Shall winds and waves their God obey,
And I refuse to hear?
Shall He, that bounds the flowing sea,
Not bind me with His fear?

5. O Thou! who rulest seas and skies,
Corruption's flood control;
Nor let the waves of passion rise
Within my troubled soul.

6. Then I, within Thy sacred mound,
Shall, in obedience blest,
Calm, gently flowing, kiss the bound,
And wait eternal rest.

* This may be sung to Arcadia page 246.

TRIALS AND TEMPTATIONS.

DUNBAR. S. M.   CORELLI.

1. When o-ver-whelm'd with grief, My heart with-in me dies,
Help-less, and far from all re-lief, To heaven I lift mine eyes.

830. S. M.

1. WHEN, overwhelmed with grief,
   My heart within me dies,
Helpless, and far from all relief,
   To heaven I lift mine eyes.

2. O, lead me to the Rock
   That's high above my head,
And make the covert of Thy wings
   My shelter and my shade.

3. Within Thy presence, Lord,
   For ever I'll abide;
Thou art the tower of my defence,
   The refuge where I hide.

4. Thou givest me the lot
   Of those that fear Thy name;
If endless life be their reward,
   I shall possess the same.
                 WATTS.

831. S. M.

1. I FAINT, my soul doth faint,
   My strength, a broken reed!
Would this so long be my complaint,
   Were I a saint indeed?

2. The sins I fancied quell'd,
   Again in arms arise;
The promise that I thought I held,
   Refuses its supplies.

3. My bosom burns with shame,
   And yet is icy cold;
Even to breathe the Saviour's name
   Seems now to be too bold.

4. So oft my soul hath trod
   The same sad path astray,
How can I turn again to God?
   What venture now to say?

5. Thou, Saviour, only Thou
   Canst meet my utter need,
And should'st Thou save the rebel now,
   It will be grace indeed!
                 MRS. GILBERT.

832. S. M.

1. JUST o'er the grave I hung;
   No pardon met my eyes;
As blessings never greet the slain,
   And hope shall never rise.

2. Sweet mercy to my soul
   Revealed no charming ray;
Before me rose a long, dark night,
   With no succeeding day.

3. I saw, beyond the tomb,
   The awful Judge appear,
Prepared to scan with strict account
   My blessings, wasted here.

4. His wrath, like flaming fire,
   Burned to the lowest hell;
And in that hopeless world of woe
   He bade my spirit dwell.

5. My friends, now friends no more,
   At infinite remove,
Left me to gain their rich reward,
   And taste forgiving love.

6. Then to the Lord I cried—
   He saved my soul from death;
To Him I'll give my heart and hands,
   And consecrate my breath.
                 DWIGHT.

CHRISTIAN EXPERIENCE.

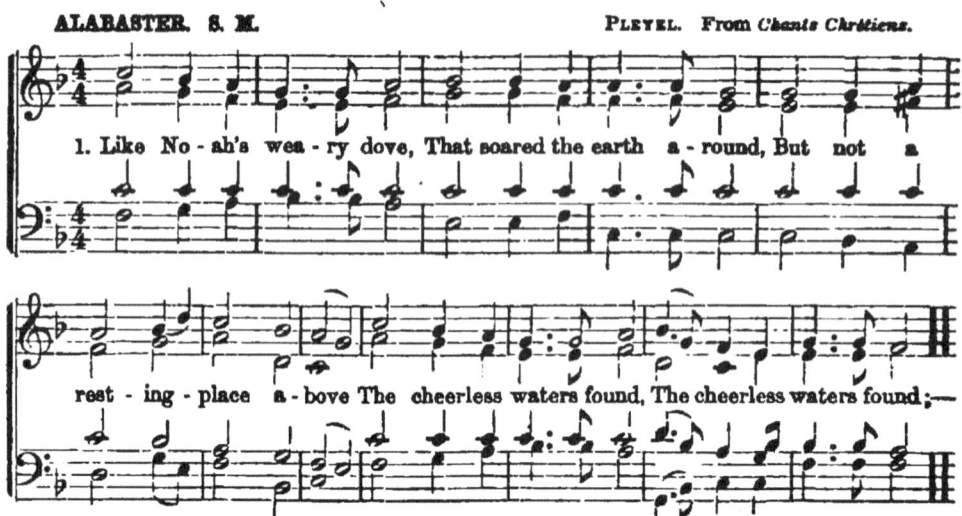

ALABASTER. S. M. — PLEYEL. From *Chants Chrétiens*.

1. Like Noah's weary dove, That soared the earth around, But not a resting-place above The cheerless waters found, The cheerless waters found;—

833. S. M.

2. O cease, my wand'ring soul,
    On restless wing to roam;
   All the wide world, to either pole,
    Has not for thee a home.

3. Behold the Ark of God,
    Behold the open door!
   Hasten to gain that dear abode,
    And rove, my soul, no more.

4. There, safe thou shalt abide,
    There sweet shall be thy rest,
   And every longing satisfied,
    With full salvation blest.

5. And when the waves of ire,
    Again the earth shall fill,
   The Ark shall ride the sea of fire,
    Then rest on Sion's hill.
                        MUHLENBERG.

834. S. M.

1. My spirit on Thy care,
    Blest Saviour, I recline,
   Thou wilt not lead me to despair,
    For Thou art love divine.

2. In Thee I place my trust,
    On Thee I calmly rest;
   I know Thee good—I know Thee just,
    And count Thy choice the best.

3. Whate'er events betide,
    Thy will they all perform;
   Safe in Thy breast my head I hide,
    Nor fear the coming storm.

835. S. M.

1. How gentle God's commands!
    How kind his precepts are!
   "Come, cast your burdens on the Lord,
    And trust His constant care."

2. Beneath His watchful eye
    His saints securely dwell;
   That hand which bears all nature up,
    Shall guard His children well.

3. Why should this anxious load
    Press down your weary mind?
   Haste to your heavenly Father's throne,
    And sweet refreshment find.

4. His goodness stands approved,
    Through each succeeding day;
   I'll drop my burden at His feet,
    And bear a song away.
                        DODDRIDGE.

836. S. M.

1. If, through unruffled seas,
    Toward heaven we calmly sail,
   With grateful hearts, O God, to Thee,
    We'll own the favoring gale.

2. But should the surges rise,
    And rest delay to come,
   Blest be the sorrow—kind the storm,
    Which drives us nearer home.

3. Soon shall our doubts and fears
    All yield to Thy control;
   Thy tender mercies shall illume
    The midnight of the soul.

4. Teach us, in every state,
    To make Thy will our own;
   And when the joys of sense depart,
    To live by faith alone.   PRATT'S COLL.

TRIALS AND TEMPTATIONS.

PLEYEL'S HYMN. 7s.   PLEYEL.

1. Jesus, lover of my soul, Let me to Thy bosom fly,
   Hide me, O my Saviour, hide, Till the storm of life is past,
   While the billows near me roll, While the tempest still is high:
   Safe into the haven guide; O receive my soul at last.

837. 7s.

2. Other refuge have I none—
     Hangs my helpless soul on Thee;
   Leave, ah! leave me not alone,
     Still support and comfort me;
   All my trust on Thee is stayed,
     All my help from Thee I bring;
   Cover my defenseless head
     With the shadow of Thy wing.

3. Thou, O Christ, art all I want,
     Boundless love in Thee I find,
   Raise the fallen, cheer the faint,
     Heal the sick, and lead the blind.
   Just and holy is Thy name,
     I am all unrighteousness;
   Vile and full of sin I am—
     Thou art full of truth and grace.

4. Plenteous grace with Thee is found—
     Grace to pardon all my sin;
   Let the healing streams abound,
     Make and keep me pure within;
   Thou of life the fountain art,
     Freely let me take of Thee;
   Spring Thou up within my heart,
     Rise to all eternity.
                                    C. WESLEY.

838. 7s.

1. When on Sinai's top I see
   God descend in majesty,
   To proclaim His holy law,
   All my spirit sinks with awe.

2. When in ecstasy sublime,
   Tabor's glorious mount I climb,
   In the too transporting light,
   Darkness rushes o'er my sight.

3. When on Calvary I rest,
   God in flesh made manifest,
   Shines in my Redeemer's face,
   Full of beauty, truth, and grace,

4. Here I would for ever stay,
   Weep and gaze my soul away:
   Thou art heaven on earth to me,
   Lovely, mournful Calvary.
                                    MONTGOMERY.

839. S. M.*

1. My sorrows, like a flood,
     Impatient of restraint,
   Into Thy bosom O my God,
     Pour out a long complaint.

2. O'ercome by dying love,
     Here at Thy cross I lie,
   Submit my soul, my all, to Thee,
     And weep, and love, and die.

3. "Rise," says the Saviour, "rise;
     Behold my wounded veins!
   Here flows a sacred, crimson flood
     To wash away thy stains."

4. See, God is reconciled!
     Behold His smiling face!
   Let sinners in His love rejoice,
     And sound aloud His grace.
                                    WATTS.

* Tune on the opposite page.

CHRISTIAN EXPERIENCE.

DOVER. S. M. — Arranged by L. Mason.

1. Give to the winds thy fears; Hope, and be undismay'd; God hears thy sighs, and counts thy tears, God shall lift up thy head.

840. S. M.

1. Give to the winds thy fears;
   Hope, and be undismay'd;
   God hears thy sighs, and counts thy tears,
   God shall lift up thy head.

2. Through waves, through clouds and storms,
   He gently clears thy way;
   Wait thou His time; so shall this night
   Soon end in joyous day.

3. Still heavy is thy heart!
   Still sink thy spirits down!
   Cast off the weight, let fear depart,
   Bid every care be gone.

4. Far, far above thy thought
   His counsel shall appear,
   When fully He the work hath wrought,
   That caused thy needless fear.

5. What, though thou rulest not!
   Yet heaven, and earth, and hell
   Proclaim, God sitteth on the throne,
   And ruleth all things well!

   GERHARD.

841. S. M.

1. Where wilt thou put thy trust?
   In a frail form of clay,
   That to its element of dust
   Must soon resolve away?

2. Where wilt thou cast thy care?
   Upon an erring heart,
   Which hath its own sore ills to bear,
   And shrinks from sorrow's dart?

3. No! place thy trust above
   This shadowy realm of night,
   In Him, whose boundless power and love
   Thy confidence invite.

4. His mercies still endure
   When skies and stars grow dim,
   His changeless promise standeth sure,—
   Go,—cast thy care on Him.

   MRS. SIGOURNEY.

842. S. M.

1. As changing as the moon
   Is man's estate below:
   To his bright day of gladness soon
   Succeeds a night of woe.

2. The night of woe resigns
   Its darkness and its grief;
   Again the morn of comfort shines,
   And brings our souls relief.

3. Yet not to fickle chance
   Is man's condition given;
   His dark and shining hours advance
   By the fixed laws of heaven.

4. God measures unto all
   Their lot of good or ill;
   Nor this too great, nor that too small,
   Ordained by wisest will.

5. Let man conform his mind
   To every changing state;
   Rejoicing now, and now resigned,
   And the great issue wait.

   T. SCOTT.

TRIALS AND TEMPTATIONS.

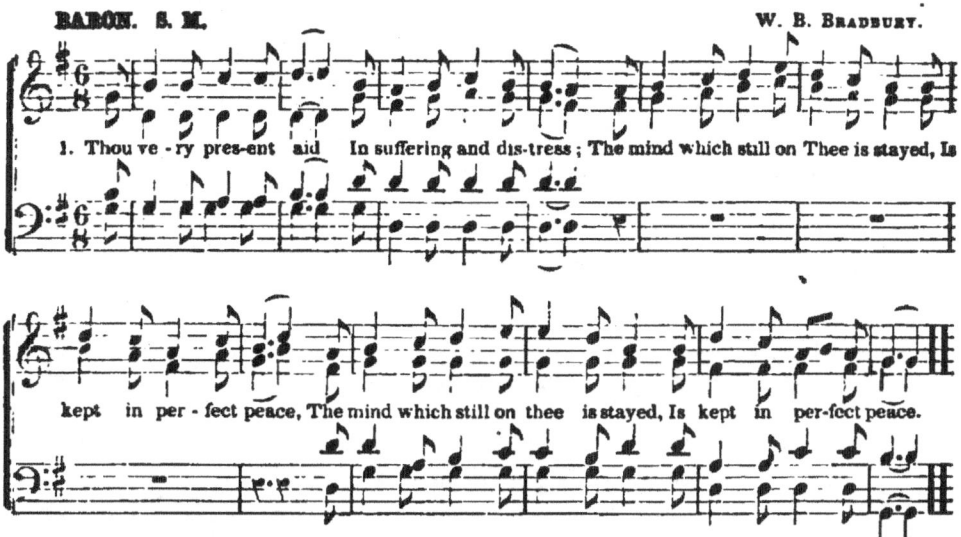

BARON. S. M. W. B. BRADBURY.

1. Thou ve-ry pres-ent aid In suffering and dis-tress; The mind which still on Thee is stayed, Is kept in per-fect peace, The mind which still on thee is stayed, Is kept in per-fect peace.

843. S. M.

2. The soul by faith reclined
    On the Redeemer's breast,
'Mid raging storms, exults to find
    An everlasting rest.

3. Sorrow and fear are gone,
    Whene'er Thy face appears;
It stills the sighing orphan's moan,
    And dries the widow's tears.

4. It hallows every cross;
    It sweetly comforts me;
Makes me forget my every loss,
    And find my all in Thee.

5. Jesus, to whom I fly,
    Doth all my wishes fill;
What though created streams are dry?
    I have the fountain still.

6. Stripp'd of each earthly friend,
    I find them all in one:
And peace and joy which never end,
    And heaven, in Christ, begun.
                        C. WESLEY.

844. S. M.

1. COMMIT thou all Thy griefs
    And ways into His hands,
To His sure trust and tender care,
    Who earth and heaven commands.

2. Who points the clouds their course,
    Whom wind and seas obey,
He shall direct thy wandering feet,
    He shall prepare thy way.

3. No profit canst thou gain
    By self-consuming care;
To Him commend thy cause,—his ear
    Attends the softest prayer.

4. Thou on the Lord rely,
    So safe shalt thou go on;
Fix on His work Thy steadfast eye,
    So shall thy work be done.
                        J. WESLEY.

845. S. M.

1. GREEN pastures and clear streams,
    Freedom and quiet rest,
Christ's flock enjoy, beneath His beams,
    Or in His shadow, blest.

2. The mountain and the vale,
    Forest and field, they range:
The morning dew, the evening gale,
    Bring health in every change.

3. Secure, amidst alarms,
    From violence or snares,
The lambs He gathers in His arms,
    And in His bosom bears.

4. The wounded and the weak
    He comforts, heals, and binds;
The lost He came from heaven to seek,
    And saves them when He finds.

5. Should storms of trouble blow,
    Warned of the coming shock,
They to the Rock of Ages go:
    Their Shepherd is their Rock.

6. Conflicts and trials done,
    His glory they behold,
Where Jesus and His flock are one—
    One Shepherd and one fold.
                        MONTGOMERY.

CHRISTIAN EXPERIENCE.

TWILIGHT. 7s. * J. ZUNDEL.

1. As the hart, with eager looks, Panteth for the water brooks,
So my soul, athirst for Thee, Pants the living God to see;
When, O when, with filial fear, Lord, shall I to Thee draw near! Lord, shall I to Thee draw near!

846. 7s.

2. Why art thou cast down, my soul?
God, thy God, shall make thee whole;
Why art thou disquieted?
God shall lift thy fallen head,
And His countenance benign
Be the saving health of thine.
MONTGOMERY.

847. 7s.

1. Holy Spirit! Lord of light!
From Thy clear celestial height,
Come, Thou Light of all that live!
Thy pure beaming radiance give!

2. Come, Thou Father of the poor!
Come with treasures which endure;
Thou, of all consolers best,
Visiting the troubled breast.

3. Thou in toil art comfort sweet;
Pleasant coolness in the heat;
Solace in the midst of woe;
Dost refreshing peace bestow.

4. Light immortal! Light divine!
Visit Thou these hearts of Thine;
If Thou take Thy grace away,
Nothing pure in man will stay.

5. Heal our wounds—our strength renew;
On our dryness pour Thy dew;
Wash the stains of guilt away;
Guide the steps that go astray.

6. Give us comfort when we die;
Give us life with Thee on high;
In Thy sevenfold gifts descend;
Give us joys which never end.
LYRA CATH.

* In 7s single, omit the repeat.

848. 7s.

1. Softly, now, the light of day
Fades upon my sight away;
Free from care, from labor free,
Lord! I would commune with Thee.

2. Soon, for me, the light of day
Shall for ever pass away;
Then, from sin and sorrow free,
Take me, Lord! to dwell with Thee.
DOANE.

849. 7s.

1. Lord! I can not let Thee go,
Till a blessing Thou bestow;
Do not turn away Thy face,
Mine's an urgent, pressing case.

2. Once, a sinner, near despair,
Sought Thy mercy-seat by prayer;
Mercy heard and set him free—
Lord! that mercy came to me.

3. Many days have passed since then,
Many changes I have seen;
Yet have been upheld till now;
Who could hold me up but Thou?

4. Thou hast helped in every need—
This emboldens me to plead;
After so much mercy past,
Canst Thou let me sink at last?

5. No—I must maintain my hold;
'T is Thy goodness makes me bold;
I can no denial take,
Since I plead for Jesus' sake.
NEWTON.

TRIALS AND TEMPTATIONS.

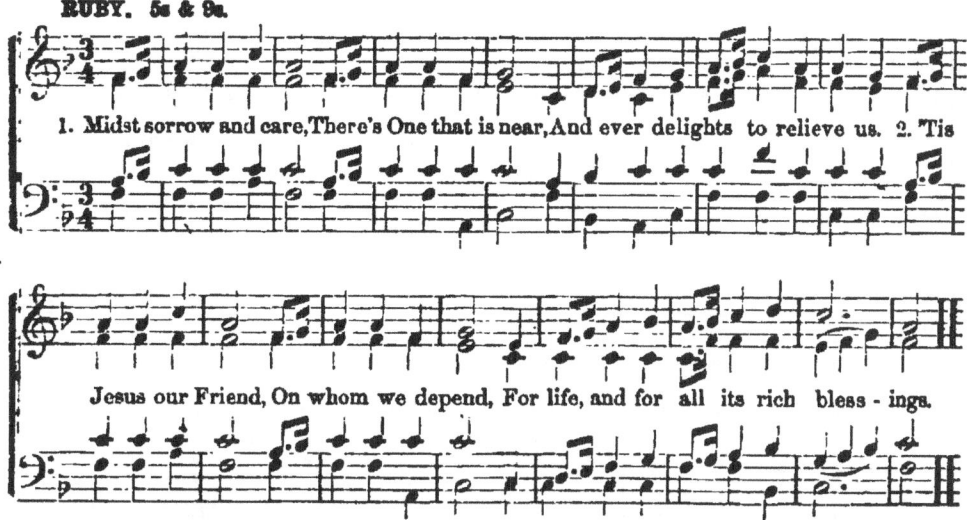

RUBY. 5s & 9s.

1. Midst sorrow and care, There's One that is near, And ever delights to relieve us. 2. 'Tis Jesus our Friend, On whom we depend, For life, and for all its rich bless-ings.

850. 5s & 9s.

1. MIDST sorrow and care
   There's One that is near,
   And ever delights to relieve us.

2. 'Tis Jesus our Friend,
   On whom we depend,
   For life and for all its rich blessings.

3. When trouble assails,
   His love never fails,
   He meets us with sweet consolation.

4. His bounties are free,
   He hears every plea,
   And welcomes the cry of the needy,

5. Blest mansions above,
   Prepared by His love,
   Are waiting at last to receive us.

6. My Saviour and Friend,
   On whom I depend,
   My heart shall for ever adore Thee.

851. 7s.*

1. HAST thou wasted all the powers
   God for noble uses gave?
   Squandered life's most golden hours?
   Turn thee, brother, God can save!

2. Is a mighty famine now
   In thy heart and in thy soul;
   Discontent upon thy brow?
   Turn thee, God will make thee whole!

* Tune on the opposite page.

3. Fall before Him on the ground,
   Pour thy sorrow in His ear,
   Seek Him while He may be found,
   Call upon Him while He's near.

   J. T. CLARKE.

852. 7s.*

1. HOLY GHOST! with light divine,
   Shine upon this heart of mine;
   Chase the shades of night away,
   Turn my darkness into day.

2. Holy Ghost! with power divine,
   Cleanse this guilty heart of mine;
   Long hath sin, without control,
   Held dominion o'er my soul.

3. Holy Ghost! with joy divine,
   Cheer this saddened heart of mine,
   Bid my many woes depart,
   Heal my wounded, bleeding heart.

4. Holy Spirit! all-divine,
   Dwell within this heart of mine;
   Cast down every idol-throne,
   Reign supreme—and reign alone.

853. 7s.*

1. CHRISTIAN brethren, ere we part,
   Every voice and every heart
   Join, and to our Father raise
   One last hymn of grateful praise.

2. Though we here should meet no more,
   Yet there is a brighter shore;
   There, released from toil and pain,
   There we all may meet again.

CHRISTIAN EXPERIENCE.

ROSEFIELD. 7s. Dr. Malan.

1. People of the living God, I have sought the world a-round,
Paths of sin and sorrow trod, Peace and comfort no where found.

854. 7s.

1. PEOPLE of the living God,
   I have sought the world around,
   Paths of sin and sorrow trod,
   Peace and comfort no where found;

2. Now to you my spirit turns,
   Turns—a fugitive unblest;
   Brethren! where your altar burns,
   O receive me into rest.

3. Lonely, I no longer roam,
   Like the cloud, the wind, the wave—
   Where you dwell shall be my home,
   Where you die shall be my grave;

4. Mine the God whom you adore,
   Your Redeemer shall be mine;
   Earth can fill my soul no more,
   Every idol I resign.
   MONTGOMERY.

855. 7s.

1. O, HOW soft that bed must be,
   Made in sickness, Lord, by Thee;
   And that rest, how calm, how sweet,
   Where Jesus and the sufferer meet.

2. It was the good Physician now,
   Soothed thy cheek, and chafed thy brow,
   Whispering, as He raised thy head—
   "It is I, be not afraid."

3. God of glory, God of grace,
   Hear from heaven, Thy dwelling-place;
   Hear, in mercy, and forgive,
   Bid Thy child believe and live.

4. Bless me, and I shall be blest,
   Soothe me, and I shall have rest;
   Fix my heart, my hopes, above;
   Love me, Lord, for Thou art love.

856. 7s.*

1. HEARKEN Lord, to my complaints,
   For my soul within me faints;
   Thee, far off, I call to mind,
   In the land I left behind,
   Where the streams of Jordan flow,
   Where the hights of Hermon glow.

2. Tempest-tost, my failing bark
   Founders on the ocean dark;
   Deep to deep around me calls,
   With the rush of waterfalls,
   While I plunge to lower caves,
   Overwhelmed by all Thy waves.

3. Once the morning's earliest light
   Brought Thy mercy to my sight,
   And my wakeful song was heard,
   Later than the evening bird;
   Hast Thou all my prayers forgot?
   Dost Thou scorn, or hear them not?

4. Why, my soul, art thou perplex'd?
   Why with faithless troubles vex'd?
   Hope in God, whose saving name
   Thou shalt joyfully proclaim,
   When His countenance shall shine
   Through the clouds that darken thine.
   MONTGOMERY.

* Repeat the first two strains.

TRIALS AND TEMPTATIONS.

857. 7s.*

1. Quiet, Lord, my froward heart,
    Make me teachable and mild,
 Upright, simple, free from art,
    Make me as a weaned child;
 From distrust and envy free,
 Pleased with all that pleases Thee.

2. What Thou shalt to-day provide,
    Let me as a child receive;
 What to-morrow may betide,
    Calmly to Thy wisdom leave;
 'T is enough that Thou wilt care—
 Why should I the burden bear?

3. As a little child relies
    On a care beyond his own;
 Knows he 's neither strong nor wise,
    Fears to stir a step alone;
 Let me thus with Thee abide,
 As my Father, Guard, and Guide.
                                NEWTON.

858. 7s.*

1. Gales from heaven, if God so will,
    Sweeter melodies can wake,
 On the lonely mountain rill,
    Than the meeting waters make.
 Who hath the Father and the Son,
 May be left, but not alone.

2. Sick or healthful, slave or free,
    Wealthy, or despised and poor—
 What is that to him or thee,
    So his love to Christ endure?
 When the shore is won at last,
 Who will count the billows past?

3. Only, since our souls will shrink
    At the touch of natural grief,
 When our earthly, loved ones sink,
    Lend us, Lord, Thy sure relief;
 Patient hearts, their pain to see,
 And Thy grace, to follow Thee.

859. 7s.

1. Gently, gently lay Thy rod
    On my sinful head, O God!
 Stay thy wrath, in mercy stay,
 Lest I sink beneath its sway.

2. Heal me, for my flesh is weak;
 Heal me, for Thy grace I seek;
 This my only plea I make—
 Heal me for Thy mercy's sake.

3. Who, within the silent grave,
 Shall proclaim Thy power to save?

* Repeat the first two strains.

Lord! my sinking soul reprieve;
Speak, and I shall rise and live.

4. Lo! He comes—He heeds my plea;
 Lo! He comes—the shadows flee;
 Glory round me dawns once more;
 Rise, my spirit, and adore!
                                LYTE.

860. 7s.

1. In the hour of my distress,
    When temptations me oppress,
    And when I my sins confess—
     Then, sweet Spirit, comfort me.

2. When I lie within my bed,
    Sick in heart, and sick in head,
    And with doubts disquieted—
     Then, sweet Spirit, comfort me.

3. When the house doth sigh and weep,
    And the world is drowned in sleep,
    Yet mine eyes the watch do keep—
     Then, sweet Spirit, comfort me.

4. When the tempter me pursueth,
    With the sins of all my youth,
    And condemns me with untruth—
     Then, sweet Spirit, comfort me.

5. When the flames and hellish cries,
    Fright mine ears, and fright mine eyes,
    And all terrors me surprise—
     Then, sweet Spirit, comfort me.

6. When the judgment is reveal'd,
    And that opened, which was seal'd,
    When to Thee I have appeal'd—
     Then, sweet Spirit, comfort me.
                                VAUGHN.

861. 7s.*

1. Center of our hopes Thou art;
    End of our enlarged desires,
 Stamp Thine image on our heart,
    Fill us now with heavenly fires;
 Joined to Thee by love divine,
 Seal our souls for ever Thine.

2. All our works in Thee be wrought—
    Leveled at one common aim;
 Every word and every thought
    Purge in the refining flame;
 Lead us through the paths of peace,
 On to perfect holiness.

3. Let us altogether rise,
    To Thy glorious life restored;
 Here regain our Paradise,
    Here prepare to meet our Lord;
 Here enjoy the earnest given;
 Travel hand in hand to heaven.
                                C. WESLEY.

HYACINTH. 7s.

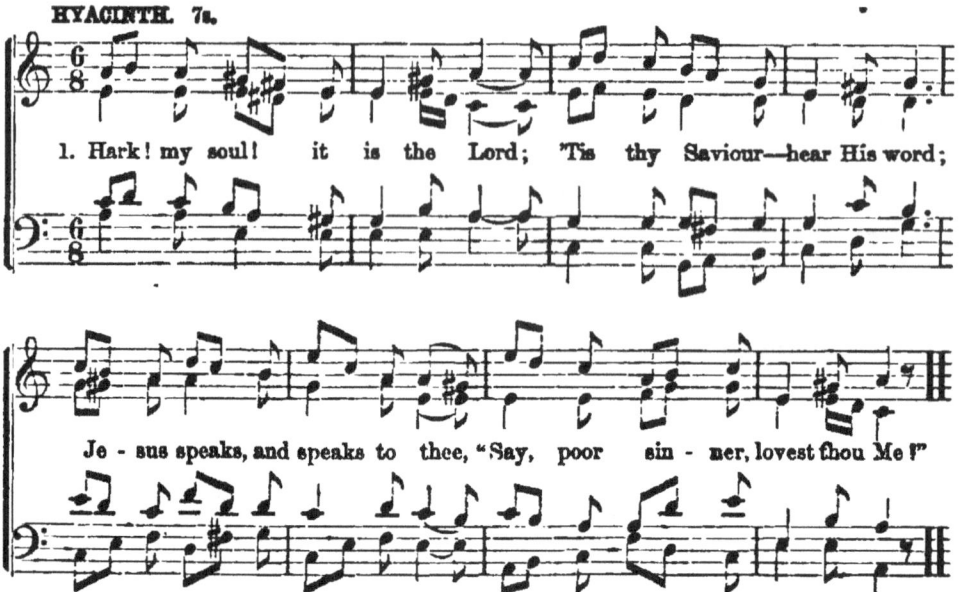

1. Hark! my soul! it is the Lord; 'Tis thy Saviour—hear His word;
Jesus speaks, and speaks to thee, "Say, poor sinner, lovest thou Me?"

862. 7s.

2. "I delivered thee when bound,
And when bleeding, healed thy wound:
Sought thee wandering, set thee right,
Turned thy darkness into light.

3. "Can a woman's tender care
Cease towards the child she bare?
Yes, she may forgetful be,
Yet will I remember thee.

4. "Mine is an unchanging love,
Higher than the heights above;
Deeper than the depths beneath—
Free and faithful—strong as death.

5. Thou shalt see My glory soon,
When the work of grace is done;
Partner of My throne shalt be;
Say, poor sinner! lovest thou Me?"

6. Lord! it is my chief complaint,
That my love is weak and faint;
Yet I love Thee, and adore;—
Oh! for grace to love Thee more.
COWPER.

863. 7s. 6 lines.

1. ABBA, Father, hear Thy child,
Late in Jesus reconciled;
Hear, and all the graces shower,
All the joy, and peace, and power;
All my Saviour asks above,
All the life and heaven of love.

2. Heavenly Father, Life divine,
Change my nature into Thine;
Move and spread throughout my soul,
Actuate and fill the whole:
Lord, I will not let Thee go
Till the blessing Thou bestow.

3. Holy Ghost, no more delay;
Come, and in Thy temple stay:
Now Thine inward witness bear,
Strong, and permanent, and clear:
Spring of life, Thyself impart;
Rise eternal in my heart.

864. 7s. 6 lines.

1. BLESSED are the sons of God;
They are bought with Jesus' blood;
They are ransomed from the grave;
Life eternal they shall have:
With them numbered may we be,
Here, and in eternity.

2. They are justified by grace,
They enjoy the Saviour's peace;
All their sins are washed away;
They shall stand in God's great day:
With them numbered may we be,
Here, and in eternity.

3. They are lights upon the earth,—
Children of a heavenly birth,—
One with God, with Jesus one;
Glory is in them begun:
With them numbered may we be,
Here, and in eternity.   HUMPHRIES.

TRIALS AND TEMPTATIONS.

COME, YE DISCONSOLATE. 11s & 10s. WEBBE, of England.

1. Come, ye dis-con-solate, where'er you languish, Come, at the shrine of God fer-vent-ly kneel; Here bring your wounded hearts, here tell your anguish, Earth has no sorrow that Heaven cannot heal. Here bring your wounded hearts, here tell your anguish; Earth has no sorrow that Heaven cannot heal.

865. 11s & 10s.

2. Joy of the desolate, light of the straying,
   Hope of the penitent, fadeless and pure!
   Here speaks the Comforter, tenderly saying,
   Earth has no sorrow that Heaven cannot cure.

3. Here see the bread of life; see waters flowing
   Forth from the throne of God, pure from above:
   Come to the feast of love; come, ever-knowing,
   Earth has no sorrow but Heaven can remove.

MOORE.

CHRISTIAN EXPERIENCE.

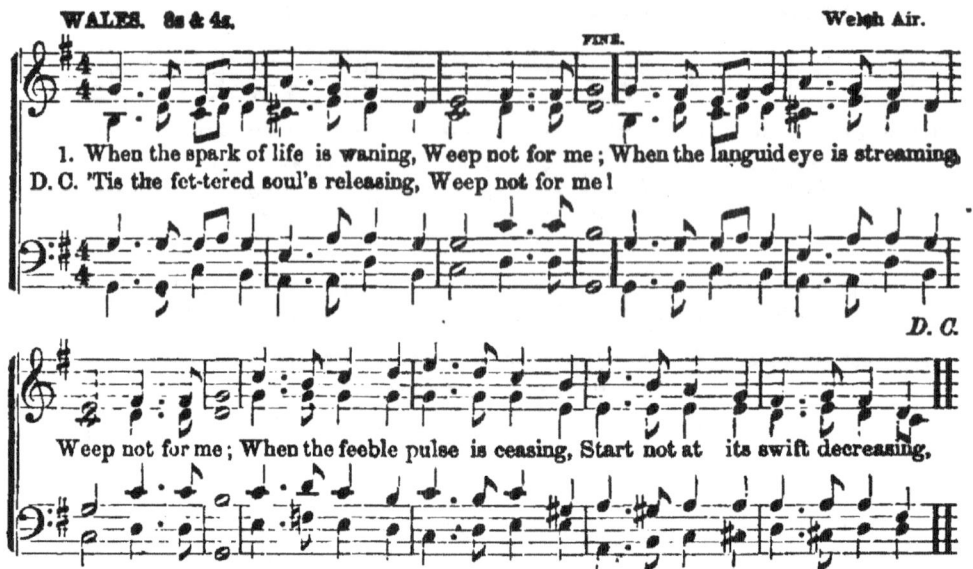

WALES. 8s & 4s.   Welsh Air.

1. When the spark of life is waning, Weep not for me; When the languid eye is streaming,
D. C. 'Tis the fettered soul's releasing, Weep not for me!
Weep not for me; When the feeble pulse is ceasing, Start not at its swift decreasing.

866. 8s & 4s.

1. WHEN the spark of life is waning,
   Weep not for me;
   When the languid eye is streaming,
   Weep not for me;
   When the feeble pulse is ceasing,
   Start not at its swift decreasing,
   'T is the fettered soul's releasing—
   Weep not for me!

2. When the pangs of death assail me,
   Weep not for me;
   Christ is mine, He can not fail me—
   Weep not for me;
   Yet though sin and doubt endeavor
   From His love my soul to sever,
   Jesus is my strength for ever:
   Weep not for me!

867. 8s & 4s.

1. THERE 's a Friend above all others,
   O how He loves!
   His is love beyond a brother's,
   O how He loves!
   Earthly friends may fail and leave us,
   This day kind, the next bereave us,
   But this Friend will ne'er deceive us—
   O how He loves!

2. Blessed Jesus!—would'st thou know Him?
   O how He loves!
   Give thyself e'en this day to Him,
   O how He loves!
   Is it sin that pains and grieves thee?
   Doubts and trials do they tease thee?
   Jesus can from all release thee,
   O how He loves!

3. Love this Friend who longs to save thee,
   O how He loves!
   Dost thou love? He will not leave thee,
   O how He loves!
   Think no more, then, of to-morrow,
   Take His easy yoke and follow,
   Jesus carries all thy sorrow,
   O how He loves!

4. All thy sins shall be forgiven,
   O how He loves!
   Backward all thy foes be driven,
   O how He loves!
   Best of blessings He 'll provide thee,
   Nought but good shall e'er betide thee,
   Safe to glory He will guide thee—
   O how He loves!

5. Pause, my soul! adore and wonder,
   O how He loves!
   Nought can cleave this love asunder;
   O how He loves!
   Neither trial, nor temptation,
   Doubt, nor fear, nor tribulation,
   Can bereave us of salvation—
   O how He loves!

6. Let us still this love be viewing,
   O how He loves!
   And, though faint, keep on pursuing,
   O how He loves!
   He will strengthen each endeavor,
   And when passed o'er Jordan's river,
   This shall be our song for ever,
   O how He loves!

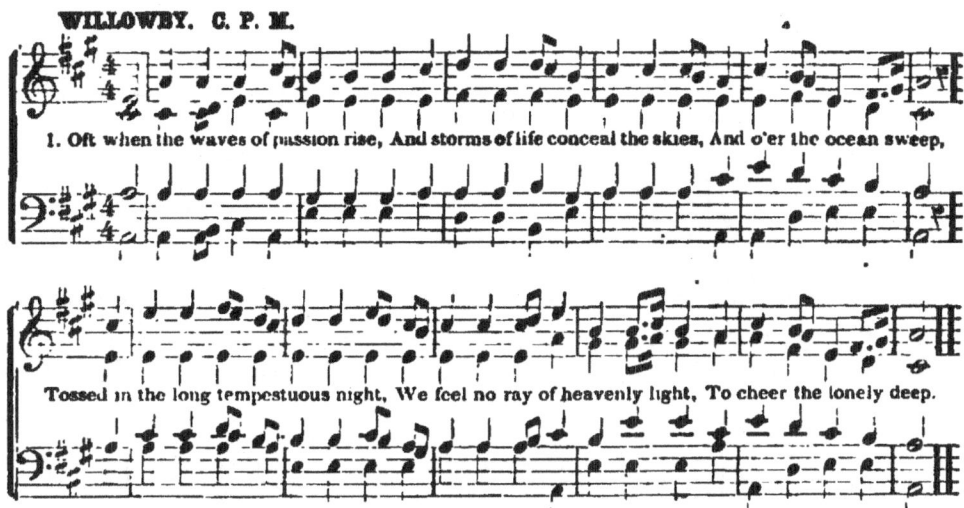

WILLOWBY. C. P. M.

1. Oft when the waves of passion rise, And storms of life conceal the skies, And o'er the ocean sweep, Tossed in the long tempestuous night, We feel no ray of heavenly light, To cheer the lonely deep.

868. C. P. M.

2. But lo! in our extremity,
   The Saviour walking on the sea!
     E'en now He passes by!
   He silences our clamorous fear,
   And mildly says, "Be of good cheer,
     Be not afraid, 't is I."

3. Ah, Lord! if it be Thou indeed,
   So near us in our time of need,
     So good, so strong to save;—
   Speak the kind word of power to me,
   Bid me believe, and come to Thee,
     Swift-walking on the wave.

4. He bids me come! His voice I know,
   And boldly on the waters go,
     And brave the tempest's shock:
   O'er rude temptations now I bound;
   The billows yield a solid ground,
     The wave is firm as rock!

5. Come in, come in, Thou Prince of peace!
   And all the storms of sin shall cease,
     And fall, no more to rise:
   O if Thy Spirit still remain,
   Our rest on distant shores we gain,
     Our haven in the skies!
                              C. WESLEY.

869. C. P. M.

1. Thy mercy heard my infant prayer,
   Thy love, with all a mother's care,
     Sustained my childish days:
   Thy goodness watched my ripening youth,
   And formed my heart to love Thy truth,
     And filled my lips with praise.

2. Then e'en in age and grief, Thy name
   Shall still my languid heart inflame,
     And bow my faltering knee:
   Oh! yet this bosom feels the fire,
   This trembling hand and drooping lyre
     Have yet a strain for Thee!

3. Yes! broken, tuneless, still, O Lord,
   This voice transported shall record
     Thy goodness, tried so long;
   Till, sinking slow, with calm decay,
   Its feeble murmurs melt away
     Into a seraph's song.
                              SIR R. GRANT.

870. C. P. M.

1. Come on, my partners in distress,
   My comrades in the wilderness,
     Who still your bodies feel;
   Awhile forget your griefs and fears,
   And look beyond this vale of tears,
     To that celestial hill.

2. Beyond the bounds of time and space,
   Look forward to that heavenly place,
     The saint's secure abode;
   On faith's strong eagle pinions rise,
   And force your passage to the skies,
     And scale the mount of God.

3. Who suffer with our Master here,
   We shall before his face appear,
     And by his side sit down:
   To patient faith the prize is sure;
   And all that to the end endure
     The cross, shall wear the crown.

CHRISTIAN EXPERIENCE.

JACINTH. 7s & 6s. Or 8s & 7s.   CH. BEECHER.

(871.) 1. Though hard the winds are blowing, And loud the billows roar; Full swiftly are we going To our dear native shore. 2. The billows breaking o'er us,

(872) 8s & 7s. 1. Tell me not, in mournful numbers, Life is but an empty dream; For the soul is dead that slumbers, And things are not what they seem. 2. Life is real! life is earnest'

The storms that round us swell, Are aiding to restore us To all we loved so well.

And the grave is not its goal; Dust thou art, to dust returnest, Was not spoken of the soul!

871. 7s & 6s.

3. So sorrow often presses
   Life's mariner along;
Afflictions and distresses
   Are gales and billows strong.

4. The sharper and severer
   The storm of life we meet,
The sooner and the nearer
   Is heaven's eternal seat.

5. Come, then, afflictions dreary,
   Sharp sickness, pierce my breast—
You only bear the weary
   More quickly home to rest.

872. 8s & 7s.
[Stanzas 1 and 2 in the music.]

3. Not enjoyment, and not sorrow,
   Is our destined end and way;
But to act, that each to-morrow
   Find us further than to-day.

4. Lives of true men all remind us
   We can make our lives sublime,
And, departing, leave behind us
   Footprints on the sands of time;

5. Footprints which perhaps another,
   Sailing o'er life's solemn main,
A forlorn and shipwrecked brother,
   Seeing, shall take heart again.

6. Let us, then, be up and doing,
   With a heart for any fate;
Still achieving, still pursuing,
   Learn to labor and to wait.
              LONGFELLOW.

873. 8s & 7s.

1. JOYFUL words,—we meet again!
Love's own language, comfort darting
Through the souls of friends at parting;
   Life in death,—we meet again!

2. While we walk this vale of tears,
Compassed round with care and sorrow,
Gloom to-day, and storm to-morrow,
   "Meet again!" our bosom cheers.

3. Far in exile, when we roam,
O'er our lost endearments weeping,
Lonely, silent vigils keeping,
   "Meet again" transports us home.

4. When this weary world is past,
Happy they, whose spirits soaring,
Vast eternity exploring,
   "Meet again" in heaven at last.

TRIALS AND TEMPTATIONS.

874. 8s & 7s.

1. FULL of trembling expectation,
    Feeling much, and fearing more,
   Mighty God of my salvation!
    I Thy timely aid implore;
   Suffering Son of Man, be near me,
    All my sufferings to sustain;
   By Thy sorer griefs to cheer me,
    By Thy more than mortal pain.

2. Call to mind that unknown anguish,
    In Thy days of flesh below;
   When Thy troubled soul did languish
    Under a whole world of woe;
   When Thou didst our curse inherit,
    Groan beneath our guilty load,
   Burdened with a wounded spirit,
    Bruised by all the wrath of God.

3. By Thy most severe temptation,
    In that dark, satanic hour;
   By Thy last, mysterious passion,
    Screen me from the adverse power.
   By Thy fainting in the garden,
    By Thy bloody sweat, I pray,
   Write upon my heart the pardon,
    Take my sins and fears away.

4. By the travail of Thy spirit,
    By Thine outcry on the tree,
   By Thine agonizing merit,
    In my pangs, remember me!
   By Thy death I Thee conjure,
    A weak, dying soul befriend;
   Make me patient to endure,
    Make me faithful to the end.
                        C. WESLEY.

875. 7s & 6s.

1. WHEN human hopes all wither,
    And friends no aid supply,
   Then whither, Lord, ah! whither
    Can turn my straining eye?
   'Mid storms of grief still rougher,
    'Midst darker, deadlier shade,
   That cross where Thou didst suffer,
    On Calvary was display'd.

2. On that my gaze I fasten,
    My refuge that I make;
   Though sorely Thou may'st chasten,
    Thou never canst forsake.
   Thou, on that cross didst languish,
    Ere glory crowned Thy head;
   And I, through death and anguish,
    Must be to glory led.

876. 8s & 7s.

1. LONE, amidst the dead and dying,
    Lord, my spirit faints for Thee;
   Longing, thirsting, drooping, sighing,—
    When shall I Thy presence see?

2. O, how altered my condition;
    Late I led the joyous throng;
   Beat my heart with full fruition,
    Flowed my lips with grateful song.

3. Now the storm goes wildly o'er me,
    Waves on waves my soul confound;
   Nought but boding fears before me,
    Nought but threat'ning foes around.

4. Save me, save me, O my Father!
    To Thy faithful word I cling;
   Thence, my soul! thy comfort gather;
    Hope! and thou again shalt sing.

877. 7s & 6s.

1. As flows the rapid river,
    With channel broad and free,
   Its waters rippling ever,
    And hastening to the sea,
   So life is onward flowing,
    And days of offered peace,
   And man is swiftly going
    Where calls of mercy cease.

2. As moons are ever waning,
    As hastes the sun away,
   As stormy winds, complaining,
    Bring on the wintry day,
   So fast the night comes o'er us.—
    The darkness of the grave;
   And death is just before us;
    God takes the life He gave.

3. Say, hath thy heart its treasure
    Laid up in worlds above?
   And is it all thy pleasure
    Thy God to praise and love?
   Beware! lest death's dark river
    Its billows o'er thee roll,
   And thou lament for ever
    The ruin of thy soul.
                        S. F. SMITH.

DOXOLOGY. 7s & 6s.

We'll praise Thy name for ever,—
    Thou glorious King of kings!
Thy wondrous love and favor
    Each ransomed spirit sings;
We'll celebrate Thy glory,
    With all Thy saints above,
And shout the joyful story
    Of Thy redeeming love.

CHRISTIAN EXPERIENCE.

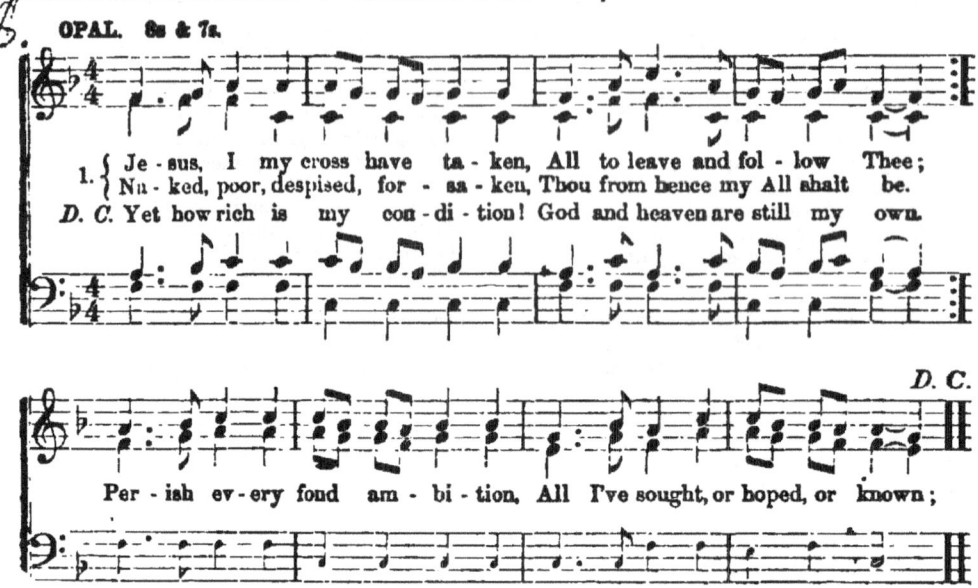

OPAL. 8s & 7s.

1. Jesus, I my cross have taken, All to leave and follow Thee;
Naked, poor, despised, forsaken, Thou from hence my All shalt be.
D.C. Yet how rich is my condition! God and heaven are still my own.
Perish every fond ambition, All I've sought, or hoped, or known;

878. 8s & 7s. Double.

1. Jesus, I my cross have taken,
　All to leave and follow Thee;
Naked, poor, despised, forsaken,
　Thou, from hence, my all shalt be.
Perish every fond ambition,
　All I've sought, or hoped, or known;
Yet how rich is my condition!
　God and heaven are still my own.

2. Let the world despise and leave me,
　They have left my Saviour, too;
Human hearts and looks deceive me,
　Thou art not, like them untrue;
And whilst Thou shalt smile upon me,
　God of wisdom, love, and might,
Foes may hate, and friends may scorn me;
　Show Thy face, and all is bright.

3. Man may trouble and distress me,
　'T will but drive me to Thy breast;
Life with trials hard may press me,
　Heaven will bring me sweeter rest.
Oh! 't is not in grief to harm me,
　While Thy love is left to me;
Oh! 'twere not in joy to charm me,
　Were that joy unmixed with Thee.

4. Soul, then know thy full salvation,
　Rise o'er sin, and fear, and care;
Joy to find in every station
　Something still to do or bear.
Think what Spirit dwells within thee;
　Think what Father's smiles are thine;
Think that Jesus died to win thee;
　Child of heaven, can'st thou repine?

5. Haste thee on from grace to glory,
　Armed by faith, and winged by prayer;
Heaven's eternal day 's before thee,
　God's own hand shall guide thee there.
Soon shall close thy earthly mission,
　Soon shall pass thy pilgrim days;
Hope shall change to glad fruition,
　Faith to sight, and prayer to praise.
　　　　　　　　　MISS GRANT.

879. 8s & 7s.

1. Cross, reproach, and tribulation,
　Ye to me are welcome guests,
When I have this consolation,
　That my soul in Jesus rests.

2. The reproach of Christ is glorious;
　Those who here His burden bear
In the end shall prove victorious,
　And eternal gladness share.

3. Bear, then, the reproach of Jesus,
　Ye who live a life of faith!
Lift triumphant songs and praises,
　E'en in martyrdom and death.

4. Bonds and stripes, and evil story,
　Are our honorable crowns;
Pain is peace, and shame is glory,
　Gloomy dungeons are as thrones.
　　　　　　　　　MORAVIAN.

880. 8s & 7s.

1. Tossed upon life's raging billow,
    Sweet it is, O Lord, to know,
   Thou did'st press a sailor's pillow,
    And canst feel a sailor's woe.
   Never slumbering, never sleeping,
    Though the night be dark and drear,
   Thou the faithful watch art keeping,
    "All, all's well," Thy constant cheer.

2. And though loud the wind is howling,
    Fierce though flash the lightnings red;
   Darkly, though the storm-cloud's scowling
    O'er the sailor's anxious head;
   Thou canst calm the raging ocean,
    All its noise and tumult still,
   Hush the tempest's wild commotion,
    At the bidding of Thy will.

3. Thus my heart the hope will cherish,
    While to Thee I lift mine eye;
   Thou wilt save me ere I perish,
    Thou wilt hear the sailor's cry.
   And though mast and sail be riven,
    Life's short voyage will soon be o'er;
   Safely moored in heaven's wide haven,
    Storm and tempest vex no more.
                        CHRISTIAN LYRE.

881. 8s & 7s.

1. Light of those whose dreary dwelling
    Borders on the shades of death!
   Rise on us, Thyself revealing—
    Rise and chase the clouds beneath.

2. Thou, of heaven and earth Creator!
    In our deepest darkness rise;
   Scatter all the night of nature,
    Pour the day upon our eyes.

3. Still we wait for Thine appearing;
    Life and joy Thy beams impart,
   Chasing all our fears, and cheering
    Every meek, benighted heart.

4. Save us, in Thy great compassion,
    O Thou mild, pacific Prince!
   Give the knowledge of salvation,
    Give the pardon of our sins.

5. By Thine all-sufficient merit,
    Every burdened soul release;
   Every weary, wandering spirit
    Guide into Thy perfect peace.
                        TOPLADY.

882. 8s & 7s.

1. In the cross of Christ I glory,
    Towering o'er the wrecks of time;
   All the light of sacred story
    Gathers round its head sublime.

2. When the woes of life o'ertake me,
    Hopes deceive, and fears annoy,
   Never shall the cross forsake me;
    Lo! it glows with peace and joy.

3. When the sun of bliss is beaming
    Light and love upon my way,
   From the cross the radiance streaming
    Adds more lustre to the day.

4. Bane and blessing, pain and pleasure,
    By the cross are sanctified;
   Peace is there that knows no measure,
    Joys that through all time abide.

5. In the cross of Christ I glory,
    Towering o'er the wrecks of time;
   All the light of sacred story
    Gathers round its head sublime.
                        BOWRING.

883. 8s, 7s & 4s.

1. Saviour, visit Thy plantation,
    Grant us, Lord, a gracious rain!
   All will come to desolation,
    Unless Thou return again;
       Lord, revive us,
    All our help must come from Thee!

*2. Keep no longer at a distance,
    Shine upon us from on high,
   Lest, for want of Thine assistance,
    Ev'ry plant should droop and die.

3. Surely, once Thy garden flourish'd,
    Ev'ry part looked gay and green;
   Then Thy word our spirits nourish'd—
    Happy seasons we have seen!

4. But a drought has since succeeded,
    And a sad decline we see;
   Lord, Thy help is greatly needed—
    Help can only come from Thee.

5. Dearest Saviour, hasten hither,
    Thou canst make them bloom again!
   O! permit them not to wither,
    Let not all our hopes be vain.

6. Break the tempter's fatal power;
    Turn the stony heart to flesh;
   And begin from this good hour
    To revive Thy work afresh.
                        NEWTON.

CHRISTIAN EXPERIENCE.

BERYL. 8s & 7s.

1. I am weary, I am weary, Of the cares and toils of life, I am weary of its sorrows, I am weary of its strife, I am weary of its flowers, That bloom so soon to die, And th' immortal spirit pineth, For its home beyond the sky, For its home, For its home beyond the sky.

884. 8s & 7s.

1. I AM weary, I am weary
   Of the cares and toils of life;
   I am weary of its sorrows;
   I am weary of its strife;
   I am weary of its flowers,
   That bloom so soon to die;
   And the immortal spirit pineth
   For its home beyond the sky.

2. I am weary of the trifles
   That occupy my days;
   I am weary of the longing
   For human love and praise;
   I am weary of thoughts that turn
   So constantly to earth,
   Fain would my spirit rise above
   Its idle joy and mirth.

3. I have seen the flowers wither;
   I have seen the loved ones die;
   I have seen the clouds of sorrow
   Overcast youth's summer sky;
   I am pining, I am pining
   For my home among the blest;
   Where the wicked cease from troubling,
   And the weary are at rest.

885. 8s & 7s.

1. O MY God, by Thee forsaken,
   Prostrate in the dust I lie;
   Faith by gloomy terrors shaken,
   All my hopes within me die;
   Yet, my soul, in Thee confiding,
   Meditates Thy mercy still;
   Though, on earth's dark coasts abiding,
   Distant far from Zion's hill.

2. Deep to deep responsive calling,
   Thunders roar, the torrents roll;
   Bursting clouds around me falling,
   Wave on wave o'erwhelms my soul:
   Yet the Lord, His grace commanding,
   Will with mercies crown my days;
   He my gurdian, near me standing,
   Cheers my nights with prayer and praise.
   PRATT'S COLL.

TRIALS AND TEMPTATIONS.

WATERBROOK. 6s & 10s.   Ch. Beecher.

1. Wilt Thou not visit me? The plant beside me feels Thy gentle dew; Each blade of grass I see, From Thy deep earth its quickening moisture drew.

886. 6s & 10s.

2. Wilt Thou not visit me?
Thy morning calls on me with cheering tone;
And every hill and tree
Lend but one voice, the voice of Thee alone.

3. Come! for I need Thy love,
More than the flower the dew, or grass the rain;
Come, like Thy holy dove,
And let me in Thy sight rejoice to live again.

4. Yes! Thou wilt visit me;
Nor plant, nor tree, Thine eye delights so well,
As when from sin set free,
Man's spirit comes with Thine in peace to dwell.

RAPHAEL. 6s & 5s.

1. My soul, go boldly forth, Forsake this sinful earth; What hath it been to thee But pain and sorrow? And think'st thou it will be More kind to-morrow?

887. 6s & 5s.

2. Thy God, thy Head's above;
There is the world of love;
Mansions there purchased are
By Christ's own merit;
For these He doth prepare
Thee by His Spirit.

3. Lord Jesus, take my spirit;
I trust Thy love and merit;
Take home Thy wandering sheep,
For Thou hast sought it;
My soul in safety keep,
For Thou hast bought it.

CHRISTIAN EXPERIENCE.

SARDIUS. 8s 7s & 4s.   Ludovick Nicholson, of Paisley, Scotland.

1. Guide me, O Thou great Je-ho-vah, Pilgrim thro' this bar-ren land: I am weak, but thou art might-y, Hold me with thy powerful hand; Bread of hea-ven, Bread of hea-ven, Feed me till I want no more. Bread of heaven, Bread of heaven, Feed me till I want no more.

888. 8s, 7s & 4s.

2. Open Thou the crystal fountain,
   Whence the healing waters flow;
Let the fiery, cloudy pillar
   Lead me all my journey through;
     Strong Deliverer,
Be Thou still my strength and shield.

3. When I tread the verge of Jordan,
   Bid the swelling stream divide;
Death of death, and hell's destruction,
   Land me safe on Canaan's side;
     Songs of praises
I will ever give to Thee.
        P. WILLIAMS, OR OLIVER.

889. 8s & 7s.

1. HOLY Father, Thou hast taught me
   I should live to Thee alone;
Year by year, Thy hand hath brought me
   On through dangers oft unknown.
When I wandered, Thou hast found me;
   When I doubted, sent me light,
Still Thine arm has been around me,
   All my paths were in Thy sight.

2. In the world will foes assail me,
   Craftier, stronger far than I;
And the strife may never fail me,
   Well, I know, before I die.
Therefore, Lord, I come, believing
   Thou canst give the power I need;
Through the prayer of faith receiving
   Strength—the Spirit's strength, indeed.

3. I would trust in Thy protecting,
   Wholly rest upon Thine arm;
Follow wholly Thy directing,
   Thou, mine only guard from harm!
Keep me from mine own undoing,
   Help me turn to Thee when tried,
Still my footsteps, Father, viewing,
   Keep me ever at Thy side!

And, O, Lord, in mer-cy give us Thy rich grace in all our fears.
O, re-fresh us— O, re-fresh us— O, re-fresh us with thy grace.

890. 8s, 7s & 4s.

2. Though ten thousand ills beset us,
   From without and from within,
Jesus says He'll ne'er forget us,
   But will save from every sin.
      Therefore praise Him—
   Praise the great Redeemer's name.

3. Though distresses now attend thee,
   And thou tread'st the thorny road;
His right hand shall still defend thee;
   Soon He'll bring thee home to God!
      Therefore praise Him—
   Praise the great Redeemer's name.

4. O that I could now adore Him,
   Like the heavenly host above,
Who for ever bow before Him,
   And unceasing sing His love!
      Happy songsters!
   When shall I your chorus join?

891. 8s & 7s.*

1. JESUS, full of all compassion,
   Hear Thine humble suppliant's cry,
Let me know Thy great salvation—
   See! I languish, faint, and die.
Guilty, but with heart relenting,
   Overwhelmed with helpless grief,
Prostrate at Thy feet repenting—
   Send, O send me quick relief!

2. Whither should a wretch be flying,
   But to Him who comfort gives?
Whither, from the dread of dying,
   But to Him who ever lives?

* Omit the repeat.

While I view Thee, wounded, grieving,
   Breathless, on the cursed tree,
Fain I'd feel my heart believing
   Thou didst suffer thus for me.

3. In the world of endless ruin,
   Let it never, Lord, be said,
"Here's a soul that perished, sueing
   For the boasted Saviour's aid!"
Saved!—the deed shall spread new glory
   Through the shining realms above;
Angels sing the pleasing story,
   All enraptured with Thy love.
                              TURNER.

892. 8s & 7s.*

1. ONWARD, Christian, though the region,
   Where thou art, be drear and lone;
God has set a guardian legion
   Very near thee,—press thou on!

2. Listen, Christian, their Hosanna
   Rolleth o'er thee,—"God is Love."
Write upon thy red-cross banner,
   "Upward ever,—heaven's above."

3. By the thorn-road, and none other,
   Is the mount of vision won;
Tread it without shrinking, brother!
   Jesus trod it,—press thou on!

4. Be this world the wiser, stronger,
   For thy life of pain and peace;
While it needs thee, O, no longer
   Pray thou for thy quick release.

5. Pray thou, Christian, daily, rather,
   That thou be a faithful son;
By the prayer of Jesus,—"Father,
   Not my will, but Thine, be done!"

CHRISTIAN EXPERIENCE.

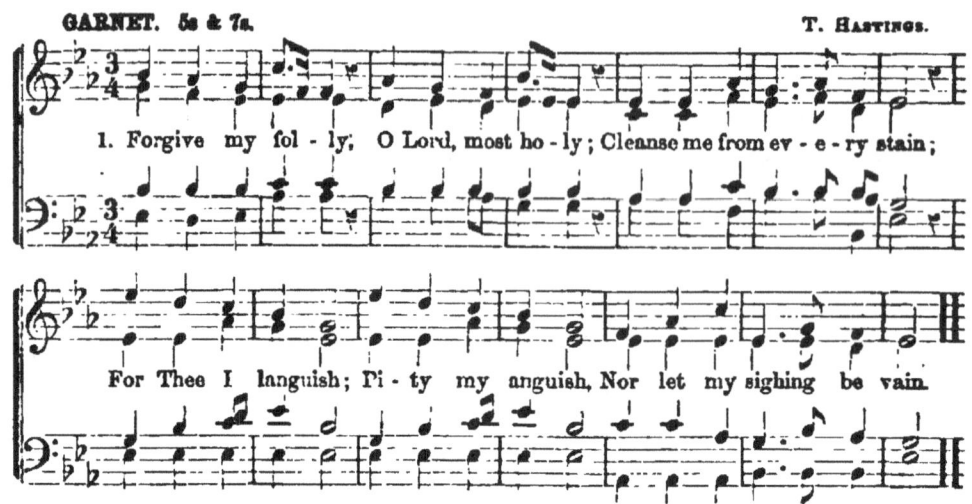

GARNET. 5s & 7s.   T. HASTINGS.

1. Forgive my fol-ly, O Lord, most ho-ly; Cleanse me from ev-e-ry stain; For Thee I languish; Pi-ty my anguish, Nor let my sighing be vain.

893. 10s & 4s.

2. Deeply repenting, sorely lamenting
All my departures from Thee·
And now returning, Thine absence mourning,
Lord, show Thy mercy to me.

3. Sinful, unworthy, trembling before Thee,
Here at Thy cross will I kneel;
Thy Love once bleeding, now interceding,
Shall for my ransom avail.

4. Through Thy rich merit, by Thy free Spirit,
Comfort my desolate soul:
Heav'nly Physician, in kind compassion,
Now bid the wounded be whole.

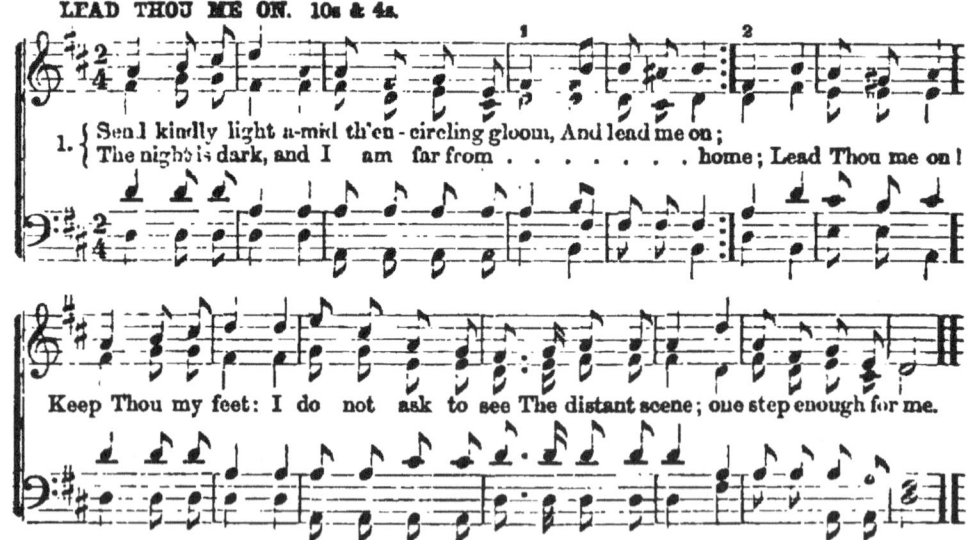

LEAD THOU ME ON. 10s & 4s.

1. { Send kindly light a-mid th'en-circling gloom, And lead me on;
The night is dark, and I am far from . . . . home; Lead Thou me on!
Keep Thou my feet: I do not ask to see The distant scene; one step enough for me.

894. 10s & 4s.

2. I was not ever thus, nor prayed that Thou
Should'st lead me on;
I loved to choose and see my path; but now
Lead Thou me on!
I loved day's dazzling light, and, spite of fears,
Pride ruled my will: remember not past years!

3. So long Thy power hath blessed me, surely still
'T will lead me on
Through dreary doubt, through pain and sorrow, till
The night is gone,
And with the morn those angel faces smile
Which I have loved long since, and lost awhile.

TRIALS AND TEMPTATIONS.

MAGDALEN. 7s & 5s. — Psalmodist.

1. Peace to thee, O favored one, Weeping thus before the throne, O'er the ills that thou hast done, With re-lent-ing sighs: While thy heart with grief is riven, All thy fol-lies are for-given: And be-neath a smiling heaven, Light will soon a-rise.

895. 7s & 5s.

1. PEACE to thee, O favored one,
   Weeping thus before the throne,
   O'er the ills that thou hast done,
     With relenting sighs:
   While thy heart with grief is riven,
   All thy follies are forgiven;
   And beneath a smiling heaven
     Light will soon arise.

2. Earthly joys to Thee are dross,
   Earthly gain is heavenly loss,
   Look upon the bleeding cross,
     View the Victim there:
   He that for thy sins hath died,
   Bids thee in His love confide;
   Trust in Him, and none beside,—
     He will hear thy prayer.

3. From the Saviour's smiling face
   Flows the plenitude of grace;
   Pardon, life, and heavenly peace,
     Like the ocean's wave:
   He the righteous law obeyed,
   He hath full atonement made,
   Let Thy soul on him be stayed,
     He is strong to save.

T. HASTINGS.

CHRISTIAN EXPERIENCE.

CHRISTUS CONSOLATOR. 7s & 6s.   CH. BEECHER.

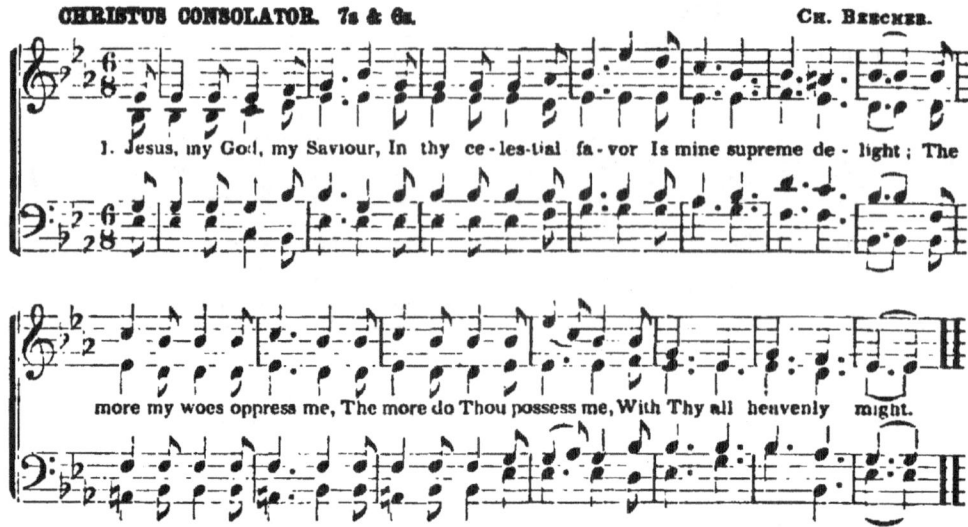

1. Jesus, my God, my Saviour, In thy celestial favor Is mine supreme delight; The more my woes oppress me, The more do Thou possess me, With Thy all heavenly might.

896. 7s & 6s.

1. Jesus my God, my Saviour,
   In Thy celestial favor
      Is my supreme delight;
   The more my woes oppress me,
   The more do Thou possess me,
      With Thy all heavenly might.

2. Whene'er my heart is broken,
   Before my grief is spoken,
      God pities my complaint:
   And though He might reject me,
   He kindly does protect me,
      Lest all my courage faint.

3. By night Thine arm attends me,
   And graciously defends me,
      And soft is my repose:
   Thine eyes, that watch my keeping,
   Are never, never sleeping—
      I can not fear my foes.

4. By day Thy hand shall lead me,
   Thy heavenly manna feed me
      Through all life's desert way;
   Thy beam my path enlightens,
   And more and more it brightens
      Unto eternal day.

5. O Jesus, my sweet Saviour,
   Soon Thy celestial favor
      Shall be my sole delight;
   With seraphs I'll adore Thee,
   And cast my crown before Thee,
      Around Thy throne of light.

897. 7s & 6s.

1. O THAT the Lord's salvation,
   Jehovah's great salvation,
      Were out of Zion come!
   To heal His ancient nation,
   His long forsaken nation—
      To lead His outcasts home!

2. How long the holy city,
   Zion, the holy city,
      Shall heathen feet profane?
   Return, O God, in pity,
   In everlasting pity,
      Rebuild her walls again.

3. Let fall Thy rod of terror,
   Thine iron rod of terror,
      Thy saving grace impart!
   Remove the vail of error,
   The midnight vail of error,
      Release the fettered heart.

4. Let Israel home returning,
   With ransom home returning,
      Their lost Messiah see!
   Give oil of joy for mourning,
   For ages long of mourning,
      And build Thy church to Thee!

DOXOLOGY. 7s & 6s.

GLORY be Thine for ever,
O Lord, of life the Giver,
   Immortal King of kings,
To Thee thrice-named be praises,
Loud as all Heaven raises,
   While earth responsive sings.

TRIALS AND TEMPTATIONS.

898. 6s & 4s. *

1. NEARER, my God, to Thee,
    Nearer to Thee!
   E'en though it be a cross
    That raiseth me;
   Still all my song shall be,—
   Nearer, my God, to Thee,
    Nearer to Thee!

2. Though, like the wanderer,
    The sun gone down,
   Darkness be over me,
    My rest a stone;
   Yet in my dreams I'd be
   Nearer, my God, to Thee,—
    Nearer to Thee!

3. There let the way appear,
    Steps unto heaven;
   All that Thou sendest me,
    In mercy given;
   Angels to beckon me
   Nearer, my God, to Thee,—
    Nearer to Thee!

4. Then with my waking thoughts,
    Bright with Thy praise,
   Out of my stony griefs,
    Bethel I'll raise;
   So by my woes to be
   Nearer, my God, to Thee,—
    Nearer to Thee!

5. Or if on joyful wing,
    Cleaving the sky,

* Omit the second repeat.

Sun, moon, and stars forgot,
 Upward I fly;
Still all my song shall be,—
Nearer, my God, to Thee,
 Nearer to Thee.

SARAH F. ADAMS.

899. 6s & 4s.

1. I'M but a stranger here:
    Heaven is my home;
   Earth is a desert drear:
    Heaven is my home;
   Danger and sorrow stand
   Round me on every hand,
   Heaven is my Father land—
    Heaven is my home.

2. What though the tempests rage:
    Heaven is my home;
   Short is my pilgrimage:
    Heaven is my home;
   And time's wild, wintry blast
   Soon will be over past,
   I shall reach home at last—
    Heaven is my home.

3. Therefore I murmur not:
    Heaven is my home;
   Whate'er my earthly lot,
    Heaven is my home;
   And I shall surely stand
   There at my Lord's right hand:
   Heaven is my Father land—
    Heaven is my home.

CHRISTIAN EXPERIENCE.

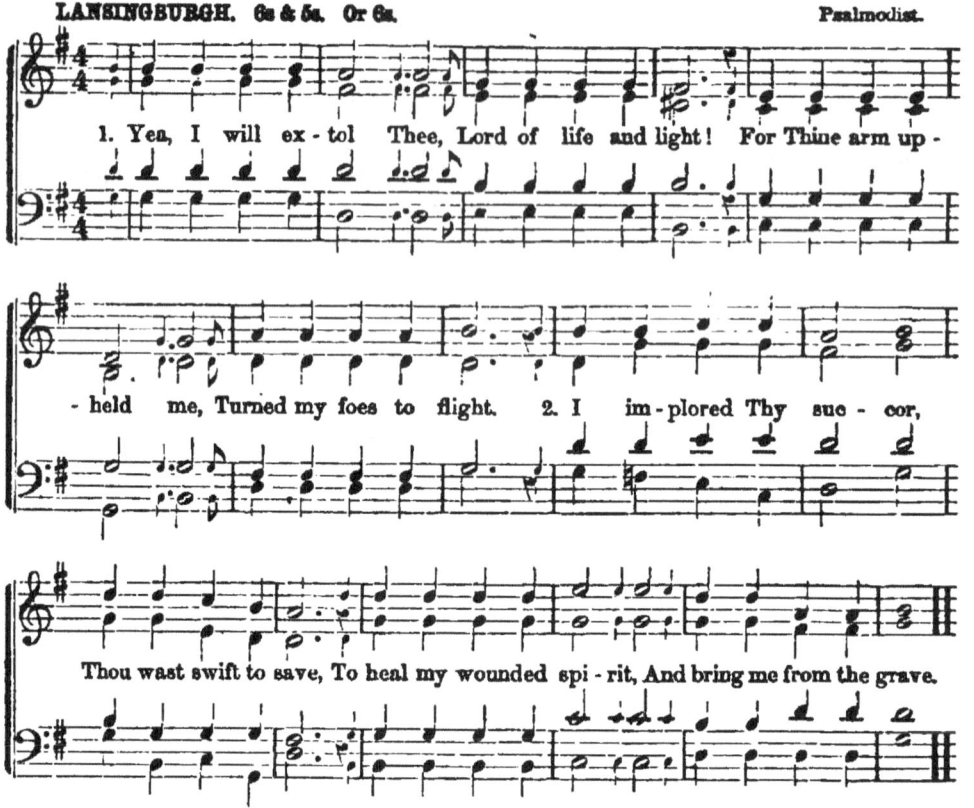

LANSINGBURGH. 6s & 5s. Or 6s. — Psalmodist.

1. Yea, I will extol Thee, Lord of life and light! For Thine arm upheld me, Turned my foes to flight. 2. I implored Thy succor, Thou wast swift to save, To heal my wounded spirit, And bring me from the grave.

900. 6s & 5s.

1. YEA, I will extol Thee,
    Lord of Life and Light;
For Thine arm upheld me,
    Turned my foes to flight.

2. I implored Thy succor,
    Thou was swift to save,
To heal my wounded spirit,
    And bring me from the grave.

3. Grief may, like the pilgrim,
    Through the night sojourn,
Yet shall joy, to-morrow,
    With the sun return.

4. Thou hast turned my mourning
    Into minstrelsy;
Girded me with gladness,
    Set from thraldom free.

5. Thee my ransomed powers
    Henceforth shall adore;
Thee, my great Deliverer,
    Bless for evermore!

MONTGOMERY.

901. 6s & 5s.

1. GOD of our salvation!
    Unto Thee we pray;
Hear our supplication,
    Be our strength and stay.

2. Wretched and unworthy,
    Poor, and sick, and blind,
Prostrate we adore Thee,
    Call Thy grace to mind.

3. He that dwelleth near Thee,
    Safely shall abide;
Ever love and fear Thee,
    In Thy strength confide.

4. Sure is Thy protection,
    Safe is Thy defence,
While in deep affliction,
    Woe, or pestilence.

5. God of our Salvation!
    Saviour, Prince of Peace!
Boundless Thy compassion,
    Infinite Thy grace.

6. While with love unceasing,
    Humbly we adore;
Grant us Thy rich blessing,
    And we ask no more.

TRIALS AND TEMPTATIONS. 285

EMILIE. 6s & 5s. Or 6s. J. ZUNDEL.

1. If life's pleasures charm thee, Give them not thy heart; Lest the gift ensnare thee From thy God to part. 2. If distress befall thee, Painful though it be, Let not grief appal thee, To thy Saviour flee.

902. 6s & 5s.

3. When earth's prospects fail thee,
   Let it not distress;
   Better comforts wait thee,
   Christ will freely bless.

4. Let not death alarm thee,
   Shrink not from his blow;
   For the conflict arm thee,
   Triumph o'er the foe.

903. 6s.*

1. I FEEL within a want
   For ever burning there,
   What I so thirst for, grant,
   O Thou who hearest prayer!

2. This is the thing I crave,
   A likeness to Thy Son;
   This would I rather have
   Than call the world my own.

3. Like Him, now in my youth,
   I long, O God, to be,
   In tenderness and truth,
   In sweet humility.

4. 'T is my most fervent prayer,
   Be it more fervent still,
   Be it my highest care,
   Be it my settled will.   FURNESS.

904. 6s.*

1. MY spirit longeth for Thee
   To dwell within my breast;
   Although I am unworthy
   Of so divine a Guest!

2. Of so divine a Guest—
   Unworthy though I be;
   Yet hath my heart no rest
   Until it come to Thee!

3. Until it come to Thee;
   In vain I look around;
   In all that I can see
   No rest is to be found!

4. No rest is to be found
   But in Thy bleeding love:
   Oh! let my wish be crown'd,
   And send it from above!

* May be sung to either tune, by using the small notes.

286. CHRISTIAN EXPERIENCE.

EASTON. L. M. — Mozart.

For God, who pities man, has shown A blessing for the eyes that weep.

905. L. M.

1. O DEEM not they are blest alone
   Whose lives a peaceful tenor keep;
   For God, who pities man, has shown
   A blessing for the eyes that weep.

2. The light of smiles shall fill again
   The lids that overflow with tears;
   And weary hours of woe and pain
   Are promises of happier years.

3. There is a day of sunny rest
   For every dark and troubled night;
   And grief may bide an evening guest,
   But joy shall come with early light.

4. Nor let the good man's trust depart,
   Though life its common gifts deny,
   Though with a pierced and broken heart,
   And spurned of men, he goes to die.

5. For God has marked each sorrowing day,
   And numbered every secret tear,
   And heaven's long age of bliss shall pay
   For all His children suffer here.

   BRYANT.

906. L. M.

1. O ZION! when I think on Thee,
   I wish for pinions like the dove,
   And mourn to think that I should be
   So distant from the place I love.

2. A captive here, and far from home,
   For Zion's sacred walls I sigh;
   Thither the ransomed nations come,
   And see the Saviour eye to eye.

3. While here I walk on hostile ground;
   The few, that I can call my friends,
   Are like myself with fetters bound,
   And weariness our steps attends.

4. But we shall yet behold the day
   When Zion's children shall return;
   Our sorrows then shall flee away,
   And we again shall never mourn.

5. The hope that such a day will come,
   Makes e'en the captives' portion sweet;
   Though now we wander far from home,
   In Zion soon we all shall meet.

   KELLY.

TRIALS AND TEMPTATIONS. 287

DIAMOND. 7s & 4s. L. MASON.

1. Head of the church triumphant, We joyfully adore Thee; Till Thou appear, Thy members here Shall sing like those in glory. We lift our heart and voices, In blest anticipation, And cry aloud, And give to God The praise of our salvation.

907. 7s, 4s & 7s.

1. Head of the church triumphant,
   We joyfully adore Thee;
     Till Thou appear,
     Thy members here
   Shall sing like those in glory.
   We lift our hearts and voices,
   In blest anticipation,
     And cry aloud,
     And give to God
   The praise of our salvation.

2. While in affliction's furnace,
   And passing through the fire,
     Thy love we praise,
     That knows our days,
   And ever brings us nigher.
   We lift our hands exulting
   In Thine almighty favor;
     The love divine,
     That made us Thine,
   Shall keep us Thine for ever.

3. Thou dost conduct Thy people
   Through torrents of temptation;
     Nor will we fear,
     While Thou art near,
   The fire of tribulation.
   The world, with sin and Satan,
   In vain our march opposes;
     By Thee we will
     Break through them all,
   And sing the song of Moses.

4. Faith now beholds the glory
   To which Thou wilt restore us;
     And earth despise,
     For that high prize
   Which Thou hast set before us.
   And if Thou count us worthy,
   We each, like dying Stephen,
     Shall see Thee stand
     At God's right hand,
   To take us up to heaven.

CLIFFORD. C. M.   Arranged from GREATOREX's Coll.

1. Daughter of Zion, from the dust Exalt thy fallen head; Again in thy Redeemer trust: He calls thee from the dead.

908. C. M.

2. Awake, awake, put on thy strength,
   Thy beautiful array;
   The day of freedom dawns at length,
   The Lord's appointed day.

3. Rebuild thy walls, thy bounds enlarge,
   And send thy heralds forth;
   Say to the south—"Give up thy charge,
   And keep not back, O north!"

4. They come, they come;—Thine exiled
   Where'er they rest or roam, [bands,
   Have heard Thy voice in distant lands,
   And hasten to their home.

5. Thus, though the universe shall burn,
   And God His works destroy,
   With songs Thy ransomed shall return,
   And everlasting joy.

MONTGOMERY.

909. C. M.

1. Jesus, immortal King! arise;
   Rise and assert thy sway;
   Till earth subdued, its tribute bring,
   And distant lands obey.

2. Ride forth, victorious Conqueror! ride,
   Till all Thy foes submit;
   And all the powers of hell resign
   Their trophies at Thy feet.

3. Send forth Thy word, and let it fly
   This spacious earth around;
   Till every soul beneath the sun
   Shall hear the joyful sound.

4. From sea to sea, from shore to shore,
   May Jesus be adored;
   And earth, with all her millions, shout
   Hosannas to the Lord.

BURDER.

910. C. M.

1. Alas, the utter emptiness!
   What life has it to give?
   O, shall it God's own fire oppress?
   Soul, wilt thou slightly live?

2. Thyself amid the silence clear,
   The world far off and dim,
   Thy vision free, the Bright One near,
   Thyself alone with Him.

3. The silence thronged gloriously
   With business how divine!
   God's glory passing unto thee—
   All heaven becoming thine.

4. The rapture, mighty, measureless,
   In each eternal thing—
   The mingling with Almightiness—
   The dwelling by Life's Spring!

5. Thus sweetly live, thus greatly watch—
   Soul, be but inly bright!
   All outer things must smile, must catch
   Thy strong, transcendent light.

6. Near Thee no darkness dares abide,
   Thou makest all things shine;
   Soul, whom the Lord has glorified,
   Is not all glory thine?

GILL.

911. C. M.

1. BEHOLD, the mountain of the Lord,
   In latter days, shall rise
   On mountain tops, above the hills,
   And draw the wond'ring eyes.

2. To this the joyful nations round,
   All tribes and tongues, shall flow;
   "Up to the hill of God," they say,
   "And to His house we'll go."

3. The beams that shine on Zion's hill
   Shall lighten every land;
   The King who reigns in Salem's towers
   Shall all the world command.

4. No longer hosts encountering hosts,
   Their millions slain deplore;
   They hang the trumpet in the hall,
   And study war no more.

5. Come, then—oh come from every land,
   To worship at His shrine;
   And, walking in the light of God,
   With holy beauties shine.
   LOGAN.

912. C. M.

1. THE Lord of glory is my light,
   And my salvation too;
   God is my strength, nor will I fear
   What all my foes can do.

2. One privilege my heart desires;
   O grant me an abode
   Among the churches of Thy saints,
   The temples of my God!

3. There shall I offer my requests,
   And see Thy beauty still;
   Shall hear Thy messages of love,
   And there inquire Thy will.

4. When troubles rise, and storms appear,
   There may His children hide;
   God has a strong pavilion, where
   He makes my soul abide.

5. Now shall my head be lifted high
   Above my foes around;
   And songs of joy and victory
   Within Thy temple sound.
   WATTS.

913. C. M.

1. O WHERE are kings and empires now
   Of old that went and came?
   But Holy Church is praying yet,
   A thousand years the same.

2. Mark ye her holy battlements,
   And her foundations strong;
   And hear within, the solemn voice,
   And her unending song.

3. For not like kingdoms of the world
   The Holy Church of God!
   Though earthquake shocks are rocking her,
   And tempests are abroad;

4. Unshaken as eternal hills,
   Unmovable she stands—
   A mountain that shall fill the earth,
   A fane unbuilt by hands.
   A. C. COXE.

914. C. M.

1. THERE is a little lonely fold,
   Whose flock One Shepherd keeps,
   Through summer's heat and winter's cold,
   With eye that never sleeps.

2. By evil beast, or burning sky,
   Or damp of midnight air,
   Not one in all that flock shall die
   Beneath that Shepherd's care.

3. For if, unheeding or beguiled,
   In danger's path they roam,
   His pity follows through the wild,
   And guards them safely home.

4. Oh, gentle Shepherd, still behold
   Thy helpless charge in me;
   And take a wanderer to Thy fold,
   That trembling turns to Thee.
   LITCHFIELD'S COLL.

915. C. M.

1. A MOTHER may forgetful be,
   For human love is frail;
   But Thy Creator's love to thee,
   O Zion! can not fail.

2. No! thy dear name engraven stands,
   In characters of love,
   On thy almighty Father's hands;
   And never shall remove.

3. Before His ever watchful eye
   Thy mournful state appears,
   And every groan, and every sigh,
   Divine compassion hears.

4. O Zion! learn to doubt no more,
   Be every fear suppressed;
   Unchanging truth, and love, and power,
   Dwell in thy Saviour's breast.
   MRS. STEELE.

THE CHURCH.

DUNDEE. C. M.

1. How sweet and awful is the place, With Christ within the doors; While everlasting love displays The choicest of her stores!

916. C. M.

2. While all our hearts, and all our songs,
   Join to admire the feast,
   Each of us cries, with thankful tongues,—
   "Lord, why was I a guest?"

3. "Why was I made to hear Thy voice,
   And enter while there's room,
   When thousands make a wretched choice,
   And rather starve than come?"

4. 'Twas the same love that spread the feast,
   That sweetly drew us in;
   Else we had still refused to taste,
   And perished in our sin.

5. Pity the nations, O our God!
   Constrain the earth to come;
   Send Thy victorious word abroad,
   And bring the strangers home.
   WATTS.

917. C. M.

1. IF human kindness meets return,
   And owns the grateful tie;
   If tender thoughts within us burn,
   To feel a friend is nigh;—

2. O, shall not warmer accents tell
   The gratitude we owe
   To Him, who died, our fears to quell—
   Who bore our guilt and woe!

3. While yet in anguish He surveyed
   Those pangs He would not flee,
   What love His latest words displayed,—
   "Meet and remember me!"

4. Remember Thee—Thy death, Thy shame,
   Our sinful hearts to share!—
   O memory! leave no other name
   But His recorded there.
   NOEL.

918. C. M.

1. LORD, may the spirit of this feast—
   The earnest of Thy love—
   Maintain a dwelling in our breast,
   Until we meet above.

2. The healing sense of pardoned sin,
   The hope that never tires,
   The strength a pilgrim's race to win,
   The joy that heaven inspires.

3. Still may their light our duties trace
   In lines of hallowed flame,
   Like that upon the prophet's face,
   When from the mount he came.

4. But if no more with kindred dear
   The broken bread we share,
   Nor at the banquet-board appear
   To breathe the grateful prayer;—

5. Forget us not,—when on the bed
   Of dire disease we waste,
   Or to the chambers of the dead,
   And bar of judgment haste.

6. Forget not,—Thou who bore the woe
   Of Calvary's fatal tree,—
   Those who within these courts below
   Have thus remembered Thee.
   MRS. SIGOURNEY.

INSTITUTIONS AND ORDINANCES.

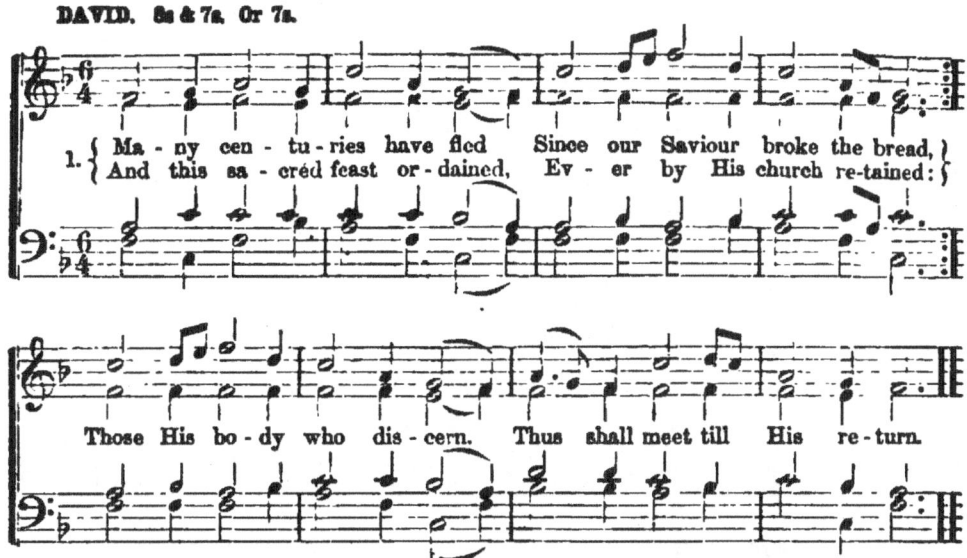

DAVID. 8s & 7s. Or 7s.

1. Many centuries have fled
Since our Saviour broke the bread,
And this sacred feast ordained,
Ever by His church retained:
Those His body who discern,
Thus shall meet till His return.

919. 7s.

1. MANY centuries have fled
Since our Saviour broke the bread,
And this sacred feast ordain'd,
Ever by His church retain'd:
Those His body who discern,
Thus shall meet till His return.

2. Through the church's long eclipse,
When, from priest or pastor's lips,
Truth divine was never heard,—
'Mid the famine of the word,
Still these symbols witness gave
To His love who died to save.

3. All who bear the Saviour's name,
Here their common faith proclaim;
Though diverse in tongue or rite,
Here, one body we unite;
Breaking thus one mystic bread,
Members of one common head.

4. Come, the blessed emblems share,
Which the Saviour's death declare;
Come, on truth immortal feed;
For His flesh is meat indeed:
Saviour! witness with the sign,
That our ransomed souls are Thine.
CONDER.

920. 8s & 7s.*

1. ON the night of that last supper,
Seated with His chosen band,
Christ, as food to all His brethren,
Gives Himself with His own hand.

2. He, as man with man conversing,
Staid the seeds of truth to sow;

* Omit repeat.

Then He closed, in solemn order,
Wondrously, His life of woe.

3. Lo! o'er ancient forms departing,
Newer rites of grace prevail;
Faith for all defects supplying,
Where the feeble senses fail.

4. To the everlasting Father,
Through the Son who reigns on high,
Be salvation, honor, blessing,
Might, and endless majesty.
BREVIARY.

921. C. M.*

1. How condescending and how kind
Was God's eternal Son!
Our misery reached His heavenly mind,
And pity brought Him down.

2. He sunk beneath our heavy woes,
To raise us to His throne;
There's ne'er a gift His hand bestows,
But cost His heart a groan.

3. This was compassion, like a God,
That when the Saviour knew
The price of pardon was His blood,
His pity ne'er withdrew.

4. Now, though He reigns exalted high,
His love is still as great;
Well He remembers Calvary,
Nor lets His saints forget.

5. Here let our hearts begin to melt,
While we His death record,
And, with our joy for pardoned guilt,
Mourn that we pierced the Lord.
WATTS.

* Sung to Dundee.

THE CHURCH.

EUCHARIST. L. M.   From the Dulcimer.

1. O, happy day that fixed my choice On Thee, my Saviour, and my God! Well may this glowing heart rejoice, And tell its raptures all abroad.

922. L. M.

2. O, happy bond that seals my vows
To Him who merits all my love!
Let cheerful anthems fill the house,
While to His altar now I move.

3. 'T is done—the great transaction 's done;
I am my Lord's, and He is mine;
He drew me, and I followed on,
Charmed to confess the voice divine.

4. Now rest, my long-divided heart!
Fixed on this blissful centre, rest;
Here have I found a nobler part,
Here heavenly pleasures fill my breast.

5. High Heaven, that hears the solemn vow,
That vow renewed, shall daily hear;
Till, in life's latest hour, I bow,
And bless in death a bond so dear.
DODDRIDGE.

923. L. M.

1. Jesus, the sinner's Friend, to Thee,
Lost and undone, for aid I flee;
Weary of earth, myself, and sin,
Open Thine arms and take me in.

2. Pity and save my sin-sick soul,
'T is Thou alone canst make me whole;
Dark, till in me Thine image shine,
And lost I am till Thou art mine.

3. At length I own it can not be,
That I should fit myself for Thee,
Here now to Thee I all resign,
Thine is the work, and only Thine.

4. What shall I say Thy grace to move?
Lord, I am sin, but Thou art love;
I give up every plea beside,—
Lord, I am lost, but Thou hast died.

924. L. M.

1. This child we dedicate to Thee,
O God of grace and purity!
Shield it from sin and threatening wrong,
And let Thy love its life prolong.

2. O may Thy Spirit gently draw
Its willing soul to keep Thy law;
May virtue, piety, and truth,
Dawn even with its dawning youth.

3. We, too, before Thy gracious sight,
Once shared the blest baptismal rite,
And would renew its solemn vow
With love, and thanks, and praises, now.

4. Grant that, with true and faithful heart,
We still may act the Christian's part,
Cheered by each promise thou hast given,
And laboring for the prize in heaven.
WEST BOSTON COLL.

925. H. M.

1. Dear Saviour, if these lambs should stray
From Thy secure inclosure's bound,
And, lured by worldly joys away,
Among the thoughtless crowd be found;

2. Remember still that they are Thine,
That Thy dear sacred name they bear;
Think that the seal of love divine,
The sign of covenant grace they wear.

3. In all their erring, sinful years,
O let them ne'er forgotten be;
Remember all the prayers and tears
Which made them consecrate to Thee.

4. And when these lips no more can pray,
These eyes can weep for them no more,
Turn Thou their feet from folly's way;
The wand'rers to Thy fold restore.

INSTITUTIONS AND ORDINANCES.

HOWARD. C. M.

1. By cool Siloam's shady rill How fair the lily grows! How sweet the breath, beneath the hill, Of Sharon's dewy rose!

926. C. M.

1. By cool Siloam's shady rill
   How fair the lily grows!
   How sweet the breath, beneath the hill,
   Of Sharon's dewy rose!

2. Lo! such the child, whose early feet
   The paths of peace have trod,
   Whose secret heart, with influence sweet,
   Is upward drawn to God.

3. By cool Siloam's shady rill
   The lily must decay;
   The rose, that blooms beneath the hill,
   Must shortly fade away.

4. And soon, too soon, the wintry hour
   Of man's maturer age
   Will shake the soul with sorrow's power,
   And stormy passion's rage.

5. O Thou, who givest life and breath,
   We seek Thy grace alone,
   In childhood, manhood, age, and death,
   To keep us still Thine own.
   HEBER.

927. C. M.

1. O say not, think not, heavenly notes
   To childish ears are vain;
   That the young mind at random floats,
   And can not reach the strain.

2. Was not our Lord, a little child,
   Taught by degrees to pray,
   By father dear, and mother mild,
   Instructed day by day?

3. And though some tones be weak and low,
   What are all prayers beneath,
   But cries of babes, that can not know
   Half the deep thought they breathe?

4. In His own words we Christ adore;
   But angels, as we speak,
   Higher above our meaning soar,
   Than we o'er children weak.
   KEBLE.

928. C. M.

1. See Israel's gentle Shepherd stand,
   With all-engaging charms;
   Hark! how He calls the tender lambs,
   And folds them in His arms!

2. "Permit them to approach," he cries,
   "Nor scorn their humble name;
   It was to bless such souls as these
   The Lord of angels came."

3. We bring them, Lord, in thankful bands,
   And yield them up to Thee;
   Joyful that we ourselves are Thine,
   Thine let our offspring be!
   DODDRIDGE.

SILVER STREET. S. M.   I. SMITH.

1. Dear Saviour, we are thine By everlasting bands;
Our hearts, our souls, we would resign Entirely to Thy hands.

929. S. M.

1. DEAR Saviour, we are Thine
By everlasting bands;
Our hearts, our souls, we would resign
Entirely to Thy hands.

2. To Thee we still would cleave
With ever-growing zeal;
If millions tempt us Christ to leave,
O, let them ne'er prevail.

3. Thy Spirit shall unite
Our souls to Thee, our Head;
Shall form us to Thy image bright,
And teach Thy paths to tread.

4. Death may our souls divide
From these abodes of clay:
But love shall keep us near Thy side,
Through all the gloomy way.

5. Since Christ and we are one,
Why should we doubt or fear?
If He in heaven hath fixed His throne,
He'll fix His members there.
          DODDRIDGE.

930. S. M.

1. JESUS, my strength, my hope,
On Thee I cast my care,
With humble confidence look up,
And know Thou hear'st my prayer.

2. Give me on Thee to wait,
Till I can all things do,
On Thee, almighty to create,
Almighty to renew.

3. I want a sober mind,
A self-renouncing will,
That tramples down, and casts behind
The baits of pleasing ill;

4. A soul inured to pain,
To hardship, grief, and loss,
Bold to take up, firm to sustain
The consecrated cross;

5. I want a godly fear,
A quick-discerning eye,
That looks to Thee when sin is near,
And sees the tempter fly;

6. A spirit still prepared,
And armed with jealous care,
For ever standing on its guard,
And watching unto prayer.
          C. WESLEY.

931. S. M.

1. MY Father bids me come,
O, why do I delay?
He calls the wandering spirit home,
And yet from Him I stay!

2. Father. the hind'rance show,
Which I have failed to see;
And let me now consent to know
What keeps me far from Thee.

3. Searcher of hearts, in mine
Thy trying powers display;
Into its darkest corners shine—
Take every veil away.

4. In me the hind'rance lies;
The fatal bar remove,
And let me see, in sweet surprise,
Thy full redeeming love.
          WESLEY.

INSTITUTIONS AND ORDINANCES.

BAPTISMAL CHANT. 932.

And Jesus said, Suffer little children, and forbid them not to come unto me; For of such is the kingdom of heaven. A-men.

1. And Jesus said, Suffer little children, and
   forbid them not to | come unto | me;
   For of | such · is the | kingdom of | heaven.

2. He shall feed His | flock · like a | shepherd:
   He shall gather the lambs with His arm
   and | carry them | in His | bosom.

3. I will pour My Spirit upon thy seed, and
   my blessing up- | on thine | offspring;
   And they shall spring up as among the
   grass, as | willows · by the | wa-ter |
   courses.

4. Go ye, therefore, and teach all nations,
   baptizing them in the name of the Father, and of the Son, and of the | Holy |
   Ghost;
   Teaching them to observe all things whatsoever I have commanded you, and lo!
   I am with you always | even · unto the |
   end · of the | world. Amen.

5. Glory be to the Father, and to the Son, and
   to the | Holy | Ghost;
   As it was in the beginning, is now, and
   ever | shall be, | world without | end. |
   Amen.

933. S. M.

1. To Him who children blest,
   And suffered | them to | come,
   To Him who took them to His breast,
   We | bring these | children | home.

2. To Thee, O God, whose face
   Their spirits | still be- | hold,
   We bring them, praying that Thy grace
   May | keep, thine | arms en- | fold.

3. And as this water falls
   On each un- | conscious | brow,
   Thy holy spirit grant, O Lord,
   To | keep them | pure as | now!
   J. F. CLARKE.

934. 7s.

1. LITTLE travelers, Zionward,
   Each one entering into rest,
   In the kingdom of your Lord,
   In the mansions | of the | blest;
   There, to welcome, Jesus waits,
   Gives the crowns his followers win—
   Lift your heads ye golden gates!
   Let the | little | travelers | in.

2. Who are they whose little feet,
   Pacing life's dark journey through,
   Now have reach'd that heavenly seat,
   They had ever | kept in | view?
   "I, from Greenland's frozen land;"
   "I, from India's sultry plain;"
   "I, from Afric's barren sand;"
   "I, from | islands | of the | main."

3. "All our earthly journey past,
   Every tear and pain gone by,
   Here together met at last,
   At the portal | of the | sky!
   Each the welcome 'Come' awaits,
   Conquerors over death and sin!"
   Lift your heads, ye golden gates!
   Let the | little | travelers | in!
   EDMESTON.

THE CHURCH.

BLENDON. L. M.   GIARDINI.

1. O, bow thine ear, Eternal One! On Thee our heart adoring calls; To Thee the followers of Thy Son Have raised, and now devote these walls.

935. L. M.

1. O, BOW Thine ear, Eternal One!
On Thee our heart adoring calls;
To Thee the followers of Thy Son
Have raised, and now devote these walls.

2. Here let Thy holy days be kept;
And be this place to worship given,
Like that bright spot where Jacob slept,
The house of God, the gate of heaven.

3. Here may Thine honor dwell; and here,
As incense, let Thy children's prayer,
From contrite hearts and lips sincere,
Rise on the still and holy air.

4. Here be Thy praise devoutly sung;
Here let Thy truth beam forth to save,
As when, of old, Thy Spirit hung,
On wings of light, o'er Jordan's wave.

5. And when the lips, that with Thy name
Are vocal now, to dust shall turn,
On others may devotion's flame
Be kindled here, and purely burn!

936. L. M.

1. WHERE ancient forests widely spread,
Where bends the cataract's ocean-fall;
On the lone mountain's silent head,
There are Thy temples, God of all!

2. All space is holy, for all space
Is filled by Thee; but human thought
Burns clearer in some chosen place,
Where Thine own words of love are taught.

3. Here be they taught; and may we know
That faith Thy servants knew of old,
Which onward bears, through weal or woe,
Till death the gates of heaven unfold.

4. Nor we alone; may those whose brow
Shows yet no trace of human cares,
Hereafter stand where we do now,
And raise to Thee still holier prayers.
NORTON.

937. L. M.

1. WHEN here, O Lord, we seek Thy face,
And dying sinners pray to live,
Hear Thou, in heaven, Thy dwelling place,
And when Thou hearest, Lord, forgive.

2. When here Thy messengers proclaim
The blessed Gospel of Thy Son,
Still by the power of His great name
Be mighty signs and wonders done.

3. When children's voices raise the song—
Hosanna! to their heavenly King—
Let heaven with earth the strain prolong;
Hosanna! let their angels sing.

4. But will, indeed, Jehovah deign
Here to abide, no transient Guest?
Here will our great Redeemer reign,
And here the Holy Spirit rest?

5. Thy glory never hence depart;
Yet choose not, Lord, this house alone;
Thy kingdom come to every heart;
In every bosom fix Thy throne.
MONTGOMERY.

INSTITUTIONS AND ORDINANCES. 297

ALL SAINTS. L. M. — WM. KNAPP.

1. The perfect world, by Adam trod, Was the first temple built to God; His fi-at laid the corner stone, And heaved its pillars one by one.

938. L. M.

1. THE perfect world, by Adam trod,
Was the first temple built by God;
His fiat laid the corner-stone,
And heaved its pillars one by one.

2. He hung its starry roof on high—
The broad, illimitable sky;
He spread its pavement, green and bright,
And curtained it with morning light.

3. The mountains in their places stood,
The sea—the sky—and "all was good;"
And when its first pure praises rang,
The "morning stars together sang."

4. Lord, 't is not ours to make the sea,
And earth, and sky, a house for Thee;
But in Thy sight our off'ring stands—
An humbler temple, "made with hands."

5. We can not bid the morning star
To sing how bright Thy glories are;
But, Lord, if Thou wilt meet us here,
Thy praise shall be the Christian's tear.
N. P. WILLIS.

939. L. M.

1. WE bid thee welcome in the name
Of Jesus, our exalted Head—
Come as a servant, so He came,
And we receive thee in His stead.

2. Come as a Shepherd; guard and keep
This fold from hell, and earth, and sin;
Nourish the lambs, and feed the sheep,
The wounded heal, the lost bring in.

3. Come as a Watchman; take thy stand
Upon thy tower amidst the sky,
And when the sword comes on the land
Call us to fight, or warn to fly.

4. Come as an Angel, hence to guide
A band of pilgrims on their way,
That, safely walking at thy side,
We fail not, faint not, turn, nor stray.

5. Come as a Teacher, sent from God,
Charged His whole counsel to declare;
Lift o'er our ranks the prophet's rod,
While we uphold thy hands with prayer.

6. Come as a Messenger of peace,
Filled with the Spirit, fired with love;
Live to behold our large increase,
And die to meet us all above.
MONTGOMERY.

DOXOLOGY. L. M.

O SAVING Victim! opening wide
The gates of Heaven to man below!
Our foes press on from every side—
Thine aid supply, Thy strength bestow.

To Thy great name be endless praise,
Immortal Godhead, One in Three!
Oh, grant us endless length of days,
In our true native land, with Thee!

THE CHURCH.

SWANWICK. C. M. — Lucas.

1. O Thou, whose own vast temple stands, Built over earth and sea, Accept the walls that human hands Have raised to worship Thee! Have raised to worship Thee!

940. C. M.

2. Lord, from Thine inmost glory send,
   Within these courts to bide,
   The peace that dwelleth, without end,
   Serenely by Thy side!

3. May erring minds that worship here
   Be taught the better way;
   And they who mourn, and they who fear,
   Be strengthened as they pray.

4. May faith grow firm, and love grow warm,
   And pure devotion rise,
   While round these hallowed walls the storm
   Of earth-born passion dies.

   BRYANT.

941. C. M.

1. THE Saviour said, "Yet one thing more,
   If thou would'st perfect be,
   Give all thou hast unto the poor,
   And come and follow me."

2. Within this temple, Christ again
   Those sacred words hath said;
   Unseen His hands to-day have been
   Laid on a young man's head.

3. Henceforth, beside him on his way
   The unseen Christ shall move,
   That he may lean on Him and say,
   "Dost Thou, dear Lord, approve?"

4. Near at the marriage feast shall be,
   To make the scene more fair;
   Near, in the dark Gethsemane,
   Of pain and midnight prayer.

5. O holy trust! O endless rest!
   Like the beloved John,
   To lean upon the Saviour's breast,
   And thus to journey on!

   ALTERED FROM LONGFELLOW.

942. C. M.

1. ANGELS, where'er we go, attend
   Our steps, whate'er betide,
   With watchful care their charge defend,
   And evil turn aside.

2. Myriads of bright cherubic bands,
   Sent by the King of kings,
   Rejoice to bear us in their hands,
   And shade us with their wings.

3. Jehovah's charioteers surround;
   The ministerial choir
   Encamp, where'er his heirs are found,
   And form our wall of fire.

4. Ten thousand offices unseen
   For us they gladly do,
   Deliver in the furnace keen,
   And safe escort us through.

5. But thronging round, with busiest love
   They guard the dying breast,
   The lurking fiend far off remove,
   And sing our souls to rest.

6. And when our spirits we resign,
   On outstretched wings they bear,
   And lodge us in the arms Divine,
   And leave us ever there.

   C. WESLEY.

MISSIONS AND REFORM.

MISSIONARY HYMN. 7s & 6s.   L. MASON.

1. From Greenland's i-cy mountains, From India's cor-al strand, Where Af-ric's sun-ny foun-tains Roll down the gold-en sand. From many an an-cient riv-er, From many a palm-y plain They call us to de-liv-er Their land from er-ror's chain.

943. 7s & 6s.

1. From Greenland's icy mountains,
   From India's coral strand,
Where Afric's sunny fountains
   Roll down their golden sand;
From many an ancient river,
   From many a palmy plain
They call us to deliver
   Their land from error's chain.

2. What though the spicy breezes
   Blow soft o'er Ceylon's isle;
Though every prospect pleases,
   And only man is vile:
In vain with lavish kindness
   The gifts of God are strown;
The heathen, in his blindness,
   Bows down to wood and stone!

3. Shall we, whose souls are lighted
   With wisdom from on high,
Shall we to men benighted
   The lamp of life deny?
Salvation, O salvation!
   The joyful sound proclaim,
Till each remotest nation
   Has learned Messiah's name.

4. Waft, waft, ye winds, his story,
   And you, ye waters roll,
Till, like a sea of glory,
   It spreads from pole to pole;
Till o'er our ransomed nature
   The Lamb for sinners slain,
Redeemer, King, Creator,
   In bliss returns to reign.   HEBER.

944. 7s & 6s.

1. Now be the gospel banner
   In every land unfurl'd;
And be the shout hosanna
   Re-echoed through the world:
Till ev'ry isle and nation,
   Till every tribe and tongue,
Receive the great salvation,
   And join the happy throng.

2. Yes, Thou shalt reign for ever,
   O Jesus, King of kings!
Thy light, Thy love, Thy favor,
   Each ransomed captive sings:
The isles for Thee are waiting,
   The deserts learn Thy praise,
The hills and valleys greeting,
   The song responsive raise.
                              HASTINGS.

CONFLICTS OF THE GOSPEL.

MISSIONARY CHANT. L. M. — CH. BEECHER.

1. Ye Christian heroes, go, proclaim Salvation thro' Immanuel's name; To distant climes the tidings bear, And plant the rose of Sharon there, And plant the rose of Sharon there.

945. L. M.

2. He'll shield you with a wall of fire,
With flaming zeal your breasts inspire;
Bid raging winds their fury cease,
And hush the tempest into peace.

3. And when your labors all are o'er,
Then we shall meet to part no more;
Meet, with the blood-bought throng to fall—
And crown our Jesus Lord of all.
PRATT'S COLL.

946. L. M.

1. TRIUMPHANT Zion! lift thy head
From dust, and darkness, and the dead!
Though humbled long—awake at length,
And gird thee with thy Saviour's strength!

2. Put all thy beauteous garments on,
And let thy excellence be known;
Decked in the robes of righteousness,
The world thy glories shall confess.

3. No more shall foes unclean invade,
And fill thy hallowed walls with dread;
No more shall hell's insulting host
Their victory and thy sorrows boast.

4. God, from on high, has heard thy prayer;
His hand thy ruins shall repair;
Nor will thy watchful Monarch cease
To guard thee in eternal peace.
DODDRIDGE.

947. L. M.

1. O SPIRIT of the living God,
In all Thy plenitude of grace,
Where'er the foot of man hath trod,
Descend on our apostate race.

2. Give tongues of fire, and hearts of love,
To preach the reconciling word;
Give power and unction from above,
Where'er the joyful sound is heard.

3. Be darkness, at Thy coming, light;
Confusion—order, in Thy path;
Souls without strength, inspire with might;
Bid mercy triumph over wrath.

4. Baptize the nations; far and nigh
The triumphs of the cross record;
The name of Jesus glorify,
Till every kindred call Him, Lord.

5. O Spirit of the Lord! prepare
All the round earth her God to meet;
Breathe Thou abroad like morning air,
Till hearts of stone begin to beat.
MONTGOMERY.

948. L. M.

1. ARM of the Lord! awake, awake!
Put on Thy strength! the nations shake!
And let the world, adoring, see
Triumphs of mercy wrought by Thee.

2. Say to the heathen, from Thy throne—
"I am Jehovah—God alone!"
Thy voice their idols shall confound,
And cast their altars to the ground.

3. Almighty God! Thy grace proclaim
In every land, of every name;
Let Zion's time of favor come;
Oh! bring the tribes of Israel home.

4. Arm of the Lord! awake, awake!
Put on Thy strength! the nations shake!
Let hostile powers before Thee fall,
And crown the Saviour Lord of all.
BURDER'S COLL.

MISSIONS AND REFORM.

URMUND. 8s & 4s. Or L. M.* L. MASON.

1. Hark! how the gospel trumpet sounds! Thro' all the world the echo bounds! And Jesus, by redeeming blood, Is bringing sinners back to God, And guides them safely by his word To endless day.

* By repeating half the last line.

949. L. M. Peculiar.

2. Hail, Jesus! all victorious Lord!
Be Thou by all mankind adored!
For us didst Thou the fight maintain,
And o'er our foes the victory gain,
That we, with Thee, might ever reign
  In endless day.

3. Fight on, ye conquering souls, fight on,
And when the conquest you have won,
Then palms of victory you shall bear,
And in His kingdom have a share,
And crowns of glory ever wear,
  In endless day.

4. There we shall in full chorus join,
With saints and angels, all combine
To sing of His redeeming love,
When rolling years shall cease to move,
And this shall be our theme above,
  In endless day.

MEDLEY.

950. L. M.

1. HARK, hark! the gospel trumpet sounds!
Thro' earth and heaven the echo bounds!
Pardon and peace by Jesus' blood,
Sinners are reconciled to God
  By grace divine.

2. Come, sinners, hear the joyful news,
Nor longer dare the grace refuse;
Mercy and justice here combine,
Goodness and truth harmonious join,
  T' invite you near.

3. Ye saints in glory, strike the lyre;
Ye mortals, catch the sacred fire;
Let both the Saviour's love proclaim—
For ever worthy is the Lamb
  Of endless praise.

951. L. M.

1. FROM day to day, before our eyes,
  Grows and extends the work begun;
When shall the new creation rise
  O'er every land beneath the sun?

2. When, in the sabbath of His love,
  Shall God from all His labors rest;
And bending from His throne above,
  Again pronounce His creatures blest?

3. As sang the morning stars of old,
  Shouted the sons of God for joy;
His widening reign while we behold,
  Let praise and prayer our tongues employ.

4. Till the redeemed in every clime,
  Yea, all that breathe, and move, and live,
To Christ, through every age of time,
  The kingdom, power, and glory give.

MONTGOMERY.

CONFLICTS OF THE GOSPEL.

PLYMOUTH. L. M.

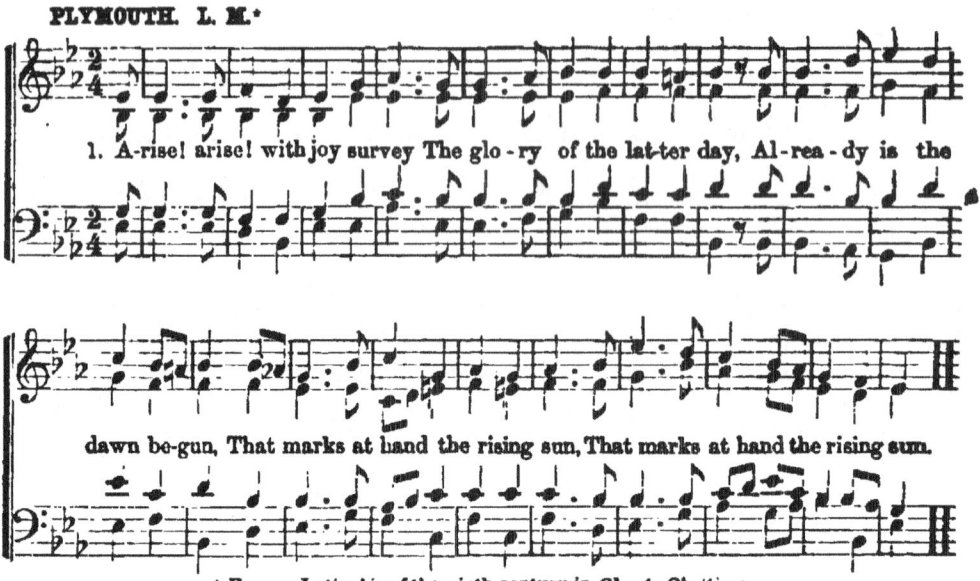

1. A-rise! arise! with joy survey The glo-ry of the lat-ter day, Al-rea-dy is the dawn be-gun, That marks at hand the rising sun, That marks at hand the rising sun.

From a Latin Air of the ninth century in Chants Chrétiens.

952. L. M.

2. The friends of truth assembled stand,
A chosen, consecrated band,
The emblem of the cross display,
And cry aloud—"Behold the way!"

3. Behold the way to Zion's hill,
Where Israel's God delights to dwell;
He fixes there His lofty throne,
And calls the sacred place His own.

4. "Behold the way!" ye heralds! cry,
Spare not, but lift your voices high,
Convey the sound from shore to shore;
And bid the captive sigh no more.

5. Auspicious dawn! thy rising ray,
With joy we view, and hail the day;
Thou Sun! arise, supremely bright,
And fill the world with purest light.

KELLY.

953. L. M.

1. Go—messenger of peace and love!
To nations plunged in shades of night;
Like angels sent from fields above,
Be Thine to shed celestial light.

2. Go—to the hungry food impart;
To paths of peace the wanderer guide,
And lead the thirsty, panting heart,
Where streams of living waters glide.

3. Go—bid the bright and morning-star,
From Bethlehem's plains resplendent shine,
And, piercing through the gloom afar,
Shed heavenly light and love divine.

4. To India's various castes proclaim
The Gospel's soft, but powerful voice;
And, at the blest Redeemer's name,
Let ocean's lonely isles rejoice.

5. From north to south, from east to west,
Messiah yet shall reign supreme;
His name by every tongue confess'd—
His praise—the universal theme.

BALFOUR.

954. L. M.

1. MARKED as the purpose of the skies,
This promise meets our anxious eyes,
That heathen lands the Lord shall know,
And warm with faith each bosom glow.

2. E'en now the hallowed scenes appear;
E'en now unfolds the promised year;
Lo! distant shores Thy heralds trace,
And bear the tidings of Thy grace.

3. 'Mid burning climes and frozen plains,
Where pagan darkness brooding reigns,
Lord! mark their steps, their fears subdue,
And nerve their arm, and clear their view.

4. When, worn by toil, their spirits fail,
Bid them the glorious future hail;
Bid them the crown of life survey,
And onward urge their conquering way.

B. NOEL.

MISSIONS AND REFORM.

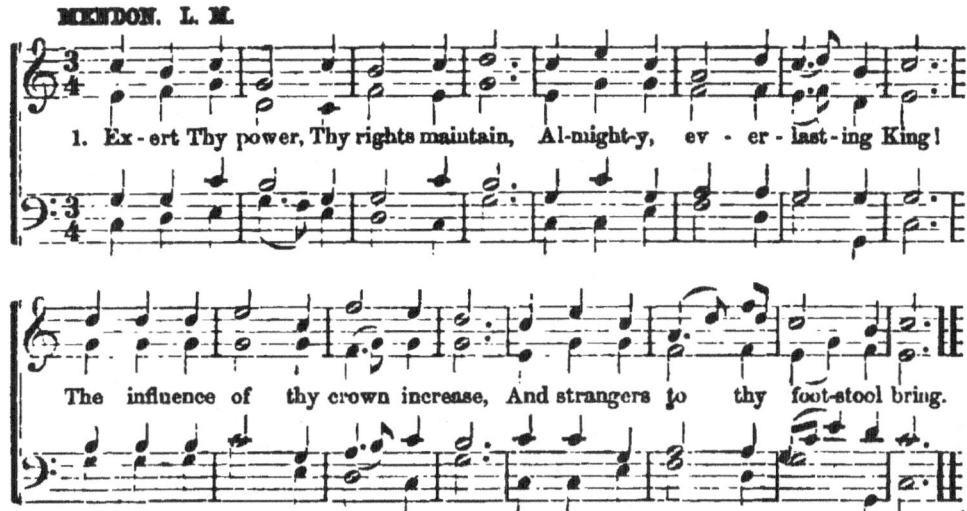

MENDON. L. M.

1. Exert Thy power, Thy rights maintain, Almighty, everlasting King! The influence of thy crown increase, And strangers to thy footstool bring.

955. L. M.

2. In one vast symphony of praise,
Gentile and Jew shall then unite,
And unbelief no longer reign,
But sink in shades of endless night.

3. Then Afric's liberated sons
Shall chant to Asia's rapturous song,
Europe resound her Saviour's fame,
And western climes the notes prolong.

4. To every land beneath the sun
Immanuel's kingdom shall extend;
And every man in every clime
Shall meet a brother and a friend.
VOKE.

956. L. M.

1. Though now the nations sit beneath
The darkness of o'erspreading death;
God will arise with light divine,
On Zion's holy towers to shine.

2. That light shall shine on distant lands,
And wandering tribes, in joyful bands,
Shall come, Thy glory, Lord, to see,
And in Thy courts to worship Thee.

3. O light of Zion, now arise!
Let the glad morning bless our eyes!
Ye nations, catch the kindling ray,
And hail the splendors of the day.
L. BACON.

957. L. M.

1. Great God, whom heaven, and earth, and sea,
With all their countless hosts obey,
Upheld by Thee the nations stand,
And empires fall at Thy command.

2. O show Thyself the Prince of Peace,
Command the din of war to cease;
With sacred love the world inspire,
And burn its chariots in the fire.

3. In sunder break each warlike spear,
Let all the Saviour's ensigns wear;
The universal Sabbath prove
The perfect rest of Christian love!
PRATT'S COLL.

958. L. M.

1. O God, beneath Thy guiding hand,
Our exiled fathers crossed the sea:
And when they trod the wintry strand,
With prayer and psalm they worshiped Thee.

2. Thou heard'st, well pleased, the song, the prayer—
Thy blessing came; and still its power
Shall onward through all ages bear
The memory of that holy hour.

3. What change! through pathless wilds no more
The fierce and naked savage roams;
Sweet praise, along the cultured shore,
Breaks from ten thousand happy homes.

4. Laws, freedom, truth, and faith in God
Came with those exiles o'er the waves,
And where their pilgrim feet have trod,
The God they trusted guards their graves.

5. And here Thy name, O God of love,
Their children's children shall adore,
Till these eternal hills remove,
And spring adorns the earth no more.
L. BACON.

CONFLICTS OF THE GOSPEL.

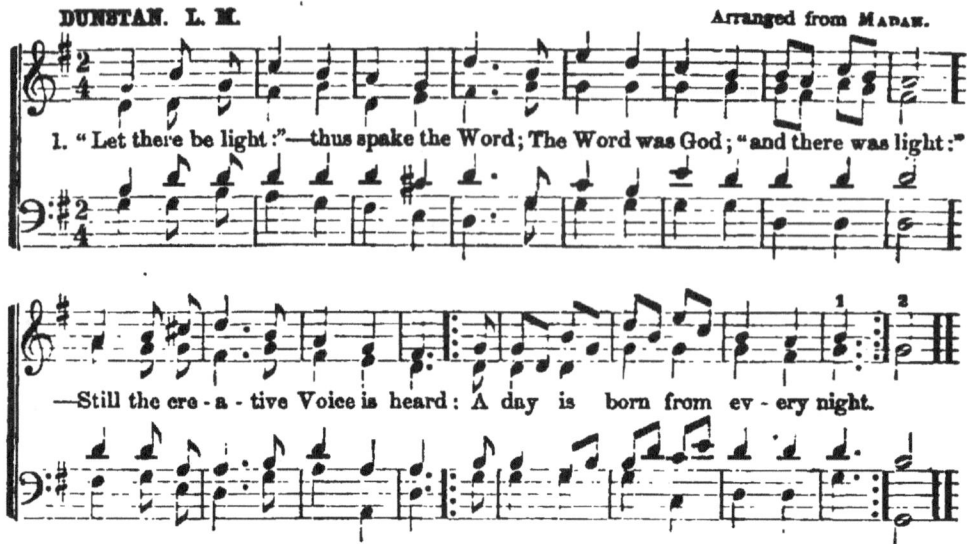

DUNSTAN. L. M.   Arranged from MADAN.

1. "Let there be light:"—thus spake the Word; The Word was God; "and there was light:" —Still the cre-a-tive Voice is heard: A day is born from ev-ery night.

959. L. M.

1. "LET there be light," thus spake the Word,
    The Word was God, "and there was light:"
    Still the creative Voice is heard:
    A day is born from every night.

2. And every night shall turn to day,
    While months, and years, and ages roll;
    But we have run a brighter ray,
    Down on the chaos of the soul.

3. Nor we alone; its wakening smiles
    Have broke the gloom of pagan sleep;
    The Word hath reached the utmost isles,—
    God's Spirit moves upon the deep.

4. Already, from the dust of death,
    Man in his Maker's image stands,
    Once more inhales immortal breath,
    And stretches forth to heaven his hands.
                MONTGOMERY.

960. L. M. Double.

1. DEPART awhile, each thought of care,
    Be earthly things forgotten all,
    And speak, my soul, thy grateful prayer,
    Obedient to the sacred call.
    For hark! the pealing chorus swells;
    Devotion chants the hymn of praise,
    And now of joy and hope it tells,
    Till, fainting on the ear, it says,—
    Glory to Thee, to Thee, O Lord!

2. Thine, wondrous Babe of Galilee!
    Fond theme of David's harp and song,
    Thine are the notes of minstrelsy,
    To Thee its ransomed chords belong.
    And hark! again the chorus swells,
    The song is wafted on the breeze,
    And to the listening earth it tells,
    In accents soft and sweet as these,—
    Glory to Thee, to Thee, O Lord!

3. My heart doth feel that still He's near,
    To meet the soul in hours like this;
    Else, why, O why, that falling tear,
    When all is peace, and love, and bliss?
    But hark! that Bethlehem chorus swells
    Anew its thrilling vesper strain;
    And still of joy and hope it tells,
    And bids creation sing again,—
    Glory to Thee, to Thee, O Lord!
                LYRA CATH.

961. L. M.

1. GREAT God, whose universal sway
    The known and unknown worlds obey,
    Now give the kingdom to Thy Son,
    Extend His power, exalt His throne.

2. Thy scepter well becomes His hands,
    All heaven submits to His commands;
    His justice shall avenge the poor,
    And pride and rage prevail no more.

3. With power He vindicates the just,
    And treads th' oppressor in the dust;
    His worship and His fear shall last,
    Till hours, and years, and time be past.

4. The heathen lands that lie beneath
    The shades of overspreading death,
    Revive at His first dawning light,
    And deserts blossom at the sight.

5. The saints shall flourish in His days,
    Dressed in the robes of joy and praise;
    Peace, like a river from His throne,
    Shall flow to nations yet unknown.

MISSIONS AND REFORM.

ANTIGUA. L. M.

1. "Go, preach my gospel," saith the Lord, "Bid the whole earth my grace receive; He shall be saved that trusts my word; And he condemned that won't believe.

962. L. M.

2. "I'll make your great commission known,
And ye shall prove My gospel true,
By all the works that I have done,
By all the wonders ye shall do.

3. "Teach all the nations My commands;
I'm with you till the world shall end;
All power is trusted in My hands;
I can destroy, and I defend."

4. He spake, and light shone round His head,
On a bright cloud to heaven He rode;
They to the farthest nations spread
The grace of their ascended God.
WATTS.

963. L. M.

1. GREAT Ruler of the earth and skies,
A word of Thine almighty breath
Can sink the world, or bid it rise:
Thy smile is life, Thy frown is death.

2. When angry nations rush to arms,
And rage, and noise, and tumult reign;
And war resounds its dire alarms,
And slaughter spreads the hostile plain;

3. Thy Sovereign eye looks calmly down,
And marks their course, and bounds their power;
Thy word the angry nations own,
And noise and war are heard no more.

4. Then peace returns with balmy wing,
Sweet peace! with her what blessings fled!
Glad plenty laughs, the valleys sing,
Reviving commerce lifts her head.

5. Thou good, and wise, and righteous Lord,
All move subservient to Thy will;
And peace and war await Thy word,
And Thy sublime decrees fulfill.
MRS. STEELE.

964. L. M.

1. O WHAT stupendous mercy shines
Around the majesty of Heaven!
Rebels He deigns to call His sons—
Their souls renewed, their sins forgiven.

2. Go, imitate the grace divine—
The grace that blazes likes a sun;
Hold forth your fair, though feeble light,
Through all your lives let mercy run.

3. Upon your bounty's willing wings
Swift let the great salvation fly;
The hungry feed, the naked clothe;
To pain and sickness help apply.

4. Pity the weeping widow's woe,
And be her counsellor and stay;
Adopt the fatherless, and smooth
To useful, happy life, his way.

5. When all is done, renounce your deeds,
Renounce self-righteousness with scorn:
Thus will you glorify your God,
And thus the Christian name adorn.
RIPPON.

CONFLICTS OF THE GOSPEL.

MEDINA. C. M.* — Psalmodist.

1, O, City of the Lord! begin Thou universal song: And let the scattered villages The joyful notes prolong. Hallelujah, hallelujah, hallelujah, Amen.

* The Hallelujah can be sung or omitted at pleasure.

965. C. M.

2. Let Kedar's wilderness afar
   Lift up the lonely voice;
   And let the tenants of the rock
   In accent rude rejoice.

3. Oh! from the streams of distant lands
   To our Jehovah sing;
   And joyful, from the mountain-tops,
   Shout to the Lord, the King.

4. Let all combined, with one accord,
   The Saviour's glories raise,
   Till in the earth's remotest bounds
   The nations sound His praise.

   LOGAN.

966. C. M.

1. Spirit of power and might, behold
   A world by sin destroyed;
   Creator, Spirit, as of old,
   Move on the formless void.

2. Give Thou the word; that healing sound
   Shall quell the deadly strife,
   And earth again, like Eden crown'd,
   Produce the tree of life.

3. If sang the morning stars for joy
   When nature rose to view,
   What strains will angel harps employ
   When Thou shalt all renew!

4. And if the sons of God rejoice
   To hear a Saviour's name,
   How will the ransomed raise their voice,
   To whom that Saviour came!

5. Lo! every kindred, tongue, and tribe,
   Assembling round the throne,
   Thy new creation shall ascribe
   To Sovereign love alone.

   MONTGOMERY.

967. C. M.

1. The mighty angel, to whose hand
   The word of life is given,
   Waves his broad wing o'er sea and land,
   And soaring, cleaves the heaven.

2. And say—shall aught oppose his flight?—
   Or cloud his flaming scroll?
   No!—not till truth with holy light
   Shall visit every soul;

3. Not till blest Peace shall spring to birth;
   And hatred sheath his sword;
   Not till the nations of the earth
   Are subject to the Lord.

   SIGOURNEY.

968. C. M.

1. Lord! send Thy servants forth
   To call the Hebrews home;
   From east, and west, and south, and north,
   Let all the wanderers come.

2. Where'er, in lands unknown,
   The fugitives remain,
   Bid every creature help them on,
   Thy holy mount to gain.

3. An offering to the Lord,
   There let them all be seen,
   Sprinkled with water and with blood,
   In soul and body clean.

4. With Israel's myriads seal'd,
   Let all the nations meet;
   And show the mystery fulfill'd,—
   Thy family complete.

   C. WESLEY.

MISSIONS AND REFORM. 307

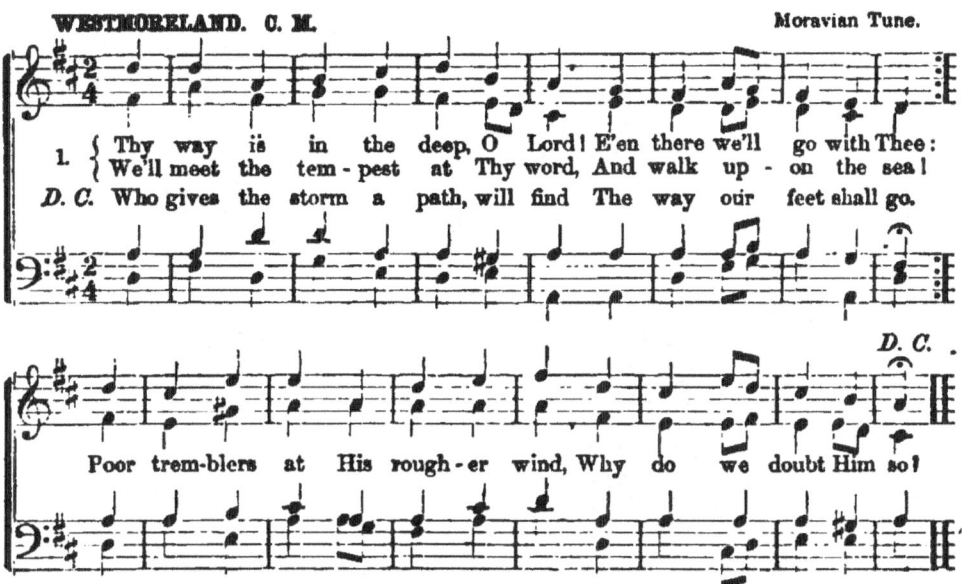

WESTMORELAND. C. M.   Moravian Tune.

1. Thy way is in the deep, O Lord! E'en there we'll go with Thee:
We'll meet the tempest at Thy word, And walk upon the sea!
D. C. Who gives the storm a path, will find The way our feet shall go.

Poor tremblers at His rougher wind, Why do we doubt Him so!

969. C. M.

1. THY way is in the deep, O Lord!
E'en there we'll go with Thee;
We'll meet the tempest at Thy word,
And walk upon the sea!

2. Poor tremblers at His rougher wind,
Why do we doubt Him so?—
Who gives the storm a path, will find
The way our feet shall go.

3. A moment may His hand be lost,—
Drear moment of delay!—
We cry, "Lord help the tempest-tost,"—
And safe we're borne away.

4. The Lord yields nothing to our fears,
And flies from selfish care;
But comes Himself, where'er He hears
The voice of loving prayer.

970. C. M.

1. GOD'S glory is a wondrous thing,
Most strange in all its ways,
And, of all things on earth, least like
What men agree to praise.

2. O blessed is he to whom is given
The instinct that can tell
That God is on the field, when He
Is most invisible!

3. Workman of God! O lose not heart,
But learn what God is like;
And in the darkest battle-field
Thou shalt know where to strike.

4. And blessed is he who can divine
Where real right doth lie,
And dares to take the side that seems
Wrong to man's blindfold eye!

5. O learn to scorn the praise of men!
O learn to lose with God!
For Jesus won the world through shame,
And beckons thee His road.
                  LYRA CATH.

971. C. M.

1. OPPRESSION shall not always reign,
There comes a brighter day,
When freedom, burst from every chain,
Shall have triumphant sway.

2. Then right shall over might prevail,
And truth, full armed in mail,
The hosts of tyrant wrong assail,
And hold eternal sway.

3. What voice shall bid the progress stay
Of truth's victorious car?
What arm arrest the growing day,
Or quench the solar star?

4. What soul shall dare, tho' stout and strong,
Restore the ancient wrong;
Oppression's guilty night prolong,
And freedom's morning bar?

5. The hour of triumph comes apace,
The fated, promised hour,
When earth upon a ransomed race
Her bounteous gifts shall shower.

6. Ring, Liberty, thy glorious bell,
On high thy banner swell,
Let trump on trump the triumph swell,
Of Heaven's redeeming power.
                  H. WARE.

CONFLICTS OF THE GOSPEL.

MORNING STAR. 7s.   CH. BEECHER.

1. Watchman! tell us of the night, What its signs of promise are. Traveler! on yon mountain's height, See that glory-beaming star! Watchman! does its beauteous ray Aught of hope or joy foretell? Traveler! yes; it brings the day, Promised day of Is-ra-el.

972. 7s.

1. WATCHMAN! tell us of the night,
   What its signs of promise are.—
   Traveler! o'er yon mountain's height,
   See that glory-beaming star!
   Watchman! does its beauteous ray
   Aught of joy or hope foretell?—
   Traveler! yes; it brings the day—
   Promised day of Israel.

2. Watchman! tell us of the night,
   Higher yet that star ascends.—
   Traveler! blessedness and light,
   Peace and truth, its course portends!—
   Watchman! will its beams alone
   Gild the spot that gave them birth?
   Traveler! ages are its own,
   See, it bursts o'er all the earth.

3. Watchman! tell us of the night,
   For the morning seems to dawn.—
   Traveler! darkness takes its flight,
   Doubt and terror are withdrawn.—
   Watchman! let thy wanderings cease;
   Hie thee to thy quiet home.—
   Traveler! lo! the Prince of Peace,
   Lo! the Son of God is come!
                   BOWRING.

973. 7s.

1. SEE how great a flame aspires,
   Kindled by a spark of grace!
   Jesus' love the nations fires—
   Sets the kingdoms on a blaze.

2. To bring fire on earth He came;
   Kindled in some heart it is:
   O that all might catch the flame,
   All partake the glorious bliss!

3. When He first the work begun,
   Small and feeble was His day:
   Now the word doth swiftly run;
   Now it wins its widening way.

4. More and more it spreads and grows,
   Ever mighty to prevail;
   Sin's strongholds it now o'erthrows—
   Shakes the trembling gates of hell.

5. Saw ye not the cloud arise,
   Little as a human hand?
   Now it spreads along the skies—
   Hangs o'er all the thirsty land.

6. Lo! the promise of a shower
   Drops already from above;
   But the Lord will shortly pour
   All the Spirit of His love.
                   C. WESLEY.

974. 7s.

1. WAKE the song of jubilee,
   Let it echo o'er the sea!
   Now hath come the promised hour;
   Jesus reigns with sovereign power.

2. All ye nations! join and sing—
   "Christ, of lords and kings, is King!"
   Let it sound from shore to shore,—
   "Jesus reigns for evermore!"

3. Now the desert lands rejoice,
   And the islands join their voice;
   Yea, the whole creation sings—
   "Jesus is the King of kings!"
                   PRATT'S COLL.

975. 7s.

1. Hark! the song of jubilee,
   Loud as mighty thunders roar,
   Or the fullness of the sea,
   When it breaks upon the shore!

2. See, Jehovah's banner's furled;
   Sheath'd His sword:—He speaks—'t is done!
   Now the kingdoms of this world
   Are the kingdom of His Son.

3. He shall reign from pole to pole
   With supreme, unbounded sway;
   He shall reign, when, like a scroll,
   Yonder heavens have passed away.

4. Hallelujah! for the Lord
   God omnipotent shall reign;
   Hallelujah!—let the word
   Echo round the earth and main.

5. Hallelujah! hark! the sound,
   From the center to the skies,
   Wakes, above, beneath, around,
   All creation's harmonies.

   MONTGOMERY.

976. 7s.

1. See the ransomed millions stand—
   Palms of conquest in their hands!
   This before the throne their strain—
   "Hell is vanquished—death is slain!

2. "Blessing, honor, glory, might,
   Are the Conqueror's native right;
   Thrones and powers before Him fall—
   Lamb of God, and Lord of all!"

3. Hasten, Lord! the promised hour;
   Come in glory and in power;
   Still Thy foes are unsubdued—
   Nature sighs to be renewed.

4. Time has nearly reached its sum;
   All things with the bride, say, "Come!"
   Jesus! whom all worlds adore,
   Come—and reign for evermore.

   CONDER.

977. 7s.

1. Go, ye messengers of God,
   Like the beams of morning fly;
   Take the wonder-working rod,
   Wave the banner-cross on high.

2. Where the lofty minaret
   Gleams along the morning skies,
   Wave it till the crescent set,
   And the "Star of Jacob" rise.

3. Go to many a tropic isle,
   In the bosom of the deep,
   Where the skies for ever smile,
   And th' oppressed for ever weep.

4. O'er the negro's night of care
   Pour the living light of heaven;
   Chase away the fiend despair,
   Bid him hope to be forgiven.

5. Where the golden gates of day
   Open on the palmy East,
   Wide the bleeding cross display,
   Spread the Gospel's richest feast.

6. Bear the tidings round the ball,
   Visit every soil and sea;
   Preach the cross of Christ to all—
   Christ, whose love is full and free.

   MARSDEN.

978. 7s.

1. Lord! Thou didst arise and say,
   To the troubled waters, "Peace!"
   And the tempest died away,
   Down they sank, the foaming seas;
   And a calm and heaving sleep
   Spread o'er all the glassy deep;
   All the azure lake serene
   Like another heaven was seen!

2. Lord! Thy gracious word repeat
   To the billows of the proud;
   Quell the tyrant's martial heat;
   Quell the fierce and changing crowd:
   Then the earth shall find repose
   From oppressions and from woes;
   And an imaged heaven appear
   On our world of darkness here.

   MILMAN.

979. 7s.

1. Sons of men, behold from far,
   Hail the long-expected star!
   Star of truth that gilds the night,
   And guides bewildered men aright.

2. Mild it shines on all beneath,
   Piercing through the shades of death;
   Scattering error's wide-spread night;
   Kindling darkness into light.

3. Nations all, remote and near,
   Haste to see your Lord appear;
   Haste, for Him your hearts prepare,
   Meet Him manifested there!

4. There behold the day-spring rise,
   Pouring light on mortal eyes;
   See it chase the shades away,
   Shining to the perfect day.

CONFLICTS OF THE GOSPEL.

HAIL TO THE BRIGHTNESS. 11 & 10s. — Spiritual Songs.

1. Hail to the brightness of Zion's glad morning! Joy to the lands that in darkness have lain; Hushed be the accents of sorrow and mourning, Zion in triumph begins her mild reign.

980. 11s & 10s.

2. Hail to the brightness of Zion's glad morning,
　Long by the prophets of Israel foretold;
Hail to the millions from bondage returning,
　Gentiles and Jews the blest vision behold.

3. Lo! in the desert rich flowers are springing,
　Streams ever copious are gliding along;
Loud from the mountain-tops echoes are ringing,
　Wastes rise in verdure and mingle in song.

4. See, from all lands—from the isles of the ocean,
　Praise to Jehovah ascending on high;
Fallen are the engines of war and commotion,
　Shouts of salvation are rending the sky.

T. HASTINGS.

MISSIONS AND REFORM.

WATTS. H. M.

1. O ye immortal throng Of angels round the throne, Join with our feeble song, To make the Saviour known! On earth ye knew His wondrous grace; His beauteous face In heaven ye view.

981. H. M.

1. O YE immortal throng
   Of angels round the throne,
   Join with our feeble song,
   To make the Saviour known!
      On earth ye knew
         His wondrous grace;
         His beauteous face
      In heaven ye view.

2. Ye saw the heaven-born Child
   In human flesh arrayed,
   Benevolent and mild,
   While in the manger laid;
      And praise to God,
         And peace on earth,
         For such a birth,
      Proclaimed aloud.

3. Ye in the wilderness,
   Beheld the tempter spoiled,
   Well known in every dress,
   In every combat foiled;
      And joined to crown
         The Victor's head,
         When Satan fled
      Before His frown.

4. Around His sacred tomb
   A willing watch ye keep,
   Till the blest moment come
   To rouse Him from His sleep;
      Then rolled the stone,
         And all adored
         Your rising Lord,
      With joy unknown.

5. When, all arrayed in light,
   The shining Conqueror rode,
   Ye hailed His rapturous flight
   Up to the throne of God;
      And waved around
         Your golden wings,
         And struck your strings
      Of sweetest sound.

6. The warbling notes pursue,
   And louder anthems raise,
   While mortals sing with you
   Their own Redeemer's praise;
      And thou, my heart,
         With equal flame,
         And joy the same,
      Perform thy part.
                                    DODDRIDGE.

DOXOLOGY. H. M.

To God the Father's throne
   Your highest honors raise;
Glory to God the Son;
   To God the Spirit praise;
With all our powers, eternal King,
Thy name we sing, while faith adores.

CONFLICTS OF THE GOSPEL.

LATTER DAY. 8s & 7s.

1. We are living, we are dwelling, In a grand and awful time, In an age on ages telling, To be living is sublime. Hark! the waking up of nations, Gog and Magog to the fray. Hark! what soundeth! is creation Groaning for its latter day!

982. 8s & 7s.

2. Will ye play, then, will ye dally,
  With your music and your wine?
Up! it is Jehovah's rally!
  God's own arm hath need of thine.
Hark! the onset! will ye fold your
  Faith-clad arms in lazy lock?
Up, O up, thou drowsy soldier;
  Worlds are charging to the shock.

3. Worlds are charging—heaven beholding;
  Thou hast but an hour to fight;
Now the blazoned cross unfolding,
  On—right onward, for the right.
On! let all the soul within you
  For the truth's sake go abroad!
Strike! let every nerve and sinew
  Tell on ages—tell for God!

  A. C. COXE.

983. 8s & 7s.

1. GLORIOUS things of thee are spoken,
  Zion, city of our God;
He, whose word can not be broken,
  Formed thee for His own abode;
On the Rock of Ages founded—
  What can shake thy sure repose?
With salvation's walls surrounded,
  Thou may'st smile on all thy foes.

2. See, the streams of living waters,
  Springing from eternal love,
Well supply thy sons and daughters,
  And all fear of want remove,
Who can faint while such a river
  Ever flows thy thirst t' assuage?
Grace, which, like the Lord, the giver,
  Never fails from age to age.

3. Round each habitation hovering,
  See the cloud and fire appear!
For a glory and a covering,
  Showing that the Lord is near—
He who gives them daily manna,
  He who listens when they cry—
Let him hear the loud hosanna
  Rising to His throne on high.

  NEWTON.

984. 8s & 7s.

1. Yes—my native land! I love thee;
All thy scenes I love them well;
Friends, connections, happy country,
Can I bid you all farewell?
Can I leave you,
Far in heathen lands to dwell?

2. Home!—thy joys are passing lovely—
Joys no stranger-heart can tell;
Happy home!—'tis sure I love thee!
Can I—can I say—Farewell?
Can I leave thee,
Far in heathen lands to dwell?

3. Scenes of sacred peace and pleasure,
Holy days and Sabbath-bell,
Richest, brightest, sweetest treasure!
Can I say a last farewell?
Can I leave you,
Far in heathen lands to dwell?

4. Yes! I hasten from you gladly,
From the scenes I love so well;
Far away, ye billows! bear me;
Lovely native land!—farewell!
Pleased I leave thee,
Far in heathen lands to dwell.

5. In the deserts let me labor,
On the mountains let me tell,
How He died—the blessed Saviour—
To redeem a world from hell!
Let me hasten,
Far in heathen lands to dwell.
S. F. SMITH.

985. 8s & 7s.

1. ONWARD, onward, men of heaven!
Bear the Gospel's banner high;
Rest not till its light is given,
Star of every pagan sky.
Send it where the pilgrim-stranger
Faints 'neath Asia's scorching ray;
Bid the red browed forest ranger
Hail it, ere he fades away.

2. Where the Arctic ocean thunders,
Where the tropics fiercely glow,
Broadly spread its page of wonders,
Brightly bid its radiance flow.
India marks its luster stealing,
Shiv'ring Greenland loves its rays,
Afric, 'mid her deserts kneeling,
Lifts the untaught strain of praise.

3. Rude in speech, or grim in feature,
Dark in spirit tho' they be,
Show that light to every creature,
Prince or vassal—bond or free.
Lo! they haste to every nation,
Host on host the ranks supply,
Onward!—Christ is your salvation,
And your death is victory.
SIGOURNEY.

986. 8s, 7s & 4s.

1. CHRISTIAN! see! the orient morning
Breaks along the heathen sky;
Lo! th' expected day is dawning—
Glorious day-spring from on high;
Hallelujah!—
Hail the day-spring from on high!

2. Heathens at the sight are singing;
Morning wakes the tuneful lays;
Precious offerings they are bringing—
First-fruits of more perfect praise;
Hallelujah!—
Hail the day-spring from on high!

3. Zion's Sun!—salvation beaming—
Gilding now the radiant hills—
Rise and shine, till brighter gleamings
All the world Thy glory fills;
Hallelujah!—
Hail the day-spring from on high!

4. Lord of every tribe and nation!
Spread Thy truth from pole to pole;
Spread the light of Thy salvation,
Till it shine on every soul;
Hallelujah!—
Hail the day-spring from on high!
LELAND'S HYMNS.

987. 8s & 7s.

1. HARK! the sounds of joy and gladness;
Whence the shout of rural mirth?
Man repents his murderous madness,
Man, the tiger of the earth!
Lo! the glittering sword descending,
Cleaves the soil it drenched before;
And the spear, the vintage tending,
Gives its work of carnage o'er.

2. Men, not now their hands imbruing,
Brother, in a brother's blood,
Sport with terror, death, and ruin,
Reckless borne on passion's flood;
Arts of peace, the nations blessing,
Clothe the hills, the valleys cheer;
While the world, its wrongs redressing,
Breathes a new, sabbatic year.

3. Lord of earth! its mournful story
Hasten, in Thy grace, to close;
Bring the days of brighter glory,
Calm its tumults, heal its woes;
All, around the cross uniting,
Blend in one harmonious throng;
Peace, the rolls of time inditing,
Love, the universal song.
MRS. GILBERT.

CONFLICTS OF THE GOSPEL.

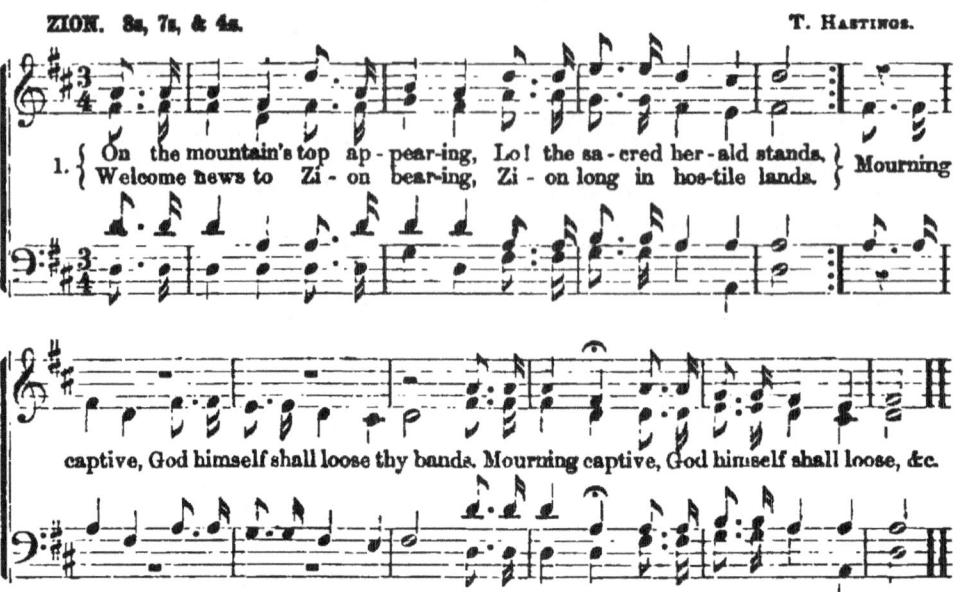

ZION. 8s, 7s, & 4s. T. HASTINGS.

1. On the mountain's top appear-ing, Lo! the sa-cred her-ald stands.
Welcome news to Zi-on bear-ing, Zi-on long in hos-tile lands. Mourning captive, God himself shall loose thy bands. Mourning captive, God himself shall loose, &c.

988. 8s, 7s & 4s.

2. Has thy night been long and mournful?
   Have thy friends unfaithful proved?
   Have thy foes been proud and scornful,
   By thy sighs and tears unmoved?
   Cease thy mourning;
   Zion still is well beloved.

3. God, thy God, will now restore thee;
   He Himself appears thy Friend;
   All thy foes shall flee before thee;
   Here their boasts and triumphs end;
   Great deliverance
   Zion's King will surely send.

4. Peace and joy shall now attend thee;
   All thy warfare now is past;
   God thy Saviour will defend thee;
   Victory is thine at last;
   All thy conflicts
   End in everlasting rest.
   KELLY.

989. 8s, 7s & 4s.

1. ZION stands with hills surrounded—
   Zion, kept by power divine:
   All her foes shall be confounded,
   Though the world in arms combine;
   Happy Zion,
   What a favored lot is thine!

2. Every human tie may perish;
   Friend to friend unfaithful prove;
   Mothers cease their own to cherish;
   Heaven and earth at last remove;
   But no changes
   Can attend Jehovah's love.

3. In the furnace God may prove thee,
   Thence to bring thee forth more bright,
   But can never cease to love thee;
   Thou art precious in His sight;
   God is with thee—
   God, thine everlasting light.
   KELLY.

990. 8s, 7s & 4s.

1. SEE, from Zion's sacred mountain,
   Streams of living water flow;
   God has opened there a fountain
   That supplies the world below;
   They are blessed
   Who its sovereign virtues know.

2. Through ten thousand channels flowing
   Streams of mercy find their way:
   Life, and health, and joy bestowing,
   Waking beauty from decay.
   O, ye nations,
   Hail the long-expected day.

3. Gladdened by the flowing treasure,
   All-enriching as it goes,
   Lo! the desert smiles with pleasure,
   Buds and blossoms as the rose;
   Lo! the desert
   Sings for joy where'er it flows.
   KELLY.

MISSIONS AND REFORM.

991. 8s, 7s & 4s.

1. MEN of God, go take your stations,
    Darkness reigns o'er all the earth—
   Go, proclaim among the nations
    Joyful news of heavenly birth—
     Bear the tidings,
   Tell the Saviour's matchless worth.

2. Go—and when exposed to dangers,
    Jesus will your souls defend;
   Go, and when 'mid foes and strangers,
    He will still appear your Friend—
     His kind presence
   Shall be with you to the end.
                                    KELLY.

992. 8s & 7s.

1. CHEEK grow pale, but heart be vigorous;
    Body fall, but soul have peace;
   Welcome, pain! thou searcher rigorous,
    Slay me, but my faith increase.

2. Sin, o'er sense so softly stealing;
    Doubt, that would my strength impair;
   Hence at once from life and feeling—
    Now my cross I gladly bear.

3. Up, my soul! with clear sedateness
    Read heaven's law, writ bright and
   Up! a sacrifice to greatness,   [broad,
    Truth, and goodness—up to God!

4. Up to labor! from thee shaking
    Off the bonds of sloth, be brave!
   Give thyself to prayer and waking;
    Toil some fainting heart to save!
                                MISS BREMER.

993. 8s, 7s & 4s.

1. YES! we trust the day is breaking,
    Joyful times are near at hand;
   God, the mighty God, is speaking
    By His word in every land;
     God is speaking—
   Darkness flies at His command.

2. With the voice of joy and singing
    Let us hail the dawning ray;
   Lo! the blessed day-star, bringing
    O'er the earth a glorious day;
     At his rising,
   Gloom and darkness flee away.
                                    KELLY.

994. 8s & 7s.

1. HARK! what mean those lamentations,
    Rolling sadly through the sky?
   'T is the cry of heathen nations—
    "Come and help us, or we die!"

2. Hear the heathen's sad complaining,
    Christians! hear their dying cry;
   And, the love of Christ constraining,
    Haste to help them, ere they die.
                                    CAWOOD.

995. 8s, 7s & 4s.

1. O'ER the realms of pagan darkness
    Let the eye of pity gaze;
   See the thronging, wandering nations,
    Lost in sin's bewildering maze:
     Darkness brooding
   On the face of all the earth.

2. Light of them that sit in darkness!
    Rise and shine! Thy blessings bring:
   Light to lighten all the Gentiles!
    Rise with healing in Thy wing;
     To Thy brightness
   Let all kings and nations come.

3. May the millions now adoring
    Idol-gods of wood and stone,
   Come, and worshiping before Him,
    Serve the living God alone:
     Let Thy glory
   Fill the earth as floods the sea.

4. Thou, to whom all power is given,
    Speak the word; at Thy command
   Let the heralds of Thy mercy
    Spread Thy name from land to land;
     Lord, be with them,
   Always, to the end of time.
                                    COTTERELL.

996. 8s, 7s & 4s.

1. O'ER the gloomy hills of darkness,
    Cheered by no celestial ray,
   Sun of righteousness! arising,
    Bring the bright, the glorious day;
     Send the gospel
   To the earth's remotest bound.

2. Kingdoms wide that sit in darkness—
    Grant them, Lord! the glorious light;
   And, from eastern coast to western,
    May the morning chase the night;
     And redemption,
   Freely purchased, win the day.

3. Fly abroad, thou mighty Gospel!
    Win and conquer, never cease;
   May thy lasting, wide dominions,
    Multiply and still increase;
     Sway Thy scepter,
   Saviour! all the world around.
                                    P. WILLIAMS.

CONFLICTS OF THE GOSPEL.

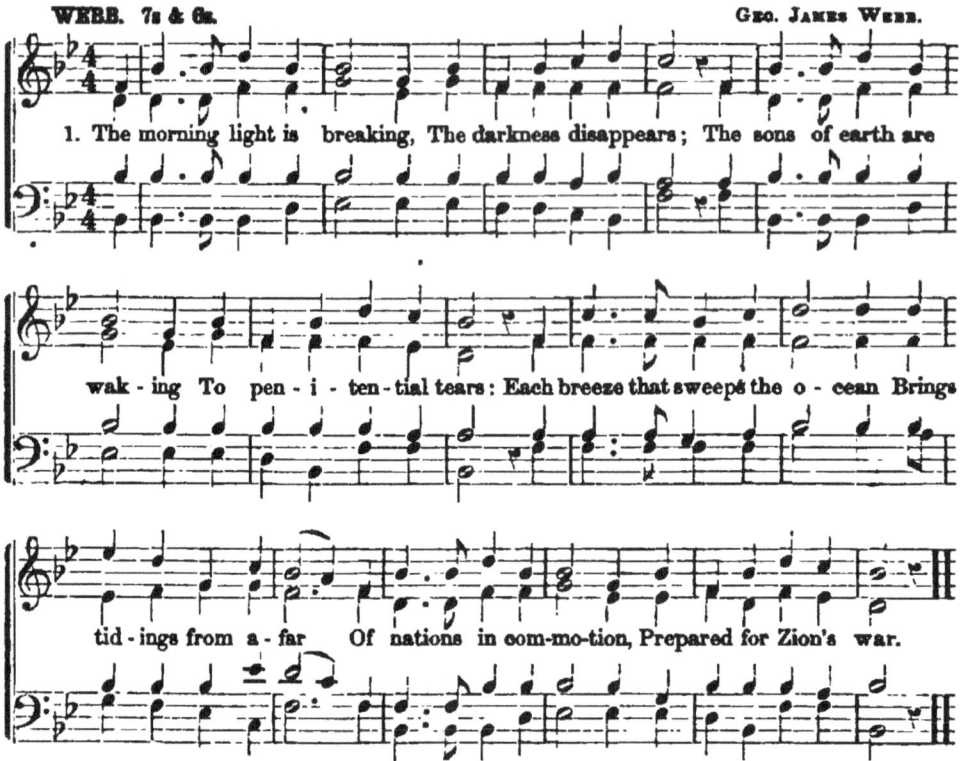

WEBB. 7s & 6s. GEO. JAMES WEBB.

1. The morning light is breaking, The darkness disappears; The sons of earth are waking To penitential tears: Each breeze that sweeps the ocean Brings tidings from afar Of nations in commotion, Prepared for Zion's war.

997. 7s & 6s.

1. THE morning light is breaking,
   The darkness disappears;
   The sons of earth are waking
   To penitential tears.
   Each breeze that sweeps the ocean
   Brings tidings from afar
   Of nations in commotion,
   Prepared for Zion's war.

2. Rich dews of grace come o'er us
   In many a gentle shower;
   And brighter scenes before us
   Are opening every hour:
   Each cry to heaven going
   Abundant answer brings;
   And heavenly gales are blowing,
   With peace upon their wings.

3. See heathen nations bending
   Before the God we love,
   And thousand hearts ascending
   In gratitude above;
   While sinners, now confessing,
   The gospel call obey,
   And seek the Saviour's blessing,—
   A nation in a day.

4. Blest river of salvation,
   Pursue thine onward way;
   Flow thou to every nation,
   Nor in thy richness stay:
   Stay not till all the lowly
   Triumphant reach their home;
   Stay not till all the holy
   Proclaim—"The Lord is come."

998. 7s & 6s.

1. ROLL on, thou mighty ocean;
   And, as thy billows flow,
   Bear messengers of mercy
   To every land below.
   Arise, ye gales, and waft them
   Safe to the destined shore;
   That man may sit in darkness,
   And death's black shade no more.

2. O Thou eternal Ruler,
   Who holdest in Thine arm
   The tempests of the ocean,
   Protect them from all harm!
   Thy presence, Lord, be with them,
   Wherever they may be;
   Though far from us, who love them,
   Still let them be with Thee.

PRATT'S COLL.

MISSIONS AND REFORM.

999. 7s & 6s.

1. WRETCHED, helpless, and distress'd,
     Ah! whither shall I fly;
   Ever gasping after rest,—
     I can not find it nigh:
   Naked, sick, and poor, and blind,—
     Fast bound in sin and misery,—
   Friend of sinners, let me find
     My help, my all in Thee.

2. Clothe me, Lord, with holiness,
     With meek humility;
   Put on me that glorious dress,—
     Endue my soul with Thee:
   Let Thine image be restored;
     Thy name and nature let me prove;
   With Thy fullness fill me, Lord,
     And perfect me in love.
                        C. WESLEY.

1000. 7s & 6s.

1. WHEN shall the voice of singing
     Flow joyfully along?
   When hill and valley, ringing
     With one triumphant song,
   Proclaim the contest ended,
     And Him, who once was slain,
   Again to earth descended,
     In righteousness to reign?

2. Then from the craggy mountains
     The sacred shout shall fly;
   And shady vales and fountains
     Shall echo the reply:
   High tower and lowly dwelling
     Shall send the chorus round,
   All hallelujah swelling
     In one eternal sound.
                    PRATT'S COLL.

1001. 7s & 6s.

1. HAIL to the Lord's Anointed,
     Great David's greater Son!
   Hail, in the time appointed,
     His reign on earth begun!
   He comes to break oppression,
     To set the captive free,
   To take away transgression,
     And rule in equity.

2. He comes, with succor speedy,
     To those who suffer wrong;
   To help the poor and needy,
     And bid the weak be strong;
   To give them songs for sighing,
     Their darkness turn to light,
   Whose souls, condemned and dying,
     Were precious in His sight.

3. He shall come down, like showers
     Upon the fruitful earth,
   And love, and joy, like flowers,
     Spring in His path to birth:
   Before Him, on the mountains,
     Shall peace, the herald, go;
   And righteousness, in fountains,
     From hill to valley flow.

4. For Him shall prayer unceasing,
     And daily vows ascend;
   His kingdom still increasing,—
     A kingdom without end:
   The tide of time shall never
     His covenant remove;
   His name shall stand for ever;
     That name to us is—Love.
                      MONTGOMERY.

1002. 7s & 6s.

1. Now, host with host assembling,
     The victory we win;
   Lo! on his throne sits trembling
     That old and giant Sin;
   Like chaff by strong winds scattered,
     His banded strength has gone,
   His charmed cup lies shattered,
     And still the cry is—"On."

2. Our fathers' God, our Keeper!
     Be Thou our strength divine!
   Thou sendest forth the reaper,—
     The harvest all is Thine.
   Roll on, roll on this gladness,
     Till, driven from every shore,
   The drunkard's sin and madness
     Shall smite the earth no more!
                       E. H. CHAPIN.

1003. 7s & 6s.

1. ON Thibet's snow-capped mountains,
     O'er Afric's burning sand,
   Where roll the fiery fountains
     Along Hawai's strand:
   In every distant nation,
     The mighty globe around,
   The heralds of salvation
     The Gospel trumpet sound.

2. In golden armor blazing,
     They press their onward way,
   And, high in air upraising,
     The glorious cross display:
   Away their weapons hurling,
     The warring nations cease,
   And hail with joy, unfurling
     The banner folds of peace.

3. What though hell's fiery legions
     Pour forth their dread array,
   Look up—angelic legions
     Attend you on your way:
   March on, ye sons of heaven,
     This precious promise sing—
   The heathen shall be given
     To Christ, our glorious King!
                       D. DUTTON, JR.

CONFLICTS OF THE GOSPEL.

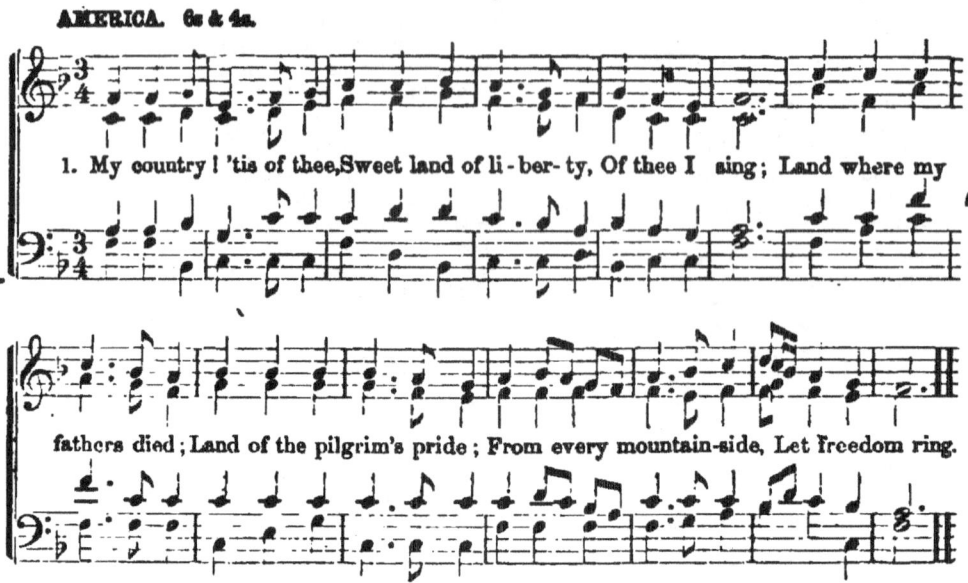

AMERICA. 6s & 4s.

1. My country! 'tis of thee, Sweet land of liberty, Of thee I sing; Land where my fathers died; Land of the pilgrim's pride; From every mountain-side, Let freedom ring.

1004. 6s & 4s.

2. My native country! thee,
   Land of the noble free,
      Thy name I love;
   I love thy rocks and rills,
   Thy woods and templed hills;
   My heart with rapture thrills,
      Like that above.

3. Let music swell the breeze,
   And ring from all the trees
      Sweet freedom's song;
   Let mortal tongues awake,
   Let all that breathes partake,
   Let rocks their silence break,
      The sound prolong.

4. Our father's God! to Thee,
   Author of liberty!
      To Thee we sing;
   Long may our land be bright
   With freedom's holy light,
   Protect us by Thy might,
      Great God, our King.
                        S. F. SMITH.

1095. 6s & 4s.

1. BREAK forth in song, ye trees,
   As, through your tops, the breeze
      Sweeps from the sea;
   For, on its rushing wings,
   To your cool shades and springs,
   That breeze a people brings,
      Exiled, though free.

2. Ye sister hills lay down
   Of ancient oaks your crown,
      In homage due;—
   These are the great of earth,
   Great, not by kingly birth,
   Great in their well-proved worth,
      Firm hearts and true.

3. These are the living lights,
   That from your bold, green heights
      Shall shine afar,
   Till they who name the name
   Of Freedom, to the flame
   Come, as the Magi came
      Towards Bethlehem's star.
                        PIERPONT.

1006. 6s & 4s.

1. GONE are those great and good
   Who here, in peril, stood
      And raised their hymn.
   Peace to the reverend dead!
   The light, that on their head
   Two hundred years have shed,
      Shall ne'er grow dim.

2. Ye temples, that to God
   Rise where our fathers trod,
      Guard well your trust,—
   The faith, that dared the sea,
   The truth, that made them free,
   Their cherished purity,
      Their garnered dust.

3. Thou high and holy One,
   Whose care for sire and son
      All nature fills;
   While day shall break and close,
   While night her crescent shows,
   O, let Thy light repose
      On these our hills!   PIERPONT.

MISSIONS AND REFORM.

PLYMOUTH ROCK. S. M. — Mrs. Brown.

1. The breaking waves dashed high, On a stern and rock-bound coast, And the woods against a stormy sky Their gi-ant branches tossed; And the heavy night hung dark The hills and waters o'er, When a band of ex-iles moored their bark On the wild New England shore.

1007. S. M.

1. The breaking waves dashed high
   On a stern and rock-bound coast,
   And the woods against a stormy sky
   Their giant branches tossed;
   And the heavy night hung dark
   The hills and waters o'er,
   When a band of exiles moored their bark
   On the wild New England shore.

2. Not as the conqueror comes,
   They, the true hearted, came;
   Not with roll of the stirring drums,
   And the trumpet that sings of fame;
   Not as the flying come,
   In silence and in fear:—
   They shook the depths of the desert gloom
   With their hymns of lofty cheer.

3. Amidst the storm they sang,
   And the stars heard, and the sea!
   And the sounding aisles of the dim woods rang
   To the anthem of the free.
   The ocean eagle soared
   From his nest by the white wave's foam,
   And the rocking pines of the forest roared—
   This was their welcome home!

4. What sought they thus afar?
   Bright jewels of the mine?
   The wealth of seas, the spoils of war?—
   They sought a faith's pure shrine!
   Ay, call it holy ground,
   The soil where first they trod!
   They have left unstained what there they found—
   Freedom to worship God.

   MRS. HEMANS.

CONFLICTS OF THE GOSPEL.

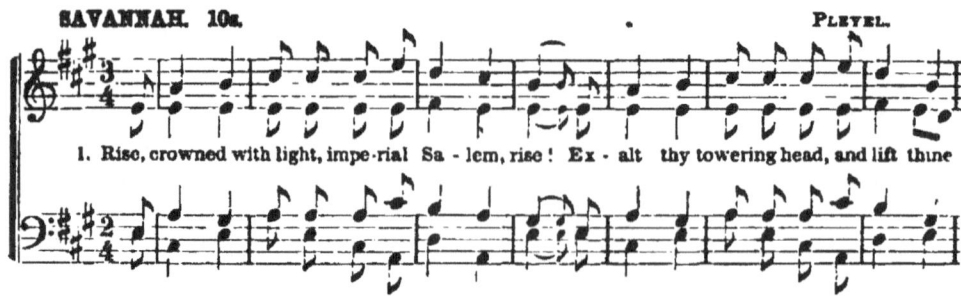
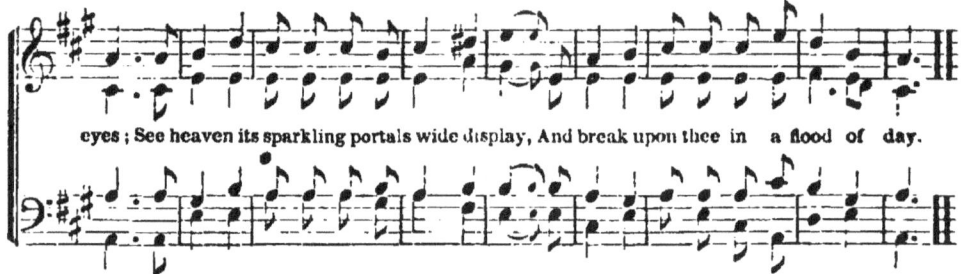

1. Rise, crowned with light, imperial Salem, rise! Exalt thy towering head, and lift thine eyes; See heaven its sparkling portals wide display, And break upon thee in a flood of day.

1008. 10s.

2. See a long race thy spacious courts adorn;
See future sons and daughters yet unborn,
In crowding ranks on every side arise,
Demanding life, impatient for the skies.

3. See barbarous nations at thy gates attend,
Walk in Thy light, and in thy temple bend;
See thy bright altars, thronged with prostrate kings,
While every land its joyous tribute brings.

4. The seas shall waste, the skies to smoke decay,
Rocks fall to dust, and mountains melt away;
But fixed His word, His saving power remains;
Thy realm shall last, thy own Messiah reigns.
POPE.

1009. 10s.

1. Pour, blessed Gospel, glorious news for man!
Thy stream of life o'er springless deserts roll:
Thy bond of peace the mighty earth can span,
And make one brotherhood from pole to pole.

2. On, piercing Gospel, on! of every heart,
In every latitude, thou own'st the key:
From their dull slumbers savage souls shall start,
With all their treasures first unlocked by thee.

3. Spread, mighty Gospel, spread thy soaring wings!
Gather thy scattered ones from every land:
Call home the wanderers to the King of kings;
Proclaim them all thine own;—'t is Christ's command!
ASHWORTH.

1010. 10s.

1. Restore, O Father! to our times restore
The peace which filled Thine infant church of yore;
Ere lust of power had sown the seeds of strife,
And quenched the new-born charities of life.

2. O, never more may different judgments part
From kindly sympathy a brother's heart!
But, linked in one, believing thousands kneel,
And share with each the sacred joy they feel.

3. From soul to soul, quick as the sunbeam's ray,
Let concord spread one universal day;
And faith by love lead all mankind to Thee,
Parent of peace, and Fount of harmony!
BEARD'S COLL.

MISSIONS AND REFORM.

MOSCOW. 11s, 10s & 9s.   Russian Air. Arranged by J. ZUNDEL.

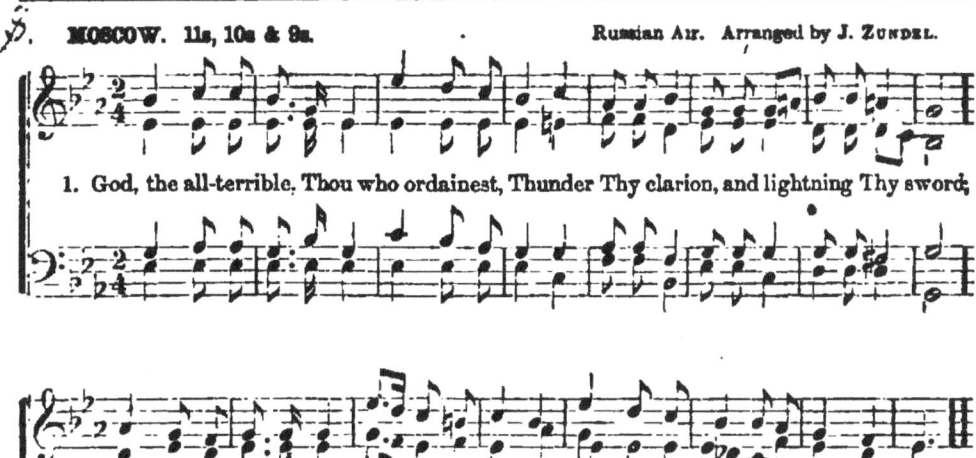

1. God, the all-terrible, Thou who ordainest, Thunder Thy clarion, and lightning Thy sword;

Show forth Thy pity on high where Thou reignest: Give to us peace in our time, O Lord!

1011. 11s, 10s & 9s.

1. GOD, the all terrible! Thou who ordainest
Thunder Thy clarion, and lightning Thy sword;
Show forth Thy pity on high where Thou reignest,
Give to us peace in our time, O Lord.

2. God, the Omnipotent! mighty Avenger,
Watching invisible, judging unheard:
Save us in mercy, O save us from danger,
Give to us peace in our time, O Lord.

3. God, the all-merciful! earth hath forsaken
Thy ways all holy, and slighted Thy word;
But not Thy wrath in its terror awaken,
Give to us pardon and peace, O Lord.

4. So will Thy people with thankful devotion,
Praise Him who saved them from peril and sword;
Shouting in chorus, from ocean to ocean,
Peace to the nations, and praise to the Lord.

1012. 11s & 10s.*

1. DOWN the dark future, through long generations,
The sounds of war grow fainter, and then cease;

* Sing to Savannah, on opposite page.

And like a bell with solemn, sweet vibrations,
I hear once more the voice of Christ say, "Peace!"

2. Peace! and no longer, from its brazen portals,
The blast of war's great organ shakes the skies:
But beautiful as songs of the immortals,
The holy melodies of love arise.

LONGFELLOW.

1013. 10s.*

1. FATHER divine! this deadening power control,
Which to the senses binds the immortal soul;
O, break this bondage, Lord! I would be free,
And in my soul would find my heaven in Thee.

2. My heaven in Thee! O God, no other heaven
To the immortal soul can e'er be given;
O, let Thy kingdom now within me come,
And as above, so here, Thy will be done!

3. My heaven in Thee, O Father, let me find,
My heaven in Thee, within a heart resigned;
No more, of heaven and bliss, my soul, despair;
For where my God is found, my heaven is there.

322 CONFLICTS OF THE GOSPEL.

BLADENBURG. S. M.

1. Lord Jesus come! for here Our path thro' wilds is laid; We watch, as for the day-spring near, Amid the breaking shade.

1014. S. M.

2. Lord Jesus, come! for hosts
   Meet on the battle-plain;
Our holiest hopes seem vainest boasts,
   And tears are shed like rain.

3. Lord Jesus, come! the slave
   Still bears his heavy chains;
Their daily bread the hungry crave,
   While teem the fruitful plains.

4. Hark! herald voices near
   Lead on Thy happier day;
Come, Lord, and our hosannas bear!
   We wait to strew Thy way.
   MISS MARTINEAU.

1015. S. M.

1. Hush the loud cannon's roar,
   The frantic warrior's call!
Why should the earth be drenched with
   Are we not brothers all?   [gore?

2. Want, from the wretch depart!
   Chains, from the captive fall!
Sweet mercy, melt the oppressor's heart—
   Sufferers are brothers all.

3. Churches and sects, strike down
   Each mean partition wall!
Let love each harsher feeling drown—
   Christians are brothers all.

4. Let love and truth alone
   Hold human hearts in thrall,
That Heaven its work at length may own
   And men be brothers all.
   JOHNS.

1016. S. M.

1. "Is this a fast for me?"
   Thus saith the Lord our God;

"A day for man to vex his soul
   And feel affliction's rod?

2. "No; is not this alone
   The sacred fast I choose—
Oppression's yoke to burst in twain,
   The bands of guilt unloose?

3. "To nakedness and want
   Your food and raiment deal,
To dwell your kindred race among,
   And all their sufferings heal?

4. "Then, like the morning ray,
   Shall spring your health and light;
Before you, righteousness shall shine,
   Behind, my glory bright!" DRUMMOND.

1017. 12s.*

1. May freedom speed onward, wherever the
      blood
   Of the wronged and the guiltless is crying
      to God;
   Wherever from kindred, torn rudely apart,
   Comes the sorrowful wail of the broken
      of heart.

2. Wherever the shackles of tyranny bind
   In silence and darkness the God-given
      mind,
   There, Lord, speed it onward! the truth
      shall be felt,
   The bonds shall be loosened, the iron will
      melt.

3. Help us turn from the cavil of words, to
      unite
   Once again for the poor in defense of the
      right,
   Unappalled by the danger, the shame of
      the pain,
   And counting each trial for truth as our
      gain.   WHITTIER.

* Sing to Burlington, page 323.

MISSIONS AND REFORM.

BURLINGTON. 12s, 11s & 8s.
Arranged from the German by L. Mason.

1. The Prince of sal-va-tion in triumph is rid-ing, And glo-ry attends Him a-long His bright way, The news of His grace on the breezes are gliding, And nations are owning His sway.

(1017) May freedom speed onward, wherever the blood Of the wronged and the guiltless is cry-ing to God; Wher-ev-er from kindred torn rude-ly a-part, (OMIT . . . .) Comes the sor-row-ful wail of the broken in heart.

1018. 12s, 11s, & 8s.

2. Ride on in Thy greatness, Thou conquering Saviour.
Let thousands of thousands submit to Thy reign,
Acknowledge Thy goodness, entreat for Thy favor,
And follow Thy glorious train.

3. Then loud shall ascend from each sanctified nation
The voice of thanksgiving, the chorus of praise,
And heaven shall re-echo the song of salvation,
In rich and melodious lays.

S. F. SMITH.

WHITTIER. 10s.
Arranged from a Jewish Chant.

1. { O, he whom Je-sus loved has tru-ly spok-en! }
   { The ho-lier wor-ship, which God deigns to bless, } Re-stores the lost, and heals the spi-rit brok-en, And feeds the wi-dow and the fa-ther-less.

1019. 11s & 10s.

2. Then, brother man, fold to thy heart thy brother!
For where love dwells, the peace of God is there;
To worship rightly is to love each other;
Each smile a hymn, each kindly deed a prayer.

3. Follow, with reverent steps, the great example
Of Him whose holy work was doing good;
So shall the wide earth seem our Father's temple,
Each loving life a psalm of gratitude.

4. Thus shall all shackles fall; the stormy clangor
Of wild war music o'er the earth shall cease;
Love shall tread out the baleful fires of anger,
And in its ashes plant the tree of peace.

WHITTIER.

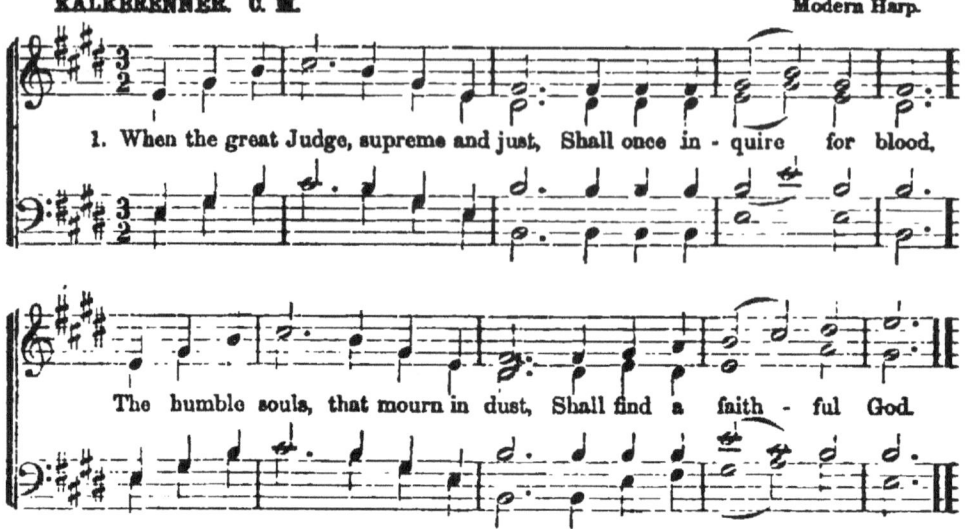

KALKBRENNER. C. M.   Modern Harp.

1. When the great Judge, supreme and just, Shall once in-quire for blood, The humble souls, that mourn in dust, Shall find a faith-ful God.

1020. C. M.

1. WHEN the great Judge, supreme and just,
Shall once inquire for blood,
The humble souls, that mourn in dust,
Shall find a faithful God.

2. He from the dreadful gates of death
Doth His own children raise;
In Zion's gates with cheerful breath
They sing their Father's praise.

3. His foes shall fall with heedless feet
Into the pit they made;
And sinners perish in the net
That their own hands have spread.

4. Though saints to sore distress are brought,
And wait, and long complain,
Their cries shall never be forgot,
Nor shall their hopes be vain.

5. Rise, great Redeemer, from Thy seat,
To judge and save the poor;
Let nations tremble at Thy feet,
And man prevail no more.
        WATTS.

1021. C. M.

1. LORD, when iniquities abound,
And blasphemy grows bold,
When faith is hardly to be found,
And love is waxing cold,—

2. Is not Thy chariot hastening on?
Hast Thou not given the sign?
May we not trust and live upon
A promise so divine?

3. "Yes," saith the Lord, "now will I rise,
And make oppressors flee;
I will appear to their surprise,
And set My servants free."

4. Thy word, like silver seven times tried,
Through ages shall endure;
The men, that in Thy truth confide,
Shall find the promise sure.
        WATTS.

1022. C. M.

1. WITH my whole heart I'll raise my song,
Thy wonders I'll proclaim;
Thou, sovereign Judge of right and wrong,
Wilt put my foes to shame.

2. I'll sing Thy majesty and grace:
My God prepares His throne
To judge the world in righteousness,
And make His vengeance known.

3. Then shall the Lord a refuge prove
For all the poor oppress'd;
To save the people of His love,
And give the weary rest.

4. The men that know Thy name will trust
In Thine abundant grace;
For Thou dost ne'er forsake the just,
Who humbly seek Thy face.

5. Sing praises to the righteous Lord,
Who dwells on Zion's hill,
Who executes His threatening word,
And doth His grace fulfill.
        WATTS.

MISSIONS AND REFORM.

HOWITT. H. M. J. ZUNDEL.

1. Gird on Thy conquering sword, Ascend Thy shining car, And march, almighty Lord, To wage Thy holy war. Before His wheels, in glad surprise, Ye valleys, rise, and sink, ye hills, Ye valleys, rise, and sink, ye hills.

1023. H. M.

1. GIRD on Thy conquering sword,
  Ascend Thy shining car,
And march, almighty Lord!
  To wage Thy holy war.
Before His wheels, in glad surprise,
Ye valleys, rise, and sink, ye hills.

2. Fair truth, and smiling love,
  And injured righteousness,
Under Thy banners move,
  And seek from Thee redress;
Thou in their cause shall prosperous ride,
And far and wide dispense Thy laws.

3. Before Thine awful face
  Millions of foes shall fall,
The captives of Thy grace—
  The grace that captures all.
The world shall know, great King of kings,
What wondrous things Thine arm can do.

4. Here to my willing soul
  Bend Thy triumphant way;
Here every foe control,
  And all Thy power display;
My heart, Thy throne, blest Jesus! see,
Bows low to Thee, to Thee alone.
  DODDRIDGE.

1024. H. M.

1. WE give immortal praise
  For God the Father's love—
For all our comforts here,
  And better hopes above;
He sent His own eternal Son
To die for sins that we had done.

2. To God the Son belongs
  Immortal glory, too,
Who bought us with His blood
  From everlasting woe;
And now He lives, and now He reigns,
And sees the fruit of all His pains.

3. To God the Spirit's name
  Immortal worship give,
Whose new-creating power
  Makes the dead sinner live;
His work completes the great design,
And fills the soul with joy divine.

4. Almighty God! to Thee
  Be endless honors done,
The undivided Three,
  And the mysterious One:
Where reason fails, with all her powers,
There faith prevails, and love adores.
  WATTS.

WASHINGTON. 6s & 4s.   J. ZUNDEL.

1. God bless our native land! Firm may she ever stand, Thro' storm and night; When the wild tempests rave, Ruler of winds and wave, Do Thou our country save By Thy great might.

1025. 6s & 4s.

2. For her our prayer shall rise
   To God above the skies;
     On Him we wait;
   Thou who hast heard each sigh,
   Watching each weeping eye,
   Be Thou for ever nigh;—
     God save the State!

1026. 6s & 4s.

1. LORD, from Thy blessed throne
   Sorrow look down upon!
     God save the poor!
   Teach them true liberty,
   Make them from tyrants free,
   Let their homes happy be!
     God save the poor!

2. The arms of wicked men
   Do Thou with might restrain,—
     God save the poor!
   Raise Thou their lowliness,
   Succor Thou their distress,
   Thou whom the meanest bless!
     God save the poor!

3. Give them stanch honesty,
   Let their pride manly be—
     God save the poor!
   Help them to hold the right,
   Give them both truth and might,
   Lord of all life and light!
     God save the poor!

                        NICOLL.

1027. 6s & 4s.

1. ROLL on, thou joyful day,
   When tyranny's proud sway,
     Stern as the grave,
   Shall to the ground be hurl'd,
   And freedom's flag, unfurl'd,
   Shall wave throughout the world
     O'er every slave.

2. Trump of glad jubilee,
   Echo o'er land and sea,
     Freedom for all;
   Let the glad tidings fly,
   And every tribe reply,
   Glory to God on high,
     At slavery's fall.

3. Free, too, the captive mind
   By darkness long confined
     In slavery's night;
   The Saviour's reign extend,
   Virtue with freedom blend,
   And full salvation send
     With freedom's light.

                        DUNCAN.

MISSIONS AND REFORM.

SUFFOLK. 8s, 7s & 4s.

1. Hark! a voice from heaven proclaiming Comfort to the mourning slave;
God has heard him long complaining, And extends His arm to save;
Proud oppression, Proud oppression Soon shall find a shameful grave.

1028. 8s, 7s & 4.

2. See, the light of truth is breaking
Full and clear on every hand,
And the voice of mercy speaking,
Now is heard through all the land;
Firm and fearless
See the friends of freedom stand.

3. Lo, the nation is arousing
From its slumber, long and deep,
And the friends of God are waking,
Never, never more to sleep
While a bondman
In his chains remains to weep.

4. Long, too long have we been dreaming
O'er our country's sin and shame;
Let us now, the time redeeming,
Press the helpless captive's claim
Till, exulting,
He shall cast aside his chain.

OLIVER JOHNSON.

1029. 8s, 7s & 4s.

1. Everlasting! changing never!
Of one strength, no more, no less:
Thine Almightiness for ever,—
All the same Thy holiness:
Thee Eternal,
Thee All-glorious we possess!

2. But we weak ones, but we sinners,
Would not in our poorness stay;
We, the low ones, would be winners
Of what holy height we may,
Ever nearer
To Thy pure and perfect day.

3. Shall things withered, fashions olden,
Keep us from life's flowing spring?
Waits for us the promise golden,—
Waits each new, diviner thing?
Onward! onward!
Why this faithless tarrying?

4. Nearer to Thee would we venture,
Of Thy truth more largely take,
Upon life diviner enter,
Into day more glorious break;
To the ages
Fair bequests and costly make.

5. By each saving word unspoken,
By Thy truth, as yet half-won,
By each idol still unbroken,
By Thy will, yet poorly done,—
Hear us! hear us!
Our Almighty, help us on!

GILL.

CONFLICTS OF THE GOSPEL.

MAY. L. M.   B. CARR.

1. Now be my heart inspired to sing The glories of my Saviour King,—Jesus the Lord; how heavenly fair His form! how bright His beauties are! His form! how bright His beauties are!

1030. L. M.

1. Now be my heart inspired to sing
The glories of my Saviour King—
Jesus the Lord; how heavenly fair
His form! how bright His beauties are!

2. O'er all the sons of human race,
He shines with a superior grace;
Love from His lips divinely flows,
And blessings all His state compose.

3. Dress Thee in arms, most mighty Lord!
Gird on the terror of Thy sword;
In majesty and glory ride,
With truth and meekness at Thy side.

4. Thine anger, like a pointed dart,
Shall pierce the foes of stubborn heart;
Or words of mercy, kind and sweet,
Shall melt the rebels at Thy feet.

5. Thy throne, O God! for ever stands;
Grace is the scepter in Thy hands;
Thy laws and works are just and right;
Justice and grace are Thy delight.

6. God, thine own God, has richly shed
His oil of gladness on thy head;
And with His sacred Spirit bless'd
His first-born Son above the rest.
                     WATTS.

1031. L. M.

1. My refuge is the God of love,
Why do my foes insult and cry,
"Fly, like a timorous, trembling dove,
To distant woods or mountains fly?"

2. If government be all destroyed—
That firm foundation of our peace—
And violence make justice void,
Where shall the righteous seek redress?

3. The Lord in heaven hath fixed His throne,
His eye surveys the world below;
To Him all mortal things are known,
His eyelids search our spirits through.

4. If He afflicts His saints so far,
To prove their love, and try their grace,
What must the bold transgressors fear?
His very soul abhors their ways.

5. On impious wretches He shall rain
Tempests of brimstone, fire, and death,
Such as He kindled on the plain
Of Sodom, with His angry breath.

6. The righteous Lord loves righteous souls,
Whose thoughts and actions are sincere;
And with a gracious eye beholds
The men that His own image bear.
                     WATTS.

MISSIONS AND REFORM.

NEWCOURT. L. P. M.   H. BOND.

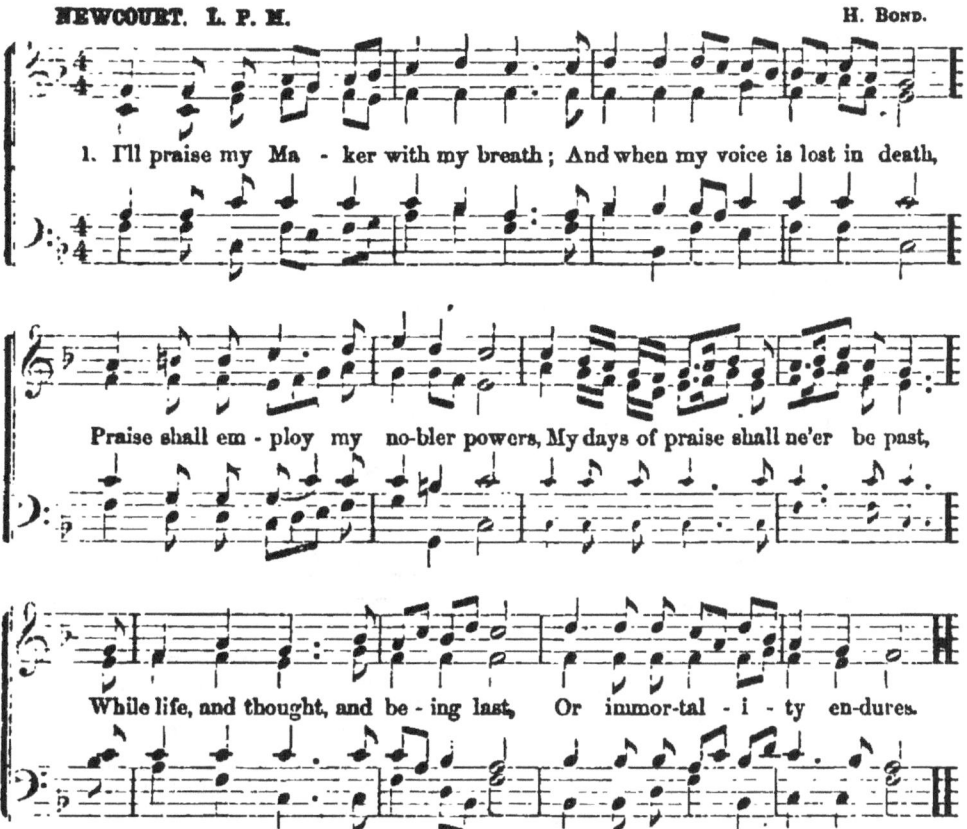

1. I'll praise my Maker with my breath; And when my voice is lost in death, Praise shall employ my nobler powers, My days of praise shall ne'er be past, While life, and thought, and being last, Or immortality endures.

1032.   L. M. 6 lines.

2. Happy the man, whose hopes rely
 On Israel's God: He made the sky,
  And earth and seas, with all their train:
 His truth for ever stands secure;
 He saves th' oppressed, He feeds the poor;
  And none shall find His promise vain.

3. The Lord hath eyes to give the blind;
 The Lord supports the sinking mind;
  He sends the laboring conscience peace;
 He helps the stranger in distress,
 The widow and the fatherless,
  And grants the prisoner sweet release.

4. He loves His saints: He knows them well;
 But turns the wicked down to hell;
  Thy God, O Zion, ever reigns;
 Let every tongue, let every age,
 In this exalted work engage;
  Praise Him in everlasting strains.
                                    WATTS.

1033.   L. P. M.

1. JUDGES, who rule the world by laws,
 Will ye despise the righteous cause,
  When the oppressed before you stands?
 Dare ye condemn the righteous poor,
 And let rich sinners go secure,
  While gold and greatness bribe your hands?

2. Have ye forgot, or never knew,
 That God will judge the judges, too?
  High in the heavens His justice reigns;
 Yet you invade the rights of God,
 And send your bold decrees abroad,
  To bind the conscience in your chains!

3. Th' Almighty thunders from the sky—
 Their grandeur melts, their titles die—
  They perish like dissolving frost;
 As empty chaff, when whirlwinds rise,
 Before the sweeping tempest flies,
  So shall their hopes and names be lost.

4. Thus shall the vengeance of the Lord
 Safety and joy to saints afford;
  And all that hear shall join and say—
 "Sure there's a God that rules on high,
 A God that hears His children cry,
  And will their sufferings well repay."
                                    WATTS.

CONFLICTS OF THE GOSPEL.

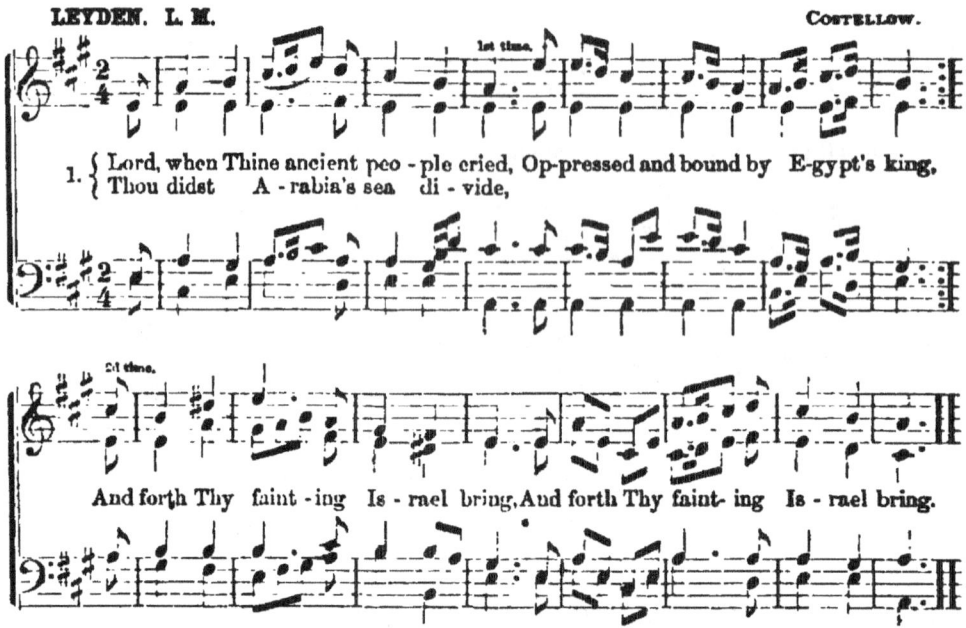

LEYDEN. L. M. COSTELLOW.

1. Lord, when Thine ancient peo-ple cried, Op-pressed and bound by E-gypt's king,
Thou didst A-rabia's sea di-vide,
And forth Thy faint-ing Is-rael bring, And forth Thy faint-ing Is-rael bring.

1034. L. M.

2. Lo, in these latter days, our land
Groans with the anguish of the slave;
Lord God of hosts! stretch forth Thy hand,
Not shortened that it can not save.

3. Roll back the swelling tide of sin,
The lust of gain, the lust of power;
The day of freedom usher in;
How long delays the appointed hour?

4. As Thou of old to Miriam's hand
The thrilling timbrel didst restore,
And to the joyful song her hand
Echoed from desert to the shore;—

5. O let Thy smitten ones again
Take up the chorus of the free—
"Praise ye the Lord! His power proclaim,
For He hath conquered gloriously!"
CAROLINE SEWARD.

1035. L. M.

1. O HOLY Father! just and true
Are all Thy works and words and ways,
And unto Thee alone are due
Thanksgiving and eternal praise!

2. As children of Thy gracious care,
We veil the eye—we bend the knee—
With broken words of praise and prayer,
Father and God, we come to Thee.

3. For Thou hast heard, O God of right!
The sighing of the hapless slave;
And stretched for him the arm of might,
Not shortened that it could not save.

4. Speed on Thy work, Lord God of hosts!
And when the bondsman's chain is riven,
And swells from all our country's coasts
The anthem of the free to heaven,

5. O, not to those whom Thou hast led,
As with Thy cloud and fire before,
But unto Thee, in fear and dread,
Be praise and glory evermore.
WHITTIER.

1036. L. M.

1. O LORD! our eyes have waited long,
But now a little cloud appears,
Spreading and swelling as it glides
Onward into the coming years.

2. Bright cloud of Liberty! full soon,
Far stretching from the ocean strand,
Thy glorious folds shall spread abroad,
Encircling our beloved land.

3. Like that sweet rain on Judah's hills,
The glorious boon of love shall fall,
And our bound millions shall arise
As at an angel's trumpet call.

4. Then shall a shout of joy go up,
The wild glad cry of freedom, come
From hearts long crushed by cruel hands,
And songs from lips long sealed and dumb.

5. And every bondsman's chain be broke,
And every soul that moves abroad
In this wide realm, shall know and feel
The blessed liberty of God.
J. H. BRYANT.

MISSIONS AND REFORM.

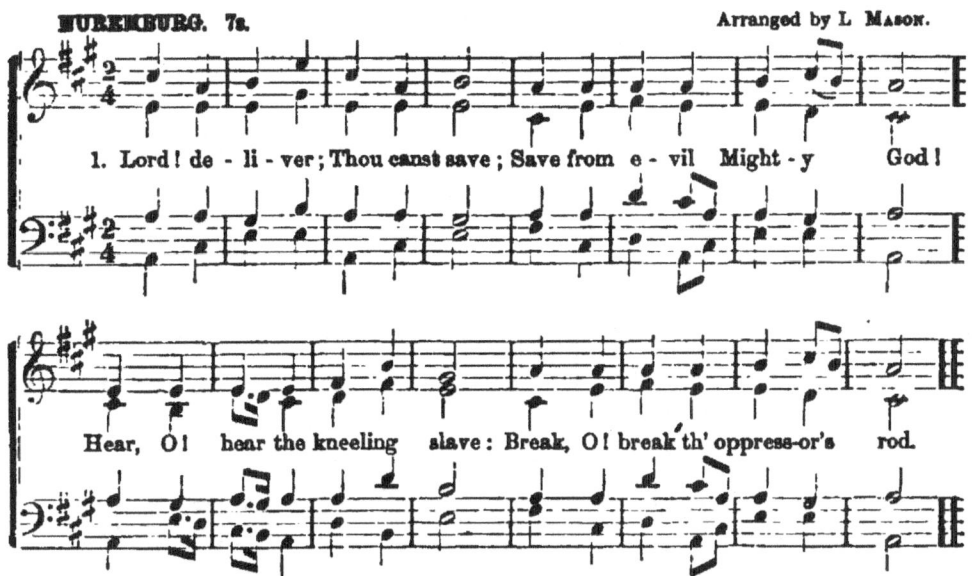

NUREMBURG. 7s. Arranged by L. Mason.

1. Lord! de-li-ver; Thou canst save; Save from e-vil Might-y God! Hear, O! hear the kneeling slave: Break, O! break th' oppress-or's rod.

1037. 7s.

2. May the captive's pleading fill
　　All the earth, and all the sky;
　Every other voice be still,
　　While he pleads with God on high.

3. He, whose ear is every where,
　　Who doth silent sorrow see,
　Will regard the captive's prayer,
　　Will from bondage set him free.

4. From the tyranny within,
　　Save thy children, Lord! we pray;
　Chains of iron, chains of sin,
　　Cast, for ever cast away.

5. Love to man, and love to God,
　　Are the weapons of our war;
　These can break th' oppressor's rod—
　　Burst the bonds that we abhor..
　　　　　　　　　　MRS. FOLLEN.

1038. 7s.

1. Men! whose boast it is, that ye
　Come of fathers brave and free,
　If there breathe on earth a slave,
　Are ye truly free and brave?
　If ye do not feel the chain
　When it works a brother's pain,
　Are ye not base slaves, indeed—
　Slaves unworthy to be freed?

2. Is true freedom but to break
　Fetters for our own dear sake,
　And with leathern hearts forget
　That we owe mankind a debt?

　No! true freedom is to share
　All the chains our brothers wear,
　And with heart and hand to be
　Earnest to make others free!

3. They are slaves, who fear to speak
　For the fallen and the weak;
　They are slaves, who will not choose
　Hatred, scoffing, and abuse,
　Rather than, in silence, shrink
　From the truth they needs must think;
　They are slaves, who dare not be
　In the right with two or three.
　　　　　　　　　JAMES R. LOWELL.

1039. 7s.

1. God made all His creatures free;
　Life itself is liberty;
　God ordained no other bands
　Than united hearts and hands.

2. Sin the primal charter broke—
　Sin, itself earth's heaviest yoke;
　Tyranny with sin began,
　Man o'er brute, and man o'er man.

3. But a better day shall be,
　Life again be liberty,
　And the wide world's only bands
　Love-knit hearts and love-linked hands.

4. So shall every slavery cease,
　All God's children dwell in peace,
　And the new-born earth record
　Love, and Love alone, is Lord.
　　　　　　　　　　MONTGOMERY.

CONFLICTS OF THE GOSPEL.

NEBO. S. M. — T. HASTINGS.

1. How beauteous are their feet, Who stand on Zion's hill! Who bring salvation on their tongues, And words of peace reveal. And words of peace reveal.

1040. S. M.

2. How charming is their voice!
   How sweet the tidings are!—
   "Zion, behold thy Saviour King!
   He reigns and triumphs here."

3. How happy are our ears,
   That hear this joyful sound,
   Which kings and prophets waited for,
   And sought, but never found!

4. How blessed are our eyes,
   That see this heavenly light!
   Prophets and kings desired it long,
   But died without the sight.

5. The watchmen join their voice,
   And tuneful notes employ;
   Jerusalem breaks forth in songs,
   And deserts learn the joy.

6. O God, make bare Thine arm
   Through all the earth abroad:
   Let every nation now behold
   Their Saviour and their Lord.

   WATTS.

1041. S. M.

1. MOURN for the thousands slain,
   The youthful and the strong;
   Mourn for the wine-cup's fearful reign,
   And the deluded throng.

2. Mourn for the tarnished gem—
   For reason's light divine,
   Quenched from the soul's bright diadem,
   Where God had bid it shine.

3. Mourn for the ruined soul—
   Eternal life and light
   Lost by the fiery, maddening bowl,
   And turned to hopeless night.

4. Mourn for the lost—but call,
   Call to the strong, the free;
   Rouse them to shun that dreadful fall,
   And to the refuge flee.

5. Mourn for the lost—but pray,
   Pray to our God above,
   To break the fell destroyer's sway,
   And show his saving love.

* 1042. C. M.

1. LORD! while for all mankind we pray,
   Of every clime and coast,
   O hear us for our native land—
   The land we love the most.

2. Our fathers' sepulchres are here,
   And here our kindred dwell;
   Our children, too: how should we love
   Another land so well?

3. O guard our shores from every foe,
   With peace our borders bless;
   With prosperous times our cities crown,
   Our fields with plenteousness.

4. Unite us in the sacred love
   Of knowledge, truth, and Thee;
   And let our hills and valleys shout
   The songs of liberty.

5. Lord of the nations! thus to Thee
   Our country we commend;
   Be Thou her Refuge and her Trust,
   Her everlasting Friend!

* May be sung to Whitfield, p. 884.

MISSIONS AND REFORM.

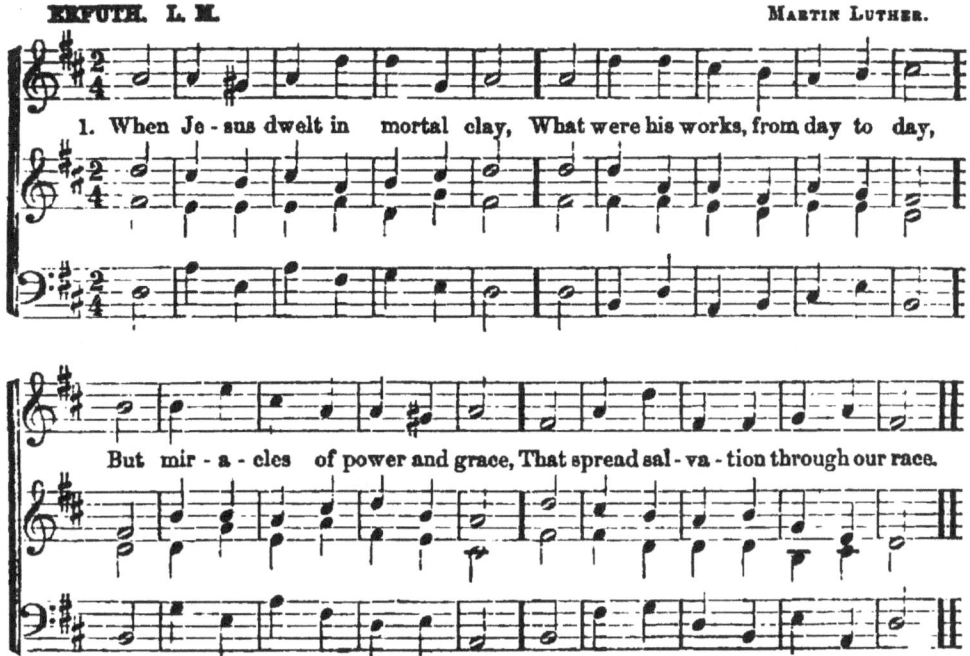

ERFURTH. L. M. — MARTIN LUTHER.

1. When Jesus dwelt in mortal clay, What were his works, from day to day, But miracles of power and grace, That spread salvation through our race.

1043. L. M.

2. Teach us, O Lord, to keep in view
Thy pattern, and Thy steps pursue;
Let alms bestowed, let kindness done,
Be witnessed by each rolling sun.

3. That man may last, but never lives,
Who much receives, but nothing gives;
Whom none can love, whom none can thank,
Creation's blot, creation's blank!

4. But he who marks, from day to day,
In generous acts his radiant way,
Treads the same path his Saviour trod,
The path to glory and to God.
GIBBONS.

1044. L. M.

1. WE praise Thee, Lord! if but one soul,
While the past year prolonged its flight,
Turned shudd'ring from the pois'nous bowl,
To health, and liberty, and light.

2. We praise Thee—if one clouded home,
Where broken hearts despairing pined,
Beheld the sire and husband come,
Erect, and in his perfect mind.

3. No more a weeping wife to mock,
Till all her hopes in anguish end—
No more the trembling mind to shock,
And sink the father in the fiend.

4. Still give us grace, Almighty King!
Unwavering at our posts to stand;
Till grateful at Thy shrine we bring
The tribute of a ransomed land.

1045. L. M.

1. SLAVERY and death the cup contains;
Dash to the earth the poisoned bowl!
Softer than silk are iron chains,
Compared with those that chafe the soul.

2. Hosannas, Lord! to Thee we sing,
Whose power the giant fiend obeys:
What countless thousands tribute bring,
For happier homes and brighter days!

3. Thou wilt not break the bruised reed,
Nor leave the broken heart unbound;
The wife regains a husband freed!
The orphan clasps a Father found!

4. Spare, Lord! the thoughtless; guide the blind;
Till man no more shall deem it just
To live, by forging chains to bind
His weaker brother in the dust.
SARGENT.

CONFLICTS OF THE GOSPEL.

WHITFIELD. C. M.   Arr. by G. Kingsley.

1. Father of mercies! send Thy grace, All-powerful from above, To form in our obedient souls The image of Thy love, To form in our obedient souls The image of Thy love.

1046. C. M.

1. FATHER of mercies! send Thy grace,
    All powerful from above,
To form, in our obedient souls,
    The image of Thy love.

2. O may our sympathizing breasts
    The generous pleasure know,
Kindly to share in others' joy,
    And weep for others' woe!

3. When the most helpless sons of grief
    In low distress are laid,
Soft be our hearts their pains to feel,
    And swift our hands to aid.

4. So Jesus looked on dying men,
    When throned above the skies;
And mid th' embraces of his God,
    He felt compassion rise.

5. On wings of love the Saviour flew,
    To raise us from the ground,
And made the richest of His blood,
    A balm for every wound.
                DODDRIDGE.

1047. C. M.

1. BLEST is the man whose softening heart
    Feels all another's pain;
To whom the supplicating eye
    Was never raised in vain:—

2. Whose breast expands with generous
    A stranger's woes to feel;   [warmth,
And bleeds in pity o'er the wound
    He wants the power to heal.

3. He spreads His kind, supporting arms,
    To every child of grief:
His secret bounty largely flows,
    And brings unasked relief.

4. To gentle offices of love
    His feet are never slow;
He views, through mercy's melting eye,
    A brother in a foe.

5. Peace from the bosom of his God
    The Saviour's grace shall give;
And when he kneels before the throne,
    His trembling soul shall live.
                MRS. BARBAULD.

1048. C. M.

1. SPEAK gently—it is better far
    To rule by love than fear;
Speak gently—let no harsh word mar
    The good we may do here.

2. Speak gently to the young—for they
    Will have enough to bear;
Pass through this life as best they may,
    'T is full of anxious care.

3. Speak gently to the aged one,
    Grieve not the careworn heart;
The sands of life are nearly run,
    Let them in peace depart.

4. Speak gently to the erring ones—
    They must have toiled in vain;
Perchance unkindness made them so;
    O, win them back again!

5. Speak gently—'t is a little thing,
    Dropped in the heart's deep well;
The good, the joy, that it may bring,
    Eternity shall tell.
                BATES.

MISSIONS AND REFORM.

1049. C. M.

1. Friends of the poor, the young, the weak!
Regard our humble train,
Compassion at your hands we seek;
Shall children plead in vain?

2. Were you not children once? Renew
The time when young as we:
Think of the friends that nourished you,
And hearken to our plea.

3. Are there not feelings from above,
In every heart that reigns?
The pulse, the voice, the look of love;
Shall nature plead in vain?

4. Have you no dear ones round your hearth
As weak and young as we?
Think, if like ours had been *their* birth
Could you resist their plea?

5. Have you not known a Saviour's grace,
For man's redemption slain?
Behold that Saviour in our place;
Shall Jesus plead in vain?

6. No! by His early griefs and tears,
When poor and young as we;
By all His woes in after years,
Accept your Saviour's plea.
MONTGOMERY.

1050. C. M.

1. Go to the pillow of disease,
Where night gives no repose,
And on the cheek where sickness preys,
Bid health to plant the rose.

2. Go where the friendless stranger lies;
To perish is his doom;
Snatch from the grave his closing eyes,
And bring his blessing home.

3. Thus what our Heavenly Father gave
Shall we as freely give:
Thus copy Him who lived to save,
And died that we might live.
LUTHERAN COLL.

1051. C. M.

1. Who is thy neighbor? he whom thou
Hast power to aid or bless;
Whose aching heart or burning brow
Thy soothing hand may press.

2. Thy neighbor? 't is the fainting poor,
Whose eye with want is dim;
O enter thou his humble door,
With aid and peace for him.

3. Thy neighbor? he who drinks the cup
When sorrow drowns the brim;
With words of high sustaining hope,
Go thou and comfort him.

4. Thy neighbor? 't is the weary slave,
Fettered in mind and limb;
He hath no hope this side the grave,
Go thou and ransom him.

5. Thy neighbor? pass no mourner by;
Perhaps thou canst redeem
A breaking heart from misery;
Go, share thy lot with him.
PEABODY.

1052. L. M.

1. Come, let us sound her praise abroad,
Sweet Charity—the child of God!
Hers, on whose kind maternal breast,
The sheltered babes of misery rest;

2. Who—when she sees the sufferer bleed—
Reckless of name, or sect, or creed,
Comes with prompt hand and look benign
To bathe his wounds in oil and wine;

3. Who in her robe the sinner hides,
And soothes and pities while she chides;
Who lends an ear to every cry,
And asks no plea but misery.

4. Her tender mercies freely fall,
Like heaven's refreshing dews, on all;
Encircling in their wide embrace
Her friends, her foes—the human race.

5. Nor bounded to the earth alone,
Her love expands to worlds unknown;
Wherever faith's rapt thought has soared,
Or hope her upward flight explored!
DRUMMOND.

1053. C. M.

1. The Lord will come, and not be slow;
His footsteps cannot err;
Before Him righteousness shall go,
His royal harbinger.

2. Mercy and Truth, that long were missed,
Now joyfully are met;
Sweet Peace and Righteousness have [kissed,
And hand in hand are set.

3. The nations all whom Thou hast made
Shall come, and all shall frame
To bow them low before Thee, Lord!
And glorify Thy name.

4. Truth from the earth, like to a flower,
Shall bud and blossom then,
And Justice, from her heavenly bower,
Look down on mortal men.

5. Thee will I praise, O Lord, my God!
Thee honor and adore
With my whole heart; and blaze abroad
Thy name for evermore!
MILTON.

CONFLICTS OF THE GOSPEL.

CHARITY. C. M. — H. E. MATHEWS.

1. Jesus, my Lord, how rich Thy grace! Thy bounties how complete! How shall I count the matchless sum? How pay the mighty debt? How pay the mighty debt?

1054. C. M.

1. JESUS, my Lord, how rich Thy grace!
   Thy bounties how complete!
   How shall I count the matchless sum!
   How pay the mighty debt?

2. High on a throne of radiant light
   Dost Thou exalted shine;
   What can my poverty bestow,
   When all the worlds are Thine?

3. But Thou hast brethren here below,
   The partners of Thy grace;
   And wilt confess their humble names,
   Before Thy Father's face.

4. In them Thou may'st be clothed and fed,
   And visited and cheered;
   And in their accents of distress,
   My Saviour's voice is heard.

5. Thy face, with reverence and with love,
   I in Thy poor would see;
   O let me rather beg my bread,
   Than keep it back from Thee.
   DODDRIDGE.

1055. C. M.

1. SHE loved her Saviour, and to Him
   Her costliest present brought;
   To crown His head, or grace His name,
   No gift too rare she thought.

2. So let the Saviour be adored,
   And not the poor despised,
   Give to the hungry from your hoard,
   But all, give all to Christ.

3. Go, clothe the naked, lead the blind,
   Give to the weary rest;
   For sorrow's children comfort find,
   And help for all distress'd;—

4. But give to Christ alone thy heart,
   Thy faith, thy love supreme;
   Then for His sake thine alms impart,
   And so give all to Him.
   CH. MIRROR.

1056. C. M.

1. O PURE reformers! not in vain
   Your trust in human kind;
   The good which bloodshed could not gain,
   Your peaceful zeal shall find.

2. The truths ye urge are borne abroad
   By every wind and tide;
   The voice of nature and of God
   Speaks out upon your side.

3. The weapons which your hands have found
   Are those which heaven hath wrought,
   Light, Truth, and Love—your battle-
     ground
   The free, broad field of Thought.

4. Press on! and if we may not share
   The glory of your fight,
   We'll ask at least, in earnest prayer,
   God's blessing on the Right.
   WHITTIER.

1057. C. M.

1. O, SEE how Jesus trusts himself
   Unto our childish love,
   As though by His free ways with us
   Our earnestness to prove!

2. His sacred name a common word
   On earth He loves to hear;
   There is no majesty in Him
   Which love may not come near.

MISSIONS AND REFORM.

3. The light of love is round His feet,
  His paths are never dim;
  And He comes nigh to us when we
  Dare not come nigh to Him.

4. Let us be simple with Him, then,
  Not backward, stiff, or cold,
  As though our Bethlehem could be
  What Sinai was of old.

1058. C. M.

1. MAKE channels for the streams of love,
  Where they may broadly run;
  And love has overflowing streams,
  To fill them every one.

2. But if at any time we cease
  Such channels to provide,
  The very founts of love for us
  Will soon be parched and dried.

3. For we must share, if we would keep
  That blessing from above;
  Ceasing to give, we cease to have;—
  Such is the law of love.
  FRENCH.

1059. C. M.

1. ALL men are equal in their birth,
  Heirs of the earth and skies;
  All men are equal when that earth
  Fades from their dying eyes.

2. God meets the throngs who pay their vows
  In courts that hands have made,
  And hears the worshiper who bows
  Beneath the plantain shade.

3. O, let man hasten to restore
  To all their rights of love;
  In power and wealth exult no more;
  In wisdom lowly move.

4. Ye great, renounce your earth-born pride,
  Ye low, your shame and fear;
  Live, as ye worship, side by side;
  Your brotherhood revere.

1060. C. M.

1. DEFEND the poor and desolate,
  And rescue from the hands
  Of wicked men the low estate
  Of him that help demands.

2. Regard the weak and fatherless,
  Dispatch the poor man's cause,
  And raise the man in deep distress
  By just and equal laws.

3. Rise, God! judge Thou the earth in might,
  The oppressed land redress;
  For Thou art He who shall by right
  The nations all possess. MILTON.

1061. C. M.

1. SCORN not the slightest word or deed,
  Nor deem it void of power;
  There's fruit in each wind-wafted seed,
  That waits its natal hour.

2. A whispered word may touch the heart,
  And call it back to life;
  A look of love bid sin depart,
  And still unholy strife.

3. No act falls fruitless, none can tell
  How vast its power may be,
  Nor what results infolded dwell
  Within it silently.

4. Work on, despair not, bring thy mite,
  Nor care how small it be,
  God is with all that serve the right,
  The holy, true, and free.

1062. C. M.

1. THINK gently of the erring one!
  O, let us not forget,
  However darkly stained by sin,
  He is our brother yet!

2. Heir of the same inheritance,
  Child of the self-same God,
  He hath but stumbled in the path
  We have in weakness trod.

3. Speak gently to the erring ones!
  We yet may lead them back,
  With holy words, and tones of love,
  From misery's thorny track.

4. Forget not, brother, thou hast sinned,
  And sinful yet may'st be;
  Deal gently with the erring heart,
  As God hath dealt with thee.
  MISS FLETCHER.

1063. C. M.

1. LORD, lead the way the Saviour went,
  By lane and cell obscure,
  And let our treasures still be spent,
  Like His, upon the poor.

2. Like Him, through scenes of deep distress,
  Who bore the world's sad weight,
  We, in their gloomy loneliness,
  Would seek the desolate.

3. For Thou hast placed us side by side
  In this wide world of ill;
  And that Thy followers may be tried,
  The poor are with us still.

4. Small are the offerings we can make;
  Yet Thou hast taught us, Lord,
  If given for the Saviour's sake,
  They lose not their reward.
  CROSWELL.

CONFLICTS OF THE GOSPEL.

DORT. 6s & 4s. L. MASON.

1. Praise ye Jehovah's name, Praise thro' his courts proclaim; Rise and adore: High o'er the heavens above, Sound His great acts of love, While His rich grace we prove, Vast as His power.

1064. 6s & 4s.

1. PRAISE ye Jehovah's name;
Praise through His courts proclaim;
Rise and adore;
High o'er the heavens above,
Sound His great acts of love,
While His rich acts we prove,
Vast as His power.

2. Now let the trumpet raise
Triumphant sounds of praise,
Wide as His fame;
There let the harp be found;
Organs, with solemn sound,
Roll your deep notes around,
Filled with His name.

3. While His high praise ye sing,
Shake every sounding string;
Sweet the accord!
He vital breath bestows;
Let every breath that flows,
His noblest fame disclose;
Praise ye the Lord.

W. GOODE.

1065. 6s & 4s.

A Temperance Hymn for Children.

1. Let the still air rejoice—
Be every youthful voice
Blended in one;
While we renew our strain
To Him, with joy again,
Who sends the evening rain,
And morning sun.

2. His hand in beauty gives
Each flower and plant that lives,
Each sunny rill;
Springs! which our footsteps meet—
Fountains! our lips to greet—
Waters! whose taste is sweet,
On rock and hill.

3. Each summer bird that sings
Drinks, from dear Nature's springs,
Her early dew;
And the refreshing shower
Falls on each herb and flower,
Giving it life and power,
Fragrant and new.

4. So let each faithful child
Drink of this fountain mild,
From early youth;
Then shall the song we raise
Be heard in future days—
Ours be the pleasant ways
Of peace and truth.

5. Now let each heart and hand,
Of all this youthful band,
United, move!
Till on the mountain's brow,
And in the vale below,
Our land may ever glow
With peace and love.

PIERPONT.

MISSIONS AND REFORM.

BRUCE. 8s, 7s & 5s.

1. Hast thou, 'midst life's empty noises, Heard the solemn steps of Time? And the low, mysterious voices Of another clime? 2. Early hath life's mighty question Thrill'd within thy heart of youth With a deep and strong beseeching, What, and where, is truth?

1066. 8s, 7s & 5s.

1. HAST thou, 'midst life's empty noises,
   Heard the solemn steps of time?
   And the low, mysterious voices
   Of another clime?

2. Early hath life's mighty question
   Thrilled within thy heart of youth,
   With a deep and strong beseeching—
   What, and where is truth?

3. Not to ease and aimless quiet
   Doth the inward answer tend;
   But to works of love and duty,
   As our being's end

4. Earnest toil, and strong endeavor
   Of a spirit which within
   Wrestles with familiar evil,
   And besetting sin;

5. And without, with tireless vigor,
   Steady heart and purpose strong,
   In the power of truth assaileth
   Every form of wrong.

   WHITTIER.

1067. 8s & 5s.

1. EVERY day hath toil and trouble,
   Every heart hath care;
   Meekly bear thine own full measure,
   And thy brother's share.
   Fear not, shrink not, though the burden
   Heavy to thee prove;
   God shall fill thy mouth with gladness,
   And thy heart with love.

2. Patiently enduring, ever
   Let thy spirit be
   Bound, by links that can not sever,
   To humanity.
   Labor, wait! thy Master perished
   Ere His task was done;
   Count not lost thy fleeting moments—
   Life hath but begun.

3. Labor! wait! though midnight shadows
   Gather round thee here,
   And the storm above thee lowering
   Fill thy heart with fear—
   Wait in hope! the morning dawneth
   When the night is gone,
   And a peaceful rest awaits thee
   When thy work is done.

   BAILEY.

1068. 8s & 6s.

1. I ASK not now for gold to gild,
   With mocking shine, an aching frame;
   The yearning of the mind is stilled—
   I ask not now for fame.

2. But, bowed in lowliness of mind,
   I make my humble wishes known;
   I only ask a will resigned,
   O Father, to Thine own.

3. In vain I task my aching brain,
   In vain the sage's thoughts I scan;
   I only feel how weak I am,
   How poor and blind is man.

4. And now my spirit sighs for home,
   And longs for light whereby to see;
   And, like a weary child would come,
   O Father, unto Thee.   WHITTIER.

TIME AND ETERNITY.

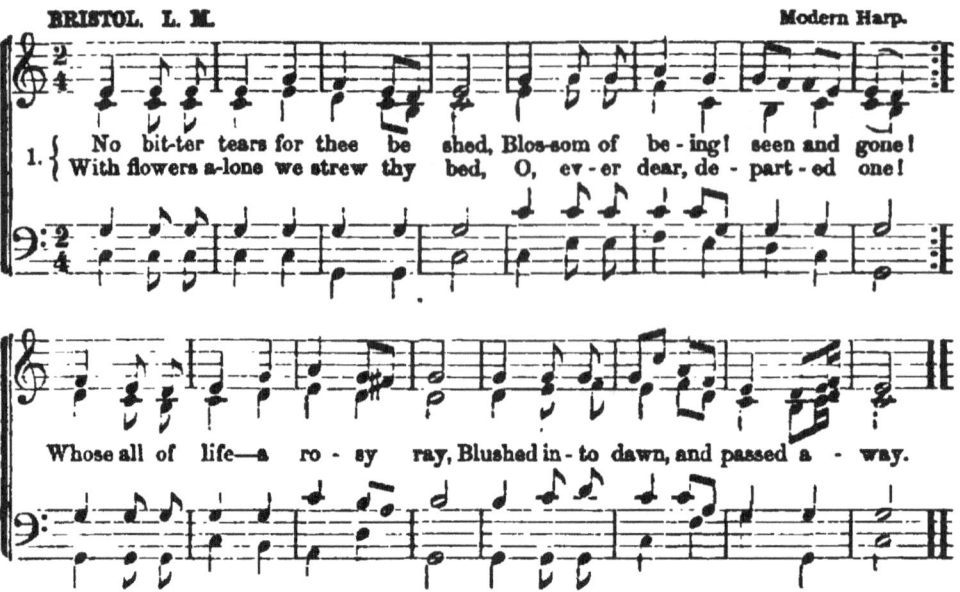

BRISTOL. L. M.   Modern Harp.

1. { No bit-ter tears for thee be shed, Blos-som of be-ing! seen and gone!
   With flowers a-lone we strew thy bed, O, ev-er dear, de-part-ed one!
Whose all of life—a ro-sy ray, Blushed in-to dawn, and passed a-way.

1069. L. M.

2. O! hadst thou still on earth remain'd,
   Vision of beauty! fair as brief!
   How soon thy brightness had been stain'd
   With passion or with grief!
   Now, not a sullying breath can rise,
   To dim thy glory in the skies.

1070. L. M.

1. Oh! if there be an hour that brings
   The breath of Heaven upon its wings,
   To light the heart, and glad the eye,
   With glimpses of eternity;
   It is the hour of mild decay,
   The sunset of the holy day.

2. For then to earth a light is given,
   Fresh flowing from the gates of heaven;
   And then on every breeze we hear
   Angelic voices whispering near;
   Through vailing shades glance seraph eyes,
   One step—and all were paradise!

1071. L. M.

1. CLOSE softly, fondly, while ye weep,
   His eyes, that death may seem like sleep,
   And fold his hands in sign of rest,
   His waxen hands, across his breast.

2. And make his grave where violets hide,
   Where star-flowers strew the rivulet's side,
   And blue-birds in the misty spring
   Of cloudless skies and summer sing.

3. But we shall mourn him long, and miss
   His ready smile, his ready kiss,
   The prattle of his little feet,
   Sweet frowns and stammered phrases sweet;

4. And graver looks, serene and high,
   A light of heaven in that young eye,
   All these shall haunt us till the heart
   Shall ache and ache—and tears will start.

5. But not his nobler part shall dwell
   A prisoner in this narrow cell;
   For he, whom now we hide from men
   In the dark ground, shall live again;

6. Shall break these clods, a form of light,
   With nobler mien and purer sight,
   And in the eternal glory stand,
   Highest and nearest God's right hand.
                             BRYANT.

1072. L. M.

1. As the sweet flower that scents the morn,
   But withers in the rising day,
   Thus lovely was this infant's dawn,
   Thus swiftly fled its life away.

2. It died ere its expanding soul
   Had ever burnt with wrong desires,
   Had ever spurned at Heaven's control,
   Or ever quenched its sacred fires.

3. Yet the sad hour that took the boy
   Perhaps has spared a heavier doom—
   Snatched him from scenes of guilty joy,
   Or from the pangs of ills to come.

4. He died to sin; he died to care;
   But for a moment felt the rod;
   Then, rising on the viewless air,
   Spread his light wings, and soared to God.
                             CUNNINGHAM.

1073. (Part 1.) L. M.

1. Of all the thoughts of God, that are
Borne inward unto souls afar,
  Along the Psalmist's music deep—
  Now tell me if that any is,
  For gift or grace surpassing this—
"He giveth His beloved sleep?"

2. His dews drop mutely on the hill—
His cloud above it saileth still—
  Though on its slope men toil and reap;
  More softly than the dew is shed,
  Or cloud is floated overhead,
"He giveth His beloved sleep."

3. And friends, dear friends! when it shall be,
That this low breath is gone from me—
  When round my bier ye come to weep;
  Let one, most loving of you all,
  Say—"Not a tear must o'er her fall,"
"He giveth His beloved sleep."
MRS. BROWNING.

1074. (Part 2.) L. M.

1. What would we give to our beloved?
The hero's heart to be unmoved—
  The poet's star-tuned harp to sweep—
  The senate's shout to patriot vows—
  The monarch's crown to light the brows?
"He giveth His beloved sleep."

2. "Sleep soft, beloved!" we sometimes say,
But have no power to charm away
  Sad dreams that through the eyelids creep;
  But never doleful dream again
  Shall break their happy slumber, when
"He giveth His beloved sleep."

3. O earth, so full of dreary noise!
O men, with wailing in your voice!
  O delved gold, the wailer's heap!
  O strife, O curse, that o'er it fall!
  God makes a silence through you all,
And giveth His beloved sleep!

4. Yea! men may wonder while they scan—
A living, thinking, feeling man
  In such a rest his heart to keep!
  But angels say—and through the word,
  I ween, their blessed smile is heard—
"He giveth His beloved sleep."
MRS. BROWNING.

1075. L. M.

1. The mourners came, at break of day,
Unto the garden sepulcher,
With saddened hearts, to weep and pray
For him, the loved one, buried there.
What radiant light dispels the gloom?
An angel sits beside the tomb.

2. The earth doth mourn her treasures lost,
All sepulchered beneath the snow,
When wintry winds and chilling frost
Have laid her summer glories low;
The spring returns, the flowrets bloom—
An angel sits beside the tomb.

3. Then mourn we not, beloved dead,
E'en while we come to weep and pray;
The happy spirit hath but fled
To brighter realms of heavenly day;
Immortal hope dispels the gloom—
An angel sits beside the tomb.
S. F. ADAMS.

1076. L. M.

1. At evening time, let there be light;
Life's little day draws near its close;
Around me fall the shades of night,
The night of death, the grave's repose;
To crown my joys, to end my woes,
At evening time, let there be light.

2. At evening time, let there be light;
Stormy and dark hath been my day;
Yet rose the morn divinely bright—
Dews, birds, and blossoms, cheered the way;
O, for one sweet, one parting ray—
At evening time, let there be light.

3. At evening time, there shall be light,
For God hath spoken—it must be;
Fear, doubt, and anguish take their flight,
His glory now is risen on me;
Mine eyes shall His salvation see;
'T is evening time—and there *is* light.

1077. L. M.

1. Oh! strange infirmity! to think
That He will leave my soul to sink
In hopeless darkness and distress—
Who has appeared in times of old,
Who saved me while the billows rolled,
And cheered me with His loving grace

2. What sweeter pledge could God bestow,
Of help in future scenes of woe,
Than grace and joy already given?
But unbelief, that hateful thing,
Oft makes me sigh, when I should sing
Of peace and confidence in heaven!

TIME AND ETERNITY.

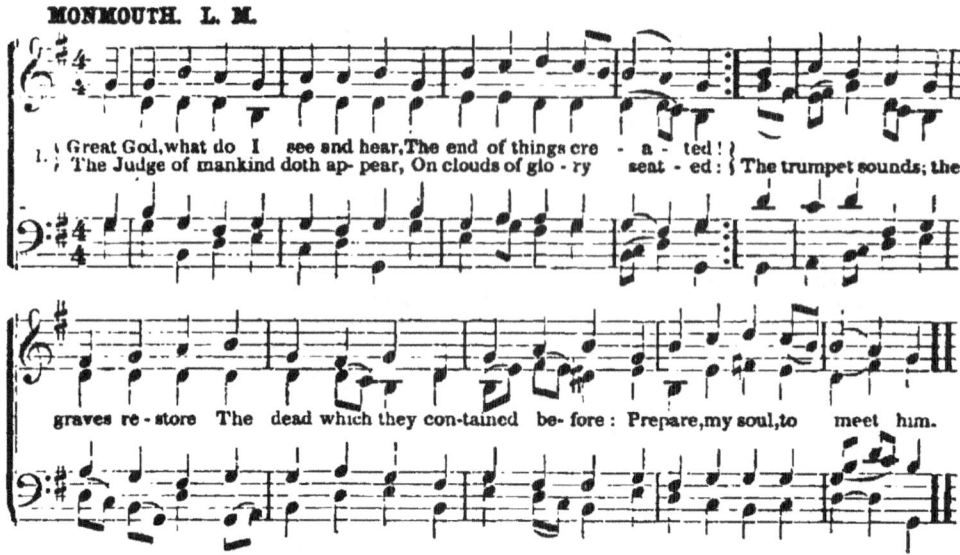

MONMOUTH. L. M.

1. Great God, what do I see and hear, The end of things cre-a-ted!
The Judge of mankind doth ap-pear, On clouds of glo-ry seat-ed: The trumpet sounds; the graves re-store The dead which they con-tained be-fore: Prepare, my soul, to meet him.

1078. L. M.

2. The dead in Christ shall first arise,
   At the last trumpet's sounding,
Caught up to meet Him in the skies,
   With joy their Lord surrounding:
No gloomy fears their souls dismay,
His presence sheds eternal day
   On those prepared to meet Him.

3. But sinners, filled with guilty fears,
   Behold His wrath prevailing;
For they shall rise, and find their tears
   And sighs are unavailing:
The day of grace is past and gone;
Trembling they stand before the throne,
   All unprepared to meet Him.

4. Great God, what do I see and hear!
   The end of things created!
The Judge of man I see appear,
   On clouds of glory seated:
Beneath His cross I view the day
When heaven and earth shall pass away,
   And thus prepare to meet Him.

1079. L. M.

1. The Lord will come; the earth shall quake,
   The hills their fixed seat forsake;
And, withering, from the vault of night
   The stars withdraw their feeble light.

2. The Lord will come, but not the same
   As once in lowly form He came:
A silent Lamb to slaughter led,
   The bruised, the suffering, and the dead.

3. The Lord will come—a dreadful form,
   With wreath of flame, and robe of storm,
On cherub wings, and wings of wind,
   Anointed Judge of human kind.

4. Can this be He who wont to stray
   A pilgrim on the world's highway,
By power oppressed, and mocked by pride?
   O God, is this the Crucified?

5. While sinners in despair shall call,
   "Rocks, hide us! mountains, on us fall!"
The saints, ascending from the tomb,
   Shall joyful sing—"The Lord is come!"
                         BISHOP HEBER.

1080. L. M.

1. Shall man, O God of light and life!
   For ever molder in the grave?
Canst Thou forget Thy glorious work,
   Thy promise, and Thy power to save?

2. In those dark, silent realms of night,
   Shall peace and hope no more arise?
No future morning light the tomb,
   Nor day-star gild the darksome skies?

3. Cease, cease, ye vain, desponding fears!
   When Christ, our Lord, from darkness
      sprang,
Death, the last foe, was captive led,
   And heaven with praise and wonder
      rang.

4. Faith sees the bright eternal doors
   Unfold to make her children way;
They shall be clothed with endless life,
   And shine in everlasting day.

5. The trump shall sound—the dead shall
      wake,
   From the cold tomb the slumberers
      spring;
Through heaven, with joy, their myriads
      rise,
   And hail their Saviour and their King.
                              DWIGHT.

1081. L. M. 6 lines.

1. O for those solitary hours,
When grace descends in silent showers;
When all the Visible withdraws
In solemn, fitful, awful pause;
And memory, like a glassy sea,
Looks up in calmness, Lord, to Thee!

2. Then, let Thine image on this heart
Be deeply felt in every part:
Each motion of the will subdue—
Inform, correct, instruct, renew;
The motives guide—the thoughts refine,
Thyself the type, from line to line!

3. Eternal, brooding, glorious Dove!
Breathe sweetly from Thy throne above:
The might of every wave control—
Be Thou the conscience of my soul;
Till self-absorbed, I sit and sing
Beneath the shadow of Thy wing.

1082. L. M.

1. He sendeth sun, He sendeth shower;
Alike they 're needful for the flower;
And joys and tears alike are sent
To give the soul fit nourishment:
As comes to me or cloud or sun,
Father, Thy will, not mine, be done!

2. Can loving children e'er reprove
With murmurs whom they trust and love?
Creator! I would ever be
A trusting, loving child to Thee:
As comes to me or cloud or sun,
Father, Thy will, not mine, be done!

3. O ne'er will I at life repine!
Enough that Thou hast made it mine;
When falls the shadow cold of death,
I yet will sing, with parting breath—
As comes to me or shade or sun,
Father, Thy will, not mine, be done!
SARAH F. ADAMS.

1083. L. M.

1. Why weep for those, frail child of woe,
Who've fled and left thee mourning here!
Triumphant o'er their latest foe,
They glory in a brighter sphere.

2. Weep not for them; beside thee now
Perhaps they watch with guardian care,
And witness tears that idly flow
O'er those who bliss of angels share.

3. Or round their Father's throne above,
With raptured voice, His praise they sing,
Or on His messages of love
They journey with unwearied wing.

4. Space can not check, thought can not bound,
The high exulting souls, whom He,
Who formed these million worlds around,
Takes to His own eternity.

5. Then weep no more—their voices raise
The song of triumph high to God,
And, wouldst thou join their song of praise,
Walk humbly in the path they trod.

1084. L. M.

1. Why should we start, and fear to die?
What timorous worms we mortals are!
Death is the gate of endless joy,
And yet we dread to enter there.

2. The pains, the groans, and dying strife,
Fright our approaching souls away;
We still shrink back again to life,
Fond of our prison and our clay.

3. O, if my Lord would come and meet,
My soul should stretch her wings in haste,
Fly, fearless, through death's iron gate,
Nor feel the terrors as she passed.

4. Jesus can make a dying bed
Feel soft as downy pillows are,
While on His breast I lean my head,
And breathe my life out sweetly there.
WATTS.

1085. L. M.

1. The great archangel's trump shall sound,
While twice ten thousand thunders roar,
Tear up the graves and cleave the ground,
And make the greedy sea restore.

2. The greedy sea shall yield her dead,
The earth no more her slain conceal;
Sinners shall lift their guilty head,
And shrink to see a yawning hell.

3. But we who now our Lord confess,
And faithful to the end endure,
Shall stand in Jesus' righteousness,
Stand as the Rock of Ages sure.

4. We, while the stars from heaven shall fall,
And mountains are on mountains hurled,
Shall stand unmoved amid them all,
And smile to see a burning world;

5. The earth and all the works therein
Dissolve, by raging flames destroyed;
While we survey the awful scene,
And mount above the fiery void.

TIME AND ETERNITY.

AZRAEL. L. M. — Ch. Beecher.

1. O, an-gel of the land of peace, When wilt thou ever come for me? I fain would be where sorrows cease, I dread no more thy kind release, I wait for thee, I wait for thee.

1086. L. M.

2. Sleep shuns mine eyes—mine inner sight
Is turning dimly heaven-ward,
To that far land of love and light,
Where angels all the silent night
   Earth's children guard.

3. My yearning soul would fain demand,
O, holy angels, pure and blest,
Where, 'mid yon happy, shining band,
In all the heavenly Father-land,
   My lost ones rest!

4. Thou, who alone, when man forgot
His heavenly innocence, and fell!
Still pitying, lingered round the spot
To soothe the anguish of his lot—
   Thou, Thou canst tell!

5. For Thou, with sweet and loving smile,
Didst gently lure them to Thy breast,
And bear them from this world of guile,
Thy pale, pure angel lips the while
   Upon them prest.

6. Dark grew my soul—till down the air
Thy seraph-smile upon me fell!
And then I know, from sin and care,
That thou my little ones didst bear
   With God to dwell!

7. O, angel of the land of peace!
When wilt Thou ever come for me?
I fain would be where sorrows cease;
I dread no more Thy kind release;
   I wait for Thee!
               MRS. C. M. SAWYER.

1087. L. M.

1. UNVEIL thy bosom, faithful tomb;
Take this new treasure to thy trust,
And give these sacred relics room
To slumber in the silent dust.

2. Nor pain, nor grief, nor anxious fear,
Invade thy bounds; no mortal woes
Can reach the peaceful sleeper here,
While angels watch the soft repose.

3. So Jesus slept; God's dying Son [bed:
Passed through the grave, and blest the
Rest here, blest saint, till from His throne
The morning break, and pierce the shade.

4. Break from His throne, illustrious morn;
Attend, O earth, His sovereign word;
Restore thy trust; a glorious form
Shall then arise to meet the Lord.
                                WATTS.

1088. L. M.

1. THE glories of our birth and state
Are shadows, not substantial things;
There is no armor against fate;
Death lays his icy hands on kings.

2. Princes and magistrates must fall,
And in the dust be equal made;
The high and mighty with the small,
Sceptre and crown with scythe and spade.

3. The laurel withers on our brow;
Then boast no more your mighty deeds:
Upon death's purple altar now
See where the victor victim bleeds!
                                SHIRLEY.

LIFE AND DEATH.

1089. L. M.

1. From his low bed of mortal dust,
   Escap'd the prison of his clay,
   The new inheritant of bliss
   To heaven directs his upward way.

2. Ye fields! that witnessed once his tears,
   Ye winds! that wafted oft his sighs,
   Ye mountains! where he breathed his prayers
   When sorrow's shadows veiled his eyes—

3. No more the weary pilgrim mourns,
   No more affliction wrings his heart;
   Th' unfettered soul to God returns—
   For ever he and anguish part!

4. Receive, O earth, his faded form,
   In thy cold bosom let it lie;
   Safe let it rest from every storm—
   Soon must it rise, no more to die.

1090. L. M.

1. So fades the lovely, blooming flower,
   Frail, smiling solace of an hour;
   So soon our transient comforts fly,
   And pleasure only blooms to die.

2. Is there no kind, no healing art,
   To soothe the anguish of the heart?
   Divine Redeemer, be Thou nigh:
   Thy comforts were not made to die.

3. Then gentle patience smiles on pain,
   And dying hope revives again;
   Hope wipes the tear from sorrow's eye,
   And faith points upward to the sky.
   MRS. STEELE.

1091. L. M.

1. Return, my roving heart! return,
   And chase those shadowy forms no more;
   Now seek, in solitude, to mourn,
   And thy forsaken God implore.

2. O Thou great God! whose piercing eye
   Distinctly marks each deep recess;—
   In these sequestered hours draw nigh,
   And with Thy presence fill the place.

3. Through all the windings of my heart,
   My search let heavenly wisdom guide,
   And still its radiant beams impart,
   Till all be cleansed and purified.

4. Oh! with the visits of Thy love,
   Vouchsafe my inmost soul to cheer;
   Till every grace shall join to prove
   That God has fixed His dwelling here.
   DODDRIDGE.

1092. L. M.

1. Earth's transitory things decay,
   Its pomps, its pleasures pass away;
   But the sweet memory of the good
   Survives in the vicissitude.

2. As, 'midst the ever rolling sea,
   The eternal isles established be,
   'Gainst which the surges of the main
   Fret, dash, and break themselves in vain:—

3. As, in the heavens, the urns divine
   Of golden light for ever shine;
   Tho' clouds may darken, storms may rage,
   They still shine on from age to age:—

4. So, through the ocean-tide of years,
   The memory of the just appears;
   So, through the tempest and the gloom,
   The good man's virtues light the tomb.
   BOWRING.

1093. L. M.

1. When life, as opening buds, is sweet,
   And golden hopes the spirits greet,
   And youth prepares his joys to meet,
   Alas! how hard it is to die.

2. When scarce is seized some borrowed prize,
   And duties press; and tender ties
   Forbid the soul from earth to rise,
   How awful, then, it is to die.

3. When, one by one, those ties are torn,
   And friend from friend is snatched forlorn,
   And man is left alone to mourn,
   Ah! then, how easy 'tis to die.

4. When trembling limbs refuse their weight,
   And films, slow gathering, dim the sight,
   And clouds obscure the mental light,
   'T is nature's precious boon, to die.

5. When faith is strong, and conscience clear,
   And words of peace the spirit cheer,
   And visioned glories half appear,
   'Tis joy, 't is triumph, then, to die.
   MRS. BARBAULD.

1094. L. M.

1. How blest are they whose transient years
   Pass like an evening meteor's flight!
   Not dark with guilt, nor dim with tears;
   Whose course is short, unclouded, bright.

2. O, cheerless were our lengthened way;
   But heaven's own light dispels the gloom,
   Streams downward from eternal day,
   And casts a glory round the tomb.

3. O, stay thy tears; the blest above
   Have hailed a spirit's heavenly birth,
   And sung a song of joy and love;
   Then why should anguish reign on earth?
   NORTON.

TIME AND ETERNITY.

ZEPHYR. L. M.   W. B. BRADBURY.

1. A-sleep in Jesus! bless-ed sleep! From which none ev-er wakes to weep:
A calm and un-disturbed re-pose, Un-broken by the dread of foes.

1095. L. M.

1. ASLEEP in Jesus! blessed sleep!
From which none ever wakes to weep;
A calm and undisturbed repose,
Unbroken by the dread of foes.

2. Asleep in Jesus! peaceful rest,
Whose waking is supremely blest;
No fear, no woes, shall dim that hour,
Which manifests the Saviour's power.

3. Asleep in Jesus! O, for me
May such a blissful refuge be;
Securely shall my ashes lie,
And wait the summons from on high.

4. Asleep in Jesus! far from thee
Thy kindred and their graves may be;
But thine is still a blessed sleep,
From which none ever wakes to weep.

5. Asleep in Jesus! O, how sweet
To be for such a slumber meet;
With holy confidence to sing,
That death has lost his venomed sting!
                MRS. MACKAY.

1096. L. M.

1. SAY, why should friendship grieve for those
Who safe arrive on Canaan's shores?
Released from all their hurtful foes,
They are not lost—but gone before.

2. How many painful days on earth
Their fainting spirits numbered o'er!
Now they enjoy a heavenly birth;
They are not lost—but gone before.

3. Dear is the spot where Christians sleep,
And sweet the strain which angels pour;
O why should we in anguish weep?
They are not lost—but gone before.

1097. L. M.

1. Go, spirit of the sainted dead,
Go to thy longed for, happy home!
The tears of man are o'er thee shed;
The voice of angels bids thee come.

2. If life be not in length of days,
In silvered locks and furrowed brow,
But living to the Saviour's praise,
How few have lived so long as thou!

3. Though earth may boast one gem the less,
May not e'en heaven the richer be?
And myriads on thy footsteps press,
To share thy blest eternity.

LIFE AND DEATH.

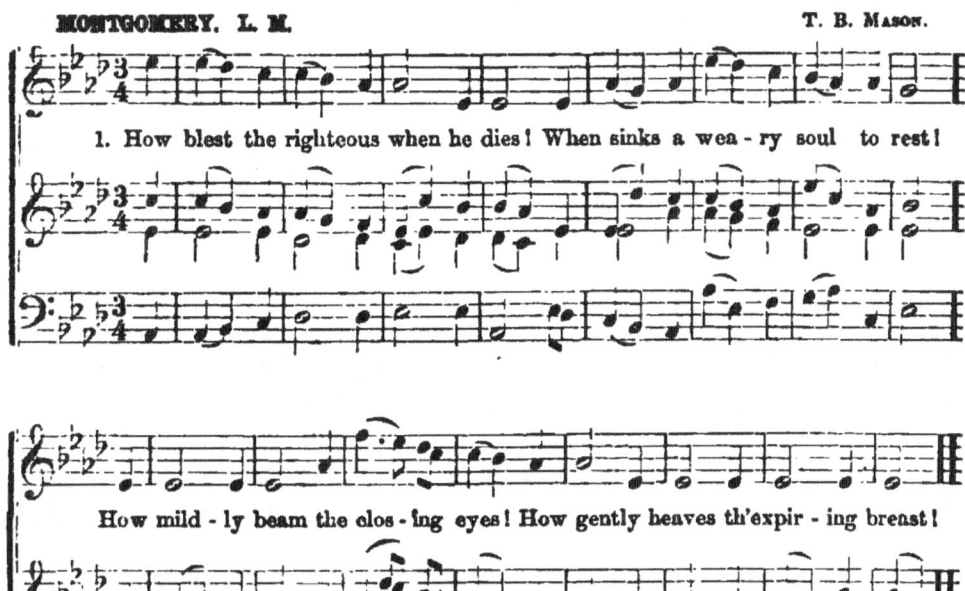

MONTGOMERY. L. M. T. B. MASON.

1. How blest the righteous when he dies! When sinks a wea-ry soul to rest! How mild-ly beam the clos-ing eyes! How gently heaves th' expir-ing breast!

1098. L. M.

1. How blest the righteous when he dies!
   When sinks a weary soul to rest!
   How mildly beam the closing eyes!
   How gently heaves th' expiring breast!

2. So fades a summer cloud away;
   So sinks the gale when storms are o'er;
   So gently shuts the eye of day;
   So dies a wave along the shore.

3. A holy quiet reigns around,
   A calm which life nor death destroys;
   And naught disturbs that peace profound
   Which his unfettered soul enjoys.

4. Farewell, conflicting hopes and fears,
   Where lights and shades alternate dwell;
   How bright the unchanging morn appears!
   Farewell, inconstant world, farewell!

5. Life's labor done, as sinks the clay,
   Light from its load the spirit flies,
   While heaven and earth combine to say,
   "How blest the righteous when he dies!"

MRS. BARBAULD.

1099. 8s & 4s.*

1. THERE is a calm for those who weep,
   A rest for weary pilgrims found;
   They softly lie, and sweetly sleep,
   Low in the ground.

2. The storm that wrecks the winter sky
   No more disturbs their sweet repose,
   Than summer evening's latest sigh,
   That shuts the rose.

3. Thou traveler in this vale of tears,
   To realms of everlasting light,
   Through time's dark wilderness of years,
   Pursue thy flight.

4. Whate'er thy lot—where'er thou be—
   Confess thy folly—kiss the rod;
   And in thy chastening sorrows see
   The hand of God.

5. Though long of winds and waves the sport,
   Condemned in wretchedness to roam,
   Thou soon shalt reach a sheltering port,
   A quiet home.

MONTGOMERY.

* L. M. by repeating the last line.

TIME AND ETERNITY.

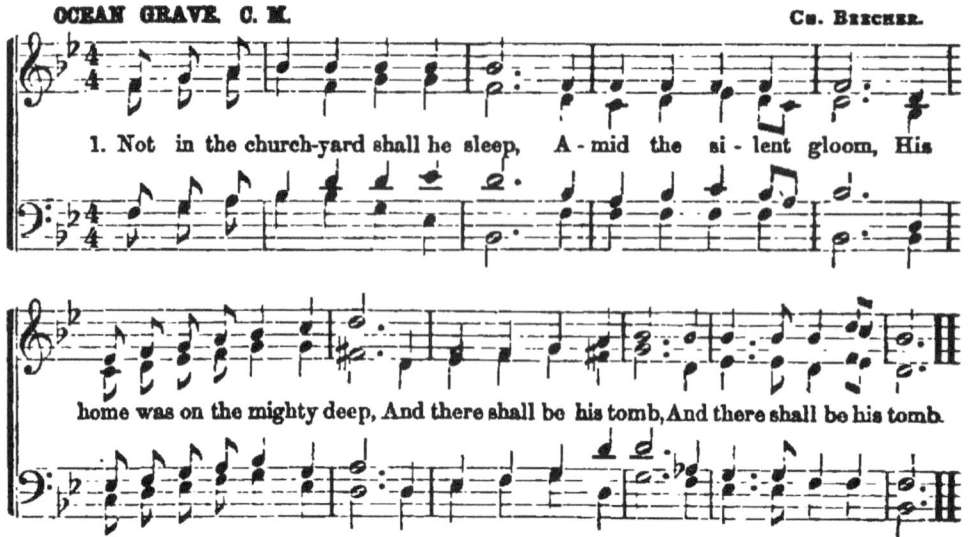

OCEAN GRAVE. C. M. — Ch. Beecher.

1. Not in the church-yard shall he sleep, Amid the silent gloom, His home was on the mighty deep, And there shall be his tomb, And there shall be his tomb.

1100. C. M.

2. He loved his own bright, deep blue sea,
   O'er it he loved to roam;
   And now his winding-sheet shall be
   That same bright ocean's foam.

3. No village bell shall toll for him
   Its mournful, solemn dirge;
   The winds shall chant a requiem
   To him beneath the surge.

4. For him, break not the grassy turf,
   Nor turn the dewy sod;
   His dust shall rest beneath the surf,
   His spirit with its God.

1101. C. M.

1. THROUGH sorrow's night, and danger's path,
   Amid the deepening gloom,
   We, followers of our suffering Lord,
   Are marching to the tomb.

2. There, when the turmoil is no more,
   And all our powers decay,
   Our cold remains in solitude
   Shall sleep the years away.

3. Our labors done, securely laid
   In this our last retreat,
   Unheeded, o'er our silent dust,
   The storms of earth shall beat.

4. Yet not thus buried, or extinct,
   The vital spark shall lie;
   For o'er life's wreck that spark shall rise
   To seek its kindred sky.

5. These ashes, too, this little dust,
   Our Father's care shall keep,
   Till the last angel rise and break
   The long and dreary sleep.

6. Then love's soft dew o'er every eye
   Shall shed its mildest rays;
   And the long silent voice awake
   With shouts of endless praise.
   H. K. WHITE.

1102. C. M.

1. BEHOLD the western evening light!
   It melts in deeper gloom;
   So calm the righteous sink away,
   Descending to the tomb.
   The winds breathe low—the yellow leaf
   Scarce whispers from the tree!
   So gently flows the parting breath,
   When good men cease to be.

2. How beautiful, on all the hills,
   The crimson light is shed!
   'T is like the peace the dying gives
   To mourners round his bed.
   How mildly on the wandering cloud
   The sunset beam is cast!
   So sweet the memory left behind,
   When loved ones breathe their last.

3. And lo! above the dews of night
   The vesper star appears!
   So faith lights up the mourner's heart,
   Whose eyes are dim with tears.
   Night falls, but soon the morning light
   Its glories shall restore;
   And thus the eyes that sleep in death
   Shall wake, to close no more.
   PEABODY.

1103. C. M.

1. Champion of Jesus!—man of God,
   Servant of Christ, well done!
   Thy path of thorns hath now been trod,
   Thy red-cross crown is won!
   No gloom of fear hath glazed thine eye,
   For though loud billows roll—
   The Aurora of eternity
   Is rising on thy soul!

2. Champion of Jesus! on that breast
   From whence Thy fervor flow'd,
   Thou hast obtained eternal rest,
   The bosom of Thy God!
   Oh! to be one, through life and death,
   In Christ, with such as thee!
   And when I yield my latest breath,
   Dear Lord, remember me!

1104. C. M.

1. In vain our fancy strives to paint
   The moment after death,
   The glories that surround a saint,
   When he resigns his breath.

2. One gentle sigh his fetters breaks;
   One effort—and he's gone!
   And lo! the willing spirit takes
   Its mansion near the throne.

3. We strive, but all our efforts fail
   To trace that upward flight;
   No eye can pierce within the vail
   Which hides the world of light.

4. Yet though we see them not—we know
   Saints are supremely blest;
   Are freed from sin, and care, and woe,
   And with their Saviour rest.

5. On harps of gold His name they praise,
   His face they always view;
   And if we here their footsteps trace,
   There we shall praise Him too.
   NEWTON.

1105. C. M.

1. Swift as the arrow cuts its way
   Through the soft yielding air;
   Or as the sun's more subtle ray,
   Or lightning's sudden glare;

2. Or as an eagle to the prey,
   Or shuttle through the loom,
   So haste our fleeting lives away,
   So pass we to the tomb!

3. Like airy bubbles, lo! we rise,
   And dance upon life's stream;
   Till soon the air that caused, destroys
   Th' attenuated frame.

4. Down the swift stream we glide apace,
   And carry death within;
   Then break, and scarcely leave a trace,
   To show that we have been.

5. The man, the wisest of our kind,
   Who length of days had seen,
   To birth and death a time assigned,
   But none to life between—

6. Yet O! what consequences close
   This transient state below!
   Eternal joys: or, losing those,
   Interminable woe!

1106. C. M.

1. Hear what the voice from heaven proclaims
   For all the pious dead;
   Sweet is the savor of their names,
   And soft their sleeping bed.

2. They die in Jesus, and are blest;
   How kind their slumbers are!
   From sufferings and from sin released,
   And freed from every snare.

3. Far from this world of toil and strife,
   They're present with the Lord;
   The labors of their mortal life
   End in a large reward.
   WATTS.

1107. C. M.

1. While through this changing world we roam
   From infancy to age,
   Heaven is the Christian pilgrim's home,
   His rest at every stage.

2. Thither, his raptured thought ascends
   Eternal joys to share;
   There, his adoring spirit bends,
   While here, he kneels in prayer.

3. From earth his freed affections rise,
   To fix on things above,
   Where all his hope of glory lies—
   Where all is perfect love.

4. There, too, may we our treasure place—
   There let our hearts be found;
   That still, where sin abounded, grace
   May more and more abound.

5. Henceforth, our conversation be,
   With Christ before the throne;
   Ere long we, eye to eye, shall see,
   And know as we are known.
   MONTGOMERY.

TIME AND ETERNITY.

CHINA. C. M. — SWAN.

1. Why do we mourn departing friends, Or shake at death's alarms!
'Tis but the voice that Jesus sends To call them to His arms.

1108. C. M.

2. Are we not tending upward, too,
   As fast as time can move?
   Nor would we wish the hours more slow,
   To keep us from our love.

3. Why should we tremble to convey
   Their bodies to the tomb?
   There the dear flesh of Jesus lay,
   And scattered all the gloom.

4. The graves of all His saints He bless'd,
   And softened every bed;
   Where should the dying members rest,
   But with the dying Head?

5. Thence He arose, ascending high,
   And showed our feet the way;
   Up to the Lord we, too, shall fly,
   At the great rising day.

6. Then let the last loud trumpet sound,
   And bid our kindred rise;
   Awake! ye nations under ground;
   Ye saints! ascend the skies.

   WATTS.

1109. C. M.

1. THE time draws nigh, when from the clouds
   Christ shall with shouts descend;
   And the last trumpet's awful voice
   The heavens and earth shall rend.

2. Then they who live shall changed be,
   And they who sleep shall wake;
   The graves shall yield their ancient charge;
   While earth's foundations shake.

3. The saints of God, from death set free,
   With joy shall mount on high;
   The heavenly hosts, with praises loud,
   Shall meet them in the sky.

4. A few short years of exile past,
   We reach the happy shore;
   Where death-divided friends, at last,
   Shall meet to part no more.

   SCOTCH PARAPHRASE.

1110. C. M.

1. MY soul, come, meditate the day,
   And think how near it stands,
   When thou must quit this house of clay,
   And fly to unknown lands.

2. Oh! could we die with those that die,
   And place us in their stead,
   Then would our spirits learn to fly,
   And converse with the dead;—

3. Then should we see the saints above,
   In their own glorious forms,
   And wonder why our souls should love
   To dwell with mortal worms.

4. We should almost forsake our clay,
   Before the summons come,
   And pray, and wish our souls away
   To their eternal home.

   WATTS.

LIFE AND DEATH.

1111. C. M.

1. When wild confusion wrecks the air,
And tempests rend the skies;
Whilst blended rain, clouds and fire
In harsh disorder rise;—

2. Safe in my Saviour's love I'll stand,
And strike a tuneful song;
My harp all trembling in my hand,
And all inspired my tongue.

3. I'll shout aloud, "Ye thunders, roll,
And shake the sullen sky;
Your sounding voice, from pole to pole,
In angry murmurs try.

4. "Let the earth totter on her base,
And clouds the heavens deform;
Blow, all ye winds, from every place,
And rush the final storm!"

5. Come quickly, blessed Lord, appear—
Bid the swift chariot fly;
Let angels tell Thy coming near,
And snatch me to the sky.

6. Around Thy wheels, in the glad throng,
I'd bear a joyful part;
All hallelujah on my tongue—
All rapture in my heart.
BYLES.

1112. C. M.

1. Awake, ye saints, and raise your eyes,
And raise your voices high;
Awake and praise the sovereign love,
That shows salvation nigh.

2. On all the wings of time it flies,
Each moment brings it near;
Then welcome, each declining day!
Welcome, each closing year!

3. Not many years their round shall run,
Nor many mornings rise,
Ere all its glories stand revealed
To our admiring eyes.

4. Ye wheels of nature, speed your course;
Ye mortal powers, decay;
Fast as ye bring the night of death,
Ye bring eternal day.
DODDRIDGE.

1113. C. M.

1. All nature dies, and lives again;
The flowers that paint the field,
The trees that crown the mountain's brow,
And boughs and blossoms yield—

2. Resign the honors of their form
At winter's stormy blast;
And leave the naked, leafless plain,
A desolated waste.

3. Yet, soon, reviving plants and flowers
Anew shall deck the plain;
The woods shall hear the voice of spring,
And flourish green again.

4. So, to the dreary grave consigned,
Man sleeps in death's dark gloom,
Until th' eternal morning wake
The slumbers of the tomb.

5. O, may the grave become to us
The bed of peaceful rest;
Whence we shall gladly rise at length,
And mingle with the blest.
LOGAN.

1114. C. M.

1. Beneath our feet and o'er our head
Is equal warning given;
Beneath us lie the countless dead,
Above us is the heaven!

2. Death rides on every passing breeze,
And lurks in every flower;
Each season has its own disease,
Its peril every hour!

3. Our eyes have seen the rosy light
Of youth's soft cheek decay;
And fate descend in sudden night
On manhood's middle day.

4. Our eyes have seen the steps of age
Halt feebly to the tomb;
And yet shall earth our hearts engage,
And dreams of days to come?

5. Then, mortal, turn! thy danger know;
Where'er thy foot can tread,
The earth rings hollow from below,
And warns thee of her dead!

6. Turn, mortal, turn! thy soul apply
To truths divinely given:
The dead, who underneath thee lie,
Shall live for hell or heaven!
HEBER.

Doxology. C. M.

Praise to the Father and the Son;
Praise to the Spirit be;
Praise to the blessed Three in One,
Through all eternity.

TIME AND ETERNITY.

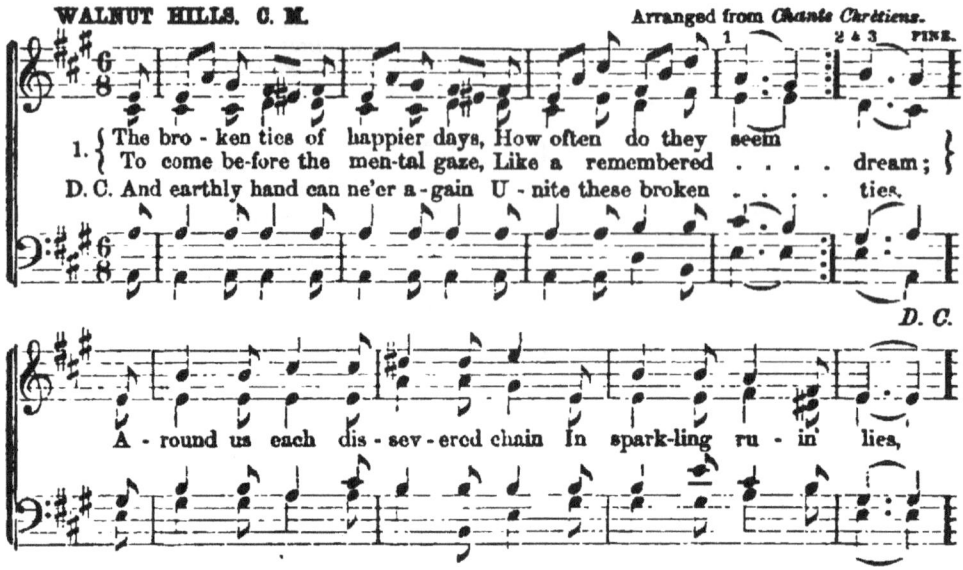

WALNUT HILLS. C. M. — Arranged from *Chants Chrétiens*.

1. The broken ties of happier days, How often do they seem
To come before the mental gaze, Like a remembered dream;
Around us each dissevered chain In sparkling ruin lies,
D. C. And earthly hand can ne'er again Unite these broken ties.

1115. C. M.

2. O, who, in such a world as this,
  Could bear their lot of pain,
Did not one radiant hope of bliss
  Unclouded yet remain?
That hope the sovereign Lord has given,
  Who reigns above the skies:—
Hope, that unites our souls to heaven,
  By faith's endearing ties.

3. Each care, each ill of mortal birth,
  Is sent in pitying love
To lift the lingering heart from earth,
  And speed its flight above.
And every pang that wrings the breast,
  And every joy that dies,
Tells us to seek a purer rest,
  And trust to holier ties.

  MONTGOMERY.

1116. C. M.

1. I TRAVEL all the irksome night,
  By ways to me unknown;
I travel like a bird in flight,
  Onward, and all alone.

2. Just such a pilgrimage is life;
  Hurried from stage to stage,
Our wishes with our lot at strife,
  Through childhood to old age.

3. The world is seldom what it seems
  To man, who dimly sees—
Realities appear as dreams,
  And dreams, realities.

4. The Christian's years, tho' slow their flight,
  When he is called away,
Are but the watches of a night,
  And death the dawn of day.

  MONTGOMERY.

1117. C. M.

1. FEW, few, and evil are thy days,
  Man, of a woman born!
Peril and trouble haunt thy ways.
  Forth, like a flower at morn,
The tender infant springs to light,
  Youth blossoms to the breeze,
Age, withering age, is cropt ere night;
  Man, like a shadow, flees.

2. And dost thou look on such a one?
  Will God to judgment call
A worm, for what a worm hath done
  Against the Lord of all?—
As fail the waters from the deep,
  As summer-brooks run dry,
Man lieth down in dreamless sleep;
  His life is vanity.

3. Man lieth down, no more to wake,
  Till yonder arching sphere
Shall with a roll of thunder break,
  And nature disappear.
O hide me till Thy wrath be past,
  Thou, who canst slay or save!
Hide me where hope may anchor fast
  In my Redeemer's grave.

  MONTGOMERY.

LIFE AND DEATH.

AXMINSTER. L. C. M.* Or 8s & 4s.

1. Alas! how poor and little worth Are all those glittering toys of earth, That lure us here! Dreams of a sleep that death must break: Alas! before it bids us wake, They disappear.

*By removing the slurs in the sixth and twelfth measures.

1118. 8s & 4s.

2. Where is the strength that spurned decay,
The step that rolled so light and gay,
   The heart's blithe tone?
The strength is gone, the step is slow,
And joy grows weariness and woe
   When age comes on.

3. Our birth is but a starting-place;
Life is the running of the race,
   And death the goal:
There all those glittering toys are brought;
That path alone, of all unsought,
   Is found of all.

4. O, let the soul its slumbers break,
Arouse its senses, and awake
   To see how soon
Life, like its glories, glides away,
And the stern footsteps of decay
   Come stealing on.   LONGFELLOW.
               FROM THE SPANISH.

1119. L. C. M.

1. O! sweet as vernal dews that fill
The closing buds on Zion's hill,
   When evening clouds draw thither—
So sweet, so heavenly 't is, to see
The members of one family
   Live peacefully together!

2. The children, like the lily flowers,
On which descend the sun and showers,
   Their hues of beauty blending;
The parents, like the willow boughs,
On which the lovely foliage grows,
   Their friendly shade extending.

3. But leaves the greenest will decay,
And flowers the brightest fade away,
   When autumn winds are sweeping;
And be the household e'er so fair,
The hand of death will soon be there,
   And turn the scene to weeping!

4. Yet leaves again will clothe the trees,
And lilies wave beneath the breeze,
   When spring comes smiling hither:
And friends, who parted at the tomb,
May yet renew their loveliest bloom,
   And meet in heaven together!

1120. L. C. M.

1. THE songs of Zion oft impart,
To each poor, lab'ring careworn heart,
   The balm of heavenly peace;
They chase away each boding fear,
And turn to joy each sorrowing tear,
   And bid the tumult cease.

2. O Thou, that fill'st the heavenly throne,
'T is not in melody alone
   To set the spirit free:
Without the breathings of Thy love,
The sweetest strains will powerless prove,
   Nor comfort bring to me.

3. But if Thy Spirit, gracious Lord,
Thy hallowed influence afford,
   My soul will upward rise;
The strain will swell with love divine,
The light of heaven around me shine,
   Beneath the bending skies.

TIME AND ETERNITY.

BARBY. C. M.

1. The once-loved form, now cold and dead, Each mournful thought employs;
And nature weeps her comforts fled, And withered all her joys.

1121. C. M.

2. Hope looks beyond the bounds of time,
When what we now deplore
Shall rise in full, immortal prime,
And bloom to fade no more.

3. Then cease, fond nature, cease thy tears;
Look to the world on high;
There everlasting spring appears,
And joys that can not die.
MRS. STEELE.

1122. C. M.

1. BLEST hour, when virtuous friends shall meet,
Shall meet to part no more,
And with celestial welcome greet,
On an immortal shore.

2. The parent finds the long-lost child;
Brothers on brothers gaze;
The tear of resignation mild
Is changed to joy and praise.

3. Each tender tie, dissolved with pain,
With endless bliss is crowned;
All that was dead revives again;
All that was lost is found.

4. Congenial minds, arrayed in light,
High thoughts shall interchange;
Nor cease, with ever-new delight,
On wings of love to range.

5. Their Father marks their generous flame,
And looks complacent down;
The smile that owns their filial claim
Is their immortal crown.
LIVERPOOL COLL.

1123. C. M.

1. How happy they, who, safely housed,
To Jesus' bosom fly,
Before the storm of wrath is roused,
O happy they who die!

2. The fury of conflicting waves
Their sleep shall not surprise;
It ruffles not their quiet graves,
It reaches not their skies.

3. Care, pain, and grief, the wild array
Of sorrows felt below;
The dread of trials' fiery day,
Of persecutions' glow.

4. All, all is o'er, with those at rest,
For Jesus' sake forgiven!
No heaving of the anxious breast,
No sickening fear, in heaven!

5. Why linger, then, with strange desire,
Where recks the deadly strife;
And shrink, unwilling to retire,
To everlasting life?
MRS. GILBERT.

1124. C. M.

1. CALM on the bosom of thy God,
Young spirit, rest thee now!
E'en while with us thy footsteps trod,
His seal was on thy brow.

2. Dust, to its narrow house beneath!
Soul, to its place on high!
They that have seen thy look in death,
No more may fear to die.

3. Lone are the paths, and sad the bowers,
Whence thy meek smile is gone;
But O. a brighter home than ours,
In heaven is now thine own.
MRS. HEMANS.

1125. C. M.

1. O, MOST delightful hour by man
    Experienced here below,
   The hour that terminates his span,
    His folly, and his woe.

2. Worlds should not bribe me back to tread
    Again life's dreary waste,
   To see again my day o'erspread
    With all the gloomy past.

3. My home henceforth is in the skies;
    Earth, seas, and sun, adieu!
   All heaven unfolded to my eyes,
    I have no sight for you.

4. So speaks the Christian, firm possessed
    Of faith's supporting rod,
   Then breathes his soul into its rest,
    The bosom of his God.
                          COWPER.

1126. C. M.

1. THE dead are like the stars by day,
    Withdrawn from mortal eye,
   Yet holding unperceived their way
    Through the unclouded sky.

2. By them, through holy hope and love,
    We feel, in hours serene,
   Connected with a world above,
    Immortal and unseen.

3. For death his sacred seal hath set
    On bright and bygone hours;
   And they we mourn are with us yet,
    Are more than ever ours;—

4. Ours, by the pledge of love and faith,
    By hopes of heaven on high;
   By trust, triumphant over death,
    In immortality.
                          BARTON.

1127. C. M.

1. ANOTHER hand is beckoning us,
    Another call is given;
   And glows once more with angel steps
    The path that leads to heaven.

2. Unto our Father's will alone
    One thought hath reconciled;
   That He whose love exceedeth ours
    Hath taken home His child.

3. Fold her, O Father, in Thine arms,
    And let her henceforth be
   A messenger of love between
    Our human hearts and Thee.

4. Still let her mild rebukings stand
    Between us and the wrong,
   And her dear memory serve to make
    Our faith in goodness strong.
                          WHITTIER.

1128. C. M.

1. DEAR as thou wast, and justly dear,
    We would not weep for thee;
   One thought shall check the starting tear—
    It is—that thou art free.

2. And thus shall faith's consoling power
    The tears of love restrain;
   O, who that saw thy parting hour
    Could wish thee here again?

3. Gently the passing spirit fled,
    Sustained by grace divine;
   O, may such grace on us be shed,
    And make our end like thine!
                          DALE.

1129. C. M.

1. THE world eludes my fond desire,
    And memory mocks my pain;
   But while the scenes of sense retire,
    The joys of faith remain.

2. Jesus, my constant friend Thou art,
    My constant Saviour Thou;
   O, fill this lorn and lonely heart
    With Thy pure presence now!

3. Thy steps have long enchanted earth,
    And now from earth to die,
   Were but the pang that marked my birth,
    To Thine own home on high.

4. If bright the world where Thou canst deign,
    Though vailed, to visit me:
   If glows the temple with Thy train,
    What must the Holiest be?

1130. C. M.

1. WHY should our tears in sorrow flow,
    When God recalls His own;
   And bids them leave a world of woe
    For an immortal crown?

2. Is not e'en death a gain to those
    Whose life to God was given?
   Gladly to earth their eyes they close,
    To open them in heaven.

3. Their toils are past, their work is done,
    And they are fully blest:
   They fought the fight, the victory won,
    And entered into rest.

4. Then let our sorrows cease to flow—
    God has recalled His own;
   And let our hearts, in every woe,
    Still say—"Thy will be done!"

TIME AND ETERNITY.

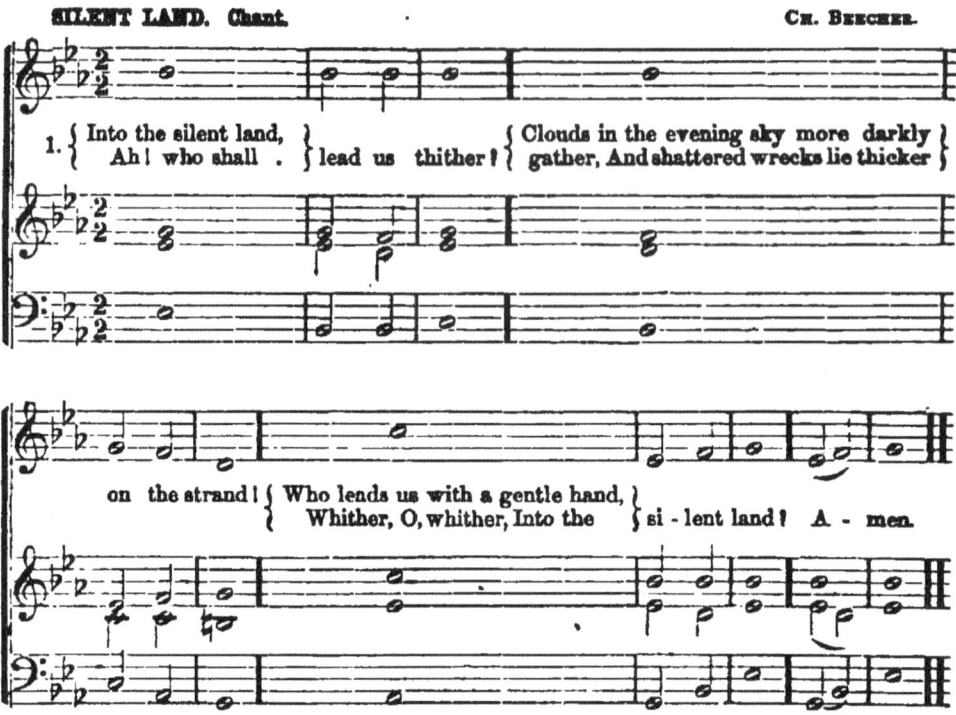

SILENT LAND. Chant.   CH. BEECHER.

1. { Into the silent land, Ah! who shall lead us thither? } { Clouds in the evening sky more darkly gather, And shattered wrecks lie thicker on the strand! } { Who leads us with a gentle hand, Whither, O, whither, Into the silent land? } A-men.

1131. (Chant.)

2. Into the silent land!
To you, ye boundless regions
Of | all per- | fection! | tender morning visions
Of beauteous souls! eterni- | ty's own | band! |
Who in life's battle firm doth stand,
Shall bear hope's tender blossoms
Into the | silent land! |

3. O land! O land!
For all the | broken- | hearted; |
The mildest herald by our fate allotted,
Beckons, and with inverted | torch doth | stand, |
To lead us with a gentle hand
Into the land of the great departed,
Into the | silent | land! |
    VAN SALIS. TR. BY LONGFELLOW.

1132. (Chant.)

1. I am the man that hath seen affliction
By the | rod of his | wrath; |
He hath builded against me,
And compassed me with | gall and | travail; |

He hath set me in dark places,
As they that be | dead of | old. |

2. Also, when I cry and shout,
He shutteth | out my | prayer;
He hath turned aside my ways, and pulled me in pieces;
He hath | made me | desolate; |
He hath made me drunken with wormwood;
He hath | covered me with | ashes.

3. Remembering mine affliction and my misery,
The | wormwood and the | gall,
My soul hath them still in remembrance,
And is | humbled | in me.
This I recall to mind,
Therefore | have I | hope.

4. For the Lord will not cast | off for | ever;
But though He cause grief, yet will He have compassion,
According to the | multitude of his | mercies;
For he doth not afflict willingly,
Nor grieve the | children of | men.

LIFE AND DEATH. 857

MOTHER'S LAMENT. 6s & 5s. Arranged from *Chants Chrétiens.*

1. Yon spot in the churchyard, How sad is the bloom That summer flings round it In flowers and perfume; It is thy dust, my darling, Gives life to each rose, 'Tis because thou hast withered, The vi-o-let blows.

1133. 6s & 5s.

1. Yon spot in the churchyard,
  How sad is the bloom
That summer flings round it,
  In flowers and perfume:
It is thy dust, my darling,
  Gives life to each rose,
'T is because thou hast withered,
  The violet blows.

2. The lilies bend meekly
  Thy bosom above,
But thou wilt not pluck them,
  Sweet child of my love:
I see the green willow
  Droop low o'er thy bed,
But I see not the ringlets
  That decked thy fair head.

3. I hear the bee humming
  Around thy bright grave:
Can he deem death is hidden
  Where sweet flow'rets wave?
From the white cloud above thee
  The lark scatters song,
But I list for thy voice,
  O, how long! O, how long!

4. Then come back, my darling,
  And come back to-day,
For the soul of thy mother
  Grows faint with delay;
The home of thy childhood
  In order is set,
The couch and the chamber—
  Why com'st thou not yet?

5. Dear child! thou wilt never
  Return unto me,
But we part not forever—
  I go unto thee.
My Saviour stands smiling
  With thee on his breast,
And in his compassion
  My heart shall find rest.

1134. (Chant.)*

1. If a man die, shall he | live a- | gain?
All the days of my appointed | time will I | wait
Till | my change | come.

2. For there is hope of a tree, if it | be cut | down,
That it will | sprout a- | gain,
And that the tender branch thereof | will not | cease.

3. Though the root thereof wax | old in the | earth,
Yet through the scent of water it will | bud,
And bring forth boughs like a | plant.

4. But man dieth and | wasteth a- | way;
Yea, man giveth | up the | ghost,
And where is | he?

5. As the waters fail from the | sea,
So man lieth down, and riseth | not
Till the | heavens be no | more

6. O that Thou would'st | hide me in the | grave,
That Thou would'st keep me in secret, till Thy | wrath be past,
That Thou would'st appoint me a set time, and re- | member | me.

7. For I know that my Re- | deemer liveth,
And that He shall stand in the latter day up- | on the earth,
And though worms destroy this body, yet in my flesh shall I | see — | God.

* Sing to Silent Land, on p. 356.

358   TIME AND ETERNITY.

ACACIA. S. M.   Arranged from *Chants Chrétiens*.

1. Go to thy rest, fair child! Go to thy dreamless bed, While yet so gentle, undefiled, With blessings on thy head. 2. Fresh ro-ses in thy hand, Buds on thy pil-low laid, Haste from this dark and fearful land, Where flowers so quickly fade, Where flowers, &c.

1135. S. M.

3. Before thy heart had learned
    In waywardness to stray;
Before thy feet had ever turned
    The dark and downward way;

4. Ere sin had seared the breast,
    Or sorrow woke the tear;
Rise to thy throne of changeless rest,
    In yon celestial sphere!

5. Because thy smile was fair,
    Thy lip and eye so bright,
Because thy loving cradle care
    Was such a dear delight;

6. Shall love, with weak embrace,
    Thy upward wing detain?
No! gentle angel, seek thy place
    Amid the cherub train.

1136. S. M.

1. What though the stream be dead,
    Its banks all still and dry!
It murmureth o'er a lovelier bed
    In air-groves of the sky.

2. What though our bird of light
    Lie mute with plumage dim;
In heaven I see her glancing bright,
    I hear her angel hymn.

3. True that our beauteous doe
    Hath left her still retreat,
But purer now, in heavenly snow,
    She lies at Jesus' feet.

4. O star untimely set!
    Why should we weep for thee?
Thy bright and dewy coronet
    Is rising o'er the sea.
                    WILSON.

1137. S. M.

1. O spirit, freed from earth,
    Rejoice, thy work is done!
The weary world's beneath thy feet,
    Thou brighter than the sun!

2. Arise, put on the robes
    That the redeemed win;
Now sorrow hath no part in Thee,
    Thou sanctified within!

3. Awake, and breathe the air
   Of the celestial clime!
Awake to love which knows no change,
   Thou who hast done with time!

4. Awake, lift up thine eyes!
   See, all heaven's host appears!
And be thou glad exceedingly—
   Thou who hast done with tears!

5. Ascend! thou art not now
   With those of mortal birth;
The living God hath touched thy lips,
   Thou who hast done with earth!
                              MARY HOWITT.

1138. S. M.

1. SERVANT of God, well done!
   Thy glorious warfare's past;
The battle's fought, the race is won,
   And thou art crowned at last.

2. In condescending love,
   Thy ceaseless prayer He heard;
And bade thee suddenly remove
   To thy complete reward.

3. With saints enthroned on high,
   Thou dost thy Lord proclaim,
And still to God salvation cry—
   Salvation to the Lamb!

5. O happy, happy soul!
   In ecstasies of praise,
Long as eternal ages roll,
   Thou seest thy Saviour's face.

6. Redeemed from earth and pain,
   Ah! when shall we ascend,
And all in Jesus' presence reign
   With our translated friend?
                              C. WESLEY.

1139. S. M.

1. SERVANT of God, well done!
   Rest from thy loved employ;
The battle fought, the victory won,
   Enter thy Master's joy.

2. The voice at midnight came;
   He started up to hear;
A mortal arrow pierced his frame,
   He fell, but felt no fear.

3. Tranquil amidst alarms,
   It found him on the field,
A veteran slumbering on his arms,
   Beneath his red-cross shield.

4. At midnight came the cry,
   "To meet thy God, prepare!"
He woke—and caught his Captain's eye;
   Then, strong in faith and prayer,

5. His spirit, with a bound,
   Left its encumbering clay;
His tent, at sunrise, on the ground,
   A darkened ruin lay.

6. The pains of death are past,
   Labor and sorrow cease:
And life's long warfare closed at last,
   His soul is found in peace.
                              MONTGOMERY.

1140. S. M.

1. IN expectation sweet,
   We wait, and sing, and pray,
Till Christ's triumphal car we meet,
   And see an endless day.

2. He comes! the Conqueror comes!
   Death falls beneath His sword;
The joyful prisoners burst their tombs,
   And rise to meet their Lord.

3. The trumpet sounds—Awake!
   Ye dead to judgment come!
The pillars of creation shake,
   While hell receives her doom.

4. Thrice happy morn for those
   Who love the ways of peace;
No night of sorrow e'er shall close,
   Or shade their perfect bliss.

1141. S. M.

1. TO-MORROW, Lord, is Thine,
   Lodged in Thy sovereign hand;
And if its sun arise and shine,
   It shines by Thy command.

2. The present moment flies,
   And bears our life away;
O, make Thy servants truly wise,
   That they may live to-day.

3. Since on this fleeting hour
   Eternity is hung,
Awake, by Thine almighty power,
   The aged and the young.

4. One thing demands our care;
   O, be that still pursued,
Lest, slighted once, the season fair
   Should never be renewed.

860 TIME AND ETERNITY.

NEWELL. S. M.   J. ZUNDEL.

1. And must this body die? This mortal frame decay? And must these active limbs of mine Lie mold'ring in the clay? Lie mold'ring in the clay?

1142. S. M.

2. Corruption, earth, and worms,
    Shall but refine this flesh,
Till my triumphant spirit comes
    To put it on afresh.

3. God, my Redeemer, lives,
    And often, from the skies,
Looks down and watches all my dust,
    Till He shall bid it rise.

4. Arrayed in glorious grace
    Shall these vile bodies shine,
And every shape, and every face,
    Look heavenly and divine.

5. These lively hopes we owe
    To Jesus' dying love;
We would adore His grace below,
    And sing His power above.

6. Dear Lord, accept the praise
    Of these our humble songs,
Till tunes of nobler sounds we raise
    With our immortal tongues.
                              WATTS.

1143. S. M.

1. AND will the Judge descend,
    And must the dead arise?
And not a single soul escape
    His all-discerning eyes?

2. How will my heart endure
    The terrors of that day,
When earth and heaven before His face
    Astonished shrink away?

3. But ere the trumpet shakes
    The mansions of the dead,
Hark, from the gospel's cheering sound
    What joyful tidings spread!

4. Ye sinners, seek His grace
    Whose wrath ye can not bear;
Fly to the shelter of His cross,
    And find salvation there.

5. So shall that curse remove,
    By which the Saviour bled;
And the last awful day shall pour
    His blessings on your head.
                            DODDRIDGE.

1144. S. M.

1. BENEATH the star-lit arch,
    Along the hallowed ground,
I see cherubic armies march,
    A camp of fire around.

2. All that I am, have been,
    All that I yet may be,
He sees as He hath ever seen,
    And shall for ever see.

3. How can I meet His eyes!
    Mine on the cross I cast,
And own my life a Saviour's prize,
    Mercy from first to last.

4. Then shall I upward fly;
    That resurrection word
Shall be my shout of victory,
    "For ever with the Lord."
                            MONTGOMERY.

1145. S. M.

1. How swift the torrent rolls,
    That bears us to the sea!
The tide that bears our thoughtless souls
    To vast eternity!

2. Our fathers, where are they,
    With all they called their own?
Their joys and griefs, and hopes and cares,
    And wealth and honor, gone!

3. And where the fathers lie,
    Must all the children dwell?
Nor other heritage possess,
    But such a gloomy cell?

4. God of our fathers, hear,
    Thou everlasting Friend!
While we, as on life's utmost verge,
    Our souls to Thee commend.

5. Of all the pious dead
    May we the footsteps trace,
Till with them, in the land of light,
    We dwell before Thy face.
                    DODDRIDGE.

1146. S. M.

1. My Father's house on high!
    Home of my soul! how near,
At times, to faith's foreseeing eye
    Thy golden gates appear!

2. Ah! then my spirit faints
    To reach the land I love,
The bright inheritance of saints,
    Jerusalem above.

3. Yet clouds will intervene,
    And all my prospect flies;
Like Noah's dove, I flit between
    Rough seas and stormy skies.

4. Anon the clouds dispart,
    The winds and waters cease;
While sweetly o'er my gladdened heart
    Expands the bow of peace.

5. I hear at morn and even,
    At noon and midnight hour,
The choral harmonies of heaven
    Earth's Babel-tongues o'erpower.

6. Then, then I feel that He—
    Remembered or forgot—
The Lord is never far from me,
    Though I perceive Him not.
                    MONTGOMERY.

1147. S. M.

1. Lord! what a feeble piece
    Is this our mortal frame!
Our life—how poor a trifle 't is,
    That scarce deserves the name!

2. Alas! the brittle clay,
    That built our body first!
And every month, and every day,
    'Tis moldering back to dust.

3. Our moments fly apace,
    Nor will our minutes stay;
Just like a flood, our hasty days
    Are sweeping us away.

4. Well, if our days must fly,
    We'll keep their end in sight;
We'll spend them all in wisdom's way,
    And let them speed their flight.

5. They'll waft us sooner o'er
    This life's tempestuous sea;
Soon we shall reach the peaceful shore
    Of blest eternity.
                    WATTS.

1148. S. M.

1. Lord! let me know mine end—
    My days, how brief their date,
That I may timely comprehend
    How frail my best estate.

2. My life is but a span,
    Mine age is naught with Thee;
What is the highest boast of man
    But dust and vanity?

3. Dumb at Thy feet I lie,
    For Thou hast brought me low;
Remove Thy judgments, lest I die;
    I faint beneath Thy blow.

4. At Thy rebuke, the bloom
    Of man's vain beauty flies;
And grief shall, like a moth, consume
    All that delights our eyes.

5. Have pity on my fears;
    Hearken to my request;
Turn not in silence from my tears,
    But give the mourner rest.

6. Oh! spare me yet, I pray,
    Awhile my strength restore,
Ere I am summoned hence away,
    And seen on earth no more.
                    MONTGOMERY.

TIME AND ETERNITY.

FULTON. 7s.   W. B. BRADBURY.

1. Brother, though from yonder sky
Cometh neither voice nor cry,
Yet we know for thee to-day,
Every pain hath passed away.

1149. 7s.

2. Well we know thy living faith,
Had the power to conquer death,
As a living rose may bloom,
By the border of the tomb.

3. Brother, in that solemn trust
We commend thee, dust to dust;
In that faith we wait, till risen,
Thou shalt meet us all in heaven.

1150. 7s.

1. Lo! the prisoner is released,
Lightened of his fleshly load;
Where the weary are at rest,
He is gathered unto God.
Lo! the pain of life is past,
And his warfare now is o'er;
Death and hell behind are cast,
Grief and suffering are no more.

2. Yes! the Christian's course is run,
Ended is the glorious strife;
Fought the fight, the crown is won,
Death is swallowed up of life.
Borne by angels on their wings,
Far from earth his spirit flies
To the Lord he loved, and sings,
Triumphing in paradise.

3. Join we, then, with one accord
In the new and joyful song;
Absent from our glorious Lord
We shall not continue long;
We shall quit the house of clay,
Better joys with Him to share;
We shall see the realms of day,
We shall meet our brethren there.
    C. WESLEY.

1151. 7s.

1. HARK! a voice divides the sky!
Happy are the faithful dead,
In the Lord who sweetly die!
They from all their toils are freed.

2. Ready for their glorious crown—
Sorrows past, and sins forgiven—
Here they lay their burthen down,
Hallowed, and made meet for heaven.

3. When from flesh the spirit, freed,
Hastens homeward to return,
Mortals cry—"A man is dead!"
Angels sing—"A child is born!"

4. Born into the world above,
They our happy brother greet;
Bear him to the throne of love,
Place him at the Saviour's feet!

5. Jesus smiles, and says—"Well done!
Good and faithful servant thou!
Enter and receive thy crown;
Reign with me triumphant now."
    C. WESLEY.

LIFE AND DEATH.

1. High in yonder realms of light,
Dwell the raptured saints above;
Far beyond our feeble sight,
Happy in Immanuel's love:
Once they knew, like us below,
Pilgrims in this vale of tears,
Torturing pain and heavy woe,
Gloomy doubts, distressing fears.

1152. 7s.

2. Oft the big, unbidden tear,
   Stealing down the furrowed cheek,
Told, in eloquence sincere,
   Tales of woe they could not speak.
But these days of weeping o'er,
   Passed this scene of toil and pain,
They shall feel distress no more—
   Never, never weep again.

3. 'Mid the chorus of the skies,
   'Mid th' angelic lyres above,
Hark, their songs melodious rise,
   Songs of praise to Jesus' love!
Happy spirits, ye are fled
   Where no grief can entrance find;
Lulled to rest the aching head,
   Soothed the anguish of the mind.

4. All is tranquil and serene,
   Calm and undisturbed repose;
There no cloud can intervene,
   There no angry tempest blows;
Every tear is wiped away,
   Sighs no more shall heave the breast,
Night is lost in endless day,
   Sorrow—in eternal rest.

                          RAFFLES.

1153. 7s.

1. "Spirit, leave thy house of clay;
   Ling'ring dust, resign thy breath;
Spirit, cast thy chains away;
   Dust, be thou dissolved in death!"—
Thus the mighty Saviour speaks,
   While the faithful Christian dies;
Thus the bonds of life He breaks,
   And the ransomed captive flies.

2. "Prisoner, long detained below,
   Prisoner, now with freedom blest,
Welcome from a world of woe;
   Welcome to a land of rest:"—
Thus the choir of angels sing,
   As they bear the soul on high,
While with hallelujahs ring
   All the regions of the sky.

3. Grave! the guardian of our dust,
   Grave! the treasury of the skies,
Every atom of thy trust
   Rests in hope again to rise!
Hark! the judgment-trumpet calls—
   "Soul, rebuild thy house of clay;
Immortality thy walls,
   And eternity thy day."

                          MONTGOMERY.

TIME AND ETERNITY.

DIES IRÆ. 8s. Or 7s.

1. Day of wrath, that day of burn-ing,
All shall melt to ash-es turn-ing,
All fore-told by seers dis-cern-ing.
O! what fear it shall en-gen-der
When the Judge shall come in splendor
Strict to mark and just to ren-der.

2. Trum-pet-scattered sound of won-der,
Rend-ing se-pul-chres a-sun-der,
Shall re-sist-less summons thun-der.
All a-ghast then Death shall shi-ver,
And great Na-ture's frame shall quiver,
When the graves their dead de-liver.

1154. 8s.

3. Think, O Jesus, for what reason,
Thou endured'st earth's spite and treason,
Nor me loss in that dread season.
Seeking me Thy worn feet hasted,
On the cross Thy soul death tasted,
Let such labor not be wasted.

4. Righteous Judge of retribution,
Grant me perfect absolution,
Ere that day of execution.
Culprit like, I—heart all broken,
On my cheek shame's crimson token—
Plead the pardoning word be spoken.

5. 'Mid the sheep a place decide me,
And from goats on left divide me,
Standing on the right beside Thee.
When th' accursed away are driven,
To eternal burnings given,
Call me with the blest to Heaven.

6. I beseech Thee, prostrate lying,
Heart as ashes, contrite, sighing,
Care for me when I am dying.

On that awful day of wailing,
When man rising, stands before Thee,
Spare the culprit, God of glory!

1155. 7s.

1. In the sun, and moon, and stars,
Signs and wonders there shall be;
Earth shall quake with inward wars,
Nations with perplexity.

2. Soon shall ocean's hoary deep,
Tossed with stronger tempests, rise;
Wilder storms the mountains sweep,
Louder thunder rock the skies.

3. Dread alarms shall shake the proud,
Pale amazement, restless fear;
And amid the thunder cloud
Shall the Judge of man appear.

4. But, though from His awful face,
Heaven shall fade, and earth shall fly;
Fear not ye, His chosen race,
Your redemption draweth nigh.

HEBER.

LIFE AND DEATH.

ANEMONE. 6s & 5s.

1. Saviour, now receive him To Thy bosom mild; For with Thee we leave him, Bless-ed, bless-ed child, Bless-ed, bless-ed child.

1156. 6s & 5s.

2. Though his eye hath brightened
Oft our weary way,
And his clear laugh lightened
Half our heart's dismay;

3. Now let thought behold him
In his angel rest,
Where those arms enfold him
To a Saviour's breast.

4. Yield we what was given,
At thy holy call;
The beautiful to heaven,
Thou who givest all!

5. Still 'mid heavy mourning,
Look thee now to God!
There, thy spirit turning,
Kneel beside the sod.

HEMANS.

ANGELS' VISITS. 11s & 4s.

1. With si-lence on-ly as their ben-e-dic-tion, God's an-gels come, Where, in the sha-dow of a great af-flic-tion, The soul sits dumb.

1157. 11s & 4s.

2. Yet would we say what every heart ap-
Our Father's will,   [proveth—
Calling to Him the dear ones whom he
Is mercy still.   [loveth,

3. Not upon us or ours the solemn angel
Hath evil wrought;

The funeral anthem is a glad evangel;
The good die not!

4. God calls our loved ones, but we lose not
What He has given;   [wholly
They live on earth in thought and deed,
As in His heaven.   [as truly

WHITTIER.

TIME AND ETERNITY.

REQUIEM. S. H. M. — PSALMODIST.

1. This place is holy ground; World, with its cares, away! A holy, solemn stillness round This lifeless, mouldering clay; Nor pain, nor grief, nor anxious fear Can reach the peaceful sleeper here.

1158. S. H. M.

1. THIS place is holy ground;
   World, with its cares, away!
   A holy, solemn stillness round
   This lifeless, mouldering clay;
   Nor pain, nor grief, nor anxious fear
   Can reach the peaceful sleeper here.

2. Behold the bed of death—
   The pale and mortal clay;
   Heard ye the sob of parting breath?
   Marked ye the eye's last ray?
   No: life so sweetly ceased to be,
   It lapsed in immortality.

3. Why mourn the pious dead?
   Why sorrows swell our eyes?
   Can sighs recall the spirit fled?
   Shall vain regrets arise?
   Though death has caused this altered mein,
   In heaven the ransomed soul is seen.

4. Bury the dead and weep
   In stillness o'er the loss;
   Bury the dead! in Christ they sleep,
   Who bore on earth His cross;
   And from the grave their dust shall rise,
   In His own image to the skies.

MONTGOMERY.

1159. S. H. M.

1. FRIEND after friend departs:
   Who hath not lost a friend?
   There is no union here of hearts
   That finds not here an end;
   Were this frail world our only rest,
   Living or dying, none were blest.

2. Beyond the flight of time,
   Beyond this vale of death,
   There surely is some blessed clime
   Where life is not a breath,
   Nor life's affections transient fire,
   Whose sparks fly upward to expire.

3. There is a world above,
   Where parting is unknown;
   A whole eternity of love,
   Formed for the good alone;
   And faith beholds the dying here
   Translated to that happier sphere.

4. Thus star by star declines,
   Till all are passed away,
   As morning high and higher shines,
   To pure and perfect day;
   Nor sink those stars in empty night—
   They hide themselves in heaven's own light.

MONTGOMERY.

LIFE AND DEATH.

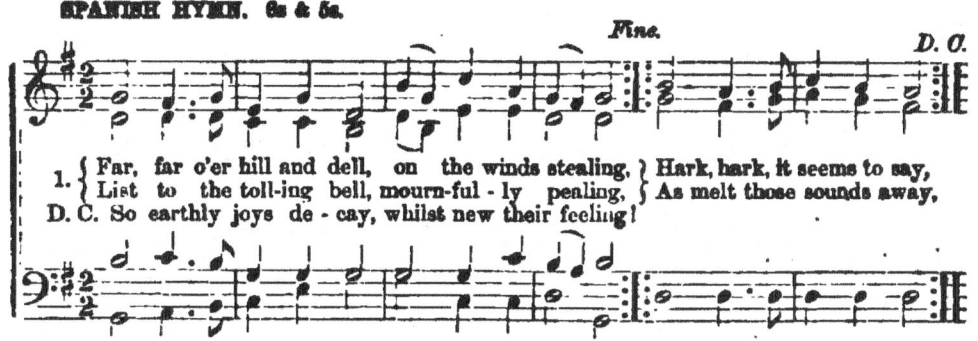

SPANISH HYMN. 6s & 5s.

1. Far, far o'er hill and dell, on the winds stealing, Hark, hark, it seems to say,
   List to the toll-ing bell, mourn-ful-ly pealing, As melt those sounds away,
   D. C. So earthly joys de-cay, whilst new their feeling!

1160. 11s & 6s.

2. Now thro' the charmed air, on the winds stealing,
   List to the mourner's prayer, solemnly bending;
   Hark, hark, it seems to say, turn from those joys away,
   To those which ne'er decay, for life is ending.

3. So when our mortal ties death shall dissever,
   Lord, may we reach the skies where care comes never,
   And in eternal day, joining the angels' lay,
   To our Creator pay homage for ever.

4. When in their lonely bed loved ones are lying;
   When joyful wings are spread to heaven flying;
   Would we to sin and pain, call back their souls again,
   Weave round their hearts the chain severed in dying!

5. No, dearest Jesus, no; to Thee, their Saviour,
   Let their free spirits go, ransomed for ever:
   Heirs of unending joy, theirs is the victory;
   Thine let the glory be, now and for ever.
   THE JUDGMENT.

1161. 6s & 5s.

1. THRO' Thy protecting care kept till the dawning,
   Taught to draw near in prayer, heed we the warning!
   O Thou great One in Three, gladly our souls would be,
   Ever more praising Thee, God of the morning.

2. God of our sleeping hours! watch o'er us waking,
   All our imperfect powers in Thine hands taking;
   In us Thy work fulfill, be with Thy children still,
   Those who obey Thy will, never forsaking

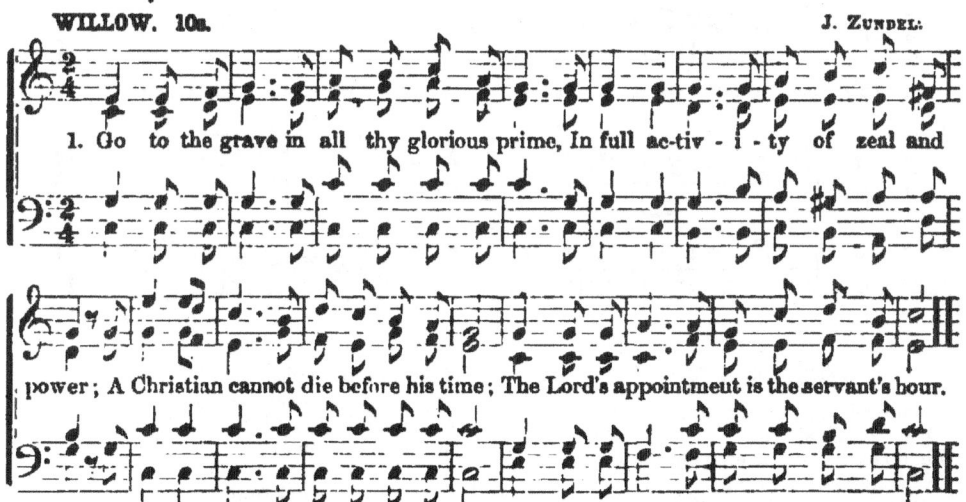

WILLOW. 10s.   J. ZUNDEL.

1. Go to the grave in all thy glorious prime, In full ac-tiv-i-ty of zeal and power; A Christian cannot die before his time; The Lord's appointment is the servant's hour.

1162. 10s. M.

2. Go to the grave; at noon from labor cease;
   Rest on thy sheaves; the harvest-task is done;
   Come from the heat of battle, and in peace,
   Soldier, go home; with thee the fight is won.

3. Go to the grave; for there thy Saviour lay
   In death's embrace, ere He arose on high;
   And all the ransomed, by that narrow way,
   Pass to eternal life beyond the sky.

4. Go to the grave;—no; take thy seat above;
   Be thy pure spirit present with the Lord,
   Where thou for faith and hope hast perfect love,
   And open vision for the written word.
   MONTGOMERY.

TIME AND ETERNITY.

LORO. 6s & 5s. *Scottish Melody.*

1. When shall we meet again? Meet ne'er to sever? When will peace wreath her chain Round us for ev-er? Our hearts will ne'er repose, Safe from each blast that blows, In this dark vale of woes, Nev-er, no, nev-er, no, no, nev-er!

1163. 6s & 5s.

2. When shall love freely flow
  Pure as life's river?
 When shall sweet friendship glow
  Changeless for ever?
 Where the joys celestial thrill,
 Where bliss each heart shall fill,
 And fears of parting chill
  Never—no, never!

3. Up to that world of light
  Take us, dear Saviour;
 May we all there unite,
  Happy for ever;
 Where kindred spirits dwell,
 There may our music swell,
 And time our joys dispel
  Never—no, never!

4. Soon shall we meet again,
  Meet ne'er to sever;
 Soon shall Peace wreath her chain
  Round us for ever;
 Our hearts will then repose
 Secure from worldly woes;
 Our songs of praise shall close.
  Never—no, never!

LIFE AND DEATH.

BASIL. 8s.

1. Let me not, thou King e-ter-nal, En-ter hell's do-mains in-fer-nal!
Where is sor-row, where is sad-ness, Where is sor-row, where is mad-ness,
D. C. Where despair is ev-er sigh-ing, Where the worm is nev-er dy-ing.

Where the shameless are as-tound-ed, Where the guilty are con-found-ed,

1164. 8s.

2. Me may Zion welcome, saved,
Tranquil city, seat of David;
God its builder, light immortal,
Orient pearl each blazing portal,
Crystal gold its streets; the nation
Of the blest its population,
Living rock the walls that bound it,
Christ the guard that dwells around it.

3. O, with what congratulations
Throng thy gates the festive nations!
What the warmth of their embracing,
What the gems thy walls enchasing!
Through that city's streets are wending
Holy throngs their anthems blending;
There may I, with myriads glorious,
Chant Thy praise in psalms victorious!

FAR, FAR AT SEA. 8s, 7s & 4. Psalmodist.

1. Star of peace, to wan-d'rers drear-y, Bright the beams that smile on me,

Cheer the pi-lot's vis-ion drear-y, Far, far at sea.

1165. 8s, 7s & 4s.

2. Star of hope! gleam on the billow,
Bless the soul that sighs for thee,
Bless the sailor's lonely pillow,
Far, far at sea.

3. Star of faith! when winds are mocking
All his toil, he flies to thee;
Save him, on the billows rocking,
Far, far at sea.

4. Star Divine! O safely guide him,
Bring the wanderer home to Thee;
Sore temptations long have tried him,
Far, far at sea.

TIME AND ETERNITY.

AMSTERDAM. 7s & 6s.

1. Rise, my soul, and stretch thy wings, Thy better portion trace;
Rise, from transitory things, Toward heaven, thy native place.
Sun, and moon, and stars decay, Time shall soon this earth remove;
Rise, my soul, and haste away To seats prepared above.

1166. 7s & 6s.

1. RISE, my soul, and stretch thy wings,
   Thy better portion trace;
   Rise, from transitory things,
   Toward heaven, thy native place:
   Sun, and moon, and stars decay,
   Time shall soon this earth remove;
   Rise, my soul, and haste away
   To seats prepared above.

2. Rivers to the ocean run,
   Nor stay in all their course;
   Fire ascending, seeks the sun,
   Both speed them to their source;
   So a soul that's born of God,
   Pants to see His glorious face,
   Upward tends to His abode,
   To rest in His embrace.

3. Cease, ye pilgrims, cease to mourn,
   Press onward to the prize;
   Soon our Saviour will return
   Triumphant in the skies;
   There we'll join the heavenly train,
   Welcomed to partake the bliss;
   Fly from sorrow, and from pain,
   To realms of endless peace.

   CENNICK.

1167. 7s & 6s.

1. TIME is winging us away
   To our eternal home;
   Life is but a winter's day—
   A journey to the tomb;
   Youth and vigor soon will flee,
   Blooming beauty lose its charms;
   All that's mortal soon shall be
   Inclosed in death's cold arms.

2. Time is bearing us away
   To our eternal home;
   Life is but a winter's day—
   A journey to the tomb;
   But the saints shall soon enjoy,
   Life—immortal life above,
   Where no worldly griefs annoy,
   Where Jesus reigns in love.

   BURTON.

LIFE AND DEATH.

KENAZ. 7s & 8s.

1. Lift not thou the wailing voice;
   Weep not—'tis a Christian dieth:
   Up, where blessed saints rejoice,
   Ransomed now, the spirit flyeth:
   High in heaven's own light she dwelleth;
   Full the song of triumph swelleth:
   Freed from earth and earthly failing,
   Lift for her no voice of wailing.

1168. 7s & 8s.

2. Pour not thou the bitter tear;
   Heaven its book of comfort opeth;
   Bids thee sorrow not, nor fear,
   But as one who always hopeth;
   Humbly here in faith relying,
   Peacefully in Jesus dying,
   Heavenly joy her eye is flushing,
   Why should thine with tears be gushing?

3. They who die in Christ are blest;
   Ours then be no thought of grieving;
   Sweetly with their God they rest,
   All their toils and troubles leaving;
   So be ours the faith that saveth,
   Hope, that every trial braveth,
   Love, that to the end endureth,
   And, through Christ, the crown secureth.
   DOANE.

1169. 7s & 8s.*

1. Jesus lives! thy terrors now
   Can no longer, Death, appall me;
   Jesus lives! and well I know,
   From the dead he will recall me;
   Better life will then commence—
   This shall be my confidence.

2. Jesus lives! to Him the throne
   Over all the world is given:
   I shall go where He is gone,
   Live and reign with Him in heaven;
   God is pledged, weak doubtings, hence!
   This shall be my confidence.

3. Jesus lives! I know full well,
   Nought from Him my heart can sever;
   Life, nor death, nor powers of hell,
   Joy, nor grief, henceforth, for ever.
   God will power and grace dispense—
   This shall be my confidence.

4. Jesus lives! henceforth is death
   Entrance into life immortal;
   Calmly I can yield my breath;
   Fearless tread the frowning portal;
   Thou, when faileth flesh and sense,
   Lord, wilt be my confidence!
   GERMAN TR. COX.

* Omit the repeat.

TIME AND ETERNITY.

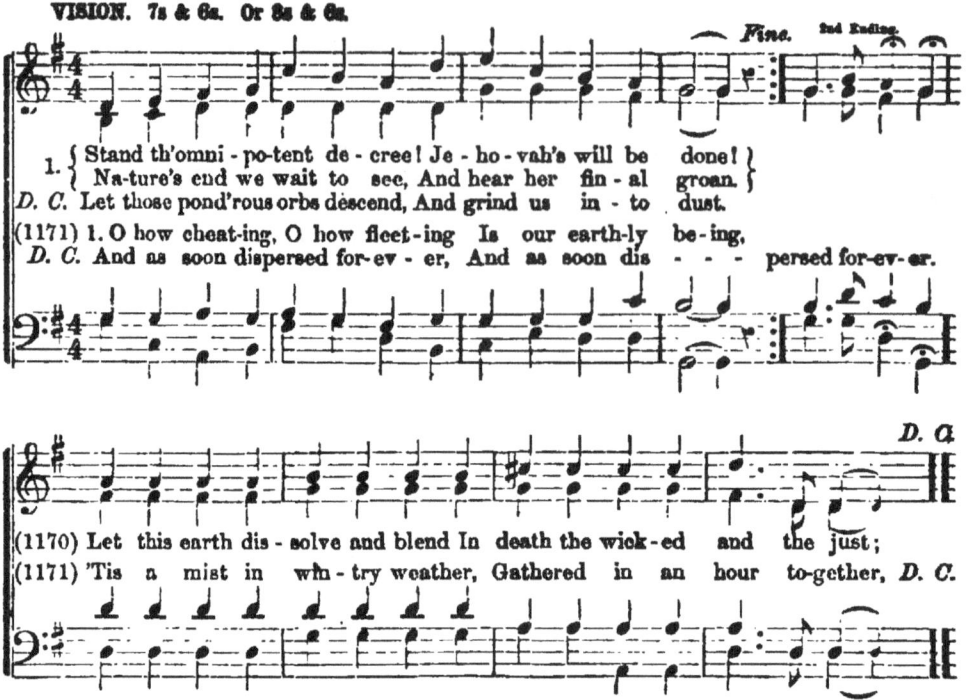

VISION. 7s & 6s. Or 8s & 6s.

1. Stand th' omni-po-tent de-cree! Jehovah's will be done!
   Nature's end we wait to see, And hear her final groan.
D. C. Let those pond'rous orbs descend, And grind us in-to dust.

(1171) 1. O how cheat-ing, O how fleet-ing Is our earth-ly be-ing,
D. C. And as soon dispersed for-ev-er, And as soon dispersed for-ev-er.

(1170) Let this earth dis-solve and blend In death the wick-ed and the just;
(1171) 'Tis a mist in win-try weather, Gathered in an hour to-gether, D. C.

1170. 7s, 6s & 8s.

2. Rests secure the righteous man;
   At his Redeemer's beck,
   Sure to' emerge and rise again,
   And mount above the wreck;
   Lo! the heavenly spirit towers,
   Like flames o'er nature's funeral pyre;
   Triumphs in immortal powers,
   And claps his wings of fire.

3. Nothing hath the just to lose,
   By worlds on worlds destroyed;
   Far beneath his feet he views,
   With smiles, the flaming void;
   Sees this universe renewed—
   The grand millennial reign begun;
   Shouts, with all the sons of God,
   Around the eternal throne.

4. Resting in this glorious hope,
   To be at last restored,
   Yield we now our bodies up
   To earthquake, plague, or sword;
   List'ning for the call divine,
   The latest trumpet of the seven,
   Soon our soul and form shall join,
   And both fly up to heaven.
   C. WESLEY.

1171. 8s & 6s.*

2. O how cheating, O how fleeting
   Are our days departing!
   Like a deep and headlong river,
   Flowing onward, flowing ever,
   Tarrying not, and stopping never.

3. O how cheating, O how fleeting
   Are the world's enjoyments;
   All the hues of change they borrow,
   Bright to-day and dark to-morrow,
   Mingled lot of joy and sorrow.

4. O how cheating, O how fleeting
   Is all earthly beauty!
   Like a summer flow'ret flowing,
   Scattered by the breezes, blowing
   O'er the bed on which 'twas growing.

5. O how cheating, O how fleeting,
   All, yes! all that's earthly!
   Every thing is fading, flying,
   Man is mortal, earth is dying,
   Christian! live, on Heaven relying.

* Omit the repeat, and sing the D. C. with 2d ending, giving the last line of each stanza twice.

LIFE AND DEATH. 373

ALL'S WELL. 8s & 8s. Western Melody.

What's this that steals, that steals up-on my frame? Is it death? Is it death?
That soon will quench, will quench this vital flame? Is it death? Is it death?
If this be death, I soon shall be from ev-ery pain and sorrow free; I shall the King of glo-ry see, All is well, All is well.

1172. 8s & 3s.

1. What's this that steals upon my frame?
   Is it death?
   That soon will quench this vital flame?
   Is it death?
   If this be death, I soon shall be
   From every pain and sorrow free,
   I shall my Lord in glory see—
   All is well!

2. Weep not, my friends, weep not for me,
   All is well;
   My sins are pardoned, I am free;
   All is well.
   There's not a cloud that doth arise,
   To hide my Saviour from my eyes;
   I soon shall mount the upper skies—
   All is well.

3. Tune, your harps, ye saints in glory,
   All is well;
   I will rehearse the pleasing story,
   All is well.
   Bright angels have from glory come,
   They're round my bed, they're in my room,
   They wait to waft my spirit home—
   All is well.

4. Hark, my Lord and Master calls me,
   All is well;
   I shall see His face in glory,
   All is well.
   Farewell dear friends, adieu, adieu,
   I can no longer stay with you—
   My glit'tring crown appears in view;
   All is well.

5. Hail, hail, all hail ye blood-washed throng,
   Saved by grace;
   I've come to join your rapturous song,
   Saved by grace.
   All, all is peace and joy divine,
   All heaven and glory now are mine;
   Oh, Hallelujah to the Lamb!
   All is well!

TIME AND ETERNITY.

AUTUMN. 8s & 7s.

1. See the leaves a-round us fall-ing, Dry and withered, to the ground.
Thus to thoughtless mortals call-ing, ... In a sad and
sol-emn sound. Sons of A-dam, once in E-den, When like him, ye bligh-ted fell,

D.C. Hear the les-son we are read-ing, ... 'Tis a-las! the
truth we tell.

1173. 8s & 7s.

2. Youth, on length of days presuming,
Who the paths of pleasure tread,
View us, late in beauty blooming,
Numbered now among the dead.

3. Though as yet no losses grieve you,
Gay with health and many a grace,
Let no cloudless skies deceive you;
Summer gives to autumn place.

4. Yearly in our course appearing,
Messengers of shortest stay,
Thus we preach in mortal hearing—
Ye, like us, shall pass away.

5. On the tree of life eternal,
O let all our hopes be laid!
This alone, for ever vernal,
Bears a leaf that shall not fade.
HORNE.

1174. 8s & 7s.

1. Cease, ye mourners, cease to languish
O'er the grave of those you love;
Pain, and death, and night and anguish,
Enter not the world above.

2. While our silent steps are straying
Lonely through night's deepening shade,
Glory's brightest beams are playing
Round the happy Christian's head.

3. Light and peace at once deriving
From the hand of God most high,
In His glorious presence living,
They shall never, never die.

4. Endless pleasure, pain excluding,
Sickness, there, no more can come;
There, no fear of woe intruding,
Shed's o'er heaven a moment's gloom.
COLLYER.

1175. 8s & 7s.

1. Cease here longer to detain me,
Fondest mother, drowned in woe,
Now thy kind caresses pain me,
Morn advances, let me go.

2. See yon orient streak appearing,
Harbinger of endless day;
Hark! a voice beyond thy hearing,
Calls my new-born soul away.

3. Yet to leave thee sorrowing pains me—
Hark! that voice again I hear;
Now thine arms no more detain me—
Follow me, my mother dear.

1176. 7s & 4s.

1. When the vale of death appears,
Faint and cold this mortal clay—
Kind Forerunner, soothe my fears,
Light me through the darksome way;
Break the shadows,
Usher in eternal day.

2. Upward from this dying state,
Bid my waiting soul aspire;
Open Thou the crystal gate,
To Thy praise attune my lyre;
Then, triumphant,
I will join the immortal choir.

3. When the mighty trumpet blown,
Shall the judgment dawn proclaim,
From the central, burning throne,
'Mid creation's final flame,
With the ransomed,
Thou wilt own my worthless name!

LIFE AND DEATH. 375

DAWN. 9s & 8s.

1. Christian, the morn breaks sweetly o'er thee, And all the midnight shadows flee, Tinged are the distant skies with glo-ry, A beacon light hung out for thee; Arise, arise! the light breaks o'er thee, Thy name is graven on the throne, Thy home is in the world of glory, Where thy Redeemer reigns alone.

1177. 9s & 8s.

1. CHRISTIAN, the morn breaks sweetly o'er thee,
    And all the midnight shadows flee,
Tinged are the distant skies with glory,
    A beacon light hung out for thee;
Arise, arise! the light breaks o'er thee;
    Thy name is graven on the throne;
Thy home is in the world of glory,
    Where thy Redeemer reigns alone.

2. Tossed on time's rude, relentless surges,
    Calmly, composed, and dauntless, stand,
For lo! beyond those scenes emerges
    The hights that bound the promised land.
Behold! behold! the land is nearing,
    Where the wild sea-storm's rage is o'er;
Hark! how the heavenly hosts are cheering,
    See in what throngs they range the shore!

3. Cheer up! cheer up! the day breaks o'er thee,
    Bright as the summer's noon-tide ray,
The star gemm'd crowns and realms of glory
    Invite thy happy soul away;
Away! away! leave all for glory,
    Thy name is graven on the throne;
Thy home is in that world of glory,
    Where thy Redeemer reigns alone.

TIME AND ETERNITY.

CASPIAN. C. P. M.

1. The fes-tal morn, my God, is come, That calls me to Thy hal-lowed dome, Thy pre-sence to a - dore:
My feet the sum-mons shall at-tend, With will-ing steps Thy courts as-cend, And tread the sa-cred floor.

1178. C. P. M.

2. With joy shall I behold the day,
That calls my thirsting soul away
  To dwell among the blest!
For, lo! my great Redeemer's power
Unfolds the everlasting door,
  And leads me to His rest!

3. E'en now, to my expecting eyes
The heaven-built towers of Salem rise;
  E'en now, with glad survey,
I view her mansions, that contain
The angel forms, a beauteous train,
  And shine with cloudless day,

4. Hither, from earth's remotest end,
Lo! the redeemed of God ascend,
  Their tribute hither bring;
Here, crowned with everlasting joy,
In hymns of praise their tongues employ,
  And hail th' immortal King.
  MERRICK.

1179. C. P. M.

1. If death my friend and me divide,
Thou dost not, Lord, my sorrow chide,
  Or frown my tears to see:
Restrained from passionate excess,
Thou bidst me mourn in calm distress
  For those that rest in Thee.

2. I feel a strong, immortal hope,
Which bears my mournful spirit up,
  Beneath its mountain load:
Redeemed from death, and grief, and pain,
I soon shall find my friend again
  Within the arms of God.

3. Pass a few fleeting moments more,
And death the blessing shall restore,
  Which death hath snatched away;
For me Thou wilt the summons send,
And give me back my parted friend,
  In that eternal day. C. WESLEY.

1180. C. P. M.

1. THE Lord into His garden comes,
The spices yield a rich perfume,
  The lilies grow and thrive;
Refreshing showers of grace divine,
From Jesus, flow to every vine,
  And make the dead revive.

2. Come, brethren, you who love the Lord,
Who taste the sweetness of His word,
  In Jesus' word go on;
Our troubles and our trials here
Will only make us richer there,
  When we arrive at home.

3. We feel that heaven is now begun,
It issues from the shining throne,
  From Jesus' throne on high;
It comes in floods we can't contain,
We drink, and drink, and drink again,
  And yet we still are dry.

4. There we shall reign, and shout, and sing,
And make the upper regions ring,
  When all the saints get home.
Come on, come on, my brethren dear,
Soon we shall meet together there,
  For Jesus bids us come.

LIFE AND DEATH.

CARMEL. C. P. M.   J. ZUNDELL.

1. How happy is the pilgrim's lot! How free from every anxious thought, From worldly hope and fear! Confined to nei-ther court nor cell, His soul disdains on earth to dwell—He on-ly so-journs here. He on-ly so-journs here.

1181.   C. P. M.

2. This happiness in part is mine,
Already saved from low design,
   From every creature-love;
Blest with the scorn of finite good,
My soul is lightened of its load,
   And seeks the things above.

3. There is my house and portion fair:
My treasure and my heart are there,
   And my abiding home;
For me my elder brethren stay,
And angels beckon me away,
   And Jesus bids me come.

4. I come, Thy servant, Lord, replies;
I come to meet Thee in the skies,
   And claim my heavenly rest!
Soon will the pilgrim's journey end;
Then, O my Saviour, Brother, Friend,
   Receive me to Thy breast!

J. WESLEY.

1182.   C. P. M.

1. We suffer with our Master here—
But shall before His face appear,
   And by His side sit down;
To patient faith the prize is sure;
And all that to the end endure
   The cross, shall wear the crown.

2. The great, mysterious Deity,
We soon with open face shall see:
   The beatific sight
Shall fill heaven's sounding courts with praise,
And wide diffuse the golden blaze
   Of everlasting light.

3. The Father, shining on His throne,
The glorious, co-eternal Son,
   The Spirit, one and seven,
Conspire our rapture to complete;
And lo! we fall before His feet,
   And silence heightens heaven.

4. In hope of that ecstatic pause,
Jesus, we now sustain the cross,
   And at Thy footstool fall;
Till Thou our hidden life reveal,
Till Thou our ravished spirits fill,
   And God be all in all!

C. WESLEY.

TIME AND ETERNITY.

KINGSLEY. 11s. G. KINGSLEY.

1. I would not live alway; I ask not to stay, Where storm after storm rises dark o'er the way.

The few lucid mornings that dawn on us here, Are enough for life's woes, full enough for its cheer.

1183. 11s.

2. I would not live alway; no—welcome the tomb,
Since Jesus has lain there, I dread not its gloom;
There, sweet be my rest, till He bid me arise
To hail Him in triumph descending the skies.

3. Who, who would live alway, away from his God;
Away from yon heaven, that blissful abode,
Where the rivers of pleasure flow o'er the bright plains,
And the noontide of glory eternally reigns:—

4. Where the saints of all ages in harmony meet,
Their Saviour and brethren transported to greet;
While the anthems of rapture unceasingly roll,
And the smile of the Lord is the feast of the soul. MUHLENBERG.

1184. 11s.

1. Oh Saviour, whose mercy, severe in its kindness,
Hath chastened my wanderings and guided my way,
Adored be the power that hath pitied my blindness,
And weaned me from phantoms that smiled to betray.

2. Enchanted with all that was dazzling and fair,
I followed the rainbow—I caught at the toy;
And still in displeasure Thy goodness was there,
Disappointing the hope, and defeating the [joy.]

3. The blossom blushed bright, but a worm was below;—
The moonlight shone fair, there was blight in the beam;
Sweet whispered the breeze, but it whispered of woe,
And bitterness flowed in the soft, flowing stream.

4. So, cured of my folly, yet cured but in part,
I turned to the refuge Thy pity displayed;
And still did this eager and credulous heart
Weave visions of promise, that bloomed but to fade.

5. I thought that the course of the pilgrim to heaven
Would be bright as the summer, and glad as the morn;
Thou show'dst me the path, it was dark and uneven,
All rugged with rock, and all tangled with thorn.

6. I dreamed of celestial rewards and renown,
I grasped at the triumph that blesses the brave;
I asked for the palm branch, the robe, and the crown,
I asked, and Thou show'dst me a cross and a grave!

7. Subdued and instructed, at length to Thy will,
My hopes, and my wishes, my all I resign;
O give me a heart that can wait and be still,
Nor know of a wish or a pleasure but Thine.

8. There are mansions exempted from sin and from woe,
But they stand in a region by mortals untrod,
There are rivers of joy—but they roll not below,
There is rest—but it dwells in the presence of God. GRANT.

LIFE AND DEATH.

SCOTLAND. 12s.   Dr. Clarke.

1. The voice of free grace cries, Escape to the mountain, For Adam's lost race Christ hath opened a fountain; { For sin and uncleanness, and ev-ery transgression, His blood flows most freely in streams of salvation, His blood flows most freely in streams, &c.
{ Halle-lu-jah to the Lamb, who hath purchased our pardon, We'll praise him again, when we pass over Jordan, We'll praise him again, when we pass over Jordan.

1185. 12s.

2. Ye souls that are wounded! O flee to the Saviour;
He calls you in mercy,—'t is infinite favor;
Your sins are increasing,—escape to the mountain,—
His blood can remove them,—it flows from the fountain.

3. O Jesus! ride onward, triumphantly glorious,
O'er sin, death, and hell, Thou art more than victorious;
Thy name is the theme of the great congregation,
While angels and men raise the shout of salvation.

4. With joy shall we stand, when escaped to the shore;
With harps in our hands, we'll praise Him the more;
We'll range the sweet plains on the bank of the river,
And sing of salvation for ever and ever!
THORNBY.

1186. 12s.

1. Thou art gone to the grave! but we will not deplore thee,
Though sorrows and darkness encompass the tomb;
The Saviour hath passed through its portals before thee,
And the lamp of His love is thy guide through the gloom.

2. Thou art gone to the grave! we no longer behold thee,
Nor tread the rough paths of the world by thy side;
But the wide arms of mercy are spread to enfold thee,
And sinners may die, for the Sinless hath died.

3. Thou art gone to the grave! and, its mansion forsaking,
What though thy weak spirit in fear lingered long;
The sunshine of Paradise beamed on thy waking,
And the sound which thou heardst, was the seraphim's song.

4. Thou art gone to the grave! but we will not deplore thee,
For God was thy ransom, thy Guardian, and Guide;
He gave thee, He took thee, and He will restore thee;
And death has no sting, for the Saviour hath died.
HEBER.

TIME AND ETERNITY.

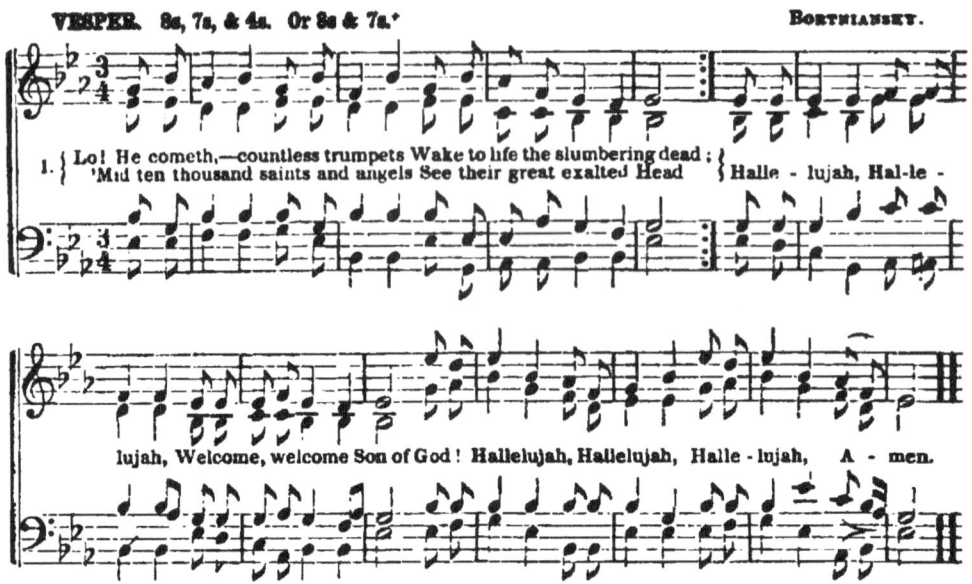

VESPER. 8s, 7s, & 4s. Or 8s & 7s.* — BORTNIANSKY.

1. Lo! He cometh,—countless trumpets Wake to life the slumbering dead;
'Mid ten thousand saints and angels See their great exalted Head
Halle-lujah, Halle-lujah, Welcome, welcome Son of God! Hallelujah, Hallelujah, Halle-lujah, A-men.

* When sung to 8s and 7s single, omit the repeat, and sing the hallelujah. To 8s and 7s double, repeat, and omit the hallelujah.

1187. 8s, 7s & 4s.

2. Full of joyful expectation,
Saints behold the Judge appear;
Truth and justice go before Him—
Now the joyful sentence hear;
Hallelujah!—
Welcome, welcome, Judge divine!

3. "Come, ye blessed of my Father!
Enter into life and joy;
Banish all your fears and sorrows;
Endless praise be your employ;"
Hallelujah!—
Welcome, welcome to the skies.

1188. 8s & 7s.

1. BROTHER! rest from sin and sorrow;
Death is o'er and life is won;
On thy slumber dawns no morrow;
Rest; thine earthly race is run.

2. Brother, wake! the night is waning;
Endless day is round thee poured;
Enter thou the rest remaining
For the people of the Lord.

3. Brother, wake! for He who loved thee,
He who died that thou mightst live,
He who graciously approved thee,
Waits thy crown of joy to give.

4. Fare thee well! though woe is blending
With the tones of earthly love,
Triumph high and joy unending
Wait thee in the realms above.

BAP. MEMORIAL.

1189. 8s, 7s & 4s.

1. Lo! the mighty God appearing—
From on high Jehovah speaks!
Eastern lands the summons hearing,
O'er the west His thunder breaks;
Earth beholds Him;
Universal nature shakes.

2. Zion, all its light unfolding,
God in glory shall display;
Lo! He comes—nor silence holding,
Fire and clouds prepare His way,
Tempests round Him
Hasten on the dreadful day.

3. To the heavens His voice ascending,
To the earth beneath He cries;
"Souls immortal now descending,
Let the sleeping dust arise!
Rise to judgment;
Let My throne adorn the skies.

4. "Gather first My saints around Me,
Those who to My covenant stood;
Those who humbly sought and found Me,
Through the dying Saviour's blood;
Blest Redeemer!
Dearest sacrifice to God!"

5. Now the heavens on high adore Him,
And His righteousness declare;
Sinners perish from before Him,
But His saints His mercies share;
Just His judgment!
God, Himself the Judge, is there.

W. GOODE.

1190. 8s & 7s.

1. Great Redeemer, Friend of sinners,
    Thou hast wondrous power to save;
Grant me grace, and still protect me,
    Over life's tempestuous wave.

2. May my soul, with sacred transport,
    View the dawn while yet afar;
And, until the sun arises,
    Lead me by the Morning Star.

3. See the happy spirits waiting
    On the banks beyond the stream;
Sweet responses still repeating,
    Jesus, Jesus is their theme.

4. Swiftly roll, ye lingering hours,
    Seraphs, lend your glittering wings;
Love absorbs my ransomed powers,
    Heavenly sounds around me ring.

5. Worlds of light! and crowns of glory!
    Far above yon azure sky;
Though by faith I now behold you,
    I'll enjoy you soon on high.
                    CHRISTIAN LYRE.

1191. 8s & 7s.

1. Happy soul! thy days are ended,
    All thy mourning days below;
Go, by angel guards attended,
    To the sight of Jesus go!
Waiting to receive thy spirit,
    Lo! the Saviour stands above;
Shows the purchase of His merit,
    Reaches out the crown of love.

2. Struggle through thy latest passion
    To thy dear Redeemer's breast,
To His uttermost salvation,
    To his everlasting rest;
For the joy He sets before thee,
    Bear a momentary pain;
Die, to live a life of glory;
    Suffer, with thy Lord to reign.
                    C. WESLEY.

1192. 8s & 7s.

1. Let me go, the day is breaking—
    Dear companions, let me go;
We have spent a night of waking
    In the wilderness below;
Upward now I bend my way;
Part we here at break of day.

2. Let me go; I may not tarry,
    Wrestling thus with doubts and fears;
Angels wait my soul to carry
    Where my risen Lord appears;
Friends and kindred, weep not so—
If ye love me, let me go.

3. We have traveled long together,
    Hand in hand, and heart in heart,
Both through fair and stormy weather,
    And 'tis hard, 'tis hard to part;
While I sigh "Farewell!" to you,
Answer, one and all, "Adieu!"

4. 'T is not darkness gathering round me
    That withdraws me from your sight,
Walls of flesh no more can bound me,
    But translated into light,
Like the lark on mounting wing,
Though unseen, you hear me sing.

5. Heaven's broad day hath o'er me broken,
    Far beyond earth's span of sky;
Am I dead? Nay, by this token,
    Know that I have ceased to die;
Would you solve the mystery,
Come up hither—come and see!
                    MONTGOMERY.

1193. 8s & 7s.

1. Parting soul! the flood awaits thee,
    And the billows round thee roar;
Yet look on—the crystal city
    Stands on yon celestial shore!
There are crowns and thrones of glory,
    There the living waters glide;
There the just, in shining raiment,
    Wander by Immanuel's side.

2. Linger not, the stream is narrow,
    Though its cold dark waters rise;
He who passed the flood before thee,
    Guides the path to yonder skies;
Hark! the sound of angels, hymning,
    Rolls harmonious o'er thine ear;
See the walls and golden portals
    Through the mist of death appear!

3. Soul, adieu! this gloomy sojourn
    Holds thy captive feet no more;
Flesh is dropped, and sin forsaken,
    Sorrow done, and weeping o'er.
Through the tears thy friends are shedding
    Smiles of hope serenely shine;
Not a friend remains behind thee,
    But would change his lot for thine.
                    EDMESTON.

TIME AND ETERNITY.

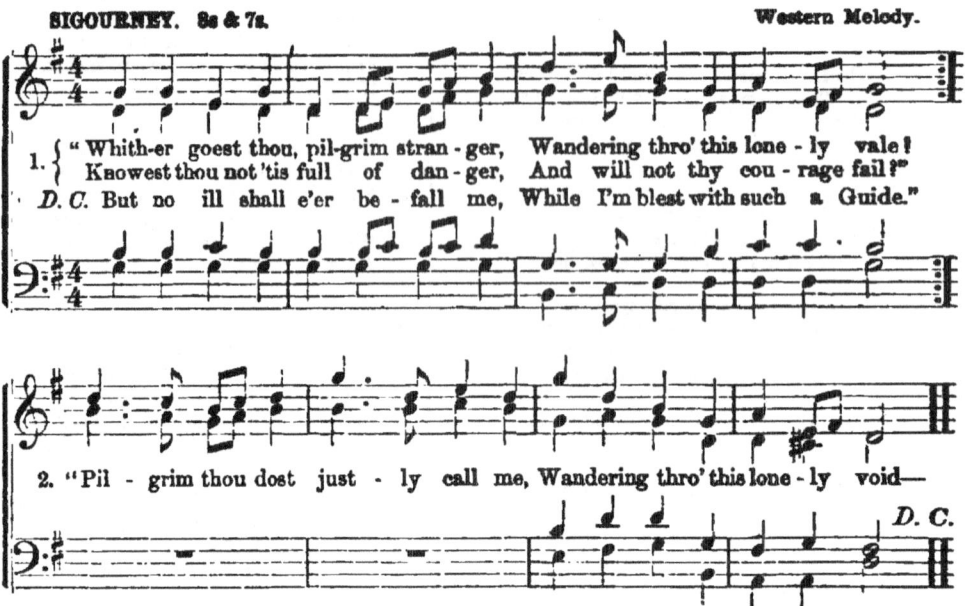

SIGOURNEY. 8s & 7s. Western Melody.

1. "Whither goest thou, pilgrim stranger,
   Wandering thro' this lonely vale?
   Knowest thou not 'tis full of danger,
   And will not thy courage fail?"
   D.C. But no ill shall e'er befall me,
   While I'm blest with such a Guide."

2. "Pilgrim thou dost justly call me,
   Wandering thro' this lonely void—

1194. 8s & 7s.

3. "Such a Guide? No guide attends thee—
   Hence for thee my fears arise:
   If some guardian power defend thee,
   'T is unseen by mortal eyes."

4. "Yes, unseen; but still, believe me,
   Such a Guide my steps attend;
   He'll in every strait relieve me,
   He will guide me to the end."

5. "Pilgrim, see that stream before thee,
   Darkly rolling through the vale;
   Should its boist'rous waves roll o'er thee,
   Would not then thy courage fail?"

6. "No, that stream has nothing frightful;
   To its brink my steps I'll bend;
   Thence to plunge will be delightful,—
   Here my pilgrimage shall end."

7. While I gazed, with speed surprising,
   Down the vale she plunged from sight;
   Gazing still, I saw her rising,
   Like an angel clothed in light.

1195. 8s & 7s.

1. HAIL, my ever blessed Jesus!
   Only Thee I wish to sing;
   To my soul Thy name is precious,
   Thou my Prophet, Priest, and King.
   O, what mercy flows from Heaven!
   O, what joy and happiness!
   Love I much, I've much forgiven—
   I'm a miracle of grace!

2. Once with Adam's race in ruin,
   Unconcerned in sin I lay;
   Swift destruction still pursuing,
   Till my Saviour passed that way.
   Witness, all ye host of heaven,
   My Redeemer's tenderness;
   Love I much, I've much forgiven—
   I'm a miracle of grace!

3. Shout, ye bright, angelic choir,
   Praise the Lamb enthroned above,
   Whilst, astonished, I admire
   God's free grace and boundless love.
   That blest moment I received Him,
   Filled my soul with joy and peace;
   Love I much, I've much forgiven—
   I'm a miracle of grace.

1196. 8s & 7s.

1. SEE the stars from heaven falling!
   Hark! on earth the doleful cry!
   Men on rocks and mountains calling,
   While the frowning Judge draws nigh;
   Hide us! hide us!
   Rocks and mountains, from His eye!

2. Lo! 't is He! our heart's desire,
   Come for His espoused below;
   Come to join us with the choir,
   Come to make our joys o'erflow;
   Palms of victory,
   Crowns of glory to bestow.

LIFE AND DEATH.

GOLDEN SHORE. 8s & 7s. Jewish Air.

1. Lo! the seal of death is breaking;
   Those who slept its sleep are waking;
   Heaven opes its portals fair!
   Hark! the harps of God are ringing,
   Hark! the seraph's hymn is flinging
   Music on immortal air.

1197. 8s & 7s.

2. There, no more at eve declining,
   Suns without a cloud are shining
   O'er the land of life and love;
   There the founts of life are flowing,
   Flowers unknown to time, are blowing
   In that radiant scene above.

3. There no sigh of memory swelleth;
   There no tear of misery welleth;
   Hearts will bleed or break no more;
   Past is all the cold world's scorning,
   Gone the night, and broke the morning,
   Over all the golden shore.
   MISS. MAG.

1198. (Part 1.) 8s & 7s.*

1. Through life's vapors dimly seeing
   Who but longs for light to break!
   O the feverish dream of being!
   When, oh when shall we awake!
   O the hour when this material
   Shall have vanished as a cloud,—
   When amid the wide ethereal
   All th' invisible shall crowd,—

2. And the naked soul, surrounded
   With realities unknown,
   Triumph in the view unbounded,
   Feel herself with God alone!
   In that sudden, strange transition,
   By what new and finer sense
   Shall she grasp the mighty vision,
   And receive its influence?

3. Angels, guard the new immortal,
   Through the wonder-teeming space,
   To the everlasting portal,
   To the spirit's resting-place.
   Till the trump, which shakes creation,
   Through the circling heavens shall roll,
   Till the day of consummation,
   Till the bridal of the soul.
   CONDER.

1198. (Part 2.) 8s & 7s.*

1. Jesus, blessed Mediator!
   Thou the airy path hast trod;
   Thou the Judge, the Consummator!
   Shepherd of the fold of God!
   Can I trust a fellow-being?
   Can I trust an angel's care?
   O Thou merciful All-seeing!
   Beam around my spirit there.

2. Blessed fold! no foe can enter;
   And no friend departeth thence;
   Jesus is their sun, their center,
   And their shield, Omnipotence.
   Blessed! for the Lamb shall feed them,
   All their tears shall wipe away,
   To the living fountains lead them,
   Till fruition's perfect day.

3. Lo! it comes, that day of wonder!
   Louder chorals shake the skies:
   Hades' gates are burst asunder;
   See! the new-clothed myriads rise.
   Thought! repress thy weak endeavor;
   Here must reason prostrate fall;
   O! th' ineffable Forever!
   And th' eternal All in All!
   CONDER.

* Sing the tune twice through to each 6 line stanza.

TIME AND ETERNITY.

MOYLE. 8s & 7s.   Ancient Irish Dirge. Arranged by CH. BEECHER.

1. Brother, thou art gone before us, Where thy saintly soul is flown: Tears are wiped away for-ever, And all sorrow is unknown; 2. From the burden of the body, From all care and fear released, Where the wicked cease from troubling, And the weary are at rest.

1199. 8s & 7s.

1. BROTHER, thou art gone before us,
   Where thy saintly soul is flown,
   Tears are wiped away for ever,
   And all sorrow is unknown;

2. From the burden of the body,
   From all care and fear released,
   Where the wicked cease from troubling,
   And the weary are at rest.

3. O'er the toilsome way thou 'st traveled,
   And endured the heavy load;
   Christ hath brought thy footsteps languid
   Safely to His blest abode.

4. Thou art resting now, like Laz'rus,
   On thy heavenly Father's breast,
   Where the wicked cease from troubling,
   And the weary are at rest.

5. Sin no more can taint thy spirit,
   Nor can doubt thy faith assail;
   Thou thy welcome hast received,
   Now thy strength shall never fail;

6. And thou 'rt sure to meet the holy,
   Whom on earth thou loved'st best,
   Where the wicked cease from troubling,
   And the weary are at rest.

7. To thy grave we sadly bear thee,
   There in dust we place thy head;
   O'er thee now the turf is pressing,
   And grows green thy narrow bed.

8. But thy spirit soars to glory,
   Free, among the faithful blest,
   Where the wicked cease from troubling,
   And the weary are at rest.

9. When the Lord shall send His summons
   Unto us who 're left behind,
   May we, by the world untainted,
   Gracious welcome with thee find;

10. Each like thee, in peace departing,
    To the kingdom of the blest,
    Where the wicked cease from troubling,
    And the weary are at rest.

ALTERED FROM MILMAN.

LIFE AND DEATH.

WILMOT. 7s.   WEBER.

1. Come, Desire of nations, come! Hasten, Lord, the general doom! Hear the Spirit and the Bride, Come, and take us to Thy side.

1260. 7s.

1. Come, Desire of nations come!
Hasten, Lord, the general doom!
Hear the Spirit and the Bride;
Come, and take us to Thy side.

2. Thou, who hast our plans prepared,
Make us meet for our reward;
Then with all Thy saints descend:
Then our earthly trials end.

3. Mindful of Thy chosen race,
Shorten these vindictive days;
Who for full redemption groan;
Hear us now, and save Thine own.

4. Now destroy the man of sin,
Now Thine ancient flock bring in!
Filled with righteousness divine,
Claim a ransomed world for Thine.

5. Plant Thy heavenly kingdom here;
Glorious in Thy saints appear:
Speak the sacred number sealed;
Speak the mystery revealed.

6. Take to Thee Thy royal power:
Reign! when sin shall be no more;
Reign! when death no more shall be;
Reign to all eternity!

1261. 7s.

1. Lord of earth! Thy forming hand
Well this beauteous frame hath planned,
Woods that wave, and hills that tower,
Ocean rolling in his power.

2. All that strikes the gaze unsought,
All that charms the lonely thought,
Friendship—gem transcending price—
Love—a flower from paradise.

3. Yet amid this scene so fair,
Should I cease Thy smile to share,
What were all its joys to me?
Whom have I on earth but Thee?

4. Lord of Heaven! beyond our sight
Rolls a world of purer light;
There in love's unclouded reign
Parted hands shall clasp again.

5. O! that world is passing fair,
Yet if Thou wert absent there,
What were all its joys to me?
Whom have I in heaven but Thee?

6. Lord of earth and heaven! my breast
Seeks in Thee its only rest;
I was lost—Thy accents mild
Homeward lured Thy wandering child.

7. I was blind—Thy healing ray
Charmed the long eclipse away;
Source of every joy I know,
Solace of my every woe!

8. O, if once Thy smile divine
Ceased upon my soul to shine,
What were earth or heaven to me?
Whom have I in *each* but Thee?

GRANT.

TIME AND ETERNITY.

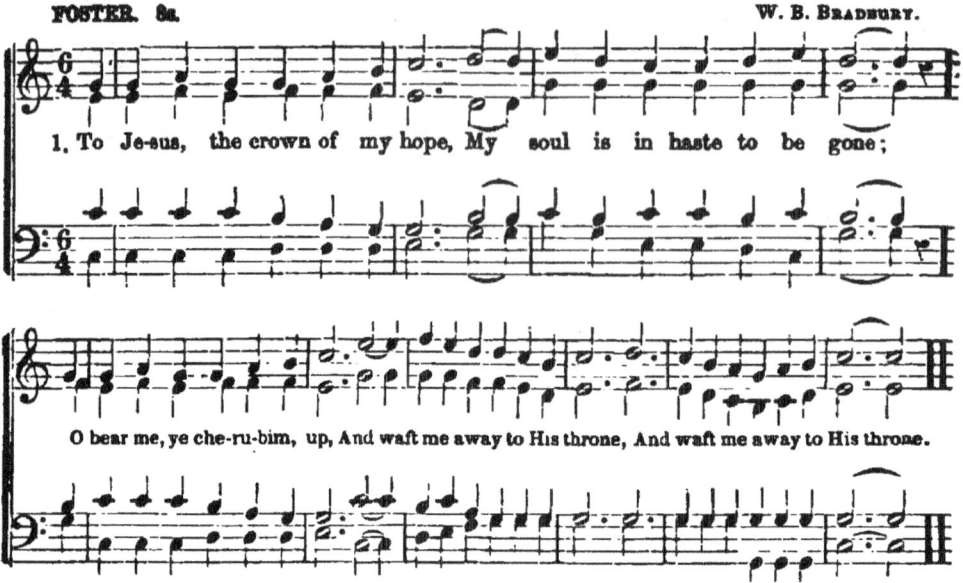

FOSTER. 8s.   W. B. BRADBURY.

1. To Jesus, the crown of my hope, My soul is in haste to be gone;
O bear me, ye cherubim, up, And waft me away to His throne, And waft me away to His throne.

1202. 8s.

1. To Jesus, the crown of my hope,
  My soul is in haste to be gone;
O bear me, ye cherubim, up,
  And waft me away to His throne.
My Saviour, whom absent I love;
  Whom, not having seen, I adore;
Whose name is exalted above
  All glory, dominion, and power.

2. Dissolve Thou these bands that detain
  My soul from her portion in Thee,
Ah! strike off this adamant chain,
  And make me eternally free.
When that happy era begins,
  When arrayed in Thy glories I shine;
Nor grieve any more, by my sins,
  The bosom on which I recline.

3. O then shall the vail be removed!
  And round me Thy brightness be poured;
I shall meet Him, whom absent I loved,
  I shall see, whom unseen I adored.
And then, never more shall the fears,
  The trials, temptations, and woes,
Which darken this valley of tears,
  Intrude on my blissful repose.
                      COWPER.

1203. 8s.

1. THIS God is the God we adore,
  Our faithful, unchangeable Friend;
Whose love is as large as His power,
  And neither knows measure nor end.

'T is Jesus, the first and the last,
  Whose Spirit shall guide us safe home;
We 'll praise Him for all that is past,
  And trust Him for all that 's to come.
                      COWPER.

1204. 8s.

1. O WHEN shall we sweetly remove,
  O when shall we enter our rest,—
Return to the Zion above,
  The mother of spirits distressed;
The city of God, the great King,
  Where sorrow and death are no more,
Where saints our Immanuel sing,
  And cherub and seraph adore?

2. But angels themselves can not tell
  The joys of that holiest place,
Where Jesus is pleased to reveal
  The light of His heavenly face:
When, caught in the rapturous flame,
  The sight beatific they prove;
And walk in the light of the Lamb,
  Enjoying the beams of His love.

3. Thou know'st in the spirit of prayer
  We long Thy appearing to see,
Resigned to the burden we bear,
  But longing to triumph with Thee:
'T is good at Thy word to be here;
  'T is better in Thee to be gone,
And see Thee in glory appear,
  And rise to a share in Thy throne.
                      C. WESLEY.

LIFE AND DEATH.

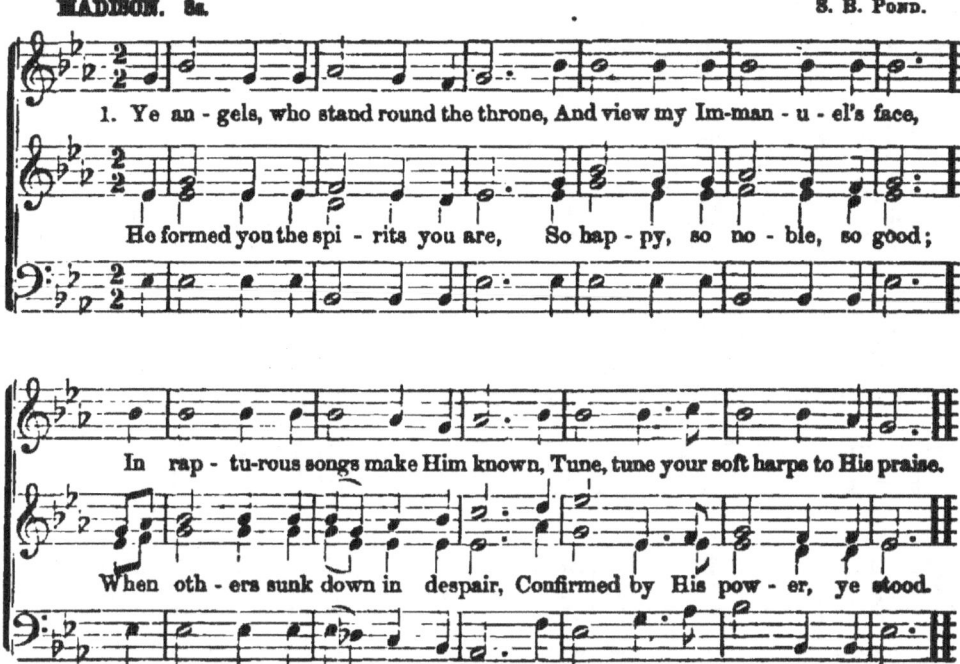

MADISON. 8s. S. B. POND.

1. Ye angels, who stand round the throne, And view my Immanuel's face,
He formed you the spirits you are, So happy, so noble, so good;
In rapturous songs make Him known, Tune, tune your soft harps to His praise.
When others sunk down in despair, Confirmed by His power, ye stood.

1205. 8s.

2. Ye saints, who stand nearer than they,
    And cast your bright crowns at His feet,
His grace and His glory display,
    And all his rich mercy repeat:
He snatched you from hell and the grave,
    He ransomed from death and despair:
For you He was mighty to save,
    Almighty to bring you safe there.

3 O, when will the period appear,
    When I shall unite in your song?
I'm weary of lingering here,
    And I to your Saviour belong!
I'm fettered and chained up in clay;
    I struggle and pant to be free;
I long to be soaring away,
    My God and my Saviour to see!

4. I want to put on my attire,
    Washed white in the blood of the Lamb;
I want to be one of Your choir,
    And tune my sweet harp to His name;
I want—O! I want to be there,
    Where sorrow and sin bid adieu—
Your joy and your friendship to share—
    To wonder, and worship with You!
                  DE FLEURY.

1206. 8s.

1. WE speak of the realms of the blest,
    Of that country so bright and so fair,
And oft are its glories confess'd;
    But what must it be to be there!

2. We speak of its pathways of gold,
    And its walls decked with jewels most rare;
Of its wonders and pleasures untold;
    But what must it be to be there!

3. We speak of its freedom from sin,
    From sorrow, temptation, and care;
From trials without and within;
    But what must it be to be there!

4. We speak of its service of love,
    Of the robes which the glorified wear;
Of the church of the first-born above;
    But what must it be to be there!

5. Then let us, 'midst pleasure and woe,
    Still for heaven our spirits prepare,
And shortly we also shall know,
    And feel what it is to be there!

TIME AND ETERNITY.

BIRMINGHAM. 8s.   English.

1. { I long to behold Him arrayed With glory and light from above;
The King in His beauty displayed—His beauty of holiest love: }
2. I languish and sigh to be there, Where Jesus hath fixed His abode; O, when shall we meet in the air, And fly to the mountain of God.

1207. 8s.

3. With Him I on Zion shall stand,
    For Jesus hath spoken the word;
  The breadth of Immanuel's land
    Survey by the light of my Lord.

4. But when, on Thy bosom reclined,
    Thy face I am strengthened to see,
  My fullness of rapture I find—
    My heaven of heavens in Thee!

5. How happy the people that dwell
    Secure in the city above!
  No pain the inhabitants feel,
    No sickness or sorrow shall prove.

6. Physician of souls! unto me
    Forgiveness and holiness give;
  And when from the body set free,
    O then to the city receive!
        C. WESLEY.

1208. 8s.

1. AWAY with our sorrow and fear,
    We soon shall recover our home;
  The city of saints shall appear,
    The day of eternity come.

2. From earth we shall quickly remove,
    And mount to our native abode;
  The house of our Father above—
    The palace of angels and God.

3. Our mourning is all at an end,
    When, raised by the life-giving word,
  We see the new city descend,
    Adorned as a bride for her Lord:

4. The city so holy and clean,
    No sorrow can breathe in the air:
  No gloom of affliction or sin;
    No shadow of evil is there.

5. By faith we already behold
    That lovely Jerusalem here:
  Her walls are of jasper and gold;
    As crystal her buildings are clear.

6. Immovably founded in grace,
    She stands as she ever hath stood,
  And brightly her Builder displays,
    And flames with the glory of God.
        C. WESLEY.

LIFE AND DEATH.

1209. 8s & 9s.

Death of a Missionary.

1. WEEP not for the saint that ascends
To partake of the joys of the sky,
Weep not for the seraph that bends
With the worshiping chorus on high.

2. Weep not for the spirit now crowned
With the garland to martyrdom given,
O weep not for him; he has found
His reward and his refuge in heaven.

3. But weep for their sorrows, who stand
And lament o'er the dead by his grave—
Who sigh when they muse on the land
Of their home, far away o'er the wave.

4. And weep for the nations that dwell
Where the light of the truth never shone,
Where anthems of praise never swell,
And the love of the Lamb is unknown.

5. Weep not for the saint that ascends
To partake of the joys of the sky;
Weep not for the seraph that bends
With the worshiping chorus on high;—

6. But weep for the mourners who stand
By the grave of their brother in tears,
And weep for the people whose land
Still must wait till the day-spring appears.
L. BACON.

1210. 8s.

1. REJOICE for a brother deceased;
Our loss is his infinite gain;
A soul out of prison released,
And freed from its bodily chain.

2. With songs let us follow his flight,
And mount with his spirit above;
Escaped to the mansions of light,
And lodged in the Eden of love.

3. Our brother the haven has gained,
Outflying the tempest and wind;
His rest he has sooner obtained,
And left his companions behind;

4. Still tossed on a sea of distress,
Hard toiling to make the blessed shore,
Where all is assurance and peace,
And sorrow and sin are no more.

5. There all the ship's company meet,
Who sailed with the Saviour beneath;
With shoutings each other they greet,
And triumph o'er trouble and death.

6. The voyage of life's at an end,
The mortal affliction is past:
The age that in heaven they spend,
For ever and ever shall last.
C. WESLEY.

1211. 8s.

1. How tedious and tasteless the hours,
When Jesus no longer I see!
Sweet prospects, sweet birds, and sweet flowers,
Have lost all their sweetness with me.

2. The mid-summer sun shines but dim,
The fields strive in vain to look gay;
But when I am happy in Him
December's as pleasant as May.

3. His name yields the richest perfume,
And sweeter than music His voice;
His presence disperses my gloom,
And makes all within me rejoice.

4. I should, were He always thus nigh,
Have nothing to wish or to fear;
No mortal so happy as I—
My summer would last all the year.

5. Dear Lord, if indeed I am Thine,
If Thou art my sun and my song,
Say, why do I languish and pine,
And why are my winters so long?

6. O drive these dark clouds from my sky,
Thy soul-cheering presence restore;
Or take me unto Thee on high,
Where winter and clouds are no more.
NEWTON.

1212. 8s.

1. O THOU, who hast spread out the skies,
And measured the depths of the sea,
'Twixt heavens and ocean shall rise
Our incense of praises to Thee.

2. We know that Thy presence is near,
While heaves our bark far from the land;
We ride o'er the deep without fear—
The waters are held in Thy hand.

3. Eternity comes in the sound
Of billows that never can sleep!
There's Deity circling us round—
Omnipotence walks o'er the deep!

4. O Father! our eye is to Thee,
As on for the haven we roll;
And faith in our Pilot shall be
An anchor to steady the soul.
H. F. GOULD.

FLORENCE. C. M. — Geo. Kingsley.

1. Father! I long, I faint to see The place of Thine abode; I'd leave Thine earthly courts, and flee Up to Thy seat, my God!

1213. C. M.

1. Father! I long, I faint, to see
The place of Thine abode;
I'd leave Thine earthly courts, and flee
Up to Thy seat, my God!

2. Here I behold Thy distant face,
And 't is a pleasing sight;
But, to abide in Thine embrace
Is infinite delight.

3. There all the heavenly hosts are seen;
In shining ranks they move;
And drink immortal vigor in,
With wonder and with love.

4. Then at Thy feet, with awful fear,
Th' adoring armies fall;
With joy they shrink to nothing there,
Before th' eternal All.

5. The more Thy glories strike my eyes,
The humbler I shall lie;
Thus while I sink, my joys shall rise
Immeasurably high.
　　　　　　　　　WATTS.

1214. C. M. Peculiar.

1. When forced to part from those we love,
Though sure to meet to-morrow,
We still a painful anguish prove—
We feel a pang of sorrow.

2. But who can e'er describe the tears
We shed when thus we sever,
If doomed to part for months, for years—
To part, perhaps, for ever?

3. Yet, if our aims are fixed aright,
A sacred hope is given,
Though here our prospects end in night,
We'll meet again in heaven.

4. Then let us form those bonds above
Which time can ne'er dissever,
Since, parting in a Saviour's love,
We part to meet for ever.

1215. C. M. Peculiar.

1. O, lay not up on this vain earth
Your hope, your joy, your treasure;
Here sorrow clouds the pilgrim's path,
And blights each opening pleasure.

2. Earth's joys, like dew-drops, fade away;
   Like clouds in visions vanish;
   Above, no night can chase the day;
   Those joys no change can banish.

3. All, all below must fade and die;
   The dearest hopes we cherish;
   Scenes touched with brightest radiancy
   Are all decreed to perish.

4. Then, man, be wise; thy constant care
   To purer joys be given,
   Nor let delusive objects share
   The place of bliss and heaven.

1216. C. M.

1. There's nothing round these painted skies,
   Or round this dusty clod,
   Nothing, my soul, that's worth thy joys,
   Or lovely as thy God.

2. 'T is heaven on earth to taste His love,
   To feel His quickening grace;
   And all the heaven I hope above
   Is but to see His face.

3. Why move my years in slow delay?
   O God of ages why?
   Let the spheres cleave, and mark my way
   To the superior sky.
                                    WATTS.

1217. C. M.

1. Jesus, to Thy dear wounds we flee,
   We seek Thy bleeding side,
   Assured that all who trust in Thee
   Shall evermore abide.

2. Then let the thundering trumpet sound,
   The latest lightning glare;
   The mountains melt; the solid ground
   Dissolve as liquid air;

3. The huge, celestial bodies roll
   Amidst that general fire,
   And shrivel as a parchment scroll,
   And all in smoke expire!

4. Sublime upon His azure throne,
   He speaks—th' Almighty Word;
   His fiat is obeyed! 't is done;
   And paradise restored.

5. So be it! let this system end,
   This ruined earth and skies;
   The New Jerusalem descend,
   The New Creation rise.

6. Thy power Omnipotent assume;
   Thy brightest majesty!
   And when Thou dost in glory come,
   My Lord! remember me.
                                    WESLEY'S COLL.

1218. C. M.

1. Bright was the guiding star, that led,
   With mild, benignant ray,
   The Gentiles to the lowly bed
   Where our Redeemer lay.

2. But, lo! a brighter, clearer light
   Now points to His abode;
   It shines through sin and sorrow's night,
   To guide us to our Lord.

3. O, haste to follow where it leads;
   The gracious call obey;
   Be rugged wilds, or flowery meads,
   The Christian's destined way.

4. O, gladly tread the narrow path,
   While light and grace are given;
   Who meekly follow Christ on earth,
   Shall reign with Him in heaven.

1219. C. M. Peculiar.

1. The silver cord in twain is snapped,
   The golden bowl is broken,
   The mortal mold in darkness wrapped,
   The words funereal spoken.
   The tomb is built, or the rock is cleft,
   Or delved is the grassy clod,
   And what for mourning man is left?
   O what is left—but God!

2. The tears are shed that mourned the dead,
   The flowers they wore are faded;
   The twilight dun hath vailed the sun,
   And hope's sweet dreamings shaded;
   The thoughts of joy that were planted deep,
   From our heart of hearts are riven;
   And what is left us when we weep?
   O what is left—but Heaven!

DOXOLOGY. C. M.

Father of mercies! hear our cry;
Hear us, coequal Son!
Who reignest with the Holy Ghost,
While ceaseless ages run.

HEAVEN.

PILGRIM'S FAREWELL. L. M.

1. Farewell, dear friends, I must be gone, I have no home nor stay with you; I'll take my staff and travel on, Till I a better world shall view.

CODA, to be sung or omitted, at pleasure.

I'll march to Canaan's land, I'll land on Canaan's shore, Where pleasures never end, And troubles come no more. Farewell, farewell, farewell, my loving friends, farewell!

1220. L. M.

2. Farewell, my friends, time rolls along,
   Nor waits for mortals' care or bliss;
   I leave you here, and travel on,
   Till I arrive where Jesus is.

3. Farewell, my brethren in the Lord,
   To you I'm bound in cords of love;
   Yet we believe His gracious word,
   We all shall meet Him soon above.

4. Farewell, old soldiers of the cross,
   You've struggled long and hard for heaven;
   You've counted all things here but dross,
   Fight on, the crown shall soon be given.

1221. L. M.

1. Farewell, bright soul, a short farewell,
   Till we shall meet again above;
   In the sweet groves where pleasures dwell,
   And trees of life bear fruits of love.

2. That glory sits on every face,
   There friendship smiles in every eye;
   There shall our tongues relate the grace
   That led us homeward to the sky.

3. O'er all the names of Christ, our King,
   Shall our harmonious voices rove;
   Our harps shall sound from every string
   The wonders of His bleeding love.

4. Come sovereign Lord! dear Saviour, come!
   Remove these separating days;
   Send Thy bright wheels to fetch us home,
   That golden hour, how long it stays?

5. How long must we lie lingering here,
   While saints around us take their flight?
   Smiling, they quit this dusky sphere,
   And mount the hills of heavenly light.

6. Sweet soul, we leave thee to thy rest,
   Enjoy thy Jesus and thy God,
   Till we, from bands of clay released,
   Spring out and climb the shining road.
   WATTS.

1222. L. M.

1. There is a harp whose thrilling sound
   Swells through the choir of heaven above;
   'Mid the blue arch the notes resound,
   While angels catch the song of love.

2. 'Tis when beyond this vale of tears,
   A sainted spirit wings its way;
   And pure before the throne appears
   In robes of bright, ethereal day.

3. Hark! the glad shout of sacred joy,
   In choral numbers, loud and long;
   Th' angel host their harps employ;
   And hallelujahs swell the song.

1223. L. M.

1. The ransomed spirit to her home,
   The clime of cloudless beauty, flies;
   No more on stormy seas to roam,
   She hails her haven in the skies;
   But cheerless are those heavenly fields,
   That cloudless clime no pleasure yields,
   There is no bliss in bowers above,
   If Thou art absent, holy Love!

2. The cherub, near the viewless throne,
   Smiteth the harp with trembling hand;
   And one, with incense-fire hath flown,
   To touch with flame the angel-band;
   But tuneless is the quivering string;
   No melody can Gabriel bring;
   Mute are its arches, when above
   The harps of heaven wake not to love!

3. Earth, sea, and sky, one language speak,
   In harmony that soothes the soul;
   'Tis heard when scarce the zephyrs wake,
   And when on thunders thunders roll;
   That voice is heard, and tumults cease;
   It whispers to the bosom peace;
   Speak, thou Inspirer from above,
   And cheer our hearts, celestial Love!
   TAPPAN.

1224. L. M.

1. Come, O Thou universal good!
   Balm of the wounded conscience, come!
   Haven to take the shipwrecked in,
   My everlasting rest from sin!

2. Come, O my comfort and delight!
   My strength, and health, and shield, and sun,
   My boast, my confidence, and might,
   My joy, my glory, and my crown!

1225. L. M.

1. Descend from heaven, immortal Dove;
   Stoop down and take us on Thy wings;
   And mount, and bear us far above
   The reach of these inferior things;

2. Beyond, beyond this lower sky,
   Up where eternal ages roll,
   Where solid pleasures never die,
   And fruits immortal feast the soul.

3. O, for a sight, a pleasing sight
   Of our Almighty Father's throne!
   There sits our Saviour, crowned with light,
   Clothed in a body like our own.

4. Adoring saints around Him stand,
   And thrones and powers before Him fall;
   The God shines gracious through the Man,
   And sheds sweet glories on them all.

5. O, what amazing joys they feel,
   While to their golden harps they sing,
   And sit on every heavenly hill,
   And spread the triumph of their King!

6. When shall the day, dear Lord, appear,
   That I shall mount, to dwell above;
   And stand, and bow, among them there,
   And view Thy face, and sing, and love!
   WATTS.

HEAVEN.

SALEM. L. M. — Psalmodist.

1. O happy saints, that dwell in light,
And walk with Jesus clothed in white,
Safe landed on that peaceful shore,
Where pilgrim's meet to part no more.

1226. L. M.

2. Released from sorrow, sin and strife,
   Death was the gate to endless life,
   And now they range the heavenly plains,
   And sing His love in melting strains.

3. They gaze upon His beauteous face,
   And tell the wonders of His grace;
   Or, overwhelmed with raptures sweet,
   Sink down, adoring at His feet.

4. Ah, Lord! with faltering steps I creep,
   And sometimes sing, and sometimes weep;
   When shall I wake in heaven to prove
   The heights and depths of Jesus' love.

1227. L. M.

1. O FOR a sweet, inspiring ray,
   To animate our feeble strains,
   From the bright realms of endless day,
   The blissful realms where Jesus reigns.

2. There, low before His glorious throne,
   Adoring saints and angels fall;
   And, with delightful worship, own   [all
   His smile their bliss, their heaven, their

3. Immortal glories crown His head,
   While tuneful hallelujahs rise,
   And love, and joy, and triumph spread
   Through all th' assemblies of the skies.

4. He smiles—and seraphs tune their songs
   To boundless rapture, while they gaze;
   Ten thousand thousand joyful tongues
   Resound His everlasting praise.

5. There all the followers of the Lamb,
   Shall join at last the heavenly choir,
   O, may the joy-inspiring theme
   Awake our faith and warm desire.

   STEELE.

1228. L. M.

1. As when the weary traveler gains
   The hight of some o'erlooking hill,
   His heart revives, if, 'cross the plains,
   He eyes his home, though distant still.

2. So when the Christian pilgrim views,
   By faith, his mansion in the skies,
   The sight his fainting strength renews,
   And wings his speed to reach the prize.

3. 'T is there, he says, I am to dwell
   With Jesus in the realms of day;
   Then shall I bid my cares farewell,
   And He will wipe my tears away.

   NEWTON.

1229. L. M.

1. THERE is a land mine eye hath seen,
   In visions of enraptured thought,
   So bright, that all which spreads between
   Is with its radiant glories fraught.

2. A land, upon whose blissful shore
   There rests no shadow, falls no stain;
   There those who meet shall part no more,
   And those long parted meet again.

3. Its skies are not like earthly skies,
   With varying hues of shade and light;
   It hath no need of suns to rise
   To dissipate the gloom of night.

4. There sweeps no desolating wind
   Across that calm, serene abode;
   The wanderer there a home may find
   Within the paradise of God.

HEAVEN.

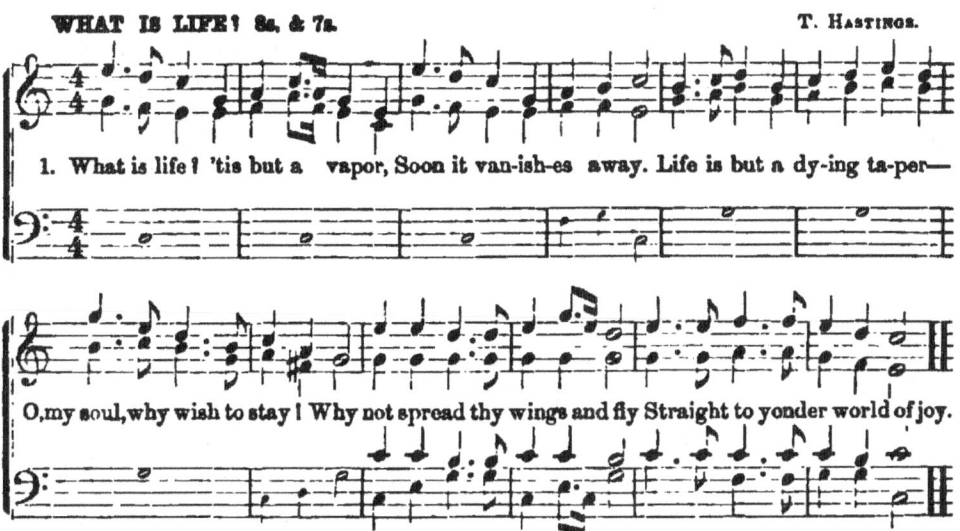

WHAT IS LIFE? 8s. & 7s. T. HASTINGS.

1. What is life? 'tis but a vapor, Soon it vanishes away. Life is but a dying taper—
O, my soul, why wish to stay! Why not spread thy wings and fly Straight to yonder world of joy.

1230. 8s & 7s.

2. See that glory, how resplendent!
   Brighter far than fancy paints;
   There, in majesty transcendent,
   Jesus reigns the King of saints.
      Why not spread, &c.

3. Joyful crowds, His throne surrounding,
   Sing with rapture of His love;
   Through the heavens His praise resound-
   Filling all the courts above.   [ing,
      Why not spread, &c.

4. Go, and share His people's glory,
   'Midst the ransomed crowd appear;
   Thine a joyful, wondrous story,
   One that angels love to hear.
      Why not spread, &c.

1231. 8s & 7s.

1. SISTER, thou wast mild and lovely,
   Gentle as the summer breeze,
   Pleasant as the air of evening,
   When it floats among the trees.

2. Peaceful be thy silent slumber—
   Peaceful in the grave so low;
   Thou no more wilt join our number;
   Thou no more our songs shalt know.

3. Dearest sister, thou hast left us,
   Here thy loss we deeply feel;
   But 't is God that hath bereft us,
   He can all our sorrows heal.

4. Yet again we hope to meet thee,
   When the day of life is fled;
   Then in heaven with joy to greet thee,
   Where no farewell tear is shed.

   S. F. SMITH.

1232. 8s, 7s & 4s.

1. HALLELUJAH! best and sweetest
   Of the hymns of praise above!
   Hallelujah! thou repeatest,
   Angel-host, these notes of love;
      This ye utter,
   While your golden harps ye move.

2. Hallelujah! church victorious,
   Join the concert of the sky!
   Hallelujah! bright and glorious,
   Lift, ye saints, this strain on high!
      We, poor exiles,
   Join not yet your melody.

3. Hallelujah! strains of gladness
   Comfort not the faint and worn;
   Hallelujah! sounds of sadness
   Best become the heart forlorn;
      Our offenses
   We with bitter tears must mourn.

4. But our earnest supplication,
   Holy God! we raise to Thee;
   Visit us with Thy salvation,
   Make us all Thy peace to see!
      Hallelujah!
   Ours at length this strain shall be.

   BREVIARY.

HEAVEN.

METROPOLIS. C. M. — Modern Harp.

1. Je-ru-sa-lem! my glorious home, Name ever dear to me! When shall my labors have an end, In joy, and peace, and Thee! 2. When shall these eyes Thy heaven-built walls And pearly gates behold! Thy bulwarks with salvation strong, And streets of shining gold!

1233. C. M.

3. There happier bowers than Eden's bloom,
   Nor sin nor sorrow know:
   Blessed seats! through rude and stormy
        scenes
   I onward press to you.

4. Why should I shrink at pain and woe?
   Or feel, at death, dismay?
   I've Canaan's goodly land in view,
   And realms of endless day.

5. Apostles, martyrs, prophets there,
   Around my Saviour stand;
   And soon my friends in Christ below
   Will join the glorious band.

6. Jerusalem! my glorious home!
   My soul still pants for Thee;
   Then shall my labors have an end,
   When I Thy joys shall see.

1234. C. M.

1. Lo! what a glorious sight appears
   To our believing eyes!
   The earth and seas are passed away,
   And the old rolling skies.

2. From the third heaven, where God resides,
   That holy, happy place,
   The new Jerusalem comes down,
   Adorned with shining grace.

3. Attending angels shout for joy,
   And the bright armies sing,—
   "Mortals, behold the sacred seat
   Of your descending King.

4. "The God of glory down to men
   Removes His blest abode;
   Men, the dear objects of His grace,
   And He the loving God.

5. "His own kind hand shall wipe the tears
   From every weeping eye;
   And pains, and groans, and griefs, and
   And death itself, shall die." [fears,

6. How long, dear Saviour, O how long
   Shall this bright hour delay?
   Fly swifter round, ye wheels of time,
   And bring the welcome day.   WATTS.

HEAVEN.

1235. C. M.

1. And let this feeble body fail,
    And let it faint or die;
  My soul shall quit this mournful vale,
    And soar to worlds on high.
  Shall join the disembodied saints,
    And find its long-sought rest:
  That only bliss for which it pants,
    In the Redeemer's breast.

2. In hope of that immortal crown
    I now the cross sustain;
  And gladly wander up and down,
    And smile at toil and pain.
  I suffer on my threescore years,
    Till my Deliverer come,
  And wipe away His servant's tears,
    And take His exile home.

3. O what hath Jesus bought for me?
    Before my ravished eye,
  Rivers of life divine I see,
    And trees of Paradise!
  I see a world of spirits bright,
    Who taste the pleasures there!
  They all are robed in spotless white,
    And conquering palms they bear.

4. O, what are all my sufferings here,
    If, Lord, Thou count me meet,
  With that enraptured host t' appear,
    And worship at Thy feet!
  Give joy or grief, give ease or pain,
    Take life or friends away;
  But let me find them all again
    In that eternal day.
                                C. WESLEY.

1236. C. M.

1. There is a state unknown, unseen,
    Where parted souls must be;
  And but a step doth lie between
    That world of souls and me.

2. I see no light, I hear no sound,
    When midnight shades are spread;
  Yet angels pitch their tents around
    And guard my quiet bed.

3. The things unseen, O God, reveal;
    My spirit's vision clear,
  Till I shall feel, and see, and know,
    That those I love are near.

4. Impart the faith that soars on high,
    Beyond this earthly strife;
  That holds sweet converse with the sky,
    And lives eternal life.
                                J. TAYLOR.

1237. C. M.

1. Ye weary, heavy-laden souls,
    Who are oppressed sore,
  Ye travelers through the wilderness,
    To Canaan's peaceful shore;
  Through chilling winds, and beating rain,
    And waters deep and cold,
  And enemies surrounding you,
    Take courage and be bold!

2. For Canaan's land is just before,
    Sweet spring is coming on,
  A few more beating winds and rains,
    And winter will be gone.
  Methinks I now begin to see
    The borders of that land;
  The trees of life, with heavenly fruit,
    In beauteous order stand.

3. O what a glorious sight appears
    To my believing eyes;
  Methinks I see Jerusalem,
    A city in the skies:
  Bright angels whispering me away—
    "O come, my brother, come!"
  And I am willing to be gone
    To my eternal home.

1238. C. M.

1. Soon in the grave my flesh shall rest,
    My soul from earth remove,
  And, in the Saviour's glory dressed,
    Shall reach the home I love.

2. My friends—the whole celestial choir;
    My every feeling—joy;
  To honor God—my one desire;
    His praise—my one employ.

3. Nor would I wait till angel-host
    Shall teach their song to raise:
  To Father, Son, and Holy Ghost,
    I'll here begin my praise.

4. Now to our God, the Father, Son,
    And Holy Spirit, sing!
  With praise to God, the Three in One,
    Let all creation ring!

Doxology. C. M.

In hope to join th' angelic host,
  And all the ransomed throng,
To Father, Son, and Holy Ghost,
  We raise the grateful song.

HEAVEN.

RHINE. C. M. — German Melody.

1. O mother dear, Jerusalem, When shall I come to thee? When shall my sorrows have an end? Thy joys when shall I see? Thy joys when shall I see?

1239. C. M.

2. O happy harbor of God's saints!
O sweet and pleasant soil!
In thee no sorrow can be found,
Nor grief, nor care, nor toil.

3. No dimly cloud o'ershadows thee,
Nor gloom, nor darksome night;
But every soul shines as the sun,
For God himself gives light.

4. Thy walls are made of precious stone,
Thy bulwarks diamond-square,
Thy gates are all of orient pearl—
O God! if I were there!

5. O my sweet home, Jerusalem!
Thy joys when shall I see?—
The King that sitteth on thy throne
In His felicity?

6. Thy gardens and thy goodly walks
Continually are green,
Where grow such sweet and pleasant
As no where else are seen. [flowers

7. Right thro' thy streets with pleasing sound
The flood of life doth flow;
And on the banks, on either side,
The trees of life do grow.

8. Those trees each month yield ripened fruit;
For evermore they spring,
And all the nations of the earth
To thee their honors bring.

9. O mother dear, Jerusalem!
When shall I come to thee?
When shall my sorrows have an end?
Thy joys when shall I see?
QUARLES.

1240. C. M.

1. Lo! I behold the scattering shades,
The dawn of heaven appears;
The sweet, immortal morning spreads
Its blushes round the spheres.

2. I see the Lord of glory come,
And flaming guards around;
The skies divide to make him room,
The trumpet shakes the ground!

3. I hear the voice—"Ye dead, arise!"
And lo! the graves obey;
And waking saints, with joyful eyes,
Salute th' expected day.

4. They leave the dust, and on the wing
Rise to the midway air;
In shining garments meet their King,
And low adore Him there.

5. O may our humble spirits stand
Among them clothed in white!
The meanest place at His right hand
Is infinite delight.

6. How will our joy and wonder rise,
When our returning King
Shall bear us homeward, through the skies,
On love's triumphant wing!
WATTS.

HEAVEN.

1241. C. M.

1. These glorious minds, how bright they shine,
   Whence all their white array?
   How came they to the happy seats
   Of everlasting day?

2. From torturing pains to endless joys,
   On fiery wheels they rode,
   And strangely washed their raiment white
   In Jesus' dying blood.

3. Now they approach a spotless God,
   And bow before His throne;
   Their warbling harps and sacred songs
   Adore the holy One.

4. The unvailed glories of His face
   Among His saints reside;
   While the rich treasure of His grace
   Sees all their wants supplied.

5. Tormenting thirst shall leave their souls,
   And hunger flee as fast;
   The fruit of life's immortal tree
   Shall be their sweet repast.

6. The Lamb shall lead His heavenly flock
   Where living fountains rise;
   And love divine shall wipe away
   The sorrows of their eyes.
   WATTS.

1242. C. M.

1. There is a place of sacred rest,
   Far, far beyond the skies,
   Where beauty smiles eternally,
   And pleasure never dies.

2. When tossed upon the waves of life,
   With fear on every side—
   When fiercely howls the gathering storm,
   And foams the angry tide—

3. Beyond the storm, beyond the gloom,
   Breaks forth the light of morn,
   Bright beaming from my Father's house,
   To cheer the soul forlorn.

4. The vision of that heavenly home,
   Shall cheer the parting soul,
   And o'er it, mounting to the skies,
   A tide of rapture roll.

5. For there, adieus are sounds unknown,
   Death frowns not on that scene,
   But life and glorious beauty shine
   Untroubled and serene.

1243. C. M.

1. Answer me, burning stars of night!
   Where is the spirit gone,
   That, past the reach of human sight,
   E'en as a breeze hath flown?

2. O many-toned and chainless wind!
   Thou art a wanderer free;
   Tell me, if thou its place canst find,
   Far over mount and sea?

3. Ye clouds, that gorgeously repose
   Around the setting sun,
   Answer! have ye a home for those
   Whose earthly race is run?

4. O speak, thou voice of God within!
   Thou of the deep, low tone!
   Answer me, through life's restless din,
   Where is the spirit flown?

5. And the voice answers, "Be thou still;
   Enough to know is given;
   Clouds, winds, and stars their part fulfill;
   Thine is to trust in Heaven!"
   HEMANS.

1244. C. M.

1. Give me the wings of faith, to rise
   Within the vail, and see
   The saints above—how great their joys!
   How bright their glories be!

2. Once they were mourning here below,
   And wet their couch with tears;
   They wrestled hard, as we do now,
   With sins, and doubts, and fears.

3. I ask them whence their victory came;
   They, with united breath,
   Ascribe their conquest to the Lamb,
   Their triumph to His death.

4. They marked the footsteps that He trod,
   His zeal inspired their breast;
   And, following their incarnate God,
   Possess the promised rest.

5. Our glorious Leader claims our praise
   For His own pattern given,
   While the long cloud of witnesses
   Show the same path to heaven.
   WATTS.

Doxology. C. M.

In hope to join th' angelic host,
And all the ransomed throng,
To Father, Son, and Holy Ghost,
We raise the grateful song.

HEAVEN.

HOLSTEIN. C. M. — Psalmodist.

1. Ye golden lamps of heaven, farewell, With all your feeble light; Farewell, thou ever changing moon, Pale empress of the night.

1245. C. M.

1. YE golden lamps of heaven, farewell,
With all your feeble light;
Farewell, thou ever-changing moon,
Pale empress of the night.

2. And thou, refulgent orb of day,
In brightest flames arrayed,
My soul, that springs beyond thy sphere,
No more demands thine aid.

3. Ye stars are but the shining dust
Of my divine abode,
The pavement of those heavenly courts,
Where I shall reign with God.

4. The Father of eternal light
Shall there His beams display;
Nor shall one moment's darkness mix
With that unvaried day.

5. No more the drops of piercing grief
Shall swell into my eyes;
Nor the meridian sun decline
Amid those brighter skies.

6. There all the millions of His saints
Shall in one song unite,
And each the bliss of all shall view,
With infinite delight.
DODDRIDGE.

1246. C. M.

1. THERE is a land of pure delight,
Where saints immortal reign:
Infinite day excludes the night,
And pleasures banish pain.

2. There everlasting spring abides,
And never-withering flowers;
Death, like a narrow sea, divides
This heavenly land from ours.

3. Sweet fields, beyond the swelling flood,
Stand dressed in living green;
So to the Jews old Canaan stood,
While Jordan rolled between.

4. But timorous mortals start and shrink
To cross this narrow sea,
And linger, shivering on the brink,
And fear to launch away.

5. Oh, could we make our doubts remove,
Those gloomy doubts that rise,
And see the Canaan that we love,
With unbeclouded eyes:—

6. Could we but climb where Moses stood,
And view the landscape o'er,—
Not Jordan's stream, nor death's cold flood,
Should fright us from the shore.
WATTS.

1247. C. M.

1. OUR country is Immanuel's ground—
We seek that promised soil;
The songs of Zion cheer our hearts,
While strangers here we toil.

2. Oft do our eyes with joy o'erflow,
And oft are bathed in tears;
Yet naught but heaven our hopes can raise,
And naught but sin our fears.

3. The flowers that spring along the road
    We scarcely stoop to pluck;
    We walk o'er beds of shining ore,
    Nor waste one wishful look.

4. We tread the path our Master trod;
    We bear the cross He bore;
    And every thorn that wounds our feet
    His temples pierced before.
                                BARBAULD.

1248. C. M.

1. ARISE, my soul, fly up, and run
    Through every heavenly street;
    And say there's nought below the sun
    That's worthy of thy feet.

2. There, on a high, majestic throne,
    Th' Almighty Father reigns,
    And sheds His glorious goodness down
    On all the blissful plains.

3. Bright, like a sun, the Saviour sits,
    And spreads eternal noon;
    No evenings there, nor gloomy nights,
    To want the feeble moon.

4. Amidst those ever-shining skies
    Behold the sacred Dove;
    While banished sin and sorrow flies
    From all the realms of love.

5. But O, what beams of heavenly grace
    Transport them all the while!
    Ten thousand smiles from Jesus' face,
    And love in every smile!

6. Jesus, and when shall that dear day,
    That joyful hour appear,
    When I shall leave this house of clay,
    To dwell among them there?
                                WATTS.

1249. C. M.

1. EARTH has engrossed my love too long!
    'Tis time I lift mine eyes
    Upward, dear Father, to Thy throne,
    And to my native skies.

2. There the blessed Man, my Saviour sits;
    The God! how bright He shines!
    And scatters infinite delights
    On all the happy minds.

3. Seraphs, with elevated strains,
    Circle the throne around;
    And move and charm the starry plains,
    With an immortal sound.

4. Jesus, the Lord, their harps employs;
    Jesus my love they sing!
    Jesus, the life of all our joys,
    Sounds sweet from every string.

5. Now let me mount and join their song,
    And be an angel, too;
    My heart, my hand, my ear, my tongue,—
    Here's joyful work for you.

6. I would begin the music here,
    And so my soul should rise;
    O for some heavenly notes to bear
    My passions to the skies!

7. There ye that love my Saviour sit,
    There I would fain have place,
    Among your thrones, or at your feet,
    So I might see His face.
                                WATTS.

1250. C. M.

1. THERE is a glorious world of light,
    Above the starry sky,
    Where saints departed, clothed in white,
    Adore the Lord most high.

2. And hark! amid the sacred songs
    Those heavenly voices raise,
    Ten thousand thousand infant tongues
    Unite in perfect praise.

3. Those are the hymns that we shall know,
    If Jesus we obey:
    That is the place where we shall go,
    If found in wisdom's way.

4. Soon will our earthly race be run,
    Our mortal frame decay;
    Parents and children, one by one,
    Must die and pass away.

5. Great God, impress the serious thought,
    This day, on every breast,
    That both the teachers and the taught
    May enter to Thy rest.
                                JANE TAYLOR.

DOXOLOGY. C. M.

Through the everlasting ages,
    Blessed Trinity, to Thee!
Father, Son, and Holy Spirit,
    Praise and endless glory be.

HEAVEN.

IVES. 7s. E. Ives, Jr. Beethoven Collection.

1. Who are these in bright ar-ray, This in-nu-mer-a-ble throng. Round the al-tar, night and day, Hymn-ing one tri-umphant song!— "Wor-thy is the Lamb once slain, Bless-ing, hon-or, glo-ry, power, Wis-dom, rich-es, to ob-tain; New do-min-ion ev-ery hour."

1251. 7s.

2. These through fiery trials trod!—
   Those from great affliction came;
Now before the throne of God,
   Sealed with His almighty name,
Clad in raiment pure and white,
   Victor palms in every hand,
Through their dear Redeemer's might,
   More than conquerors they stand.

3. Hunger, thirst, disease unknown,
   On immortal fruits they feed;
Them, the Lamb amid the throne,
   Shall to living fountains lead;
Joy and gladness banish sighs;
   Perfect love dispels all fears;
And for ever from their eyes
   God shall wipe away the tears.
MONTGOMERY.

1252. 7s.

1. Palms of glory, raiment bright,
   Crowns that never fade away,
Gird and deck the saints in light;
   Priests, and kings, and conquerors, they.

2. Yet the conquerors bring their palms
   To the Lamb amid the throne;
And proclaim, in joyful psalms,
   Victory through His cross alone.

3. Kings for harps their crowns resign,
   Crying, as they strike the chords—
   "Take the kingdom; it is thine,
   King of kings, and Lord of Lords."

4. Round the altar priests confess,
   If their robes are white as snow,
   'T was their Saviour's righteousness,
   And His blood, that made them so.

5. Who are these? On earth they dwelt,
   Sinners once of Adam's race;
   Guilt, and fear, and suffering felt,
   But were saved by sovereign grace.

6. They were mortal, too, like us;
   Ah! when we, like them, shall die,
   May our souls, translated thus,
   Triumph, reign, and shine, on high!
   MONTGOMERY.

1253. 7s.

1. WHO are these arrayed in white,
   Brighter than the noon-day sun?
   Foremost of the sons of light;
   Nearest the eternal throne?
   These are they that bore the cross;
   Nobly for their Master stood;
   Sufferers in His righteous cause;
   Followers of the dying God.

2. Out of great distress they came;
   Washed their robes, by faith, below,
   In the blood of yonder Lamb—
   Blood that washes white as snow;
   Therefore are they next the throne;
   Serve their Maker day and night;
   God resides among His own,
   God doth in His saints delight.
   C. WESLEY.

1254. 7s.

1. DEATHLESS principle, arise;
   Soar, thou native of the skies;
   Pearl of price, by Jesus bought,
   To His glorious likeness wrought,
   Go to shine before His throne,
   Deck His mediatorial crown;
   Go, His triumphs to adorn,
   Born of God—to God return.

2. Burst thy shackles, drop thy clay,
   Sweetly breathe thyself away;
   Singing, to thy crown remove,
   Swift of wing, and fired with love.
   Shudder not to pass the stream;
   Venture all thy care on Him;
   Him, whose dying love and power
   Stilled its tossing, hushed its roar.

3. Saints in glory perfect made,
   Wait thy passage through the shade;
   Ardent for thy coming o'er,
   See, they throng the blissful shore;
   Mount, their transports to improve,
   Join the longing choir above;
   Swiftly to their wish be given,
   Kindle higher joy in heaven.
   TOPLADY.

1255. 7s.

1. LIFT your eyes of faith, and see
   Saints and angels joined in one;
   What a countless company
   Stand before yon dazzling throne!
   Each before his Saviour stands,
   All in milk-white robes arrayed;
   Palms they carry in their hands,
   Crowns of glory on their head.

2. Saints, begin the endless song;
   Cry aloud, in heavenly lays—
   Glory doth to God belong;
   God the glorious Saviour praise;
   All salvation from Him came—
   Him who reigns enthroned on high;
   Glory to the bleeding Lamb—
   Let the morning stars reply.

3. Angel powers the throne surround;
   Next the saints in glory they;
   Lulled with the transporting sound,
   They their silent homage pay;
   Prostrate on their face, before
   God and His Messiah fall;
   Then in hymns of praise adore—
   Shout the Lamb that died for all.
   C. WESLEY.

1256. 7s.

1. MUCH in sorrow, oft in woe,
   Onward, Christians, onward go;
   Fight the fight; and, worn with strife,
   Steep with tears the bread of life.

2. Onward, Christians, onward go;
   Join the war, and face the foe;
   Faint not; much doth yet remain;
   Dreary is the long campaign.

3. Shrink not, Christians,—will ye yield?
   Will ye quit the battle-field?
   Fight till all the conflict's o'er,
   Nor your foes shall rally more.

4. But when loud the trumpet blown,
   Speaks their forces overthrown,
   Christ, your Captain, shall bestow
   Crowns to grace the conqueror's brow.
   H. K. WHITE.

HEAVEN.

I'M A PILGRIM.   Hymn 1257. P. M.

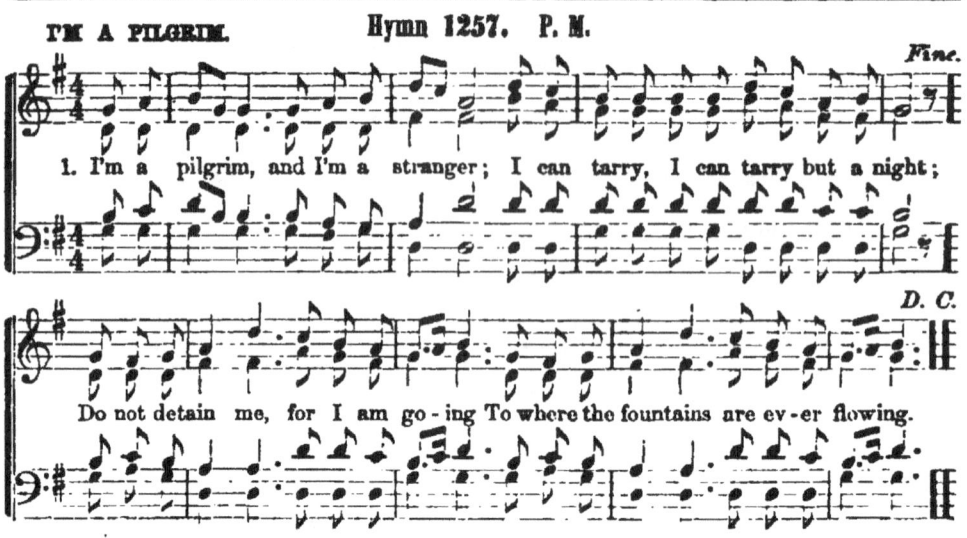

1. I'm a pilgrim, and I'm a stranger; I can tarry, I can tarry but a night;
Do not detain me, for I am going To where the fountains are ev-er flowing.

2. There the glory is ever shining!
O, my longing heart, my longing heart is there;
Here in this country so dark and dreary,
I long have wandered forlorn and weary.

3. There's the city to which I journey;
My Redeemer, my Redeemer is its light!
There is no sorrow, nor any sighing,
Nor any tears there, nor any dying!

MERDIN. 7s, 6s & 7s.   Hymn 1258.   L. MASON.

1. Burst, ye emerald gates, and bring To my raptured vision,
All the ecstatic joys that spring Round the bright elysian:
Lo! we lift our longing eyes,
Break, ye intervening skies! Sons of righteousness, arise, Ope the gates of Paradise.

2. Floods of everlasting light!
   Freely flash before Him:
Myriads, with supreme delight,
   Instantly adore Him;
Angelic trumps resound His fame;
Lutes of lucid gold proclaim
All the music of His name;
Heaven echoing the theme.

3. Four and twenty elders rise
   From their princely station;
Shout His glorious victories,
   Sing the great salvation;
Cast their crowns before His throne,
Cry, in reverential tone,
Glory be to God alone,
Holy! Holy! Holy One.

4. Hark! the thrilling symphonies
   Seem, methinks, to seize us;
Join we too the holy lays—
   Jesus, Jesus, Jesus!
Sweetest sound in seraph's song,
Sweetest note on mortal tongue,
Sweetest carol ever sung—
Jesus, Jesus, flow along.

HEAVEN.

PARADISE. 6s.

1. Oh, exiled Paradise, Oh, how we long for thee! When wilt thou robe the earth! When plant life's healing tree! Thou hast fresh blooming vales, Where glittering fountains play, And sweet sequestered dales Hid in thy groves away!

D.C. Oh, for thy smiling hills, With gush of clear cascade! For ever flowing rills, By living waters made!

1259. 6s.

2. Oh for thy fragrant flowers,
   That bloom through all the year!
   Oh for thy rosy bowers,
   The wilderness to cheer!
   To thee we shall return,
   And to Mount Zion come!
   With songs sing joyfully,
   And shout the harvest home!
   Awake the harp and lute,
   In praises to the King
   Who reigns on David's throne,
   To Him hosannas bring!

3. Jesus shall ever reign!
   When His bright kingdom comes
   The sun shall be ashamed
   Before His dazzling thrones!
   The moon confounded, then,
   Shall hide her silver ray,
   And saints of every age,
   Rejoice in glorious day!
   Oh, exiled Paradise,
   Oh, how we long for thee!
   Robe thou anew the earth—
   Bring back Life's healing tree.

1260. 7s & 6s.*

1. In the broad fields of heaven,
   In the immortal bowers
   By life's clear river side,
   Amid undying flowers—
   There hosts of beauteous souls,
   Fair children of the earth,
   Linked in bright bands of love,
   Sing of their human birth.

2. They sing of earth and heaven—
   Divinest voices rise
   To God, their gracious Lord,
   Who called them to the skies:
   They all are there—in heaven—
   Safe, safe, and sweetly blest;
   No cloud of sin can dim
   Their bright and holy rest.

* Repeat the last half of the stanza for the D C.

HEAVEN.

HOLY CITY. 7s & 6s.   Arr. from a Western Melody.

1. There is a ho-ly ci-ty, A hap-py world above, Be-yond the starry re-gions, Built by the God of love; An ev-er-last-ing tem-ple, And saints arrayed in white, There serve their great Redeemer, And dwell with Him in light.

1261.   7s & 6s.

1. There is a holy city,
    A happy world above,
Beyond the starry regions,
    Built by the God of love;
An everlasting temple,
    And saints arrayed in white,
There serve their great Redeemer,
    And dwell with Him in light.

2. The meanest child of glory
    Outshines the radiant sun;
But who can speak the splendor
    Of that eternal throne,
Where Jesus sits exalted,
    In godlike majesty?
The elders fall before Him,
    The angels bend the knee.

3. Is this the Man of sorrows,
    Who stood at Pilate's bar,
Condemned by haughty Herod,
    And by his men of war?
He seems a mighty conqueror,
    Who spoiled the powers below,
And ransomed many captives
    From everlasting woe!

4. The hosts of saints around Him
    Proclaim His work of grace;
The patriarchs and prophets,
    And all the godly race,
Who speak of fiery trials
    And tortures on their way—
They came from tribulation
    To everlasting day.

5. And what shall be my journey,
    How long I'll stay below,
Or what shall be my trials,
    Are not for me to know;
In every day of trouble,
    I'll raise my thoughts on high;
I'll think of the bright temple,
    And crowns above the sky.

HEAVEN.

MT. BLANC. 6s & 7s.

1. We are on our journey home, Where Christ our Lord is gone; We shall meet around His throne, When He makes His people one In the new, In the new Jerusalem. In the new Jerusalem.

1262. 7s & 6s.

2. We can see that distant home,
   Tho' clouds rise dark between;
   Faith views the radiant dome,
   And a luster flashes keen
      From the new Jerusalem.

3. O glory shining far
   From the never setting Sun!
   O trembling morning star!
   Our journey's almost done
      To the new Jerusalem.

4. O holy, heavenly home!
   O, rest eternal there!
   When shall the exiles come,
   Where they cease from earthly care,
      In the new Jerusalem.

5. Our hearts are breaking now
   Those mansions fair to see;
   O Lord! Thy heavens bow,
   And raise us up with Thee
      To the new Jerusalem.

CH. BEECHER.

GLORY. 7s & 6s.

1. We shall see a light appear, By and by, when He comes; We shall see him full and clear, By and by, when he comes; Ride on, Jesus, O ride on! We are on our journey home.

1263. 7s & 6s.

2. We shall have a mighty shout,
      By and by, when He comes;
   We shall like the stars shine out,
      By and by, when He comes.

3. Then shall blaze earth's funeral pyre,
      By and by, when He comes;
   We shall shout above the fire,
      By and by, when He comes.

HEAVEN.

HOME. 11s.

1. 'Mid scenes of confusion and creature complaints,
How sweet to my soul is communion with saints;
To find at the banquet of mercy there's room,
And feel in the presence of Jesus at home.
Home, home, sweet, sweet home;
Prepare me, dear Saviour, for glory, my home.

1264. 11s.

2. Sweet bonds that unite all the children of peace!
And thrice precious Jesus, whose love can not cease!
Though oft from Thy presence in sadness I roam,
I long to behold Thee in glory, at home.

3. I sigh from this body of sin to be free,
Which hinders my joy and communion with Thee:
Though now my temptation like billows may foam,
All, all will be peace, when I'm with Thee at home.

4. While here in the valley of conflict I stay,
O give me submission, and strength as my day;
In all my afflictions to Thee would I come,
Rejoicing in hope of my glorious home.

5. Whate'er Thou deniest, O give me Thy grace.
The Spirit's sure witness, and smiles of Thy face;
Endue me with patience to wait at Thy throne,
And find, even now, a sweet foretaste of home.

6. I long, dearest Lord, in Thy beauties to shine;
No more as an exile in sorrow to pine;
And in Thy dear image arise from the tomb,
With glorified millions to praise Thee at home.

1265. 10s.

1. O WHERE can the soul find relief from its foes!
A shelter of safety, a home of repose!
Can earth's highest summit, or deepest hid vale,
Give a refuge, nor sorrow nor sin can assail!
No, no! there's no home!
There's no home on earth—the soul has no home

2. Shall it leave the low earth, and soar to the sky,
And seek for a home in the mansions on high!
In the bright realms of bliss will a dwelling be given,
And the soul find a home in the glory of heaven!
Yes, yes! there's a home!
There's a home in high heaven—the soul has a home.

3. O! holy and sweet its rest shall be there!
Free for ever from sin, and from sorrow and care;
And the loud hallelujahs of angels shall rise,
To welcome the soul to its home in the skies!
Home, home!—home of the soul!
The bosom of God is the home of the soul!

DEODATUS DUTTON.

1266. 11s.*

1. My home is in heaven, my rest is not here,
Then why should I murmur when trials appear!
Be hushed, my dark spirit, the worst that can come,
But shortens thy journey, and hastens thee home.

2. It is not for thee to be seeking thy bliss.
And building thy hopes in a region like this;
I look for a city which hands have not piled;
I pant for a country by sin undefiled.

3. The thorn and the thistle around me may grow,
I would not recline upon roses below;
I ask not my portion, I seek not my rest,
Till I find them for ever on Jesus's breast.

* Sing either to Home or to Eden, on the opposite page.

HEAVEN.

EDEN. 12s & 11s.

1. How sweet to reflect on the joys that await me In yon blissful region, the haven of rest.
Where glorified spirits with welcome shall greet me, And lead me to mansions prepared for the blest;
Encircled with light, and with glory enshrouded, My happiness perfect, my mind's sky unclouded,
I'll bathe in the ocean of pleasure unbounded, And range with delight thro' the Eden of Love.

1267. 11s & 12s.

2. While angelic legions, with harps tuned celestial,
   Harmoniously join in the concert of praise,
The saints as they flock from the regions terrestrial,
   In loud hallelujahs their voices will raise;
Then songs to the Lamb shall re-echo thro' heaven,
My soul will respond, To Immanuel be given
All glory, all honor, all might and dominion,
   Who brought us thro' grace to the Eden of Love.

3. Then hail, blessed state! hail, ye songsters of glory!
   Ye harpers of bliss, soon I'll meet you above!
And join your full choir in rehearsing the story,
   "Salvation from sorrow, through Jesus's love;"
Though 'prisoned in earth, yet by anticipation,
Already my soul feels a sweet prelibation
Of joys that await me, when freed from probation;
   My heart's now in Heaven, the Eden of Love.

HEAVEN.

1268. 5s.

1. There's rest in the grave,
Life's toils are all past,
Night cometh at last:
How calmly I rest
In the sleep of the blest,
Nor hear life's storm rave
O'er my green, grassy grave.

2. No rest in the grave—
Heaven's dawn purples fast,
Morn's splendors are cast
Like shafts through the gloom
Of the dark, silent tomb;
Heaven's fair bowers wave—
No rest in the grave!

3. Arise from the grave!
Heaven's bright, burning throng
Come rushing along;
They gird me about,
And triumphant shout,
As myriad palms wave,
"Ascend from the grave."

CH. BEECHER.

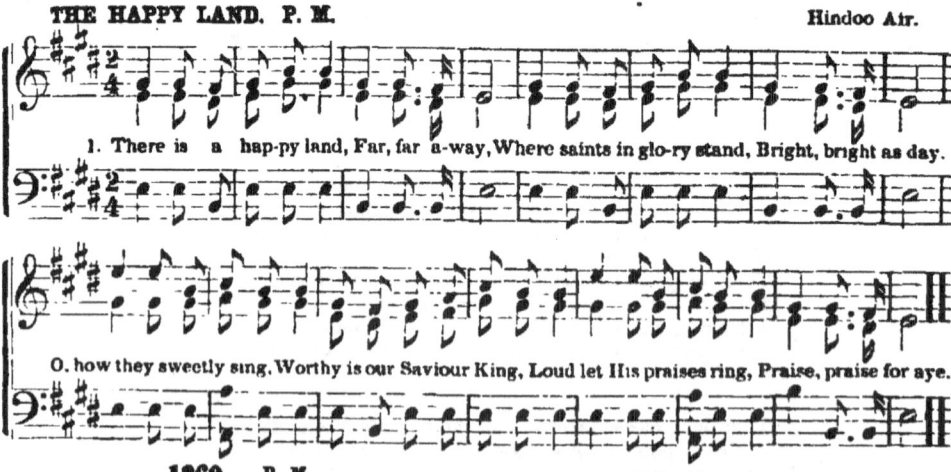

1269. P. M.

2. Come to that happy land, come, come away;
Why will ye doubting stand, why still delay?
Oh, we shall happy be,
When from sin and sorrow free!
Lord, we shall live with Thee,
Blest, blest for aye.

3. Bright, in that happy land, beams every eye;
Kept by a Father's hand, love cannot die.
Oh, then, to glory run;
Be a crown and kingdom won;
And bright, above the sun,
We reign for aye.

HEAVEN.

CHRISTIAN VICTOR. 10s.

Joy-ful-ly, joy-ful-ly on-ward I move, Bound to the land of bright spi-rits a-bove;
An-gel-ic chor-is-ters sing as I come, Joy-ful-ly, joy-ful-ly haste to thy home!
Soon with my pil-grimage end-ed be-low, Home to the land of bright spi-rits I go;
Pilgrim and stranger no more shall I roam, Joy-ful-ly, joy-ful-ly rest-ing at home.

1270. 10s.

1. JOYFULLY, joyfully onward I move,
Bound to the land of bright spirits above;
Angelic choristers, sing as I come—
Joyfully, joyfully haste to thy home!
Soon with my pilgrimage ended below,
Home to the land of bright spirits I go;
Pilgrim and stranger no more shall I roam:
Joyfully, joyfully resting at home.

2. Friends, fondly cherished, have passed on before;
Waiting, they watch me approaching the shore;
Singing to cheer me thro' death's chilling gloom:
Joyfully, joyfully haste to thy home.
Sounds of sweet melody fall on my ear;
Harps of the blessed, your voices I hear!
Rings with the harmony heaven's high dome—
Joyfully, joyfully haste to thy home.

3. Death, with thy weapons of war lay me low,
Strike, king of terrors! I fear not the blow;
Jesus hath broken the bars of the tomb!
Joyfully, joyfully will I go home.
Bright will the morn of eternity dawn,
Death shall be banished, his scepter be gone;
Joyfully, then, shall I witness his doom,
Joyfully, joyfully, safely at home.

1271. 10s.

1. HAPPY the spirit released from its clay;
Happy the soul that goes bounding away;
Singing, as upward it hastes to the skies,
Victory! victory! homeward I rise.
Many the toils it has passed through below,
Many the seasons of trial and woe;
Many the doubtings it never should sing,
Victory! victory! thus on the wing.

2. How can we wish them recalled from their home,
Longer in sorrowing exile to roam!
Safely they passed from their troubles beneath,
Victory! victory! shouting in death.
Thus let them slumber, till Christ from the skies,
Bids them in glorified body arise;
Singing, as upward they spring from the tomb,
Victory! victory! Jesus hath come.

HEAVEN.

TAPPAN. C. M. — Geo. Kingsley.

1. On Jordan's rug-ged banks I stand, And cast a wish-ful eye To Canaan's fair and hap-py land, To Canaan's fair and hap-py land, Where my pos-sess-ions lie.

1272. C. M.

2. O, the transporting, rapturous scene,
   That rises to my sight!
   Sweet fields arrayed in living green,
   And rivers of delight!

3. O'er all those wide extended plains
   Shines one eternal day;
   There God, the Sun, for ever reigns,
   And scatters night away.

4. No chilling winds, or poisonous breath,
   Can reach that healthful shore:
   Sickness and sorrow, pain and death,
   Are felt and feared no more.

5. When shall I reach that happy place,
   And be for ever blest?
   When shall I see my Father's face,
   And in His bosom rest?

6. Filled with delight, my raptured soul
   Can here no longer stay;
   Though Jordan's waves around me roll,
   Fearless I'd launch away.

   STENNETT.

1273. C. M.

1. A STRANGER in the world below,
   I calmly sojourn here;
   Nor can its happiness or woe
   Provoke my hope or fear;
   Its evils in a moment end;
   Its joys as soon are past;
   But O, the bliss to which I tend
   Eternally shall last!

2. To that Jerusalem above,
   With singing I repair;
   While in the flesh, my hope and love,
   My heart and soul, are there.
   There my exalted Saviour stands,
   My merciful High Priest;
   And still extends His wounded hands
   To take me to His breast.

   C. WESLEY.

1274. C. M.

1. O, THE delights, the heavenly joys,
   The glories of the place,
   Where Jesus sheds the brightest beams
   Of His o'erflowing grace!

2. Sweet majesty and awful love
   Sit smiling on His brow;
   And all the glorious ranks above
   At humble distance bow.

3. Archangels sound His lofty praise
   Through every heavenly street,
   And lay their highest honors down
   Submissive at His feet.

4. This is the Man, th' exalted Man,
   Whom we, unseen, adore;
   But when our eyes behold His face,
   Our hearts shall love Him more.

5. And while our faith enjoys this sight,
   We long to leave our clay;
   And wish Thy fiery chariots, Lord,
   To bear our souls away.

   WATTS.

HEAVEN.

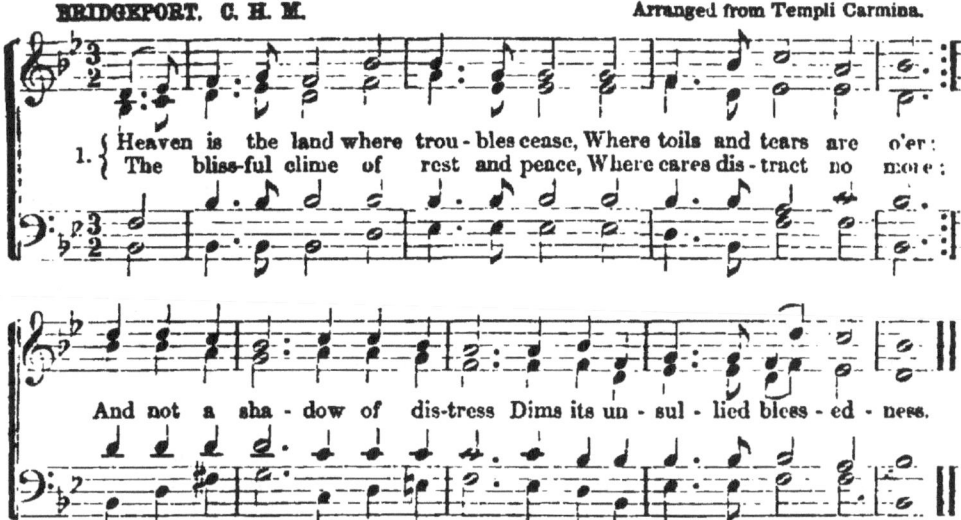

BRIDGEPORT. C. H. M.
Arranged from Templi Carmina.

1. Heaven is the land where troubles cease, Where toils and tears are o'er:
The blissful clime of rest and peace, Where cares distract no more:
And not a shadow of distress Dims its unsullied blessedness.

1275. C. H. M.

1. Heaven is the land where troubles cease,
   Where toils and tears are o'er;
   The blissful clime of rest and peace,
   Where cares distract no more;
   And not a shadow of distress
   Dims its unsullied blessedness.

2. Heaven is the place where Jesus dwells,
   And pleads His dying blood,
   While to His prayers His Father gives
   An unknown multitude—
   Whose harps and tongues, through endless days,
   Shall crown His head with songs of praise.

3. Heaven is the dwelling-place of joy,
   The home of light and love,
   Where faith and hope in rapture die,
   And ransomed souls above
   Enjoy, before their Father's throne,
   Bliss everlasting and unknown.

1276. C. M.*

1. AROUND the throne of God in heaven,
   Thousands of children stand;
   Children, whose sins are all forgiven,
   A holy, happy band.

2. What brought them to that world above,
   That heaven so bright and fair—
   Where all is peace, and joy, and love?
   How came those children there?

* Sing Tappan.

3. Because the Saviour shed His blood
   To wash away their sin;
   Bathed in that pure and precious flood,
   Behold them white and clean!

4. On earth they sought their Saviour's grace,
   On earth they loved His name;
   So now they see His blessed face,
   And stand before the Lamb.

1277. C. M.*

1. BRIGHT glories rush upon my sight,
   And charm my wondering eyes—
   The regions of immortal light,
   The beauties of the skies!

2. All hail! ye fair, celestial shores,
   Ye lands of endless day!
   A rich delight your prospect pours,
   And drives my griefs away.

3. There's a delightful clearness now;
   My clouds of doubt are gone;
   Fled is my former darkness, too;
   My fears are all withdrawn.

4. Short is the passage, short the space,
   Between my home and me;
   There, there behold the radiant place
   How near the mansions be!

5. Immortal wonders! boundless things
   In those dear worlds appear!
   Prepare me, Lord, to stretch my wings,
   And in those glories share.

VILLAGE HYMNS.

TIMES AND SEASONS.

NIGHT THOUGHT. L. M.   CH. BEECHER.

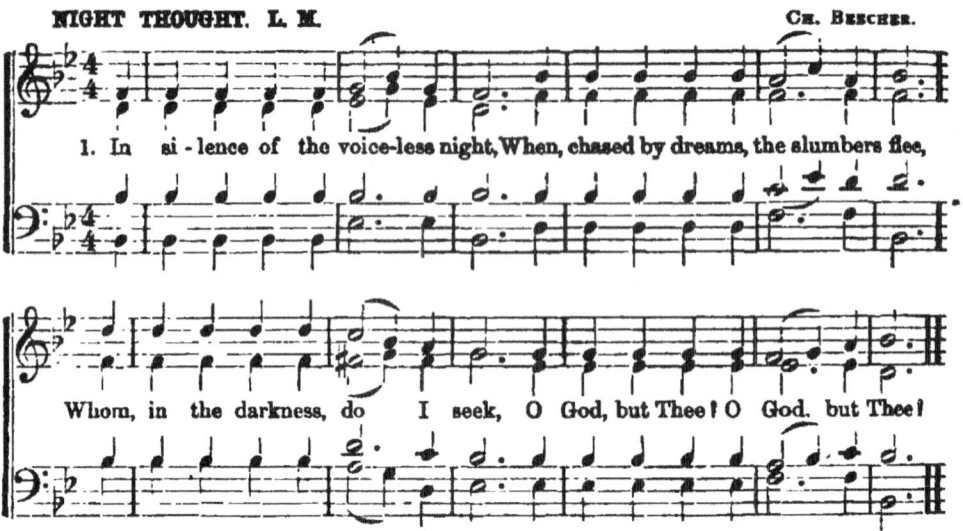

1. In silence of the voiceless night, When, chased by dreams, the slumbers flee,
Whom, in the darkness, do I seek, O God, but Thee! O God, but Thee!

1278. L. M.

2. And if there weigh upon my breast
Vague memories of the day forgone,
Scarce knowing why, I fly to Thee,
   And lay them down.

3. Or, if it be the gloom that comes,
In token of impending ill,
My bosom heeds not what it is
   Since 'tis Thy will.

4. For, O! in spite of constant care,
Or aught beside, how joyfully
I pass that solitary hour,
   My God, with Thee!

5. More tranquil than the stilly night,
More peaceful than that voiceless hour,
Supremely blest, my bosom lies
   Beneath Thy power.

6. For what on earth can I desire,
Of all it hath to offer me?
Or whom in heaven do I seek,
   O God, but Thee?

1279. L. M.

1. THE dawn is sprinkling in the east
   Its golden shower, as day flows in;
Fast mount the pointed shafts of light;—
   Farewell to darkness and to sin!

2. Away, ye midnight phantoms all!
   Away, despondence and despair!
Whatever guilt the night has brought,
   Now let it vanish into air.

3. So, Lord, when that last morning breaks,
   Which shrouds in darkness earth and
May it on us, low bending here,   [skies,
   Arrayed in joyful light arise!
                    LYRA CATH.

1280. L. M.

1. FORTH in Thy name, O Lord, we go,
   Our daily labor to pursue;
Thee, only Thee, resolved to know,
   In all we think, or speak, or do.

2. Still would we bear Thy easy yoke,
   And every moment watch and pray;
Would still to things eternal look,
   And hasten to Thy glorious day.

3. For Thee alone we would employ
   Whate'er Thy bounteous grace hath
      given;
Would run our course with even joy,
   And closely walk with Thee to heaven.
                    C. WESLEY.

1281. L. M.

1. O BACKWARD-LOOKING son of time!—
   The new is old, the old is new,
The cycle of a change sublime
   Still sweeping through.

2. Take heart!—the waster builds again—
   A charmed life old goodness hath;
The tares may perish—but the grain
   Is not for death.

3. God works in all things; all obey
   His first propulsion from the night;
Ho, wake and watch!—the world is gray
   With morning light!
                    WHITTIER.

TIMES AND SEASONS.

1282. L. M.

1. Eternity! Eternity!
   How long art thou, Eternity!
   Yet onward still to thee we speed,
   As to the fight th' impatient steed.

2. As ship to port, or shaft from bow,
   Or swift as couriers homeward go;
   Mark well, O man, Eternity!
   Eternity! Eternity!

3. Eternity! Eternity!
   How long art thou, Eternity!
   As in a ball's concentric round
   Nor starting-point nor end is found;

4. So thou, Eternity, so vast,
   No entrance and no exit hast;
   Mark well, O man, Eternity!
   Eternity! Eternity!
   COXE. FROM THE GERMAN.

1283. L. M.

1. I cannot always trace the way
      Where Thou, Almighty One, dost move;
   But I can always, always say,
      That God is love.

2. When fear her chilling mantle throws
      O'er earth, my soul to heaven above,
   As to her native home, upsprings,
      For God is love.

3. When mystery clouds my darkened path,
      I'll check my dread, my doubts reprove,
   In this my soul sweet comfort hath,
      That God is love.

4. Yes, God is love;—a thought like this
      Can every gloomy thought remove,
   And turn all tears, all woes, to bliss,
      For God is love.

1284. L. M.

1. Thy will be done! In devious way
      The hurrying stream of life may run;
   Yet still our grateful hearts shall say,
      Thy will be done!

2. Thy will be done! If o'er us shine
      A gladdening and a prosperous sun,
   This prayer shall make it more divine:—
      Thy will be done!

3. Thy will be done! Though shrouded o'er
      Our path with gloom, one comfort, one,
   Is ours—to breathe, while we adore,
      Thy will be done!
   BOWRING.

1285. L. M.

1. Rocked in the cradle of the deep,
   I lay me down in peace to sleep;
   Secure I rest upon the wave,
   For Thou, O Lord! hast power to save.

2. I know Thou wilt not slight my call!
   For Thou dost mark the sparrow's fall!
   And calm and peaceful is my sleep,
   Rocked in the cradle of the deep.

3. And such the trust that still were mine,
   Though stormy winds swept o'er the brine,
   Or though the tempest's fiery breath
   Roused me from sleep to wreck and death!

4. In ocean caves still safe with Thee,
   The germs of immortality;
   And calm and peaceful is my sleep,
   Rocked in the cradle of the deep.
   MRS. WILLARD.

1286. L. M.

1. Glory to Thee, whose powerful word
      Bids the tempestuous winds arise!
   Glory to Thee, the sovereign Lord
      Of air, and earth, and sea, and skies!

2. Let air, and earth, and skies obey,
      And seas Thine awful will perform;
   From them we learn to own Thy sway,
      And shout to meet the gathering storm.

3. What though the floods lift up their voice;
      Thou hearest, Lord, our louder cry;
   They can not damp Thy children's joys,
      Or shake the soul when God is nigh.

4. Headlong we cleave the yawning deep,
      And back to highest heaven are borne;
   Unmoved, though rapid whirlwinds sweep,
      And all the watery world upturn.

5. Roar on, ye waves: our souls defy
      Your roaring to disturb our rest;
   In vain t' impair the calm ye try—
      The calm in a believer's breast.

6. Rage, while our faith the Saviour tries,
      Thou sea, the servant of His will;
   Rise, while our God permits thee, rise,
      But fall, when He shall say,—Be still.
   C. WESLEY.

DOXOLOGY. L. M.

To God the Father, glory be,
   And to His sole-begotten Son;
The same, O Holy Ghost! to Thee,
   While everlasting ages run.

TIMES AND SEASONS.

TALLIS EVENING HYMN. L. M. Th. Tallis. 1650.

1. Glory to Thee, my God, this night, For all the blessings of the light: Keep me, O, keep me, King of kings, Beneath Thine own almighty wings.

1287. L. M.

2. Forgive me, Lord, for Thy dear Son,
The ill which I this day have done;
That with the world, myself, and Thee,
I, ere I sleep, at peace may be.

3. Teach me to live, that I may dread
The grave as little as my bed;
Teach me to die, that so I may
Rise glorious at Thy judgment-day.

4. O let my soul on Thee repose,
And may sweet sleep mine eyelids close!
Sleep, which shall me more vigorous make,
To serve my God when I awake.

5. Be Thou my guardian, while I sleep,
Thy watchful station near me keep;
My heart with love celestial fill,
And guard me from th' approach of ill.

6. Lord, let my soul for ever share
The bliss of Thy paternal care:
'T is heaven on earth, 't is heaven above,
To see Thy face, and sing Thy love!
KENN.

1288. L. M.

1. O BLEST Creator of the light!
Who dost the dawn from darkness bring,
And, framing nature's depth and hight,
Didst with the new-born light begin;

2. Who, gently blending eve with morn,
And morn with eve, didst call them day:
Thick flows the flood of darkness down:
O, hear us as we weep and pray!

3. Keep Thou our souls from schemes of crime;
Nor guilt remorseful let them know;
Nor, thinking but on things of time,
Into eternal darkness go.

4. Teach us to knock at heaven's high door;
Teach us the prize of life to win;
Teach us all evil to abhor,
And purify ourselves within.
LYRA CATH.

1289. L. M.

1. 'Tis gone, that bright and orbed blaze,
Fast fading from our wistful gaze;
Yon mantling cloud has hid from sight
The last faint pulse of quivering light.

2. Sun of my soul! Thou Saviour dear!
It is not night if Thou be near;
O, may no earth-born cloud arise
To hide Thee from Thy servant's eyes.

3. When the soft dews of kindly sleep
My wearied eyelids gently steep,
Be my last thought, how sweet to rest
For ever on my Saviour's breast.

4. Abide with me from morn till eve,
For without Thee I can not live;
Abide with me when night is nigh,
For without Thee I dare not die.

5. Come near and bless us when we wake,
Ere through the world our way we take:
Till in the ocean of Thy love
We lose ourselves in heaven above.
KEBLE.

TIMES AND SEASONS.

STONEFIELD. L. M.   STANLEY

1. Throughout the hours of darkness dim, Still let us watch and raise the hymn; And in deep mid-night's aw-ful calm, Pour forth the soul in deepest psalm.

1290. L. M.

2. Amid the silence, else so drear,
Think the Almighty leans to hear;
Well pleased to list, at such a time,
The wakeful heart, in praise sublime.

3. Still watch and pray, and raise the hymn,
Throughout the hours of darkness dim!
God will not spurn the humblest guest,
But give us of His holy rest.

4. Glory to God, who is in heaven!
Praise to His blessed Son be given!
Thee, Holy Spirit, we implore,
Be with us now and evermore!
BREVIARY.

1291. L. M.

1. ANOTHER fleeting day is gone;
Slow o'er the west the shadows rise;
Swift the soft-stealing hours have flown,
And night's dark mantle vails the skies.

2. Another fleeting day is gone;
In solemn silence rest, my soul!
Bow down before His awful throne,
Who bids the morn and evening roll.

3. Soon shall a darker night descend,
And vail from me yon azure skies;
And soon shall death's oppressive hand
Lie heavy on these languid eyes.

4. Yet when beneath the dreadful shade
I lay my weary frame to rest,
That night shall not make me afraid;
That bed the dying Saviour pressed.

5. Again emerging from the night,
I, like my risen Lord, shall rise;
Again drink in the morning light,
Pure at its fount above the skies.
COLLYER.

1292. L. M.

1. NOT worlds on worlds, in phalanx deep,
Need we to prove a God is here;
The daisy, fresh from winter's sleep,
Tells of His hand in lines as clear.

2. For who but He that arched the skies,
And pours the day-spring's living flood;
Wondrous alike in all He tries,
Could rear the daisy's purple bud;

3. Mold its green cup, its wiry stem,
Its fringed border nicely spin;
And cut the gold embossed gem,
That, set in silver, gleams within;

4. Then fling it, unrestrained and free,
O'er hill and dale, and desert sod,
That man, whene'er he walks, may see
In every step the stamp of God.
J. M. GOOD.

1293. C. M.

1. O THOU, the heaven's eternal King!
Lord of the starry spheres!
Who with the Father equal art
From everlasting years;

2. Eternal Shepherd! who Thy flock
In Thy pure Font dost lave,
Where souls are cleansed, and all their
Buried as in a grave;   [guilt

3. Anoint me with Thy heavenly grace,
Adopt me for Thine own—
That I may see Thy glorious face,
And worship at Thy throne!
LYRA CATH.

TIMES AND SEASONS.

HEBRON. L. M. — L. MASON.

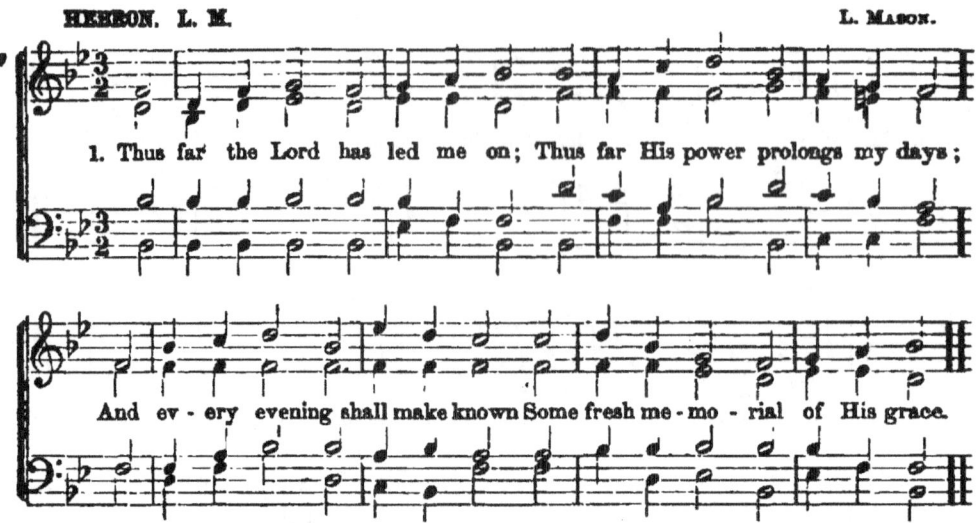

1. Thus far the Lord has led me on; Thus far His power prolongs my days; And every evening shall make known Some fresh memorial of His grace.

1294. L. M.

2. Much of my time has run to waste,
   And I, perhaps, am near my home;
   But He forgives my follies past;
   He gives me strength for days to come.

3. I lay my body down to sleep;
   Peace is the pillow for my head;
   While well-appointed angels keep
   Their watchful stations round my bed.

4. Thus, when the night of death shall come,
   My flesh shall rest beneath the ground,
   And wait Thy voice to rouse my tomb,
   With sweet salvation in the sound.
   WATTS.

1295. L. M.

1. GREAT God! to Thee my evening song
   With humble gratitude I raise;
   O let Thy mercy tune my tongue,
   And fill my heart with lively praise.

2. My days unclouded as they pass,
   And every gentle, rolling hour,
   Are monuments of wondrous grace,
   And witness to Thy love and power.

3. And yet this thoughtless, wretched heart,
   Too oft regardless of Thy love,
   Ungrateful, can from Thee depart,
   And, fond of trifles, vainly rove.

4. Seal my forgiveness in the blood
   Of Jesus; His dear name alone
   I plead for pardon, gracious God!
   And kind acceptance at Thy throne.

5. Let this blest hope mine eyelids close;
   With sleep refresh my feeble frame;
   Safe in Thy care may I repose,
   And wake with praises to Thy name.
   MRS. STEELE.

1296. L. M.

1. MY God! how endless is Thy love!
   Thy gifts are every evening new;
   And morning mercies from above,
   Gently distill, like early dew.

2. Thou spread'st the curtains of the night,
   Great Guardian of my sleeping hours!
   Thy sovereign word restores the light,
   And quickens all my drowsy powers.

3. I yield my powers to Thy command;
   To Thee I consecrate my days;
   Perpetual blessings from Thy hand
   Demand perpetual songs of praise.
   WATTS.

1297. L. M.

1. GOD of my life, to Thee belong,
   The grateful heart, the joyful song;
   Touched by Thy love, each tuneful chord
   Resounds the goodness of the Lord.

2. Yet why, dear Lord, this tender care!
   Why does Thy hand so kindly rear
   A useless cumberer of the ground,
   On which so little fruit is found?

3. Still let the barren fig-tree stand,
   Upheld and fostered by Thy hand;
   And let its fruit and verdure be
   A grateful tribute, Lord, to Thee.

1298. L. M.

1. Awake, my soul, and with the sun
Thy daily stage of duty run;
Shake off dull sloth, and joyful rise
To pay thy morning sacrifice.

2. Wake, and lift up thyself, my heart,
And with the angels bear thy part,
Who all night long unwearied sing
High praises to th' eternal King.

3. All praise to Thee, who safe hast kept,
And hast refreshed me while I slept;
Grant Lord, when I from death shall wake,
I may of endless life partake.

4. Lord! I my vows to Thee renew;
Scatter my sins as morning dew;
Guard my first springs of thought and will,
And with Thyself my spirit fill.

5. Direct, control, suggest, this day,
All I design, or do, or say;
That all my powers, with all their might,
In Thy sole glory may unite.
KENN.

1299. L. M.

1. In sleep's serene oblivion laid,
I safely passed the silent night;
Again I see the breaking shade—
I drink again the morning light.

2. New-born, I bless the waking hour,
Once more, with awe, rejoice to be;
My conscious soul resumes her power,
And springs, my guardian God, to Thee!

3. O guide me through the various maze
My doubtful feet are doomed to tread;
And spread Thy shield's protecting blaze,
When dangers press around my head.

4. A deeper shade will soon impend;
A deeper sleep mine eyes oppress:
Yet then Thy strength shall still defend,
Thy goodness still delight to bless.

5. That deeper shade shall break away;
That deeper sleep shall leave mine eyes;
Thy light shall give eternal day—
Thy love, the rapture of the skies.
HAWKESWORTH.

1300. L. M.

1. Sweet evening hour! sweet evening hour!
That calms the air, and shuts the flower,
That brings the wild bee to its rest,
The infant to its mother's breast!

2. O season of soft sounds and hues,
Of twilight walks among the dews,
Of feelings calm, and converse sweet,
And thoughts too shadowy to repeat!

3. Yes, lovely hour! thou art the time
When feelings flow, and wishes climb;
When timid souls begin to dare,
And God receives and answers prayer.

4. Then, trembling through the dewy skies,
Look out the stars, like thoughtful eyes
Of angels, calm reclining there,
And gazing on the world of care.

5. Sweet hour! for heavenly musing made,
When Isaac walked, and Daniel prayed;
When Abraham's offering God did own,
And Jesus loved to be alone.

1301. L. M.

1. New every morning is the love
Our wakening and uprising prove:
Through sleep and darkness safely brought,
Restored to life, and power, and thought.

2. New mercies, each returning day,
Hover around us while we pray;
New perils past, new sins forgiven,
New thoughts of God, new hopes of heaven.

3. Old friends, old scenes will lovelier be,
As more of heaven in each we see;
Some softening gleam of love and prayer
Shall dawn on every cross and care.

4. Only, O Lord, in Thy dear love,
Fit us for perfect rest above,
And keep us this, and every day,
To live more nearly as we pray.
KEBLE.

1302. C. M.

1. Be Thou, O God, by night, by day,
My Guide, my Guard from sin,
My Life, my Trust, my Light divine,
To keep me pure within.

2. Pure as the air, when day's first light
A cloudless sky illumes;
And active as the lark that soars
Till heaven shines round its plumes—

3. So may my soul, upon the wings
Of faith, unwearied rise,
Till at the gate of heaven it sings,
'Midst light from Paradise.
CHAPEL HYMNS.

NORTHAMPTON. L. M.
Arranged by Geo. Kingsley.

When, on the midnight of the East, At the dead moment of repose, The planet of salvation rose, The planet of salvation rose, Like Hope on Misery's darkened breast, The planet of salvation rose;

1303. L. M.

1. When, on the midnight of the East,
   At the dead moment of repose,
   Like Hope on Misery's darkened breast,
   The planet of salvation rose,—

2. The shepherd, leaning o'er his flock,
   Started, with broad and upward gaze,—
   Kneeled,—while the star of Bethlehem broke
   On music wakened into praise!

3. Shall we, for whom that star was hung
   In the dark vault of frowning heaven,—
   Shall we, for whom that strain was sung,
   That song of peace and sin forgiven,—

4. Shall we, for whom the Saviour bled,
   Careless His banquet's blessings see,
   Nor heed the parting word that said,
   "Do this in memory of Me?"

1304. L. M.

1. How sweet the hour of closing day,
   When all is peaceful and serene,
   And when the sun, with cloudless ray
   Sheds mellow luster o'er the scene!

2. Such is the Christian's parting hour;
   So peacefully he sinks to rest;
   When faith, endued from heaven with power,
   Sustains and cheers his languid breast.

3. Mark but that radiance of his eye,
   That smile upon his wasted cheek;
   They tell us of his glory nigh
   In language that no tongue can speak.

4. A beam from heaven is sent to cheer
   The pilgrim on his gloomy road;
   And angels are attending near
   To bear him to their bright abode.

5. Who would not wish to die like those
   Whom God's own Spirit deigns to bless?
   To sink into that soft repose,
   Then wake to perfect happiness?

1305. L. M.

1. O fairest-born of Love and Light!
   Yet bending brow and eye severe
   On all which pains the holy sight,
   Or wounds the pure and perfect ear,—

2. Beneath Thy broad, impartial eye,
   How fade the lines of caste and birth!
   How equal in their sufferings lie
   The groaning multitudes of earth!

3. Still to a stricken brother true,
   Whatever clime hath nurtured him;
   As stooped to heal the wounded Jew,
   The worshipper of Gerizim.

4. In holy words which can not die,
   In thoughts which angels leaned to know,
   Christ gave Thy message from on high,
   Thy mission to a world of woe.

5. That voice's echo hath not died;
   From the blue lake of Galilee,
   From Tabor's lonely mountain side,
   It calls a struggling world to Thee.

WHITTIER.

CUBA. 10s.
Templi Carmina.

1. Now, when the dusky shades of night, retreating Before the sun's red banner, swiftly flee;
Now, when the terrors of the dark are fleeting, O Lord! we lift our thankful hearts to Thee.

1306. 11s & 10s.

1. Now, when the dusky shades of night, retreating
Before the sun's red banner, swiftly flee;
Now, when the terrors of the dark are fleeting,
O Lord! we lift our thankful hearts to Thee.

2. To Thee, whose word, the fount of light unsealing,
When hill and dale in thickest darkness lay,
Awoke bright rays across the dim earth stealing,
And bade the even and morn complete the day.

3. Look from the tower of heaven, and send to cheer us
Thy light and truth, to guide us onward still;
Still let Thy mercy, as of old, be near us,
And lead us safely to Thy holy hill.

4. So, when that morn of endless light is waking,
And shades of evil from its splendors flee,
Safe may we rise, the earth's dark breast forsaking,
Through all the long bright day to dwell with Thee.

1307. 10s.

1. Quiet from God! how beautiful to keep
This treasure, the All-merciful hath given;
To feel, when we awake and when we sleep,
Its incense round us, like a breath from heaven!

2. To sojourn in the world, and yet apart;
To dwell with God, and still with man to feel;
To bear about for ever in the heart
The gladness which His spirit doth reveal!

3. Who shall make trouble, then? Not evil minds,
Which, like a shadow, o'er creation lower;
The soul which peace hath thus attuned finds
How strong within doth reign the Calmer's power.

4. What shall make trouble? Not slow-wasting pain,
Nor even the threatening, certain stroke of death;
These do but wear away, then break, the chain
Which bound the spirit down to things beneath.

1308. 10s.

1. Again returns the day of holy rest,
Which, when He made the world, Jehovah blest;
When, like His own, He bade our labors cease,
And all be piety, and all be peace.

2. Let us devote this consecrated day
To learn His will, and all we learn obey;
So shall He hear, when fervently we raise
Our supplications and our songs of praise.

3. Father of heaven! in whom our hopes confide,
Whose power defends us, and whose precepts guide,
In life our Guardian, and in death our Friend,
Glory supreme be Thine, till life shall end.

REV. WM. MASON

TIMES AND SEASONS.

DEVIZES. C. M.   TUCKER.

1. When morning's first and hallowed ray Breaks, with its trembling light, To chase the pearl-y dews a-way, Bright tear-drops of the night,—Bright tear-drops of the night,—

1309. C. M.

1. WHEN morning's first and hallowed ray
   Breaks, with its trembling light,
   To chase the pearly dews away,
   Bright tear-drops of the night,—

2. My heart, O Lord! forgets to rove,
   But rises gladly free,
   On wings of everlasting love,
   And finds its home in Thee.

3. When evening's silent shades descend,
   And nature sinks to rest,
   Still, to my Father and my Friend,
   My wishes are addressed.

4. Though tears may dim my hours of joy,
   And bid my pleasures flee,
   Thou reign'st where grief can not annoy;
   I will be glad in Thee.

5. And e'en when midnight's solemn gloom
   Above, around is spread,
   Sweet dreams of everlasting bloom
   Are hovering o'er my head.

6. I dream of that fair land, O Lord!
   Where all Thy saints shall be;
   I wake to lean upon Thy word,
   And still delight in Thee.

1310. C. M.

1. LORD of the world, who hast preserved
   Us safely through this day,
   Now guard us in the silent night,
   And in all time, we pray!

2. Be present, in Thy peace, to those
   Who as Thy suppliants wait;
   Blot out the record of our sin;
   Our gloom illuminate!

3. Let not, amid our hours of sleep,
   Life's enemy steal in;
   Let not a vision of the night
   Have power to whisper sin.

4. Guard every avenue from guile,
   When slumber seals our eyes;
   And guiltless as we laid us down,
   So guiltless let us rise.

   BREVIARY.

1311. C. M.

1. HOSANNA, with a cheerful sound,
   To God's upholding hand;
   Ten thousand snares attend us round,
   And yet secure we stand.

2. That was a most amazing power,
   That raised us with a word;
   And every day, and every hour,
   We lean upon the Lord.

3. The evening rests our weary head,
   And angels guard the room;
   We wake; and we admire the bed,
   That was not made our tomb.

4. God is our sun, whose daily light
   Our joy and safety brings;
   Our feeble flesh lies safe at night
   Beneath His shady wings.

   WATTS.

1312. C. M.

1. Soil not thy plumage, gentle dove,
    With sublunary things—
Till in the fount of light and love
    Thou shalt have bathed thy wings.

2. Shall Nature from her couch arise,
    And rise for Thee in vain?
While heaven, and earth, and seas, and skies,
    Such types of truth contain.

3. See—where the Sun of Righteousness
    Unfolds the gates of day;
Go—meet Him in His glorious dress,
    And quaff the orient ray!

4. There, where ten thousand seraphs stand,
    To crown the circling hours—
Soar thou—and from that blissful land
    Bring down unfading flowers.

5. Some Rose of Sharon, dyed in blood,
    Some spice of Gilead's balm,
Some lily washed in Calvary's flood,
    Some branch of heavenly palm!

6. And let the drops of sparkling dew,
    From Siloa's spring be shed,
To form a fragrance fresh and new—
    A halo round thy head.

7. Spread then Thy plumes of faith and prayer,
    Nor fear to wend away;
And let a glow of heavenly air
    Gild every earthly day!
                        BRYDGES.

1313. C. M.

1. We wait in faith, in prayer we wait,
    Until the happy hour
When God shall ope the morning gate,
    By His almighty power.

2. We wait in faith, and turn our face
    To where the day-light springs;
Till He shall come earth's gloom to chase,
    With healing on His wings.

3. And even now, amid the gray,
    The East is brightening fast,
And kindling to that perfect day
    Which never shall be past.

4. We wait in faith, we wait in prayer,
    Till that blest day shall shine,
When earth shall fruits of Eden bear,
    And all, O God, be Thine!

5. O, guide us till our night is done!
    Until, from shore to shore,
Thou, Lord, our everlasting sun,
    Art shining evermore!

1314. C. M.

1. Once more, my soul, the rising day
    Salutes thy waking eyes;
Once more, my voice, thy tribute pay
    To Him that rules the skies.

2. Night unto night His name repeats,
    The day renews the sound,
Wide as the heaven on which He sits,
    To turn the seasons round.

3. 'Tis He supports my mortal frame;
    My tongue shall speak His praise;
My sins would rouse His wrath to flame,
    And yet His wrath delays.

4. A thousand wretched souls are fled
    Since the last setting sun;
And yet Thou lengthenest out my thread,
    And yet my moments run.

5. Great God, let all my hours be Thine,
    While I enjoy the light;
Then shall my sun in smiles decline,
    And bring a pleasant night.
                        WATTS.

1315. C. M.

1. Now that the sun is gleaming bright,
    Implore we, bending low,
That He, the uncreated light,
    May guide us as we go.

2. No sinful word, nor deed of wrong,
    Nor thoughts that idly rove;
But simple truth be on our tongue,
    And in our hearts be love.

3. And while the hours in order flow,
    O Christ, securely fence
Our gates beleaguered by the foe,
    The gate of every sense.

4. And grant that to Thine honor, Lord,
    Our daily toil may tend;
That we begin it at Thy word,
    And in Thy favor end.

DOXOLOGY. C. M.

Now to our God—the Father, Son,
    And Holy Spirit, sing!
With praise to God, the Three in One,
    Let all creation ring.

TIMES AND SEASONS.

SOUTHPORT. C. M.   *Templi Carmina.*

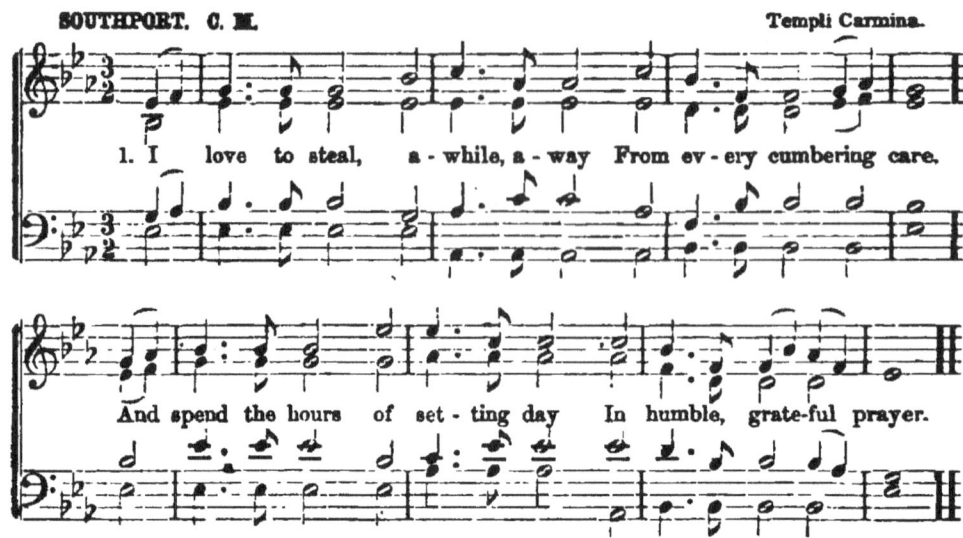

1. I love to steal, a-while, a-way From ev-ery cumbering care,
And spend the hours of set-ting day In humble, grate-ful prayer.

1316. C. M.

2. I love, in solitude, to shed
The penitential tear;
And all His promises to plead,
When none but God is near.

3. I love to think on mercies past,
And future good implore;
My cares and sorrows all to cast
On Him whom I adore.

4. I love, by faith, to take a view
Of brighter scenes in heaven;
The prospect doth my strength renew,
While here by tempests driven.

5. And when life's toilsome day is o'er,
May its departing ray
Be calm as this impressive hour,
And lead to endless day.
                 MRS. BROWNE.

1317. C. M.

1. God of the sunlight hours, how sad
Would evening shadows be;
Or night, in deeper shadows clad,
If aught were dark to Thee!

2. How mournfully that golden gleam
Would touch the thoughtful heart,
If, with its soft, retiring beam,
We saw Thy light depart!

3. But though the sun-set hours may hide
These gentle rays awhile;
And deep thro' ocean's wave may glide
The slumber of their smile.

4. Enough, while these dull heavens may
   lower,
If here Thy presence be;

Then midnight shall be morning hour,
And darkness light to me.

5. Through the deep gloom of mortal things,
Thy light of love can throw
That ray which gilds an angel's wings,
To soothe a pilgrim's woe.
                 LEIFCHILD'S COLL.

1318. C. M.

1. O Lord, another day is flown;
And we, a lonely band,
Are met once more before Thy throne,
To bless Thy fostering hand.

2. And, Jesus, Thou Thy smiles wilt deign,
As we before Thee pray;
For Thou didst bless the infant train,
And we are less than they.

3. And wilt Thou bend a listening ear
To praises low as ours?
Thou wilt! for Thou dost love to hear
The song which meekness pours.

4. Thy heavenly grace to each impart;
All evil far remove;
And shed abroad in every heart
Thy everlasting love.

5. Thus chastened, cleansed, entirely Thine,
A flock by Jesus led,
The Sun of holiness shall shine
In glory on our head.

6. And Thou wilt turn our wandering feet,
And Thou wilt bless our way;
Till worlds shall fade, and faith shall greet
The dawn of lasting day.
                 H. K. WHITE.

1319. C. M.

1. Dread Sovereign, let my evening song
    Like holy incense rise;
   Assist the offerings of my tongue
    To reach the lofty skies.

2. Through all the dangers of the day
    Thy hand was still my guard;
   And still to drive my wants away
    Thy mercy stood prepared.

3. Perpetual blessings from above
    Encompass me around;
   But O! how few returns of love
    Hath my Creator found!

4. What have I done for Him that died
    To save my wretched soul?
   How are my follies multiplied,
    Fast as the minutes roll!

5. Lord, with this guilty heart of mine,
    To Thy dear cross I flee,
   And to Thy grace my soul resign,
    To be renewed by Thee.

6. Sprinkled afresh with pardoning blood,
    I lay me down to rest,
   As in th' embraces of my God,
    Or on my Saviour's breast.
                                WATTS.

1320. C. M.

1. Unheard the dews around me fall,
    And heavenly influence shed;
   And, silent on this earthly ball,
    Celestial footsteps tread.

2. Night reigns in silence o'er the pole,
    And spreads her gems unheard;
   Her lessons penetrate the soul,
    Yet borrow not a word.

3. Noiseless the sun emits his fire,
    And pours his golden streams;
   And silently the shades retire
    Before his rising beams.

4. O, grant my soul an ear to hear
    Thy deep and silent voice;
   To bend in lowly, filial fear,
    And in Thy love rejoice.
                                DODDRIDGE.

1321. C. M.

1. Hail, tranquil hour of closing day!
    Begone, disturbing care!
   And look, my soul, from earth away,
    To Him who heareth prayer.

2. How sweet the tear of penitence,
    Before His throne of grace,
   While, to the contrite spirit's sense,
    He shows His smiling face.

3. How sweet, through long-remembered years,
    His mercies to recall;
   And, pressed with wants, and griefs, and fears,
    To trust His love for all.

4. How sweet to look, in thoughtful hope,
    Beyond this fading sky,
   And hear Him call His children up
    To His fair home on high.

5. Calmly the day forsakes our heaven
    To dawn beyond the west;
   So let my soul, in life's last even,
    Retire to glorious rest.
                                L. BACON.

1322. C. M.

1. Lord, Thou wilt hear me when I pray;
    I am for ever Thine;
   I fear before Thee all the day,
    Nor would I dare to sin.

2. And while I rest my weary head,
    From cares and business free,
   'T is sweet conversing on my bed
    With my own heart and Thee.

3. I pay this evening sacrifice;
    And when my work is done,
   Great God! my faith and hope relies
    Upon Thy grace alone.

4. Thus, with my thoughts composed to peace,
    I give mine eyes to sleep;
   Thy hand in safety keeps my days,
    And will my slumbers keep.
                                WATTS.

1323. C. M.

1. Jesus, the Lord of glory, died,
    That we might never die;
   And now He reigns supreme, to guide
    His people to the sky.

2. Weak though we are, He still is near
    To lead, console, defend;
   In all our sorrow, all our fear,
    Our all-sufficient Friend.

3. And from His love's exhaustless spring
    Joys like a river come,
   To make the desert bloom and sing,
    O'er which we travel home.

4. O Jesus, there is none like Thee,
    Our Saviour and our Lord!
   Through earth and heaven exalted be,
    Beloved, obeyed, adored!

TIMES AND SEASONS.

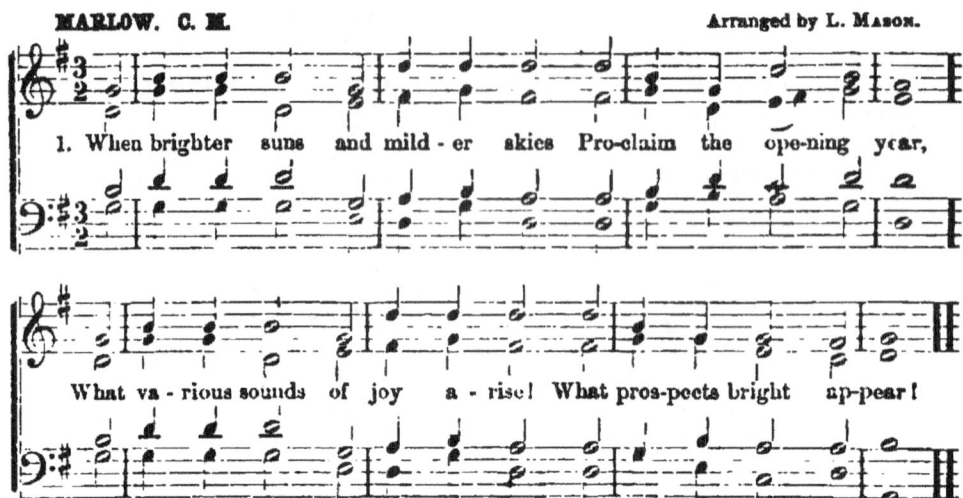

MARLOW. C. M. — Arranged by L. Mason.

1. When brighter suns and milder skies Proclaim the opening year, What various sounds of joy arise! What prospects bright appear!

1324. C. M.

2. Earth and her thousand voices give
    Their thousand notes of praise;
   And all, that by His mercy live,
    To God their offering raise.

3. The streams, all beautiful and bright,
    Reflect the morning sky;
   And there, with music in his flight,
    The wild bird soars on high.

4. Thus, like the morning, calm and clear,
    That saw the Saviour rise,
   The spring of heaven's eternal year
    Shall dawn on earth and skies.

5. No winter there, no shades of night
    Obscure those mansions blest,
   Where, in the happy fields of light,
    The weary are at rest.

1325. C. M.

1. WITH songs and honors sounding loud,
    Address the Lord on high;
   Over the heaven He spreads His cloud,
    And waters vail the sky.

2. He sends His showers of blessings down
    To cheer the plains below;
   He makes the grass the mountains crown,
    And corn in valleys grow.

3. His steady counsels change the face
    Of the declining year;
   He bids the sun cut short his race,
    And wintry days appear.

4. His hoary frost, His fleecy snow,
    Descend and clothe the ground:
   The liquid streams forbear to flow,
    In icy fetters bound.

5. He sends His word, and melts the snow,
    The fields no longer mourn;
   He calls the warmer gales to blow,
    And bids the spring return.

6. The changing wind, the flying cloud,
    Obey His mighty word;
   With songs and honors sounding loud,
    Praise ye the sovereign Lord.
                                    WATTS.

1326. C. M.

1. 'T is by Thy strength the mountains stand,
    God of eternal power!
   The sea grows calm at Thy command,
    And tempests cease to roar.

2. Thy morning light and evening shade
    Successive comforts bring;
   Thy plenteous fruits make harvest glad;
    Thy flowers adorn the spring.

3. Seasons and times, and moons and hours,
    Heaven, earth, and air are Thine;
   When clouds distill in fruitful showers,
    The author is divine!

4. Those wandering cisterns in the sky,
    Borne by the winds around,
   With watery treasures well supply
    The furrows of the ground.

5. The thirsty ridges drink their fill,
    And ranks of corn appear;
   Thy ways abound with blessings still—
    Thy goodness crowns the year.
                                    WATTS.

TIMES AND SEASONS. 427

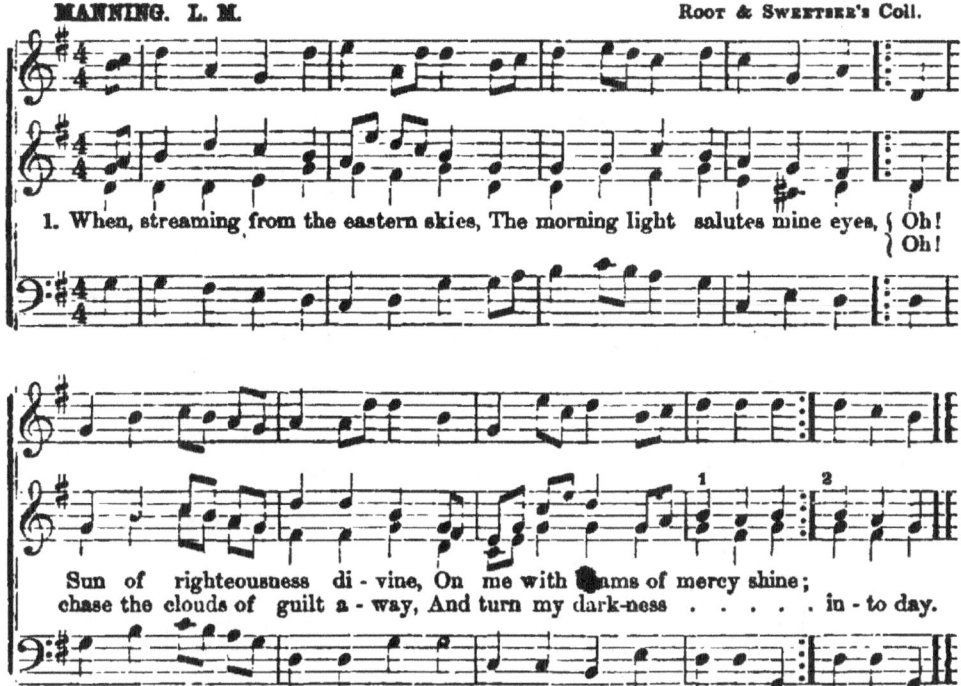

MANNING. L. M.   Root & Sweetser's Coll.

1. When, streaming from the eastern skies, The morning light salutes mine eyes, Oh! Oh! Sun of righteousness di-vine, On me with beams of mercy shine; chase the clouds of guilt a-way, And turn my dark-ness in-to day.

1327. L. M.

1. WHEN, streaming from the eastern skies,
The morning light salutes mine eyes,
Oh! Sun of righteousness divine,
On me with beams of mercy shine;
Oh! chase the clouds of guilt away,
And turn my darkness into day.

2. When to heaven's great and glorious King
My morning sacrifice I bring,
And, mourning o'er my guilt and shame,
Ask mercy, in my Saviour's name;
Then, Jesus, sprinkle with Thy blood,
And be my Advocate with God.

3. When each day's scenes and labors close,
And wearied nature seeks repose,
With pardoning mercy, richly blest,
Guard me, my Saviour, while I rest!
And as each morning sun shall rise,
O lead me onward to the skies!

4. And at my life's last setting sun,
My conflicts o'er, my labors done,
Jesus! Thy heavenly radiance shed,
To cheer and bless my dying bed—
And from death's gloom my spirit raise,
To see Thy face, and sing Thy praise.

          SIR R. GRANT.

1328. L. M.

1. GREAT God, as seasons disappear,
And changes mark the rolling year;
As time with rapid pinions flies,
May every season make us wise.

2. Long has Thy favor crowned our days,
And summer shed again its rays;
No deadly cloud our sky has vailed;
No blasting winds our path assailed.

3. Our harvest months have o'er us rolled,
And filled our fields with waving gold;
Our tables spread, our garners stored!
Where are our hearts to praise the Lord?

4. The solemn harvest comes apace,
The closing day of life and grace:
Time of decision, awful hour!
Around it let no tempests lower!

5. Prepare us, Lord, by grace divine,
Like stars in heaven to rise and shine;
Then shall our happy souls above
Reap the full harvest of Thy love!

DOXOLOGY. L. M.

Now to the Father, and the Son
  Who rose from death, be glory given;
With Thee, O holy Comforter,
  Henceforth by all in earth and heaven.

TIMES AND SEASONS.

EUPATOR. S. M. — T. B. Mason.

1. The day is past and gone, The evening shades appear; O may I ever keep in mind, The night of death draws near.

1329. S. M.

2. I lay my garments by,
   Upon my bed to rest;
So death will soon disrobe us all,
   And leave my soul undressed.
3. Lord, keep me safe this night,
   Secure from all my fears;
May angels guard me while I sleep,
   Till morning light appears.
4. And when I early rise,
   To view th' unwearied sun,
May I set out to win the prize,
   And after glory run—
5. That when my days are past,
   And I from time remove,
I then may in Thy bosom rest,
   The bosom of Thy love.
   HARTFORD SELECTION.

1330. S. M.

1. COME at the morning hour,
   Come, let us kneel and pray;
Prayer is the Christian pilgrim's staff
   To walk with God all day.
2. At noon, beneath the Rock
   Of Ages, rest and pray;
Sweet is that shelter from the sun
   In the weary heat of day.
3. At evening, in Thy home,
   Around its altar, pray;
And finding there the house of God,
   With heaven then close the day.
4. When midnight vails our eyes,
   O, it is sweet to say,
I sleep, but my heart waketh, Lord!
   With Thee to watch and pray.
   BRIGG'S COLL.

1331. S. M.

1. THE swift declining day,
   How fast its moments fly!
While evening's broad and gloomy shade
   Gains on the western sky.
2. Ye mortals, mark its pace,
   And use the hours of light;
And know, its Maker can command
   At once eternal night.
3. Give glory to the Lord,
   Who rules the whirling sphere;
Submissive at His footstool bow,
   And seek salvation there.
4. Then shall new luster break
   Through death's impending gloom,
And lead you to unchanging light,
   In your celestial home.
   DODDRIDGE.

1332. S. M.

1. SEE how the mounting sun
   Pursues his shining way;
And wide proclaims his Maker's praise,
   With every brightening ray.
2. Thus would my rising soul
   Its heavenly Parent sing;
And to its great Original
   The humble tribute bring.
3. Serene, I laid me down
   Beneath His guardian care;
I slept, and I awoke, and found
   My kind Preserver near!
4. Dear Saviour, to Thy cross
   I bring my sacrifice;
Cleansed by Thy blood, it shall ascend
   With fragrance to the skies.
   E. SCOTT.

TIMES AND SEASONS.

IOWA. S. M. — Western Melody.

1. Another day is past, The hours forever fled; And time is bearing me away, To mingle with the dead.

1333. S. M.

2. My mind in perfect peace
My Father's care shall keep;
I yield to gentle slumber now,
For Thou canst never sleep.

3. How blessed, Lord, are they
On Thee securely stayed!
Nor shall they be in life alarmed,
Nor be in death dismayed.

CURTIS'S COLL.

1334. S. M.

1. SWEET Sabbath of the year!
While evening lights decay,
Thy parting steps methinks I hear
Steal from the world away!

2. Amid thy silent bowers,
'Tis sad, but sweet to dwell;
Where falling leaves and drooping flowers
Around me breathe—Farewell.

3. Along Thy sunset skies,
Their glories melt in shade;
And, like the things we fondly prize,
Seem lovelier as they fade.

4. A deep and crimson streak
The dying leaves disclose;
As on consumption's waning cheek,
Mid ruin, blooms the rose.

5. Thy scene each vision brings
Of beauty in decay;
Of fair and early-faded things,
Too exquisite to stay;

6. Of joys that come no more;
Of flowers whose bloom is fled;
Of farewells wept upon the shore;
Of friends estranged or dead;—

7. Of all that now may seem,
To memory's tearful eye,
The vanished beauty of a dream,
O'er which we gaze and sigh.

1335. S. M.

1. SWEET is the time of spring,
When nature's charms appear;
The birds with ceaseless pleasure sing,
And hail the opening year;
But sweeter far the spring
Of wisdom and of grace,
When children bless and praise their King,
Who loves the youthful race.

2. Sweet is the dawn of day,
When light just streaks the sky;
When shades and darkness pass away,
And morning's beams are nigh;
But sweeter far the dawn
Of piety in youth;
When doubt and darkness are withdrawn
Before the light of truth.

3. Sweet is the early dew,
Which gilds the mountain tops,
And decks each plant and flower we view
With pearly, glittering drops;
But sweeter far the scene
On Zion's holy hill,
When there the dew of youth is seen
Its freshness to distill.

EMERALD. 8s & 7s. English Melody.

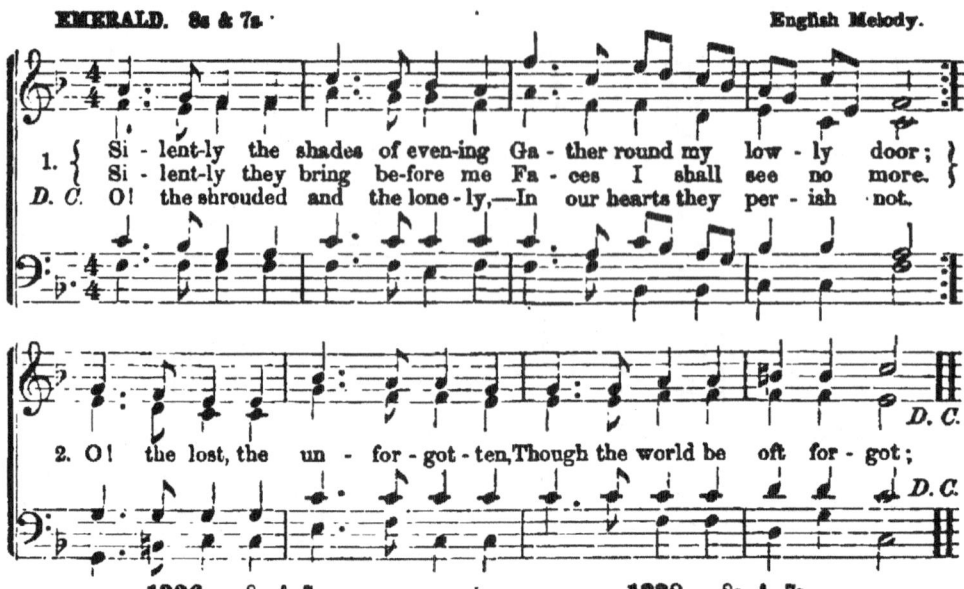

1. { Si - lent-ly the shades of even-ing Ga-ther round my low-ly door;
   { Si - lent-ly they bring be-fore me Fa-ces I shall see no more.
D. C. O! the shrouded and the lone-ly,—In our hearts they per-ish not.

2. O! the lost, the un - for - got - ten, Though the world be oft for - got;

1336. 8s. & 7s.

3. Living in the silent hours,
   Where our spirits only blend,
   They, unlinked with earthly trouble,
   We, still hoping for its end.

4. How such holy memories cluster,
   Like the stars when storms are past;
   Pointing up to that far heaven
   We may hope to gain at last.

1337. 8s. & 7s.

1. TARRY with me, O my Saviour,
   For the day is passing by;
   See! the shades of evening gather,
   And the night is drawing nigh.

2. Many friends were gathered round me
   In the bright days of the past;
   But the grave has closed above them,
   And I linger here at last.

3. Deeper, deeper grow the shadows;
   Paler now the glowing West;
   Swift the night of death advances;
   Shall it be the night of rest?

4. Feeble, trembling, fainting, dying,
   Lord, I cast myself on Thee;
   Tarry with me through the darkness!
   While I sleep, still watch by me.

5. Tarry with me, O my Saviour!
   Lay my head upon Thy breast
   Till the morning; then awake me—
   Morning of eternal rest!

1338. 8s. & 7s.

1. SAVIOUR! breathe an evening blessing,
   Ere repose our eyelids seal;
   Sin and want we come confessing;
   Thou canst save, and Thou canst heal.

2. Though destruction walk around us,
   Though the arrows past us fly,
   Angel-guards from Thee surround us—
   We are safe, if Thou art nigh.

3. Though the night be dark and dreary,
   Darkness can not hide from Thee:
   Thou art He who, never weary,
   Watcheth where Thy people be.

4. Should swift death this night o'ertake us,
   And our couch become our tomb,
   May the morn in heaven awake us,
   Clad in bright and deathless bloom.
   EDMESTON.

1339. 8s. & 7s.

1. ON the dewy breath of even
   Thousand odors mingling rise,
   Borne like incense up to heaven—
   Nature's evening sacrifice.

2. Thou, whose favors without number
   All our days with gladness bless,
   Let Thine eye, that knows no slumber,
   Guard our hours of helplessness.

3. Then, though conscious we are sleeping
   In the outer courts of death,
   Safe beneath a Father's keeping,
   Calm we rest in perfect faith.
   MARTINEAU'S COLL.

TIMES AND SEASONS.

NORWICH. 7s. — L. MASON.

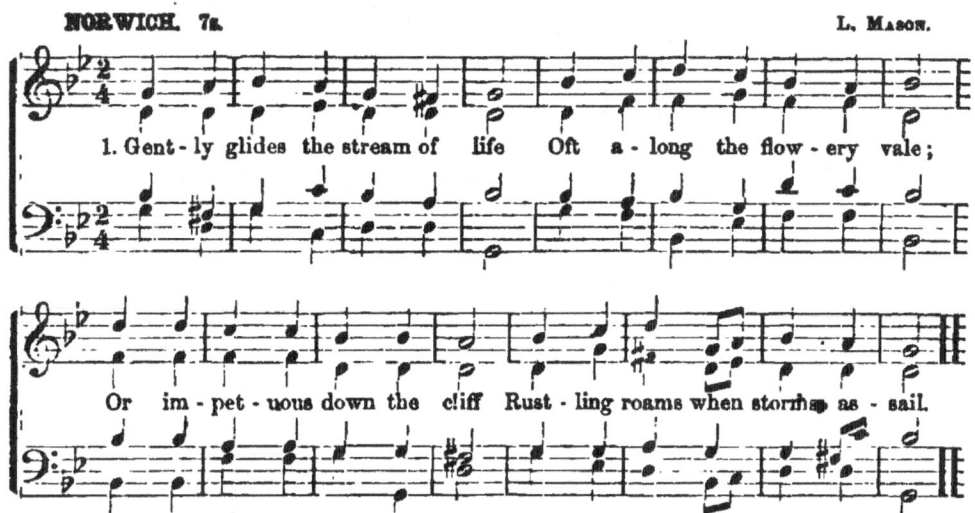

1. Gently glides the stream of life
Oft along the flowery vale;
Or impetuous down the cliff
Rustling roams when storms assail.

1340. 7s.

2. Tis an ever varied flood,
Always rolling to its sea,
Slow, or quick, or mild, or rude,
Tending to Eternity.

3. Mortal, what has life for thee,
Like the visions faith can see?
Is thy path of fading flowers,
Half so bright, so sweet as ours?

4. Doth a skillful, healing Friend
On thy daily path attend,
And, where thorns and stings abound,
Shed a balm on every wound?

5. When the tempest rolls on high,
Hast thou still a refuge nigh?
Can, O can thy dying breath
Summon one more strong than death?

6. Canst thou, in that awful day,
Fearless tread the gloomy way,
Plead a glorious ransom given,
Burst from earth, and soar to heaven?

1341. 7s.

1. SLOWLY, by God's hand unfurled,
Down around the weary world
Falls the darkness; O, how still
Is the working of His will!

2. Mighty Spirit, ever nigh!
Work in me as silently;
Vail the day's distracting sights,
Show me heaven's eternal lights.

3. Living stars to view be brought
In the boundless realms of thought;
High and infinite desires,
Flaming like those upper fires!

4. Holy Truth! Eternal Right,
Let them break upon my sight!
Let them shine serene and still,
And with light my being fill.

FURNESS.

1342. 7s.

1. THOU that dost my life prolong,
Kindly aid my morning song;
Thankful from my couch I rise,
To the God that rules the skies.

2. Gently, with the dawning ray,
On my soul Thy beams display;
Sweeter than the smiling morn,
Let Thy cheering light return.

EDYFIELD.

1343. 7s.

1. IN a land of strange delight
My transported spirit strayed:—
I awake—where all is night,
Silence, solitude, and shade.

2. Is the dream of nature flown?
Is the universe destroyed?—
Man extinct, and I alone
Breathing through the formless void?

3. No; my soul, in God rejoice;
Through the gloom His light I see,
In the silence hear His voice,
And His hand is over me.

4. When I slumber in the tomb,
He will guard my resting-place;
Fearless, in the day of doom,
May I see Him face to face.

MONTGOMERY.

1344. H. M.

1. How pleasing is Thy voice,
   O Lord, our heavenly King!
   That bids the frosts retire,
   And wakes the lovely spring!
   The rains return, the ice distills,
   And plains and hills forget to mourn.

2. The morn with glory crowned,
   Thy hand arrays in smiles;
   Thou bid'st the eve decline,
   Rejoicing o'er the hills.
   Soft suns ascend; the mild wind blows;
   And beauty glows to earth's far end.

3. Thy showers make soft the fields;
   On every side behold
   The ripening harvests wave
   Their loads of richest gold!
   The laborers sing with cheerful voice,
   And, blest, rejoice in God, their King.

4. The thunder is His voice;
   His arrows blazing fires;
   He glows in yonder sun,
   And smiles in starry choirs.
   The balmy breeze His breath perfumes:
   His beauty blooms in flowers and trees.

5. With life He clothes the spring;
   The earth with summer warms;
   He spreads the autumnal feast,
   And rides in wintry storms.
   His gifts divine through all appear,
   And round the year His glories shine.

DWIGHT.

TIMES AND SEASONS.

LUCAS. 5s, 6s & 11s.

1. Come, let us anew Our journey pursue, Roll round with the year, And never stand still, till the Master appear; His adorable will Let us gladly fulfill, And our talents improve, By the patience of hope, and the labor of love, By the patience of hope, and the labor of love.

1345. 5s, 6s & 11s.

2. Our life is a dream; our time, as a stream,
   Glides swiftly away,
 And the fugitive moment refuses to stay;
   The arrow is flown; the moment is gone;
   The millennial year
 Rushes on to our view, and eternity's near.

3. O, that each, in the day of His coming,
     may say,
   "I have fought my way through;
 I have finished the work Thou didst give
     me to do;"
 O, that each from his Lord may receive the
     glad word,
   "Well and faithfully done;
 Enter into my joy, and sit down on my
     throne."
                                        C. WESLEY.

1346. 11s & 9s.

1. Come, let us ascend, my companion and
     friend,
   To a taste of the banquet above:

 If thy heart be as mine, if for Jesus it pine,
   Come up into the chariot of love.

2. We in Jesus confide, and are bold to out-
     ride
   The storms of affliction beneath;
 With the prophet we soar to the heavenly
     shore,
   And outfly all the arrows of death.

3. By faith we are come to our permanent
     home;
   By hope we the rapture improve:
 By love we still rise, and look down on
     the skies,
   For the heaven of heavens is love.

4. What a rapturous song, when the glorified
     throng
   In the spirit of harmony join!—
 Join all the glad choirs, hearts, voices,
     and lyres,
   And the burden is—Mercy divine!
                                        C. WESLEY.

1347. 7s & 6s.

1. Go, when the morning shineth,
   Go, when the noon is bright,
   Go, when the eve declineth,
   Go, in the hush of night;
   Go, with pure mind and feeling,
   Put earthly thoughts away,
   And, in God's presence kneeling,
   Do thou in secret pray.

2. Remember all who love thee,
   All who are loved by thee;
   Pray, too, for those who hate thee,
   If any such there be;
   Then for thyself, in meekness,
   A blessing humbly claim;
   And blend with each petition
   Thy great Redeemer's name.

3. Or, if 't is e'er denied thee
   In solitude to pray,
   Should holy thoughts come o'er thee,
   When friends are round thy way,
   E'en then, the silent breathing
   Thy spirit lifts above,
   Will reach His throne of glory,
   Where dwells eternal love.

1348. 7s & 6s.

1. THE mellow eve is gliding
   Serenely down the west;
   So, every care subsiding,
   My soul would sink to rest.

2. The woodland hum is ringing
   The daylight's gentle close;
   May angels round me, singing,
   Thus hymn my last repose.

3. The evening star has lighted
   Her crystal lamp on high;
   So, when in death benighted,
   May hope illume the sky.

4. In golden splendor dawning,
   The morrow's light shall break;
   O, on the last bright morning
   May I in glory wake!

SACRED SONGS.

TIMES AND SEASONS. 485

DE CALL. 7s & 6s.   Arranged by J. Zundel.

1. When spring unlocks the flow-ers to paint the laughing soil, When summer's balmy show-ers re-fresh the mow-er's toil; When win-ter binds in frosty chains the fal-low and the flood, In God the earth re-joic-eth still, and owns his Ma-ker good.

1349. 14s.

1. When spring unlocks the flowers to paint the
   laughing soil,
   When summer's balmy showers refresh the
   mower's toil;
   When winter binds in frosty chains the fallow
   and the flood,
   In God the earth rejoiceth still, and owns his
   Maker good.

2. The birds that wake the morning, and those that
   love the shade;
   The winds that sweep the mountain, or lull the
   drowsy glade;
   The sun that from his amber bower rejoiceth on
   his way,
   The moon and stars their Maker's name in silent
   pomp display.

3. Shall man, the lord of nature, expectant of the
   sky,
   Shall man, alone unthankful, his little praise
   deny?
   No, let the year forsake his course, the seasons
   cease to be,
   Thee, Father, must we always love,—Creator!
   honor Thee.

4. The flowers of spring may wither, the hope of
   summer fade;
   The autumn droop in winter, the birds forsake
   the shade;
   The winds be lulled,—the sun and moon forget
   their old decree;
   But we in nature's latest hour, O Lord, will cling
   to Thee!
               HEBER.

1350. 7s & 6s.

1. The leaves, around me falling,
   Are preaching of decay;
   The hollow winds are calling,
   "Come, pilgrim, come away!"
   The day, in night declining,
   Says I must, too, decline;
   The year, its life resigning,—
   Its lot foreshadows mine.

2. The light my path surrounding,
   The loves, to which I cling,
   The hopes within me bounding,
   The joys that round me wing,—
   All melt, like stars of even,
   Before the morning's ray,—
   Pass upward into heaven,
   And chide at my delay.

3. The friends, gone there before me,
   Are calling from on high;
   And joyous angels o'er me,
   Tempt sweetly to the sky.
   "Why wait," they say, "and wither
   'Mid scenes of death and sin?
   O, rise to glory, hither,
   And find true life begin."

4. I hear the invitation,
   And fain would rise and come—
   A sinner to salvation;
   An exile to his home:
   But, while I here must linger,
   Thus, thus let all I see
   Point on, with faithful finger,
   To heaven, O Lord, and Thee.

TIMES AND SEASONS.

NEWBURY. H. M.   MICHAEL HAYDN.

1. Lord of the worlds below! On earth Thy glories shine; The changing seasons show Thy skill and power divine. The rolling years are full of Thee; In all we see, a God appears.

1351. H. M.

2. Forth in the flowery spring,
   We see Thy beauty move;
   The birds on branches sing
   Thy tenderness and love;
   Wide flush the hills; the air is balm;
   Devotion's calm our bosom fills.

3. Then come, in robes of light,
   The summer's flaming days;
   The sun Thine image bright,
   Thy majesty, displays;
   And oft Thy voice in thunder rolls;
   But still our souls in Thee rejoice.

4. In autumn, a rich feast
   Thy common bounty gives
   To man, and bird, and beast,
   And every thing that lives.
   Thy liberal care at morn and noon,
   And harvest moon, our lips declare.

5. In winter, awful Thou!
   With storms around Thee cast!
   The leafless forests bow
   Beneath Thy northern blast.
   While tempests lower, to Thee, dread King,
   We homage bring, and own Thy power.
   FREEMAN.

1352. H. M.

1. YE boundless realms of joy,
   Exalt your Maker's fame;
   His praise your song employ
   Above the starry frame:
   Your voices raise, ye cherubim
   And seraphim, to sing His praise.

2. Thou moon, that rul'st the night,
   And sun, that guid'st the day,
   Ye glittering stars of light,
   To Him your homage pay:
   His praise declare, ye heavens above,
   And clouds that move in liquid air.

3. Let them adore the Lord,
   And praise His holy name,
   By whose almighty word
   They all from nothing came:
   And all shall last, from changes free;
   His firm decree stands ever fast.

4. United zeal be shown,
   His wondrous fame to raise,
   Whose glorious name alone
   Deserves our endless praise:
   Earth's utmost ends His power obey;
   His glorious sway the sky transcends.

CHILDREN.

CANAAN. Peculiar. H. E. MATTHEWS. Arranged.

1. Here we meet to part again, Here we meet to part again, But when we meet on Ca-naan's plain, There'll be no parting there. In that bright world a-bove, In that bright world a-bove; Shout! shout the victory, we're on our journey home.

1354. 8s & 7s.

2. Here we meet to part again,
   But there we shall with Jesus reign,
   There 'll be, &c.

3. Here we meet to part again,
   But when we join the heavenly train,
   There 'll be, &c.

SUNSHINE. 6s & 5s. Arr. from the German by J. ZUNDEL.

1. See the shining dewdrops On the flowers strewed, Proving as they sparkle God is ever good.

2. See the morning sunbeams Lighting up the wood, Silently proclaiming God is ev-er good.

1355. 6s & 5s.

3. Hear the mountain streamlet
   In the solitude,
   With its ripple saying
   God is ever good.

4. In the leafy tree tops,
   Where no fears intrude,
   Merry birds are singing
   God is ever good.

5. Bring, my heart, thy tribute,
   Songs of gratitude,
   While all nature utters
   God is ever good.

CHILDREN.

EVENING. 6s & 5s.

1. See, the light is fading From the western sky; Day, thou art departing, Night is drawing nigh.

1356. 6s & 5s.

2. Evening winds are breathing
Through the forest green,
Crimson clouds are wreathing
In the sky serene.

3. See the stars appearing
All around so bright,
Emblems ever cheering
Of eternal light.

SUMMER MORNING. 7s, 6s & 8s.   L. Mason.

1. How beau-ti-ful the morning, When summer days are long; O we will rise be-times, and hear The wild-bird's happy song—For when the sun pours down his ray, The bird will cease to sing; She'll seek the cool and silent shade, And sit with folded wing.

1357. 7s, 6s & 8s.

1. How beautiful the morning,
When summer days are long;
O we will rise betimes, and hear
The wild-bird's happy song—
For when the sun pours down his ray,
The bird will cease to sing;
She'll seek the cool and silent shade,
And sit with folded wing.

2. Up in the morning early—
'Tis Nature's gayest hour!
While pearls of dew adorn the grass,
And fragrance fills the flowers—
Up in the morning early,
And we will bound abroad,
And fill our hearts with melody,
And raise our songs to God.

440 CHILDREN.

YOUTH. 7s. Hymn 1358. J. ZUNDEL.

1. Young and hap-py while thou art, Not a fur-row on thy brow, Not a sorrow in thy heart, Seek the Lord thy Saviour now. In its freshness bring the flower, While the dew up-on it lies, In the cool and cloudless hour Of the morn-ing sa-cri-fice.

2. Life will have its evil years, When its skies are overcast, All the present, thronged with fears, And with vain re-grets, the past. Let him trem-ble, who his heart Brings not in an hour like this, Lest Je-ho-vah say—"Depart, You shall nev-er taste my bliss."

ROSE. 8s & 7s. Hymn 1359.

1. O how pure-ly, O how sure-ly, Live the in-no-cent in heart; Ev-er lightly, Ev-er brightly, Ev-ery hour doth joy im-part.

2. Angels standing, where we're wandering,
   Watch our walk and guard our way;
   Like the showers on the flowers,
   So fall blessings all the day.

3. Day's declining, stars are shining,
   Gleaming through the tranquil night;
   Eyelids closing, safe reposing,
   Rest we till the morning light.

4. Father! holy, pure and lowly,
   May Thy children ever be;
   Anthems swelling, with Thee dwelling,
   Here and in eternity.

CHILDREN.

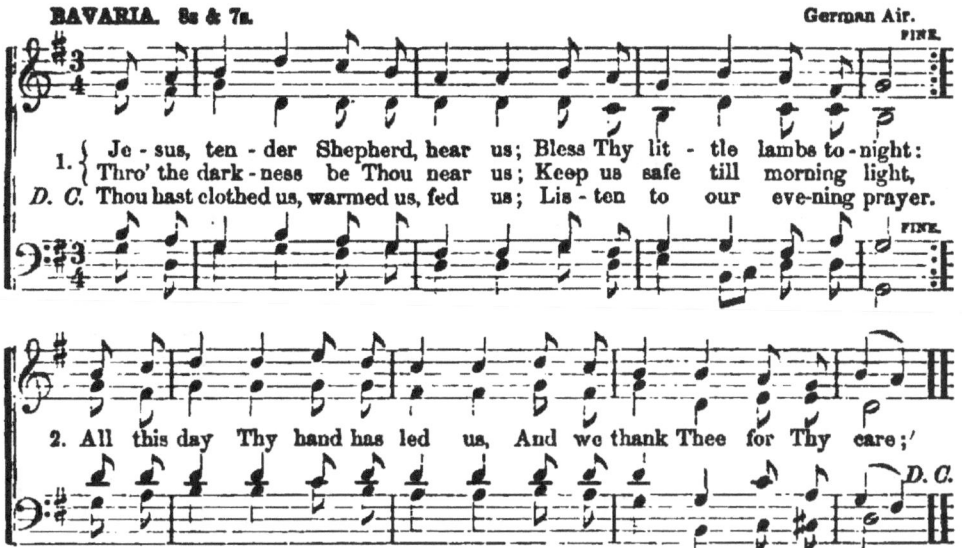

BAVARIA. 8s & 7s.   German Air.

1. Jesus, tender Shepherd, hear us; Bless Thy little lambs to-night:
   Thro' the darkness be Thou near us; Keep us safe till morning light,
   D. C. Thou hast clothed us, warmed us, fed us; Listen to our evening prayer.

2. All this day Thy hand has led us, And we thank Thee for Thy care;

1360. 8s & 7s.

2. All this day Thy hand has led us,
   And we thank Thee for Thy care;
   Thou hast clothed us, warmed us, fed us,
   Listen to our evening prayer!

3. May our sins be all forgiven;
   Bless the friends we love so well;
   Take us, when we die, to heaven,
   Happy there with Thee to dwell.

   MARY LUNDIE DUNCAN.

1361. 8s & 7s.
Cradle Hymn.

1. Hush, my dear, lie still and slumber,
   Holy angels guard thy bed,
   Heavenly blessings without number
   Gently falling on thy head.

2. Sleep, my babe, thy food and raiment,
   House and home thy friends provide;
   All, without thy care or payment,
   All thy wants are well supplied.

3. How much better thou 'rt attended
   Than the Son of God could be,
   When from heaven He descended,
   And became a child like thee.

4. Soft and easy is thy cradle—
   Coarse and hard the Saviour lay,
   When His birth-place was a stable,
   And His softest bed was hay.

5. Blessed Babe, what glorious features,
   Spotless, fair, divinely bright!
   Must He dwell with brutal creatures?—
   How could angels bear the sight!

6. Was there nothing but a manger
   Cursed sinners could afford
   To receive the heavenly Stranger?
   Did they thus affront their Lord?

7. Soft, my child—I did not chide thee,
   Tho' my song might sound too hard;
   'Tis thy mother sits beside thee,
   And her arm shall be thy guard.

8. Yet, to read the shameful story
   How the Jews abused their King;
   How they served the Lord of glory,
   Makes me angry while I sing.

9. See the kinder shepherds round Him,
   Telling wonders from the sky;
   There they sought Him, there they found Him,
   With his virgin mother by.

10. See the lovely Babe a-dressing,
    Lovely Infant, how He smiled!
    When He wept, the mother's blessing
    Soothed and hushed the holy Child.

11. Lo, He slumbers in His manger,
    Where the horned oxen feed—
    Peace, my darling, here's no danger,
    Here's no ox a-near thy bed.

12. 'Twas to save thee, child, from dying,
    Save my dear from burning flame,
    Bitter groans, and endless crying,
    That thy blest Redeemer came.

13. Mayst thou live to know and fear Him,
    Trust and love Him all Thy days!
    Then go dwell for ever near Him,
    See His face, and sing His praise.

14. I could give thee thousand kisses,
    Hoping what I most desire;
    Not a mother's fondest wishes
    Can to greater joys aspire.

    WATTS.

CHILDREN.

SWEET STORY. 11s & 9s.

1. I think when I read that sweet story of old, When Jesus was here among men, How He called little children as lambs to His fold, I should like to have been with them then.

1362. P. M.

2. I wish that His hands had been placed on my head,
That His arm had been thrown around me,
And that I might have seen His kind look when He said,
"Let the little ones come unto me."

3. Yet still to His footstool in prayer I may go,
And ask for a share in His love;
And if I thus earnestly seek Him below,
I shall see Him and hear Him above;

4. In that beautiful place he is gone to prepare
For all who are washed and forgiven:
And many dear children are gathering there,
"For of such is the kingdom of heaven."

CHILD'S PRAYER. 6s & 5s.   L. MASON.

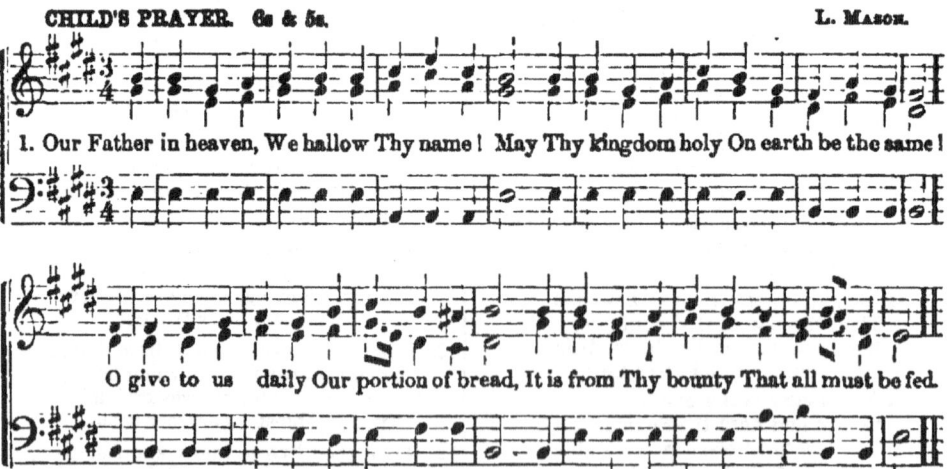

1. Our Father in heaven, We hallow Thy name! May Thy kingdom holy On earth be the same! O give to us daily Our portion of bread, It is from Thy bounty That all must be fed.

1363. 6s & 5s.

2. Forgive our transgressions,
And teach us to know
That humble compassion
That pardons each foe;

Keep us from temptation,
From weakness and sin,
And Thine be the glory
For ever—Amen!

CHILDREN.

VIOLET. 8s & 7s.

1. Jesus Christ my Lord and Saviour, Once became a child like me,
O that in my whole behavior, He my pattern still might be!
D.C. But the Lord was meek and lowly, And was never known to sin.

2. All my nature is unholy, Pride and passion dwell within;

1364. 8s & 7s.

1. Jesus Christ, my Lord and Saviour,
   Once became a child like me;
   O that in my whole behavior
   He my pattern still might be.

2. All my nature is unholy,
   Pride and passion dwell within;
   But the Lord was meek and lowly,
   And was never known to sin.

3. While I'm often vainly trying
   Some new pleasure to possess,
   He was always self-denying,
   Patient in His worst distress.

4. Let me never be forgetful
   Of His precepts any more:
   Idle, passionate, and fretful,
   As I've often been before.

5. Help me, by Thy word to measure
   Every deed and every thought,
   Thinking it my greatest pleasure
   There to learn what Thou hast taught.

1365. 8s & 7s.

1. Lord, a little band, and lowly,
   We are come to sing to Thee;
   Thou art great, and high, and holy—
   O how solemn should we be!

2. Fill our hearts with thoughts of Jesus,
   And of heaven, where He is gone;
   And let nothing ever please us
   He would grieve to look upon.

3. For we know the Lord of glory
   Always sees what children do,
   And is writing now the story
   Of our thoughts and actions, too.

4. Let our sins be all forgiven;
   Make us fear whate'er is wrong;
   Lead us on our way to heaven,
   There to sing a nobler song.

1366. 8s & 7s.

1. What a strange and wondrous story,
   From the Book of God is read—
   How the Lord of life and glory
   Had not where to lay His head.

2. How He left His throne in heaven,
   Here to suffer, bleed, and die,
   That my soul might be forgiven,
   And ascend to God on high.

3. Father! let Thy Holy Spirit
   Still reveal a Saviour's love,
   And prepare me to inherit
   Glory where He reigns above;

4. There, with saints and angels dwelling,
   May I that great love proclaim,
   And with them be ever telling,
   All the wonders of His name.

CHILDREN.

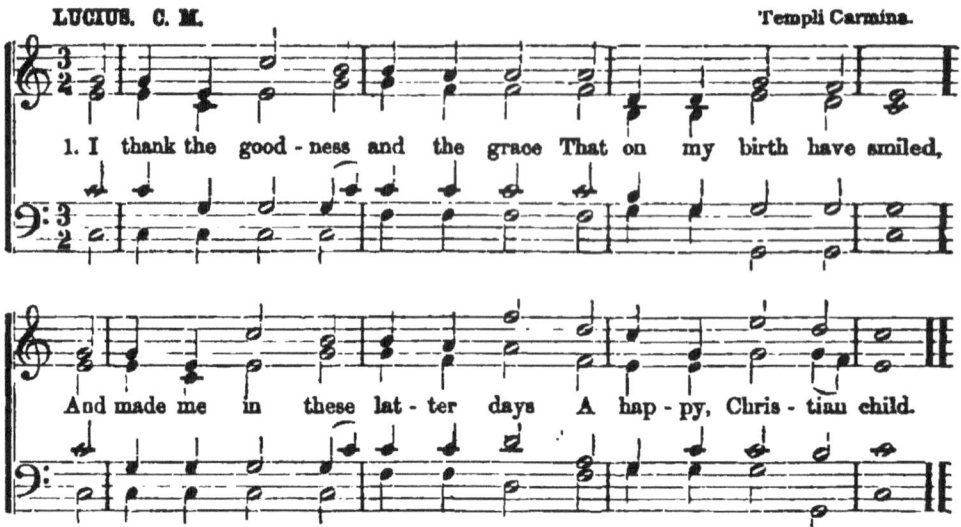

LUCIUS. C. M. — Templi Carmina.

1. I thank the good-ness and the grace That on my birth have smiled, And made me in these lat-ter days A hap-py, Chris-tian child.

1367. C. M.

1. I THANK the goodness and the grace
That on my birth have smiled,
And made me, in these latter days,
A happy, Christian child.

2. I was not born as thousands are,
Where God is never known,
And taught to say a useless prayer
To gods of wood and stone.

3. I was not born without a home,
In some poor broken shed,
A gipsy baby, taught to roam,
And steal my daily bread.

4. I was not born a little slave,
To labor in the sun,
And wish I were but in my grave,
And all my labor done.

5. My God, I thank Thee, who hast planned
A better lot for me,
And placed me in this favored land,
Where I may hear of Thee.

1368. C. M.

1. ALMIGHTY God! Thy piercing eye
Strikes thro' the shades of night,
And our most secret actions lie
All open to Thy sight.

2. There's not a sin that we commit,
Nor wicked word we say,
But in Thy dreadful book 'tis writ
Against the judgment-day.

3. Lord, at Thy foot ashamed I lie;
Upwards I dare not look;
Pardon my sins before I die,
And blot them from Thy book.

5. Remember all the dying pains,
Thou, my Redeemer felt,
And let Thy blood wash out my stains,
And answer for my guilt.

6. O may I now for ever fear
To indulge a sinful thought,
Since the great God can see and hear,
And writes down every fault.
WATTS.

1369. C. M.

1. WHY should I join with those in play,
In whom I've no delight,
Who curse and swear, but never pray,
Who call ill names and fight.

2. I hate to hear a wanton song,
Their words offend my ears;
I should not dare defile my tongue
With language such as theirs.

3. Away from fools I'll turn my eyes,
Nor with the scoffers go;
I would be walking with the wise,
That wiser I may grow.

4. From one rude boy that's used to mock,
They learn the wicked jest,
One sickly sheep infects the flock,
And poisons all the rest.

5. My God, I hate to walk or dwell
With sinful children here,
Then let me not be sent to hell,
Where none but sinners are.
WATTS.

1370. C. M.

1. How doth the little busy bee
    Improve each shining hour,
   And gather honey all the day
    From every opening flower!

2. How skillfully she builds her cell!
    How neat she spreads her wax!
   And labors hard to store it well,
    With the sweet food she makes.

3. In works of labor or of skill,
    I would be busy, too,
   For Satan finds some mischief still
    For idle hands to do.

4. In books, or work, or healthful play,
    Let my first years be past,
   That I may give for every day
    Some good account at last.
   WATTS.

1371. C. M.

1. WHATEVER brawls disturb the street,
    There should be peace at home,
   Where sisters dwell, and brothers meet,
    Quarrels should never come.

2. Birds in their little nests agree,
    And 't is a shameful sight
   When children of one family
    Fall out, and chide, and fight.

3. Hard names at first, and threatening words,
    That are but noisy breath,
   May grow to clubs and naked swords,
    To murder and to death.

4. The wise will make their anger cool,
    At least before 't is night;
   But in the bosom of a fool
    It burns till morning light.

5. Pardon, O Lord, our childish rage,
    Our little brawls remove,
   That, as we grow to riper age,
    Our hearts may be all love.
   WATTS.

1372. C. M.

1. WHENE'ER I take my walks abroad,
    How many poor I see;
   What shall I render to my God
    For all his gifts to me?

2. Not more than others I deserve,
    Yet God hath given me more,
   For I have food while others starve,
    Or beg from door to door.

3. How many children in the street
    Half naked I behold,
   While I am clothed from head to feet,
    And covered from the cold.

4. While some poor wretches scarce can tell
    Where they may lay their head,
   I have a home wherein to dwell,
    And rest upon my bed.

5. While others early learn to swear,
    And curse, and lie and steal,
   Lord, I am taught Thy name to fear,
    And do Thy holy will.

6. Are these Thy favors day by day,
    To me above the rest,
   Then let me love Thee more than they,
    And try to serve Thee best.
   WATTS.

1373. C. M.

1. WHAT blessed examples do I find
    Writ in the word of truth,
   Of children that began to mind
    Religion in their youth.

2. Jesus who reigns above the sky,
    And keeps the world in awe,
   Once was a child as young as I,
    And kept his Father's law.

3. At twelve years old he talked with men—
    The Jews in wonder stand,
   Yet he obeyed his mother then,
    And came at her command.

4. Children a sweet hosanna sung,
    And blest their Saviour's name;
   They gave him honor with their tongue,
    While scribes and priests blaspheme.

5. Then why should I so long delay
    What others learn so soon;
   I would not pass another day,
    Without this work begun.
   WATTS.

1374. C. M.

1. WE miss thee in thy place at school,
    And on thy homeward way,
   Where violets by the reedy pool,
    Peep out so shyly gay.

2. And many a tearful, longing look
    In silence seeks thee yet,
   Where, in its own familiar nook,
    Thy fireside chair is set.

3. And oft, when little voices dim
    Are feeling for the note
   In chanted prayer, or psalm, or hymn,
    And wav'ring wildly float—

4. Comes gushing o'er a sudden thought
    Of her who led the strain,
   How oft, such music home she brought,
    But ne'er shall bring again.

5. O say not so! the spring-tide air
    Is fraught with whisperings sweet,
   Who knows, but heavenly carols there
    With ours may duly meet?
   LYRA INNOCENTIUM.

DOXOLOGIES.

1. L. M.

To God the Father, God the Son,
And God the Spirit, Three in One,
Be honor, praise, and glory given,
By all on earth, and all in heaven.

2. L. M.

Praise God, from whom all blessings flow!
Praise Him, all creatures here below!
Praise Him above, ye heavenly host!
Praise Father, Son, and Holy Ghost.

3. L. M. Double.

1. Worthy the Lamb of boundless sway,—
   In earth and heaven the Lord of all!
   Let all the powers of earth obey,
   And low before His footstool fall.

2. Higher—still higher swell the strain;
   Creation's voice the note prolong!
   Jesus, the Lamb, shall ever reign:
   Let hallelujahs crown the song.

4. L. M.

All glory while the ages run
Be to the Father, and the Son
Who rose from death; the same to Thee,
O Holy Ghost, eternally.

5. L. M.

Praise to the Father, with the Son,
And Holy Spirit, Three in One;
As ever was in ages past,
And shall be so while ages last.

6. C. M.

Let God the Father, and the Son,
  And Spirit, be adored,
Where there are works to make Him
    known,
  Or saints to love the Lord.

7. C. M.

To Father, Son, and Holy Ghost,
  One God, whom we adore,
Be glory as it was, is now,
  And shall be evermore.

8. C. M.

To God the Father glory be,
  And to His only Son;
The same, O Holy Ghost! to Thee,
  While ceaseless ages run.

9. C. M.

In hope to join th' angelic host,
  And all the ransomed throng,
To Father, Son, and Holy Ghost,
  We raise the grateful song.

10. C. M.

Thou art the first, and Thou the last;
  Time centers all in Thee,
The Almighty God who was, and is,
  And evermore shall be.

To Thee let every tongue be praise
  And every heart be love;
All grateful honors paid on earth,
  And nobler songs above.

11. C. M.

We raise our shouts, O God, to Thee,
  And send them to Thy throne;
All glory to th' united Three,
  The undivided One.
Hosanna! let the earth and skies
  Repeat the joyful sound;
Rocks, hills, and vales reflect the voice
  In one eternal round.

12. S. M.

1. Ye angels round the throne,
    And saints that dwell below,
  Worship the Father, praise the Son,
    And bless the Spirit, too.

13. H. M.

To God the Father's throne
  Your highest honors raise;
Glory to God the Son;
  To God the Spirit, praise;
With all our powers, Eternal King,
Thy name we sing, while faith adores.

14. 7s.

Sing we to our God above
Praise eternal as His love;
Praise Him, all ye heavenly host—
Father, Son, and Holy Ghost.

15. 7s.

Praise the name of God most high,
Praise him, all below the sky,
Praise him, all ye heavenly host,
Father, Son, and Holy Ghost;
As through countless ages past,
Evermore his praise shall last.

16. L. P. M.

Now to the great and sacred Three,
The Father, Son and Spirit, be
Eternal praise and glory given—
Through all the worlds where God is known,
By all the angels near the throne,
And all the saints in earth and heaven.

17. C. P. M.

To Father, Son, and Holy Ghost,
Be praise amid the heavenly host,
And in the church below;
From whom all creatures draw their breath,
By whom redemption blessed the earth,
From whom all comforts flow.

18. 8s & 7s.

Praise the Father, earth, and heaven,
Praise the Son, the Spirit praise,
As it was, and is, be given,
Glory through eternal days.

19. 8s & 7s.

Praise the God of all creation,
  Praise the Father's boundless love;
Praise the Lamb, our expiation;
  Praise the Spirit from above:
Praise the fountain of salvation,
  Him by whom our spirits live;
Undivided adoration
  To the one Jehovah give.

20. 6s & 4s.

To the great One in Three,
The highest praises be,
  Hence evermore;
His sovereign majesty
May we in glory see,
And to eternity
  Love and adore.

21. 7s & 6s.

To Thee be praise for ever,
  Thou glorious King of kings:
Thy wondrous love and favor
  Each ransomed spirit sings:
We'll celebrate Thy glory,
  With all Thy saints above,
And shout the joyful story
  Of Thy redeeming love.

22. 8s, 7s & 4s.

Great Jehovah, we adore Thee,
  God the Father, God the Son,
God the Spirit, joined in glory
  On the same eternal throne;
    Endless praises
  To Jehovah, Three in One.

23. 8s, 7s & 4s.

Father, Son, and Holy Spirit,
  Thou, the God whom we adore,
May we all thy love inherit,
  To thine image us restore,
    Vast Eternal!
  Praises to Thee evermore.

24. 5s & 6s.

By angels in heaven
  Of every degree,
And saints upon earth,
  All praise be addressed
To God in three persons—
  One God ever-blessed:
As hath been, and now is,
  And always shall be.

25. 11s.

O Father Almighty, to thee be addressed,
With Christ and the Spirit, one God ever bless'd,
All glory and worship, from earth and from heaven,
As was, and is now, and shall ever be given.

26. 8s & 7s.

1. May the grace of Christ the Saviour,
    And the Father's boundless love,
  With the Holy Spirit's favor,
    Rest upon us from above.

2. Thus may we abide in union,
    With each other, and the Lord,
  And possess, in sweet communion,
    Joys which earth cannot afford.

INDEX OF SUBJECTS.

THE FIGURES REFER TO THE HYMNS.

ANGELS—*Visits of, to the Christian*, 164. 942.—*Mission of, to earth*, 967.—*Praises to God by*, 1223. 1232. 1260.

BENEVOLENCE—*Duty of*, 964. 1043. 1050. 1051. 1052. 1063. See CHRISTIAN LOVE.

BIBLE, the—*Influence of*, 46. 74. 75. 76. 77. 78. 79. 80.—*Gratitude for*, 74. 78. See GOSPEL.

CALVARY and SINAI, 838.
CHILDREN—*In heaven*, 934. 1276.—*Baptism of*, 924. 928. 930. 931.—*Prayer for*, 925.—*Christ's love for*, 596. 928. 932.—*Exhortations to*, 1358.—*Hymns for the use of*, 596. 1355. 1359. 1360. 1362. 1363. 1364. 1365. 1366. 1367. 1369. 1370. 1371. 1372. 1373. 1374.

CHRIST—*Birth of*, 1861.—*Rejoicings in the birth of*, 2. 3. 2[•]4. 2[•]6. 2[•]7. 208. 209. 210. 214. 215. 216. 217. 218. 219. 220. 221. 222. 223. 282.—*Life of, on earth*, 226. 227. 60. 772.—*Character of, on earth*, 230. 536. 537.—*Teachings of*, 229.—*Miracles of*, 224. 431. 595.—*Sufferings of*, 231. 282. 283. 239. 240. 245. 246. 247. 249. 250. 896.—*Sufferings and death of*, 241. 242. 248. 260. 318. 317. 412. 417. 666.—*Death of*, 830.—*Cross of*, 832.—*Dying love of*, 528. 571. 573. 574. 917. 921.—*Death and resurrection of*, 235. 236. 237. 238. 351. 392. 496.—*Resurrection and glory of*, 252. 253. 254. 255. 256. 261. 264. 267. 666.—*Victory of*, 234. 259. 273. 276. 909.—*Triumph of the cross of*, 257.—*Ascension of*, 253. 255. 256. 260. 278. 279. 280. 283. 234. 287. 668.—*Glory of*, 263. 270. 513.—*In heaven*, 437. 640.—*Worshiped in heaven*, 286. 283. 784. 1221. 1230. 1251. 1253. 1255. 1258. 1262. 1263.—*Salvation through*, 465. 466. 473. 498. 548. 599. 627. 642. 839. 1217. 1218.—*A mediator*, 514. 520. 669.—*A refuge*, 846. 400. 401. 409. 516. 537. 543.—*Sympathizing love of*, 265. 270. 271. 272. 852. 881. 407. 408. 419. 579. 590. 596. 627. 647. 649. 665. 837. 839. 916. 1046. 1057. 1366. 1305.—"*Loving-kindness*" *of*, 545.—*A shepherd*, 281. 914.—"*Our righteousness*," 550.—*A "hiding-place*," 548.—*A friend*, 665. 857.—*Characters of*, 939.—*The Christian's communion with*, 225. 643. 802. 861. 1202.—*Joy in*, 242. 439. 524. 525. 527. 540. 553. 591. 650. 663. 786. 1211.—*Trust in*, 529. 548. 544. 568. 668. 837. 1837.—*Comfort in*, 531. 532. 850. 1129. 1169. 1837.—*Love toward*, 917.—*The Christian "not ashamed" of*, 492.—"*Nearer to*," 438. See JESUS.

CHRISTIAN LIFE—*The daily duties of*, 521. 622.—*The difficulties of*, 568. 679.—*Exhortation to*, 519. 526. 565. 566. 567. 626. 633. 697. 823. 872. 887. 892. 1256. 1345.—*Courage in*, 557. 564. 612. 808. 999. 1067. 1280.

CHRISTIAN LOVE, *duty of—toward our fellow-men*, 1043. 1051. 1061. 1062.—*Toward the poor*, 1046. 1047. 1049.—*Toward the sick*, 1050. See BENEVOLENCE.

CHURCH, the—*Uniting with*, 922. 941.—*Stability of*, 913. 1008. See SANCTUARY.

COMMUNION OF CHRISTIANS—*With God*, 678. 689. 693. 695. 789. 782.—*With Christ*, 225. 643. 802. 861. 1202.—*With each other*, 680. 681. 685. 703. 704. 705. 706. 708. 709. 710. 711. 713. 716. 718. 719. 720. 721. 722. 854.

CONSECRATION—*of the soul to Christ*, 398. 899. 400. 404. 411. 413. 418. 421. 428. 424. 426. 427. 428. 429. 441. 452. 453. 454. 547. 549. 608. 671. 929. 930.—*Of the soul to God*, 414. 416. 422. 425. 449. 450. 5[•]3. 580. 589. 619. 656. 981. See ORDINANCES. ORDINATION.

CONSOLATION—*in affliction*, 742. 746. 749. 774. 775. 776. 777. 778. 779. 780. 781. 787. 789. 790. 791. 792. 793. 799. 800. 801. 804. 805. 810. 855. 856. 858. 860. 862. 865. 868. 871. 874. 879. 880. 890. 895. 896. 900. 902. 905. 907. 1115. 1132—*In sickness*, 806. 867.—*For death of friends*, 868. 873. 1138. 1174. 1179. 1210. See RESIGNATION.

DEATH—1076. 1084. 1088. 1094. 1101. 1114. 1126. 1131.—*Of friends*, 1069. 1073. 1074. 1075. 1083. 1089. 1091. 1096. 1108. 1119. 1121. 1127. 1128. 1129. 1148. 1157. 1159. 1160. 1186. 1188. 1199.—*Of children*, 1071. 1072. 1185. 1186. 1156.—*Of the Christian*, 1102. 1103. 1104. 1106. 1128. 1124. 1125. 1187. 1188. 1139. 1150. 1151. 1153. 1158. 1162. 1168. 1191. 1220. 1271. 1804.—*Of magistrates*, 1088.—*Of a missionary*, 1209.—*Longing for*, 1086.—*Approach of*, 1172. 1175. 1176. 1177. 1190. 1192. 1193. 1194. 1198.—*Peaceful*, 1095. 1098. 1099.—*At sea*, 1100.—*Vanquished by Christ*, 1828.

DEPRAVITY—*Human*, 315. 836. 480. 620. 1041. See PENITENCE.

DOXOLOGIES—*pages* 11. 18. 17. 25. 29. 49. 59. 117. 185. 155. 185. 187. 191. 193. 199. 203. 217. 221. 237. 243. 251. 273. 297. 811. 891. 897. 899. 401. 415. 423. 427. 446. 447.

ETERNITY—*Compared with time*, 114.—*Duration of*, 1282.

EVENING—1287. 1289. 1291. 1294. 1295. 1300. 1304. 1309. 1316. 1317. 1318. 1321. 1322. 1329. 1331. 1333. 1336. 1337. 1338. 1339. 1341. 1345. 1353. 1356. See SABBATH—*Evening of the*.

FREEDOM—971. 972. 1004. 1016. 1017. 1019. 1027. 1028. 1033. 1034. 1035. 1036. 1037. 1038. 1039. 1059. 1060.

FRIENDS—*Parting from*, 1214.—*Loss of*, 1231. 1884. See CONSOLATION—*For death of friends*.

FUNERAL HYMNS—1219. 1221. 1231. See DEATH. FRIENDS—*Loss of*. FUTURE PUNISHMENT. See WARNING.

GOD—*Discerned in nature*, 82. 84. 86. 87. 89. 90. 91. 106. 145. 176. 177. 735. 936. 958. 1243. 1293.—*Eternal existence of*, 117. 120. 121. 621.—*Attributes of*, 112. 495.—*Power of*, 108. 123. 124. 126. 146. 159. 183.—*Creative power of*, 142. 938. 959.—*Omniscience of*, 100. 122. 1868—*Power and omniscience of*, 107.—*Omnipresence of*, 192.—*Justice of*, 141.—*Goodness of*, 115.—"*Is good*," 1855.—*Benevolence of*, 50. 113. 141. 178. 182. 629. 963.—*Glory of*, 110.—*Worshiped in Heaven*, 1238.—*Majesty of*, 44. 69. 129. 130. 132. 133. 134. 135. 138. 139. 154. 155. 165.—*Sovereignty of*, 152. 179.—*Miraculous providences of*, 160. 478.—*Providence of, mysterious*, 193. 410.—*Upon Mt. Sinai*, 290.—*Protecting care of, over the Christian*, 60. 85. 86. 92. 93. 139. 173. 174. 175. 180. 181. 184. 185. 186. 187. 188. 494. 522. 629. 670. 673. 687. 689. 692. 727. 728. 818. 845. 869. 1814. 1319. 1832.—*Providential government of, over the world*, 1031. 1032. 1325. 1326. 1328. 1344.—*Decrees of*, 111.—*Forgiving love of*, 140. 483. 555.

INDEX OF SUBJECTS.

915.—*Pity of,* 102.—"*Is love,*" 128. 438. 631. 670. 1388.—*Present at our worship,* 153.—*Grace of,* 570. 531.—*A refuge,* 178. 912.—*A shepherd,* 781. 782.—*Comfort in,* 119. 846.—*Joy in,* 508. 510. 575. 582. 586. 587. 597. 617. 676. 677. 678. 714. 729. 797. 1218. 1216.—*Trust in,* 127. 144. 189. 190. 191. 342. 397. 445. 463. 477. 594. 619. 623. 673. 693. 725. 755. 756. 757. 734. 735. 736. 793. 808. 813. 834. 835. 836. 840. 841. 842. 1077. 1134. 1224. 1273. 1321.—*Trust in, at sea,* 1235. 1236.—*Trust in the promises of,* 172.—"*As my day my strength shall be,*" 765.—*Our dependence upon,* 499. 515. 623.—*Love toward,* 585. 599. 600.—*Submission to,* 809. 811. 1068. 1082.—*Nearness to,* 585. 533. 1081.—"*Nearer to,*" 893.—*The sinner called by,* 875.
GOSPEL, *the—Rejoicings in the spread of,* 949. 950. 951. 952. 1009. 1010.—*Ultimate success of, certain,* 1084. 1040. See MISSIONS.
PRAISE—*To God and Christ, for the conversion of the world.*
GRACE—*In the heart,* 608.—*Of God,* 615. 687.—*Manifested through Christ,* 635. 636. See PRAYER—*for grace.*
GRACES, *the—Love,* 415. 508. 580. 1058. See also, CHRISTIAN LOVE. —*Faith,* 602. 748.—*Joy,* 641.—*Charity,* 1052. See BENEVOLENCE. —*Faith, Hope, and Charity,* 498.
GRAVE, *the—*1087. 1101. 1118. See DEATH.

HAPPINESS—*of the Christian,* 430. 484. 645. 712. 864. 910.—*Of Heaven,* 1244. 1245. 1253. 1260. 1261. 1312.
HEAVEN—*Anticipations of,* 468 497. 499. 509. 594. 613. 614. 616. 644. 808. 870. 1112. 1146. 1152. 1163. 1164. 1166. 1178. 1179. 1180. 1181. 1182. 1133. 1197. 1198. 1204. 1205. 1206. 1217. 1228. 1223. 1226. 1227. 1229. 1233. 1234. 1239. 1240. 1242. 1246. 1247. 1248. 1249. 1250. 1251. 1252. 1254. 1255. 1257. 1261. 1262. 1264. 1265. 1266. 1267. 1269. 1270. 1271. 1272. 1273. 1274. 1275. 1277. 1346. 1354.—*Aspirations toward,* 482. 493. 530. 519. 1018. 1221. 1235. 1237. 1238. 1259.—*Waiting for,* 1813.—*Meeting of friends in,* 1132.—*Rest in,* 844. 1107.—"*Cross and Crown,*" 770.—"*My home,*" 899.
HOLY SPIRIT, *The—Offices of,* 197. 289.—*Bestowed upon the disciples,* 291.—*Power of the influences of,* 488. See PRAYER—*and* PRAISE—*to the Holy Spirit.*
HUMAN LIFE—*Trials of,* 737. 738. 743. 744. 750. 751. 752. 753. 755. 759. 760. 763. 768. 765. 767. 768. 769. 814. 815. 816. 817. 824. 842. 843. 844. 876. 884.—*Temptations of,* 741. 754. 760. 761. 871.—*Uncertainty of,* 825. 896. 1230.—*Shortness of,* 97. 117. 821. 1340.—*Close of,* 683. 848.

IMMORTALITY—*Of the soul,* 1254.
INVITATION—*To receive the Gospel,* 320. 322. 340. 341. 363. 364. 365. 386. 391. 610.—*To repentance* 316. 340. 353.—*To return to God,* 324. 325. 443.—*To accept Christ,* 356. 357. 362. 366. 367. 368. 369. 371. 372. 377. 878. 380. 381. 387. 389. 403. 667.—*To "come to me,"* 742.—*To heaven,* 889. 882.—"*To the ark,*" 778. 888.

JESUS—*Name of,* 588. 598. 605. 607. See CHRIST.
JUDGMENT—*Day of,* 802. 1065. 1143. 1154. 1196.—*Approach of,* 343. 1078. 1079. 1109. 1111. 1140. 1155.—*Anticipations of,* 876. 890. 1060. 1189. 1240. See WARNING.

LIBERTY. See FREEDOM.
LORD'S DAY, *the.* See SABBATH.
LORD'S PRAYER, *the,* 1368.

MISSIONARIES—*Encouragement to,* 945. 953. 977. 984. 985. 991.—*Prayer for,* 954.—*Ordained by Christ,* 962.
MISSIONS.—943. 944. 945. 946. 947. 948. 949. 950. 953. 954. 956. 957. 962. 963. 984. 985. 986. 993. 994. 995. 996. 997. 998. 1000. 1008.
MORNING—1161. 1279. 1298. 1296. 1298. 1299. 1301. 1306. 1309. 1314. 1315. 1327. 1392. 1342. 1358. See SABBATH.—*Morning of the.*
MUSIC—187.—*Of heaven,* 285. 1222. See PRAISE.

NATURE — *Teachings of,* 88. 101. 1243. See GOD—*Discerned in nature.*
NEW YEAR—*The,* 455.
NIGHT—1278. 1285. 1290. 1291. 1310. 1320. 1343.

ORDINANCES—*The Lord's Supper,* 244. 918. 919. 920. 921. See COMMUNION OF CHRISTIANS. *Baptism,* 924. 928. 932. 933. See CHILDREN—*Baptism of.*
ORDINATION—941.—*Of a missionary,* 953.

PATRIOTIC HYMNS—958. 1004. 1025. 1027. 1042.
PEACE—*The spread of,* 972. 987. 1000. 1012. 1015. 1019—*Prayer for,* 978. 1011. 1015.
PILGRIM FATHERS—*the,* 958. 1005. 1006. 1007.
PENITENCE—*for natural depravity,* 480. 523. 601. 620.—*For human weakness,* 374. 440. 442. 471. 592. 627. 857. 903. 1297.—*For past sins,* 461.—*For backsliding,* 433. 434. 444. 459. 479. 812. 831.—*In view of the death of Christ,* 328. 327. 351. 354. 482. 446. 447. 448. 461. 634.—*And pardon,* 487. 647.
PRAISE—*To God,* 96. 97. 98. 99. 100. 103. 104. 105. 116. 118. 131. 142. 143. 146. 147. 148. 149. 150. 151. 156. 157. 158. 161. 162. 163. 166. 167. 168. 170. 171. 202. 487. 495. 505. 506. 509. 511. 702. 546. 552. 569. 630. 1029. 1064. 1195. 1187. 1201. 1208. 1212. 1352.—*To Christ,* 200. 211. 212. 213. 232. 258. 259. 260. 262. 263. 266. 267. 274. 275. 292. 293. 294. 295. 296. 297. 299. 299. 301. 402. 467. 489. 491. 501. 502. 507. 512. 513. 517. 551. 556. 558. 560. 561. 562. 576. 577. 578. 606. 618. 644. 652. 654. 655. 658. 659. 660. 663. 664. 665. 666. 734. 882. 907. 909. 981. 1195.—*To the Holy Spirit,* 196.—*To the Trinity,* 201. 223.—*For salvation,* 487. 572. 726.—*To God for the conversion of the world,* 961. 965. 966. 975. 980. 995. 1022. 1024. 1080. 1082.—*To Christ for the conversion of the world,* 960. 973. 974. 976. 979. 1001. 1002. 1018. 1024. —*On earth to be continued in heaven,* 486.—*Exhortations to,* 632. 638. 639. 672.—*Appropriate to the Sabbath,* 40. 41. 42. 62. 64. 65. 66. 67.—*Appropriate to the Sanctuary,* 39. 44. 57. 72. 985. 986. 987.
PRAYER—*Nature of,* 694.—*Worth of,* 686. 696. 715. 783.
PRAYER, *Hymns of—For grace,* 88. 90. 94. 436. 440. 530. 602. 926. 1298. —*For holiness,* 205. 305. 874. 483. 523. 631. 674. 683. 690. 700. 740. 819. 863. 903. 904. 999. 1302. 1352.—*For guidance in a Christian life,* 888. 889. 890. 894.—*For strength and support in duty,* 622. 623. 631. *For the presence of God,* 451. 475. 525. 621. 653. 876. 1091. 1200.—*For mercy,* 406. 435. 849. 891. 893.—*For rest,* 456.—*For submission,* 420. 723. 795. 796. 822. 827. 829. 857.—*For consolation,* 476. 691. 701. 794. 859. 874. 875. 886. 901. 961. 969.—*For divine protection,* 224. 653. 657. 724. 880. 885. 969. 1833.—*For preparation for Heaven,* 95. 674. 691. 888. 889.—*For preparation for judgment,* 845. 853. 884.—*For the Holy Spirit* 198. 405. 472. 481. 624. 674. 847. 1120. 1225.— "*Oh Lord remember me,*" 820. —*To Christ for salvation,* 346. 398. 419. 457. 468. 524. 661. 662. 837. 891. 928. 1298.—*Litany to Christ,* 454.—*For the poor,* 1026. *—For the sailor,* 1165.—*For the divine blessing upon the church,* 684. 717. 888.—*For a revival of religion,* 883.—*For the salvation of the Jews,* 897.—*For the conversion of the world,* 955. 956. 957. 1014. 1020. 1021. 1023. 1900.—*For the divine blessing upon the world,* 881. 947. 948. 963.—*Appropriate to the Sabbath,* 23. 54. —*Appropriate to the sanctuary,* 7. 17. 18. 19. 34. 37. 49. 58. 699. 987.

REFORMS—1041.—*Work of God in,* 970. 1053.—*Urgent duty of the Christian in,* 982. 992. 1066.—*Ultimate success of, certain,* 1044. 1058.—*The right not always popular,* 970.
REPENTANCE. See PENITENCE.
RESIGNATION—*Under trials,* 458. 764. 771. 745. 747.—*To the will of God,* 1284. See CONSOLATION.
REST—*In God,* 675. 1307.—*In Heaven,* 1268.
RESURRECTION—*Of the body,* 1242. 1244. 1270.
REWARD—*Of Christian labors,* 686.

SABBATH, *The—As an anniversary of Christ's resurrection,* 30. 40. 41. 42. 507.—*A type of Heaven,* 4. 9. 15. 19. 26. 28. 29. 52.—*Universal observance of,* 11.—*Sacredness of,* 6. 8. 9. 1306.—*Spiritual in-*

fluences of, 45.—*Usefulness of*, 30.—*Worship of*, 1. 5.—*Enjoyments of*, 15. 20. 29.—*Morning of*, 3. 25. 45. 56. 61. 62. 65. 70. 72.—*Evening of*, 55. 670.—"*Drawing on*," 56.

SANCTUARY, The—*Dedication of*, 939.—*Invitation to*, 51.—*Opening of worship in*, 52.—*Enjoyments of*, 2. 12. 13. 23. 24. 31. 32. 36. 38. 43. 48. 58. 68. 935.—*Sacredness of*, 10. 31.—*Exercises proper for*, 14. 33. 47. 71. 169. 935.—*Spiritual influences of*, 35. 39. 936.—*Close of worship in*, 21. 22. 34. 54. 59. 63.—*Detention from*, 16. 783.

SEASONS—1325. 1351.—*Spring*, 1324. 1335. 1349.—*Autumn*, 1334. 1350.

"STAR OF BETHLEHEM," 588.
SUBMISSION. See RESIGNATION.

TE DEUM, 157. 506.
TEMPERANCE, 1044. 1045. 1065.
TIME—*Flight, of*, 455. 468. 625. 1092. 1105. 1117. 1141. 1145. 1147. 1148. 1167. 1173. 1280. 1340. 1345. 1351.
TRINITY—*The*, 194. 195. 199.

WARNING—*From the evanescence of nature*, 317. 829. 1359.—*From the flight of time*, 3. 8. 326. 330. 394. 1350.—*From the approach of death*, 308. 309. 313. 328. 337. 338. 359. 386. 388. 832.—*From the certainty of future punishment*, 829. 844. 879. 462. 829.—*From the approach of the judgment*, 332. 333.

334. 335. 347. 350. 359. 360. 361. 363. 373. 383. 396.—*From the fate of the wicked*, 312. 314. 335. 1020. —*From the numbers of the lost*, 310. 311. 395.
WORLDLY PLEASURES—*Evanescence of*, 370. 497. 733. 1116. 1113. 1171. 1215.
WORSHIP—*Always seasonable*, 1350. 1347.—*Private*, 504. 1335. See SANCTUARY.

YEAR OF JUBILEE, 364. 365.

ZION—*Daughter of*, 726. 908.—*Captivity of*, 908.—*God protects*, 983. 988. 989. 990.—*Triumph of*, 911. 946. 980. 990.

INDEX OF FIRST LINES.

First Line	Page
Abba, Father hear thy child	268
Abide with me, fast falls the eventide	215
Abide with us, the evening shades	169
Above, below, where'er I gaze	24
A charge to keep I have	195
Affliction is a stormy deep	249
Again returns the day of holy rest	421
Again the Lord of life and light	10
Ah guilty sinner, ruin'd by transgression	120
Ah whither should I go	152
Alas and did my Saviour bleed	144
Alas how poor and little worth	353
Alas the utter emptiness	288
Alas what hourly dangers rise	179
All from the sun's uprise	18
All hail the power of Jesus' name	174
All men are equal in their birth	337
All mortal vanities begone	234
All nature dies and lives again	351
All ye nations praise the Lord	27
Almighty God thy piercing eye	444
Almighty Maker God	31
Along the mountain track of life	142
Altho' the vine its fruit deny	38
Amazing grace, how sweet the sound	180
Am I a soldier of the cross	178
Amid thy wrath, remember love	141
A mother may forgetful be	289
And are we yet alive	231
And can my heart aspire so high	255
And Jesus said, Suffer little children	295
And let this feeble body fail	397
And must I part with all I have	139
And must this body die	360
And now another week begins	10
And will the Judge descend	360
And will the Lord thus condescend	141
Angel of God, whate'er betide	255
Angels assist to sing	50
Angels from the realms of glory	65
Angels rejoiced and sweetly sung	63
Angels roll the rock away	89
Angels where'er we go attend	298
Another day has passed along	4
Another day is past	429
Another fleeting day is gone	417
Another hand is beckoning us	355
Another six days work is done	3
Answer me, burning stars of night	399
A poor way-faring man of grief	169
Approach my soul the mercy-seat	145
Arise, arise, with joy survey	302
Arise my soul, arise	211
Arise my soul, fly up and run	401
Arise my soul, my joyful powers	174
Arise ye people, and adore	46
Arm of the Lord awake, awake	300
Around Bethesda's healing wave	137
Around the Saviour's lofty throne	161
Around the throne of God in heaven	413
As changing as the moon	262
As down in the sunless retreats of the	206
As flows the rapid river	273
Asleep in Jesus' blessed sleep	346
As oft with worn and weary feet	243
As once the Saviour took his seat	191
As pants the hart for cooling streams	56
As the hart with eager looks	264
As the sweet flower that scents the morn	340
A stranger in the world below	412
As when the weary traveler gains	394
At anchor laid remote from home	156
At evening time let there be light	341
At the cross her station keeping	75
Author of good, we rest on thee	247
Awake and sing the song	192
Awake, awake, the sacred song	63
Awaked by Sinai's awful sound	148
Awake my heart, arise my tongue	181
Awake my soul and with the sun	419
Awake my soul in joyful lays	172
Awake my soul, lift up thine eyes	166
Awake my soul, stretch every nerve	178
Awake our drowsy souls	18
Awake our souls, away our fears	165
Awake ye saints and raise your eyes	351
Away with our sorrow and fear	388
Before Jehovah's awful throne	40
Begin my soul th' exalted lay	28
Begin my tongue some heavenly theme	47
Behold a stranger at the door	98
Behold my soul the narrow bound	104
Behold the day is come	109
Behold the glories of the Lamb	182
Behold the Lamb	79
Behold the man, how glorious he	76
Behold the morning sun	12
Behold the mountain of the Lord	289
Behold the path that mortals tread	101
Behold the Saviour of mankind	80
Behold the western evening light	343

INDEX OF FIRST LINES.

	PAGE
Behold what wondrous grace	199
Behold where in a mortal form	80
Be joyful in God all ye lands of the earth	20
Beneath our feet and o'er our head	351
Beneath the star-lit arch	360
Be still, be still, for all around	3
Be still my heart, these anxious cares	236
Be thou O God by night by day	419
Beyond, beyond that boundless sea	32
Beyond the starry skies	92
Beyond where Cedron's waters flow	131
Blessed are the sons of God	268
Blest be the tie that binds	227
Blest by the dear uniting love	224
Blest day of God most calm, most bright	7
Blest hour when mortal man retires	4
Blest hour when virtuous friends shall	354
Blest is the man whose softening heart	334
Blest morning whose young dawning ray	10
Blow ye the trumpet blow	116
Both heaven and earth do worship thee	162
Break forth in song ye trees	318
Brethren, while we sojourn here	229
Brightest and best of the sons of the	90
Bright glories rush upon my sight	413
Bright was the guiding-star that led	391
Bright were the mornings first impearl'd	251
Broad is the road that leads to death	100
Brother, rest from sin and sorrow	380
Brother, tho' from yonder sky	362
Brother, thou art gone before us	384
Burst ye emerald gates and bring	404
By cool Siloam's shady rill	293
Call Jehovah thy salvation	16
Calm on the bosom of thy God	354
Calm on the listening ear of night	69
Cease here longer to detain me	374
Cease ye mourners, cease to languish	374
Center of our hopes thou art	267
Champion of Jesus! man of God	349
Cheek grow pale, but heart be vigorous	315
Child of sin and sorrow	126
Children of God who faint and slow	255
Children of the heavenly king	228
Christian brethren, ere we part	265
Christian, see the orient morning	313
Christian, the morn breaks sweetly o'er	375
Christ leads me thro' no darker rooms	249
Christ, of all my hopes the ground	201
Christ the Lord is risen to-day	89
Christ whose glory fills the skies	201
Close softly, fondly, while ye weep	340
Come all ye saints of God	222
Come at the morning hour	428
Come, children, drink the balmy dew	99
Come, dearest Lord, and feed thy sheep	7
Come, desire of nations, come	385
Come every pious heart	210
Come, gracious Spirit, heav'nly dove	59
Come hither all ye weary souls	98

	PAGE
Come, Holy Spirit, come	195
Come, Holy Spirit, heav'nly dove	153
Come in thou blessed of our God	216
Come let us anew our journey pursue	433
Come let us ascend my companion and	433
Come let us gladly sing	35
Come let us join our cheerful songs	181
Come let us join our songs of praise	180
Come let us lift our joyful eyes	177
Come let us sound her praise abroad	335
Come my fond, flattering heart	211
Come my soul thy suit prepare	219
Come now ye wanderers to your God	133
Come O Creator Spirit blest	58
Come O my soul in sacred lays	41
Come on my partners in distress	271
Come O thou traveler unknown	170
Come O thou universal good	393
Come! said Jesus' sacred voice	113
Come shout aloud the Father's grace	183
Come sinner to the Gospel feast	103
Come thou Almighty King	60
Come thou desire of all thy saints	9
Come thou fount of every blessing	204
Come thou long-expected Jesus	209
Come to the ark, come to the ark	245
Come to the house of prayer	13
Come to the land of peace	108
Come trembling sinner in whose breast	138
Come wandering sheep, O come	123
Come weary souls, with sins distressed	99
Come ye disconsolate	269
Come ye sinners heavy laden	118
Come ye sinners poor and needy	118
Come ye souls by sin afflicted	119
Come ye that know and fear the Lord	39
Come ye that love the Lord	199
Come ye that love the Saviour's name	176
Come ye weary souls oppressed	113
Commit thou all thy griefs	263
Cross, reproach and tribulation	274
Crown his head with endless blessing	209
Daughter of Zion, awake from thy sadness	230
Daughter of Zion from the dust	288
Day of judgment day of wonders	114
Day of wrath that day of burning	364
Dear as thou wer't and justly dear	355
Dearest of all the names above	188
Dear friend, whose presence in the house	187
Dear is the hallowed morn to me	5
Dear Jesus ever at my side	187
Dear refuge of my weary soul	245
Dear Saviour if these lambs should stray	292
Dear Saviour we are thine	294
Dear Saviour, when my thoughts recall	140
Deathless principle arise	403
Defend the poor and desolate	337
Depart awhile each thought of care	304
Depth of mercy can there be	111
Descend from heaven immortal dove	393

INDEX OF FIRST LINES.

First Line	PAGE
Dismiss us with thy blessing Lord	5
Does the Gospel word proclaim	147
Do I not love thee O my Lord!	188
Down the dark future thro' long	321
Doxologies	446 & 447
Dread sovereign let my evening song	425
Drooping souls no longer mourn	117
Dying souls fast bound in sin	117
Early my God without delay	6
Earth has engrossed my love too long	401
Earth's transitory things decay	345
Earth with her ten thousand flowers	27
Enthron'd is Jesus now	92
Ere to the world again we go	5
Eternal Spirit we confess	59
Eternity, eternity	415
Everlasting, changing never	327
Every day hath toil and trouble	339
Exert thy power, thy rights maintain	303
Fading, still fading	437
Fairest Lord Jesus	207
Fairest of all the lights above	37
Fair shines the morning star	116
Faith, hope and charity, these three	159
Farewell bright soul a short farewell	393
Farewell dear friends I must be gone	392
Far, far o'er hill and dell	367
Far from mortal cares retreating	16
Far from my thoughts vain world begone	235
Far from the world O Lord I flee	220
Father divine this deadening power	321
Father, how wide thy glory shines	33
Father I long I faint to see	390
Father of mercies send thy grace	334
Father, they who thee receive	27
Father, whate'er of earthly bliss	250
Few are thy days and full of woe	257
Few, few and evil are thy days	352
Firm as the earth thy Gospel stands	247
For a season call'd to part	229
Forever with the Lord	194
Forgive my folly	280
For the mercies of the day	15
Forth from the dark and stormy sky	5
Forth in thy name O Lord we go	414
Fountain of grace, rich full and free	167
Friend after friend departs	366
Friends of the poor the young the weak	335
From all that dwell below the skies	163
From Calvary a cry was heard	76
From day to day before our eyes	301
From every earthly pleasure	151
From every stormy wind that blows	234
From Greenland's icy mountains	299
From his low bed of mortal dust	345
From the cross uplifted high	111
From thee my God my joys shall rise	184
From the recesses of a lowly spirit	120
Full of trembling expectation	273
Gales from heaven if God so will	267
Gently, gently lay thy rod	267
Gently glides the stream of life	431
Gently Lord, O gently lead us	279
Gird on thy conquering sword	324
Give me the wings of faith to rise	399
Give thanks to God most high	51
Give to the Lord ye sons of fame	44
Give to the winds thy fears	263
Glorious in thy saint appear	27
Glorious things of thee are spoken	312
Glory, glory to our King	89
Glory to God on high	60
Glory to God whose witness train	187
Glory to thee my God this night	416
Glory to thee whose powerful word	415
God bless our native land	326
God in His temple let us meet	2
God in the high and holy place	30
God is a name my soul adores	58
God is gone up on high	83
God is love, his mercy brightens	204
God is the refuge of his saints	51
God made all his creatures free	331
God moves in a mysterious way	51
God my supporter and my hope	57
God named Love, whose fount thou art	157
God of eternity from thee	98
God of my life and all my powers	255
God of my life through all its days	157
God of my life thy boundless grace	132
God of my life, to thee belong	418
God of my life to thee I call	237
God of my life whose gracious power	159
God of our salvation	284
God of the sunlight hours how sad	424
God's glory is a wondrous thing	307
God the all-terrible, thou who ordainest	321
God the eternal awful name	45
God the Lord a King remaineth	97
Go messenger of peace and love	302
Gone are those great and good	318
Go preach my Gospel saith the Lord	305
Go, spirit of the sainted dead	346
Go to dark Gethsemane	110
Go to the grave in all thy glorious prime	367
Go to the pillow of disease	335
Go to thy rest fair child	358
Go tune thy voice to sacred song	176
Go watch and pray, thou can'st not tell	126
Go when the morning shineth	434
Go ye messengers of God	309
Grace, like an uncorrupted seed	191
Grace, 'tis a charming sound	193
Gracious Jesus Lord most dear	147
Great God as seasons disappear	427
Great God how infinite art thou	32
Great God thy penetrating eye	33
Great God to thee my evening song	418
Great God we sing, that mighty hand	164
Great God what do I see and hear	342

INDEX OF FIRST LINES.

	PAGE		PAGE
Great God, whom heaven, and earth, and.	303	Here cares and angry passions cease....	9
Great God whose universal sway........	304	He reigns, the Lord the Saviour reigns...	41
Great Redeemer, friend of sinners.......	381	Here we meet to part again............	438
Great ruler of all nature's frame.........	56	He sendeth sun, he sendeth............	343
Great ruler of the earth and skies.......	305	He who on earth as man was known....	87
Great shepherd of thine Israel..........	217	High in the heavens eternal God........	53
Great shepherd of thy people hear.......	221	High in yonder realms of light..........	363
Great source of being and of love........	23	High on a hill of dazzling light.........	41
Green pastures and clear streams.......	263	Holy Father thou hast taught me.......	278
Guide me O thou great Jehovah........	278	Holy Ghost with light divine...........	265
		Holy, holy, holy Lord, Be thy..........	88
Hail morning known among the blest....	84	Holy, holy, holy Lord, Live............	88
Hail my ever-blessed Jesus.............	382	Holy Saviour, friend unseen...........	241
Hail sovereign love that form'd the plan..	173	Holy Spirit Lord of light..............	264
Hail sweetest, dearest tie that binds.....	223	Hosanna to the living Lord............	84
Hail the day that sees him rise..........	89	Hosanna to the Prince of light..........	177
Hail thou happy morn so glorious.......	97	Hosanna with a cheerful sound.........	422
Hail thou once despised Jesus..........	97	How are thy servants blessed O Lord....	55
Hail to the brightness of Zion's glad.....	310	How beauteous are their feet...........	332
Hail to the Lord's anointed.............	317	How beauteous were the marks divine....	72
Hail to the Prince of life and peace......	85	How beautiful the morning.............	439
Hail tranquil hour of closing day........	425	How blest are they whose transient.....	345
Hallelujah best and sweetest...........	395	How blest is he whose tranquil mind....	216
Happy soul thy days are ended.........	381	How blest the righteous when he dies...	347
Happy the heart where graces reign.....	183	How blest the sacred tie that binds.....	216
Happy the spirit released from its clay...	411	How blest thy creature is O God........	13
Hark a voice divides the sky...........	362	How calm and beautiful the morn.......	91
Hark a voice from heaven proclaiming...	327	How charming is the place.............	226
Hark, hark the Gospel trumpet sounds...	301	How condescending and how kind......	291
Hark, hark the notes of joy.............	70	How dear is the thought that the angels.	48
Hark how the Gospel trumpet sounds....	301	How deep and tranquil is the joy.......	218
Hark how the watchmen cry............	198	How did my heart rejoice to hear.......	8
Hark my soul it is the Lord............	268	How doth the little busy bee...........	445
Hark ten thousand harps and voices....	96	How dread are thine eternal years......	175
Hark the glad sound the Saviour comes..	69	How firm a foundation ye saints of the...	230
Hark the herald angels sing............	62	How gentle God's commands...........	260
Hark the song of jubilee...............	309	How happy are the new-born race......	203
Hark the sounds of joy and gladness....	313	How happy every child of grace........	225
Hark the voice of love and mercy.......	97	How happy is the pilgrim's lot..........	377
Hark those happy voices saying........	129	How happy they who safely hous'd......	354
Hark what celestial sounds............	70	How heavy is the night................	194
Hark what mean those holy voices......	64	How high thou art, our songs can own...	159
Hark what mean those lamentations....	315	How long sometimes a day appears......	34
Haste O sinner to be wise..............	113	How lost wast my condition............	150
Hast thou midst life's empty noise......	339	How oft, alas, this wretched heart.......	143
Hast thou wasted all the powers........	265	How pleasant, how divinely fair.........	1
Hath God, cast off forever.............	154	How pleased and blest was I...........	11
Have we no tears to shed for him.......	73	How pleasing is thy voice..............	432
Head of the Church triumphant........	287	How precious is the book divine........	21
Head of the hosts in glory.............	94	How rich thy favors God of grace.......	54
Health of the weak to make them strong..	137	How short and hasty is our life.........	105
Hearken Lord to my complaints........	266	How sweet and awful is the place.......	290
Hear, O sinner, mercy hails you........	115	How sweet and heavenly is the sight....	225
Hear the heralds of the Gospel.........	115	How sweet, how calm this Sabbath morn.	9
Hearts of stone relent, relent..........	112	How sweetly flow'd the Gospel sound....	72
Hear what the voice of heaven proclaims.	349	How sweet the hour of closing day......	420
Heaven is the land where troubles cease.	413	How sweet the melting lay.............	226
He dies the friend of sinners dies........	74	How sweet the name of Jesus sounds....	191
He knelt, the Saviour knelt and pray'd...	78	How sweet to leave the world awhile....	4
He lives, the great Redeemer lives......	164	How sweet to reflect on the joys that....	409
Here at thy cross my dying Lord........	135	How swift the torrent rolls............	361

INDEX OF FIRST LINES.

First Line	Page
How tedious and tasteless the hours	389
How vain are all things here below	254
Hush, my dear, lie still and slumber	441
Hush, the loud cannon's roar	322
I am the man that hath seen affliction	356
I am weary I am weary	276
I asked the Lord that I might grow	135
I ask not now for gold to gild	339
I can not always trace the way	415
I can not call affliction sweet	248
I faint, my soul doth faint	259
If a man die shall he live again	357
If death my friend and me divide	376
I feel within a want	285
If human kindness meets return	290
If life in sorrow must be spent	239
If life's pleasures charm thee	285
If on our daily course our mind	165
If through unruffled seas	260
I left the God of truth and light	155
I'll praise my Maker with my breath	329
I long to behold him array'd	388
I love thy kingdom, Lord	227
I love to steal awhile away	424
I'm a pilgrim and I'm a stranger	404
I'm but a stranger here	283
I'm not ashamed to own my Lord	177
In a land of strange delights	431
In all my Lord's appointed ways	179
In evil long I took delight	102
In expectation sweet	359
Infinite leagues beyond the sky	45
In God's own house pronounce his	8
I now have found abiding rest	168
In silence of the voiceless night	414
In sleep's serene oblivion laid	419
Inspirer and hearer of prayer	205
In sweet exalted strains	51
In the broad fields of heaven	405
In the cross of Christ I glory	275
In the hour of my distress	267
In the sun and moon and stars	364
In time of fear, when trouble's near	246
In time of tribulation	154
Into the silent land	356
In trouble and in grief O Lord	249
In true and patient hope	108
In vain our fancy strives to paint	349
In Zion's sacred gates	50
I send the joys of earth away	161
I sing of God, the mighty source	28
I sing th' almighty power of God	34
I stand on Zion's mount	193
Is this a fast for me	322
Is this the kind return	152
I thank thee uncreated sun	137
I thank the goodness and the grace	444
I think when I read that sweet story of	442
I thirst, but not as once I did	167
It is the Lord enthron'd in light	249
I travel all the irksome night	352
I want a heart to pray	197
I was a wand'ring sheep	196
I worship thee sweet will of God	247
I would not live alway	378
Jehovah reigns, he dwells in light	37
Jehovah reigns, his throne is high	53
Jerusalem my glorious home	396
Jesus and didst thou condescend	144
Jesus and shall it ever be	159
Jesus at thy command	211
Jesus blessed mediator	383
Jesus Christ, my Lord and Saviour	443
Jesus full of all compassion	279
Jesus I love thy charming name	190
Jesus immortal King arise	288
Jesus I my cross have taken	274
Jesus in sickness and in pain	252
Jesus lives and so shall I	200
Jesus lives, thy terrors now	371
Jesus Lord we look to thee	228
Jesus lover of my soul	261
Jesus my all to heaven is gone	172
Jesus my God and Saviour	282
Jesus my Lord how rich thy grace	336
Jesus my Lord, my God, my all	158
Jesus my strength my hope	294
Jesus our Lord ascend thy throne	81
Jesus shall reign where'er the sun	163
Jesus tender shepherd hear us	441
Jesus the Lord of glory died	425
Jesus the name high over all	183
Jesus the sinner's friend to thee	292
Jesus the very thought of thee	142
Jesus thou art the sinner's friend	144
Jesus thou everlasting King	161
Jesus thy boundless love to me	171
Jesus thy love shall we forget	244
Jesus thy robe of righteousness	173
Jesus to thy dear wounds we flee	391
Jesus' transporting name	83
Jesus' tremendous name	193
Jesus united by thy grace	251
Jesus where'er thy people meet	3
Jesus who knows full well	226
Jesus who on Calvary's mountain	209
Jesus whose glory streaming rays	166
Jews were wrought to cruel madness	75
Join all the glorious names	83
Joyfully joyfully onward I move	411
Joyful words we meet again	272
Joy to the world the Lord is come	68
Joy to those that love the Lord	201
Judges who rule the world by laws	329
Just as I am without one plea	132
Just o'er the grave I hung	259
Keep silence all created things	33
Kindred in Christ for his dear sake	217
Kingdoms and thrones to God belong	37

INDEX OF FIRST LINES.

	PAGE		PAGE
Laden with guilt and full of fears	21	Lord thou hast search'd and seen me	37
Lamb of God whose bleeding love	149	Lord thou hast won at length I yield	203
Lamp of our feet whereby we trace	21	Lord thou wilt hear me when I pray	425
Let every mortal ear attend	191	Lord thy glory fills the heaven	65
Let God arise in all his might	43	Lord 't is an infinite delight	183
Let me go, the day is breaking	381	Lord what a feeble piece	361
Let me not thou, King Eternal	369	Lord what a heaven of saving grace	77
Let others boast how strong they be	257	Lord what a thoughtless wretch was I	101
Let party names no more	227	Lord what a wretched land is this	257
Let saints below in concert sing	223	Lord when iniquities abound	324
Let there be light, thus spoke the word	304	Lord when I quit this earthly stage	161
Let the still air rejoice	338	Lord when my raptured thought surveys	34
Let us awake our joys	95	Lord when thine ancient people cried	330
Let us with a joyful mind	27	Lord where shall guilty souls retire	57
Let worldly minds the world pursue	139	Lord while for all mankind we pray	332
Let Zion and her sons rejoice	57	Lord with glowing heart I'll praise thee	17
Let Zion in her King rejoice	45	Lo! the mighty God appearing	380
Life is the time to serve the Lord	100	Lo! the prisoner is releas'd	362
Lift not thou the wailing voice	371	Lo! the seal of death is breaking	383
Lift your eyes of faith and see	403	Loud Hallelujahs to the Lord	40
Lift your glad voices in triumph on high	90	Love divine all love excelling	208
Light of life seraphic fire	14	Love, love on earth appears	123
Light of the soul, O Saviour blest	235	Lo! what a glorious corner-stone	162
Light of those whose dreary dwelling	275	Lo! what a glorious sight appears	396
Like morning when her early breeze	156	Lowly and solemn be	222
Like Noah's weary dove	260		
Like sheep we went astray	153	Majestic sweetness sits enthron'd	190
Little travelers Zionward	295	Make channels for the streams of love	337
Lo! God is here let us adore	45	Man has a soul of vast desires	101
Lo! he comes with clouds descending	114	Many centuries have fled	291
Lo! he cometh countless trumpets	380	Marked as the purpose of the skies	302
Lo I beheld the scattering shades	398	Mary to the Saviour's tomb	112
Lone amidst the dead and dying	273	May freedom speed onward wherever	322
Lo! on a narrow neck of land	125	May the grace of God our Saviour	16
Look ye saints the sight is glorious	96	Meet and right it is to sing	61
Loosed from my God, and far removed	136	Men of God go take your stations	315
Lord a little band and lowly	443	Men whose boast it is that ye	331
Lord at this closing hour	13	Mercy alone can meet my case	141
Lord deliver, thou canst save	331	Mercy O thou Son of David	204
Lord dismiss us with thy blessing	17	Messiah at thy glad approach	69
Lord forever at thy side	147	Mid scenes of confusion and creature	408
Lord from thy blessed throne	326	Midst sorrow and care	265
Lord how secure and blest are they	156	Mighty God while angels bless thee	65
Lord I am vile, conceiv'd in sin	155	Mighty one before whose face	26
Lord I can not let thee go	264	Morning breaks upon the tomb	88
Lord in the morning thou shalt hear	6	Mortals awake, with angels join	68
Lord in thy garden agony	73	Mourn for the thousands slain	332
Lord I will bless thee all my days	172	Much in sorrow oft in woe	403
Lord Jesus come for here	322	Must Jesus bear the cross alone	244
Lord lead the way the Saviour went	337	My country 'tis of thee	318
Lord let me know mine end	361	My days, my weeks, my months, my	130
Lord may the spirit of this feast	290	My faith looks up to thee	222
Lord may thy truth upon the heart	5	My Father bids me come	294
Lord of earth thy forming hand	385	My Father God, how sweet the sound	153
Lord of the Sabbath and its light	3	My Father's house on high	361
Lord of the worlds above	19	My Father to thy mercy-seat	257
Lord of the worlds below	436	My feet are worn and weary with the	215
Lord of the world who hast preserved	422	My former hopes are fled	258
Lord see what floods of sorrow rise	142	My God accept my early vows	161
Lord send thy servants forth	306	My God how endless is thy love	418
Lord thou didst arise and say	309	My God I love and I adore	53

INDEX OF FIRST LINES.

First Line	Page
My God in whom are all the springs	44
My God my Father, blissful name	250
My God my King thy various praise	40
My God, my life, my love	197
My God, my portion and my love	185
My God permit me not to be	217
My God the covenant of thy love	143
My God the spring of all my joys	188
My gracious Lord I own thy right	173
My gracious Redeemer I love	205
My heart lies dead and no increase	239
My home is in heaven my rest is not	408
My Lord if thou one moment leave	158
My opening eyes with rapture see	2
My refuge is the God of love	328
My Sabbath suns may all have set	7
My Saviour can I follow thee	145
My Saviour let me hear thy voice	185
My Saviour my Almighty friend	182
My Saviour thou thy love to me	171
My Shepherd's name is Love	211
My sorrows like a flood	261
My soul be on thy guard	192
My soul come meditate the day	350
My soul go boldly forth	277
My soul, repeat His praise	31
My soul review the trembling days	145
My spirit longeth for thee	285
My spirit on thy care	260
My spirit sinks within me Lord	240
My sufferings all to thee are known	135
My thoughts on awful subjects roll	107
My times of sorrow and of joy	253
Nature hath seasons of repose	23
Nearer my God to thee	283
New every morning is the love	419
No bitter tears for thee be shed	340
No change of time shall ever shock	43
None loves me Saviour with thy love	168
Not all the blood of beasts	198
Not for the pious dead we weep	251
Not in the church-yard shall he sleep	348
No track is on the sunny sky	93
Not seldom clad in radiant vest	235
Not to the terrors of the Lord	223
Not worlds on worlds in phalanx deep	417
Now all chafing fears shall cease	15
No war nor battle's sound	67
Now begin the heavenly theme	206
Now be my heart inspired to sing	328
Now be the Gospel banner	299
Now for a tune of lofty praise	85
Now I have found the ground wherein	171
Now host with host assembling	317
Now in the heat of youthful blood	101
Now let our cheerful eyes survey	87
Now let our souls on wings sublime	160
Now let our voices join	193
Now that the sun is gleaming bright	423
Now the Saviour standeth pleading	119
Now to the haven of thy breast	244
Now to the Lord a noble song	163
Now when the dusky shades of night	421
O angel of the land of peace	344
O backward looking son of time	414
O blest Creator of the light	416
O bow thine ear eternal One	296
O city of the Lord begin	306
O come loud anthems let us sing	44
O could I find from day to day	184
O could I speak the matchless worth	202
O could our thoughts and wishes fly	184
O dearest Lamb, take thou my heart	189
O deem not they are blest alone	286
O'er the dark wave of Galilee	72
O'er the gloomy hills of darkness	315
O'er the realms of pagan darkness	315
O exil'd paradise, O how we long for	405
O fairest born of love and light	420
Of all the joys we mortals know	163
Of all the thoughts of God that are	341
O for a closer walk with God	220
O for a glance of heavenly day	166
O for a shout of sacred joy	86
O for a sweet inspiring ray	394
O for a thousand tongues to sing	177
O for the happy days gone by	186
O for those solitary hours	343
Oft when the waves of passion rise	271
O gift of gifts, O grace of faith	189
O God beneath thy guiding hand	303
O God by whom the seed is given	8
O God my refuge hear my cries	249
O God of Bethel by whose hand	218
O God our help in ages past	56
O God thou art my God alone	240
O God we praise thee and confess	46
O happy day that fix'd my choice	292
O happy saints that dwell in light	394
O he whom Jesus loved has truly spoken	323
O holy Father just and true	330
O holy, holy, holy, Lord—Bright	58
O holy, holy, holy, Lord—Thou	162
O how cheating, O how fleeting	372
O how happy are they	232
O how purely, O how surely	440
O how soft that bed must be	266
O how the thought of God attracts	189
O if my Lord would leave the skies	166
O if my soul were form'd for woe	103
O if there be an hour that brings	340
O it is joy in one to meet	225
O Jesus, life-spring of the soul	165
O Jesus, light of all below	187
O lay not up on this vain earth	390
O let my trembling soul be still	242
O Lord another day is flown	424
O Lord had'st thou been here, but when	250
O Lord how happy should we be	131
O Lord I would delight in thee	250
O Lord my best desires fulfill	253

INDEX OF FIRST LINES.

First line	Page
O Lord our eyes have waited long	330
O Lord thy counsels and thy care	240
O love divine how sweet thou art	203
O love of pure and heav'nly birth	136
O most delightful hour by man	355
O mother dear Jerusalem	398
O my dear Saviour when thy cares	143
O my God by thee forsaken	276
Once I thought my mountain strong	147
Once more my soul the rising day	423
One prayer I have, all prayers in one	253
One sole baptismal sign	19
One there is above all others	209
On Jordan's rugged banks I stand	412
O no we can not sing the song	252
On the dewy breath of evening	430
On the mountains' top appearing	314
On the night of that last supper	291
On Thibet's snow-capp'd mountains	317
Onward Christian thro' the region	279
Onward, onward men of heaven	313
Oppression shall not always reign	307
O praise ye the Lord prepare your glad	48
O pure reformers not in vain	336
O render thanks to God above	41
O sacred day of peace and joy	2
O sacred head now wounded	78
O Saviour whose mercy severe in its	378
O say not think not heav'nly notes	293
O see how Jesus trusts himself	336
O sing unto my soul my love	91
O sinner bring not tears alone	189
O source divine and life of all	25
O spirit freed from earth	358
O spirit of the living God	300
O strange infirmity to think	341
O sweet as vernal dews that fill	353
O tell me thou life and delight of my soul	233
O that I could forever dwell	133
O that I knew the secret place	139
O that my load of sin were gone	135
O that the Lord's salvation	282
O the delights the heavenly joys	412
O the immense the amazing height	42
O there will be mourning	128
O the sweet wonders of that cross	133
O thou Almighty Father	213
O thou by long experience tried	36
O thou eternal King most high	81
O thou eternal source of love	255
O thou from whom all goodness flows	256
O thou holy God come down	62
O thou in whose presence	232
O thou the first the greatest friend	256
O thou that hear'st the prayer of faith	130
O thou the heaven's eternal King	417
O thou to whose all-searching sight	157
O thou who driest the mourner's tears	245
O thou who hast spread out the skies	389
O thou whose own vast temple stands	298
O thou whose tender mercy hears	254
O throw away thy rod	258
O turn ye, O turn ye, for why will ye die	121
O 'twas a joyful sound to hear	8
Our blest Redeemer ere he breathed	93
Our Christ hath reached his heavenly	141
Our country is Immanuel's ground	400
Our Father in heaven we hallow thy	442
Our heavenly Father calls	197
Our Lord is risen from the dead	84
Our pathway oft is wet with tears	245
Our souls by love together knit	224
Our willing feet shall stand	13
O what amazing words of grace	103
O what stupendous mercy shines	305
O when shall I see Jesus	150
O when shall we sweetly remove	386
O where are kings and empires now	289
O where can the soul find relief	408
O where shall rest be found	109
O worship the King all glorious above	49
O ye immortal throng	311
O Zion tune thy voice	212
O Zion when I think of thee	286
Palms of glory raiment bright	402
Parting soul the flood awaits thee	381
Peace to thee O favor'd one	281
Peace troubled soul, whose plaintive	243
People of the living God	266
Perfect in love Lord, can it be	243
Pilgrim burden'd with thy sin	112
Plung'd in a gulf of dark despair	182
Pour blessed Gospel, glorious news for	320
Praise, everlasting praise be paid	45
Praise the Lord who reigns above	61
Praise the Lord ye heavens adore him	65
Praise ye Jehovah's name	338
Praise ye the Lord immortal choir	30
Prostrate dear Jesus at thy feet	104
Prayer is the soul's sincere desire	220
Quiet from God how beautiful to keep	421
Quiet Lord my froward heart	267
Raise your triumphant songs	199
Rejoice for a brother deceas'd	389
Rejoice in God alway	193
Rejoice the Lord is King	18
Repent the voice celestial cries	105
Restore O Father to our times restore	320
Return my roving heart return	345
Return O wand'rer return	104
Return O wand'rer to thy home	104
Ride on ride on in majesty	74
Rise crown'd with light, imperial Salem	320
Rise glorious conqu'ror rise	94
Rise my soul and stretch thy wings	370
Rise O my soul pursue the path	178
Rock'd in the cradle of the deep	415
Rock of ages cleft for me	110

INDEX OF FIRST LINES.

First line	PAGE
Roll on thou joyful day	326
Roll on thou mighty ocean	316
Safely thro' another week	14
Salvation O the joyful sound	181
Saviour breathe an evening blessing	430
Saviour now receive him	364
Saviour of all what hast thou done	137
Saviour visit thy plantation	275
Saviour when in dust to thee	146
Saw ye my Saviour, saw ye, etc.	129
Say how may earth and heav'n unite	42
Say sinner hath a voice within	101
Say why should friendship grieve for	346
Scorn not the slightest word or deed	337
See daylight is fading o'er earth and o'er	71
See from Zion's sacred mountain	314
See how great a flame aspires	308
See how the mounting sun	428
See Israel's gentle shepherd stand	293
See the clouds upon the mountain	17
See the leaves around us falling	374
See the light is fading	439
See the Lord of glory dying	75
See the ransom'd millions stand	309
See the shining dew-drops	438
See the stars from heaven falling	382
See th' eternal judge descending	115
Self love no grace in sorrow sees	203
Send kindly light amid the encircling	280
Servant of God well done	359
Shall man O God of life and light	342
She lov'd her Saviour, and to Him	336
Shepherds hail the wondrous stranger	62
Show pity Lord, O Lord forgive	134
Silently the shades of evening	430
Since first thy word awaken'd my heart	23
Since o'er thy footstool here below	29
Sing, sing his lofty praise	95
Sing to the Lord Jehovah's name	47
Sing to the Lord most high	35
Sing to the Lord that built the skies	43
Sing ye redeemed of the Lord	176
Sin like a venomous disease	107
Sinner art thou still secure	111
Sinner come mid thy gloom	122
Sinner hear the Saviour's call	127
Sinners the voice of God regard	105
Sister thou wast mild and lovely	395
Slavery and death the cup contains	333
Slowly by God's hand unfurl'd	431
So fades the lovely blooming flower	345
Soft be the gentle breathing notes	167
Softly fades the twilight ray	15
Softly now the light of day	264
Soil not thy plumage gentle dove	423
Soldiers of Christ arise	192
Some seraph lend your heavenly tongue	32
Songs of praise the angels sang	200
Son of the carpenter receive	138
Sons of men behold from far	309
Soon as I heard my Father say	54
Soon in the grave my flesh shall rest	397
Source of being source of light	26
Speak gently it is better far	334
Speak with us Lord, thyself reveal	153
Spirit leave thy house of clay	363
Spirit of power and might behold	306
Stand the omnipotent decree	372
Stand up and bless the lord	31
Stand up my soul shake off thy fears	165
Star of peace to wand'rers dreary	369
Stay thou insulted spirit stay	134
Still, still with thee	214
Stoop down my thoughts, that use to rise	107
Stop poor sinner stop and think	127
Sweet day so cool, so calm, so bright	102
Sweet evening hour	419
Sweet is the prayer whose holy stream	221
Sweet is the task O Lord	12
Sweet is the time of spring	429
Sweet is the work my God my King	1
Sweet Sabbath bells I love your voice	5
Sweet Sabbath of the year	429
Sweet the moments rich in blessing	209
Sweet was the time when first I felt	140
Swift as the arrow cuts its way	349
Tarry with me O my Saviour	430
Teach me my God and King	195
Tell me not in mournful numbers	272
Tell us wand'rer wildly roving	118
That awful day will surely come	106
That day of wrath that dreadful day	98
That man in life wherever placed	55
That mystic word of thine O Sovereign	215
That warning voice O sinner hear	148
The Almighty reigns exalted high	43
The billows swell, the winds are high	239
The bird let loose in eastern skies	185
The breaking waves dash'd high	319
The broken ties of happier days	352
The bud will soon become a flower	221
The chariot, the chariot, its wheels	121
The darkened sky how thick it lowers	237
The dawn is sprinkling in the east	414
The day approacheth O my soul	106
The day is past and gone	428
The dead are like the stars by day	355
The deluge at the Almighty's call	164
Thee we adore eternal name	107
Thee will I love O Lord my strength	241
Thee with the tribes assembled	154
The festal morn, my God is come	376
The floods O Lord lift up their voice	240
The glories of our birth and state	344
The glorious universe around	225
The great Archangel's trump shall sound	343
The harvest dawn is near	195
The head that once was crown'd with	86
The heavens declare thy glory Lord	22
The leaves around me falling	435

INDEX OF FIRST LINES.

First Line	Page
The Lord descended from above	46
The Lord how fearful is his name	47
The Lord how wondrous are his ways	42
The Lord into his garden comes	376
The Lord is great, ye hosts of heaven	49
The Lord is King, lift up thy voice	45
The Lord is my shepherd, he makes me	233
The Lord is my shepherd, no want shall I	90
The Lord is risen indeed	92
The Lord Jehovah reigns, And royal	11
The Lord Jehovah reigns, His throne	19
The Lord my pasture shall prepare	24
The Lord my shepherd is	197
The Lord of glory is my light	289
The Lord our God is full of might	39
The Lord the Judge before His throne	106
The Lord will come and not be slow	335
The Lord will come, the earth shall	342
The Lord will happiness divine	143
The mighty angel to whose hand	306
The mighty God who rolls the spheres	38
The mellow eve is gliding	434
The morning dawns upon the place	77
The morning light is breaking	316
The mourners came at break of day	341
The once lov'd form, now cold and dead	354
The perfect world by Adam trod	297
The pity of the Lord	31
The prince of salvation in triumph is	323
The promises I sing	51
The ransomed spirit to her home	393
There is a calm for those who weep	347
There is a fountain filled with blood	181
There is a glorious world of light	401
There is a happy land far, far, away	410
There is a harp whose thrilling sound	393
There is a holy city	406
There is a land my eye hath seen	394
There is a land of pure delight	400
There is a little lonely fold	289
There is an hour of peaceful rest	248
There is a place of sacred rest	399
There is a state unknown, unseen	397
There's a friend above all others	270
There's nothing bright above, below	53
There's nothing round these painted	391
There's rest in the grave	410
The rosy light is dawning	20
The Saviour calls let every ear	103
The Saviour what a noble flame	80
The Saviour said yet one thing more	298
The scene around me disappears	66
These glorious minds how bright they	399
The silver chord in twain is snapp'd	391
The songs of Zion oft impart	353
The spacious firmament on high	25
The spirit in our hearts	108
The starry firmament on high	22
The sun of righteousness on me	170
The swift declining day	428
The tempter to my soul hath said	241
The time draws nigh when from the	350
The turf shall be my fragrant shrine	234
The voice of free grace	379
The waters of Bethesda's pool	237
The winds were howling o'er the deep	140
The winter is over and gone	205
The word descending from above	159
The world eludes my fond desire	355
They pass refresh'd the thirsty vale	9
They that have made their refuge God	53
They who seek the throne of grace	219
Thine earthly Sabbaths Lord we love	2
Think gently of the erring one	337
This child we dedicate to thee	292
This God is the God we adore	386
This is the day the Lord hath made	6
This place is holy ground	366
This world is poor from shore to shore	248
Tho' all the world my choice deride	133
Tho' faint and sick and worn away	246
Tho' hard the winds are blowing	272
Tho' now the nations sits beneath	303
Tho' sorrows rise and dangers roll	169
Thou art gone to the grave	379
Thou art my hiding-place O Lord	221
Thou art O God the life and light	24
Thou art the way and he who	165
Thou dear Redeemer dying Lamb	175
Thou hast been called to God rebellious	120
Thou hidden love of God whose bright	137
Thou hidden source of calm repose	171
Thou judge of quick and dead	109
Thou Lamb once slain, whose flaming	139
Thou Lord who rear'st the mountain's	43
Thou O Lord in tender love	149
Thou O my Jesus thou did'st me	139
Thou only sovereign of my heart	131
Thousands O Lord of hosts to-day	247
Thou sweet gliding Kedron by thy silver	71
Thou that dost my life prolong	431
Thou very present aid	263
Thou who art enthron'd above	15
Thou whom my soul admires above	158
Tho' waves and storms go o'er my head	243
Thro' all the changing scenes of life	179
Thro' every age eternal God	36
Thro' life's vapors dimly seeing	388
Thro' sorrow's night and danger's path	348
Thro' the day thy love has spared us	207
Thro' thy protecting care	367
Throughout the hours of darkness dim	417
Thus far the Lord hath led me on	418
Thy gracious presence O my God	145
Thy happy ones a strain begin	167
Thy home is with the humble Lord	185
Thy mercy heard my infant prayer	271
Thy way is on the deep O Lord	307
Thy will be done in devious way	415
Thy will be done I will not fear	239
Time is winging us away	370
'Tis by the faith of joys to come	238

INDEX OF FIRST LINES.

First Line	Page
'Tis by thy strength the mountains stand.	426
'Tis finish'd so the Saviour cried	76
'T is gone that bright and orbed blaze	416
'Tis midnight, and on Olive's brow	76
'Tis my happiness below	147
'Tis not the skill of human heart	162
To-day the Saviour calls	128
To God the only Wise	199
To heaven I lift mine eyes	212
To heaven I lift my waiting eyes	219
To Him who little children blest	295
To Jesus the crown of my hope	386
To keep the lamp alive	231
To-morrow, Lord, is thine	359
To our Redeemer's glorious name	181
Toss'd upon life's raging billow	275
To thee my God and Saviour	151
To thee my shepherd and my Lord	190
To thy pastures fair and large	27
To weary hearts, to mourning homes	242
To your Creator God	50
Trembling before thine awful throne	157
Triumphant Christ ascends on high	86
Triumphant Zion lift thy head	300
'T was God who hurl'd the rolling spheres	33
'T was in the watches of the night	247
'T was on that dark that doleful night	77
Unheard the dews around me fall	425
Unite my roving thoughts unite	185
Unshaken as the sacred hill	250
Unveil thy bosom faithful tomb	344
Upon the Gospel's sacred page	22
Up to the fields where angels lie	156
Up to the hills I lift mine eyes	52
Wait O my soul thy maker's will	237
Wake the song of Jubilee	308
Walk in the light so thou shalt know	257
Watchman tell us of the night	308
We are living we are dwelling	312
Wearied with earthly toil and care	7
Weary of wandering from my God	136
Weary souls that wander wide	112
We bid thee welcome in the name	297
Weep not for the saint that ascends	389
We give immortal praise	325
Welcome delightful morn	19
Welcome O Saviour to my heart	145
Welcome sweet day of rest	12
Welcome welcome dear Redeemer	208
Welcome welcome quiet morning	17
We love thee, Lord, and we adore	55
We miss thee in thy place at school	445
We praise thee Lord if but one soul	333
Were not the sinful Mary's tears	102
We're on our journey home	407
We're traveling home to heaven above	124
We shall see a light appear	407
We speak of the realms of the blest	387
We suffer with our Master here	377
We've no abiding city here	160
We wait in faith, in prayer we wait	423
What a strange and wondrous story	443
What blessed examples do I find	445
What equal honors shall we bring	163
Whatever broils disturb the street	445
What glory gilds the sacred page	21
What is life, 'tis but a vapor	395
What is our God, or what his name	37
What is the world, a wildering snare	130
What poor despised company	225
What shall I render to my God	138
What sinners value I resign	160
What's this that steals upon my frame	373
What tho' the stream be dead	358
What various hind'rances we meet	217
What would we give to our beloved	341
When adverse winds and waves arise	243
When all thy mercies O my God	54
When as returns this solemn day	4
When brighter suns and milder skies	426
Whence do our mournful thoughts arise	253
Whene'er I take my walks abroad	445
When forced to part from those we love	390
When forth from Egypt's trembling	47
When gath'ring clouds around I view	242
When God of old came down from	93
When God reveal'd his gracious name	175
When grief and anguish press me down	245
When groves by moonlight silence keep	235
When here O Lord we seek thy face	296
When human hopes all wither	273
When I can read my title clear	251
When Israel of the Lord beloved	165
When I survey the wond'rous cross	74
When I the holy grave survey	85
When Jesus dwelt in mortal clay	333
When Jesus' friend had ceas'd to be	134
When Jordan hush'd his waters still	72
When languor and disease invade	252
When life as opening buds is sweet	345
When marshall'd on the mighty plain	168
When morning's first and hallowed ray	422
When musing sorrow weeps the past	253
When my Saviour shall I be	229
When on Sinai's top I see	261
When on the giddy cliff I stand	258
When on the midnight of the east	420
When overwhelm'd with grief	259
When power divine in mortal form	238
When shall the voice of singing	317
When shall we all meet again	228
When shall we meet again	368
When sins and fears prevailing rise	167
When spring unlocks the flowers	435
When streaming from the eastern skies	427
When the great judge supreme and just	324
When the harvest is past and the summer	122
When the spark of life is waning	270
When the vale of death appears	374
When the worn spirit wants repose	7

First line	PAGE
When thou my righteous Judge shalt	125
When thro' the torn sail the wild	71
When thy mortal life is fled	111
When waves of trouble round me swell	246
When we our wearied limbs to rest	238
When wild confusion wrecks the air	351
When winds are raging o'er the upper	214
Where ancient forests widely spread	296
Where high the heav'nly temple stands	85
Where O my soul, O where	152
Where shall the child of sorrow find	246
Where wilt thou put thy trust	262
While life prolongs its precious light	100
While nature was sinking in stillness to	71
While now upon the Sabbath eve	5
While shepherds watch'd their flocks by	63
While through this changing world we	349
While to its grief my soul gave way	239
While with ceaseless course the sun	146
Whilst thee I seek protecting power	218
Whither goest thou pilgrim stranger	382
Who are these arrayed in white	403
Who are these in bright array	402
Who is this fair one in distress	236
Who is thy neighbor? he whom thou	335
Why do we mourn departing friends	350
Why is my heart so far from thee	141
Why is thy face so lit with smiles	81
Why should I join with those in play	444
Why should our tears in sorrow flow	355
Why should the children of a King	55
Why should we start and fear to die	343
Why weep for those, frail child of woe	343
Wilt thou not visit me	277
With all my powers of heart and tongue	42
With glory clad with strength array'd	37
With his rich gifts the heav'nly dove	9
Within thy courts have millions met	3
With joy we meditate the grace	87
With my whole heart I'll raise my	324
With silence only as their benediction	365
With songs and honors sounding loud	426
With tearful eyes I look around	236
With tears of anguish I lament	143
Witness ye men and angels now	139
Would Jesus have the sinner die	136
Wretched helpless and distress'd	317
Yea I will extol thee	284
Ye angels who stand round the throne	387
Ye boundless realms of joy	436
Ye Christian heroes go proclaim	300
Ye dying sons of men	210
Ye golden lamps of heaven farewell	400
Ye hearts with youthful vigor warm	105
Ye humble souls that seek the Lord	87
Ye lands and isles of ev'ry sea	177
Ye nations round the earth rejoice	36
Ye saints your music bring	83
Ye servants of God your Master proclaim	48
Ye servants of the Lord	195
Yes my native land I love thee	313
Yes the Redeemer rose	82
Yes we trust the day is breaking	315
Ye trembling captives hear	108
Ye trembling souls dismiss your fears	254
Ye weary heavy-laden souls	397
Ye wretched hungry starving poor	103
Yield to me now for I am weak	170
Yon spot in the church-yard	357
Young and happy while thou art	440
Your harps ye trembling saints	194
Zion stands with hills surrounded	314

INDEX OF HYMNS

BY ANY VERSE BUT THE FIRST.

A.

Hymn	Page
A beam from heaven is sent to	420
Abide in me—o'ershadow by	215
Abide in me: there have been	215
Abide with me from morn till	416
Abide with us, amazed they	169
Abide with us, and still unfold	169
Abide with us, Thou heavenly	169
A broken heart, a fount of tears	73
A captive here, and far from	286
A cloud of witnesses around	178
A country far from mortal	225
Across the waves around the	53
A deep and crimson streak	429
A deeper shade will soon	790
Admit Him, ere His anger	98
Adoring angels at His birth	177
Adoring angels tuned their	63
Adoring saints around Him	893
A dying, risen Jesus	151
A faith that seems not faith, a	186
A few short years of exile past	859
Again emerging from the	417
Against the God that rules the	178
A glance of Thine runs through	58
A glimpse of glories far more	237
Agonizing in the garden	118
A hand divine shall lead you on	176
A heart that, when my days	168
Ah, grace! into unlikeliest	189
Ah, Lord! if it be Thou indeed	271
Ah, Lord! with faltering steps	894
A holy quiet reigns around	847
A hope so much divine	199
A horror of great darkness fell	76
Ah! then my spirit faints	861
Ah, those are of a royal line	225
Ah! whither shall I fly?	258
A land, upon whose blissful	894
Alas, I knew not what I did	102
Alas! the brittle clay	861
All, all below must fade and	891
All, all is o'er, with those at	854
All-bounteous Lord! Thy	84
All glory be to God on high	68
All-gracious Lord, whate'er my	249
All hail the glorious day	95
All hail, triumphant Lord	82
"All hail, triumphant Lord!"	18
All hail! ye fair, celestial	413
All His creatures God doth	27
All honor to His name	198
All is tranquil and serene	863
All may of Thee partake	195
All my capacious powers can	190
All my desire to Thee is known	141
All my nature is unholy	443
All our earthly journey past	295
All our works in Thee be	267
All power to Him is given	198
All power to our great Lord	83
All praise to Thee, who safe	419
All scenes alike engaging prove	86
All space is holy, for all space	296
All that have motion, life, and	8
All that I am, have been	860
All that strikes the gaze	885
All the assembling saints	284
All the hopes and fears that	27
All this day Thy hand has led	441
All thy sins shall be forgiven	270
All who bear the Saviour's	291
All-wise, all-mighty, and	253
All ye nations! join and sing	808
Almighty God! Thy grace	800
Almighty God! to Thee	825
Almighty grace! Thy healing	143
Almighty Lord! the sun shall	22
Alone with Thee—amid the	214
Along Thy sunset skies	429
Already, from the dust of death	804
Also, when I cry and shout	856
Although I fail, I weep	258
Amazing grace! that kept my	107
Amazing knowledge, vast and	87
Amazing love that yet will	165
Ambition, stop thy panting	126
Amid a thousand snares, I	42
Amid the roaring of the sea	289
Amid those ever-shining	41
Amid the silence, else so drear	417
Amid the splendors of His	86
Amid the storm they sang	819
Amid thy silent bowers	429
A moment may His hand seem	847
Among a thousand harps and	85
Among the saints on earth	227
Among the saints that fill Thy	139
Among Thy saints let me be	125
And as He rose with all His	81
And as this water falls	295
And ate, but gave me part	109
And at my life's last setting sun	427
And blessed is he who can	807
And, bursting through the	255
And canst Thou—wilt Thou	148
And can this mighty King	19
And dear to me the loud Amen	5
And dear to me the winged	5
And death, which sets the	78
And didst Thou pity mortal	144
And dost Thou look on such a	852
And e'en when midnight's	422
And even now, amid the gray	423
And every bondsman's chain	880
And every night shall turn to	804
And every virtue we possess	93
And friends, dear friends! when	841
And from His love's exhaustless	425
And grant that to Thine honor	428
And graver looks, serene and	840
And griefs and torments	189
And hark! amid the sacred	401
And here are comrades in the	9
And here Thy name, O God of	808
And His that gentle voice we	98
And if no evening visit's paid	161
And if there weigh upon my	414
And if the sons of God rejoice	806
And, in every grace complete	27
And, Jesus, Thou Thy smiles	424
And, lest the shadow of a spot	181
And let the drops of sparkling	428
And let those eyes, with	184
And like a den most dark He	46
And lo! above the dews of	848
And make his grave where	840
And many a tearful, longing	445
And may Thy Gospel's joyful	231
And must I, from the cheerful	101
And must my body faint and	107
And not a prayer, a tear, a sigh	3
And now Christ is ready your	121
And now his conquering	10
And now my spirit sighs for	889
And oft as the tumult of life's	71
And oft, when little voices dim	445
And O, when gathers on our	165
And, O! when I have safely	249
And O, when the whirlwind of	71
And palms shall wave, and	244
And say—shall aught oppose	806
And shall man alone be dumb	200
And shall my guilty fears	254
And shall the soul thou bid'st	28
And since, by passion's force	247
And so, 'mid boundless time	25
And soon the harvest of thy	221
And soon, too soon, the	293
And such the trust that still	415
And the naked soul	882
And then was heard afar	94
And the voice answers, "Be	399
And though loud the wind is	275
And though some tones be	298
And though Thy wisdom takes	253
And thou, refulgent orb of day	400
And thou 'rt sure to meet the	884
And Thou wilt turn our	424
And thus shall faith's	855
And was His mortal hour	78
And weep for the nations	889
And what is life, 'mid toil and	246
And what shall be my journey	406
And when before Thy Throne	256
And when, dear Saviour! I	187
And when he stooped to earth	92
And, when I close my eyes in	144
And when I early rise	428
And when life's toilsome day is	424
And when my Saviour calls me	179
And when nature sinks in	15
And when our spirits we resign	298
And when the gleams of day	162
And when the last dread hour	288
And when the lips that with	296
And when the Master seems to	251
And when these lips no more	292
And when the shades of	91
And when the waves of ire	260
And when Thou mak'st Thy	924
And when Thy awful voice	221
And when your labors all are	300
And where the fathers lie	361
And while I rest my weary	425
And while our faith enjoys this	412
And while the hours in order	422
And while Thy bleeding glories	80
And while upon my restless	185

	PAGE		PAGE		PAGE
And while we pass this vale	216	A thousand wretched souls are	428	Be this world the wiser	279
And wilt Thou bend a listening	424	At length I own it can not be	292	Be Thou exalted, O my God!	44
And without, with tireless	389	At length, this great Physician	151	Be Thou my guardian while I	416
And ye of meaner birth!	50	At midnight came the cry	359	Be Thou my shield and hiding	145
And yet ten thousand	108	At noon, beneath the Rock	428	Be Thou, O Lord, my Father	246
And yet the songs I frame	31	A trusting heart, a yearning	189	Better than life itself Thy love	240
And yet this thoughtless	418	At Salem's courts we must	8	Beyond, beyond this lower sky	393
Angel of patience! sent to	242	Attending angels shout for joy	396	Beyond my highest joy	227
Angel powers the throne	408	At this hour, lo! from their	15	Beyond the bounds of time and	271
Angels! archangels! glorious	95	At thy approaching dawn	18	Beyond the flight of time	366
Angels! assist our mighty joys	182	At Thy rebuke, the bloom	361	Beyond the storm, beyond the	399
Angels, guard the new	383	At twelve years old he talked	445	Beyond this vale of tears	109
Angels, in bright attire	109	Auspicious dawn! thy rising	362	Birds in their little nests agree	445
Angels standing, where we 're	440	Author and Guardian of my	220	Blessed Babe, what glorious	441
An offering to the Lord	306	A voice from the shepherd now	233	Blessed be the voice that	236
Anoint me with Thy	417	Awake, and breathe the air	359	Blessed fold! no foe can enter	383
Anon the clouds dispart	361	Awake, awake, my tuneful	182	Blessed is the man, whose	93
Another day, more awful	107	Awake, awake, put on thy	288	Blessed Jesus!—would'st thou	270
Another fleeting day is gone	417	Awake, lift up thine eyes!	359	Blessing, honor, glory, might	302
A pilgrim through the earth I	258	Awake, my soul, thy way	101	Blessings abound where er He	163
Apostles join the glorious	162	Awake, then, my harp, and my	205	Blessings for ever on the Lamb	163
Apostles, martyrs, prophets	396	Away from fools I'll turn my	444	Bless me, and I shall be blest	266
Approach, ye saints! this God	161	Away, ye false, delusive toys	105	Bless the Lord of earth and	129
Archangels sound His lofty	412	Away, ye midnight phantoms	414	Bless the Lord of life for ever	129
Are there no foes for me to	178	A whispered word may touch	337	Bless the Lord of thy salvation	129
Are there not feelings from	335	A word of His almighty breath	47	Bless the Lord, whose love	129
Are these Thy favors day by	445			Blest are the men whose hearts	1
Are they not all Thy servants	41	B.		Blest are the souls that find a	1
Are we not tending upward	350	Bane and blessing, pain and	275	Blest be the Father of our Lord	84
A rill, a stream, a torrent	224	Baptize the nations; far and	300	Blest be the Lord who comes	6
Arise from the grave!	410	Bear, bear the tidings round	70	Blest day! thine hours too	7
Arise into Thy resting-place	2	Bear, then, the reproach of	274	Blest hour, for where the Lord	4
Arise, my soul! awake, my	174	Bear the tidings round the ball	302	Blest hour when earthly cares	4
Arise, my soul, from deep	139	Be earth, with all her scenes	217	Blest hour when God himself	4
Arise, put on the robes	358	Because the Saviour shed His	418	Blest is the man, O God	194
Arm me with jealous care	195	Because thy smile was fair	358	Blest Jesus, come, and rule my	184
Arm of the Lord! awake	300	Be Christ our pattern and our	80	Blest mansions above	265
Around Him angels fair	92	Be daily dearer to my heart	133	Blest river of salvation	316
Around His sacred tomb	311	Be darkness, at Thy coming	300	Blest Saviour, introduced by	173
Around Thy wheels, in the glad	351	"Be faithful unto death	193	Blest Saviour! what delicious	235
Arrayed in glorious grace	360	Before His ever-watchful eye	289	Blest with this fellowship	241
Art Thou not touched with	135	Before His throne a volume	33	Blind unbelief is sure to err	57
A sacred spring at Thy	23	Before its splendid hour, the	257	Bonds, and stripes, and evil	274
As a little child relies	267	Before me place, in dread	125	Born by a new celestial birth	160
As by the light of opening day	139	Before our Father's throne	227	Borne upon the latest breath	200
Ascend! thou art not now	359	Before the hills in order stood	56	Born into the world above	362
As children of Thy gracious	380	Before the mountains heaved	256	Born, Thy people to deliver	209
A second look He gave, that	102	Before the mournful scene	77	Boundless wisdom, power	27
Ashamed of Jesus! sooner far	159	Before Thine awful face	325	Bowed down beneath a load of	145
Ashamed of Jesus! that dear	159	Before thy heart had learned	358	Bread of our souls! whereon	21
Ashamed of Jesus! yes, I may	159	Before we quite forsake our	183	Break from His throne	344
Ashamed to lift her streaming	191	Begirt with Thee, my fearless	83	Break the tempter's fatal	273
As in the dawning, o'er the	214	Behold Him rise from Olive's	99	Break off the yoke of inbred	135
As, in the heavens, the urns	345	Behold His loving-kindness	89	Break off your tears, ye saints	74
Asleep in Jesus! far from thee	346	Behold! the aged sinner goes	101	Break, Sovereign Grace, O	145
Asleep in Jesus! O, for me	346	Behold the Ark of God	260	Breathe, O breathe Thy loving	209
Asleep in Jesus! O, how sweet	346	Behold the bed of death	366	Brightest and best of the sons	163
Asleep in Jesus! peaceful rest	346	Behold the blest assembly	223	Bright angels, strike your	177
As, 'midst the ever-rolling sea	345	Behold the body in the tomb	99	Bright cloud of Liberty I full	330
As moons are ever waning	278	Behold the innumerable host	228	Bright garlands of immortal	176
As o'er a parched and weary	244	Behold the Lamb	79	Bright heralds of th' Eternal	157
A soul inured to pain	294	Behold the Lamb on Calvary	99	Bright, in that happy land	410
A spirit still prepared	294	Behold the Man! by all	76	Bright, like a sun, the Saviour	401
As sang the morning stars of	301	Behold the Man! He stands	76	Bright seraphs, dispatched	205
As ship to port, or shaft from	415	Behold the Man! though	76	Bright the star of your	62
Assist me, gracious God!	50	Behold the way to Zion's hill	362	Bring, my heart, thy tribute	128
As some rare perfume in a vase	215	"Behold the way!" ye	362	Brother, in that solemn trust	363
As spring the winter—day the	243	Behold Thy prisoner, loose my	247	Brother, wake! for He who	390
As still to the star of its	206	Behold your King, your	176	Brother, wake! the night is	390
Assure my conscience of her	55	Being of beings! may our	45	Brought forth to judgment	77
As the waters fall from the sea	357	Believe the heavenly word	210	Brought safely by His hand	236
As Thou of old to Miriam's	330	Believing, we rejoice	198	Burdened with a load of sin	147
A stranger, lonely here I roam	248	Below He washed our guilt	180	Burdened with a world of	113
As welcome as the water-spring	244	Be near when I am dying	79	Buried in sorrow and in sin	181
At birth, our brother He	159	Beneath His watchful eye	260	Burst thy shackles, drop thy	402
At evening, in Thy home	428	Beneath Thy broad, impartial	420	Burst wide, ye heavenly	213
At evening time, let there be	341	Be present, in Thy peace, to	422	Bury the dead and weep	366
At evening time, there shall be	341	"Be still—and learn that I am	45	But a better day shall be	331
At His call, the dead awaken	114	Bestow on every joyous thrill		But above all lay hold	192
At His presence nature shakes	111	Bethesda's pool has lost its	187	But a celestial voice I heard	173
A thousand ages in Thy sight	56	Be this my one great business	125	But a drought has since	275

ANY VERSE BUT THE FIRST. 465

First Line	Page
But, ah! my inward spirit	253
But angels themselves can not	396
But, bowed in lowliness of	339
But charity, serene, sublime	159
But, chiefest, in our cleansed	84
But chief 'tis joy to think that	225
But Christ, the heavenly Lamb	193
But drops of grief can ne'er	144
But dry your tears, and tune	87
But ere one fleeting hour is	141
But ere the trumpet shakes	360
But ere this spacious world was	87
But even years are passing by	84
But fairer shone the tears of	251
But fixed for everlasting years	22
But flowers of paradise	193
"But gather all my saints," He	106
But give to Christ alone thy	336
But God shall raise His head	153
But hark! He prays: 'tis for	77
But He, for His own mercy's	140
But her sorrows quickly fled	113
But he that turns to God shall	105
But he who marks, from day to	333
But he whose blossom buds in	55
But high she shoots through air	185
But hush, my soul, nor dare	160
But I amid your choirs shall	157
But I am jealous of my heart	236
But I am Thine, my ransom	189
But if at any time we cease	337
But if Immanuel's face appear	158
But if it hath been sin of mine	186
But if no more with kindred	290
But if this weariness hath come	186
But if Thy Spirit, gracious Lord	353
But, if you trifle with His	120
But I have felt Thee in my	187
But I'll confess my guilt to	141
But in His looks a glory stands	163
But I shall share a glorious part	1
But leaves the greenest will	353
But let us hasten to the day	224
But lo! a brighter, clearer	391
But lo! in our extremity	271
But man dieth and wasteth	357
But man, weak man, is born	86
But mightier than the mighty	240
But no such sacrifice I plead	105
But not his nobler part shall	340
But now, a prisoner of the	5
But now I am a soldier	150
But no worship, song, or glory	75
But of all the foes we meet	229
But O! from human tongues	50
But O! my Saviour, be Thou	240
But O! their end, their	101
But O, the soul that never	107
But our earnest supplication	395
But out of all, the Lord	231
But O, what beams of heavenly	401
But O! when gloomy doubts	245
But O! when that last	157
But Power Divine can do the	166
But shall my soul be then	130
But should the surges rise	260
But since Thou hast Thy love	203
But sinners, filled with guilty	342
But some of them seem poor	225
But soon He'll break death's	80
But speak, my Lord, and calm	135
But sweeter far the still small	221
But those visions never blessed	119
But Thou art not in tempest	32
But Thou art true, incarnate	235
But, though from his awful	361
But, though the sun-set hours	424
But Thou hast brethren here	336
But Thou wilt heal the broken	245
But thronging round, with	293
But thy spirit soars to glory	384
But timorous mortals start and	430
But 't is in vain they strive to	258
But 't is our God supports our	257
But to draw near to Thee, my	57
But to sing the rest of glory	119
But to those who have	114
But to Thy house will I resort	6
But we are come to Sion's hill	223
But weep for their sorrows, who	389
But weep for the mourners	389
But we shall mourn him long	340
But we shall yet behold the	286
But we weak ones, but we	327
But we who now our Lord	343
But what to those who find?	142
But when He came the second	93
But when its troubled waters	237
But when loud the trumpet	403
But when, on Thy bosom	388
But when we view Thy strange	83
But where the Gospel comes	12
But while I thus in anguish	148
But while untroubled, they	237
But who can e'er describe tho	390
But who can speak Thy	40
But why keep they that narrow	225
But will He prove a friend	98
But will, indeed, Jehovah	296
By all Hell's host withstood	193
By all its joys I charge my heart	185
By cool Siloam's shady rill	293
By day, along th' astonished	165
By day, by night, at home	164
By day Thy hand shall lead	282
By each saving word unspoken	327
By evil beast, or burning sky	289
By faith I see the land	211
By faith we already behold	388
By faith we are come to our	433
By Him who bowed to take	222
By night Thine arm attends me	282
By Thee must come, Thou	165
By Thee, my prayers	191
By Thee observed, by Thee	83
By Thee, through life	151
By them, through holy hope	355
By the thorn-road, and none	279
By the travail of Thy spirit	273
By Thine agonizing pain	149
By Thine all-sufficient merit	275
By Thine hour of dark despair	146
By Thine own eternal Spirit	209
By Thy birth and early years	146
By Thy deep expiring groan	146
By Thy most severe temptation	273
By Thy reconciling love	228

C.

First Line	Page
Call me away from flesh and	217
Call to mind that unknown	273
Calmly the day forsakes our	425
Calvary's mournful mountain	110
"Can a woman's tender care	268
Can I, with hopes so firmly built	249
Can loving children e'er	343
Canst thou, in that awful day	431
Can this be He who wont to	342
Captives of sin and shame	116
Careful without care I am	149
Careless, through outward	138
Care, pain, and grief, the wild	354
Cease, cease, ye vain	342
Cease, ye pilgrims, cease to	370
Celestial choirs, from courts	69
Celestial King! Thy blazing	42
Champion of Jesus! on that	349
Chance and change are busy	204
Changed from glory into glory	203
Cheered by a signal so divine	158
Cheerful they walk with	1
Cheerful we tread the desert	238
Cheerful, where'er Thy hand	185
Cheer up! cheer up! the day	375
"Chief of ten thousand!" now	4
Childhood's preceptor!	21
Child of sin and sorrow	126
Children a sweet hosanna sang	445
Christ, by prophets long	62
Christian! dry your flowing	389
"Christ is born, the great	64
Christ, the Lord, is risen to-day	89
Christ, when Thou shalt call	75
Churches and sects, strike	322
Close by its banks in order fair	23
Clothed with our nature still	180
Clothe me, Lord, with	317
Cold on His cradle the dew	90
Come, Almighty to deliver	308
Come, and with humble souls	47
Come as a Messenger of peace	297
Come as an Angel, hence to	297
Come as a Shepherd; guard	297
Come as a Teacher, sent from	297
Come as a Watchman; take	297
Come, bless the Lord, whose	8
Come, brethren, you who love	376
Come, for all else must fail and	237
Come, for all things now are	119
Come! for I need Thy love	277
Come, freely come, by sin	243
Come give us your hand, and	121
Come, holy Comforter	60
Come, Holy Spirit, come	195
Come, Holy Spirit, heavenly	158
Come in, come in, Thou Prince	271
Come, in this accepted hour	14
Come, kneel before His throne	35
Come, Lord! God's image can	184
Come, Lord! Thy love alone	9
Come, Lord, when grace hath	249
Come, magnify the Lord with	172
Come, make your wants, your	45
"Come, my Beloved, haste	286
Come near and bless us when	416
Come, O my comfort and	393
Come quickly, blessed Lord	351
Come, sacred Spirit, seal the	153
Come, saints, and adore Him	71
Comes gushing o'er a sudden	445
Come, sinner, drink the balmy	99
Come, sinners, hear the joyful	301
Come, sovereign Lord! dear	396
Come, the blessed emblems	291
Come, then, afflictions dreary	272
Come then—oh come from	239
Come, then, with all your	103
Come, then, ye saints! and	10
Come, thou incarnate Word	60
Come, thou Father of the poor	264
Come to that happy land	410
Come to the ark—all, all that	245
Come to the bright and blest	108
Come to the house of praise	13
Come, visit us! and when dull	187
"Come, wanderers, to my	72
"Come, ye blessed of my	380
Come, ye weary, heavy laden	113
Compelled by bleeding love	210
Conflicts and trials done	268
Congenial minds, arrayed in	354
Constant to my latest end	27
Contented now, upon my thigh	170
Convince us of our sin	195
Corruption, earth, and worms	360
Could I be cast where Thou art	86
Could I command the spacious	9
Could we but climb where	400
Could we but kneel, and cast	131
Countless bands of angels	97
Create my soul anew	81
Creation's mighty fabric all	246
Creatures no more divide my	139

	PAGE		PAGE		PAGE
Creatures that borrow life from	84	Each tender tie, dissolved with	854	Far in exile, when we roam	273
Crown Him, ye martyrs of our	174	Early, at the break of day	15	Father Almighty, how faithful	49
Crown Him, ye morning stars	174	Early hasten to the tomb	110	Father and Saviour! plant	128
Crown the Saviour, angels	96	Early hath life's mighty	339	Father! forgive the heart that	229
Crushed is the haughty foe	192	Earnest toil, and strong	339	Father, God, Thy love we	61
		Earth and her thousand voices	426	Father! holy, pure, and lowly	440
D.		Earth has a joy unknown in	157	Father in heaven, O hear when	437
Dangers stand thick through	107	Earthly joys to Thee are dross	281	Father, King, whose heavenly	26
Dark and cheerless is the morn	201	Earth, sea, and sky, one	393	Father let Thy Holy Spirit	443
Dark grew my soul—till down	344	Earth's joys, like dew-drops	391	Father of heaven! in whom our	421
Darkness prevailed, darkness	129	Earth quakes before that	93	Father of Jesus! love's reward	175
Daughter of Zion! the Power	230	Earth, with its caverns dark	47	Father, now one prayer I raise	17
Day's declining, stars are	440	E'en down to old age all My	239	Father, the hindrance show	294
Days, months, and years must	84	E'en now, above, there's	289	Fear hath no dwelling here	108
Deal gently, Lord! with souls	250	E'en now the hallowed scenes	302	Fear Him, ye saints! and ye	179
Dear are thy peaceful hours to	2	E'en now, to my expecting	376	Fearless of hell, and ghastly	188
Dear child! thou wilt never	357	E'en the hour that darkest	294	Fear not, brethren, joyful stand	223
Dear Comforter! Eternal Love!	185	E'er since, by faith I saw the	181	Fear not, I am with thee, Oh!	230
Dear, dying Lamb, Thy	181	E'en so I love Thee, and will	189	Fear not, said he—for mighty	63
Dearest Saviour, hasten hither	275	Empires decay, and nations die	248	Fear not that He will e'er	254
Dearest sister, thou hast left us	394	Enchanted with all that was	378	Fear not the powers of earth	254
Dear is the spot where	346	Endless pleasure, pain	374	Fear not the terrors of the	254
Dear Lord, accept the praise	360	Endow me with my Saviour's	136	Fear not the want of outward	254
Dear Lord, and shall we ever	153	Engraved, as in eternal brass	47	Feeble, trembling, fainting	198
Dear Lord, if indeed I am	339	Enlightened by thy heavenly	50	Fight on, my soul, till death	193
Dear Lord, while we, adoring	181	Enough, while these dull	424	Fight on, ye conquering souls	301
Dear Saviour, draw reluctant	103	Enter His courts with joy	85	Filled with delight, my	412
Dear Saviour! let Thy beauties	254	Enter his gates with songs of	86	Fill our hearts with thoughts of	443
Dear Saviour! let Thy glory	9	Enter, Incarnate God	94	Finish then Thy new creation	308
Dear Saviour! let Thy	99	Enter thine ark, while patience	164	Firm are the words His	45
Dear Saviour, to Thy cross	429	Enthroned amid the radiant	41	Firm as His throne, His	177
Dear Shepherd! I hear, and	232	Ere sin had scared the breast	358	Firmly trusting in Thy blood	201
Death, and the terrors of the	241	Eternal are Thy mercies, Lord	131	Fixed on this ground will I	243
Death, like an overflowing	86	Eternal, brooding, glorious	343	Fix, O fix my wavering mind	27
Death may our souls divide	294	Eternal glory to the King	257	Floods of everlasting light	404
Death rides on every passing	351	Eternal God! who shall not fear	38	Flow to restore, but not	22
Death, with thy weapons of	411	Eternal King! I fear Thy name	101	Flow, wondrous stream with	23
Decay, then, tenements of dust	72	Eternal life thy words impart	132	Fly abroad, thou mighty	315
Deep are His counsels, and	41	Eternal Shepherd! who Thy	417	Fold her, O Father, in Thine	355
Deeper, deeper grow the	430	Eternal wisdom has prepared	191	Follow to the judgment-hall	110
Deep horror then my vitals	163	Eternity comes in the sound	8-9	Follow, with reverent steps, the	323
Deep in the shades of gloomy	85	Eternity! Eternity	415	Fond youth, while free from	126
Deep in unfathomable mines	57	Eternity, with all its years	82	Foolish, and impotent, and	150
Deeply repenting, sorely	280	Evening winds are breathing	439	Fools never raise their	1
Deep to deep responsive calling	276	Ever thus in God's high praises	65	Footprints which, perhaps	273
"Deny thyself, and take thy	100	Every eye shall then behold	114	Forbid it, Lord, that I should	74
Depart in peace, the Saviour	191	Every human tie may perish	814	For Canaan's land is just	397
Descend, celestial Dove	19	Every mournful sinner cheer	14	For death his sacred seal hath	85
Descend, O Spirit of the Lord!	84	Every stain of guilt abhorring	16	Forerunner of the sun	253
Determined are the days that	257	Exalt the Lamb of God	116	For ever firm Thy justice	53
Did ever mourner plead with	237	Exposed continually to shame	158	For ever reign, victorious	85
Did ever trouble yet befall	236	Extend to me that favor, Lord	41	For ever shall Thy throne	87
Didst Thou regard the beggar's	144			For ever with the Lord	195
Didst Thou regard Thy	144	**F.**		For ever thirsty, longing	108
Did the solid earth ordain	27	Fain with them our souls	88	For friends and brethren dear	13
Direct, control, suggest, this	419	Fain would I lay the burden	7	Forget not, brother, thou hast	337
Dissolve Thou these bands	386	Fain would I learn of Thee, my	185	Forget not—Thou who bore	290
Dole not thy duties out to God	159	Fain would I mount, fain would	156	Forget us not—when on the	290
Do sickness, feebleness, or pain	243	Fain would I trace the	53	For good is the Lord	90
Dost Thou not dwell in all the	55	Fair are the meadows	207	Forgive me, Lord, for Thy dear	416
Doth a skillful, healing Friend	431	Fair is the sunshine	207	Forgiveness, love, and peace	108
"Do this," He cried, "till time	77	Fair truth, and smiling love	325	Forgive our transgressions	443
Doth sickness fill the heart with	167	Faith grasps the blessing she	221	For God has marked each	286
Do thy best always—do it now	221	Faith is our only business here	239	For God, that God the good	55
Down from the shining seats	182	Faith now beholds the glory	287	For God the Lord, both sun	9
Down stooped a silver cloud	81	Faith sees the bright eternal	342	Forgotten be each wordly	217
Down the swift stream we	349	Faith, that in prayer can never	159	For her my tears shall fall	227
Down through the portals of	63	Fall before him on the ground	265	For her our prayer shall rise	326
Draw us, O God! with	105	Fare thee well! though woe is	340	For him, break not the grassy	348
Dread alarms shall shake the	364	Far, far above all mortal things	218	For Him shall endless prayer	163
Dress Thee in arms, most	328	Far, far above thy thoughts	262	For Him shall prayer	317
Dumb at Thy feet I lie	361	Far, far away, the roar of	214	For His truth and mercy stand	97
Dust, to its narrow house	354	Far, far beneath, the noise of	214	For if, unheeding or beguiled	239
Dying Redeemer, to Thy	7	Far, far to distant lands	108	For I know that my	357
		Far from her home, fatigued	241	For not like kingdoms of the	239
E.		Far from this world of toil and	349	For O! in spite of constant care	414
Each care, each ill of mortal	359	Far from us drive the foe we	58	For, sure as olden sages tell	91
Each following minute, as it	161	Farewell, conflicting hopes and	347	For surely we may weep to	134
Each like thee, in peace	384	Farewell, my brethren in the	392	For sure, of all the plants that	167
Each place alike is holy	5	Farewell, my friends, time rolls	392	For Thee alone we would	414
Each summer bird that sings	396	Farewell, old soldiers of the	392	For Thee, my God, the living	56

ANY VERSE BUT THE FIRST. 467

	PAGE		PAGE		PAGE
For the grandeur of Thy	65	Give me one kind assuring	106	Great God, subdue this vicious	101
For the Lord will not cast off	356	Give me on Thee to wait	294	Great God, the work is all divine	162
For then to earth a light is	841	Give thanks aloud to God	51	Great God, what do I see and	342
For there adieus are sounds	392	Give them staunch honesty	326	Great God, whom heavenly	217
For there is hope of a tree, if it	357	Give Thou the word; that	846	"Great is the work," my	175
Forth, in the flowery spring	436	Give tongues of fire, and hearts	300	Great Paraclete! to Thee we	58
For this Thy temple, Lord, we	107	Give us comfort when we die	264	Great Prophet of our God	83
For Thou hast heard, O God of	330	Gladdened by the flowing	814	Great Shepherd of thy chosen	8
For Thou hast placed us side by	337	Glad shouts aloud—wide	46	Great Source of wisdom, teach	98
For Thou, within no walls	8	Glad, we trace th' amazing	62	Great Sun of Righteousness	29
For Thou, with sweet and	844	Glory to God, in full anthems	90	Grief may, like the pilgrim	294
For Thy dear mercy's sake	255	Glory to God, on high	70	Guard every avenue from guile	422
For Thy rich, Thy free	65	"Glory to God!" the sounding	69	
For we must share, if we	337	Glory to God! who deigns to	9	**H.**
For we know the Lord of Glory	443	Glory to God, who dwells on	63	Had I a glance of Thee, my	156
For what on earth can I desire	414	Glory to God, who is in heaven	417	Hail, great Immanuel, all	235
For when self-seeking turns to	137	Glory to Jesus, who returns	81	Hail, hail, all hail ye blood	373
For who but He that arched the	417	Glory to Jesus, who returns	165	"Hail, hail, auspicious morn	67
For whom didst Thou the cross	135	Glory to Thee, O God most	162	Hail Him, ye heirs of David's	174
Found guilty of excess of love	73	Go, and share His people's	304	Hail, Jesus! all victorious	301
Fountain of o'erflowing grace	201	Go—and when exposed to	315	Hail, mighty Saviour! Hail	129
Four and twenty elders rise	404	Go—bid the bright and	302	Hail, mighty Saviour! Thee	10
Frail children of dust, and	49	Go, clothe the naked, lead the	336	Hail, Prince of life! for ever	68
Free from anger and from	228	God calls our loved ones, but	365	"Hail, Prince of life!" they	92
Free, too, the captive mind	326	God, from on high, has heard	300	Hail! the heaven-born Prince	62
Fresh as the grass our bodies	257	God, from on high, invites us	105	Hail to the brightness of Zion's	310
Fresh roses in thy hand	353	God hath pronounced a firm	51	Hallelujah! church victorious	395
Friend of the friendless and the	287	God, in Israel, sows the seeds	147	Hallelujah! for the Lord	309
Friends, fondly cherished, have	411	God is our strength and song	31	Hallelujah! hark! the sound	309
From all eternity with love	171	God is our sun, whose daily	422	Hallelujah! strains of gladness	395
From all thy wanderings now	104	God measures unto all	262	Happy, if with my latest breath	183
From busy scenes we now	4	God meets the throngs who	337	Happy the man, whose hopes	329
From day to day, O Lord, do	162	God, my Redeemer, lives	360	Happy they who never rest	88
From earth his freed affections	349	God of glory, God of grace	266	Hard names at first, and	445
From earth we shall quickly	383	God of my strength, how long	56	Hark! I from the midnight hills	72
From east to west the sun	8	God of our fathers, hear	361	Hark, hark, my Lord and	378
From everlasting is His might	83	God of our salvation	294	Hark! hark!—the sound draws	70
From fear to hope, from hope	142	God of our sleeping hours	357	Hark! hark! to God the	168
From Heaven He came, of	72	God only is the creature's	189	Hark! herald voices near	322
From Jesus and His love, who	168	God only knows the love of	243	Hark! how He groans, while	80
From marble domes and	4	God pities all our griefs	197	Hark, how the angels sweetly	10
From men great skill	150	God shall preserve my soul	249	Hark! how the choirs above	222
From north to south, from east	802	God ruleth on high, almighty	43	Hark, it is the Saviour's voice	112
From one rude boy that's used	444	God's spirit will not always	101	Hark! the cherubic armies	63
From parent's eye and paths of	255	God, the all-merciful, earth	321	Hark! the glad shout of sacred	398
From sea to sea, from shore to	283	God, the eternal, mighty God	183	Hark! the thrilling symphonies	404
From sea to sea, through all	45	God, the Omnipotent! mighty	321	Hark! those bursts of	96
From sorrow, toil, and pain	227	God, thine own God, has richly	328	Harmonious accents to my	185
From soul to soul, quick as the	320	God, thy God, will now restore	314	Has cheered the nations with	13
From strength to strength go	192	God, whom we serve, our God	187	Haste, and mercy now implore	118
From strife of tongues and	221	God will exalt His glorious	81	Haste, my Beloved, fetch my	184
From the burden of the body	334	God works in all things; all	414	Hasten, Lord! the promised	309
From the cross uplifted high	147	Go, imitate the grace divine	345	"Haste, ye mortals, to adore	64
From the dark grave He rose	210	Go, man of pleasure, strike thy	5	Haste, O sinner! now return	118
From Thee, the overflowing	165	Good is the Lord our God	85	Haste, O sinner! to the	115
From the highest throne of	65	Good-will to men, and zeal for	80	Haste thee on from grace to	274
From thence He'll quickly	210	Good-will to men; ye fallen	63	Haste while yet thou canst be	118
From the provisions of Thy	53	Go to many a tropic isle	849	Hast found the pearl of price	176
From the Saviour's smiling	281	Go to the grave: at noon from	367	Has thy night been long and	814
From the sword, at noonday	16	Go to the grave; for there thy	367	Hast Thou a lamb in all Thy	183
From the third heaven where	306	Go to the grave;—no; take thy	367	Hast thou no tears, like those	157
From the tyranny within	331	Go—to the hungry food impart	303	Hast Thon not pledged Thy	212
From Thy house when we	15	Go up with Christ your Head	193	Hath He his loving kindness	154
From Thy works our joys	15	Go where the friendless	335	Have pity on my fears	361
From torturing pains to endless	339	Grace all the work shall crown	193	Have we forgot the almighty	258
Full of joyful expectation	389	Grace first contrived a way	193	Have ye forgot, or never knew	329
Full oft wast thou found afar	71	Grace led my roving feet	193	Have you no dear ones round	335
Fully in my life express	229	Grace! 't is a sweet, a charming	163	Have you not known a	335
		Grace will complete what grace	43	Have you no words? Ah	217
G.		Grant, Oh grant Thy Spirit's	209	Headlong we cleave the	415
Gather first My saints around	380	Grant that, with true and	293	Head of Thy church beneath	19
Gay is the morning: flattering	257	Graves have yawned in	114	He all His foes shall quell	18
Gay mirth shall deepen into	187	Grave, the guardian of our	368	Heal me, for my flesh is weak	287
Gently the passing spirit fled	355	Great Advocate, almighty	164	Heal our wounds—our strength	264
Gently with the dawning ray	431	Great All in All, Eternal King	156	He always wins who sides with	247
Gethsemane can we forget	244	Great God! a creature can not	84	Heart-broken, friendless, poor	155
Gird on, great God, Thy sword	13	Great God, create my heart	155	Hear the cries he now is	115
Give glory to the Lord	423	Great God, how infinite art	33	Hear the heathen's sad	315
Give me a calm, a thankful	250	Great God, impress the serious	401	Hear the mountain streamlet	438
Give me a faith shall never fail	168	Great God, let all my hours be	423	Hear them tell the wondrous	64
Give me, O Lord, a place	226	Great God! on what a slender	107	He, as man with man	291

	PAGE		PAGE		PAGE
Heathen at the sight are	313	Here it is I find my heaven	209	His name yields the richest	389
Heaven and earth must pass	200	Here let my faith unshaken	167	His nature, truth, and love	326
Heaven from above His call	106	Here let our hearts begin to	291	His own kind hand shall wipe	396
Heaven is the dwelling-place	413	Here let Thy holy days be kept	296	His piercing eye at once	88
Heaven is the place where	413	Here may Thine honor dwell	296	His power subdues our sins	81
Heavenly Father, life divine	368	Here mercy's boundless ocean	99	His presence sinks the proudest	177
Heaven's bright melodious	75	Here, O my soul, thy trust	167	His providence unfolds the	83
Heaven's broad day hath o'er	381	Here on the mercy-seat	226	His purposes will ripen fast	57
Heaven unfolds its portals wide	89	Here see the bread of life; see	269	His rising form on Olivet	81
He bears their buffeting and	77	Here's love and grief beyond	74	His sacred name a common	336
He bids me come! His voice	271	Here, then, my God, be pleased	153	His sanctuary is the heart	5
He bows beneath the sins of	131	Here the whole Deity is	83	His sovereign power, without	40
He bows His gracious ear	226	Here to my willing soul	325	His spirit, with a bound	359
He bows the heavens; the	80	Here we come Thy name to	14	His standard-bearers now	198
He breaks the captive's heavy	43	Here we meet to part again	438	His steady counsels change the	426
He breaks the power of	177	Here will we rest, here build	249	His terrors keep the world in	58
He called Himself my covenant	145	He rides and thunders through	43	His very word of grace is	47
He came in tongues of living	93	He rides upon the winged wind	55	His voice sublime is heard afar	89
He came, sweet influence to	93	Her portion in those realms of	145	His work my hoary age shall	178
He comes, arrayed in burning	43	Her tender mercies freely fall	335	His wrath, like flaming fire	259
He comes, from thickest films	69	He rules the world with truth	68	Hither come, for here is found	113
He comes! He comes! that	93	He sat serene upon the floods	46	Hither, from earth's remotest	376
He comes! He comes! Tho	153	He saw me as He passed	123	Hither, then, your tribute	206
He comes, the broken heart to	69	He saw me plunged in deep	190	Ho! all ye hungry, starving	191
He comes! the Conqueror	359	He saw the nations lie	51	Holiness becomes Thy dwelling	17
He comes, the prisoner to	69	He sends His showers of	426	Holy Ghost, no more delay	268
He comes to cheer the	72	He sends His word, and melts	426	Holy Ghost! with joy divine	265
He comes, with succor speedy	317	He sent His only Son	51	Holy Ghost! with power divine	265
He comes, your souls to save	70	He shakes the heavens with	87	Holy pilgrim! what for thee	112
He darts along the burning	83	He shall come down, like	317	Holy Spirit! all divine	265
He died to sin; he died to care	340	He shall reign from pole to pole	309	Holy Truth! Eternal Right	431
He ever lives above	211	He sits a Sovereign on His	57	Home—thy joys are passing	313
He formed the seas, and formed	43	He smiles—and seraphs tune	394	Honor immortal must be paid	168
He freely redeemed, with His	205	He spake, and light shone	305	Hope looks beyond the bounds	354
He frees the souls condemned	57	He spake, and my poor name	169	Hosanna in the highest strains	6
He from the dreadful gates of	324	He spake the wondrous word	87	Hosanna, Lord! Thine angels	84
He gave the mountains birth	85	He speaks, and at His fierce	55	Hosannas, Lord! to Thee we	333
He gilds thy mourning face	212	He speaks, and lo! all nature	42	Hosanna to th' anointed King	6
He guards thy soul, He keeps	219	He spreads His kind	334	How awful is the sight!	109
He guides our feet, he guards	52	He strengthens my spirit, He	233	How beautiful, on all the hills	343
He has pardons, full and free	117	He sunk beneath our heavy	291	How blessed are our eyes	332
He hears our praises and	8	He that dwelleth near Thee	284	How blessed, Lord, are they	429
He hung its starry roof on high	297	He to eternal glory calls	54	How can I meet His eyes	360
He in the days of feeble flesh	87	He vanquished sin and hell	95	How can we wish them	411
He in the thickest darkness	237	He was extended, He was	129	How charming is their voice	332
Heir of the same inheritance	337	He whispers me—"I 'm wholly	168	How damp were the vapors	71
He knew them all—the doubt	73	He who has helped me	296	How did love seize me—that	189
He leads me to the place	197	He, whose ear is every where	331	How dreadful was the hour	153
He left His starry crown	210	He will present our souls	199	How far from this our daily	181
He lives! again He lives	123	He will sustain our weakest	219	How far this heavenly robe	181
He lives—the everlasting God	52	He with earthly cares	244	How glorious He! How happy	87
Hell and the powers infernal	75	High as the heavens are raised	81	How glorious was the grace	158
Hell and the grave unite their	10	High God, and pure, and	159	How happy all Thy servants	185
Hell and thy sins resist thy	165	High Heaven, that hears the	292	How happy are our ears	332
He'll shield you with a wall of	300	High o'er th' angelic band He	87	How happy are the saints	244
He looks! and ten thousands	282	High o'er the earth His mercy	44	How happy the people that	388
He, Lord of all the world is on	105	High on a throne His glories	40	How He left His throne in	443
He loved His own bright, deep	348	High on a throne of radiant	336	How kind Thou art! Thou	159
He loves His saints; He knows	329	High on His holy seat	83	How large His bounties are	197
He loves to come when others	251	Him, in whom they move and	61	How little of that road, my soul	189
Help me by Thy word to	443	His bounties are free	265	How long, dear Saviour, O how	396
Help me to watch and pray	195	His dearest flesh He makes my	158	How long, dear Saviour, shall I	143
Help us turn from the evil of	322	His dews drop mutely on the	341	How long must we lie lingering	393
He met that glance so	140	His enemies, with sore dismay	41	How long the holy city	252
Henceforth, beside Him on His	293	His foes shall fall with heedless	324	Howl, winds of night, your force	39
Henceforth, our conversation	349	His foes shall tremble at the	177	How many children in the	445
Hence, gloomy doubts and	222	His goodness stands approved	260	How many hearts thou mightst	189
Hence, then, ye black	164	His grace will to the end	194	How many painful days on	346
He raised me from the deeps of	174	His hand in beauty gives	338	How mighty is His hand	51
Her dust and ruins that remain	57	His hand no thunder bears	199	How mournfully that golden	424
Here, before Thee, fallen	147	His hands provide our food	85	How much better thou 'rt	441
Here be they taught; and may	296	His hands the wheels of nature	87	How much is mercy thy	138
Here be Thy praise devoutly	296	His hoary frost, His fleecy	426	How oft my mournful thoughts	79
Here fix, my roving heart	197	His holy angels pitch their	172	How oft they look to heavenly	156
Here I behold Thy distant face	390	His honor is engaged to save	247	How perfect is Thy word	12
Here I 'll sit for ever viewing	209	His kingdom can not fail	18	How pure Thou art! Our	159
Here I raise my Ebenezer	204	His love exceeds your highest	10	How shall weak eyes of flesh	166
Here I would for ever stay	261	His love in my heart shed	205	How shall we tune our voice	238
Here, in the body pent	194	His love what mortal thought	181	How should our songs, like	9
Here in their house of	225	His mercies still endure	262	How skillfully she builds her	445
Here in Thy courts I leave my	188	His name the sinner hears	88	How slowly does His wrath	42

ANY VERSE BUT THE FIRST.

First Line	Page
How straight the path appears	193
How strong Thou art! We...	159
How such holy memories	430
How sure established is Thy	87
How sweet the tear of	425
How sweet, through long	425
How sweet to look, in	425
How sweet was that moment	71
How sweet will be the	7
How swift to save me didst	244
How tranquil now the rising	91
How vain the delusion, that	421
How we deserve the deepest	195
How will my heart endure	360
How will my lips rejoice to tell	182
How will our joy and wonder	398
Ho! ye that pant for living	191
Huge troubles, with	240
Humble as a little child	147
Hunger, thirst, disease	402

I.

First Line	Page
I am weary of the trifles	276
I ask a foretaste of the peace	7
I ask them whence their	399
I bent before Thy gracious	235
I beseech Thee, prostrate	364
I call to recollection	154
I can but perish if I go	138
I can not feel Thee touch my	187
I can not live contented here	161
I cast my burdens on the Lord	249
I come, I wait, I hear, I pray	7
I come, Thy servant, Lord	377
I come to join that countless	132
I could give thee thousand	441
"I delivered thee when bound	268
"I die for thee," He said	123
I dreamed of bliss in pleasure's	155
I dreamed of celestial rewards	878
I dream of that fair land, O	422
I'd sing the characters He	202
I'd sing the precious blood He	202
I'd tell Him how my sins arise	139
If aught should tempt my soul	242
If bright the world where Thou	855
If burning beams of noon	53
If distress befall thee	285
If done beneath Thy laws	195
I feel a strong, immortal hope	876
I feel throughout my evil day	153
If e'er I go astray	197
If e'er I heedless stray	211
If, for Thy sake, upon my	255
If God hath made this world so	30
If government be all destroyed	828
If He afflicts His saints so far	828
If He withdraws a moment's	163
If I, a wretch, should leave	79
I find Thee in the noon of night	24
If in my Father's love	199
If in this darksome wild I stray	157
If I to mention Thee forbear	289
If life be not in length of days	346
If love, that mildest flame, can	139
If my immortal Saviour lives	167
If night's blue curtain of the	29
If o'er my sins I think to draw	57
If sang the morning stars for	806
If Satan tempt our hearts to	213
If such the sweetness of the	252
If tears of sorrow would suffice	105
If there's a fervor in my soul	189
If this drear change be Thine	186
If Thou art my shield and my	205
If Thou hadst bid Thy	203
If Thou should'st take them all	253
If vapors with malignant breath	53
If winged with beams of	57
If ye have wept at yonder cross	87
I had no power to ask His	163
I hate to hear a wanton song	444
I have long withstood His grace	111
I have no argument beside	221
I have no cares, O blessed Will	247
I have no skill the snare to shun	159
I have seen the flowers wither	276
I have sinned, but Oh, restore	209
I hear at morn and even	361
I hear, but seem to hear in vain	143
I heard His people shout	145
I heard the law its thunders	143
I hear the bee humming	357
I hear Thee in the stormy wind	24
I hear the voice—"Ye dead	893
I hear the invitation	435
I hoped that in some favored	185
I implored Thy succor	284
I know Thee, Saviour, who	170
I know the soul that trusts in	246
I know Thou wilt not slight	415
I laid me down and slept:—I	241
I languish and sigh to be there	883
I lay my body down to sleep	418
I lay my garments by	428
I'll cast myself before His feet	240
I'll go to Jesus, though my sin	188
I'll make your great	85
I'll seek, by day, some glade	284
I'll shout aloud, "Ye thunders	851
I'll sing Thy majesty and grace	824
I'll speak the honors of Thy	190
Ill, that God blesses, is our	247
I long, dearest Lord, in Thy	408
I love, by faith, to take a view	424
I love her gates, I love the road	8
I love, in solitude, to shed	424
I love Thy church, O God	227
I love to meet Thy people now	125
I love to think on mercies past	424
I may not to Thy courts	217
Immortal glories crown His	894
Immortal glory forms His	47
Immortal light, and joys	43
Immortal wonders! boundless	413
Immovably founded in grace	888
I'm now on my journey to	71
Impart the faith that soars on	897
Impossible!—for Thine own	161
In all my ways Thy hand I own	159
In all our Maker's grand	41
In all their erring, sinful years	292
In all the times of my distress	244
In autumn, a rich feast	436
In books, or work, or healthful	445
In condescending love	359
Increase my faith—increase my	179
In darkest shades if He appear	188
In darkest skies, though storms	246
In each event of life, how clear	219
I need not tell Thee who I am	170
I need Thy presence every	215
In every dark, distressful hour	164
In every joy that crowns my	213
In every pang that rends the	65
Infinite joy, or endless woe	107
In foreign realms, and lands	55
In Gilead there is balm	211
In God my strength, howe'er	89
In golden armor blazing	817
In golden pomp, when autumn	233
In golden splendor dawning	434
In heaven, and earth, and air	187
In heaven the rapturous song	68
In His own words we Christ	293
In holy duties let the day	8
In holy words which can not	429
In honor to His name	219
In hope of that ecstatic pause	877
In hope of that immortal	397
In Israel stood His ancient	86
In Jesus is our store	231
In life, Thy promises of aid	164
In me the hinderance lies	297
In me, Lord, Thyself reveal	62
In midst of dangers, fears, and	55
In my distress I called my God	241
In ocean caves still safe with	415
In one fraternal bond of love	225
In one vast symphony of	813
In our sickness and our health	219
In prayer, my soul drew near	140
In prison I saw Him next	169
In reason's ear they all rejoice	25
In riches when I sought for joy	155
In robes of judgment, lo! He	41
In scenes exalted or depressed	164
In secret foldings they contain	237
In shame and anguish once He	85
In shining white they stand	92
In sight of all my foes	197
Instead of this He bade me feel	185
Instead of wine and cheerful	217
In such society as this	223
In suff'ring be Thy love my	171
In sunder break each warlike	858
In that beautiful place he is	442
In that lone land of deep	100
In the ark the weary dove	147
In the cold prison of the tomb	10
In the cross of Christ I glory	275
In Thee I place my trust	26
In the deserts let me labor	843
In the furnace God may prove	814
In the last hour of deep distress	89
In the leafy tree-tops	433
In the midst of affliction my	90
In them Thou may'st be	336
In the way a thousand snares	229
In the world of endless ruin	279
In the world will foes assail me	278
In Thine all-gracious	247
In this divine abode	103
In those dark, silent realms of	843
In Thy fair book of life and	83
In Thy word I hear Thee saying	209
In Thy strength may we be	229
In vain I ask my aching brain	839
In vain on earth we hope to	101
In vain the bright, the burning	185
In vain the noisy crowd	11
In vain the tempter's flattering	166
In vain thou strugglest to get	179
In vain we tune our formal	193
In want, my plentiful supply	171
In weakness, help us to	73
In whom but Thee, in heaven	240
In winter, awful Thou	433
In works of labor or of skill	415
I pay this evening sacrifice	425
I perish, and my doom were	141
I ran and raised the Sufferer up	169
I rest upon Thy word	197
Is a mighty famine now	265
I saw, beyond the tomb	259
I saw One hanging on a tree	163
I saw thee stray forlorn	123
I saw the opening gates of hell	241
I see no light, I hear no sound	397
I see, or think I see	259
I see the Lord of glory come	893
I shall His goodness see	193
I shield thee from alarms	123
I should, were He always thus	389
I sigh from this body of sin to	403
I sigh to think of happier days	56
I sing the goodness of the Lord	84
I sing the wisdom that	84
Is not e'n death a gain to those	835
Is not Thy chariot hastening on	824
Is not Thy name melodious	183
I spied Him where a fountain	169
Israel, a name divinely blest	59

	PAGE		PAGE		PAGE
Israel, now and evermore	147	Jesus lives, and God extends	200	Let all combined, with one	306
Israel rejoice and rest secure	219	Jesus lives, and I am sure	200	Let all that dwell above the	181
Israel's strength and consolation	209	Jesus lives and reigns supreme	200	Let all your lamps be bright	195
Is that He who died on Calvary	97	Jesus lives! henceforth is death	371	Let all your secret passions	8
Is the dream of nature flown	481	Jesus lives! I know full well	371	Let cares like a wild deluge	251
Is there a thing beneath the	187	Jesus lives! to Him the throne	371	Let clouds, and winds, and	40
Is there no guide to show that	180	Jesus, my all in all Thou art	171	Let day and dusky night	56
Is there no kind, no healing art	845	Jesus, my constant friend Thou	855	Let distant times and nations	40
Is this the Man of sorrows	4 6	Jesus, my God, but rather	168	Let each unholy passion cease	9
I strive to mount Thy holy hill	247	Jesus, my God!—I know His	177	Let earth's alluring joys	132
Is true freedom but to break	831	Jesus, my God, Thy blood alone	155	Let elders worship at His feet	132
It died ere its expanding soul	840	Jesus, my hope, my rock, my	132	Let everlasting thanks be Thine	21
It hallows every cross	263	Jesus! my Shepherd, Guardian	191	Let every act of worship be	161
I thank Thee, God's beloved	168	Jesus my Shepherd is	198	Let every creature join	50
I thought that the course of the	878	Jesus, once numbered with the	85	Let every creature rise and	163
"It is finished!" Oh what	97	Jesus, our God, ascends on	86	Let every creature sing	50
It is; it is; and I adore	66	Jesus, our great High Priest	116	Let every kindred, every tribe	174
It is not for thee to be seeking	408	Jesus, our great High Priest	83	Let every step, let every	142
It is that heaven-born faith	233	Jesus, our living Head	197	Let fall Thy rod of terror	232
It is the Lord—my covenant	249	Jesus, our Lord, descend	60	Let floods and nations rage	11
It is the Lord—who gives me	249	Jesus, our Priest, for ever lives	81	Let goodness and mercy, my	90
It makes the wounded spirit	191	Jesus, our shadowy path illume	251	Let him that heareth say	108
I told Him all my silent grief	172	Jesus shall ever reign	405	Let Israel home returning	283
I, too, at the season ordained	205	Jesus smiles, and says—"Well	362	Let Israel to the Prince of	69
It passed not, through the	78	Jesus sought me when a	204	Let Kedar's wilderness afar	306
Its dewy morn, its glowing	8	Jesus! Thee our Saviour	209	Let love and truth alone	323
It seems as if the Christian's	9	Jesus, the hinderance show	152	Let man conform his mind	263
Its pleasures now no longer	139	Jesus, the Lord, their harps	401	Let me go; I may not tarry	331
Its skies are not like earthly	394	Jesus the Lord will hear	226	Let me mingle tears with thee	75
It sweetly cheers our fainting	21	Jesus! the name that calms our	177	Let me never be forgetful	443
It tells me of a place of rest	236	Jesus—the name to sinners	183	Let me to some wild desert go	249
It was heaven below	232	Jesus! Thou art all compassion	208	Let me to Thee, in all my	132
It was my guide, my light, my	108	Jesus, Thou everlasting King	161	Let mountains from their seats	52
It was the good Physician now	266	Jesus, Thou Friend divine	227	Let music swell the breeze	318
It was the sight of Thy dear	167	Jesus! Thy feast we celebrate	77	Let noise and flame confound	42
I've not a secret care or pain	246	Jesus, to Thee I fly	106	Let no sense of guilt prevent	118
I've seen Thy glory and Thy	6	Jesus, to Thy dear faithful hand	107	Let not, amid our hours of	422
I want a godly fear	294	Jesus, to whom I fly	263	Let not conscience make you	118
I want a sober mind	294	Jesus! we come at Thy	98	Let not death alarm thee	285
I want a true regard	197	Jesus, who reigns above the	445	Let not Thy face be hid from	54
I want that grace that springs	167	Join, all ye ransomed race	60	Let others stretch their arms	185
I want to put on my attire	887	Joined in one Spirit to our	224	Let our sins be all forgiven	448
I was blind—Thy healing ray	885	Join we then with one accord	362	Let past ingratitude	152
I was not born as thousands	444	Joy e'en here—a budding flower	201	Let princes hear, let angels	47
I was not born without a home	444	Joyful, all ye nations! rise	62	Let rivers of salvation	20
I was not born a little slave	444	Joyful crowds, His throne	394	Let the dumb world its silence	76
I was not ever thus, nor	280	Joy of the desolate, light of the	269	Let the earth totter on her	851
I welcome all Thy sovereign	148	Joy to the world—the Saviour	68	Let them adore the Lord	486
I will forgive them	129	Judge not the Lord by feeble	57	Let them His great name	48
I will not fear, though armed	241	Just as I am—and waiting not	132	Let these earthly Sabbaths	15
I wish that His hands had been	442	Just as I am—poor, wretched	132	Let the sweet hope that Thou	250
I wooed ambition, climbed the	155	Just as I am—though tossed	132	Let the world despise and	274
I would begin the music here	401	Just as I am—Thou wilt	132	Let this blest hope mine	419
I would, but Thou must give	185	Just as I am—Thy love	132	Let those refuse to sing	199
I would for ever speak His	188	Just such a pilgrimage is life	352	Let those that sow in sadness	175
I would not ask to climb the	166	Just such as I, this earth He	243	Let Thy blood, by faith	149
I would not breathe for worldly	173			Let us altogether rise	267
I would not live alway; no	873	**K.**		Let us be simple with Him	337
I would submit to all Thy will	255	Keep no longer at a distance	275	Let us devote this consecrated	421
I would trust in Thy protecting	278	Keep Thou our souls from	416	Let us for each other care	228
I yield my powers to Thy	418	Kindled His relentings are	111	Let us still this love be	270
		Kindle our senses from above	53	Let us take up the cross	231
J.		Kingdoms wide that sit in	815	Let us, then, be up and doing	272
Jehovah is God, and Jehovah	20	King of glory, reign for ever	96	Let us, then, with angels sing	62
Jehovah's awful voice is heard	185	Kings for harps their crowns	403	Let us, then, with joy remove	229
Jehovah's charioteers surround	298	Knowing as I am known	195	Let us Thy dear example, Lord	251
Jehovah—'tis a glorious word	40	Knowledge, alas, 'tis all in vain	183	Life, death, and hell, and	38
Jerusalem! my glorious home	896	Known to all to be Thy	203	Life is real, life is earnest	272
Jerusalem! thy banished ones	252			Life, like a fountain, rich and	56
Jesus, and when shall that dear	401	**L.**		Life's brightest joys we may	244
Jesus can make a dying bed	343	Labor! wait! though mid night	389	Life's labor done, as sinks the	347
Jesus, for this to Thee I cry	158	Lame as I am, I take the prey	170	Life will have its evil years	440
Jesus—full of truth and love	113	Laws, freedom, truth, and faith	303	Lift up thy voice to heaven	20
Jesus, hail! enthroned in glory	97	Lead me, O Spirit, to the Son	187	Lift up your eyes, ye sons of	85
Jesus, hail! whose glory	96	Lead on, dear Shepherd!—led	190	Light and peace at once	874
Jesus, hear our humble prayer	229	Lead us to God, our final rest	59	Light immortal! Light divine	264
Jesus is from the proud	235	Lead us to holiness, the road	59	Light of them that sit in	815
Jesus is worthy to receive	181	Leave, Lord, Thy vigil there	226	Light on thy hills, Jerusalem	69
Jesus, I throw my arms around	106	Leave no unguarded place	192	Like airy bubbles, lo! we rise	349
Jesus lives, and by His grace	200	Lest when thy struggling soul	120	Like arrows went those	98
Jesus lives, and death is now	200	Let air, and earth, and skies	415	Like flames of fire His	45

ANY VERSE BUT THE FIRST.

First Line	Page
Like floods the angry nations	87
Like Him, now in my youth	285
Like Him, through scenes of	387
Like Him whose fetters dropp'd	23
Like that sweet rain on Judah's	330
Like the rough sea that can	105
Linger not in all the plain	117
Linger not, the stream is	381
Ling'ring about these mortal	107
Lion of Judah—Hail!	94
Listen, Christian, their	279
Little, then, myself I knew	117
Lives of true men all remind	272
Living in the silent hours	430
Living stars to view be	431
Lo! every kindred, tongue	306
Lo! glad I come, and Thou	172
Lo, God is here! Him, day and	45
Lo! He comes—He heeds my	267
Lo, he receives a sealed book	231
Lo! He rises, mighty King!	89
Lo, He slumbers in His manger	441
Lo! His triumphal chariot	84
Lo! in the desert rich flowers	310
Lo, in these latter days, our	830
Lo! it comes, that day of	388
Lo! it dawns, the Sabbath	17
Lo, Jehovah, we adore Thee	209
Lo! Jesus, who invites	103
Lone are the paths, and sad the	854
Lonely, I no longer roam	266
Long hadst Thou reigned ere	35
Long has Thy favor crowned	427
Long have we roamed in want	5
Long, too long have we been	827
Lo! o'er ancient forms	291
Look from the tower of heaven	421
Look! how we grovel here	153
Loose all your bars of massy	84
Loose me from the chains of	62
Lord, at Thy foot ashamed I lie	444
Lord! at Thy threshhold I	9
Lord, bring these precious	73
Lord, from Thine inmost glory	293
Lord God of truth and praise	109
Lord, grant me grace for every	243
Lord! how Thy wonders are	84
Lord, I address Thy heavenly	191
Lord, I adore Thy matchless	161
Lord! I am guilty—I am vile	144
Lord, I come to Thee for rest	219
Lord, I desire with Thee to live	184
Lord! I obey, my hopes	239
Lord! if Thine arm support us	187
Lord! I my vows to Thee	419
Lord! I ceaseless	240
Lord! it is my chief complaint	268
Lord Jesus, come! for hosts	322
Lord Jesus, come! the slave	823
Lord Jesus, take my spirit	277
Lord, keep me safe this night	428
Lord, let my soul forever	416
Lord! let not all my hopes be	100
Lord, make these faithless	131
Lord, may I ever keep in view	178
Lord! not in sepulchres alone	134
Lord, not in sorrow's hour	251
Lord, not my will, but Thine	245
Lord of earth and heaven! my	845
Lord of earth! its mournful	813
Lord of every tribe and nation	313
Lord of Heaven! beyond our	885
Lord of the nations! thus to	332
Lord of the patriarchs gone	187
Lord! on Thy cross I fix mine	76
Lord, prepare us by Thy grace	111
Lord, remove this grievous	204
Lord! rise in Thine	141
Lord, send a beam of light	184
Lord! send the gracious tidings	68
Lord! shall the breathings of	145
Lord, submissive make us go	223
Lord! the water-floods have	97
Lord! the words Thy lips are	97
Lord, this bosom's ardent	17
Lord, Thy glory fills the	65
Lord! Thy gracious word	309
Lord! Thy mercies never fail	83
Lord, 't is not ours to make the	297
Lord, we adore Thy ways	194
Lord, we obey Thy call	199
Lord, we return Thee what we	80
"Lord, why is this," I	185
Lord, with this guilty heart of	425
Lo! such a child, whose early	298
Lo! the angelic bands	82
Lo! the heavens are bursting	75
Lo! the last long separation	114
Lo, the nation is arousing	327
Lo! the promise of a shower	848
Lo! th' incarnate God	118
Lo, through the gloom of guilty	155
Lo! 't is He! our heart's	882
Loud hallelujahs to Thy name	162
Loud let the pealing organ	79
Loud is the song, the heavenly	157
Loud may the troubled ocean	59
Love and grief my heart	209
Love as I loved you—was the	157
Love eternal moved tho	69
Love is my Master; when it	169
Love is my teacher; He can	169
Love is the golden chain that	225
Love sits in His eyelids	232
Love this Friend who longs to	270
Love thou the path of sorrow	215
Love to God, and to our	17
Love to man, and love to God	381
Low at Thy feet my soul	132
Lo, we come to Thee for ease	118

M.

First Line	Page
Madness by nature reigns	107
Make haste, my days, to reach	141
Make us of one heart and mind	228
Make us into one spirit drink	251
Man drew from man his birth	13
Mankind shall be one	23
Man lieth down, no more to	852
Man may trouble and distress	274
Man's weakness, waiting upon	247
Man's wisdom is to seek	281
Many days have passed since	264
Many for His crying chid Him	204
Many friends were gathered	430
March on in your Redeemer's	176
Mark but that radiance of His	420
Mark ye her holy battlements	289
Martyrs! whose mystic legions	95
May erring minds that worship	293
May faith grow firm, and love	293
May He, by whose kind care	217
May I remember that to Thee	253
May my soul, with sacred	381
May our sins be all forgiven	441
May peace attend thy gate	11
May prayer now lift her sacred	5
Mayst thou live to know and	441
Mayst the captive's pleading	331
May the Gospel's joyful sound	14
May the great truths we here	5
May the millions now adoring	315
May Thy rich grace impart	229
May we, a little band of love	224
May we in faith receive Thy	221
Meekly may my soul	147
Me may Zion welcome, saved	369
Men, not now their hands	313
Mercy and Truth, that long	335
Mercy looked down with	84
Mere mortal power shall fade	253
Me to Thy suffering self	255
'Mid burning climes and frozen	302
'Midst keen reproach, and cruel	80
'Mid the chorus of the skies	863
'Mid the sheep a place decide	364
Mighty Spirit, ever nigh	431
Mild He lays His glory by	62
Mild it shines on all beneath	309
Millions of pilgrims throng	130
Millions of years my wondering	184
Millions of sinners, vile as you	103
Mindful of Thy chosen race	885
"Mine is an unchanging love	269
Mine the God whom you adore	266
Mix'd with those beyond the	88
Mold its green cup, its wiry	417
Money was not what he	204
More and more it spreads and	308
More glorious still as centuries	22
More tranquil than the stilly	414
Mortal, what has life for thee	431
Mourn for the lost—but call	332
Mourn for the lost—but pray	882
Mourn for the ruined soul	882
Mourn for the tarnished gem	882
Mourning souls dry up your	206
Much of my time has run to	418
Must I be carried to the skies	178
My best desires are faint and	148
My bosom burns with shame	259
My cheerful hope can never	257
My choir shall be the moonlit	234
My crimes are great, but don't	184
My days unclouded as they	418
My eyes are weary looking at	215
My fainting flesh had died with	54
My faith would lay her hand	198
My Father, God, and may these	183
My Father O permit my	255
My feet shall never slide	436
My feet shall travel all the	182
My flesh is hastening to decay	240
My flesh shall slumber in the	160
My flesh would rest in thine	1
My friendship's utmost zeal to	169
My friends, now friends no	259
My friends—the whole celestial	397
My garments, travel-worn and	215
My God! and can an humble	161
My God! forgive my follies	141
My God, how excellent Thy	53
My God, I hate to walk or	444
My God, I thank Thee who	444
My God, what inward	145
My God is reconciled	211
My God, I would not long to	83
My gracious God, how plain	12
My gracious Master and my	177
My great Protector and my	257
My hands are weary, toiling on	215
My heart and flesh cry out for	9
My heart doth feel that still	304
My heart grows warm with	235
My heart is fixed: my song	44
My heart is weary of its own	215
My heart, O Lord, forgets to	422
My heart shall triumph in my	1
My heart with grief is breaking	154
My heaven in Thee, O Father	321
My heaven in Thee! O God	321
My home henceforth is in the	355
My knowledge of that life is	249
My life is but a span	361
My life, my joy, my hope, I now	190
My lifted eye, without a tear	218
My lips with shame my sins	184
My mind in perfect peace	429
My native country! thee	318
My prayer hath power with God	170
My reason tells me Thy	143
Myriads of bright cherubic	293
My Saviour and Friend	285

	PAGE		PAGE		PAGE
My Saviour bids me come	152	Nor we alone; its wakening	804	O angels and archangels	218
My Saviour, every smile of	184	Nor we alone; may those whose	296	O believe the record true	112
My Saviour's face made thee to	7	Nor will our days of toil be long	4	O bid this trifling world retire	2
My sins a heavy load appear	141	Nor would I drop a murmuring	253	O blessed be this darkness then	186
My song for ever shall record	241	Nor would I wait till angel-host	897	O blessed is he to whom is given	807
My soul is desolate and drear	8	Nor wreck, nor ruin, there is	164	O break, O break, hard heart of	78
My soul, attend the solemn	130	No sculptured wonders meet	9	O! break the fatal chain	159
My soul looks back, to see	193	No sinful word, nor deed of	423	O, by the pangs Thyself hast	169
My soul rejoices to pursue	21	No sin to cloud, no lure to stay	185	O cease, my wand'ring soul	260
My soul, repeat His praise	81	No sun shall smite thy head by	52	O, cheerless were our	845
My soul shall pray for Zion	8	Not all that tyrants think or	185	O come, and with His children	108
My soul would leave this heavy	188	Not all the harps above	197	O come! for Thou dost know	239
My soul would rise and sing	31	Not as the conqueror comes	819	O come, Thou Holy Spirit	218
My suffering, slain, and risen	155	Not by the terrors of a slave	191	O come, Thou living Saviour	218
My thoughts, before they are	87	Not enjoyment, and not sorrow	272	O could I hear some sinner say	124
My tongue repeats her vows	11	Notes to heaven's high mansions	15	O! could we die with those	850
My wearied soul was all resign'd	248	Not half so far has nature placed	42	O could we learn that sacrifice	165
My willing soul would stay	12	Not half so high His power	42	O, could we make our doubts	400
My yearning soul would fain	844	No, that stream has nothing	852	O do not at a distance stand	158
		Nothing hath the just to lose	872	O drive these dark clouds from	889
N.		Nothing in my hand I bring	110	O earth, before the Lord, the	47
Nations all, remote and near	809	Nothing more can we require	14	O earth! grow flowers beneath	158
Naught else I feel, or hear, or	23	No! Thy dear name engraven	289	O earth, so full of dreary noise	841
Near at the marriage feast shall	298	Not life itself, with all its joys	6	O! enter his gates with	20
Nearer to Thee would we	327	Not many years their round	851	O'er all the names of Christ	393
Near Thee no darkness dares	2-8	Not more than others I deserve	445	O'er all the sons of human race	823
Ne'er think the victory won	192	No touching tale of anguish	157	O'er all the strait and narrow	21
New-born, I bless the waking	419	Not the fair palaces	226	O'er all those wide extended	413
New mercies, each returning	419	Not the labors of my hands	110	O'ercome by dying love	261
Night her solemn mantle	15	Not till blest Peace shall spring	806	O'er the blue depths of Galilee	69
Night reigns in silence o'er the	425	Not to ease and aimless quiet	839	O'er the negro's night of care	809
Night unto night His name	423	Not upon us or ours the solemn	865	O'er the toilsome way thou'st	854
No act falls fruitless	337	Not what we wish, but what we	247	O! evermore may all our bliss	5
No bleeding bird, nor bleeding	155	Not walls, nor hills, could guard	250	Of all that now may seem	429
No bliss I'll seek, but to fulfill	239	Not with the hope of gaining	189	Of all the pious dead	861
No burning heats by day	212	No village bell shall toll for him	845	O F ther, in that hour	222
No! by His early griefs and	835	Now behold Him high	89	O Father! our eye is to Thee	889
No chilling winds, or poisonous	412	Now cheerful to the house of	91	Of His deliverance I will boast	179
No, dearest Jesus, no; to Thee	867	Now, despisers, look and	115	Of joys that come no more	429
No dimly cloud o'ershadows	898	Now destroy the man of sin	8-5	O for a sight, a pleasing sight	893
No earthly father loves like	175	Now, from His high, imperial	43	O for a strong, a lasting faith	45
No good in creatures can be	250	Now God invites; how blest	100	O for a trumpet voice	83
No guile within His mouth is	77	Now He's waiting to be gracious	110	O for grace our hearts to soften	240
No—I must maintain my hold	264	Now I am Thine, for ever	138	O for the coming of the end	23
Noiseless the sun emits his fire	425	Now I esteem their mirth an	101	O for the day, the glorious day	176
No; is not this alone	322	Now in the grave He's laid	123	O for the living flame	31
No lingering look, no parting	223	No winter there, no shades of	426	O for the times when on my	156
No longer hosts encountering	289	Now let each heart and hand	333	O for this love let rocks and	182
No longer now delay	210	Now let me mount and join	401	O for thy fragrant flowers	405
No more a wand'ring sheep	196	Now let the Lord for ever	47	O! from the streams of distant	396
No more a weeping wife to	333	Now let the trumpet raise	349	Of so divine a Guest	285
No more fatigue, no more	2	Now let thought behold him	365	Oft do our eyes with joy	400
No more let sin and sorrow	63	Now, Lord, I would be Thine	203	Often I feel my sinful heart	173
No more shall bold blasphemers	106	Now may the King descend	19	Oft has He called thee, but thou	120
No more shall foes unclean	800	Now rest my long-divided	293	Oft has the Lord whole nations	55
No more shall peevish passion	47	Now safely moored, my perils	168	Oft the big, unbidden tear	363
No more the drops of piercing	400	Now shall my head be lifted	289	Oft when beneath the work of	253
No more the sovereign eye of	105	Now, sinners, dry your tears	199	Oft, when I seem to tread	241
No more the weary pilgrim	845	Now the desert lands rejoice	808	Oft when the world, with iron	5
No mortal can with Him	190	Now the feast is spread before	129	O garden of Olivet, thou dear	71
No, my soul, in God rejoice	431	Now the full glories of the Lamb	83	O gentle Shepherd, still	289
No! place thy trust above	262	Now the gay world with	189	O gladly tread the narrow path	891
No profit canst thou gain	263	Now the heavens on high adore	880	O! glorious hour! O! blest	160
Nor accents flow, nor words	221	Now the storm goes wildly o'er	273	O glory, shining far	407
No! rather let me freely yield	253	Now they approach a spotless	899	O God, make bare Thine arm	828
Nor bounded to the earth alone	835	Now, though He reigns exalted	291	O God, mine inmost soul	125
Nor death nor hell shall e'er	247	Now thro' the charmed air, on	867	O God of glory, God of love	87
Nor doth it yet appear	199	Now to our God, the Father	897	O God! our help in ages past	56
Nor earth, nor all the sky	197	Now to the Lamb that once was	182	O God Triune, to Thee we owe	58
No rest in the grave	410	Now to the shining realms	161	O gracious God! in whom I live	179
No rest is to be found	285	Now to you my spirit turns	266	O grant my soul an ear to hear	425
Nor from the seat of scornful	55	Now we may bow before His	177	O grant that nothing in my soul	171
Nor let the good man's trust	286	Now when the evening shade	140	O grant us, in this solemn hour	4
Nor let thou life's delightful	25	Now, ye needy, come and	118	O guard our shores from every	339
Nor pain, nor grief, nor anxious	844	Now, ye saints, His power	249	O guide me through the various	419
Nor scorching sun, nor sickly	219	Now, ye saints, lift up your	89	O guide us till our night is	423
Nor shall the glowing flame	216			O! guilty sinner, hear the	120
Nor shall Thy spreading Gospel	23	**O.**		O! hadst thou still on earth	340
Nor time, nor distance, e'er	189	O all-sufficient Saviour! be	167	O happy bond that seals my	292
No rude alarms of raging foes	2	O all ye Christian heroes	213	O happy, happy soul!	850
Nor voice can sing, nor heart	143	O angel of the land of peace	844	O happy, happy that I am	180

ANY VERSE BUT THE FIRST.

	PAGE		PAGE		PAGE
O happy harbor of God's saints	398	O may the sweet, the blissful	181	Or round their Father's throne	343
O happy scenes above the sky	145	O may Thine own Bride and	114	O sacred hope! O blissful hope	223
O happy servant he	195	O may Thy Spirit gently draw	292	O Salem! our once happy seat	288
O happy souls! O glorious state	191	O may Thy Spirit guide my	6	O saving Leader! opening wide	159
O happy souls that pray	19	O may we all, while here	89	O Saviour! with protecting care	84
O haste to follow where it leads	391	O may we ne'er forget His	180	O say not so! the spring-tide	445
O! hast thou felt a Saviour's	176	O may we thus be found	109	O season of soft sounds and hues	419
O hear it, sinner—hear that	120	O may we thus insure	109	O see those waters streaming	20
O! holy and sweet its rest shall	408	O may we ever hear Thy voice	175	O, shall not warmer accents tell	290
O holy, heavenly home	407	O memory! can those strains on	253	O shine on this benighted	254
O holy, holy, holy Lord	46	O messenger of dear delight	208	O shout, ye people, and adore	46
O Holy Spirit from above	58	O! methinks I hear Him	204	O show Thyself the Prince of	308
O holy trust! O endless rest!	298	O might I hear Thy heavenly	47	O sinners! in His presence bow	105
O hope of every contrite heart	142	O might I once mount up and	156	O! spare me yet, I pray	361
O how altered my condition	273	O might some dream of vision'd	25	O speak, thou voice of God	399
O how cheating, O how	372	O mother dear, Jerusalem	398	O Spirit of the Lord! prepare	300
O how I hate those lusts of	103	O move us—Thou hast power	157	O spread Thy covering wings	218
O how long-suffering, Lord!	120	O my sweet home, Jerusalem	398	O star untimely set	358
O how sad and sore distressed	75	O my unsteadfast mind	152	O, stay thy tears; the blest	345
O how shall these dim eyes	29	On all the wings of time it flies	351	O stay with us, and still	160
O how tremendous is the	33	On angels, with unveiled face	47	O sweet abode of peace and love	160
O! if my Lord would come and	343	Once, a sinner, near despair	264	O! tell me the place where Thy	233
O! if my soul, when death	7	Once, like thee, by joys	118	O! tell me that my worthless	106
O, if once Thy smile divine	385	Once more our welcome we	216	O tell of His might, and sing of	49
O, in Thy light be mine to go	73	Once on the raging seas I rode	168	O that a dying world might	188
O Jesus, full of grace the sighs	166	Once the morning's earliest	266	"O! that all the blind but	204
O Jesus, full of truth and grace	186	Once they were mourning here	399	O, that each, in the day of His	488
O Jesus, Lamb once crucified	53	Once when my scanty meal was	169	O that I could for ever sit	208
O! Jesus, let me ever hail	8	Once with Adam's race in ruin	382	O that I could now adore Him	279
O Jesus, my sweet Saviour	282	On cherub and on cherubim	46	O that I could, with favor d	208
O Jesus, once rocked on the	71	One army of the living God	223	O that I, like a little child	171
O Jesus! ride onward	379	On earth they sought their	413	O that our thoughts and thanks	8
O Jesus, there is none like	425	One day, amid the place	12	O that Thou wouldst hide me in	357
O Jesus! Thou the beauty art	187	One family, we dwell in Him	223	O that we now might see our	228
O keep me in Thy heavenly	179	One gentle sigh His fetters	349	O that with yonder sacred	174
O land! O land	356	O ne'er will I at life repine	343	O! that world is passing fair	385
Old friends, old scenes will	419	One look of mercy from Thy	142	O the lost, the unforgotten	430
Old friends, old scenes will	165	One moment, and the silentness	173	O then let wrath remove	258
O lead me to the Rock	259	One moment—and the Spirit	93	O then shall the vail be removed	886
O learn to scorn the praise of	807	One privilege my heart desires	289	O, there will be mourning	128
O let man hasten to restore	337	One thing demands our care	359	O the rapturous height	239
O let me wing my hallowed	253	One trial more must yet be	243	Other refuge have I none	261
O let my hand forget her	234	O never let my soul remove	257	O, the rich depths of love	66
O let my name engraven	236	O, never more may different	820	O, the transporting, rapturous	412
O let my soul on Thee repose	416	One thing alone, dear Lord! I	186	O thou Almighty Lord	68
O let the dead now hear Thy	173	On harps of gold His name they	849	O Thou eternal Ruler	316
O let the soul its slumbers	353	On Him the Spirit largely	69	O Thou great God! whose	345
O let Thy smitten ones again	330	On Him the weight of	173	O Thou, that fill'st the heavenly	358
O let Thy star of love but	145	On Him, with rapture then I'll	225	O Thou, who givest life and	298
O let us then with heartfelt	159	On impious wretches He shall	328	O thou, who mournest on thy	242
O let us to His courts repair	44	Only a sweet and holy soul	102	O Thou! who rulest seas and	258
O light of Zion, now arise	308	Only, O Lord, in Thy dear love	419	O throw away thy rod	258
O Lord! amidst this mental	243	Only, since our souls will shrink	267	O! to grace how great a	204
O Lord! ascend Thy throne	95	Only Thee content to know	229	Our beauty and our strength	107
O Lord! I cast my care on Thee	250	Only to sit and think of God	175	Our birth is but a starting place	356
O Lord, my weary soul release	184	On me Thy providence hath	34	Our brother the haven has	339
O Lord of hosts, Almighty	45	On mightier wing, in loftier	22	Our Captain leads us on	193
O Lord of life and truth	141	On my heart each stripe be	147	Our cautioned souls prepare	109
O Lord, prevent it by Thy	125	O noblest brow and dearest	79	Our days are numbered; let us	239
O Lord, the pilot's part perform	239	O, not to those whom Thou	330	Our days run thoughtlessly	105
O! lovely attitude—He stands	98	On, piercing Gospel, on! of	320	Our dearest joys, and nearest	254
O Lord! ascend Thy throne	95	On that my gaze I fasten	278	Our eyes have seen the rey	351
O Love, Thy sov'reign aid	137	On Thee alone, my hope relies	86	Our eyes have seen the steps of	351
O! madder than the raving	140	On thee foul spirits have no	52	Our fathers' God, our Keeper	317
O! magnify the Lord with me	179	On the tree of life eternal	374	Our fathers' God! to Thee	316
O! make but trial of His love	179	On us He bids the sun	152	Our fathers' sepulchres are here	332
O! make this heart rejoice or	143	Onward, Christians, onward go	403	Our fathers, where are they	361
O many-toned and chainless	399	On wheels of light, on wings of	72	Our fellow-sufferer yet retains	85
O may He walk among us here	141	On wings of love the Saviour	334	Our flesh, our reins, our spirits	255
O! may I bear some humble	83	O, on that day, that dreadful	98	Our glad hosannas, Prince of	69
O! may I feel Thy worth	211	Open Thou the crystal fountain	278	Our glorious Leader claims our	399
O may I live to reach the place	163	Oppressed with sin and sorrow's	191	Our guilty spirits dread	194
O! may I never turn aside	145	O pray we then for Salem's	8	Our hopes that when with joy	456
O may I now for ever fear	414	O precious cross! O glorious	244	Our harvest months have o'er	427
O may our humble spirits stand	393	Or as an eagle to the prey	349	Our hearts are breaking now	407
O may our sympathizing breasts	334	O render thanks to God above	41	Our hearts have often burned	234
O may that faith our hearts	197	O Rest of rests! O Peace, serene	214	Our hearts leap up; our	156
O may the grave become to us	351	O righteous Judge, if Thou wilt	189	Our journey is a thorny maze	237
O may the influence of this day	5	Or, if it be the gloom that comes	414	Our kindred and our friends are	101
O may the righteous, when I	161	Or if on joyful wing	283	Our labors done, securely laid	849
O may these thoughts possess	87	Or, if 't is e'er denied thee	434	Our life contains a thousand	257

	PAGE		PAGE		PAGE
Our life is a dream; our time	433	Plenteous grace with Thee is	261	Rich is the grace we sing	95
Our life, whilst Thou preserv'st	55	Poor souls! that know not how	187	Ride forth, victorious	288
Our lives through various	32	Poor tho' I am—despised	237	Ride on in Thy greatness, Thou	323
Our moments fly apace	361	Poor tremblers at His rougher	307	Ride on, ride on in majesty	74
Our mirth is not afraid of Thee	167	Pour not thou the bitter tear	371	Righteous Judge of retribution	364
Our mourning is all at an end	388	Praise Him, ye celestial choirs	89	Right thro' thy streets with	398
Our sacrifice is one	19	Praise Him, ye who know His	27	Ring, Liberty, thy glorious bell	307
Our Saviour shall be still our	175	Praise, my soul, the God that	17	Rise, God! judge Thou the	337
Ours, by the pledge of love and	355	Praise the Creator of the skies	37	Rise, great Redeemer, from Thy	324
Our sorrows and our sins were	244	Praise the God of our salvation	65	Rise, my soul, the day is	17
Our souls are faint, our hearts	169	Praise the Lord—for He hath	65	Rise, Saviour! help me to	140
Our voices join the heavenly	234	Praise the Lord—for He is	65	"Rise," says the Saviour	261
Our vows, our prayers, we now	218	Prayer is the burden of a sigh	220	Rise, touched with gratitude	98
Out of great distress they came	403	Prayer is the Christian's vital	220	Rivers of love and mercy, here	191
O utter but the name of God	189	Prayer is the contrite sinner's	220	Rivers to the ocean run	370
O voice of mercy! voice of love	237	Prayer is the simplest form of	220	Roar on, ye waves; our souls	415
O wash my soul from every sin	184	Prayer makes the darkened	217	Roll back the swelling tide of	320
O watch and fight, and pray	192	Pray thou, Christian, daily	279	Room in the Saviour's bleeding	103
O wavering, wretched state	152	Precious is the Saviour's name	117	Round each habitation hovering	312
O! weak to know a Saviour's	255	Prepare us, Lord, by grace	427	Round the altar priests confess	403
O were I like some gentle dove	249	Press on! and if we may not	336	Rude in speech, or grim in	313
O what a blessed hope is ours	225	Preserve it from the passing	8	
O what a glorious sight appears	397	Princes and magistrates must	344	**S.**
O what amazing joys they feel	393	"Prisoner, long detained below	363	Sad be the notes, the plaintive	253
O what a night was that which	10	Prisoners of hope, in gloom	116	Sad to his toil he goes	195
O, what are all my sufferings	397	Proclaim abroad His name	95	Safe the dreary vale I tread	27
O what hath Jesus bought for	397	Proclaim Him King, pronounce	37	Safe in my Saviour's love I'll	351
O, when His wisdom can	45	Proclaim His wonders from the	45	Sages, leave your contemplations	65
O! when shall my foes and my	233	Proclaim the glories of your	87	Saints and angels, joined in	113
O, when will the period appear	387	Prone to wander, Lord, I feel	204	Saints, before the altar bending	65
O! when wilt Thou, my Life	138	Prostrate before the mercy seat	135	Saints, begin the endless song	403
O while I breathe to Thee	140	Prostrate bow; confess your	117	Saints below, with heart and	200
O, while the soul unruffled lies	237	Prostrate I'll lie before His	138	Saints! in fair circles, casting	95
O, who hath lock'd those	196	Protect me from the furious	244	Saints in glory perfect made	403
O, who, in such a world as this	352	Publish—spread to all around	61	Salvation and immortal praise	10
O, who like Thee—so calm, so	73	Pure as the air, when day's first	419	Salvation!—let the echo fly	181
O, who like Thee so humbly	73	Pure as the sun's enliv'ning	167	Salvation to God, who sits on	48
O, who would bear life's stormy	245	Put all thy beauteous garments	300	Satan may vent his sharpest	174
O! why should I stray with the	233	Put on the armor from above	167	Save me, for none beside can	141
O! why should I wander	232			Save me, save me, O my	273
O! with the visits of Thy love	345	**Q.**		Save us, in Thy great	275
O, with what congratulations	369	Quick as their thoughts their	156	Saviour, hasten Thine appearing	96
O! wondrous Love—to bleed	145			Saviour in glory beaming	95
O, would He of all of heaven	225	**R.**		Saviour, may our Sabbaths be	15
O, wretched state of deep	106	Rage, while our faith the	415	Saviour! shine, and cheer my	147
O, ye angels, hovering round us	115	Raised on devotion's lofty wing	41	Saviour, Thy love is still the	187
O ye that love His holy name	43	Raise thy downcast eyes, and	127	Saviour, where'er Thy steps I	157
O Zion! learn to doubt no more	259	Raise your devotion, mortal	177	Saw ye not the cloud arise	308
"O Zion, lift thy raptured eye	72	Ready for their glorious crown	362	Say, hath thy heart its treasure	273
		Reason, I hear, her counsels	143	Say—live forever, glorious	74
P.		Rebel ye waves, and o'er the	89	Say, O sinner, that livest at rest	129
Pardon, and grace, and heaven	137	Rebuild thy walls, thy bounds	288	Say, shall we yield Him in	90
Pardon, O Lord, our childish	445	Receive, O earth, his faded	345	Say to the heathen, from Thy	300
Partakers of the Saviour's grace	224	Redeemed from earth and	359	Scarce morning twilight had	84
Pass a few fleeting moments	376	Regard the weak and fatherless	337	Scenes of sacred peace and	313
Patience, poor soul! the	215	Rehearse His praise, with awe	86	Seal my forgiveness in the	415
Patiently enduring, ever	339	Rejoice in glorious hope	19	Searcher of hearts, in mine	294
Pause, my soul! adore and	270	Rejoice in hope and fear	193	Season of rest! the tranquil soul	4
Peace and joy shall now attend	814	Rejoice when care and woe	193	Seasons and times, and moons	436
Peace! and no longer, from its	321	Rejoice, ye righteous, and	43	Secure, amidst alarms	263
Peace be within this sacred	8	Released from sorrow, sin and	394	Secure from danger and from	225
Peaceful be thy silent slumber	395	Remember all the dying pains	444	See a long race thy spacious	321
Peace from the bosom of his	334	Remember all who love thee	434	See barbarous nations at thy	320
Peace is on the world abroad	15	Remembered songs of gladness	154	See, from all lands—from the	310
"Peace on earth, good-will	64	Remembering mine affliction	356	See, from His head, His hands	74
Peace to our brethren give	13	Remember still that they are	292	See, God is reconciled	261
People and realms of every	163	Remember Thee—Thy death	290	See heathen nations bending	316
Perhaps, before the morning	249	Remember Thy pure word of	144	See how the Conqueror mounts	177
Perhaps He will admit my plea	138	Renew'd, the earth a robe of	69	See, Jehovah's banner furled	309
"Permit them to approach," He	293	Repeated crimes awake our	164	See, Jesus stands with open	103
Perpetual blessings from above	425	Resign the honors of their form	351	See, low before Thy throne of	254
Physician of souls! unto me	388	Rest for my soul I long to find	185	"See, Mercy, from her golden	72
"Pilgrims, see that stream	382	Resting in this glorious hope	373	See on the mountain top	193
Pilgrims through this world and	207	Restraining prayer, we cease to	217	See Salem's golden spires	193
Pilgrim thou dost justly call me	723	Rests secure the righteous man	373	See that glory, how resplendent	395
Pillar of fire, through watches	21	Retreat beneath His wings	231	See the happy spirits waiting	381
Pity and save my sin-sick soul	292	Return, O holy Dove, return	220	See, the heaven its Lord	89
Pity the nations, O our God!	290	Return, O wanderer, return	104	See the Judge our nature	114
Pity the weeping widow's woe	305	Return, O wand'rer, to thy	104	See the kind angels at the gates	257
Plant Thy heavenly kingdom	385	Revive our drooping faith	195	See the kinder shepherds round	441
		Rich dews of grace come o'er us	316	

	PAGE		PAGE		PAGE
See, the light of truth is	827	Sinners, see your ransom paid	69	Soul, adieu! this gloomy	381
See the lovely Babe a-dressing	441	Sinners, whose love can ne'er	174	Soul, then know thy full	274
See the morning sunbeams	488	Sinners, will you scorn the	115	Sounds among the vales and	27
See the rocks and mountains	75	Sinners, wrung with true	65	Sounds of so sweet a tone	67
See the stars appearing	489	Sin no more can taint thy	834	Source of light, Thou bid'st the	26
See! the storm of vengeance	115	Sin, o'er sense so softly stealing	315	Source of truth, whose rays	26
See, the streams of living	812	Sin the primal charter broke	831	So, when a raging fever burns	101
See the universe in motion	114	Slain in the guilty sinner's	130	So when my latest breath	195
See where it shines in Jesus'	163	Sleep, my babe, thy food and	441	So when our mortal ties death	367
See where rebellious passions	166	Sleep shuns mine eyes—mine	844	So when the Christian pilgrim	394
See—where the Sun of	423	"Sleep soft, beloved!" we	841	So, when that morn of endless	421
See yon orient streak appearing	874	Small are the offerings we can	837	So, when the transient storm is	216
Selfish pursuits, and nature's	186	So Abra'm, by divine command	288	So will Thy people with	321
Send forth Thy word, and let	288	So before Thy presence fading	17	Space cannot check, thought	343
Seraphs, with elevated strains	401	So be it! let this system end	391	Spared to see another year	146
Serene, I laid me down	428	So, cured of my folly, yet cured	878	Spare, Lord! the thoughtless	888
Servant of all, to toil for man	138	So deep were His sorrows, so	71	Speak, for you feel His burning	45
Shall aught beguile us on the	160	So fades a summer cloud away	847	Speak gently—'t is a little thing	884
Shall break these clods, a form	840	So fast eternity comes on	104	Speak gently to the aged one	884
Shall every creature around	205	Soft and easy is thy cradle	441	Speak gently to the erring ones	884
Shall it leave the low earth, and	408	Soft as the morning dews	167	Speak gently to the erring ones	837
Shall Jesus for admittance	141	Soft, my child—I did not chide	441	Speak gently to the young	884
Shall love like Thine be thus	140	So, gracious Saviour, on my	87	Speak of the wonders of that	40
Shall love, with weak embrace	853	So grant me, Lord, from every	185	Speed on Thy work, Lord God	880
Shall man, the lord of nature	435	So in the dreary grave confined	671	Spirit of glory and of God	132
Shall Nature from her couch	423	So, in the last and dreadful day	84	Spirit of purity and grace	98
Shall things withered, fashions	827	So in this darkness I can learn	186	"Spread for thee the festal	111
Shall we, for whom that star	420	So Jesus looked on dying men	834	Spread, mighty Gospel, spread	820
Shall we, for whom the Saviour	420	So Jesus rose to pray	226	Spread then Thy plumes of	428
Shall we Thy life of grief forget	244	So Jesus slept; God's dying	344	Sprinkled afresh with pardoning	425
Shall we, whose souls are	299	So Jesus still doth pray	226	"Sprinkled now with blood	111
Shall winds and waves their	253	So let each faithful child	838	Spurn not the call to life and	101
Sharing now Thy wounds, I	147	So let our souls, benighted	20	Stand, then, in His great might	192
Shed on those who in Thy	26	So let the Saviour be adored	836	Stand up, and bless the Lord	81
Shepherds, in the field abiding	65	So live for ever, glorious Lord	85	Star Divine! O safely guide	869
Short is the passage, short the	413	So, Lord, when that last	414	Star of faith! when winds are	869
Should earth against my soul	251	So long Thy power hath blessed	280	Star of hope! gleam on the	869
Should earth and hell with	52	So I may sing, in Jesus safe	164	Stay with us, Lord, and with	157
Should friends and kindred	54	Some Rose of Sharon, dyed in	423	Stern and awful are its tones	201
Should I suppress my vital	57	Some to their everlasting home	223	Still as the light of morning	8
Should storms of trouble blow	263	Son of the Father! Lord most	285	Still for us He intercedes	89
Should strong temptations	252	Songs of praise awoke the	209	Still give us grace, Almighty	833
Should sudden vengeance seize	134	So oft my soul hath trod	259	Still heavy is thy heart	262
Should swift death this night	430	Sons of Adam, once in Eden	874	Still let her mild rebukings	855
Should worlds conspire to drive	135	Soon as the evening shades	25	Still let the barren fig-tree	418
Shout to the Lord, ye surging	80	Soon as the morn the light	140	Still let the Spirit cry	199
Shout, ye bright, angelic choir	382	Soon as the morn with roses	151	Still may their light our duties	290
Shout, ye little flock, and blest	228	Soon as we draw our infant	155	Still 'mid heavy mourning	865
Shout, ye saints, with	75	Soon, borne on time's most	100	Still near the lake, with weary	72
Shout, ye seraphs; Gabriel	59	Soon, for me, the light of day	264	Still restless nature dies and	58
Show me what I have to do	219	Soon must we change our place	60	Still, still with Thee! as to each	214
Show me Thy face, and I'll	188	Soon night comes on with	148	Still tossed on a sea of distress	889
Show us some token of Thy	221	Soon relentless death will come	127	Still the Spirit lingers near	15
Shrink not, Christians; will ye	408	Soon shall a darker night	417	Still to a stricken brother true	420
Sick or healthful, slave or free	267	Soon shall I pass the gloomy	172	Still watch and pray, and raise	417
Silence, and solitude, and	100	Soon shall ocean's hoary deep	834	Still we wait for Thine	275
Silent and slow, they glide	98	Soon shall our doubts and fears	194	Still will I hope for voice and	255
Silent our harps o'er Babel's	252	Soon shall our doubts and fears	260	Still would we bear Thy easy	414
Since Christ and we are one	294	Soon shall we hear Him say	198	Stop, thoughtless sinner, stop	120
Since from His bounty I receive	190	Soon shall we meet again	865	Strangely, my soul, art thou	181
Since on this fleeting hour	859	"Soon the days of life shall end	111	Strike, strike the harps again	70
Since Thou, the everlasting	143	Soon will the awful trumpet	105	Stripp'd of each earthly friend	263
Since, with pure and firm	16	Soon will our earthly race be	401	Stronger His love than death or	208
Sinful, unworthy, trembling	280	So pilgrims on the scorching	5	"Stronger than death Thy love	286
Sing how eternal love	199	Sorrow and fear are gone	263	Strong in the Lord of hosts	192
Sing, how He left the worlds of	85	Sorrow and Love go side by	203	Strong were thy foes; but the	230
Sing of the Lamb that once was	176	So shall every slavery cease	831	Struggle through thy latest	881
Sing, on your heavenly way	193	So shall it be at last, in that	214	Stung by the scorpion sin	83
Sing praises to the righteous	824	So shall my walk be close with	220	Subdued and instructed at	878
Sing, till we feel our heart	193	So shall that curse remove	360	Sublime upon His azure throne	891
Sinner! can you hate this	119	So shall their course more	104	"Such a Guide? No guide	888
Sinner! come, ere thy doom	122	So sleeps the soul, till Thou, O	156	Such blessings from Thy	218
Sinner! come to thy home	122	So sorrow often presses	272	Such is pleasure's transient	118
Sinner! come, while there	122	So speaks the Christian, firm	355	Such is the Christian's parting	420
Sinner! haste, time fleets fast	122	So thou, Eternity, so vast	415	Such was the lot He freely	72
Sinner! hear your God and	119	So, though our path is steep	193	Sun, moon, and stars convey	22
Sinner! it was a heavenly	101	So, through the ocean-tide of	345	Sun of my soul! Thou Saviour	416
Sinner! perhaps this very day	101	So to the heart that knows Thy	214	Sure as Thy truth shall last	227
Sinners in derision crowned	96	So, trusting in Thy love, I	242	Sure I must fight, if I would	178
Sinners rejoice, and saints	163			Sure is Thy protection	264

Hymn	Page
Surely, once Thy garden	275
Sure never, till my latest	102
Sure there was ne'er a heart so	148
Sweet as home to pilgrims	119
Sweet, at the dawning hour	12
Sweet bonds that unite all the	408
Sweet drops of grace, the	251
Sweet fields, beyond the	400
Sweet hour! for heavenly	419
Sweet in the confidence of	252
Sweet is the dawn of day	429
Sweet is the day of sacred rest	1
Sweet is the early dew	429
Sweet is the light of Sabbath	4
Sweet is the vision of Thy face	133
Sweet majesty and awful love	412
Sweet mercy to my soul	259
Sweet on His faithfulness to	252
Sweet, on this day of rest	12
Sweet rose! in air whose odors	102
Sweet soul, we leave thee to	393
Sweet spring! of days and	102
Sweet the day of sacred rest	15
Sweet to look inward, and	252
Swift as an eagle cuts the air	165
Swift to its close ebbs out life's	215
Swiftly roll, ye lingering hours	381
Swift through the vast	68

T.

Hymn	Page
Take down thy long-neglected	289
Take heart!—the waster builds	414
Take His easy yoke, and wear it	119
Take the rest this day is	17
Take to Thee Thy royal power	385
Tarry with me, O my Saviour	430
Teach all the nations My	305
Teach me some melodious	264
Teach me to live, that I may	416
Teach us, in every state	260
Teach us, O Lord, how frail is	86
Teach us, O Lord, to keep in	333
Teach us that not a leaf can	43
Teach us to knock at heaven's	416
Tell how He shows His smiling	45
Tell of His wondrous	47
Tell them, I AM, Jehovah said	23
Tempest-tost, my failing bark	266
Temptations fled at His rebuke	241
Tempted souls, they bring you	115
Tend'rer is the form it wears	261
Ten thousand offices unseen	298
Ten thousand thousand precious	54
Ten thousand thousand voices	10
Ten thousand worlds, ten	189
Thanks for mercies past receive	146
Thanks to my God for every	183
Thanks we give, and adoration	17
That awful Word, that sovereign	68
That deeper shade shall break	419
That every human word and	43
That glory sits on every face	393
That, having all things done	192
That light shall shine on distant	303
That long as life itself shall last	139
That man may last, but never	333
That man shall flourish like the	55
That Power, which raised, and	256
That prize with peerless glories	178
That sacred stream, Thine holy	52
That Upper Room is heaven on	93
That voice's echo hath not died	420
That warning voice, O sinner	148
That was a most amazing	422
That when my days are past	428
The Almighty thunders from	329
The angel host appears	192
The angelic hosts descend	70
The angels come at dawn	123
The answering hills of Palestine	69
The apostles' glorious company	46
The arms of everlasting love	174
The arms of wicked men	326
The beams of noon, the	57
The beams that shine on Zion's	289
The bending angels stooped to	78
The billows breaking o'er us	272
The birds that wake the morn'g	435
The blossom blushed bright, but	378
The bounties of Thy love	197
The breezes waft their cries	226
The brightest things below the	254
The calm retreat, the silent	220
The changing wind, the flying	426
The cheerful tribute will I give	157
The cherub, near the viewless	393
The children, like the lily	358
The Christian's years, though	352
The city of my blest abode	174
The city so holy and clean	388
The clouds disperse, the light	248
The clouds shot hail, they	154
The consecrated cross I'll bear	244
The cross hath power to save	53
The cross—the cross alone	53
The crowd of cares, the	159
The crown that my Saviour	205
The day glides swiftly o'er their	156
The day of bright glory is	71
The day of small and feeble	185
The days of old, in vision	154
The dazzling sun at noonday	29
The dead in Christ shall first	342
The dearest idol I have known	220
The depths of earth are in His	44
The dew lies thick on all the	247
The dust returns to dust again	101
The dying thief rejoiced to see	151
The earth and all the works	343
The earth doth mourn her	341
The earth shall soon dissolve	180
The earth, the ocean and the sky	225
Thee in these works of power	32
Thee, in the watches of the	240
Thee my ransomed powers	284
Thee, the first-born sons of light	61
The evening rests our weary	422
The evening star has lighted	434
Thee, while dust and ashes	88
Thee will I love, my joy, my	137
Thee will I praise, O Lord, my	385
The Father heard; and angels	181
The Father of eternal light	400
The Father, shining on His	377
The fearful soul that tires	100
The fires that rushed on Sinai	93
The first-fruits oft a blessing	7
The floods, O Lord, lift up their	87
The flowers of spring may	435
The flowers that spring along	401
The fondness of a creature's love	254
The footsteps of Thy flock I see	158
The forests in His strength	80
The friends, gone there before	435
The friends of truth assembled	302
The fury of conflicting waves	354
The gladness of that happy day	161
The glorious orb, whose golden	13
The glory! the glory! around	121
The God of glory down to men	396
The gospel trumpet hear	116
The grave is near the cradle	180
The graves of all His saints He	350
The great, mysterious Deity	377
The greedy sea shall yield her	343
The guiltless shame, the sweet	138
The hand that gave it still	21
The happy gates of gospel-grace	191
The healing sense of pardoned	290
The hearing ear, the watchful	221
The heathen lands that lie	304
The heavenly Babe you there	68
The heavens His rightful power	177
The highest place that heaven	86
The hill of Zion yields	199
The holy church throughout the	46
The holy triumphs of my soul	184
The hopes that holy word	22
The hope that such a day will	286
The hosts of God encamp	179
The hosts of saints around Him	406
The hour of triumph comes	307
The hours of pain have yielded	249
The house of mourning He	251
The huge, celestial bodies roll	391
The incense of the spring	69
Their fancied joys—how fast	101
Their Father marks their	354
Their feet shall never slide to	219
Their harmony shall sound	51
Their hatred, and their love	100
Their peace is sealed, their rest	251
Their streaming eyes together	216
Their toils are past, their work	355
Their worship no interval	205
The joy of all who dwell above	86
The joy, the shout, the harmony	284
The judgment! the judgment!	121
The King himself comes near	12
The king of terrors then would	180
The Lamb shall lead His	399
The landscape, lately shrouded	20
The lark mounts up the sky	31
The laurel withers on our brow	344
The light my path surrounding	435
The light of love is round His	237
The light of smiles shall fill	246
The light of truth to us display	59
The light, the dark, where'er I	53
The lilies bend meekly	357
The limpid stream with sudden	28
The little cloud increases still	224
The living know that they must	100
The lofty hills and towers	193
The Lord can clear the darkest	175
The Lord has promised good	160
The Lord hath eyes to give the	329
The Lord in heaven hath fixed	328
The Lord is God; 'tis He alone	36
The Lord is good, the Lord is	36
The Lord is great; His majesty	49
The Lord is great; His mercy	49
The Lord is King! child of the	45
The Lord is risen indeed	92
The Lord of glory builds His	45
The Lord proclaims His power	44
The Lord sits sovereign on the	44
The Lord's unsparing hand	231
The Lord will come—a dreadful	342
The Lord will come, but not the	342
The Lord will raise Jerusalem	57
The Lord yields nothing to our	307
The madman in a tomb had	140
The majesty of God ne'er broke	187
The man, the wisest of our kind	349
The meanest child of glory	406
The men of grace have found	199
The men that know Thy name	324
The midsummer sun shines but	359
The mighty God, whose	165
The moment we believe, 'tis	208
The more I strove against their	172
The more Thy glories strike my	390
The morning star is lost in light	159
The morn with glory crowned	432
The mountain and the vale	263
The mountains in their places	297
The mountains melt away	51
Then Afric's liberated sons	303
Then all the chosen seed	190

	PAGE		PAGE		PAGE
Then, all the day long	232	Then, to thy courts when I	2	There's not a plant or flower	34
Then all the earth, renewed	83	Then, trembling through the	419	There's not a sin that we	444
The names of all His saints He	87	Then weep no more—their	348	There's nothing bright, above	234
The nations all whom Thou hast	385	Then what my thoughts design	100	There's nothing dark, below	53
Then at Thy feet, with awful	390	Then whene'er the signal's	17	There's room around thy	103
Then back to heaven they fly	82	Then when I knelt to meditate	86	There's room in God's eternal	103
Then, brother man, sold to thy	323	Then, while a voice of pardon	148	There's room in heaven among	103
Then cease, fond nature, cease	354	Then who would choose to	225	There's room within the church	103
Thence He arose, ascending	350	Then, why, O blessed Jesus	189	There's the city to which I	404
Then, Christian, dry the falling	255	Then why should I so long	445	There sweeps no desolating	394
Then, come back, my darling	357	Then will He own my	177	There the blessed man, my	401
Then, come, in robes of light	436	Then will I tell to sinners	172	There the glorious triumph	89
Then, e'en in age and grief	271	Then with my waking thoughts	283	There the glory is ever shining	404
Then fling it, unrestrained and	417	The oak strikes deeper as it	249	There, there, on eagle wings, we	234
Then, fly, my song, an endless	37	The ocean that in mountains	23	There, too, may we our	349
Then from the craggy mountains	317	The o'erwhelming power	183	There we shall in full chorus	301
Then gentle patience smiles on	345	The opening heavens around	188	There we shall reign, and shout	376
Then gladly will I follow Thee	145	The orb of light thro' clouds	255	There, when the turmoil is no	348
Then hail, blessed state! hail	409	The pains of death are past	359	There, where my blessed Jesus	184
The night of woe resigns	262	The pains, the groans, and	343	There, where ten thousand	423
Then, in a moment, to my view	169	The parent finds the long lost	354	There, with eternal glory	86
Then in a nobler, sweeter song	181	The peaceful gates of heavenly	177	There, with saints and angels	448
Then I shall end my sad	249	The perfect way is hard to flesh	189	There, with united heart and	103
Then I, within Thy sacred	253	The pity of the Lord	81	There, ye that love my Saviour	401
Then keep me, Lord	246	The poor in spirit thou hast fed	8	The righteous Lord loves	328
Then let me mount and soar	172	The powers of darkness leagued	10	The rising God forsakes the	74
Then let my soul march boldly	165	The powers of hell agree	194	The rocks can rend; the earth	166
Then let our humble faith	87	The present moment flies	359	The rolling ocean's vast abyss	44
Then let our songs abound	199	The prophet of the cross may	7	The rolling sun, the changing	22
Then let our sorrows cease to	355	The rapture, mighty,	288	The saints I heard with rapture	148
Then let the last loud trumpet	85	There all the followers of the	394	The saints of God, from death	350
Then let the noisy world pursue	218	There all the heavenly hosts	390	The saints on earth and all the	223
Then let the price be what it	136	There all the millions of His	400	The saints shall flourish in His	304
Then let the thundering	391	There all the ship's company	389	The saints shall mount on	253
Then, let Thine image on this	343	There are mansions exempted	378	The Saviour smiles upon my	157
Then let us adore, and give Him	48	There are no acts of pardon	100	The scourge, the thorns, the	76
Then let us earnest be	226	There behold the day-spring	309	The sea beheld, and struck	47
Then let us form those bonds	390	There endless crowds of sinners	107	These are the living lights	318
Then let us make our boast	231	There everlasting spring abides	400	These are the sweet and	7
Then let us, 'midst pleasure and	357	There faith lifts up her cheerful	248	These ashes, too, this little dust	349
Then, like the morning ray	322	Therefore I murmur not	283	The seas shall waste, the skies	320
Then loud shall ascend from	323	There for me the Saviour stands	111	The seeds of ecstasy unknown	237
Then love's soft dew o'er every	348	There fragrant flowers	243	The seeds of joy and glory	177
Then, man, be wise; thy	391	There from the bosom of my	161	The seeing eye, the feeling	133
Then mighty God, I'd sing and	156	There happier bowers than	396	These inward trials I employ	135
Then, mortal, turn! thy danger	351	There interceding, there	129	These lively hopes we owe	360
Then mourn we not, beloved	341	There His triumphal chariot	64	These speak of Thee with loud	82
Then, my soul, in every strait	219	There if thy Spirit touch the	220	These through fiery trials trod	402
The noble and victorious host	162	There is a dark and fearful vale	246	These were but seasons	215
Then One, amid their thick	47	There is a day of sunny rest	286	The sharper and severer	273
Then peace returns with balmy	305	There is a death whose pang	109	The shepherd, leaning o'er his	420
Then raise the song of gladness	95	There is a gulf that must be	246	The shepherds on the lawn	67
Then right shall over might	307	There is a home for weary	248	The Shepherd sought His sheep	196
Then save me from eternal	130	There is a place where Jesus	234	The silence thronged gloriously	258
Then, Saviour, then my soul	125	There is a scene where spirits	234	The silver cloud hath sailed	81
Then shall a shout of joy go up	330	There is a soft, a downy bed	243	The sins I fancied quell'd	259
Then shall blaze earth's funeral	407	There is a stream whose gentle	52	The smoothest seas will	235
Then shall I see, and hear, and	1	There is a world above	366	The social talk, the evening fire	187
Then shall I upward fly	360	There is my house and portion	377	The solemn harvest comes	427
Then shall my cheerful spirit	145	There joys unseen by mortal	184	The solemn, midnight cry	109
Then shall new luster break	428	There let the way appear	283	The songs of everlasting years	54
Then, shall on faith's sublimest	184	There, like the nightingale, she	220	The soul, a dreary province	18
Then shall our hearts	9	There, low before his glorious	394	The soul alone, like a neglected	215
Then shall the Lord a refuge	324	There, no more at eve declining	383	The soul by faith reclined	263
Then shall the mourner at Thy	140	There no sigh of memory	383	The soul that longs to see My	105
Then shall the trembling	237	There, on a green and flowery	257	The soul that on Jesus hath	230
Then shone Almighty power	63	There, on a high, majestic	401	The spacious worlds of	87
Then should the earth's old	45	There on His holy hill	213	The sparrow for her young	19
Then should we see the saints	350	There our exalted Saviour	177	The spacious earth and	163
Then sorrow touched by Thee	245	The reproach of Christ is	274	The Spirit calls to-day	128
Then swift and dreadful she	107	There's a delightful clearness	413	The Spirit wrought my faith	181
Then take your golden lyres	92	There, safe thou shalt abide	260	The stars of Heaven are	239
Then the great, the rich, the	111	There, seated in Thy majesty	81	The storm is laid, the winds	55
Then, then I feel that He	361	There shall I bathe my weary	251	The storm that wrecks the	347
Then they might fight, and rage	156	There shall I offer my requests	239	The stormy winds are hushed	23
Then they who live shall	350	There shall I wear a starry	165	The streams all beautiful and	426
Then, though conscious we are	430	There shall no doubts disturb	239	The sun and rain will ripen	221
Then, though it be in accents	221	There shall our raptured tongue	193	The sun went down in fearful	78
Then to his portals press	18	There shall the conqueror rest	192	The tears are shed that	301
Then to the Lord I cried	259	There shed Thy choicest love	191	The things unseen, O God	397

	PAGE		PAGE		PAGE
The thirsty ridges drink their.	426	Thine essence is a vast abyss..	82	Though rocks and quicksands..	211
The thorn and the thistle	408	Thine, wondrous Babe of	304	Though rough and thorny be..	236
The thunder is His voice	432	Think how on the cross He	127	Though saints to sore distress..	324
The thunder of that dismal	106	Think of Thy sorrows, dearest	105	Though seed lie buried long in	175
The thunders of His hand	19	Think, O Jesus, for what reason	364	Though Sinai's curse, in	169
The tide of creatures ebbs and	87	This can my every care control	145	Though sin defile our worship	161
The time how lovely and how.	4	This day be grateful homage	10	Though tears may dim my	423
The trivial round, the common	165	This day I must to God appear	7	Though tempest-tossed, and half	229
The troubled conscience knows	59	This empty tomb shall now	85	Though ten thousand ills beset	279
The trumpet's martial voice...	50	This freezing heart, O Lord	186	Though the night be dark and	430
The trumpet sounds. Awake...	359	This glorious hope revives	227	Though the root thereof wax old	357
The trumpet! the trumpet	121	This happiness in part is mine.	377	Though unworthy, Lord, Thine	88
The trump shall sound—the...	842	This heavenly calm within the	8	Though waves and storms go	171
The truths ye urge are borne..	336	This hour, with flowing tears.	152	Though we are guilty. Thou art	5
The umbrageous oak in pomp.	235	This is my body, broke for sin	77	Though we here should meet to	265
The unvailed glories of His....	399	This is the field where hidden	21	Though your heart be made of	127
The unwearied sun from day to	25	This is the grace that lives and	183	Thou givest me the lot	259
The vaulted heavens shall fall..	193	This is the hidden life I prize..	138	Thou giv'st the word; Thy...	256
The vision of the heavenly	399	This is the judge that ends....	21	Thou good, and wise, and	305
The voice at midnight came...	359	This is the Man, th' exalted...	412	Thou hast been called when by	120
The volume of my Father's...	21	This is the spouse of Christ....	236	Thou hast been called when o'er	120
The voyage of life's at an end	839	This is the thing I crave	285	Thou hast helped in every need	264
The want of right she well....	285	This is the way I long had....	172	Thou hast redeemed our souls	183
The warbling notes pursue....	811	This lamp through all the dreary	21	Thou hast turned my mourning	284
The watchmen join their voice	382	This life's a dream—an empty	160	Thou heard'st, well pleased, the	343
The waves obey thy dread....	82	This only can my fears control	230	Thou heaven of heavens, His..	23
The way the holy prophets....	172	This pilgrim-path by Thee was	142	Thou high and holy One	313
The way to heaven is straight..	124	This precious truth His word..	39	Thou in that sign the rebel....	165
The wise will make their anger	445	This shall be known when we	57	Thou in toil art comfort sweet	264
The weapons which your hands	336	This spotless robe the same ...	173	Thou knowest I love Thee...	183
The weary bird hath left the..	72	This spring with living water	108	Thou know'st in the spirit of..	886
The whole creation groans....	109	This was compassion, like a	291	Thou know'st the way to bring	186
The whole creation join in one	181	Thither, his raptured thought..	349	Thou layest them, with all....	256
The widow and the fatherless..	48	Thither the tribes repair	18	Thou lovely Chief of all my joys	106
The wings of every hour shall	40	Those are the hymns that we..	401	Thou loving, all-atoning Lamb	186
The woodland hum is ringing..	434	Those characters shall fair abide	67	Thou moon that rul'st the night	436
The work begun is carried on.	89	Those gentle whispers let me..	56	Thou my Deliv'rer art, my God	43
The world and Satan I forsake	145	Those joys which earth cannot	216	Thou, O Christ, art all I want..	261
The world beheld the glorious	175	Those mighty orbs proclaim..	33	Thou, of heaven and earth....	275
The world can never give....	169	Those nighty periods of years	256	Thou on the Lord rely	263
The world is seldom what it...	852	Those trees each month yield..	308	Thou restless globe of golden..	80
The world is tempting still my	299	Those wandering cisterns in the	426	Thou, Saviour, only Thou....	259
The world shut out from all my	133	Thou aged man, life's wintry	126	Thou seest my heart's desire..	256
The worlds of nature and of....	132	Thou art a God before whose..	6	Thou shalt see My glory soon..	268
The world, the clustering	28	Thou art gone to the grave! and	379	Thou spread'st the curtains of.	418
The worst of all diseases.....	150	Thou art gone to the grave! but	379	Thou that hast slept in error's	109
The wounded and the weak....	263	Thou art gone to the grave! we	379	Thou that to will in me hast..	7
They are justified by grace....	263	Thou art my everlasting trust	182	Thou, through the starry orbs,	81
They are lights upon the earth	268	Thou art my Pilot—wise	211	Thou, tossed upon the waves...	3
They are slaves, who fear to....	831	Thou art resting now, like....	384	Thou, to whom all power is..	315
They bid us be in mirthful....	252	Thou art the earnest of His love	55	Thou traveller in this vale of..	347
They come as half-forgotten..	91	Thou art the sea of love	197	Thou treadest on enchanted..	167
They come, on the wings of the	48	Thou callest me to seek Thy...	153	Thou, who alone, when man...	344
They come, they come; Thine	288	Thou didst the meek example..	137	Thou who art mourning o'er..	3
They come when we wander..	48	Thou dost conduct Thy people	287	Thou who hast dear ones far..	3
They die in Jesus, and are blest	349	Though as yet no losses grieve	374	Thou who hast laid within the	3
The year rolls round, and steals	107	Though buried deep, or thinly	8	Thou, who hast our plans	385
They find access at every hour	191	Though dead, they speak in..	178	Thou, who homeless and	113
They flourish like the morning	256	Though destruction walk around	431	Thou, whose benignant eye....	12
They gaze upon His beauteous	394	Though distresses now attend	279	Thou, whose favors without ...	430
They go from strength to	19	Though earth may boast one..	346	Thou wilt not break a bruised .	185
They journey on from strength	9	Though earth-born shadows...	245	Thou wilt not break the bruised	333
They leave the dust, and on the	398	Though faith and hope may oft	241	Thou wilt not, Lord, our smiles	167
They'll waft us sooner o'er....	361	Though fields, in verdure once	38	Thou wilt! Thou dost!—a still	142
They marked the footsteps that	399	Though for a time I hid My face	230	Thou wondrous Advocate with	144
They saw a glorious light	67	Though from the fold the flock	88	Thrice happy morn for those..	359
They saw Him on the cross...	99	Though furiously their heads..	258	Thro' all my weak and fainting	145
They scorn to seek our golden	156	Though high above all praise	31	Throned on a cloud our God...	106
They shall find rest who learn	98	Though his eye hath brightened	365	Through all eternity to Thee...	54
They sing of death and hell...	46	Though His majesty be great.	127	Through all His works what...	53
They sing of earth and heaven	405	Though I have most unfaithful	134	Through all my pilgrimage....	259
They sing the Lamb of God..	92	Though in a bare and rugged...	24	Through all the dangers of the	425
They sing Thy deeds, as I have	247	Though in the paths of death I	24	Through all the storms that....	18
They spoke in tender love....	196	Though in a foreign land	194	Through all the windings of my	345
They suffer with their Lord..	86	Though in the dust I lay my .	85	Through changes bright or....	13
They thronged His chariot....	92	Though, like the wanderer ...	283	Through David's city I am led	68
They were mortal, too, like us	408	Though long of winds and...	347	Through duty and through....	179
They who die in Christ are...	371	Though now ascended up on..	85	Through each perplexing path	218
Thine anger, like a pointed dart	328	Though on foreign shore we .	228	Through every period of my...	54
Thine earthly Sabbaths, Lord..	2	Though raised to a superior...	57	Through floods and flames if...	179

ANY VERSE BUT THE FIRST.

	PAGE
Through many dangers, toils	180
Through ten thousand channels	314
Through the deep gloom of	424
Through the churches' long	291
Through the valley and shadow	90
Through the wild sea Thou	154
Through Thy rich merit, by	299
Through waves, through clouds	262
Thunder, and hail, and fire, and	80
Thus as the moments pass	217
Thus chastened, cleansed	424
Thus glorious, will He	53
Thus, like the morning, calm	426
Thus low the Lord of life was	87
Thus may we abide in union	16
Thus might I hide my blushing	144
Thus my heart the hope will	275
Thus, O thus an entrance give	201
Thus present still, though now	165
Thus shall all the shackles fall	323
Thus shall the God our Saviour	42
Thus shall the vengeance of the	329
Thus shall this moving engine	43
Thus spake the seraph, and	63
Thus star by star declines	366
Thus sweetly live, thus greatly	283
Thus, though the universe shall	283
Thus, till my last expiring	184
Thus, till my last expiring day	6
Thus to the Lord I raised my	241
Thus what our heavenly	335
Thus, when the night of death	418
Thus, while the meaner	80
Thus, while they prayed, at	169
Thus will the church below	227
Thus, with my thoughts	425
Thus would I live till nature	133
Thus would my rising soul	428
Thy beautiful and shining face	187
Thy bountiful care, what	49
Thy bright example I pursue	138
Thy choice and mine shall be	203
Thy church is in the desert	217
Thy counsels, Lord, shall guide	57
Thy covenant in the darkest	148
Thy deeds, O Lord, are wonder	154
Thy dew came down—my	255
Thy dew doth every morning	239
Thy face, with reverence and	336
Thy favor, all my journer	253
Thy gardens and thy goodly	393
Thy glory never hence depart	296
Thy glory shines immensely	32
Thy God, thy Head's above	277
Thy golden sceptre from above	166
Thy grace can send its	156
Thy grace, O Holy Ghost	93
Thy grace still dwells upon my	190
Thy gracious promise now	246
Thy hand, great God, sustains	53
Thy heavenly grace to each	424
Thy heaven, on which 'tis bliss	234
Thy judgments, too, which	166
Thy light and truth shall guide	240
Thy love, a sea without a shore	183
Thy love can cheer the	255
Thy love the powers of thought	213
Thy mercy-seat is open still	245
Thy mercy stretches o'er my	247
Thy mercy tempers every blast	56
Thy ministering spirits descend	205
Thy morning light and evening	426
Thy name my inmost powers	132
Thy names, how infinite they	32
Thy neighbor? he who drinks	335
Thy neighbor? pass no	335
Thy neighbor? 'tis the fainting	335
Thy neighbor? 'tis the weary	335
Thy noblest wonders here we	23
Thy pard'ning love—so free, so	143

	PAGE
Thy power and glory work	59
Thy power Omnipotent	391
Thy promise is my only plea	145
Thy promises are true	11
Thy providence is kind and	58
Thy risen Lord, my soul	85
Thy saints are comforted, I	143
Thy saints, in all this glorious	178
Thyself amid the silence clear	283
Thy scene each vision brings	420
Thy scepter well becomes His	804
Thy secret voice invites me	137
Thy shining grace can cheer	197
Thy showers make soft the	432
Thy Sovereign eye looks calmly	305
Thy Spirit shall unite	294
Thy steps have long enchanted	355
Thy suffering life I cannot trace	143
Thy sufferings I embrace with	133
Thy thousand thousand hosts	165
Thy throne eternal ages stood	32
Thy throne, O God, for ever	823
Thy voice produced the sea and	53
Thy walls are made of precious	338
Thy way is in great waters	154
Thy will be done! If o'er us	415
Thy will be done! Though	415
Thy winged troops, O God of	41
Thy word is true, Thy promise	240
Thy word, like silver seven	324
Tidings, glad tidings from above	66
Till, by Thine own triumphant	73
Till David touched his sacred	156
Till God in human flesh I see	188
Till then, I would Thy love	191
Till then, nor is my boasting	159
Till the redeemed in every	801
Time has nearly reached its	309
Time is bearing us away	370
Time, like an ever-rolling	56
'Tis a joy, that seated deep	201
'Tis an ever varied flood	431
'Tis by the merits of Thy death	188
'Tis done—the great transaction	292
'Tis finished!—let the joyful	76
'Tis finished! now the ransom's	80
'Tis God's all-animating voice	178
'Tis He adorned my naked	181
'Tis heaven on earth to taste His	189
'Tis here the troubled springs of	218
'Tis He supports my mortal	423
'Tis His almighty love	199
'Tis in the silence of the shade	219
'Tis Jesus, our Friend	265
'Tis Jesus, the first and the last	886
'Tis joy to think the angel	225
'Tis love! 'tis love! Thou	170
'Tis mercy all, that Thou hast	187
'Tis midnight—and for others'	76
'Tis midnight—and from all	76
'Tis midnight, and, from ether	76
'Tis my most fervent prayer	285
'Tis not darkness gathering	381
'Tis not that murmuring	251
'Tis not the trump of war	103
'Tis sin, alas! with tyrant power	141
'Tis the joy of pardoned sin	201
'Tis there he says I am to dwell	394
'Tis Thine to cleanse the heart	195
'Tis to my Saviour I would live	173
'Tis when beyond this vale of	393
To be encompassed round	33
To bring fire on earth He came	309
To damp our earthly joys	109
To-day, her glimmering light	152
To-day He rose and left the	6
To-day the Saviour calls	128
To dwell with God, to feel His	160
To dwell with misery here	63
To each, the soul of each, how	216

	PAGE
To earth He bends His throne	51
To every land beneath the sun	309
To gaze on His glories divine	205
To gentle offices of love	334
Together oft they seek the	216
To give my weakness strength	246
To God I cried when troubles	42
To God, our great Father	71
To God, the Only Wise	18
To God the Son belongs	325
To God the Spirit's name	325
To bear the sorrows Thou hast	166
To heaven, the place of His	190
To Him I owe my life and	190
To Him their prayers and cries	226
To India's various castes	309
To leave my Saviour I disdain	255
To Lebanon He turns His voice	44
To nakedness and want	329
To our Redeemer God	199
Tormenting thirst shall leave	399
To scorn the senses' sway	195
To serve the present age	195
To shine with the angels in	205
To sit one day beneath Thine	9
To smite the breast, the clothes	189
To sojourn in the world, and	421
To songs of praise and joy	12
To speak, and think, and will	137
To spread the rays of heavenly	80
Tossed on time's rude	375
To that Jerusalem above	412
To the desert or the cell	149
To Thee, all angels cry aloud	46
To Thee all angels loudly cry	162
To Thee, and Thee alone	197
To Thee, great One in Three	60
To Thee I owe my wealth and	185
To Thee I tell each rising grief	245
To Thee I will address my	43
To Thee my trembling spirit	190
To Thee, O God, whose face	295
To Thee, O Lord, my tender	255
To Thee, ten thousand thanks	177
To Thee, Thee only will I	141
To the everlasting Father	291
To Thee we still would cleave	294
To Thee, whose word the	421
To the heavens His voice	330
To them remains nor place, nor	86
To them the cross is life and	86
To them the cross with all its	86
To this the joyful nations	289
To thy grave we sadly bear	334
To Thy great name, almighty	10
Touch'd by the loadstone of	251
Touched with a sympathy	87
To what a stubborn frame	152
To you, in David's town, this	63
Tranquil amidst alarms	359
Treasures of everlasting	253
Tremble, ye who Him rejected	97
Trials make the promise sweet	147
Trials must and will befall	147
True as the magnet to the pole	167
True that our beauteons doc	359
True, 't is a straight and thorny	165
Truly blessed is this station	209
Trumpet scattered sound of	364
Trump of glad jubilee	328
Truth from the earth, like to a	335
Tune, tune your harps	373
Tune your harps anew	97
Turn, mortal, turn! thy soul	351
Turn, turn us, mighty God	152
'Twas for my sins my dearest	103
'Twas grace that taught my	180
'Twas mercy filled the throne	199
'Twas the same love that spread	290
'Twas through the Lamb's most	178

U.

Hymn	Page
'Twas to save thee, child, from	441
Under Thy protection take	62
Unholy and impure	194
United zeal be shown	436
Unite us in the sacred love	332
Unnumbered comforts on my	64
Unshaken as eternal hills	259
Until it come to Thee	235
Unto our Father's will alone	355
Upheld by Thy commands	11
Uphold me in the doubtful race	137
Up in the morning early	439
Up, my soul! with clear	315
Upon the crystal pavement	244
Upon your bounty's willing	305
Up to her courts, with joys	8
Up to labor! from thee	315
Up to that world of light	368
Up to the heavens I send my	44
Up to the hills where Christ is	6
Up to Thy dwelling-place	13
Upward from this dying state	374
Unwearied may I this pursue	171

V.

Hymn	Page
Vainly we offer each ample	90
Vain, sinful man! creation's	4
Victor o'er death and hell	94
Visit, then, this soul of mine	201

W.

Hymn	Page
Waft, waft, ye winds, His story	299
Wait on the Lord, ye trembling	54
Wait, then, my soul	237
Wake, and lift up thyself, my	419
Waken, O God! my trifling	104
Waken, O Lord, our drowsy	107
Walk in the light! and e'en	257
Walk in the light! and thou	257
Walk in the light! thy path	257
Want, from the wretch	322
Warm our hearts with sacred	15
Wash out its stains, refine its	157
Was it for crimes that I had	144
Was not our Lord, a little child	293
Was there nothing but a	441
Watchman! tell us of the night	308
Watch o'er my lips, and guard	161
Watch—'t is your Lord's	195
Weak is the effort of my heart	191
Weak though we are, He still	425
We are His people; we His care	40
Weary of this war within	113
We bring them, Lord, in	293
We can not bid the morning	297
We can not trust Him as we	131
We can see that distant home	407
Weep not for them; beside the	343
Weep not for the saint that	389
Weep not for the spirit now	859
Weep not, my friends, weep not	373
We feel that heaven is now	376
We feel the resurrection near	225
We fly to our eternal Rock	55
We give our souls the wounds	107
We hail the church built high	141
We have traveled long together	381
We in Jesus confide, and are	438
We know that Thy presence is	359
Welcome, and precious to my	7
Welcome, sweet hour of full	169
We lick the dust, we grasp the	107
We'll catch the note of lofty	10
We'll crowd Thy gates, with	40
Well, if our days must fly	361
Well might the sun in darkness	144
We'll talk of all He did and said	217
Well, the delightful day will	202
Well we know thy living faith	362
Well, we shall quickly pass the	77
We praise Thee—if one clouded	383
We 're going to join the	124
We 're going to see the bleeding	124
Were half the breath thus	217
Were I in heaven without my	57
Were I possessor of the earth	185
Were not those sweets so	102
Were the whole realm of nature	74
Were you not children once?	335
We see Thy hand; it leads us	120
We shall have a mighty shout	407
We share our mutual woes	227
We should almost forsake our	350
We shrink before Thy vast	25
We speak of its freedom from	387
We speak of its pathways of	387
We speak of its service of love	887
We strive, but all our efforts	349
We, too, before Thy gracious	292
We tread the path our Master	401
We trust not in our native	139
We turn to Thee a smiling face	107
"We've no abiding city here,"	160
We wait in faith, and turn our	423
We wait in faith, we wait in	423
We, while the stars from	343
We would no longer lie	199
What ailed thee, O thou mighty	47
What am I, Lord, that Thou so	143
What a rapturous song, when	433
What brought them to that	413
What change! through pathless	303
Whate'er events betide	260
Whate'er Thou deniest, O give	408
Whate'er thy lot—where'er	347
Whate'er Thy providence	220
Whate'er Thy sacred will	250
What Friend have I in heaven	246
What have I done for Him that	425
What if the springs of life were	57
What in Thy love possess I not	171
What is my being, but for Thee	173
What language shall I borrow	79
What object, Lord, my soul	105
What peaceful hours I once	220
What shall I say Thy grace to	292
What shall make trouble? Not	421
What shall soothe thy bursting	111
What sought they thus afar?	319
What soul shall dare, tho' stout	307
What sweeter pledge could God	341
What thanks I owe Thee, and	220
What though hell's fiery	317
What though in solemn silence	25
What though our bird of light	358
What, though parted from our	69
What though the floods lift up	415
What though the northern	228
What though the spicy breezes	299
What though the tempests	288
What, though thou rulest not	262
What Thou shalt to-day provide	267
What though we are but	151
What troubles have we seen	231
What vain disturbing thoughts	7
What voice shall bid the	307
What was Thy crime, my	73
What wonders shall Thy	81
What worldly tie must break	152
When all arrayed in light	311
When all created streams are	250
When all I am I clearly see	138
When all is done, renounce	305
When angry nations rush to	305
When anxious cares would	157
When black the threatening	246
When, bringing every balmy	102
When by the dreadful tempest	55
When cares and sorrows	252
Whence comes it, that, your	136
When children's voices raise	296
When darkness, and when	249
When day, with farewell beam	24
When death invades my	245
When death o'er nature shall	157
When death shall interrupt	164
When dreadful guilt is done	185
When each can feel his brother	227
When each day's scenes and	427
When earthly cares engross the	161
When earth's prospects fail	255
Whene'er becalm'd I lie	211
Whene'er my heart is broken	282
Whene'er you meet with	150
When ends life's transient	223
When evening's silent shades	422
When faith is strong, and	345
When fear her chilling mantle	415
When first before His mercy	236
When from flesh the spirit	362
When from the dust of death	173
When gladness wings my	218
When God, our leader, shines	55
When He first the work begun	305
When He lived on earth	209
When here Thy messengers	296
When I am filled with sore	182
When I behold them pressed	161
When I can say, my God is	77
When I faint with summer's	27
When I lie within my bed	267
When in ecstasy sublime	261
When infancy at evening tries	285
When in His earthly courts	176
When in their lonely bed loved	367
When, in the sabbath of His	301
When in the slippery path of	54
When, in the solemn hour of	256
When in the sultry glebe I	24
When I review my ways	258
When I slumber in the tomb	431
When I touch the blessed shore	291
When I tread the verge of	273
When joy no longer soothes	245
When love in one delightful	225
When, lo! with ravished ears	67
When men in ships far off at sea	23
When mercy points where	235
When midnight vails our eyes	423
When mounted on Thy	242
When mourning o'er some stone	243
When my forgetful soul	141
When mystery clouds my	415
When nature shudders, loth to	237
When night with wings of	84
When obstacles and trials	247
When on Calvary I rest	261
When, one by one, those ties	345
When our earthly comforts	219
When raging foes surround	211
When rising floods my soul	157
When round Thy courts by	163
When scarce is seized some	345
When shall earth's blest	15
When shall I reach that happy	413
When shall love freely flow	368
When shall the day, dear Lord	393
When shall these eyes thy	396
When should not they rejoice	193
When, shriveling like a	98
When sinks the soul, subdued	214
When storms of fierce	221
When storms of sorrow round	131
When tempest clouds are dark	245
When that illustrious day shall	175
When the dreams of life are	229
When the flames and hellish	267
When the holy have gone to	123

ANY VERSE BUT THE FIRST. — 481

First Line	Page
When the house doth sigh and	267
When the Judge descends in	111
When the judgment is reveal'd	267
When the Lord shall send His	384
When the mighty trumpet	374
When the morning paints the	15
When the most helpless	334
When the pangs of death assail	270
When the rich gales of mercy	122
When the soft dews of kindly	416
When the sun of bliss is beaming	275
When the tempest rolls on high	431
When the tempter me pursueth	267
When the woes of life o'ertake	275
When the world has passed	111
When this weary world is past	272
When Thou shinest on the	81
When through fiery trials thy	280
When through the deep waters	230
When to heaven's great and	427
When tossed upon the waves	399
When trembling limbs refuse	345
When trouble assails	265
When trouble, like a gloomy	172
When troubles, like a burning	87
When troubles rise, and storms	289
When we appear in yonder	175
When we asunder part	227
When we in darkness walk	191
When will my pilgrimage be	7
When, with sad footsteps	243
When, worn by toil, their	302
When worn with pain, disease	256
When youthful Spring around	24
Where are the vows which	243
Where dost Thou, dear	232
Where'er I turn my gazing eyes	84
Where'er, in lands unknown	306
Where is the blessedness in	220
Where is the shadow of that	158
Where is the strength that	353
Where the arctic ocean	318
Where the golden gates of day	309
Where the lofty minaret	309
Where the saints of all ages in	378
Wherever the shackles of	322
Where wilt thou cast thy care	263
Where the worm dies not, and	120
Which of all our friends, to	209
While all our hearts, and all	290
While all the stars that round	25
While angelic legions with	449
While angels shout and praise	56
While guilt disturbs and breaks	155
While He affords His aid	197
While harps unnumbered	67
While here in the valley of	408
While here I walk on hostile	286
While His high praise ye sing	388
While I am a pilgrim here	219
While I am held in Thine	163
While I draw this fleeting	110
While I gazed, with speed	332
While I lay resting on my bed	247
While I'm often vainly trying	443
While in affliction's furnace	257
While Jews on their own law	188
While life's dark maze I tread	222
While of Thy absence we	163
While on earth ordained to stay	68
While others early learn to	443
While our silent steps are	374
While passing a garden I	71
While place we seek, or place	86
While sinners in despair shall	342
While some poor wretches	445
While such a scene of sacred	77
While the bright nation sounds	188
While the Holy Ghost is nigh	111
While the wounds of woe are	119
While Thy word is heard with	15
While to Thee our prayers	15
While we seek supplies	14
While we walk this vale of	272
While with a melting, broken	108
While with love unceasing	284
While yet in anguish He	290
While yet the life-proclaiming	7
Whither, ah! whither shall I	132
Whither, O whither should	159
Whither should a wretch be	279
Who are these? On earth	403
Who are they whose little feet	295
Who bow to Christ's command	198
Who can His mighty deeds	41
Who, gently blending eve	416
Who in heart on Thee believes	27
Who in her robe the sinner	385
Who is the King of glory	64
Who made this beating heart	185
Who may share this great	16
Who paints the clouds their	263
Whose breast expands with	334
Who shall make trouble, then	421
Who suffer with our Master	271
Who—when she sees the	385
Who, who would live alway	378
Who, within the silent grave	267
Who would not wish to die like	420
Why art thou cast down, my	264
Why art thou afraid to come	127
Why linger, then, with strange	354
Why mourn the pious dead	366
Why move my years in slow	391
Why move ye thus, with	255
Why must they shun the	225
Why, my soul, art thou	266
Why restless, why cast down	56
Why seeks He not a home of	72
Why should I shrink at pain	396
Why should I shrink at Thy	258
Why should my passions mix	217
Why should this anxious load	260
Why should thy bride appear	158
Why should we tremble to	350
Why was I made to hear Thy	290
Why will you in the crooked	105
Wide as His vast dominion lies	40
Wide as the world is Thy	40
Wide as they sweep their	56
Will ye play, then, will ye	312
Wilt thou let Him bleed in vain	112
Wilt Thou not visit me	277
Wilt Thou not yet to me reveal	170
Winds, ye shall bear His name	80
Wisdom and mercy guide my	258
With all His sufferings full in	80
With all tones of waters	97
With boldness, therefore, at the	65
With faith I plunge me in this	171
With forests huge, of dateless	43
With gentle resignation still	131
With gentle smiles call me Thy	185
With glory adorned, His	48
With grateful hearts the past	164
With Him I on Zion shall	388
With these walls let holy	221
Within these walls may peace	18
Within this temple, Christ	293
Within Thy circling power I	87
Within Thy presence, Lord	259
With Israel's myriads seal'd	306
With it the thoughtless sons of	98
With joy shall I behold the day	376
With joy shall we stand, when	379
With life He clothes the spring	432
With my burden I begin	219
With pitying eyes the Prince of	182
With power He vindicates the	304
With righteousness Thy saints	2
With saints enthroned on high	389
With songs let us follow his	389
With speed He flew to my	241
With thanks approach His	47
With Thee conversing, we	153
With the voice of joy and	315
Workman of God! O lose not	307
Work on, despair not, bring	337
Worlds are charging—heaven	312
Worlds of light and crowns of	381
Worlds should not bribe me	355
Worship, honor, power, and	97
Worthy is He that once was	168
"Worthy the Lamb that died,"	161
Worthy Thy hand to hold the	85
Would not my heart pour forth	188
Wretched and unworthy	284
Wretched wanderer, now return	104
Wretch that I am to wander	141

Y.

First Line	Page
Yea, Amen! Let all adore Thee	114
Ye aged, hither come	13
Yea! men may wonder while	341
Yea more, with His own hand	185
Ye angels above; His glories	48
Ye are traveling home to God	228
Yearly in our course appearing	374
Ye chosen seed of Israel's race	174
Ye clouds, that gorgeously	399
Ye daughters of Zion	232
Ye deeps, with roaring billows	28
Ye fair, enchanting throng	211
Ye fearful saints, fresh courage	57
Ye fields! that witnessed once	345
Ye great, renounce your	387
Ye in the wilderness	311
Ye mortals, catch the sound	82
Ye mortals, mark its pace	428
Ye mourning saints! dry every	91
Ye nations! bend—in	39
Ye palaces, scepters, and	205
Ye saints in glory strike	301
Ye saints, who stand nearer	387
Ye saw of old, on chaos rise	157
Ye saw the heaven born Child	311
Yes! broken, tuneless, still, O	271
Yes, God is love; a thought	415
Yes! I hasten from you gladly	313
Yes, I'm secure beneath	135
Ye sinners, come; 'tis mercy's	103
Ye sinners, seek His grace	360
Ye sister hills lay down	318
Ye slaves of sin and hell	116
Yes, let it go! One look from	189
Yes, lovely hour! thou art the	419
Yes, my Redeemer—they shall	103
Ye souls that are wounded! O	379
"Yes," saith the Lord "now	324
Ye stars are but the shining	400
Yes! the Christian's course is	362
Yes!—Thou art precious to my	190
Yes, Thou shalt reign for ever	299
Yes! Thou wilt visit me	277
Yes, thy sins have done the	112
Yes, unseen; but still, believe	382
Yes! when I pray, Thou	187
Yes, when this flesh and heart	160
Yes, whosoever will	108
Yet a few days to me, perhaps	142
Yet again we hope to meet thee	395
Yet amid this scene so fair	385
Yet clouds will intervene	361
Yet could I hear Him once	140
Yet dear the awful thought to	32
Yet does one short preparing	107
Ye temples, that to God	318
Ye tempting sweets! forbear	211
Yet, glorious Lord, Thy	45
Yet, gracious God, where shall	245

INDEX OF HYMNS.

First line	Page
Yet, if our aims are fixed aright	390
Yet I may love Thee too, O	175
Yet leaves again will clothe	353
Yet let the sons of Grace	237
Yet, like an idle tale, we spend	104
Yet, Lord, Thy wronged love	157
Yet Noah, humble, happy saint	164
Yet not thus buried, or extinct	349
Yet not to fickle chance	202
Yet O! the chief of sinners	134
Yet O! what consequences	349
Yet, save a trembling sinner	134
Yet see the sign among the	99
Yet, soon, reviving plants and	351
Yet sovereign mercy calls	143
Yet still to His footstool in	442
Yet sweetly as they glide	3
Yet the conquerors bring	402
Yet the dear path to Thine	267
Yet the sad hour that took the	349
Yet though we see them not	349
Yet through the stormy clouds	142
Yet, through this rough and	240
Yet to leave thee sorrowing	374
Yet, to read the shameful	441
Yet when beneath the dreadful	417
Yet when God's justice rose in	173
Yet, when the sound shall tear	43
Yet, who are those behind	91
Yet why, dear Lord, this	418
Yet will the Lord command	240
Ye twinkling stars, who gild	87
Yet would we say what every	365
Ye vile seducers! hence	141
Ye weary, heavy-laden, come	124
Ye wheels of nature, speed your	351
Ye, who are of death afraid	89
Ye who see the Father's grace	206
Ye who surround the throne	60
Ye, who tossed on beds of pain	113
Ye, who yourselves have sold	116
Ye worlds, with ev'ry living	33
Ye young! before His throne	13
Yield we what was given	365
Yonder azure vault on high	26
Yonder sits my slighted	115
You, in His wisdom, power	254
Your streams were floating	161
Your way is dark, and leads to	105
Youth, on length of days	374

Z.

First line	Page
Zion, all its light unfolding	389
Zion enjoys her Monarch's	52
Zion's Sun!—salvation	313
Zion, thrice happy place	11

INDEX OF PSALMS.

Psalm	Hymn
I =	184
IV =	1322
V =	28
IX =	1020, 1022
XI =	1031
XVII =	497
XVIII =	144, 155, 760
XIX =	46, 73, 87
XXIII =	85, 92, 628
XXIV =	260
XXVII =	181, 912
XXIX =	148
XXXIV =	546, 569
XXXVI =	173
XXXVIII =	434
XLII =	188, 758
XLV =	1030
XLVI =	152, 173
XLVII =	156, 267
L =	333, 1189
LI =	406
LV =	794
LVII =	147
LXI =	830
LXIII =	94, 755, 782
LXVIII =	124
LXXI =	578
LXXII =	513, 961, 1001
LXXIII =	191, 212
LXXVII =	476, 477, 478
LXXX =	684
LXXXIV =	2, 68
LXXXV =	1058
LXXXVII =	983
LXXXVIII =	309, 1090
XC =	117, 137, 821, 1147
XCII =	1
XCIII =	44, 121, 120, 163
XCV =	146, 156
XCVII =	134, 143
XCVIII =	216
C =	115, 118, 139
CII =	190
CIII =	102, 140
CVI =	133
CVII =	185
CX =	258
CXVI =	422
CXVII =	96, 511
CXVIII =	25, 507, 664
CXXI =	673, 692
CXXII =	31, 32, 43, 1173
CXXV =	793
CXXVI =	554
CXXXVI =	93, 170
CXXXVII =	717, 747
CXXXVIII =	133
CXXXIX =	117, 192
CXLI =	504
CXLV =	131
CXLVI =	1069
CXLVII =	1325
CXLVIII =	97, 130
CXLIX =	166
CL =	36

INDEX OF AUTHORS.

	HYMN.
Adams, Sarah F.	893. 1075. 1083
Addison	85. 87. 180. 185
Allen	368
Allen, G. N.	770
Ambrose, St.	506
Ancient Hymns	211. 709
Bacon, L.	956. 958. 1209. 1331.
Bailey	1067
Bakewell	299
Balfour	953
Baptist Memorial	1133
Barbauld, Mrs.	14. 40. 857. 526. 680. 909. 1047. 1093. 1098. 1247.
Bowring	79. 229. 374. 651. 882. 972. 1092. 1234.
Barton	76. 419. 746. 776. 823. 1126.
Bates	1043
Baxter, R.	791
Beard's Collection	1010
Beatty	663
Beddome	343. 423. 429. 624. 713. 745. 810. 813.
Beecher, Charles	1262. 1263
Bernard, St.	430
Blacklock	136
Boden	667
Bourne's Collection	449
Bowdler	816
Bradley	443
Bremer	993
Breviary	496. 601. 920. 1282. 1290. 1810.
Briggs' Collection	839. 1337
Browne, Mrs.	609. 1316
Browne	193
Browning, Mrs.	401. 483. 496. 1073. 1074.
Bryant, W. C.	90. 905. 940. 1071
Bryant, J. H.	1036
Brydges	243. 292. 298. 359. 1312
Bunting, W. M.	27
Burder	68. 198. 909
Burder's Collection	948
Burgess, G.	160. 625. 756.
Burns	184. 821
Burton	1167
Byles	1111
Campbell's Collection	571
Campbell, T.	223
Caswell	819
Cawood	309. 994
Christian Lyre	778. 880. 1190
Christian Psalmist	24
Clark, J. F.	595. 851. 933
Codman's Collection	80
Cennick	547. 730. 1168
Chapel Hymns	1312
Chapin	19. 1002.
Church Psalmody	165
Collyer	62. 276. 325. 598. 1174. 1291
Conder	106. 151. 505. 799. 919. 976. 1199.
Cotterell	995
Cotton	793

	HYMN.
Cowper, T.	50. 74. 198. 249. 442. 458. 530. 573. 696. 698. 695. 723. 744. 750. 811. 823. 862. 1126. 1202. 1203.
Cox, A. C.	230. 913. 982. 1169. 1282
Croswell	1063
Cunningham	20. 1072
Curtis's Collection	1333
Cutter, W.	1051. 1055
Dale	1123
Doddridge	4. 81. 172. 182. 189. 218. 255. 266. 271. 273. 303. 326. 328. 331. 334. 445. 453. 474. 486. 515. 516. 549. 557. 564. 590. 591. 593. 605. 615. 616. 626. 629. 672. 743. 835. 922. 923. 929. 946. 931. 1028. 1046. 1064. 1091. 1112. 1143. 1145. 1245. 1320. 1331.
Doane	848. 1169
Drummond	1016. 1052.
Dutton, Deodatus	1003. 1265
Duncan	551. 1027
Duncan, Mary Lundie	1360
Dwight	115. 169. 309. 717. 831. 1080. 1344.
Eastburne, I. W.	194
Edmeston	15. 29. 934. 1193. 1333
Edyfield	1343
Enfield	250
Evans	800
Faber	254. 291. 593. 596. 600
Fawcett	329. 716
Furness	903. 1341
Fitch, E. T.	49
Fitzgerald's Collection	726
Fletcher, Miss	1063
Fleury, Marie de	236. 1205
Follen, Mrs	1037
Francis, B.	171. 652
Freeman	1351
French	1058
Frothingham	437
Gallaudet, T. H.	805
Gellert	640
Gems	167
Gerhardt, P.	247. 840
Gibbons	277. 493. 1043
Gilbert, Mrs.	831. 937. 1123
Gill, T. H.	527. 910. 1329
Gisborne	733
Good, J. M.	1292
Goode, W.	1064. 1139
Gould, H. F.	1212
Grant	1184. 1211
Grant, Miss	878
Grant, Sir R.	80. 454. 762. 869. 1327
Greene, T.	792
Green	894
Gregg	304. 492
Guion, Madame	415. 508. 645. 648. 758.
Hammond	632

	HYMN.
Hart	22. 369. 523
Hartford Selection	585. 1329
Hastings, T.	72. 254. 324. 885. 462. 732. 778. 895. 944. 930.
Hatfield	116. 670.
Hawes	343. 467. 654. 820
Hawksworth	1299
Hayward	70
Heath	611
Heber	228. 261. 289. 431. 936. 942. 1079. 1114. 1155. 1156. 1349.
Hemans	246. 1007. 1124. 1156. 1248
Herbert	517. 623. 754
Higginbotham	54. 606
Hillhouse	497
Horne	1173
Howitt, Mary	1137
Humphries	864
Huntingdon	822
Hurn	203
Hyde	813
Hymns for the Sanctuary	61
Johns	1015
Jones	421
Judkin	283
Keble	290. 927. 1299. 1301
Kelly	13. 41. 209. 279. 287. 296. 297. 499. 502. 641. 950. 954. 958. 959. 990. 991. 993.
Kenn	1257. 1298
Kennedy	725
Key, S. F.	64
Kingsbury	293
Kirkham	725
Langford	655
Leifchild's Collection	56. 450. 1317
Leland's Hymns	936
Litchfield Collection	914
Liverpool Collection	213. 1122
Logan	230. 265. 683. 826. 911. 965. 1118.
Longfellow	872. 941. 1012. 1118. 1131
Lowell, James R.	1036
Lutheran Collection	1050
Lyra Catholica	196. 232. 259. 490. 491. 517. 555. 589. 598. 602. 618. 794. 847. 960. 970. 1279. 1288. 1298
Lyra Innocentium	1374
Lytte	678. 859
Mackay, Mrs.	1095
Madan	199. 280. 553. 661
Marsden	977
Martineau's Collection	1339
Martineau, Miss	1014
Mason	23. 1308
Medley	217. 320. 545. 644. 949
Merrick	92. 755. 1178
Methodist	205
Miller	706
Milman	234. 876. 973. 1199
Milton	85. 93. 215. 1058. 1060
Missionary Magazine	1197

INDEX OF AUTHORS.

	HYMN.
Montgomery,	5. 11. 48. 54. 60. 78. 96. 101. 104. 210. 214. 241. 245. 281. 344. 347. 364. 395. 435. 460. 476. 477. 478. 479. 498. 586. 621. 639. 694. 709. 755. 761. 782. 789. 809. 838. 843. 846. 854. 856. 900. 903. 937. 939. 947. 951. 959. 966. 975. 1001. 1039. 1049. 1099. 1107. 1115. 1116. 1117. 1189. 1144. 1146. 1148. 1153. 1158. 1159. 1162. 1192. 1251. 1252. 1343.
Moore,	82. 84. 176. 316. 433. 588. 656. 735. 774. 865.
Moravian,	414. 423. 426. 441. 543. 608. 879.
Muhlenberg	883. 1183
Needham	565
Newton	887
Nicoll	1025
Noel, Baptist	807. 917. 954
Noel's Collection	39
Newton,	52. 59. 270. 318. 349. 360. 387. 388. 410. 427. 480. 452. 455. 456. 459. 465. 570. 607. 646. 649. 665. 685. 690. 699. 724. 741. 751. 849. 857. 888. 963. 1104. 1211. 1228.
New York Collection	18
Norton, Mrs.	875. 936. 1094
Ockum	461
Ogilvie	97
Oliver	883
Onderdonk, H. U.	127. 840
Ovington's Collection	883
Oxford Psalter	801
Palmer, Ray	700
Parkinson's Collection	447
Patrick	157
Peabody	1102
Pierpont	1005. 1006. 1065
Pope	1008
Pratt's Collection,	841. 664. 703. 836. 885. 945. 957. 974. 998. 1000
Quarles	1239
Raffles	12. 698. 1152
Reed	257. 362. 401. 689
Reed's Collection	222
Rippon	67. 964
Rippon's Collection	75
Robinson	71. 212. 650
Roscoe, J.	752
Russell	227
Ryland	567. 797
Sacred Songs	898. 1348
Salisbury Collection	221. 275

	HYMN.
Sandys	57. 66
Sargent	1045
Sawyer, Mrs. C. M.	1086
Scotch Paraphrase	1109
Scott, E.	65. 109. 1332
Scott, T.	358. 471. 843
Scott, Sir Walter	802. 322
Sears, E. H.	219
Seward, Caroline	1034
Shirley	1083
Sigourney, Mrs.	701. 765. 841. 918. 967. 985.
Smart	99
Smith, J. E.	749
Smith, S. F.,	55. 850. 879. 896. 877. 1004. 1018. 1231.
Songs in the Night	16
Southey, Mrs.	831
Spirit of the Psalms	47. 156. 289
Spiritual Songs	386. 543
Steele, Mrs.,	37. 113. 168. 207. 263. 307. 319. 321. 400. 432. 436. 443. 451. 514. 529. 558. 568. 574. 584. 777. 795. 796. 812. 817. 822. 915. 963. 1090. 1121. 1227. 1295.
Stennett,	9. 242. 327. 440. 444. 604. 666. 714.
Sterling	68. 145
Sternhold	155
Stowe, Mrs. H. B.	675. 676. 677
Stowell	733
Strain	614. 710
Sutton	708
Tappan, W. B.	787. 1223
Tate	206
Tate & Brady,	121. 144. 146. 162. 188. 569. 747.
Taylor, E.	51
Taylor, J.,	53. 126. 671. 1236. 1250
Taylor	114
Teasdegan, G.	404
Thornby	1185
Tortont's Collection	854
Toplady,	846. 865. 893. 619. 658. 863. 876. 881. 1254.
Turner	236. 891
Vaughn	860
Very, Jones	697
Village Hymns	1277
Voke	955
Wallin	264
Ware, H.	971
Wardlaw	261. 811
Watts,	1. 2. 23. 24. 25. 31. 33. 39. 42. 43. 44. 45. 46. 68. 69. 77. 78. 100. 102. 103. 105. 107. 108. 110. 111. 112. 117. 118. 120. 122. 123.

	HYMN.
	124. 125. 130. 131. 132. 134. 135. 139. 140. 141. 142. 143. 147. 148. 149. 150. 152. 154. 158. 159. 161. 170. 173. 174. 178. 179. 181. 183. 186. 187. 190. 191. 192. 196. 197. 216. 233. 235. 243. 244. 253. 258. 263. 267. 272. 305. 308. 310. 312. 314. 315. 323. 330. 332. 333. 335. 336. 337. 338. 402. 406. 409. 422. 425. 433. 434. 446. 469. 472. 473. 480. 482. 484. 489. 497. 500. 501. 503. 504. 507. 509. 510. 511. 512. 513. 518. 519. 525. 546. 552. 554. 559. 560. 561. 563. 566. 572. 575. 576. 577. 578. 579. 580. 582. 586. 587. 597. 599. 618. 610. 620. 624. 630. 634. 635. 636. 637. 638. 678. 683. 684. 692. 705. 734. 739. 740. 743. 758. 760. 762. 766. 794. 793. 803. 808. 814. 824. 825. 830. 839. 913. 916. 921. 962. 1020. 1021. 1022. 1024. 1030. 1081. 1082. 1083. 1040. 1084. 1087. 1106. 1108. 1110. 1142. 1147. 1213. 1216. 1221. 1225. 1234. 1240. 1241. 1244. 1246. 1248. 1249. 1274. 1294. 1296. 1311. 1314. 1319. 1322. 1325. 1326. 1361. 1363. 1369. 1370. 1371. 1472. 1373.
Weber	17
Wesley, C.,	201. 256. 259. 260. 274. 342. 345. 351. 355. 354. 443. 445. 470. 475. 485. 490. 494. 538. 539. 540. 541. 542. 544. 550. 562. 563. 612. 613. 623. 631. 633. 643. 647. 660. 669. 704. 707. 712. 721. 723. 727. 771. 802. 815. 818. 837. 843. 861. 868. 930. 942. 968. 973. 999. 1138. 1150. 1151. 1170. 1179. 1182. 1191. 1204. 1207. 1209. 1210. 1230. 1258. 1255. 1278. 1280. 1236. 1345. 1346. 1347.
Wesley, J.,	53. 89. 153. 416. 418. 524. 767. 844. 931. 1181. 1217.
West Boston Collection	924
Weston	715
White, H. K.,	129. 533. 1101. 1256. 1318.
Whittier,	763. 1017. 1019. 1085. 1056. 1066. 1068. 1127. 1157. 1251. 1305.
Willard, Mrs.	1283
Williams, P.	683. 994
Williams, Miss H. M.	687
Willis, N. P.	938
Wilson	1186
Windham	649
Wordsworth	737
Xavier	494

SUPPLEMENTARY HYMNS,

ADDED BY

THE CHURCHES

OF THE

MIAMI CONFERENCE

TO THE

PLYMOUTH COLLECTION.

1856.

SUPPLEMENT.

1375. C. M.

1. Arise! O King of grace, arise,
    And enter to Thy rest.:
Behold, Thy church with longing eyes
    Waits to be owned and blest.

2. Enter with all Thy glorious train,
    Thy Spirit and Thy word;
All that the ark did once contain,
    Could no such grace afford.

3. Here, mighty God, accept our vows,
    Here let Thy praise be spread;
Bless the provisions of Thy house,
    And fill Thy poor with bread.

4. Here let the Son of David reign,
    Let God's Anointed shine;
Justice and truth His court maintain,
    With love and power divine.

5. Here let Him hold a lasting throne,
    And as His kingdom grows,
Fresh honors shall adorn His crown,
    And shame confound His foes.

1376. L. M.

1. The praise of Zion waits for Thee,
    My God! and praise becomes Thy house;
There shall Thy saints Thy glory see,
    And there perform their public vows.

2. O Thou, whose mercy bends the skies,
    To save when humble sinners pray!
All lands to Thee shall lift their eyes,
    And every yielding heart obey.

3. Blest is the man whom Thou shalt choose,
    And give him kind access to Thee;
Give him a place within Thy house,
    To taste Thy love divinely free.

4. With dreadful glory God fulfills
    What His afflicted saints request;
And with almighty wrath reveals
    His love, to give His churches rest.

5. Then shall the flocking nations run
    To Zion's hill, and own their Lord;
The rising and the setting sun
    Shall see the Saviour's name adored.

1377. H. M.

1. To spend one sacred day
    Where God and saints abide,
Affords diviner joy,
    Than thousand days beside;
        Where God resorts,
            I love it more
            To keep the door,
        Than shine in courts.

2. God is our sun and shield,
    Our light and our defence;
With gifts His hands are filled,
    We draw our blessings thence;
        He shall bestow,
            On Jacob's race,
            Peculiar grace
        And glory too.

3. The Lord His people loves,
    His hand no good withholds
From those His heart approves,
    From pure and pious souls:
        Thrice happy he,
            O God of hosts!
            Whose spirit trusts
        Alone in Thee.

1378. S. M.

1. Sweet is the work, O Lord!
    Thy glorious name to sing,
To praise and pray, to hear Thy word,
    And grateful offerings bring.

2. Sweet—at the dawning light,
    Thy boundless love to tell;
And when approach the shades of night,
    Still on the theme to dwell.

3. Sweet—on this day of rest,
    To join, in heart and voice,
With those who love and serve Thee best,
    And in Thy name rejoice.

4. To songs of praise and joy
    Be every Sabbath given,
That such may be our blest employ
    Eternally in heaven.

1379. H. M.

1. Lord, to Thy sacred house
   I turn my willing feet,
   Where saints, with morning-vows,
   In full assembly meet:
      Thy power divine
         Shall here be shown,
         And from Thy throne
      Thy mercy shine.

2. Oh! send Thy light abroad;
   Thy truth with heavenly ray
   Shall lead my soul to God,
   And guide my doubtful way;
      I'll hear Thy word
         With faith sincere,
         And learn to fear
      And praise the Lord.

3. Here reach Thy gracious hand,
   And all my sorrows heal,
   Here health and strength divine,
   Oh! make my bosom feel;
      Like balmy dew,
         Shall Jesus' voice
         My heart rejoice
      And strength renew.

4. Now in Thy holy hill,
   Before Thine altar, Lord!
   My harp and song shall sound
   The glories of Thy word:
      O God of grace!
         Henceforth to Thee
         My life shall be
      A hymn of praise.

1380. L. M.

1. Great God! attend while Zion sings
   The joy that from Thy presence springs;
   To spend one day with Thee on earth
   Exceeds a thousand days of mirth.

2. Might I enjoy the meanest place
   Within Thy house, O God of grace!
   Not tents of ease, nor thrones of power,
   Should tempt my feet to leave Thy door.

3. God is our sun, He makes our day;
   God is our shield, He guards our way
   From all th' assaults of hell and sin,
   From foes without, and foes within.

4. All needful grace will God bestow,
   And crown that grace with glory too;
   He gives us all things, and withholds
   No real good from upright souls.

1381. S. M.

1. Great is the Lord our God,
   And let His praise be great;
   He makes His churches His abode,
   His most delightful seat.

2. These temples of His grace,
   How beautiful they stand!
   The honors of our native place,
   And bulwarks of our land.

3. In Zion, God is known,
   A refuge in distress;
   How br.ght hath His salvation shone
   Through all her palaces!

4. Oft have our fathers told,
   Our eyes have often seen,
   How well our God secures the fold
   Where His own sheep have been.

5. In every new distress
   We'll to His house repair,
   We'll think upon His wondrous grace,
   And seek deliverance there.

1382. L. M.

1. 'Twas by an order from the Lord,
   The ancient prophets spoke His word;
   His Spirit did their tongues inspire, [fire.
   And warmed their hearts with heavenly

2. The works and wonders which they
      wrought,
   Confirmed the messages they brought;
   The prophet's pen succeeds his breath,
   To save the holy words from death.

3. Great God, mine eyes with pleasure look
   On the dear volume of Thy book;
   There my Redeemer's face I see,
   And read His name who died for me.

4. Let the false raptures of the mind
   Be lost, and vanish in the wind:
   Here I can fix my hope secure:
   This is Thy word, and must endure.

1383. C. M.

1. Lord! I have made Thy word my choice,
   My lasting heritage;
   There shall my noblest powers rejoice,
   My warmest thoughts engage.

2. I'll read the hist'ries of Thy love,
   And keep Thy laws in sight,
   While through the promises I rove,
   With ever fresh delight.

3. 'Tis a broad land of wealth unknown,
   Where springs of life arise;
   Seeds of immortal bliss are sown,
   And hidden glory lies:—

4. The best relief that mourners have;
   It makes our sorrows blest:—
   Our fairest hope, beyond the grave,
   And our eternal rest.

1384. C. M.

1. Oh! how I love Thy holy law!
   'Tis daily my delight;
   And thence my meditations draw
   Divine advice by night.

2. My waking eyes prevent the day
   To meditate Thy word:
   My soul with longing melts away
   To hear Thy gospel, Lord!

3. How doth Thy word my heart engage!
   How well employ my tongue!
   And, in my tiresome pilgrimage,
   Yields me a heavenly song.

4. Am I a stranger, or at home!
   'Tis my perpetual feast;
   Not honey, dropping from the comb,
   So much delights my taste.

5. No treasures so enrich the mind;
   Nor shall Thy word be sold
   For loads of silver well refined,
   Nor heaps of choicest gold.

6. When nature sinks, and spirits droop,
   Thy promises of grace
   Are pillars to support my hope,—
   And there I write Thy praise.

1385. C. M.

1. Through endless years Thou art the same,
   O Thou eternal God!
   Ages to come shall know Thy name,
   And tell Thy works abroad.

2. The strong foundations of the earth,
   Of old by Thee were laid;
   By Thee, the beauteous arch of heaven,
   With matchless skill was made.

3. Soon shall this goodly frame of things,
   Formed by Thy powerful hand,
   Be like a vesture laid aside,
   And changed at Thy command.

4. But Thy perfections all divine,
   Eternal as Thy days,
   Through everlasting ages shine,
   With undiminished rays.

5. Thy children's children still Thy care,
   Shall own their fathers' God;
   To latest times Thy favor share,
   And spread Thy praise abroad.

1386. C. M.

1. In all my vast concerns with Thee,
   In vain my soul would try
   To shun Thy presence, Lord! or flee
   The notice of Thine eye.

2. Thine all-surrounding sight surveys
   My rising and my rest,
   My public walks, my private ways,
   And secrets of my breast.

3. My thoughts lie open to the Lord,
   Before they're formed within;
   And ere my lips pronounce the word,
   He knows the sense I mean.

4. Oh! wondrous knowledge, deep and high,
   Where can a creature hide!
   Within Thy circling arms I lie,
   Inclosed on every side.

5. So let Thy grace surround me still,
   And like a bulwark prove,
   To guard my soul from every ill,
   Secured by sovereign love.

1387. C. M.

1. God is a Spirit, just and wise;
   He sees our inmost mind;
   In vain to heaven we raise our cries,
   And leave our souls behind.

2. Nothing but truth before His throne
   With honor can appear;
   The painted hypocrites are known,
   Through the disguise they wear.

3. Their lifted eyes salute the skies,
   Their bended knees the ground;
   But God abhors the sacrifice,
   Where not the heart is found.

4. Lord, search my thoughts, and try my ways,
   And make my soul sincere;
   Then shall I stand before Thy face,
   And find acceptance there.

1388. L. M.

1. Shall the vile race of flesh and blood
   Contend with their Creator, God!
   Shall mortal worms presume to be
   More holy, wise, or just, than He!

2. Behold, He puts His trust in none
Of all the spirits round His throne;
Their natures, when compared with His,
Are neither holy, just, nor wise.

3. But how much meaner things are they
Who spring from dust, and dwell in clay!
Touched by the finger of Thy wrath,
We faint, and vanish like the moth.

4. From night to day, from day to night,
We die by thousands in Thy sight:
Buried in dust whole nations lie,
Like a forgotten vanity.

5. Almighty Power, to Thee we bow;
How frail are we! how glorious Thou!
No more the sons of earth shall dare
With an eternal God compare.

1389. S. M.

1. Oh! bless the Lord, my soul!
Let all within me join,
And aid my tongue to bless His name,
Whose favors are divine.

2. Oh! bless the Lord, my soul!
Nor let His mercies lie
Forgotten in unthankfulness,
And without praises die.

3. 'Tis He forgives thy sins,
'Tis He relieves thy pain,
'Tis He who heals thy sicknesses,
And makes thee young again.

4. He crowns thy life with love,
When ransomed from the grave;
He, who redeemed my soul from hell,
Hath sovereign power to save.

5. He fills the poor with good;
He gives the sufferers rest;
The Lord hath judgments for the proud,
And justice for th' oppressed.

6. His wondrous works and ways
He made by Moses known;
But sent the world His truth and grace
By His beloved Son.

1390. C. M.

1. Long as I live, I'll bless Thy name,
My King, my God of love;
My work and joy shall be the same,
In brighter worlds above.

2. Great is the Lord—His power unknown,
Oh let His praise be great;
I'll sing the honors of Thy throne,
Thy works of grace repeat.

3. Thy grace shall dwell upon my tongue,
And while my lips rejoice,
The men who hear my sacred song,
Shall join their cheerful voice.

4. Fathers to sons shall tell Thy name,
And children learn Thy ways;
Ages to come Thy truth proclaim,
And nations sound Thy praise.

5. The world is governed by Thy hand,
Thy saints are ruled by love;
And Thine eternal kingdom stands,
Though rocks and hills remove.

1391. C. M.

1. 'Tis by Thy strength the mountains stand,
God of eternal power!
The sea grows calm at Thy command,
And tempests cease to roar.

2. Thy morning-light and evening-shade
Successive comforts bring;
Thy plenteous fruits make harvest glad,
Thy flowers adorn the spring.

3. Seasons and times, and moons and hours,
Heaven, earth, and air are Thine;
When clouds distill in fruitful showers,
The author is divine.

4. Those wandering cisterns in the sky,
Borne by the winds around,
With watery treasures well supply
The furrows of the ground.

5. The thirsty ridges drink their fill,
And ranks of corn appear;
Thy ways abound with blessings still,
Thy goodness crowns the year.

1392. C. M.

1. Sweet is the mem'ry of Thy grace,
My God! my heavenly King!
Let age to age Thy righteousness
In sounds of glory sing.

2. God reigns on high,—but ne'er confines
His goodness to the skies;
Through the whole earth His bounty shines,
And every want supplies.

3. With longing eyes, Thy creatures wait
On Thee for daily food:
Thy lib'ral hand provides their meat,
And fills their mouth with good.

4. How kind are Thy compassions, Lord!
How slow Thine anger moves!
But soon He sends His pard'ning word
To cheer the souls He loves.

5. Creatures with all their endless race,
    Thy power and praise proclaim;
But saints, who taste Thy richer grace,
    Delight to bless Thy name.

1393. 7s.

1. Praise the Lord—His power confess;
Praise Him in His holiness;
Praise Him as the theme inspires;
Praise Him as His fame requires.

2. Let the trumpet's lofty sound
Spread its loudest notes around;
Let the harp unite, in praise,
With the sacred minstrel's lays.

3. Let the organ join to bless
God—the Lord of righteousness;
Tune your voice to spread the fame
Of the great Jehovah's name.

4. All who dwell beneath His light!
In His praise, your hearts unite;
While the stream of song is poured—
Praise and magnify the Lord.

1394. L. P. M.

1. Let all the earth their voices raise,
    To sing the choicest psalm of praise;
    To sing and bless Jehovah's name:
His glory let the heathen know;
His wonders to the nations show;
    And all His saving works proclaim.

2. He framed the globe, He built the sky,
He made the shining worlds on high,
    And reigns complete in glory there;
His beams are majesty and light;
His beauties—how divinely bright!
    His temple—how divinely fair!

3. Come the great day, the glorious hour,
When earth shall feel His saving power,
    And barb'rous nations fear his name!
Then shall the race of man confess
The beauty of His holiness,
    And, in His courts, His grace proclaim.

1395. C. M.

1. Let children hear the mighty deeds
    Which God performed of old;
Which in our younger years we saw,
    And which our fathers told.

2. He bids us make His glories known,—
    His works of power and grace;
And we'll convey His wonders down
    Through every rising race.

3. Our lips shall tell them to our sons,
    And they again to theirs,
That generations yet unborn
    May teach them to their heirs.

4. Thus shall they learn, in God alone
    Their hope securely stands;
That they may ne'er forget His works,
    But practice His commands.

1396. L. M.

1. Lord, in Thy great, Thy glorious name,
    I place my hope, my only trust;
Save me from sorrow, guilt, and shame,
    Thou ever gracious, ever just.

2. Thou art my rock—Thy name alone
    The fortress where my hopes retreat;
Oh make Thy power and mercy known
    To safety guide my wandering feet.

3. Blest be the Lord—forever blest,
    Whose mercy bids my fear remove,
Those sacred walls, which guard my rest
    Are His almighty power and love.

4. Ye humble souls, who seek his face,
    Let sacred courage fill your heart!
Hope in the Lord—and trust His grace,
    And He will heavenly strength impart.

1397. C. M.

1. I love the Lord;—He heard my cries,
    And pitied every groan;
Long as I live, when troubles rise,
    I'll hasten to His throne.

2. I love the Lord;—He bowed His ear,
    And chased my griefs away;
Oh! let my heart no more despair
    While I have breath to pray.

3. My flesh declined, my spirits fell,
    And I drew near the dead;
While inward pangs and fears of hell
    Perplexed my wakeful head.

4. "My God," I cried, "Thy servant save,
    Thou ever good and just!
Thy power can rescue from the grave—
    Thy power is all my trust."

5. The Lord beheld me sore distressed,
    He bade my pains remove;
Return, my soul! to God Thy rest,
    For thou hast known His love.

6. My God hath saved my soul from death,
    And dried my falling tears;
Now to His praise I'll spend my breath,
    And my remaining years.

1398. L. M.

1. From deep distress and troubled thoughts,
   To Thee, my God! I raise my cries:
   If Thou severely mark our faults,
   No flesh can stand before Thine eyes.

2. But Thou hast built Thy throne of grace,
   Free to dispense Thy pardons there;
   That sinners may approach Thy face,
   And hope and love, as well as fear.

3. As the benighted pilgrims wait,
   And long and wish for breaking day,
   So waits my soul before Thy gate;—
   When will my God His face display!

4. My trust is fixed upon Thy word,
   Nor shall I trust Thy word in vain;
   Let mourning souls address the Lord,
   And find relief from all their pain.

5. Great is His love, and large His grace,
   Through the redemption of His Son;
   He turns our feet from sinful ways,
   And pardons what our hands have done.

1399. C. M.

1. God of my childhood and my youth!
   The guide of all my days,
   I have declared Thy heavenly truth,
   And told Thy wondrous ways.

2. Wilt thou forsake my hoary hairs,
   And leave my fainting heart?
   Who shall sustain my sinking years,
   If God, my strength, depart?

3. Let me Thy power and truth proclaim
   To the surviving age,
   And leave a savor of Thy name,
   When I shall quit the stage.

4. The land of silence and of death
   Attends my next remove;
   Oh! may these poor remains of breath
   Teach the wide world Thy love.

1400. C. M.

1. My God, how many are my fears!
   How fast my foes increase!
   Conspiring my eternal death,
   They break my present peace.

2. The lying tempter would persuade
   There's no relief in heaven;
   And all my swelling sins appear
   Too great to be forgiven.

3. I cried, and from His holy hill
   He bowed a listening ear;
   I called my Father and my God,
   And He subdued my fear.

4. What though the hosts of death and hell,
   All armed, against me stood;
   Terrors no more shall shake my soul,—
   My refuge is my God.

5. Salvation to the Lord belongs,
   His arm alone can save;
   Blessings attend Thy people here,
   And reach beyond the grave.

1401. C. M.

1. O Lord, our Lord, how wondrous great
   Is thine exalted name!
   The glories of Thy heavenly state
   Let men and babes proclaim.

2. When I behold Thy works on high,
   The moon that rules the night,
   And stars that well adorn the sky,
   Those moving worlds of light:—

3. Lord, what is man, or all his race,
   Who dwells so far below,
   That Thou shouldst visit him with grace,
   And love his nature so!

4. That Thine eternal Son should bear
   To take a mortal form,
   Made lower than His angels are,
   To save a dying worm.

5. Jesus, our Lord, how wondrous great
   Is Thine exalted name!
   The glories of Thy heavenly state,
   Let the whole earth proclaim.

1402. H. M.

1. Thy mercy, oh! our God,
   To all Thy church display;
   Proclaim Thy grace abroad,
   And spread the gospel day
     High on thy throne,
       Our prayers attend;
     And quickly send
   Salvation down.

2. Jesus the Saviour's nigh
   To those who fear His name
   He comes!—His praise on high
   Let all His church proclaim!
     His footsteps still
       On earth shall stand,
     And all the land
   His glory fill.

3. Now truth and mercy meet
In Jesus' face they shine;
And peace and justice greet,
With smiles of love divine:
With heavenly grace,
Midst sons of men,
They join again
Their kind embrace.

4. The Lord His blessing pours,
Around our favored land;
His grace, like gentle showers,
Descends at His command:
O'er all the plains
Blest fruits arise,
In rich supplies—
Since Jesus reigns.

5. His righteousness alone
Prepares His wondrous way;
He rises to His throne
In realms of endless day!
His steps we trace,
His path pursue;
And, heaven in view,
Adore His grace.

1403. S. M.

1. Did Christ o'er sinners weep!
And shall our cheeks be dry?
Let floods of penitential grief
Burst forth from every eye.

2. The Son of God in tears,
Angels with wonder see!
Be thou astonished, O my soul,
He shed those tears for thee.

3. He wept that we might weep,
Each sin demands a tear;
In heaven alone no sin is found,
And there's no weeping there.

1404. C. M.

1. In vain we seek for peace with God,
By methods of our own;
Nothing, O Saviour! but Thy blood
Can bring us near the throne.

2. The threatenings of Thy broken law
Impress the soul with dread:
If God His sword of vengeance draw,
It strikes the spirit dead.

3. But thine illustrious sacrifice
Hath answered these demands;
And peace and pardon from the skies
Are offered by Thy hands.

4. 'Tis by Thy death we live, O Lord!
'Tis on Thy cross we rest:
Forever be Thy love adored,
Thy name forever blessed.

1405. L. M.

1. Deep in our hearts, let us record
The deeper sorrows of our Lord;
Behold the rising billows roll,
To overwhelm His holy soul!

2. Yet, gracious God! Thy power and love
Have made the curse a blessing prove;
Those dreadful sufferings of Thy Son
Atoned for sins that we had done.

3. The pangs of our expiring Lord
The honors of Thy law restored;
His sorrows made Thy justice known,
And paid for follies not His own.

4. Oh! for His sake, our guilt forgive,
And let the mourning sinner live:
The Lord will hear us in His name,
Nor shall our hope be turned to shame.

1406. S. M.

1. I saw, beyond the tomb,
The awful Judge appear,
Prepared to scan, with strict account,
The blessings wasted here.

2. His wrath, like flaming fire,
In hell for ever burns;
And, from that hopeless world of woe,
No fugitive returns.

3. Ye sinners! fear the Lord,
While yet 'tis called to-day;
Soon will the awful voice of death
Command your souls away.

4. Soon will the harvest close,
The summer soon be o'er;
O sinners! then your injured God
Will heed your cries no more.

1407. S. P. M.

1. When God in wrath shall come
To tell the sinner's doom,
What anguish shall the wicked tear!
The men that slight His name,
That boast of sin and shame,
No more shall ask—"What God can hear?"

2. Thou hearest, omniscient Lord!
Each curse and idle word
Of men who scoff with lips profane:

And when the hand of death
Shall stop their impious breath,
  Their souls shall seek for peace in vain.

3. Oh! how will sinners need
An advocate to plead,
  Accepted at Thine awful throne!
How, in that solemn hour,
Would faith's transcendent power
  Outweigh all things beneath the sun!

4. Yet save their souls, O Lord!
Subdue them by Thy word,
  Though all their powers oppose Thy reign,
Now may Thy foes submit,
And bow beneath Thy feet,
  Nor let them read Thy wrath in vain.

1408. S. M.

1. Can sinners hope for heaven,
     Who love this world so well;
   Or dream of future happiness,
     While in the road to hell!

2. Shall they hosannas sing,
     With an unhallowed tongue;
   Shall psalms adorn the guilty hand
     Which does its neighbor wrong?

3. Can sin's deceitful way,
     Conduct to Zion's hill;
   Or those expect with God to reign,
     Who disregard His will?

4. Thy grace, O God, alone,
     Can a good hope afford!
   The pardoned and renewed shall see,
     The glory of the Lord.

1409. L. M.

1. Why will ye waste on trifling cares
   That life which God's compassion spares,
   While, in the various range of thought,
   The one thing needful is forgot!

2. Shall God invite you from above!
   Shall Jesus urge His dying love!
   Shall troubled conscience give you pain!
   And all these pleas unite in vain!

3. Not so your eyes will always view
   Those objects which you now pursue;
   Not so will heaven and hell appear,
   When death's decisive hour is near.

4. Almighty God, Thy grace impart,
   Fix deep conviction on each heart:
   Then we no more on trifling cares
   Shall waste that life Thy mercy spares.

1410. C. M.

1. Blest is the man who shuns the place
     Where sinners love to meet;
   Who fears to tread their wicked ways,
     And hates the scoffer's seat.

2. But in the statutes of the Lord
     Has placed his chief delight;
   By day he reads or hears the word,
     And meditates by night.

3. He, like a plant of generous kind
     By living waters set,
   Safe from the storms and blasting wind,
     Enjoys a peaceful state.

4. Green as the leaf, and ever fair,
     Shall his profession shine;
   While fruits of holiness appear,
     Like clusters on the vine.

5. Not so the impious and unjust:
     What vain designs they form!
   Their hopes are blown away like dust,
     Or chaff before the storm.

6. Sinners in judgment shall not stand
     Among the sons of grace,
   When Christ, the Judge, at His right hand,
     Appoints His saints a place.

1411. 7s double.

1. Sinners, turn, why will ye die!
   God your Maker asks you why!
   God, who did you being give,
   Made you with Himself to live;
   He, the fatal cause demands,
   Asks the work of His own hands;
   Why, ye thankless creatures, why
   Will ye cross His love, and die!

2. Sinners, turn, why will ye die!
   God your Saviour asks you why;
   He who did your souls retrieve—
   Died Himself that ye might live.
   Will ye let Him die in vain!
   Crucify your Lord again!
   Why, ye ransomed sinners, why
   Will ye slight his grace, and die!

3. Sinners, turn, why will ye die!
   God the Spirit asks you why;
   Now His influence from above,
   Moves you to embrace His love:
   Will ye not His grace receive!
   Will ye still refuse to live!
   Why, ye long-sought sinners, why
   Will ye grieve your God, and die!

1412. 7s.

1. Come, ye weary sinners, come,
    All who feel your heavy load:
   Jesus calls the wanderers home;
    Hasten to your pardoning God:
   Come, ye guilty souls oppressed,
    Answer to the Saviour's call:
   "Come, and I will give you rest;
    Come, and I will save you all."

2. Jesus, full of truth and love,
    We Thy kindest call obey,
   Faithful let Thy mercies prove,
    Take our load of guilt away:
   Weary of this war within,
    Weary of this endless strife,
   Weary of ourselves and sin,
    Weary of a wretched life.

3. Burdened with a world of grief,
    Burdened with our sinful load,
   Burdened with this unbelief,
    Burdened with the wrath of God,
   Lo, we come to Thee for ease,
    True and gracious as Thou art;
   Now our weary souls release,
    Write forgiveness on our heart.

1413. L. M.

1. No more, my God, I boast no more,
   Of all the duties I have done;
   I quit the hopes I held before,
   To trust the merits of Thy Son.

2. Now, for the love I bear His name,
    What was my gain, I count my loss:
   My former pride I call my shame,
    And nail my glory to His cross.

3. Yes, and I must and will esteem
    All things but loss for Jesus' sake;
   Oh, may my soul be found in Him,
    And of His righteousness partake!

4. The best obedience of my hands
    Dares not appear before Thy throne;
   But faith can answer Thy demands,
    By pleading what my Lord has done.

1414. L. M.

1. Though I have grieved Thy Spirit, Lord!
   His help and comfort still afford;
   And let a wretch come near Thy throne,
   To plead the merits of Thy Son.

2. A broken heart, my God! my King!
    Is all the sacrifice I bring;
   The God of grace will ne'er despise
    A broken heart for sacrifice.

3. My soul lies humbled in the dust,
    And owns Thy dreadful sentence just;
   Look down, O Lord! with pitying eye,
    And save the soul condemned to die.

4. Then will I teach the world Thy ways;
    Sinners shall learn Thy sovereign grace;
   I'll lead them to my Saviour's blood,
    And they shall praise a pard'ning God.

5. Oh! may Thy love inspire my tongue;
    Salvation shall be all my song;
   And all my powers shall join to bless
    The Lord, my strength and righteousness.

1415. C. M.

1. Now shall my solemn vows be paid
    To that almighty Power,
   Who heard the long requests I made,
    In my distressful hour.

2. My lips and cheerful heart prepare
    To make His mercies known;
   Come, ye who fear my God, and hear
    The wonders He has done.

3. When on my head huge sorrows fell,
    I sought His heavenly aid;
   He saved my sinking soul from hell,
    And death's eternal shade.

4. Had sin lain covered in my heart,
    While prayer employed my tongue,
   The Lord had shown me no regard,
    Nor I His praises sung.

5. But God—His name be ever blessed—
    Has set my spirit free;
   Nor turned from Him my poor request,
    Nor turned His heart from me.

1416. C. M.

1. I waited patient for the Lord,—
    He bowed to hear my cry;
   He saw me resting on His word,
    And brought salvation nigh.

2. He raised me from a horrid pit,
    Where, mourning, long I lay;
   And from my bonds released my feet—
    Deep bonds of miry clay.

3. Firm on a rock He made me stand,
    And taught my cheerful tongue
   To speak the wonders of His hand,
    In praise thankful song.

4. I'll spread His works of grace abroad;
    The saints with joy shall hear;
   And sinners learn to make my God
    Their only hope and fear.

1417. C. M.

1. In vain we lavish out our lives
   To gather empty wind;
   The choicest blessings earth can yield
   Will starve a hungry mind.

2. Our God can every want supply,
   And fill our hearts with peace:
   He gives by covenant, and by oath,
   The riches of His grace.

3. Come—and He'll cleanse our guilty souls,
   And wash away our stains
   In that pure fountain which his Son
   Poured from his dying veins.

4. His spirit in our hearts shall dwell,
   And deep engrave His law;
   And every motion of our souls
   To swift obedience draw.

5. Thus will He pour salvation down,
   And we shall render praise:
   We, the dear people of His love,
   And he, our God of grace.

1418. L. M.

1. Blest be the Lord, who heard my prayer,
   The Lord my shield, my help my song,
   Who saved my soul from sin and fear,
   And tuned with praise my thankful tongue.

2. In the dark house of deep distress,
   By foes beset, of death afraid,
   My spirit trusted in His grace,
   And sought, and found, His heavenly aid.

3. O blest Redeemer of mankind!
   Thy shield, Thy saving strength, shall be,
   The shield, the strength of every mind,
   That loves Thy name and trusts in Thee.

4. Remember, Lord, Thy chosen seed;
   Israel defend from guilt and woe;
   Thy flock in richest pastures feed,
   And guard their steps from every foe.

5. Zion exalt, her cause maintain,
   With peace and joy her courts surround:
   In showers let endless blessings rain,
   And saints eternal praise resound.

1419. L. M.

1. Who shall the Lord's elect condemn?
   'Tis God that justifies their souls,
   And mercy, like a mighty stream,
   O'er all their sins divinely rolls.

2. Who shall adjudge the saints to hell?
   'Tis Christ that suffered in their stead;
   And, their salvation to fulfill,
   Behold Him rising from the dead!

3. He lives! He lives! and sits above,
   Forever interceding there:
   Who shall divide us from His love,
   Or what should tempt us to despair?

4. Faith hath an overcoming power,
   It triumphs in the dying hour;
   He that hath loved us, bears us through,
   And makes us more than conquerors too.

5. Not all that men on earth can do,
   Nor powers on high, nor powers below,
   Shall cause His mercy to remove,
   Or wean our hearts from Christ our love.

1420. 8s.

1. A debtor to mercy alone,
   Of covenant mercy I sing;
   Nor fear, with Thy righteousness on,
   My person and off rings to bring:
   The terrors of law and of God
   With me can have nothing to do;
   My Saviour's obedience and blood
   Hide all my transgressions from view.

2. The work which His goodness began,
   The arm of His strength will complete;
   His promise is Yea and Amen,
   And never was forfeited yet;
   Things future, nor things that are now,
   Not all things below or above,
   Can make Him His purpose forego,
   Or sever my soul from His love.

3. My name from the palms of His hands
   Eternity will not erase;
   Impressed on His heart it remains,
   In marks of indelible grace:
   Yes—I to the end shall endure,
   As sure as the earnest is given;
   More happy, but not more secure,
   The glorified spirits in heaven.

1421. L. M.

1. How oft have Sin and Satan strove
   To rend my soul from thee, my God!
   But everlasting is Thy love,
   And Jesus seals it with His blood.

2. The oath and promise of the Lord
   Join to confirm the wondrous grace;
   Eternal power performs the word,
   And fills all heaven with endless praise.

3. Amidst temptations, sharp and long,
   My soul to this dear refuge flies;
   Hope is my anchor, firm and strong,
   While tempests blow, and billows rise.

4. The gospel bears my spirit up;
   A faithful and unchanging God,
   Lays the foundation for my hope,
   In oaths, and promises, and blood.

1422. C. M.

1. I wait for Thy salvation, Lord,
   With strong desires I wait;
   My soul, invited by Thy word,
   Stands watching at Thy gate.

2. Just as the guards that keep the night
   Long for the morning skies,
   Watch the first beams of breaking light,
   And meet them with their eyes:—

3. So waits my soul to see Thy grace,
   And, more intent than they,
   Meets the first openings of Thy face,
   And finds a brighter day.

4. Then in the Lord let Israel trust,
   Let Israel seek His face;
   The Lord is good as well as just,
   And plenteous is His grace.

5. There's full redemption at His throne
   For sinners long enslaved;
   The great Redeemer is His Son,
   And Israel shall be saved.

1423. 8s.

1. The moment a sinner believes,
   And trusts in his crucified God,
   His pardon at once he receives—
   Redemption in full through His blood.
   'Tis faith that still leads us along,
   And lives under pressure and load,
   That makes us in weakness more strong,
   And draws the soul upward to God.

2. It treads on the world and on hell,
   It vanquishes death and despair;
   And oh! let us wonder to tell,
   It wrestles and conquers by prayer;
   Permits a vile worm of the dust,
   With God to commune as a friend;
   His promise of mercy to trust,
   And look for His love to the end.

3. It says to the mountains, "Depart,"
   That stand between God and the soul;—
   It binds up the broken in heart,
   And makes wounded consciences whole;
   Bids sins of a crimson like dye
   Be spotless as snow and as white:
   And raises the sinner on high,
   To dwell with the angels of light.

1424. C. M.

1. My soul lies cleaving to the dust;
   Lord, give me life divine;
   From vain desires, and every lust,
   Turn off these eyes of mine.

2. I need the influence of Thy grace
   To speed me in Thy way,
   Lest I should loiter in my race,
   Or turn my feet astray.

3. Are not Thy mercies sovereign still,
   And Thou a faithful God?
   Wilt Thou not grant me warmer zeal
   To run the heavenly road?

4. Does not my heart Thy precepts love,
   And long to see Thy face?
   And yet, how slow my spirits move
   Without enlivening grace!

5. Then shall I love Thy gospel more,
   And ne'er forget Thy word,
   When I have felt its quickening power
   To draw me near the Lord.

1425. 8s.

1. Encompassed with clouds of distress,
   Just ready all hope to resign,
   I pant for the light of Thy face,
   And fear it will never be mine;
   Disheartened with waiting so long,
   I sink at Thy feet with my load;
   All plaintive I pour out my song,
   And stretch forth my hands unto God.

2. If sometimes I strive, as I mourn,
   My hold on Thy promise to keep,
   The billows more fiercely return,
   And plunge me again in the deep:
   While harassed and cast from thy sight,
   The tempter suggests with a roar,
   "The Lord has forsaken thee quite:
   Thy God will be gracious no more."

3. Shine, Lord, and my terrors shall cease;
   The blood of atonement apply;
   And lead me to Jesus for peace,
   The rock that is higher than I.
   Almighty to rescue Thou art
   Thy grace is my shield and my tower
   Come, succor and gladden my heart,
   Let this be the day of Thy power.

1426. L. M.

1. Lord, I can suffer Thy rebukes,
   When Thou with kindness dost chastise;
   But Thy fierce wrath I cannot bear,
   Oh, let it not against me rise!

2. See how in sighs I pass my days,
   And waste in groans the weary night;
   My bed is watered with my tears,
   My grief consumes and dims my sight.

3. Look how the powers of nature mourn!
   How long, Almighty God, how long!
   When shall Thine hour of grace return,—
   When shall I make Thy grace my song?

4. I feel my flesh so near the grave,
   My thoughts are tempted to despair:
   The grave can never praise the Lord,
   For all is dust and silence there.

5. Depart, ye tempters, from my soul,
   And all despairing thoughts, depart;
   My God, who hears my humble moan,
   Will ease my flesh and cheer my heart.

1427. L. M.

1. How long, O Lord, shall I complain,
   Like one that seeks his God in vain?
   Wilt Thou Thy face forever hide?
   Shall I still pray and be denied?

2. Hear, Lord, and grant me quick relief,
   Before my death conclude my grief;
   If Thou withhold Thy heavenly light,
   I sleep in everlasting night.

3. How will the powers of darkness boast
   If but one praying soul be lost!
   But I have trusted in Thy grace,
   And shall again behold thy face.

4. Whate'er my fears or foes suggest,
   Thou art my hope, my joy, my rest;
   My heart shall feel Thy love, and raise
   My cheerful voice to songs of praise.

1428. C. M.

1. My drowsy powers, why sleep ye so?
   Awake, my sluggish soul;
   Nothing has half thy work to do,
   Yet nothing's half so dull.

2. The little ants for one poor grain,
   Labor, and tug, and strive;
   Yet we, who have a heaven to obtain,
   How negligent we live!

3. We, for whose sake all nature stands,
   And stars their courses move—
   We, for whose guard the angel-bands
   Come flying from above—

4. We for whom God the Son came down
   And labored for our good—
   How careless to secure that crown
   He purchased with His blood!

5. Lord, shall we lie so sluggish still,
   And never act our parts?
   Come, Holy Spirit, come and fill,
   And wake and warm our hearts.

6. Then shall our active spirits move;
   Upward our souls shall rise:
   With hands of faith and wings of love,
   We'll fly and take the prize.

1429. C. M.

1. How helpless guilty nature lies,
   Unconscious of its load!
   The heart unchanged, can never rise
   To happiness and God.

2. Can aught beneath a power divine
   The stubborn will subdue?
   'Tis Thine, Almighty Saviour, Thine
   To form the heart anew.

3. 'Tis Thine the passions to recall,
   And upward bid them rise,
   And make the scales of error fall
   From reason's darkened eyes.

4. To chase the shades of death away,
   And bid the sinner live;
   A beam of heaven, a vital ray,
   'Tis Thine alone to give.

5. Oh, change these wretched hearts of ours,
   And give them life divine;
   Then shall our passions and our powers,
   Almighty Lord, be Thine.

1430. S. M.

1. Mine eyes and my desire
   Are ever to the Lord;
   I love to plead His promises,
   And rest upon His word.

2. Turn, turn Thee to my soul;
   Bring Thy salvation near;
   When will Thy hand release my feet
   Out of the deadly snare?

3. When shall the sovereign grace
   Of my forgiving God,
   Restore me from those dangerous ways
   My wandering feet have trod?

CHARITY, FORGIVENESS, HOLINESS, ETC.

4. With every morning light,
    My grief anew begins;
  Look on my anguish and my pain,
    And pardon all my sins.

5. O keep my soul from death,
    Nor put my hope to shame;
  For I have placed my only trust
    In my Redeemer's name.

6. With humble faith I wait
    To see Thy face again;
  Of Israel it shall ne'er be said,
    He sought the Lord in vain.

1431. L. M.

1. Great God, how oft did Israel prove
  By turns Thine anger and Thy love!
  There in a glass our hearts may see
  How fickle and how false are we.

2. How soon the faithless Jews forgot
  The dreadful wonders God had wrought!
  Then they provoke Him to His face,
  Nor fear His power nor trust His grace.

3. Oft when they saw their brethren slain,
  They mourned and sought the Lord again;
  Called Him the Rock of their abode,
  Their high Redeemer and their God.

4. Their prayers and vows before Him rise
  As flattering words or solemn lies;
  While their rebellious tempers prove
  False to His covenant and His love.

5. Yet did His sovereign grace forgive
  The men who ne'er deserved to live;
  His anger oft away He turned,
  Or else with gentle flame it burned.

6. He saw their flesh was weak and frail,
  He saw temptation still prevail;
  The God of Abra'm loved them still,
  And led them to His holy hill.

1432. L. M.

1. Blest is the man whose heart doth move,
    And melt with pity to the poor;
  Whose soul, by sympathizing love,
    Feels what his fellow-saints endure.

2. His heart contrives for their relief
    More good than his own hands can do;
  He, in the time of general grief,
    Shall find the Lord has pity too.

3. His soul shall live secure on earth,
    With secret blessings on his head,
  When drought, and pestilence, and dearth,
    Around him multiply their dead.

4. Or, if he languish on his couch,
    God will pronounce his sins forgiven;
  Will save him with a healing touch,
    Or take his willing soul to heaven.

1433. C. M.

1. When sunk in guilt, our souls approached
    The borders of despair,
  Thy grace, through Jesus' blood, proclaimed
    A free salvation near.

2. What shall we render, bounteous God,
    For all the grace we see?
  Alas, the goodness we can yield
    Extendeth not to Thee.

3. To tents of woe, to beds of pain,
    We cheerfully repair;
  And with the gift Thy hand bestows
    Relieve the sufferers there.

4. The widow's heart shall sing for joy;
    The orphan's tear be dry;
  The sinner hear the call of love,
    And find a Saviour nigh.

5. Thus passing through the vale of tears,
    Our useful light shall shine;
  And others learn to glorify
    Our Father's name divine.

1434. H. M.

1. How beautiful the sight,
    Of brethren who agree
  In friendship to unite,
    And bonds of charity!
  'Tis like the precious ointment, shed
  O'er all his robes, from Aaron's head.

2. 'Tis like the dews that fill
    The cups of Hermon's flowers;
  Or Zion's fruitful hill,
    Bright with the drops of showers;
  When mingling odors breathe around,
  And glory rests on all the ground.

3. For there the Lord commands
    Blessings, a boundless store,
  From his unsparing hands—
    E'en life for evermore:
  Thrice happy they who meet above,
  To spend eternity in love.

1435. C. M.

1. When, in the form of mortal man,
    God's Son on earth was found,
  With cruel slanders, false and vain,
    Foes compassed Him around.

2. Their miseries His compassion move,
   Their peace He still pursued;
   They render hatred for His love,
   And evil for His good.

3. Their malice raged without a cause;
   Yet, with His dying breath,
   He prayed for murderers on His cross,
   And blessed His foes in death.

4. Lord! shall Thy bright example shine
   In vain before my eyes?
   Give me a soul akin to Thine,
   To love mine enemies.

1436. C. M.

1. O God! my sins are manifold,
   Against my life they cry,
   And all my guilty deeds foregone
   Up to Thy temple fly.

2. Wilt Thou release my trembling soul,
   That to despair is driven?
   "Forgive!" a blessed voice replied,
   "And thou shalt be forgiven!"

3. My foemen, Lord, are fierce and fell,
   They spurn me in their pride,
   They tender evil for my good,
   My patience they deride.

4. Arise, O King! and be the proud
   To righteous ruin driven!
   "Forgive!" an awful answer came,
   "As thou wouldst be forgiven!"

5. Seven times, O Lord! I pardoned them,
   Seven times they sinned again:
   They practice still to work me woe,
   They triumph in my pain.

6. But let them dread my vengeance now,
   To just resentment driven!
   "Forgive!" the voice of thunder spake,
   "Or never be forgiven."

1437. L. M.

1. So let our lips and lives express
   The holy gospel we profess:
   So let our works and virtues shine,
   To prove the doctrine all divine.

2. Thus shall we best proclaim abroad
   The honors of our Saviour God;
   When the salvation reigns within,
   And grace subdues the power of sin.

3. Our flesh and sense must be denied,
   Passion and envy, lust and pride:
   While justice, temperance, truth and love,
   Our inward piety approve.

4. Religion bears our spirits up,
   While we expect that blessed hope,
   The bright appearance of the Lord,
   And faith stands leaning on His word.

1438. C. M.

1. O for a heart to praise my God,
   A heart from sin set free;
   A heart that's sprinkled with the blood
   So freely shed for me!

2. A heart resigned, submissive, meek,
   My dear Redeemer's throne;
   Where only Christ is heard to speak,
   Where Jesus reigns alone:—

3. An humble, lowly, contrite heart,
   Believing, true, and clean,
   Which neither life nor death can part
   From Him that dwells within:—

4. A heart in every thought renewed,
   And filled with love divine;
   Perfect, and right, and pure, and good,—
   An image, Lord, of Thine.

5. Thy nature, gracious Lord, impart;
   Come quickly from above;
   Write Thy new name upon my heart,—
   Thy name, O God, is Love.

1439. C. M.

1. Oh that the Lord would guide my ways
   To keep His statutes still!
   Oh that my God would grant me grace
   To know and do His will!

2. Oh send Thy Spirit down, to write
   Thy law upon my heart;
   Nor let my tongue indulge deceit,
   Nor act the liar's part.

3. From vanity turn off my eyes;
   Let no corrupt design,
   Nor covetous desire arise
   Within this soul of mine.

4. Order my footsteps by Thy word,
   And make my heart sincere;
   Let sin have no dominion, Lord,
   But keep my conscience clear.

5. My soul hath gone too far astray—
   My feet too often slip:
   Yet since I keep in mind Thy way,
   Restore Thy wandering sheep.

6. Make me to walk in Thy commands—
   'Tis a delightful road;
   Nor let my head, nor heart, nor hands,
   Offend against my God.

CHARITY, FORGIVENESS, HOLINESS, ETC.

1440. S. M.

1. Shall we go on to sin
   Because free grace abounds!
   Or crucify the Lord again,
   And open all His wounds!

2. Forbid it, mighty God!
   Nor let it e'er be said,
   That we whose sins are crucified
   Should raise them from the dead.

3. We will be slaves no more,
   Since Christ has made us free;
   Has nailed our tyrants to the Cross,
   And bought our liberty.

1441. 7s.

1. Who, O Lord, when life is o'er,
   Shall to heavenly mansions soar?
   Who, an ever welcome guest,
   In Thy holy place shall rest?

2. He whose heart Thy love has warmed;
   He whose will, to Thine conformed,
   Bids his life unsullied run;
   He whose thoughts and words are one;—

3. He who shuns the sinner's road,
   Loving those who love their God;
   Who with hope and faith unfeigned,
   Treads the path by Thee ordained;—

4. He who trusts in Christ alone,
   Not in aught himself hath done;—
   He, great God, shall be Thy care,
   And Thy choicest blessings share.

1442. S. M.

1. Oh! blessed souls are they
   Whose sins are covered o'er;
   Divinely blest—to whom the Lord
   Imputes their guilt no more.

2. They mourn their follies past,
   And keep their hearts with care;
   Their lips and lives, without deceit,
   Shall prove their faith sincere.

3. While I concealed my guilt,
   I felt the festering wound;
   But I confessed my sins to Thee,
   And ready pardon found.

4. Let sinners learn to pray;
   Let saints keep near the throne;
   Our help, in times of deep distress,
   Is found in God alone.

1443. L. M.

1. Blest is the man, forever blest,
   Whose guilt is pardoned by his God;
   Whose sins with sorrow are confessed,
   And covered with his Saviour's blood.

2. From guile his heart and lips are free;
   His humble joy, his holy fear,
   With deep repentance well agree,
   And join to prove his faith sincere.

3. How glorious is that righteousness
   That hides and cancels all his sins!
   While a bright evidence of grace
   Through his whole life, appears and shines.

1444. 7s.

1. Gracious Spirit—Love divine,
   Let Thy light within me shine;
   All my guilty fears remove,
   Fill me with Thy heavenly love.

2. Speak Thy pardoning grace to me,
   Set the burdened sinner free;
   Lead me to the Lamb of God,
   Wash me in His precious blood.

3. Life and peace to me impart;
   Seal salvation on my heart;
   Breathe Thyself into my breast,
   Earnest of immortal rest.

4. Let me never from Thee stray,
   Keep me in the narrow way;
   Fill my soul with joy divine;
   Keep me, Lord, forever Thine.

1445. H. M.

1. O Thou who hearest prayer,
   Attend our humble cry;
   And let Thy servants share
   Thy blessing from on high:
   We plead the promise of Thy word;
   Grant us Thy Holy Spirit, Lord.

2. If earthly parents hear
   Their children when they cry;
   If they with love sincere
   Their varied wants supply,
   Much more wilt Thou thy love display,
   And answer when Thy children pray.

3. Our Heavenly Father, Thou,
   We children of Thy grace—
   Oh let Thy Spirit now
   Descend, and fill the place;
   That all may feel the heavenly flame,
   And all unite to praise Thy name.

1446. L. M.

1. Sure the blest Comforter is nigh,
   'Tis He sustains my fainting heart;
   Else would my hope forever die,
   And every cheering ray depart.

2. Whene'er to call the Saviour mine,
   With ardent wish my heart aspires,
   Can it be less than power divine
   Which animates these strong desires?

3. What less than Thine almighty word
   Can raise my heart from earth and dust,
   And bid me cleave to Thee, my Lord,
   My Life, my Treasure, and my Trust!

4. And when my cheerful hope can say,
   I love my God, and trust His grace,
   Lord, is it not Thy blissful ray,
   Which brings this dawn of sacred peace?

5. Let thy kind Spirit in my heart
   Forever dwell, O God of love,
   And light, and heavenly peace impart,
   Sweet earnest of the joys above.

1447. L. M.

1. The Spirit, like a peaceful dove,
   Flies far from realms of noise and strife;
   Why should we vex and grieve His love,
   Who seals our souls to heavenly life!

2. Clamor, and wrath, and war begone;
   Envy and strife forever cease;
   Let bitter words no more be known
   Among the saints, the sons of peace.

3. Tender and kind be all our thoughts,
   Through all our lives let mercy run;
   So God forgives our numerous faults,
   For the dear sake of Christ, his Son.

1448. C. M.

1. Where shall we go to seek and find
   A habitation for our God!
   A dwelling for the eternal mind,
   Among the sons of flesh and blood!

2. The God of Jacob chose the hill
   Of Zion for His ancient rest;
   And Zion is His dwelling still;
   His church is with His presence blest.

3. Here will He meet the hungry poor,
   And fill their souls with living bread;
   Sinners, that wait before His door,
   With sweet provision shall be fed.

4. Here will I fix my gracious throne,
   And reign forever—saith the Lord;
   Here shall my power and love be known,
   And blessings shall attend my word.

1449. S. M.

1. Far as Thy name is known
   The world declares Thy praise;
   Thy saints, O Lord, before Thy throne,
   Their songs of honor raise.

2. With joy Thy people stand
   On Zion's chosen hill,
   Proclaim the wonders of Thy hand,
   And counsels of Thy will.

3. Let strangers walk around
   The city where we dwell,
   Compass and view Thine holy ground,
   And mark the building well;—

4. The order of Thy house,
   The worship of Thy court,
   The cheerful songs—the solemn vows;—
   And make a fair report.

5. How decent, and how wise!
   How glorious to behold!
   Beyond the pomp that charms the eyes,
   And rites adorned with gold.

6. The God we worship now
   Will guide us till we die;
   Will be our God, while here below,
   And ours above the sky.

1450. S. M.

1. Sing to the Lord aloud,
   And make a cheerful noise;
   God is our strength, our Saviour-God;
   Let Israel hear His voice:—

2. "From vile idolatry
   Preserve my worship clean;
   I am the Lord who set thee free
   From slavery and from sin.

3. "Stretch thy desires abroad,
   And I'll supply them well;
   But if ye will refuse your God,
   If Israel will rebel;—

4. "I'll leave them," saith the Lord,
   "To their own lusts a prey,
   And let them run the dangerous road;—
   'Tis their own chosen way.

5. "Yet, oh! that all my saints
   Would hearken to my voice;
   Soon I would ease their sore complaints,
   And bid their hearts rejoice.

6. "While I destroyed their foes,
     I'd richly feed my flock,
   And they should taste the stream that flows
     From their eternal Rock."

1451. L. M.

1. We are a garden walled around,
   Chosen and made peculiar ground;
   A little spot inclosed by grace,
   Out of the world's wide wilderness.

2. Awake, O heavenly wind, and come,
   Blow on this garden of perfume;
   Spirit divine, descend and breathe
   A gracious gale on plants beneath.

3. Make our best spices flow abroad,
   To entertain our Saviour God:
   And faith, and love, and joy appear,
   And every grace be active here.

4. Our Lord into His garden comes,
   Well pleased to smell our poor perfumes;
   And calls us to a feast divine,
   Sweeter than honey, milk, or wine.

5. Jesus, we will frequent Thy board,
   And sing the bounties of our Lord:
   But the rich food on which we live,
   Demands more praise than tongue can give.

1452. L. M.

1. Lord, Thou hast planted with Thy hands
   A lovely vine in this our land;
   Did not Thy power defend it round,
   And heavenly dews enrich the ground!

2. How did the spreading branches shoot,
   And bless the nations with the fruit!
   But now, O Lord, look down and see
   Thy mourning vine, that lovely tree.

3. Why is her beauty thus defaced?
   Why hast Thou laid her fences waste?
   Strangers and foes against her join,
   And every beast devours the vine.

4. Return, Almighty God, return;
   Nor let Thy bleeding vineyard mourn:
   Turn us to Thee, Thy love restore,
   We shall be saved and sigh no more.

1453. S. M.

1. Now Christ ascends on high,
     And asks to rule the earth;
   The merit of His blood He pleads,
     And pleads His heavenly birth.

2. He asks, and God bestows,
     A large inheritance;
   Far as the world's remotest ends,
     His kingdom shall advance.

3. The nations that rebel
     Must feel His iron rod;
   He'll vindicate those honors well,
     Which He received from God.

4. Be wise, ye rulers, now,
     And worship at His throne;
   With trembling joy, ye people, bow
     To God's exalted Son.

5. If once His wrath arise,
     Ye perish on the place;
   Then blessed is the soul that flies
     For refuge to His grace.

1454. 8, 7, & 4.

1. Who, but Thou, Almighty Spirit,
     Can the heathen world reclaim?
   Men may preach, but till Thou favor,
     Heathens will be still the same:
       Mighty Spirit!
     Witness to the Saviour's name.

2. Thou hast promised by the prophets,
     Glorious light in latter days:
   Come, and bless bewildered nations,
     Change our prayers and tears to praise:
       Promised Spirit!
     Round the world diffuse Thy rays.

3. All our hopes, and prayers, and labors,
     Must be vain without Thine aid:
   But Thou wilt not disappoint us—
     All is true that Thou hast said:—
       Faithful Spirit!
     O'er the world Thine influence shed.

1455. C. M.

1. Sing to the Lord, ye distant lands!
     Ye tribes of every tongue!
   His new-discovered grace demands
     A new and nobler song.

2. Say to the nations,—"Jesus reigns,
     God's own almighty Son;
   His power the sinking world sustains,
     And grace surrounds His throne."

3. Let heaven proclaim the joyful day,
     Joy through the earth be seen,
   Let cities shine in bright array,
     And fields in cheerful green.

4. Let an unusual joy surprise
    The islands of the sea;
  Ye mountains! sink, ye valleys! rise,
    Prepare the Lord His way.

5. Behold, He comes,—He comes to bless
    The nations, as their God;
  To show the world His righteousness,
    And send His truth abroad.

6. But when His voice shall raise the dead,
    And bid the world draw near,
  How will the guilty nations dread
    To see their Judge appear!

1456. C. M.

1. Fools, in their hearts, believe and say
    That all religion's vain;—
  There is no God who reigns on high,
    Or minds the affairs of men.

2. The Lord, from His celestial throne,
    Looked down on things below,
  To find the man that sought His grace,
    Or did His justice know.

3. By nature all are gone astray,
    Their practice all the same;
  There's none that fears his Maker's hand,—
    There's none that loves His name.

4. Their tongues are used to speak deceit,—
    Their slanders never cease:
  How swift to mischief are their feet,
    Nor know the paths of peace.

5. Such seeds of sin, that bitter root,
    In every heart are found;
  Nor can they bear diviner fruit,
    Till grace refine the ground.

1457. S. M.

1. Sure there's a righteous God,
    Nor is religion vain;
  Though men of vice may boast aloud,
    And men of grace complain.

2. I saw the wicked rise,
    And felt my heart repine,
  While haughty fools, with scornful eyes,
    In robes of honor shine.

3. The tumult of my thought
    Held me in hard suspense,
  Till to Thy house my feet were brought
    To learn Thy justice thence.

4. Thy word with light and power,
    Did my mistake amend;
  I viewed the sinners' life before,
    But here I learned their end.

5. On what a slippery steep
    The thoughtless wretches go!
  And oh! that dreadful fiery deep
    That waits their fall below!

6. Lord! at Thy feet I bow;
    My thoughts no more repine;
  I call my God my portion now,
    And all my powers are Thine.

1458. S. M.

1. Ah! how shall fallen man
    Be just before his God?
  If He contend in righteousness,
    We fall beneath His rod.

2. If He our ways should mark
    With strict inquiring eyes,
  Could we for one of thousand faults
    A just excuse devise?

3. All-seeing, powerful God,
    Who can with Thee contend?
  Or who that tries the unequal strife
    Shall prosper in the end?

4. The mountains, in Thy wrath,
    Their ancient seats forsake;
  The trembling earth deserts her place,
    Her rooted pillars shake.

5. Ah! how shall guilty man
    Contend with such a God?
  None, none can meet Him and escape
    But through the Saviour's blood.

1459. L. M.

1. Oh! let me, gracious Lord! extend
    My view, to life's approaching end:
  What are my days?—a span their line;
    And what my age, compared with Thine!

2. Our life advancing to its close,
    While scarce its earliest dawn it knows,
  Swift, through an empty shade, we run,
    And vanity and man are one.

3. God of my fathers! here, as they,
    I walk, the pilgrim of a day;
  A transient guest, Thy works admire,
    And instant to my home retire.

4. Oh! spare me, Lord! in mercy, spare,
    And nature's failing strength repair;
  Ere, life's short circuit wandered o'er,
    I perish, and am seen no more

1460. S. M.

1. O for the death of those
  Who slumber in the Lord!
  O be like theirs my last repose,
  Like theirs my last reward.

2. Their bodies in the ground
  In silent hope may lie,
  Till the last trumpet's joyful sound
  Shall call them to the sky.

3. Their ransomed spirits soar
  On wings of faith and love,
  To meet the Saviour they adore,
  And reign with Him above.

4. With us their names shall live
  Through long succeeding years,
  Embalmed with all our hearts can give,
  Our praises and our tears.

5. O for the death of those
  Who slumber in the Lord!
  O be like theirs my last repose,
  Like theirs my last reward.

1461. C. M.

1. O for an overcoming faith,
  To cheer my dying hours;
  To triumph o'er the monster Death,
  And all his frightful powers!

2. Joyful, with all the strength I have,
  My quivering lips should sing,—
  "Where is thy boasted victory, grave?
  And where's the monster's sting?"

3. If sin be pardoned, I'm secure;
  Death has no sting beside;
  The law gives sin its damning power;
  But Christ my ransom died.

4. Now to the God of victory
  Immortal thanks be paid;—
  Who makes us conquerors while we die,
  Through Christ, our living Head.

1462. C. M.

1. Nor eye hath seen, nor ear hath heard,
  Nor sense, nor reason known,
  What joys the Father has prepared
  For those who love the Son.

2. But the good Spirit of the Lord
  Reveals a heaven to come;
  The beams of glory in His word
  Allure and guide us home.

3. Pure are the joys above the sky,
  And all the region peace;
  No wanton lip nor envious eye
  Can see or taste the bliss.

4. Those holy gates forever bar
  Pollution, sin, and shame;
  None shall obtain admittance there
  But followers of the Lamb.

5. He keeps the Father's book of life;
  There all their names are found;
  The hypocrite in vain shall strive
  To tread the heavenly ground.

1463. L. M.

1. Come, dearest Lord, descend and dwell
  By faith and love in every breast;
  Then we shall know, and taste, and feel,
  The joys that cannot be expressed.

2. Come, fill our hearts with inward strength;
  Make our enlarged souls possess,
  And learn the height, and breadth, and length,
  Of Thine immeasurable grace.

3. Now to the God whose power can do
  More than our thoughts or wishes know,
  Be everlasting honors done
  By all the Church—through Christ, His Son.

1464. 11s.

JEHOVAH TSIDKENU—*The Lord our Righteousness.*

1. I once was a stranger to grace and to God,
  I knew not my danger and felt not my load;
  Though friends spoke in rapture of Christ on the tree,
  Jehovah Tsidkenu was nothing to me.

2. I oft read with pleasure, to soothe or engage,
  Isaiah's wild measure and John's simple page;
  But e'en when they pictured the blood-sprinkled tree,
  Jehovah Tsidkenu seemed nothing to me.

3. Like tears from the daughters of Zion that roll,
  I wept when the waters went over His soul;
  Yet thought not that my sins had nailed to the tree
  Jehovah Tsidkenu—'twas nothing to me.

4. When free grace awoke me, by light from on high,
  Then legal fears shook me—I trembled to die;
  No refuge, no safety in self could I see—
  Jehovah Tsidkenu my Saviour must be.

5. My terrors all vanished before the sweet name;
  My guilty fears banished, with boldness I came
  To drink at the Fountain, life-giving and free,—
  Jehovah Tsidkenu is all things to me.

6. Jehovah Tsidkenu! my treasure and boast—
  Jehovah Tsidkenu! I ne'er can be lost;
  In Thee I shall conquer by flood and by field,
  My Cable, my Anchor, my Breastplate and Shield!

7. Even treading the valley, the shadow of death,
  This watchword shall rally my faltering breath;
  For while from life's fever my God sets me free,
  Jehovah Tsidkenu, my death-song shall be.

INDEX OF SUBJECTS.

	HYMNS.
Sabbath and Sanctuary	1375—1381
Bible	1382—1384
God;	
Attributes of	1385—1392
Adoration of	1393—1395
Confidence in	1396—1400
Christ	1401—1406
Warnings and Invitations	1407—1413
Christian Experience;	
Consciousness of Sin	1414—1415
Praise, Joy, Conflict	1416—1432
Charity, Forgiveness, Holiness, &c.	1433—1448
The Church and Missions	1449—1456
Miscellaneous	1457—1464